ANGLO-SAXON POETRY

*An anthology of Old English poems
in prose translation
with introduction and headnotes
by*

S. A. J. Bradley

Department of English and Related Literature
University of York

Dent: London, Melbourne and Toronto
EVERYMAN'S LIBRARY

© Introduction, translation and notes, J. M. Dent & Sons Ltd, 1982

Phototypeset in 10/11½ VIP Sabon by
D. P. Media Limited, Hitchin, Hertfordshire
Printed in Great Britain by
Richard Clay (The Chaucer Press) Ltd, Bungay, Suffolk for
J. M. Dent & Sons Ltd
Aldine House, 33 Welbeck Street, London W1M 8LX
First published in Everyman's Library 1982

British Library Cataloguing in Publication Data

Anglo-Saxon poetry. – (Everyman's library)
  1. Anglo-Saxon poetry – Translations into
  English
  2. English poetry – Translations from
  Anglo-Saxon
  I. Bradley, S. A. J.
  829'.1   PR1502

ISBN 0-460-10794-1
ISBN 0-460-11794-7 Pbk

Contents

Preface vii
Introduction xi
Abbreviations xxiv
Bibliography xxv

Three Early Poems 1
Cædmon's Hymn 3
The Ruthwell Cross Inscription 4
Bede's Death-song 6

Junius 11 7
Genesis 10
Exodus 49
Daniel 66
Christ and Satan 86

The Vercelli Book 107
Andreas 110
The Fates of the Apostles 154
The Dream of the Rood 158
Elene 164

The Exeter Book 199
Christ I (The Advent Lyrics) 203
Christ II (The Ascension) 216
Christ III (The Judgment) 228
Guthlac A 248
Guthlac B 269
The Phoenix 284
Juliana 301
The Wanderer 320
The Gifts of Men 325
The Seafarer 329

Widsith   336
The Fortunes of Men   341
Maxims I   344
The Panther (Physiologus)   352
The Whale (Physiologus)   355
Soul and Body II   358
Deor   362
Wulf and Eadwacer   365
Riddles 3, 5, 9, 25, 26, 29, 30a, 35, 38, 42–8, 53   367
The Wife's Lament   382
Resignation   386
The Descent into Hell   390
Alms-giving   395
Riddle 60   397
The Husband's Message   398
The Ruin   401
Riddles 61, 66, 69, 76, 86   403

Cotton Vitellius A xv   405
Beowulf   408
Judith   495

Poems from Other Manuscripts   505
The Battle of Finnsburh   507
Waldere   510
Maxims II   512
The Battle of Brunanburh   515
The Battle of Maldon   518
Judgment Day II   528
The Benedictine Office (Prime): The Lord's Prayer;
   The Creed; Fragments of Psalms   536
The Metrical Charms: For unfruitful land;
   A journey charm   543

A Check-list of Old English Poetry   551

Preface

Ælfric, most accomplished of the Anglo-Saxon prose-writers and a scholarly translator of Scriptures from Latin into West Saxon, had a word – *hefigtyme*, 'oppressive, vexatious, toilsome' – for the translator's burden, and in the preface to his rendering of Genesis, looking over what he had managed to accomplish, he asked his patron plainly not to bid him translate anything more ever again. Whoever presumes to take the poetry of Ælfric's day and render it into contemporary English must soon come to feel the frustration and trepidation which Ælfric voices. So much of the sense and the artistry of the original resists the metamorphosis of language and literary form, and the compromise which no translator can avoid stands vulnerable to complaint from the expert reader of Old English and the expert speaker of modern English alike. Yet, as the long life of Professor R. K. Gordon's distinguished precursor to this volume testifies, the demand for translations of the oldest English poetry abides; and, as Ælfric also acknowledges (*mutatis mutandis*), where there is modest hope of enlarging the community of the faithful, toil and frustration become a privilege. Infelicities and plain errors doubtless do abound in a work so broad as this in scope. I shall be glad to hear of them in the hope of making future corrections. To family, friends and colleagues for their long tolerance of my preoccupation with this task I now offer my thanks. So I do to the many of my students at York who have wittingly or unwittingly contributed to the translations. I also gladly record the gratitude I owe to Dr Graham Caie of the University of Copenhagen for his valued judgments and encouragement; to my editor, Jocelyn Burton, for the meticulous care she has devoted to the production of this book, for constant and unstinted support and, in her dealings with an oft-distracted author, for her almost flawless patience; but above all to my wife Mette, whose least contribution to the accomplishment of this task was to prepare a large part of the typescript, and who, in this as in my every toilsome undertaking, has always lightened what was *hefigtyme* with ministrations not available to Abbot Ælfric. It ought to be any translator's last word to wish his readers well in coming to know the source-works at first hand, free from the interpreter's mediation. In helping its readers to an appreciation and enjoyment of Anglo-Saxon poetry in its Old English form it is hoped that this book will prove to be of some transitional aid.

Forth I go: may I meet with friends! (*A journey charm*).

21 February 1982

S. A. J. Bradley
Alne
North Yorkshire

Introduction

A familiar anecdote told of King Alfred by his contemporary biographer, Asser, Bishop of Sherborne (*The Life of Alfred*, ch.23), witnesses to the king's affection for the traditional poetry of his people, and celebrates his ability as a child to win an attractive book from his mother by memorizing and repeating to her the poems which it contained; for though, as Asser says (ch.22), Alfred remained illiterate until he was twelve years old or more, he was a zealous listener to the Saxon poems on those frequent occasions when he could hear them recited in the hall, and, being readily taught, he retained them in his memory with evident ease. The story may well be authentic. Certainly, it accords with other demonstrations Alfred made of his concern for the distinctive identity of the English people and the English language. The fact that Einhard had earlier attributed such interest in vernacular (Frankish) poetry to Charlemagne in his Life of the King of the Franks may be taken as independent evidence of a similar enlightenment in two great kings, rather than of any imitative intention on Asser's part to make his Life conform with Einhard's; but either way, the anecdote revealingly assumes the propriety of kings patronizing, and themselves cultivating, the native poetic arts of their people.

A thousand years on, the surviving poetry of the Anglo-Saxons, along with their prose (itself an abiding monument to Alfred's royal initiatives in the cultural life of his nation), constitutes a legacy yet more precious for its antiquity. The poems are voices carrying over moral values, thought and sentiment from a period of English history which began with the fifth-century migration to Britain of Germanic tribesmen from beyond the north-west boundary of the Roman empire and ended, at least in formal terms of chronology and political sovereignty, with the Norman Conquest. By the end of this span, the nation was characterized by the effects of its long-nurtured and conscious aspiration towards assimilation of Mediterranean-centred culture, not only in religious and ecclesiastical spheres but in the intellectual and artistic traditions which were the gift of Roman Christianity to converted nations. By this time, there had long been a sense of commercial, political and cultural community with Western Europe; a consciousness of one nation of the English long established, ruled according to written codes of law by one sovereign king, the deputy of God consecrated to office and aided in government by the Church through a complex central and local administration; a distinctive insular culture, deeply indebted to, but not enslaved by influences from abroad, which had achieved excellence by international standards in such diverse areas as manuscript drawing and painting, book-making, ecclesiastical building, sculpture and needlework; and a literary language independent of Latin, rich in accomplishments and healthily evolving. Recognition of this state of affairs increasingly persuades scholars that already in late Anglo-Saxon England the tap-roots of English medieval culture are to be found, drawing from the Anglo-Saxon earth some considerable part of that 'licour, of which vertu engendred is the flour'.

The six centuries' span of Anglo-Saxon history is equivalent to that from the Norman Conquest to the restoration of the monarchy in 1660 and the publication of *Paradise Lost*, or from the Peasants' Revolt and the writing of *Canterbury Tales* to the present day: a span in which it would be inconceivable not to find change. The notion of kingship embodied in the writings of Wulfstan and in the tenth-century ordering of the Coronation represents a radical shift from the kingship practised in the days of the settlement. The superb art of the tenth- and eleventh-century Benedictine missals, benedictionals or calendars expresses concepts and objectives markedly different from those of the equally superb art of the seventh-century Lindisfarne Gospels. So, we must surely believe, the poetry of the later Anglo-Saxon period sought different objectives and served different tastes from those of the traditional lays which the first generations of settlers doubtless brought with them in their cultural baggage. We may indeed assume that throughout this period of cultural evolution the poets had a main part to play in conserving the traditional and mediating the new. But here we run into a problem in English literary history: the chronology of the surviving Anglo-Saxon poems.

The fact that the unique text of *Beowulf*, like most other Old English poems, is known to us only in a manuscript written towards the end of the period continues to challenge those who would like to argue that the actual *composition* of the poem belongs, say, to the century of the Sutton Hoo ship burial (*c*.625). On the other hand, the late manuscript text of *The Dream of the Rood* incorporates lines of alliterative verse which are also found inscribed in runes on the eighth-century Ruthwell Cross. Again, *The Battle of Maldon* appears to embody heroic sentiment leading straight back to the world of Germanic antiquity as it was described in the *Germania* of Tacitus in the first century after Christ; and yet the poem cannot have been composed before the battle was actually fought in 991. Neither manuscript nor sentiment nor tone are very reliable guides to the chronology of composition – and specific dates on poems are very few.

The problem is a complex one. The *Beowulf*-poet's apparently well furnished memory of traditional Germanic subject-matter – Scandinavian royal dynasties and heroes, humanoid monsters and dragons – seems to support arguments for an early date of composition. But the relationship of the Ruthwell Cross poem to the later manuscript poem *The Dream of the Rood* advises us of the likelihood of early poems undergoing a later reworking, in which quite different purposes or emphases, even different interpretations, might assert themselves over the old material, according to the demands of a different audience and changing tastes and preoccupations among the poets. Indeed, the widely held theory of the essentially *oral* mode of composition and transmission of Anglo-Saxon poetry, in which written composition and manuscript recording with their fossilizing effect have no functional place, implies that *written* texts are of prime relevance only to the historical period of the manuscript date. Since, by definition of the theory, the poem is reconstituted with each retelling, only with great circumspection may the *written* text be made to yield conclusions about any speculative period earlier in the unstable life of what is only notionally the 'same' poem. Again, if the ancient pre-migratory sentiments of *The Battle of Maldon* suggest an extreme conservatism spanning the centuries, the poet's equally explicit approval of Byrhtnoth's stand for God and the Christian faith, for his king and his country, for the values of an English aristocracy secure in its life-style and its context of family, hereditary land and a hierarchical social order, with exemplary responsibilities as well as privileges, should all serve to establish that in some major respects the poem is significantly nearer to the world of the *Chanson de Roland* than to that of the lost lays of Weland, Eormanric and Sigmund. Thus it may be mistaken to construe the antique tone of this poem as a symptom of entrenched ethical and technical conservatism among late Anglo-Saxon poets; it is conceivably a cultivated antiquarianism, perhaps even a deliberate tool of propaganda, best judged in the light of contemporary prose propaganda such as that echoed in the late tenth- and eleventh-century annals of the *Anglo-Saxon Chronicle*, and thumped out loud and clear in Archbishop Wulfstan's sermon, the *Sermo Lupi ad Anglos*, addressed to the English nation in 1014.

The manuscript texts, then, give rather equivocal guidance as to the age or sequence of composition of the Old English poems. Nor can the names of the poets be used to secure firm association between the extant poems and the age in which they were composed, for it is a natural consequence of the oral conditions of composition and transmission that the original composer of a poem is forgotten as it passes into popular circulation – each singer himself assuming for the duration of the performance the 'I'-personality through which the action of these poems is so often narrated, and freely recreating the substance of the poem, untrammelled by the existence of a definitive written version of it. Only Cynewulf, as far as is known, took care to build into his poems an explicit identification of the 'I'-speaker of the narrative with himself, the author, by incorporating a signature in runes – and even of

Cynewulf no certain historical documentation exists, so we can give him no sure dates. Otherwise, there is no named poet to whom a corpus of extant poetry in Old English can be assigned – neither Aldhelm, Bishop of Sherborne (died 709), nor Cædmon, recipient, according to Bede, of a miraculous faculty for composing Christian poetry at Whitby between 657 and 680, both of whom have claims to be the first poet to treat Christian subject-matter in the English language.

Yet the poets' role, we may think, was potentially a prominent and honoured one. Diverse tokens suggest this was so: the implication of Tacitus that among the early Germanic peoples poets were the sole formal keepers of their nation's history – a function which probably continued with increasing importance once the Anglo-Saxons had become immigrants in Britain, and even after the Church had introduced the Roman alphabet and the scriptorium; the presence of the lyre in the symbolically furnished seventh-century royal ship-burial at Sutton Hoo; the prominence and space given to the miracle of Cædmon in Bede's *History of the English Church and People*; Asser's attention to King Alfred's patronage of poetry; the fact that the Church devoted such resources to the preserving of vernacular poetry in the tenth and eleventh centuries; and, though the evidence is hardly impartial, the fact that the poets themselves speak of their profession with pride in their acknowledged worth as repositories of tradition, arbiters of the motives and deeds of men and women, and advocates for good and for God. Above all is the intrinsic evidence of the content and quality of surviving poetry. Without significant exception, it occupies itself with serious matters of philosophy, the history and truths of the faith, public and private ethics and issues of social responsibility, in a manner regularly prescriptive and didactic.

Secular patronage, by royal persons or wealthy families, certainly developed in Anglo-Saxon England, as the poetry itself implies (see particularly *Widsith* and *Deor*), and is known to account for the making of at least a few manuscripts. But through most of the Anglo-Saxon period the monasteries held the real advantages in literacy – those of favourably organized conditions, of surplus wealth, of time, of institutional continuity, of reputable learning, of teaching, and of the practical means of recording and copying and preserving for repeated access vernacular poetry as well as the Latin works proper to the Church. Inevitably, the monopoly of literacy was accompanied by censorship. What we now read as the literary legacy of Anglo-Saxon society is to a large extent the Anglo-Saxon *ars poetica* as it was adapted and adopted by a favoured section of that society – by the heirs, though more rigorously institutionalized than he, of Cædmon (whom Hilda perciperiently received into the Whitby community as a fully professed monk once his special talent had been revealed).

Censorship by selection, then, has surely occurred in the monastic scriptoria where poems were written down, and in the refectories where they were recited. But in other respects too the monks were arbiters over what has survived to represent the Anglo-Saxon poetic achievement. Almost certainly they had among their numbers men of literary judgment who could and did *edit* existing poetry in order to achieve special emphases within one poem or to develop complex cross-relationships between poems anthologized in a codex; and among their numbers too they doubtless had original poets who met directly the community's special poetic tastes and needs. Alcuin's repeatedly cited reproof (letter, dated 797) to Higbald and the monks of Lindisfarne for preferring barbarian songs about fictitious heroes to the truths of Christ – 'Quid Hinieldus cum Christo?' (What has Ingeld [see *Beowulf*] to do with Christ?) – certainly states one orthodox Christian attitude to vernacular poetry of pagan origins. But equally well known to the monks of Lindisfarne, no doubt, was the wide licence afforded by Augustine's judgment upon the Greek and Roman philosophical writers, in a text of the greatest importance to those who study early literature whether in Latin or in the vernacular (*CI*, Bk.II, ch.40, pp.112–13) – an authorization far more influential in all likelihood than the limited mandate given by Pope Gregory to Abbot Mellitus on his departure to join the mission to the English in 601 (*HE*, Bk.I, ch.30). As Augustine said of the Platonists so the monks were entitled to say of their native poets: that 'if [they] have said things by chance that are truthful and conformable to our faith, we must not only have no fear of them, but even appropriate them for our own use from those who are, in a sense, their illegal possessors'. The people of Israel, when they rejected the Egyptian idols and threw off the burden of their bondage to cross the Red Sea towards the Promised Land, did not disdain to take with them the gold and silver of the Egyptians, to put them to a better use, at God's commandment. In the same way, while the 'counterfeit and superstitious notions' of pagan writings must be spurned by Christians aspiring to heaven, any 'liberal instruction more adapted to the service of truth' and 'useful principles about morals' may by all means be plundered from them. 'These are, in a sense, their gold and silver. They themselves did not create them, but excavated them, as it were, from some mines of divine Providence', and all this 'it is also right for us to receive and possess, in order to convert it to a Christian use.' Among many great Christian writers who have thus despoiled the Egyptians, Augustine cites Lactantius – to whom is attributed the poem translated and elaborated by one of the Anglo-Saxons poets as *The Phoenix*. But the example, he repeats, was set by Moses, and 'what happened in the exodus is undoubtedly a figure that signified the present' (see the Old English *Exodus* and its headnotes, and note the treasure-gathering in *Exodus* as well as in *Judith* and *Beowulf*).

Here, then, was a construable legitimization of an *ars poetica* which was, in origin, the vehicle of the ideas and values of a heathen people; and to Cædmon is traditionally attributed the realization that this ancient native craft could be salvaged and converted to Christian uses, at God's commandment.

Teachers of Anglo-Saxon literature are familiar with the disappointment students sometimes express when, having hoped to encounter the pagan, the mythological, that which embodies the stoical Anglo-Saxon warrior-farmer confronting his environment and his foes, they are pressed to acknowledge the Christian motivation and subject-matter of so much Anglo-Saxon poetry. But the teacher may not dissimulate: the search for Anglo-Saxon paganism has led to positions of academic fecklessness, to the disreputable, to the sinister (see, for example, evidence presented in E. G. Stanley, *The Search for Anglo-Saxon Paganism*, Cambridge and Totowa, 1975). Of actively heathen thought very little indeed survives to speak of the structure and content of the creed of Coifi and his antecedents (*HE*, Bk.II, ch.13). Of formulaic wisdom of a more secular kind which derives from the pre-Christian period, rather more probably survives, though it is not easy to identify for want of any other truly comparable corpus of literature by which the supposedly distinctive hallmarks of 'Germanic' tradition might be verified. But the *heroic* aspect of Anglo-Saxon poetry, often taken to be the most characteristic legacy of the Anglo-Saxons' continental Germanic past, is surely not demeaned by its adaptation to Christian purpose. Not inconceivably, the very dynamic of Cædmon's poetic revolution may have been his realization that the traditional heroic mode was in fact little compromised by the constraints of Christian action and sentiment – that, indeed, the heroic idiom may prove a didactic tool in mediating a whole host of Christian concepts, such as that of spiritual warfare.

Whether or not one accepts the presence of any mystical truth in the world view presented by the Christian poetry of the Anglo-Saxons, one could not wish away the enrichment which came with the dowry of the Mediterranean-Christian intellectual tradition – both the older Roman-Hellenic and the newer patristic legacy. This latter body of material – no mere store of scholastic subtleties, but a source of profound influence upon the very way in which reality was perceived and communicated in much of the poetry – was popularized even among the relatively unlearned through *florilegia* (anthologies of sayings from the Fathers of the Church, such as the *Liber Scintillarum*), or through the daily liturgy of the Church, and the prose sermons, often in the vernacular language, which served throughout the Middle Ages to familiarize the illiterate laity with the Scriptures and their interpretation by the Fathers. Repeatedly, when we come to analyse the mode in which an Anglo-Saxon poet has chosen to portray the Christian truths he perceives, we find ourselves dealing with psychological and aesthetic issues fundamental to any theory of the way in which literature, particularly poetry, actually works. The poet's awareness of the psychology of the relationship between narrator and audience, his ability to exploit the human faculty of responding to literary *imitation* of reality as authentically as to the reality itself, and to manipulate the listener's capacity to perceive the symbolic in the literal and to augment out of his own resources that which is expressly stated with that which is implicit, these among others are trained skills which are integral not only (as the Anglo-Saxon poets saw it) to the cultivation of a Christian spiritual response to literature, but also (as we may see it) to the *modus operandi* of the literary art itself, in any period of literary history.

The poetry produced in this Christian tradition has its flaws. We may regret the self-effacing way in which the poets so often settle for expressing themselves in orthodox terms of Christian thought and imagery, or deplore the general obsession with hell and punishment or Cynewulf's Christian antisemitism in *Elene*. But at its frequent best, the poetry has an abiding relevance and what may fairly be called a nobility of purpose. It shows a deep awareness of the integrity and worth of the individual and of organized human society – as well as a humane concern for their tragic frailty. Much of its thought stands, of course, in the mainstream of the western Christian cultural tradition of the Middle Ages – an affinity which, in varying degrees, it shares, fruitfully for the student of ideas and their artistic images, with Anglo-Saxon pictorial and plastic art. But the poetry is not devoid of humour, as the *Judith*-poet's relish in his narrative proves. The riddles show the poets' pleasure in wit, whimsy and ribaldry; and the still-obscure *Wulf and Eadwacer* suggests that the Anglo-Saxon poet was not inhibited from exploring sexual passion, nor indeed was the episcopal donor of the codex (the Exeter Book) inhibited from letting his monks read such things – though, as already indicated, we may believe that there was much more of this blatantly secular poetry which was not so admitted into codices destined for preservation, and which consequently perished.

Accordingly, despite problems of chronology, the study of Anglo-Saxon poetry affords insights into spiritual, intellectual, social and artistic preoccupations of the Anglo-Saxons, and the opportunity to consider their distinctive formulation of issues which are even now of relevance to us, articulated in the language of which we are heirs and in literary forms amenable to our formal literary-critical approaches.

The description of the basic pattern of the Anglo-Saxon verse line – a line divided by a caesura into two sub-units each commonly containing two principal stressed elements (but quite often three) and a varying number of unstressed elements, the whole line being bound together by an alliterative scheme crossing the caesura – belies the complex of poetic effects open to the inventive poet's manipulation.

Within each sub-unit a variety of metrical patterns was attainable, and thus opportunities were created for the poet to give calculated metrical pointing to his main sense-words. The overall metrical shape and weight of the first half-line created a certain range of expectations (in the mind of the audience) for the metrical shape and weight of the second half-line, and in the way in which the poet proceeded to structure his statement while meeting these aesthetic expectations there again lay great scope for inventive *poetic* pointing of the *sense* relationship between these two sub-units. The latitude for creating dynamic correlations of metrical patterning and of sense between the two half-lines was further increased by the alliterative scheme spanning the whole line. Either or both stresses in the *first* sub-unit could partake in the alliterative scheme; but in the *second* sub-unit only the first stress was allowed to do so, and it was required to do so: it was therefore a point of maximum rhetorical significance in the whole line. It was the moment of audible resolution of the alliterative rhyme-scheme; it was a peak of metrical emphasis in the profile of the line; and the competent poet would regularly exploit this dramatic potential by making this 'head-stave' also a key *sense*-word, so that there often occurred in the head-stave a resolution of the metrical, rhyme and sense scheme of the whole construct.

To all this was added the modulation which the caesura could effect, ranging as it did from the slightest notional rest between the half-lines – so that perhaps the alliterating words expressed the continuous accumulation or swift onward progress of narrative elements – to a full syntactic stop, one which might indeed be even more emphasized by the opening of the new sentence, in the second half-line, with words expressing dramatic contrast to those in the first half-line. By this latter device, for example, the poet of *Beowulf* embodies in the *form* of his poem his philosophical belief that sudden reversal of fortune tragically characterizes the human lot. Nor was the complex of effects confined within the boundaries of the single line. It might be extended at the poet's judgment from one line to the next, into a series of lines, into whole verse paragraphs; and the paragraphs themselves, in the best poetry, could stand in significant relationships of rhetorical characteristics and content of meaning – as in the superbly managed shifts of mood and narrative pace in *Beowulf*, or in the popular narrative device of threefold incremental repetition used, for example, in the narration of Grendel's advance upon Heorot in *Beowulf*, and fundamental to the structure of *Guthlac*.

Beyond this technical management of metre, rhyme, sense deployment and rhetorical architectonics lay the poet's art of exploiting the traditional vocabulary and formulaic store of the Old English poetic language – a topic too large to handle here, further than observing that the existence of lexical conventions and norms, while offering the hack poet mechanical salvation, challenged the creative poet with scope for playing off modulations of conventions and norms against the trained expectations of the audience – which is indeed a significant part of the poetic art in almost any age. The richly didactic irony in *Judith*, as a simple example, functions first by stimulation of the audience's conventional response to heroic terminology, before exposure of its incongruity when applied to the raucous Holofernes, and recognition of its worthier application to the supposedly vulnerable woman, Judith. The role of the heroic lexis in *The Dream of the Rood* is altogether more complex and fundamental to the didacticism of that poem.

Of this sophisticated, subtle artistry, in which so often the *form* of the poem is essentially an aspect of its *meaning*, modern English translations whether in prose or in verse can hardly catch a half. For every translation is a tissue of compromises, a partial realization, merely, of some of the achievement of the original, recreated or replicated in new words which capture one thing only by sacrificing another. The translations in this book are constrained by the objective of remaining recognizably close, if not rigidly so, to the syntax and vocabulary of the Old English texts, while trying to avoid the no-man's-language into which translators can easily slip; and since translation into verse, and especially into alliterative verse, imposes dire restriction and compulsion on language, forcing one away from such closeness, these translations are in prose and therefore make no effort systematically to replicate the aural effects of the original, beyond making casual echo of the alliterative manner. They were undertaken with issues of literary history and literary critical interpretation primarily in mind. To this end, manuscript readings have been judged afresh in cases of proposed editorial emendation, and as a general principle translations have been sought which allow the manuscript reading to stand wherever possible.

It has furthermore seemed to accord with these aims that the poems should be located for discussion purposes in their manuscript context, and grouped by codex in this book. This is done partly in order to avoid the false suggestion of a definable evolution in Anglo-Saxon poetry from pagan towards Christian, from early towards late, which can be the result of grouping poems according to subject-matter or speculative dates. But it is also done, more positively, to draw attention to the importance of considering the literary phenomenon of the codex. As much has been included as space would allow of the contents of the Junius manuscript, which is undoubtedly the most coherently organized and thematically integrated of the four main codices. To the Exeter Book too, space has been given as its supreme importance merits; though some of the poems have been omitted from the translation, a brief note marks the position of each one at the proper point in the codex and characterizes the omitted text so that a reasonably complete impression may be conveyed of the whole content and structure of this Anglo-Saxon anthology of poetry. So too in the case of the other codices and remaining individual poems, note has been made, more or less extensively, of the context in which the poetry is recorded.

The codices are, after all, evidence as palpable as any that serves to illuminate the crucial association between the poetry and its patrons. We may *speculate* endlessly, and to some extent usefully, about the likelihood of this poem or that being sung in the market-place, mead-hall or monastery in the eighth century or the ninth or tenth; but in, say, the Exeter Book we have a palpable document, a book presented to an eleventh-century monastery by a bishop, an act of cultural choice, of literary discrimination, an expression of intent and an analysable motive. Whatever life the poems may have enjoyed before they were collected into the codex, we are in most cases allowed to *know* only this fact of their existence, that they are uniquely recorded in this codex and met the purposes of this patron. For each one of the four main codices as for the lesser poetic manuscripts, it is both practical and proper to investigate the organizational principles governing their compilation – a procedure involving examination of the reciprocal relationships of theme, emphasis, imagery, verbal formulations, sometimes of editing in the process of compilation, between the component poems (and prose pieces, in some cases), and the context of the whole collection. The best interpretation of a poem will take into account the implications of its context in the collection, while any attempt to define the organizational principles of a codex must depend partly upon the interpretation given to individual poems.

Thus we may become more clearly aware of the intentions and tastes of that rather small number of codex-compilers who have determined almost all that we are allowed to know of the place of poetry, with its special craft of giving voice to mind and spirit, in the vernacular literary history of the Anglo-Saxons.

Abbreviations

The abbreviated references to poems follow F. P. Magoun Jr., 'Abbreviated titles for the poems of the Anglo-Saxon poetic corpus', *Études Anglaises*, T. viii, 2(1955). (See also the Check-list of Old English Poetry.)

Alm — Alms-giving; And — Andreas; BDS — Bede's Death Song; Brb — Battle of Brunanburh; Bwf — Beowulf; Cæd — Cædmon's Hymn; Chr I — Christ I (Advent Lyrics); Chr II — Christ II (Ascension); Chr III — Christ III (Judgment); Crd — Creed; Dan — Daniel; Deo — Deor; DHl — Descent into Hell; DrR — Dream of the Rood; Ele — Elene; Exo — Exodus; FAp — Fates of the Apostles; Fnb — Battle of Finnsburh; FPs — Fragments of Psalms; FtM — Fortunes of Men; Gen — Genesis; GfM — Gifts of Men; Glc — Guthlac; HbM — Husband's Message; Jud — Judith; Jln — Juliana; LPr III — Lord's Prayer III; MCh — Metrical Charms; Mld — Battle of Maldon; Mxm I — Maxims I; Mxm II — Maxims II; Phx — Phoenix; Pnt — Panther; Rsg — Resignation; Rdl — Riddles; Rui — Ruin; RCr — Ruthwell Cross; Sfr — Seafarer; SlB II — Soul and Body II; Wan — Wanderer; Whl — Whale; Wid — Widsith; WfL — Wife's Lament; Wld — Waldere; WlE — Wulf and Eadwacer; XSt — Christ and Satan.

Bibliography

(a) WORKS CITED

ASPR   *The Anglo-Saxon Poetic Records*: vol.I *The Junius Manuscript*, ed. G. P. Krapp (New York, 1931); vol. II *The Vercelli Book*, ed. G. P. Krapp (New York, 1932); vol.III *The Exeter Book*, ed. G. P. Krapp and E. V. K. Dobbie (New York, 1936); vol.IV *Beowulf and Judith*, ed. E. V. K. Dobbie (New York, 1953); vol.V *The Paris Psalter and The Metres of Boethius*, ed. G. P. Krapp (New York, 1933); vol.VI *The Anglo-Saxon Minor Poems*, ed. E. V. K. Dobbie (New York, 1942).

CG   *Saint Augustine: The City of God*: Bks.I–VII tr. D. B. Zema and G. G. Walsh (Washington, 1950); Bks.VIII–XVI tr. G. G. Walsh and G. Monahan (New York, 1952); Bks.XVII–XXII tr. G. G. Walsh and D. J. Honan (New York, 1954). Vols.VIII, XIV and XXIV respectively in *The Fathers of the Church: a New Translation*.

CI   *Saint Augustine: Christian Instruction*, tr. J. J. Gavigan (New York, 1950). Vol.II in *The Fathers of the Church: a New Translation*.

EHD   *English Historical Documents*, vol.I (500–1042), tr. D. Whitelock (London, 1953).

HE   *Bede's History of the English Church and People*, tr. L. Sherley Price (revised ed., London, 1968).

Ker   *Catalogue of Manuscripts containing Anglo-Saxon*, N. R. Ker (Oxford, 1957); see also 'A supplement to Catalogue etc.', *Anglo-Saxon England 5* (1976).

LSc   *Defensor's Liber Scintillarum*, ed. E. W. Rhodes (London, 1889; repr. 1973).

NCBEL   *New Cambridge Bibliography of English Literature*, vol.I, ed. G. Watson (Cambridge, 1974).

NEB   *The New English Bible with Apocrypha* (Oxford and Cambridge, 1970) from which quotations are taken unless otherwise stated.

PL   *Patrologiæ Cursus Completus . . . Series (Latina) Prima*, ed. J. P. Migne (Paris, 1844–64).

(b) FOR FURTHER REFERENCE

Sources and Analogues of Old English Poetry, tr. M. J. B. Allen and D. G. Calder (Cambridge and Totowa, New Jersey, 1976).

Old English Literature: a Select Bibliography, Fred C. Robinson (Toronto, 1970).

A Bibliography of Publications of Old English Literature to the End of 1972, S. B. Greenfield and F. C. Robinson (Toronto and Manchester, 1980).

International Bibliography of Books and Articles on the Modern Languages and Literatures (New York, 1970 onwards; annual listings of current publications).

Anglo-Saxon England (Cambridge, 1972 onwards; contains annual bibliography of current publications).

(c) FOR FURTHER READING

A Critical History of Old English Literature, S. B. Greenfield (New York, 1965; London, 1966).

A Study of Old English Literature, C. L. Wrenn (London, 1967).

Old English Verse, T. A. Shippey (London, 1972).

The Art and Background of Old English Poetry, Barbara C. Raw (London, 1978).

THREE
EARLY POEMS

Three Early Poems

The dating of OE poems is a notorious problem in AS literary scholarship. The following three poems, however, are of fairly certain antiquity. Two of them have from early times been traditionally and plausibly associated with historical personages of the later seventh and earlier eighth centuries, and one is carved in runes on an artefact generally agreed to belong to the earlier eighth century. The fact that all three are expressly Christian statements witnesses to the infinitely greater chance Christian poetry had over secular poetry of being written down; for literacy, material resources and patronage were from the start the Church's to command.

Cædmon's Hymn

[Cambridge, University Library Kk.5.16, fol.128^b and many other MSS]

The miracle by which Cædmon, an elderly and untutored lay-brother of the religious house at Whitby, mastered the traditional *ars poetica* of vernacular English and so became the first poet to adapt it to Christian subject-matter, is told by Bede (*HE*, Bk.IV, ch.22) as part of his account of the reign of abbess Hilda (657–80). Poetry is claimed as a divine gift in many cultures and ages but there is no good reason to doubt Cædmon's existence, especially as the miracle itself may plausibly be rationalized in terms of the psychology and mechanics of the oral-formulaic mode of composition; though it may be that Cædmon is only the figure-head for a more diffuse experimentalism among contemporary English poets, for Aldhelm (*c*.640–709), according to William of Malmesbury's twelfth-century life of the saint, was winning congregations by similarly singing of Christ in the language and poetry of the Anglo-Saxons. Wherever the innovatory credit is to be placed, the achievement is a momentous one in English literary annals. The ancient vernacular poetry, which might well have been abandoned on account of its unredeemed worldiness or paganism, was successfully sanctified. Indeed, the poets quickly perceived new scope for semantic virtuosity, in exploiting both correspondences and antitheses between Mediterranean-Christian and Germanic-secular concepts and terminology. The way was cleared for centuries of vernacular religious poetry in a direct line of descent.

Though Cædmon composed poems upon Genesis, Exodus and other Old Testament historical books, the gospels and the apostles' teachings, the Last Judgment, heaven and hell and the blessings and judgments of God, none of his work is known to survive except this traditionally ascribed fragment, associated with Bede's narrative where it is represented as the first lines of Christian poetry ever to be composed in the English language.

Now we must laud the heaven-kingdom's Keeper, the Ordainer's might and his mind's intent, the work of the Father of glory: in that he, the Lord everlasting, appointed of each wondrous thing the beginning; he, holy Creator, at the first created heaven for a roof to the children of men; he, mankind's Keeper, Lord everlasting, almighty Ruler, afterwards fashioned for mortals the middle-earth, the world.

Cædmon first sang this song.

The Ruthwell Cross Inscription

[Ruthwell Church, Dumfries]

Whether or not this was the primary purpose of the Ruthwell Cross, it possessed through its location, its shape, its iconographic programme and its inscriptions the power to assert to the meditative beholder in the wilderness of undominated nature and of heathenism the contemporary or suprachronological efficacy of Christ's historical triumph over Satan and death in the desert and upon the Cross – that victorious struggle with the devil in the wilderness which the saints' lives (such as *Glc*) repeat over the ensuing generations. The artefact is in material terms an imitation of the true historic Cross, but the artist goes so far in encouraging a metaphysical identification between the two as to give this stone imitation the personality and the voice itself of the true Cross – needing only a reader of runes to articulate it. The runic verse inscription which shares in this dynamic and didactic relationship between reality and imitation and between word and image apparently belongs with the Cross in the century following Edwin's conversion to Christianity in 627. There has been time for synthesis. The topic of the verses is Mediterranean-Christian; their vernacular language, poetic idiom, metre, alliteration and runic letter-forms belong to the Germanic heritage of Anglian Northumbria. Deliberate damage to the Cross and weathering account for the incompleteness of the text, which nonetheless shows a very close affinity to lines used later in *DrR* (39–64).

He stripped himself there, God almighty, when he willed to climb the gallows, bloody in front of all the people. I did not dare to give way. . .

5   I raised up the powerful King, the Lord of heaven. I did not dare to topple. They humiliated us both together. I was soaked with blood, poured forth. . .

10   Christ was on the Cross. But diligent and noble men came there from afar to the lonely one. All this I witnessed. I was sorely oppressed by anxieties, nonetheless I bowed. . .

15   . . . wounded by sharp points. They laid down the man weary of limb. They stood at his body's head. There they gazed upon the Lord of heaven. . .

Bede's Death-song

[Switzerland, St Gallen Stiftsbibliothek 254 and many other MSS]

The letter *Epistola Cuthberti de obitu Bedae* from Cuthbert, pupil of Bede and probably that Cuthbert, abbot of Wearmouth, who called himself 'disciple of the priest Bede' (Letter to bishop Lul, 764, *EHD*, p.765), gives a touching account of Bede's last days which was offered, and doubtless accepted by many succeeding generations, as a true example of saintliness in living and in dying. It was in the final days of his last sickness in 735 that this great scholar of early Christendom, whose competence in Latin poetry is attested by his hymn in honour of Etheldreda (*HE*, Bk.IV, ch.20) and his *De die judicii*, composed this short verse in English; for he was also skilled, as Cuthbert records, in the poesy of his own native language. It is an echo of the theme of his Latin poem on the Day of Judgment, the likely source for *JgD II*. Cuthbert gives only a Latin paraphrase. The earliest MS to include the OE text dates from the ninth century. Twenty-nine MSS of Cuthbert's letter, from every century thereafter through to the sixteenth, contain Bede's OE poem.

Before the inevitable journey no man shall grow more discerning of thought than his need is, by contemplating before his going hence what, good or evil, will be adjudged to his soul after his death-day.

JUNIUS 11

The Junius Manuscript

[Oxford, Bodleian Library, Junius 11 (5123)]

Four different hands are usually identified in the writing of this codex, palaeographically assigned to a short period of time over the turn of the tenth century into the eleventh. *Gen*, *Exo* and *Dan* (together designated Liber I in the MS) are in one hand, the earlier one, while *XSt* (Liber II in the MS) is written in three later hands – so it is not unanimously agreed that this last poem was part of the original design. Furthermore, the poems are divided into sections of varying length, which are marked by large capitals and spacing, and are sporadically numbered. Throughout Liber I the numbering is consecutive, overriding the separate identities of the poems; but Liber II is separately numbered. There are various stylistic and organizational indications such as the obviously composite nature of *Gen* to suggest that the compiler of the book was not the original author of all the poetry in it; indeed it is possible that his function was that of a judicious editor alone – though the continuity of theme and consistency of diction through much of the contents might argue at least for a close-knit school of poets if not for one creatively presiding redactor. As is the case with the poems of the other codices, the dating of the poems, as distinct from that of the MS, must depend mainly upon stylistic assessments which themselves rest upon somewhat arbitrary 'evolutionary' assumptions as to a chronological progress in poetry from early classical correctness to late evolved licence. Great uncertainty must be admitted in this area.

Because of its exclusively poetical content and its thematic devotion to scriptural topics, this codex was long popularly regarded as being part of the corpus of the poet Cædmon who, Bede says, received the gift of poetry directly from God and forthwith set about turning the whole of the sacred history into English poetry. The belief is no longer tenable, for want of any supporting evidence, though critics still find it useful to refer to a Cædmonian school of poetics, in which material from this codex has its place.

In fact, the scriptural poems here are far from being plain translations or paraphrases or merely the abandoned beginnings of a versified Bible. They are free reworkings, designed with greater or lesser thoroughness to intimate the significance of those events in terms of a Christian synthesis of Old and New Testament revelation of God's purpose for man and of man's duty in view of that purpose. This exegetical motive embraces, and is indeed enhanced by the inclusion of, *XSt* – whether or not that poem was part of the original scheme. More precisely, the subject-matter selected for such treatment is broadly that which the Church reflected upon during the liturgical season of Lent. It seems likely indeed that the anthology offered a series of readings appropriate to the needs of a religious community over Lent and Easter. Through all the poems run sustained themes, topics and imagery, often in polarized pairs, such as those of the covenant with God and the tyranny of evil, righteousness and unrighteousness, exile and the homeward journey, the earthly city and the heavenly, light and darkness, water and fire – all of which recur, sometimes more allusively, in other OE poems. In these respects, the Junius codex may be judged the most clearly unified and planned of the four principal books of AS poetry. It also contains, particularly in the Fall of the Angels section of *Gen* and in *Exo*, some of the most qualitatively impressive and intellectually strenuous poetry in the AS corpus.

What conspicuously distinguishes Junius 11 is the large number of fine ink drawings in a programme of illustrations, unfortunately not completed. Their presence as part of the didactic function of the book, their composition and pictorial imagery relative to the rhetorical structure and verbal imagery of the episodes they match, prompt important issues within the whole field of responses between art and literature in AS England.

Genesis

[Oxford, Bodleian Library, Junius 11, pp.1–142]

There are generally held to be at least two originally separate poems in *Gen*. Lines 1–234 and 852–2935, often called *Genesis A* or *The Earlier Genesis*, differ markedly in style from lines 235–851 and are usually dated, on somewhat tenuous grounds, as early as the beginning of the eighth century. Licence to seek rhetorical effect beyond the austere metrical constraint of *Gen A* distinguishes the style of lines 235–851 which, with their self-contained account of the fall of the angels and the fall of man, have often been handled as a separate poem, *Gen B* or *The Later Genesis*, dated speculatively in the mid-ninth century. Characteristics of metre and vocabulary seem to confirm that *Gen B* is translated from an Old Saxon original – of which, indeed, a portion (corresponding to lines 791–817 of the OE poem) survives, composed in a region which was converted to Christianity by AS missionaries in the eighth century. But despite its composite structure, the poem is offered by the compiler of the codex as a coherent and consecutive work; a work conceived not as a mere vernacular translation of the scriptural narratives, nor only as a rhetorical elaboration upon them, but as an exegetical survey of the history of that love of God for mankind which ennobles man and transcends the justified wrath that human nature has at times incurred. Nowithstanding its exclusive address to the Old Testament texts (augmented by the apocryphal matter of the fall of the angels), the poem is distinctly Messianic in its careful delineation of the recurring model of the man found righteous, for whose sake God refrains from abandoning mankind to destruction. The Messianic theme of righteousness is of course explicit in the Old Testament, especially in the prophets Amos, Isaiah, Hoseah and Micah, and is fundamental to the orthodox Christian reading of the Old Testament; and this was signalized from early times in the Church's lectionary – the programme of scriptural texts appointed to be read at divine service. There the narratives of the fall of man, of the first murder, of the subsequent division of humanity into the righteous and the wilfully unrighteous, and of the patriarchs who led the people of the covenant towards righteousness – which are the subject of much of the poetry in Junius 11 – are covered in the weeks leading from Septuagesima up to Easter. It has therefore been plausibly suggested that the codex was compiled to serve as a lectionary in the vernacular for the less formal environment of the refectory of a religious house. In this view, the single New Testament poem in the codex, *XSt*, dealing directly as it does with the Messiah and having primary relevance to the liturgical seasons of Lent and Easter, appropriately affirms the consummation in divine love of the human faith and hope of *Gen*. Thus understand, the OE *Gen* also has its value as a context to which the *Bwf*-poet's assertion of his hero's righteousness and his references to Cain, Abel, the Flood and the giants may be referred for a fuller understanding of their suggestiveness to an AS Christian audience.

The postulation that Milton may have discussed the poem with his acquaintance Junius, the one-time owner of the manuscript, is not necessary to account for broad similarities between parts of *Gen* and of *Paradise Lost*. Both poets, as a direct consequence of opting for an epic heroic genre, risk counterproductively investing the rebel angel with an admirable dignity and heroic appeal which are inherent in the traditional diction and manner of the genre. But surely neither poet fails to control the hazard. Though individual speeches of the AS Lucifer may ring with Beowulf's courage and Byrhtnoth's defiance, they are set off in context by implicit and explicit statements of the Satanic presumption, blasphemy and malicious treachery involved; and the juxtaposition of the story of the fall of man is calculated to force an audience to recognize that they are themselves the direct and continuing victims of this evil. The nature of evil is proved unequivocally to be darkness and self-delusion such as the *Bwf*-poet assigns to Grendel, the dark death-shadow, and such as the composer of the *Mxm* knows to be the proverbial distinction between the guilty man and the innocent who belongs in the light. Conversely, much sympathy is shown for man who, though he must take responsibility for his free choosing, was foully deceived by Satan. This humane warmth of fellow-sympathy for man culminates in the moving scenes of the harrowing of hell in *XSt*. Many themes later to be developed in medieval poetry are first explored in English in this richly complex work.

LIBER I

I

A great duty is ours: that we should praise with our words and love with our hearts the Guardian of the heavens, the glorious King of hosts. He is plenitude of powers, sovereign of all his sublime creations, the Lord almighty. Of him was never beginning nor origin nor will there come hereafter an end to the everlasting Lord but he will ever remain mighty above the thrones of heaven.

8   With powers sublime, steadfast in truth and abounding in plenty, he ruled the plains of heaven which were established in their width and breadth by God's command for the children of glory, the guardians of souls. Joyfulness and happiness they had, those angel hosts, and sheer bliss in their begetter; great bounty was theirs. Majestic servants, they lauded their Prince and willingly spoke his praise and glorified their Lord of life; greatly were they blessed with the benefits of the Lord God. They had no knowledge of the commission of sins and of crimes, but they lived eternally in peace with their Prince.

20   In the heavens they exalted nothing else but right and truth – until the chief of the angels strayed through pride into perversity. No longer were they willing to pursue their own best interest, but they turned aside from God's loving friendship. They had the great arrogance to boast that they could partition with God that mansion, glorious in the majesty of the multitude, broad and ethereally bright: thereupon the wound took effect in them, the envy and the presumption and the pride of that angel who first forwarded, contrived and encouraged that folly when, thirsting for trouble, he outspokenly declared that he meant to have a home and a throne in the northern part of the kingdom of heaven.

34   Then God grew angry and irate against the multitude whom he had previously dignified with beauty and splendour. He fashioned for the renegade a home – one in exile – as reward for his effort: the howlings of hell and harsh afflictions. That outcasts' prison, deep and cheerless, our Lord commanded the guardians of souls to suffer when he knew it to be ready, enveloped in endless night, filled with torment, inundated with fire and intense cold, smoke and ruddy flame. He then commanded the punitive horrors to multiply throughout that desolate abode. Unrelentingly they had mustered a league of enmity against God, for which an unrelenting reward befell them.

47   Violent of mood, they declared that they meant to have a kingdom and that they could easily do so. This hope played

them false when the Ruler, the high King of the heavens, raised up his most sublime hands against that army. They were not competent, those rash and wicked beings, to share power with the ordaining Lord, but glorious God put a stop to their pride and humbled their bombast. One he was angered he balked the evil-doers of victory and of rule, of dignity and of wealth, and he despoiled the foe of happiness, of peace and of all pleasure and of shining glory, and by the powers of his own self he vigorously avenged his injury upon his adversaries by forcible dispossession. He had a stern heart, unrelentingly provoked; with hostile hands he snatched up his enemies and crushed them in his grasp, irate in his heart, and cut off his adversaries from their native home, from the heavenly mansions.

65   So our Creator thrust out and cut off the presumptuous clan of angels from the heavens, a traitorous throng. The Ruler dispatched the rebellious army, those miserable spirits, upon a long journey. Their bragging was broken, their boasting shattered, their splendour humbled and their beauty blotted. Thereafter they languished dismally in distress; no cause they had to laugh loud at the escapade, for they were living damned in the tortures of hell and experiencing affliction, pain and grief and they suffered torment, muffled in darkness, and strict retribution, because they had striven against God.

78   Then as before there was true concord in the heavens, the pleasant virtues of peace, and the Lord loved by all, the King by his servants. The splendours increased of the hosts enjoying happiness with the Lord.

II

82   They were in accord then, those who should inhabit the sky, the celestial homeland. Strife had ceased and enmity among the angels and martial hostility after the warmongers left heaven, deprived of the light. In their wake there stood abroad in God's kingdom thrones abounding in heavenly riches, increasing in endowments, resplendent and prosperous, lacking incumbents

ever since the damned spirits abjectly departed to their place of punishment in hell-dungeon.

92   Then our Lord meditated in his mind how he might resettle that glorious creation, its dwelling-places and its thrones ethereally bright, with a better company since the braggart wreckers had abandoned them high in the heavens. Therefore holy God with his mighty powers willed that under the ambit of the skies should be established for him an earth and a sky and a broad ocean, a created world in compensation for those revolted aggressors whom he sent out of his protection.

103   Nothing but darkness was as yet come into being here, but this wide abyss stood deep and dim, remote from the Lord, desolate and fallow. Purposive of spirit, the King looked upon it with his eyes and surveyed the cheerless place and saw the dark murk lowering in endless night, black beneath the skies, gloomy and waste until this created world came into being by the word of the King of glory. Here the everlasting Lord, Protector of all beings, the Lord almighty, first created heaven and earth, raised aloft the sky and founded this spacious land by his mighty powers.

116   The ground was not as yet green with grass. Dark endless night far and wide muffled the ocean and its gloomy waves. Then the celestially shining Spirit of heaven's Keeper was very quickly extended over the deep. The ordaining Lord of the angels, the Giver of life, commanded light to issue forth across the vast abyss. Swiftly the high King's bidding was fulfilled; there was holy light for him throughout the void as the Maker decreed.

126   When the Arbiter over victorious achievements divided the light from the darkness, the shadow from the radiance, above the watery flood, then the Giver of life shaped names for them both. By the Lord's behest was light, that bright and beautiful creation, first named Day. The Lord was well pleased with that fruitful period at the beginning, the first day. He saw the dark shadow vanish black across the vast abyss.

III

135   When this period went slipping by above the framework of middle-earth, after the sheer radiance the ordaining Lord our Creator set in motion the first evening. In its wake hastened and advanced the gloom of darkness for which the Prince himself shaped the name Night. Our Saviour divided them; ever afterwards they have fulfilled and performed the will of the Lord unceasingly upon the earth.

143   Then came the second day, light after darkness. Then the Protector of life commanded that there be in the midst of the flood the auspicious framework of the sky. Our Ruler divided the oceans and then built the firmament of the sky; the mighty Lord omnipotent by his own word raised it up from the earth. The flood below the empyrean was divided by his holy powers, that water from those waters which still remain beneath the firmament of the roof of mortals.

154   Then over the earth advancing eagerly came the third glorious morning. As yet neither wide lands nor waves were profitable to the Lord but the earth stood constantly covered by the flood. The Lord of angels commanded by his word that the waters should be joined in one, which now keep their course beneath the skies, confined in their place. Then the broad ocean beneath the heavens swiftly stood gathered together; then the sea was divided from the land. So the Guardian Lord of life, the Shepherd of the angelic multitudes, observed a dry place – far and wide it appeared – which he named Earth. He defined to the waves and to the spacious ocean their proper compass and confined. . .

At this point, between the pages now numbered 8 and 9 in the MS, there is an obvious break in the narrative. Three MS leaves may be missing which may have contained as much as 200 lines of verse. In the lost ending to the poem's third section the poet presumably completed the account of the seven days of creation, and he may have reserved the account of man's creation for the lost opening of the fourth section. It is noteworthy, though, that the text as it stands seems to conflate the two alternative accounts of man's creation in Genesis 1 and 2, with the prime result of establishing that Eve has already been made from Adam's rib, and is thus present to hear the charge at first hand, when God forbids man to eat from the tree of the knowledge of good and evil.

IV

169   ... It did not seem apt then to the Guardian of the skies that Adam should long remain the lonely tender and keeper of Paradise, the new creation. Therefore the high King, the almighty Lord, ordained for him help; the Author of light and of life brought woman into being and bestowed this helpmate upon the cherished man. The substance he removed from Adam's body and skilfully he drew from his side a rib. He was deep in repose and quietly slept; he felt no pain and not a scrap of discomfort, nor did there come any blood from the wound, but the Ruler of angels drew from his body the living bone – the man being unhurt – from which God wrought a lovely woman. He instilled in her life and an immortal soul. They were comparable with the angels once Eve, bride of Adam, was furnished with a spirit. In youthfulness they both were born, radiantly beautiful, into the world by the ordaining Lord's might. They knew nothing of committing or practising evil but in the bosoms of them both was a burning love of the Lord.

192   Then the benign-hearted King, the ordaining Lord of all his creatures, blessed those first two of humankind, the father and the mother, the female and the male. He spoke these words:

196   'Be fruitful now and increase and fill the all-verdant earth with your offspring, your family, with sons and with daughters. The salt water shall abide under your dominion, and all the worldly creation. Enjoy days of harvest and sea's repletion and the birds of heaven. Into your dominion are the cattle consecrated and the wild beasts given and the living things which tread the land and the life-endowed species that swim the ocean along the whale's track. All belong to you.'

206   Then our Creator looked upon the bounty of his fruits, and
of his fresh creations. Goodly and hospitable, Paradise stood
filled with the everlasting benefits of his favours. Running
water, a welling spring, pleasantly irrigated the gentle land-
scape. Not as yet did dark clouds carry with the wind rain-
storms across the spacious plain, but the ground stood covered
with crops. Four noble rivers kept their onward course from
out of the new Paradise. They had been separated by the
powers of the Lord, when he shaped this earth, all from the one
radiantly beautiful fount and sent forth into the world. People,
folk dwelling on the earth, call that one Pishon which broadly
encircles with gleaming currents the region of land, Havilah. In
that country the people, sons of men, find near and far gold and
the finest precious stones, as books tell us. Then the second
encompasses the land and country of Ethiopia, that vast realm;
the name of it is Gihon. The third is Tigris, the full-flowing river
which runs hard by the kingdom of Asshur. And there is the
fourth, which men throughout many a nation now widely call
Euphrates. . .

*Between the pages now numbered 12 and 13 there occurs in the
narrative another break due, it is assumed, to the loss of at least one
MS leaf. The missing matter was not necessarily extensive for the
biblical verses (Genesis 2: 15–17) relating to man's establishment
in Eden and God's injunction concerning the tree (with which the
poem resumes after the lacuna) follow immediately upon those nam-
ing the four rivers (Genesis 2: 10–14). The essentials of the story are
intact, moreover. That Adam and Eve are now in Eden is obviously
implicit in the following speech and confirmed in the narrative a few
lines later; and God's opening injunction serves aptly as a kind of text
prefacing the fifth section of the poem, which is itself a prelude to the
account of the revolt and revenge of the angels.*

V

235   '. . . but enjoy all the rest. Leave untouched that one tree and
guard yourselves against that fruit. No want will be yours of
needful things.'

237   Then they bowed their heads devoutly to the heaven-King and spoke their thanks for all, for his skills and for those precepts. He left them to inhabit that land and then the holy Lord, the King purposive of spirit, returned to the heavens. The creatures of his making remained together on the ground. They knew nothing of cares to be bemoaned, only that they should for ever fulfil the will of God. They were precious to God while they were willing to keep his holy commandments.

VI [*Genesis B*]

246   The Ruler of all, the holy Lord, by the might of his hand had ordained ten orders of angels in whom he firmly trusted that they would follow in his fealty and work his will since he, the holy Lord, had given them intelligence and shaped them with his hands. So blessedly had he established them, and a certain one he had made so strong and so powerful in his intellect, so much he allowed him to command, the highest after himself in the realm of the heavens, so dazzling had he made him, so winsome was his person in the heavens which came to him from the Lord of the angel multitudes – he was comparable to the incandescent stars – he ought to have done homage to the Lord, he ought to have prized his pleasures in the heavens and he ought to have thanked his Lord for the bounty he had allotted him in that existence: then he would have let him rule it in perpetuity. But he turned it to his own worse purpose: he began to stir up trouble against the supreme Ruler of heaven who sits upon the holy throne.

261   He was dear to our Lord; it could not be concealed from him that his angel began to grow presumptuous, set himself up against his Master, resorted to malicious talk and boasting against him. He would not wait upon God. He declared that his body was radiant and shining, bright and dazzlingly beautiful. He could not find it in his self-esteem to be willing to wait upon God, his Prince, in a status of fealty. To himself it seemed that he had a greater force and strength of fellow-fighters than the holy God could command. Many words of presumption this

angel spoke. He contemplated how, through his sole strength, he might create for himself a more powerful throne, more exalted in the heavens. He declared that his self-esteem persuaded him that he should start building in the west and in the north and fortify the construction. He declared that it seemed to him doubtful that he would remain subordinate to God.

278　'Why must I labour?' he declared. 'There is no need at all for me to have a master. I can work just as many marvels with my hands. I have plenty of power to furnish a goodlier throne, one more exalted in heaven. Why must I wait upon his favour and defer to him in such fealty? I can be a god as well as he. Strong comrades stand by me, heroes hardy of spirit, who will not fail me in the fight. They have chosen me as their master, those confident warriors; with such fellow-fighters one can think out a strategy and with such achieve it. They are my eager friends, loyal in the disposition of their hearts. I can be their master and govern in this realm. So it does not seem to me fitting that I need flatter God at all for any advantage. No longer will I be his subordinate.'

292　When the Ruler of all heard all this, that his angel had promoted a great presumption against his Master and rashly voiced conceited talk against his Lord, then he had to pay for the deed and share in the suffering of this strife, and he had to receive his punishment – the greatest of all torments. So does each man who attempts to strive with iniquity against his Ruler, against the glorious Lord. Then the mighty and supreme Ruler of heaven grew angered and threw him down from the lofty throne. He had won from his Master hate; he had forfeited his favour. The good God was grown hostile to him in his heart, for which cause he would have to go to the abyss of hell's harsh punishment, because he fought against heaven's Ruler. He banished him then from his favour and threw him down into hell, into those deep pits where he turned into a devil, the fiend with all his companions.

306　Then they fell from on high, from out of the heavens, for as long as three nights and days, those angels, from out of the heavens into hell, and the Lord transformed them all into devils. Because they were not willing to esteem his deed and word the almighty God therefore deposited them, thwarted of their triumph, in a worse existence underneath the earth in black hell. There during nights inordinately long they endure, each and every one of those fiends, ever-replenished fire; then with the dawn comes an east wind and frost intensely cold. Fire or piercing cold, they constantly had to endure some harsh wringing torment: it had been created in the first instance for their punishment – their world was changed – and hell was filled with those conflicting elements. From then on, the angels who had previously maintained their allegiance towards God possessed the heights of the heavenly kingdom.

VII [Genesis B]

322   The others, the fiends, lay in the fire, who had once maintained so much strife against their Ruler. They suffer punishment – the hot fierce turbulence in the midst of hell, burning and broad flames and acrid fumes too and smoke and darkness – because they disregarded their duty towards God. Their arrogance and the angel's presumption betrayed them. They had been unwilling to esteem the word of the Ruler of all: they received a heavy punishment. They were then prostrated in the depth of the fire in hot hell for their recklessness and for their presumption. They sought another country: it was devoid of light and was filled with flame and the heavy onslaught of fire. The fiends realized that they had got in exchange an infinitude of punishments through their great boldness and through God's power and most of all through pride.

338   Then spoke the presumptuous king who had once been the most radiant of the angels, the brightest in heaven and loved by his Master, dear to his Lord, until they grew too rash so that because of their arrogance the mighty God himself grew angry at heart. He precipitated him into that torment, down into that death-bed and devised for him a name thereafter. The supreme Lord said that he should ever after be called Satan and he

commanded him to take charge of black hell's abyss, in no way to strive against God.

347   Satan held forth; sorrowing he spoke who in future was to rule hell and have care of the abyss. Once he had been an angel of God, bright in heaven, until his ambition and his presumption most of all deluded him so that he was not willing to respect the word of the Lord of the multitudes. Within him ambition welled about his heart; without was hot and bitter torment. He uttered these words:

356   'This confining place is very unlike that other which once we knew high in the heaven-kingdom and which my Lord granted me – though we were not allowed by the Ruler of all to keep it and to extend our realm. Yet he has not done right in having toppled us into the depth of the fire, into this scorching hell, robbed of our heavenly realm – which he has designated to be peopled with humankind. That to me is the greatest of my griefs, that Adam, who was made out of earth, is to occupy my mighty throne and be in bliss, and we suffer this torment and the pain in this hell. Alas and alack! if I had the use of my hands and could be out of here a single while, be out for one winter's space, then I, with this army –

371   'But bonds of iron encircle me; a halter of chain yokes me. I am powerless, such hard hell fetters have fast laid hold of me. There is a great fire here, above and below. Never have I seen a landscape more hostile. The flame, hot throughout hell, will not die down. Fetters of links, a cruel chain, have impeded my movement, deprived me of my motion. My feet are shackled, my hands tethered. The ways are blocked through these hell-gates so that I cannot escape at all from these trammels. Great bars of tough iron forged in fire surround me and with them God has tethered me by the neck: thus I know that he was aware of my purpose, and this he has also realized, Lord of the multitudes, that it needs must turn out evilly between Adam and me over that realm in heaven if I had the use of my hands.

VIII [*Genesis B*]

389 'But we are now in hell suffering oppressions – they are the darkness and the burning – fierce and fathomless. God himself has swept us into these black mists. Although he cannot charge us with any sin, or that we did him any harm in that country, yet he has cut us off from the light and cast us down into the severest of all punishments. May we not take vengeance for this and pay him back with some harm, because he has cut us off from the light?

395 'Now, he has marked out a middle-earth, where he has made man after his likeness. Through him he means to resettle the realm of the heavens with pure souls. This we must earnestly think upon: that, if ever we can, we should make good our grudge upon Adam and upon his heirs as well and frustrate him of his will in this, if we can at all contrive it.

401 'No longer now shall I myself aspire to that heavenly existence, that blessed state, which he means long to enjoy with the strength of his angels. Never in eternity can we succeed in weakening the resolution of mighty God. Let us then subvert it from the children of men, that heavenly kingdom, now that we cannot have it, and see to it that they forgo his favour, that they transgress against what he has commanded by his word. Then he will grow angry with them in his heart and reject them from his favour. Then they will have to seek out this hell and these grim depths. Then we shall be able to have them as our subordinates, the children of men, in these tight bonds. Let us start now to think about the campaign.

409 'If of old I bestowed princely treasures upon any follower while we were happily situated in that pleasant realm and had control of our thrones, then never at a more welcome time could he pay me back with returns for my liberality, if any one of my followers would now prove agreeable to this – that he might escape out and up and away from this dungeon and had the strength in him so that he could fly with his wings and soar into the sky to where Adam and Eve stand created in the

kingdom of earth, surrounded by riches, and we are cast down here into these deep pits. Now they are much more precious to the Lord and they are allowed to keep for themselves that prosperity and the realm which in fairness we should have in the heavenly kingdom: that benefit is reserved for humankind. It is so agonizing to me in my heart and it irks me in my pride, that they will own to eternity the kingdom of heaven.

427 'If any one of you can somehow bring it about that they repudiate the words and precepts of God they will straightway become more repugnant to him. If they violate his prerogative then he will grow enraged with them; then that prosperous state will be reversed for them and punishment, some cruel penalty, will be prepared for them. All of you give thought to this, how you can betray them. Then I can rest easily in these shackles if that realm is lost to them.

435 'For the one who achieves that, will ever afterwards be at the ready the reward of such profits as we inside here can in future obtain within this fire.

IX [Genesis B]

438 'Him I shall allow to sit by my own self, whosoever shall enter this scorching hell to say that they have contemptuously repudiated in words and deeds the precepts of the heaven-King.'

The sentence ending p.22 of the MS lacks a verb (guessed at in 'repudiated') and shows metrical insufficiency; and, as p.23 begins with a new sentence which, according to the system of sectional division, ought to be section XI, it is certain that something is missing here from an originally longer text. A simple explanation is that some leaves, including the whole of section X, have been lost from the MS since it was made. However, the jump in the narrative as it now stands is not so drastic as to cause an audience any perplexity: it is immediately clear on p.23 that the 'adversary of God' has come forward in response to the promise made by Satan in the opening of section IX on p.22. In fact, Satan's promise makes an apt thematic

preface to the action which immediately follows it in the present text.
Upon this evidence, then, it could as well be argued that the compiler
of the MS himself deliberately shortened the original narrative,
perhaps in the very process of copying it into his own MS, and that
nothing has been inadvertently lost beyond a few words.

XI [Genesis B]

442 Then an adversary of God eager in his accoutrements got
himself ready: he had an evil sense of purpose. He set on his
head a concealing helm and fastened it very tightly and secured
it with clasps. He had in him knowledge of plenty of speeches
of perverse words. From there he wound his way upwards and
passed through the gates of hell – he had a strong sense of
purpose – and hovered aloft, malevolent-minded. He beat
down the fire on both sides with his fiend's strength: he meant
surreptitiously to seduce, to lead astray and to pervert with
wicked deeds the followers of the Lord, men, so that they
would become repugnant to God.

453 He journeyed on then with his fiend's strength until in the
kingdom of earth he came upon the perfected Adam, God's
wisely created handiwork, and his wife also, a most beautiful
woman, so that they could accomplish much good whom
mankind's ordaining Lord himself had appointed as his subor-
dinates.

460 And near them stood two trees which were laden with a crop
and covered with fruit according as God the Ruler, the high
King of heaven, had planted them with his hands in order that
thereby the children of men, each person, might choose be-
tween good and evil, well-being and woe. Their fruit was not
alike. The one was so pleasant, beautiful and radiant, graceful
and admirable – that was the tree of life. He would be allowed
thereafter to live on and to exist in the world in eternity who ate
of that fruit, so that age did not harm him after that nor severe
sickness, but he would be allowed from then on always to live
among pleasures and to have his existence and the heaven-
King's favour here in the world and to have as his pledge

assured honours in that high heaven when he should journey there. Then there was the other, entirely black, obscure and dark — that was the tree of death which brought forth much bitterness. Each man soever that tasted of what grew on that tree must needs become aware of the two things, the divergent ways of good and of evil in this world, and thereafter he would have to live by his sweat and in sorrows, forever under punishment. Old age must needs rob him of valorous deeds, of pleasures and of authority, and death be decreed him. For a little while he would enjoy his life and then go to the darkest of realms, into the fire, and would have to minister to fiends there where there will exist for an infinite duration the greatest of all perils for men. That the malignant creature, the devil's secret messenger who was contending against God, well knew.

491   He turned himself then into the form of a snake and then wound himself about the tree of death with the cunning of a devil; there he plucked a fruit and went thence back again to where he perceived the heaven-King's handiwork. Then in his first utterance the malignant creature began to question him with lies:

496   'Do you long for anything, Adam, from God above? I have journeyed here from far away on his business; it was not long since that I sat by his very self. He then commanded me to go on this mission. He commanded that you should eat of this fruit and he declared that your strength and skill and your mind would grow greater, and your body much more beautiful, your limbs more handsome, and he declared that to you there would prove no want of any wealth in the world. You have now done the will of the heaven-King and your loyal duty to him and served your Master to his satisfaction and you have made yourself precious to the Lord. I heard him in his splendour praise your deeds and your words and speak about your way of life. Accordingly, you are to carry out what his messengers bring word of here into this country. Broad are the green regions in the world and God, the Ruler of all, sits above in the most exalted realm of the heavens. The Lord of men is unwill-

ing himself to have the hardships of travelling on this mission; rather he sends his subordinate to speak with you. Now he has commanded me to teach you by messages cunning skills. Carry out his bidding confidently. Take this fruit into your hand, bite it and taste it. Within your breast you will become untrammelled and your outward form will become the more beautiful. God the Ruler, your Lord, has sent you this help from the heaven-kingdom.'

522   Adam, the self-determined man, standing there on the earth, spoke out:

523   'When I heard the triumphant Lord, mighty God, speak with stern voice, and when he commanded me to establish myself here and to keep his behests and gave me this wife, this lovely woman, and commanded me take heed that I should not be brought to ruin or utterly betrayed over that tree of death, he declared that he would have to inhabit black hell who of his own volition did anything evil. I do not know whether you come with lies from a hidden motive or whether you are the messenger of the Lord from heaven. You see, I cannot make any sense of your suggestions, of your words and reasons, your mission and declarations. I do know what he, our Saviour, himself enjoined upon me when I saw him last: he commanded me to honour and keep well his word and carry out his precepts. You are not like any of his angels whom I saw before, nor have you shown me any token that my Master has sent to me out of his favour and out of his grace. Therefore I cannot obey you, and you may go your way. I have a firm trust above in the almighty God who fashioned me here with his arms and with his hands. He is capable of endowing me with every advantage from his high kingdom, even if he did not send his subordinate.'

XII [*Genesis B*]

547   He turned himself, the malevolent creature, to where in earth's domain he saw the woman Eve standing, beautifully

formed; and he declared to her that it would prove the greatest harm in the world to all their children thereafter:

551   'I am certain that the Lord God will be incensed against the two of you when I return from this journey along the lengthy road if I personally tell him this message, that you two do not properly act upon whatever message he sends here from the east on this occasion. Now he himself will have to make the journey, according to your answer. His spokesman is not allowed to speak his business, therefore I am certain that in his heart he, the mighty God, is going to be incensed against you. But if you, a compliant woman, will listen to my words then you will be able to think circumspectly about a remedy for it. Consider in your heart that you can fend off punishment from the pair of you, as I shall show you.

564   'Eat of this fruit. Then your eyes will become so clear that you will afterwards be able to see as widely as beyond the whole world and the throne of your Master himself, and henceforth to enjoy his favour. You will be able moreover to manipulate Adam if you command his desire and he trusts in your words. If you tell him truly what an exemplary precept you yourself hold in your bosom, because you have carried out God's bidding and counsel, he will abandon in his heart this distasteful antagonism and his ill response, if we two both talk to him with effect. Coax him carefully so that he carries out your counsel, lest you should both be forced to prove abhorrent to God your Ruler.

578   'If you achieve that design, most excellent lady, I will conceal from your Master that Adam spoke so much insult and so many contemptible words to me. He accuses me of lies and says that I am a messenger intent upon malicious and hostile things, and not an angel of God. But I know the whole race of angels and the lofty roofs of the heavens so well, so long has been the time I have eagerly served God, my Master, the Lord himself, with loyal resolution. I am not like a devil.'

588   So he led her on with lies and by cunning coaxed on the woman in that mischief until the snake's thinking began to seethe up inside her – the ordaining Lord had defined for her a frailer resolution – so that she began to let her mind go along with those counsels. Therefore she received from the abhorrent foe, against the word of the Lord, the tree of death's injurious fruit. A deed more evil was not defined for men. It is a great wonder that eternal God, the Prince, would ever tolerate it that so many a servant should be led astray by lies as happened because of those counsels.

599   She ate of the fruit then and violated the word and the will of the Ruler of all. Then through the gift of the abhorrent foe who betrayed her with lies and subtly defrauded her, which came to her because of his doings, she was enabled to see far afield so that heaven and earth seemed brighter to her and all this world more beautiful and God's work great and mighty – although she did not view it by means of a human perception, but the destroyer who had lent her the vision assiduously deluded her in her spirit so that she could gaze so widely over the heavenly domain.

609   Then the apostate spoke out of his malevolence; he did not teach her anything at all of profit:

611   'Now you can see for yourself, so I do not need to tell you it, virtuous Eve, that appearances and forms are different since you trusted in my words and carried out my counsels. Now light shines out before you and gracious radiance towards you which I have brought from God, gleaming from out of the heavens. Now you can lay hold on it. Tell Adam what powers of vision you possess through my coming. If even now he carries out my counsels in modest manner, then I shall give him abundance of this light with which, so virtuous, I have adorned you. I shall not reproach him for those blasphemies, even though he is not worthy of being excused for he expressed much that was abhorrent to me.'

623 So must her children live in their turn: when they do some-
thing abhorrent they must achieve an amicable settlement,
make good the blaspheming of their Master and enjoy his
favour from then on.

626 To Adam then she went, the most lovely of women, the most
beautiful of wives that might come into the world, because she
was the work of the hand of the heaven-King, even though she
had then been subtly corrupted and led astray by lies so that
they were to prove abhorrent to God through the enemy's
scheming and were to lose the esteem and favour of their
Master through the devil's devices and to forfeit the kingdom
of heaven for many a season. Misery replete will befall the man
who does not keep on his guard while he enjoys self-
determination.

636 One unblessed apple she carried in her hand, one lay at her
heart, the fruit of the tree of death which the Lord of lords had
previously forbidden her; and the Prince of glory had uttered
this pronouncement, that men, his servants, lay under no
necessity of suffering that great death, but he, the holy Lord,
granted to each one of his people the kingdom of heaven and
copious wealth if they would let be that one fruit which the
abhorrent tree bore on its boughs, filled with bitterness: it was
death's tree which the Lord forbade them. Her, then, and the
mentality of Eve, the frail mind of woman, he seduced who was
hostile to God and in hatred of the heaven-King, so that she
believed in his words, carried out his counsels, and accepted in
trust that he had brought those precepts from God which he so
carefully communicated to her in his words and showed her a
sign and gave assurance of his good faith and honest intent.
Then she spoke to her master:

655 'Adam, my lord, this fruit is so sweet and delectable in my
breast, and this handsome messenger is God's good angel: I see
by his apparel that he is the envoy of our Master, the King of
heaven. His favour is better for us to win than his enmity. If you
spoke anything hurtful to him today he will nevertheless for-

give it, if we two are willing to pay him deference. What will it avail you, such detestable quarrelling with your Master's messenger? We need his favour. He can intercede for us with the Ruler of all, the King of heaven. I can see from here where he himself is sitting – it is to the south-east – surrounded with wealth, who shaped the world. I see his angels moving about him on their wings, the hugest of all throngs, of multitudes the most joyous. Who could give me such discernment if God, the Ruler of heaven, had not sent it directly to me? I can hear amply and see so widely into all the world and beyond this spacious creation, I can hear the ethereal merriment in the heavens. My mind has become enlightened within and without since I ate the fruit. I have some of it here in my hands now, virtuous master. I give it to you gladly. I believe that it has come from God, brought by his command – so this messenger has told me with truthful words. It is like nothing else on earth except that, as this envoy says, it has come directly from God.'

XIII [Genesis B]

684   She talked to him repeatedly and coaxed him the whole day towards the dismal act, that they should violate their Lord's will. The malignant messenger stayed; he foisted desires upon them, enticed them with cunning and audaciously dogged them. The fiend remained very close, who had travelled on the audacious journey along the lengthy road: he meant to make man fall into that great and mortal sin, to misguide people and lead them astray so that they should forgo God's benefaction, the Almighty's gift, possession of the kingdom of heaven. Indeed, the hellish mischief-maker well knew that they must be subject to God's wrath and imprisonment in hell and of necessity undergo that forcible oppression once they had broken God's command, when with lying words he misguided the lovely woman, the most beautiful of wives, into that indiscretion, so that she spoke under his will and became as an instrument to him in misguiding God's handiwork.

704   She talked quite often to Adam, then, this most lovely of women, until the man's mind was changed, so that he put his

trust in the promise which the woman expressed to him in her words. Yet she did it out of loyal intent. She did not know that there were to follow so many hurts and terrible torments for humankind because she took to heart what she heard in the counsellings of that abhorrent messenger; but rather she thought that she was gaining the favour of the heavenly King with those words which she presented to the man as a sign, and gave assurance of her good faith until within his breast Adam's determination wavered and his heart began to incline towards her desire. From the woman he accepted hell and departure hence, though it was not so called, but had the name of fruit. Yet it was the sleep of death and the yoke of the devil, hell and death, and the perdition of men, the murder of mankind, that unholy fruit which they took as their food.

723   As it entered within him and touched him at the heart, then the cruel-minded messenger laughed and skipped and declared thanks to his master for the two things:

726   'Now I have deserved your certain favour towards me and fulfilled your desire for very many a day. The human beings, Adam and Eve, are led astray. The Ruler's disfavour towards them is certain now that they have forsaken his spoken word and his counsel. No longer therefore will they be allowed to inhabit the heavenly kingdom but they will have to go on the dark journey to hell. So you need not endure the misery of it in your bosom, where you lie enchained, nor grieve in your mind that here men are occupying the high heaven yet we are presently suffering pains and misery and a land of darkness and many, through your great pride, have forfeited lofty edifices and pleasant courts in the heavenly kingdom. God grew angry with us because in heaven we were not willing to bow our heads to him, the holy Lord, in subordination; but it was not acceptable to us that we should minister to him in vassalage. The Ruler therefore grew furious in mind with us, cruel of purpose, and drove us into hell, toppled the hugest of throngs into the fire and with his hands restored again the celestial

thrones in the kingdom of heaven and granted that realm to mankind.

750 'Your heart can be happy in your bosom, for both things are here accomplished: both that the sons of men, humanity, must forfeit the kingdom of heaven and pass scorching into the flame, to you; and also an injury, a heartfelt grief, is done to God. Whatever torment we suffer here it is now all recompensed in Adam, with his Master's hatred and with the perdition of men and, in human beings, with the pain of mortality. My mind is therefore healed, the broodings about my heart are voided; all our injuries are avenged in respect of the odium that we have long endured. I will go back now towards the fire and there I will seek out Satan – he is shackled in black hell with a yoke of chains.'

762 The most cruel of messengers once more departed downwards. He meant to make his way to the broad flames, those canopies of hell, where his master lay bound in chains.

765 The couple, Adam and Eve, were both suffering remorse, and between them anxious words often passed. They dreaded the punishment of God their Master and greatly feared the hostility of the King of heaven. They realized themselves that his word had been transgressed. The woman grieved and lamented, repentant at heart – she had forfeited the favour and counsel of God – when she saw slip elsewhere away that radiance which he who had prompted them into that calamity, so that they were to receive the affliction of hell and countless humiliations, had by false means shown her as a sign. Therefore heartfelt sorrows smouldered in their breasts.

777 At intervals the wedded pair fell to praying together and addressed the virtuous Lord of victories and called on God, Ruler of heaven, and begged him that they might receive and willingly undergo the penalty for it, since they had broken God's command. They saw their bodies were naked. As yet they did not have fixed dwelling-places in the land and they did

not know anything of the misery of toil, but they could have lived well in that land if they had been willing always to follow God's advice. They spoke many sorrowing words together then, the two consorts.

790   Adam spoke up and said to Eve:

791   'See, Eve; you, by your wickedness, have sealed the destiny of our two selves. Do you now see that dark hell, greedy and voracious? Now you can hear it raging from here. The kingdom of heaven is not like that fire; rather, it is the best of realms, which by the grace of our Master we two could have had if you had not listened to him who prompted us into this offence, that we broke the command of the Ruler, the King of heaven.

799   'Now we have cause to grieve, remorseful, over this destiny, for he himself enjoined us that we should be on our guard against pain, the greatest of afflictions. Now hunger and thirst gnaw me cruelly in my breast, for both of which we were once without a care through all time. How shall we now survive or exist in this land if wind comes here from west or east, south or north? Dark cloud will loom up, a hailstorm will come pelting from the sky and frost will set in along with it, which will be wickedly cold; at times the bright sun will glare and gleam down hotly from the heavens and we stand here naked, unprotected by clothing. There is nothing in front of us as a defence against the storm nor any provision made for food, but mighty God the Ruler is in angry mood towards us. What must become of us now? Now I have cause to regret that I prayed the God of heaven, the virtuous Ruler, that he should fashion you here for me, out of my limbs, now you have led me astray into my Master's hatred. So now I have cause to regret for ever to eternity that I looked upon you with my eyes.'

XIV [*Genesis B* ends at line 851]

821   Then Eve replied, the most lovely of women, most beautiful of wives, for she was God's creation even though she had by then been brought to ruin under the devil's cunning:

824 'You have cause, Adam, my friend and lord, to reproach me for this with your words; and yet it cannot grieve you worse in your mind than it does me in my heart.'

827 Adam then answered her:

828 'If I knew the Lord's pleasure, what I was to receive from him as punishment, even though the God of heaven should command me from now on to journey away upon the sea and travel the main, however horribly deep it were, however vast the ocean, you would never the sooner see that my heart ever questioned it; rather, I would go to the bottom of the sea if I could achieve God's pleasure. Not for me will there be the joy of rendering any service in the world now that I have forfeited the favour of my Prince, so that I may not enjoy it. But by no means can we remain, both of us together, thus naked. Let us go into this forest, into the shelter of this wood.'

840 They turned away, the two of them, and walked sorrowing into the green forest and sat apart to await the provisions of the King of heaven himself, since they could not keep those things which almighty God had previously given them. They then covered their bodies with leaves and dressed themselves with greenery, since they did not have clothes. But they prostrated themselves in prayer, the two of them together, each morning and prayed the mighty God that he, God almighty, should not forget them and that the virtuous Ruler should show them how they were to survive henceforth in that existence.

852 Then the Lord almighty, the glorious Prince, came after the midst of the day to walk in Paradise for his pleasure. Our Redeemer, the merciful Father, wanted to find out what his children were doing: he knew that they were ruined, to whom he had previously given form. Then they went hurrying away under cover of the trees, wretched at heart, stripped of their dignity. They hid themselves in the gloom when they heard the holy voice of the Lord and they were afraid of him. Then at once the Lord of heaven summoned the keeper of the world's

creatures; the powerful Prince commanded his son to come instantly to him. Then the man himself, abject, being in need of apparel, answered him and said:

867   'I am hiding myself here, lacking clothes, my Lord, and covering myself with leaves. My conscience, full of guilt, disturbed, is cruelly oppressive upon my spirit. I dare not come out before your presence. I am completely naked.'

XV

872   Then God quickly answered him:

873   'Tell me, my son, why do you seek obscurity, feeling ashamed? You took from me no sense of shame at first, rather wholly that of joy. Why are you aware of misery and why do you clothe your shame and experience grief and yourself cover up your body with leaves and, abject and wretched in mind, voice the worldly worry that you lack apparel – unless you have eaten an apple from that tree which I forbade you by my words?'

882   Then Adam answered him back:

883   'The woman, the beautiful female, gave the fruit into my hand, my Lord, which, in your despite, I took. Now I carry the clear mark of it upon myself. I am the more aware of miseries.'

887   Then the almighty God questioned Eve about it:

888   'What have you profited, daughter, from the ample splendours and the new-created things of Paradise and its abounding endowments, since you have covetously grasped at the tree, plucked fruit from the tree's branches and eaten that bane in my despite and given to Adam those fruits which were strictly forbidden you by my orders?'

895   Then the beautiful female, the woman, answered him abashed:

897   'The snake tricked me, the glittering serpent with his fair words, and urged me eagerly to that ill-conceived act and to that sin of greed, until I wickedly committed that hasty act of hostility and perpetrated a deed of enmity and robbed the tree in the forest then, which it was not right to do, and ate the fruit.'

903   Then our Saviour, the almighty Lord, decreed for the snake, the guilty serpent, far-flung wanderings, and these words he spoke:

906   'You shall for ever tread, weary in your heart, the bosom of the wide earth and fare footless while life and spirit remain within you. You shall eat dust for the days of your life. Because you evilly instigated discord, the woman shall persecute you and hate you here below the heavens and will tread down your guilty head with her feet. You shall lie in wait of her heels in ever-renewed hostility. There shall be mutual enmity between your offspring and hers as long as ever the world beneath the skies remains. Now, abhorrent enemy of men, you know and understand how you are to live.'

XVI

918   Then to Eve God angrily spoke:

919   'Set yourself aside from happiness: you are to be in the power of the male, strictly constrained by your awe of the man, and to suffer, abject, the error of your actions and to experience death and in sorrow and lamentation to bring forth with great pain sons and daughters into the world.'

925   To Adam also the eternal Lord, the radiant Lord of life, announced unwelcome tidings:

927   'You are to seek out another homeland, a dwelling-place devoid of happiness, and wander in exile, a naked and needy destitute deprived of the privileges of Paradise; divorce of body and soul is ordained for you. See; you have detestably

perpetrated a crime: therefore you shall struggle and provide for your own sustenance upon earth, wear a sweating countenance and eat your own bread as long as you live here, until the disagreeable disease which you yourself once swallowed in the apple grips you hard at the heart – and consequently you shall die.'

939   Listen; now we shall hear where bitter tribulations and the misery of the world were born to us.

941   Heaven's Keeper, our Creator, dressed them with clothes; the Lord commanded them cover their shame with rudimentary apparel and commanded them to depart from Paradise into a more straitened existence. Behind them at the Lord's behest a holy angel with a fiery sword closed the hope-filled home of joys and pleasures, No mortal, wicked and guilty of sin, can pass by there, but the keeper has power and strength who guards for the Lord that glorious existence, precious in its privileges.

952   But the almighty Father did not intend at the first to take away all favours from Adam and Eve, even though they had defected from him, but instead, for their consolation, he allowed to continue in being the dome of the sky adorned with holy stars, and granted to them the spacious bounty of earth. He commanded each of the teeming species of sea and of land to yield their fruits for the couple's worldly use.

961   Following their sin, then, they settled in a land fraught with cares, a country and a homeland less abounding with every advantage than was that original seat from which they had been driven in consequence of their deed.

965   Then at God's behest they started to beget children, as the ordaining Lord had bidden them. Of Adam and Eve were born the first children, two handsome sons, Cain and Abel. Books inform us how those toilers, amicable brothers, augmented their resources, their well-being and their sustenance. The one

zealously provided for himself from the earth: he was the firstborn. The other looked after the livestock in support of his father, until a considerable part of their tally of days was past. Then both of them brought gifts to the Lord. The Ruler of angels, King of all beings, looked with his eyes upon Abel's sacrifice; but Cain's offering he would not view. To the man this was at heart a grievous insult. Indignation surged up in the man's bosom, a livid fury, anger out of envy. Then he did a rash thing with his hands: he killed his kinsman, his brother, and he shed his blood, Cain that of Abel. This earth soaked up the spillage of murder, the blood of man.

987   Evil was exalted, a brood of troubles, in consequence of that murderous stroke. From that seedling subsequently grew — the longer the more vigorously — malignant and violent fruit. The tendrils of that crime reached far and wide throughout the communities of man; its injurious branches lashed the children of men hard and painfully — they still do so — and from them the ample fruits of every kind of atrocity began to burgeon. Not without reason we may lament that history, that deadly grim event, with weeping; for the lovely woman severely harmed us by the first sin which men, the inhabitants of earth, ever committed against the ordaining Lord, after Adam was animated by the breath of God's mouth.

XVII

1002   Then the Lord of heaven asked Cain in converse where in the earth Abel might be. Quickly thereupon the worthless deviser of murder then answered him:

1006   'I do not know the coming and going and the roaming of my kinsman Abel, nor was I my brother's keeper.'

1008   Then the King of angels, the Spirit abounding in virtue, again addressed him:

1010   'Behold; you with your incensed hands have buried in his mortal resting-place a man steadfast in faith, your brother, and his blood calls out and cries to me. For this murder you shall receive punishment and wander in exile, accursed into eternity. The earth will not yield you her fair fruits for your worldly use, for she has soaked up the holy blood of violence from your hands; therefore the green ground will withhold from you its benefits and beauty. Miserable, deprived of grace, you shall depart out of your native land because you became Abel's killer: for that you shall roam far-flung paths, a fugitive, abhorrent to your kinsmen.'

1022   Then Cain replied to him at once:

1023   'I need expect no grace in the world, but I have forfeited your favour, exalted King of the heavens, your love and protection; therefore I must bend my footsteps abroad, in expectation of trouble when someone meets me, the criminal, who, far or near, may remind me of this violence, of this brother-murder. I shed his blood, his gore upon the earth. For this you banish me today from community and expel me from my native land. Some incensed person will become my killer. Being accursed, Lord, I shall pass out of your sight.'

1036   Then the Lord of victories himself answered him:

1037   'You need not as yet fear the terror of death and extinction, although you must go a marked man far from your kinsmen. If any person robs you of life with his hands, a sevenfold vengeance shall come upon him for that sin and punishment following that deed.'

1043   The Ruler, the glorious Ordainer and Lord, set a mark upon him, a sign of immunity, lest some enemy far or near should dare to touch him with hostile violence. Then he ordered the criminal to depart from his mother, his kinsmen and his family.

1049   Cain, then, went wandering away, morbid of mood, out of God's sight, a friendless exile, and afterwards chose for himself a settling-place in lands to the east, a home far from the dwellings of his father, where a noble woman, a lady, according to kind bore him children. The first was called Enoch, the firstborn child of Cain. Later, together with those members of the family, they built a stronghold, a city – this was the first beneath the skies of all the walled strongholds that sword-bearing princes have ordered to be founded.

The poet, following a tradition which takes considerable liberties with scriptural narrative, is now set upon polarizing the kin of Cain and the kin of Seth (Abel's replacement). By distinguishing two name-forms, Lameh and Lamech, he rationalizes the inconsistency of the biblical genealogies (which assign the single figure of Lamech to the lineage of both Cain and Seth) and makes Lameh not merely the murderer he is in the Scriptures, but the slayer of his own near kinsman, Cain. Lameh, then, compounds Cain's crime, violating the earth, as Cain did, by spilling upon it human blood; while Lamech, born of the lineage of Seth, is represented as a good ruler of his people and becomes the father of the righteous man, Noah. (Lines 1061–1245.)

XX

1245   As yet the family of Seth, the cherished lord of his people, remained very much within the Lord's love, dear to him and blessed with good repute – until the children of God began to seek brides among the kin of Cain, that accursed race, in defiance of God's consent, and there the sons of men chose themselves wives, beautiful and fair women, from among those guilt-ridden people.

1253   Then the Ruler of the skies spoke, angry with humankind, and said these words:

1255   'The tribe of Cain have not gone from my mind free men, for that family has sorely enraged me. Now the children of Seth renew the anger in me and are taking to themselves women as their mates from among my foes; there the beauty of females, the appearance of the women, and the eternal fiend have malevolently insinuated themselves into the nation of men who were previously in concord.'

1263   After one hundred and twenty years in the world, told by tally, acts of vengeance afflicted the doomed people when the Lord willed to impose a punishment upon the renegades and to strike down in death those guilty in their actions, the giant sons displeasing to God, the huge wicked wreckers, abhorrent to the Lord.

1270   Then the Wielder of victories saw for himself what human wickedness there was in the earth, and that they were shameless in their sins and full of evil. He resolved hideously to avenge this upon the nations of men and grimly and painfully to overwhelm humanity with his harsh powers. He very much repented that he, the Paragon of princes, had stirred to life the firstborn of the nations when he created Adam; and he declared that because of men's sins he would destroy everything that was upon the earth and exterminate every body which enfolded in its bosom the spirit of life. All this the Lord intended to kill in that imminent hour which was approaching the children of men.

1285   Noah was a virtuous man, loved by the Saviour and much blessed, the son of Lamech and a righteous man and meek. The Lord was aware that this noble man's fortitude would hold good in the thoughts of his heart. Therefore the holy King and protecting Lord of all beings told him in his own voice what he, being hostile to men, meant to do. He saw the earth full of wrong, its broad plains burdened with sins and polluted by abominations. The Ruler spoke then, our Saviour, and said to Noah:

1296   'I mean to destroy with a flood the folk and each of the species of living beings that air and water bring forth and nurture, beasts and birds. You shall have sanctuary together with your sons when murky waters and dark deadly torrents engulf the multitudes, the guilt-ridden wreckers. Start building yourself a ship, a great sea-going vessel. In it you are to clear resting-places and proper living-quarters for the many off-spring of the earth, each after its own kind. Make a deck amidships. Build the vessel fifty ell-measures wide, thirty high and three hundred long and build the joints strong against the waves. There into that wooden fortress the progeny of every species alive, the issue of earth's offspring, must be led: to this end the ark must be the bigger.'

1314   Noah did as the Saviour commanded him; he obeyed the holy heaven-King and began to build the vessel, a great sea-going ark. He told his family that a calamitous thing was about to befall the people, a dire punishment. To this they gave no heed. Then after many years the ordaining Lord, true to his pledge, saw the most enormous ocean-going home towering in readiness, Noah's vessel, secured within and without against the tide by the finest mortar of earth. It is a special kind: it gets ever the harder as the rough waters, the murky sea-currents, buffet it the more severely.

XXI

1327   Then our Saviour said to Noah:

1328   'Most beloved of men, I give you my pledge upon this, that you and the progeny of the beasts that you must transport will make your way across the deep water for many days in the bosom of your craft. Lead inside the ark, as I have commanded you, your children, those three patriarchs, and your four wives. And take into this floating tabernacle seven, tallied by number, of each of those species which are food for humans and two of each of the others. You are also to take into the vessel provisions of all the fruits of the earth for the numbers which are to survive with you the flood. Freely feed the progeny of living creatures until I am willing once more to furnish sustenance here below the skies for the survivors from these seafarings.

1345   'Now, set about getting aboard the vessel, together with the sorts and the throng of living things. I know you to be a good man, steadfast of purpose; you are worthy of being saved together with your children, and of favours.

1351   'For forty days I will wreak vengeance upon men and by means of a deluge destroy all chattels and their owners that are outside the bulwarks of the ark, when the dark cloud-rack begins to amass.'

1356   Then Noah went, as the Saviour commanded him, aboard the ark, leading his children, the menfolk, into the buoyant timber ship, and their wives together with them; and everything that the Lord almighty wished to have by way of progeny passed under its roof to their provider, just as the Almighty, the Lord of the multitudes, enjoined him by his word. The Keeper of the kingdom of heaven, the Lord presiding over victories, locked the ocean vessel's entrance behind them with his own hands, and he, our Saviour, blessed the ark within with his personal bounties.

1367   Noah, son of Lamech, was six hundred years old when with his sons he climbed aboard, a sage amidst the young, amidst his cherished people, at God's behest. The Lord sent rain from the skies and also caused the capacious well-springs in the world to surge from their every course, and dark cataracts to roar. The seas mounted up above the bastions of the shore. Strong he was and severe who wielded the waters; he engulfed and enveloped the children of the earth's iniquity and the hereditary land of humans with a sombre flood. The ordaining Lord laid waste their dwellings and wreaked purposeful enmity upon men. Inundation clutched violently at the doomed population for forty days and as many nights besides. Severe and deadly fierce was the attack upon mortals; the King of glory's waves flushed the lives of the impious from out of their fleshly carcasses. The flood, tempestuous beneath the heavens, engulfed all the lofty mountains across the spacious earth and the ark lifted afloat from the ground and that family with it which the Lord himself, our Maker, blessed when he closed up the ship.

1392   Then wide across the ambit of the ocean that most excellent shelter rode under the skies and voyaged with its cargo. The water's terror was not permitted violently to touch the seafaring vessel, but holy God piloted and saved them. Fifteen ells deep above the mountains stood the inundating flood: it is a remarkable fact. Finally there was no one for it to destroy nor was there lamentation raised up in the lofty air when the ravaging flood had killed all the offspring of the earth – excepting that the Lord of the heavens preserved the ship of the ark – when the holy and everlasting God, the stern-hearted King, caused the obedient flood to amass in cataracts.

XXII

1407   Then God, the Lord presiding over victories, kept in mind the seafaring son of Lamech and all that stock which he, the Lord of light and life, had locked away against the water in the bosom of the ship. Then the Lord of hosts led his champion by his word across the wide land. The compliant flood began to subside again. The inundation ebbed away, dark beneath the sky. The true ordaining Lord had turned back the sea and its gleaming flux for his children, and stilled the rain.

1417   One hundred and fifty days the foamy ship was voyaging beneath the skies from when the flood first lifted up that most excellent vessel, the ship of rivetted timber, until the full tally of the terrible span of days passed by. Then Noah's ark, greatest of ocean-going abodes, settled with its cargo high on the mountains which are called Armenia. There the saintly man, Lamech's son, for a long while awaited authentic orders, as to when the Guardian Lord of life, the Lord almighty, would grant him rest from his perilous journeyings which he had protractedly endured when the sombre waves had carried him abroad, afloat across the wide earth.

1431   The ocean went on receding. The hero, the seafarers and their wives likewise yearned for when they might step from out of their cramped state across the rivetted ship's side and across the water's edge and bring their chattels out from confinement. Then the ship's pilot tested whether as yet the flood was sinking, there below the skies. So a number of days after the lofty

slopes had received that precious cargo and also the families of
the offspring of earth, Lamech's son let a black raven fly from
out of the house across the deep flood. Noah reckoned that if he
did not find land on that journey he would in duty return to him
on the ship across the wide water. His hope subsequently
played him false, for he perched exulting upon a floating
corpse; the dun-feathered bird was unwilling to return.

1449   Then seven days later he let fly from the ark after the black
raven a grey dove to test whether the deep foamy sea had as yet
yielded up any portion of green earth. She sought with a will
widely about her and flew far afield. She found no resting-place
however, because she could not touch the ground with her feet
for the flood, nor land in the leaves of a tree for the eddying
currents; rather, the steep slopes were covered by the waters. In
the evening the wild bird went seeking the ark across the
sombre sea, descending weary and hungry into the hands of the
saintly man.

1464   Then after a week the wild dove was again dispatched from
the ark. She flew abroad until, dazed by the spaciousness, she
found a pleasant resting-place and then landed with her feet
upon a tree; blithe of mood she enjoyed being able to sit,
extremely weary, in the beautiful boughs of a tree. She shook
her feathers and went flying back with her presents: the travel-
ler brought a twig from an olive-tree, a green sprig, to his
hands. Then the lord of the mariners quickly realized that
comfort was come, relief from their toilsome journeyings.

1476   Once more the blessed man, after the third week, dispatched
a wild dove. She did not come flying back to the ship, but she
found land and green woods. Never again would she gladly
present herself aboard the black-painted ship, in the plank-
built refuge, now there was no necessity upon her.

XXIII

1483   Then our Saviour, the Keeper of the heavenly kingdom,
spoke to Noah with holy voice:

1485 'For you a patrimony is once more extended, peace ashore and a pleasant resting-place on land from your sea-journeyings. Go in safekeeping from out of the ark, and into the lap of earth from out of that lofty abode lead the kinds and all the progeny which I mercifully saved in the throes of the waves when the ocean in its power held the third homeland engulfed.'

1493 Thus he did and obeyed the Lord; he went ashore as the voice enjoined him with great pleasure, and then he led out of the ship the survivors of the angry waves. Then Noah, unwavering in good sense, set about preparing a sacrifice to the Saviour, and, prudent man, quickly took a portion from among all his chattels, those which the Lord had given him to his profit, as the offering; and then, noble-minded man, he dedicated the sacrifice to God himself, King of the angels.

1503 Truly our Saviour made it clear when he blessed Noah and his children together, that he had given that offering willingly and that by good works in his youth he had already deserved it that almighty God, just in his gifts, was liberal of all favours towards him. Once more the Lord, the Prince of glory, spoke words to Noah:

1512 'Be fruitful now and increase and enjoy your glory and security with gladness; fill the earth and multiply all things. Into your authority is given the patrimony and the contents of the ocean and the birds of heaven and the wild beasts and the earth all verdant and its teeming wealth.

1518 'Never disgracefully eat the meat at your table together with the blood polluted with sin by the life-blood. Everyone will be robbing himself in advance of the benefits of the spirit, who extinguishes the life of another with the spear's point. He will have no cause to rejoice in the retribution, but I shall much more sternly seek the requital of a human life from the slayer and the brother-murderer, if the letting of blood and the killing of a man by weapons and murder with the hands prove to prosper. Man was first moulded in the image of God. Everyone shall have the kindred likeness of the Lord and of the angels, who is willing to hold to holy virtues.

1532   'Thrive and flourish; enjoy your desires and favours on earth; fill the expanses of the land with your noble issue, your descendants and offspring. I give you my pledge to this, that never again shall I bring a deluge upon the world and water over the broad earth. Of this you will often and again be able to see a token in the clouds when I show forth my rainbow: that I shall keep this promise with men while the world remains.'

The poem continues to line 2936, broadly following the narrative of the Bible, in which the principal figure of interest is the righteous patriarch Abraham. Notable is the poet's freely amplified and stirring account of the battles (Genesis 14) between the four kings and the five and between Abraham and the captors of Lot in which he skilfully draws upon the formulas, the terminology and the images of conventional Germanic battle-poetry (lines 1982–2005 and 2039–95). There is much effective dialogue freely developed from the scriptural narrative, such as that between Abraham and the king of Sodom and between Abraham and God (lines 2120–215); and the destruction of Sodom and Gomorrah is told in lively fashion with much supplied descriptive detail and homiletic commentary (lines 2541–90). The poem ends, perhaps incompletely – but, if so, aptly – with Abraham sacrificing the ram which God had given in place of Isaac, and expressing gratitude to God, the Lord of benefactions, for his unceasing generosity to those who have stood firm in faith and truth, who have proved, in the extremity of the test, their righteousness. The Old Testament story of Abraham and Isaac was accepted as a foreshadowing of the Redemption. Thus the poem which opens with the rebellion of the angels and the fall of man closes with an anticipation of the salvation of mankind from the power of Satan.

Exodus

[Oxford, Bodleian Library, Junius 11, pp.143–71]

'The Lord watches over the way of the righteous, but the way of the wicked is doomed' (Ps.1:6). The story of the Israelites' crossing of the Red Sea was already understood in the Hebrew Bible itself not merely as the narration of a historic event but as a 'riddle of things past' (Ps.78:2) to be expounded as a permanently abiding token of God's patience and steadfastness in truth to the covenant. 'They were not loyal to him in their hearts nor were they faithful to his covenant. Yet he wiped out their guilt and did not smother his own natural affection' (Ps.78:37–8). In the New Testament, St Paul cites Moses, as leader of the exodus, among those – Abel, Enoch, Noah, Abraham and the many others – who made good their claim to 'the righteousness which comes of faith' (Hebrews 11:7); though he sees faith in the post-Messianic age as demanding more than simple observance of the old law and the covenant. 'And what is faith? Faith gives substance to our hopes, and makes us certain of realities we do not see. It is for their faith that the men of old stand on record. . . By faith they crossed the Red Sea as though it were dry land, whereas the Egyptians, when they attempted the crossing, were drowned. . . And what of ourselves? With all these witnesses to faith around us like a cloud we must throw off every encumbrance, every sin to which we cling, and run with resolution the race for which we are entered, our eyes fixed on Jesus, on whom faith depends from start to finish' (Hebrews 11:1, 2, 29 and 12:1–2). Elsewhere, Paul speaks of the events of the exodus as 'symbols'. '. . . Our ancestors were all under the pillar of cloud, and all of them passed through the Red Sea; and so they all received baptism into the fellowship of Moses . . . they all drank from the supernatural rock that accompanied their travels – and that rock was Christ. . . These events happened as symbols to warn us. . .' (I Corinthians 10:1–6). This is the range of significations of the exodus – treating history as veiled revelation full of intimations, mutually confirmative, of an ever-present divine plan – which is adopted and extended in the medieval tradition of scriptural exegesis. Thus the fiery pillar pointing a way through the inundating waters of the Red Sea, like the ark and the waters of Noah before it, is a deliberate foreshadowing and promise of man's redemption by the Cross from perdition, and of that salvation which is available to the individual Christian through the waters of baptism, from the world, the flesh, the devil and the doom of the unrighteous.

The poet of *Exo* himself speaks of the 'keys of the spirit' by which a willing soul may unlock the mystery of the Lord's authentic words given through Moses (523–30) – a plain injunction to read the Scriptures as allegory, and very likely an invitation to treat his own poetic narrative to the same kind of exegesis. Doubtless, the digression (362–446) to the voyage of Noah's family across the Flood and to Abraham's obviated sacrifice of Isaac upon Mount Zion (Jerusalem) is intended to serve an exegetical purpose precisely within the scope of Paul's interpretation of the record of 'the men of old'. How much further the poet goes in this allegorical-typological method is a matter of scholarly dispute. It was, for example, a commonplace of exegesis that the rod of Moses prefigured the Cross; such may appear to be the poet's implication here, where his choice of terminology, as in his references to the pillar of fire, seems deliberately ambivalent so as to provoke a parallel consciousness of the Cross as consummation of these portents and promises. Even if the poem is not the tissue of multi-layered meanings and technical masterstrokes which its most enthusiastic expositors depict, it is without doubt a work of major intellectual stature matched with a high order of poetic skill – attested particularly in the versatility of the poet's rhetoric, his imaginative use of metaphor and the dramatic force of his narrative of the destruction of the Egyptians.

The references to Noah and Abraham link *Exo* by subject-matter as well as by theme with the preceding poem in the manuscript, *Gen*. No educated Anglo-Saxon (not necessarily literate but, for the later period at least, merely well versed in such homilies as were regularly preached in the vernacular language) would have failed to perceive in this collocation of 'men of old' the figure of the righteous man fulfilled in perfection in Christ. *Exo* also shares with the other poems of Junius 11 a link with the liturgy of Lent and Holy Week – in particular, with the liturgy of Holy Saturday.

A number of verbal correspondences of compound words and of phrases between *Exo* and *Bwf* has prompted debate over the relative dating of the poems and over the likelier direction of any borrowing. However, oral formulaic theory must be allowed to challenge here, as in the case of *And* and *Bwf*, the very premises of a theory of literary indebtedness. It remains an open question whether such correspondences even indicate a common period of origin or only a common period of final reshaping of the poems involved.

XLII

Listen! far and near throughout the world we have heard worthies tell of the decrees of Moses and of exilic promises to the generations of mortals – of the reward of life in heaven for each of the blessed after the hazardous journey, and of everlasting profit for each living soul. Let him who will, give heed.

8   Him the Lord of the heavenly hosts, the King steadfast in truth, distinguished in the desert with his own authority, and the eternal Ruler of all put many miraculous powers at his disposal. He was loved by God, a shrewd and wise elder of his people, leader of the army and a bold commander. He curbed the nation of Pharaoh, God's adversary, by chastisement with the rod, when the Lord of victories vouchsafed to him, their courageous mentor, the life of his compatriots, and to the sons of Abraham the habitation of a homeland. Divine was the retribution of his hand and loyal his Lord: he granted him supremacy of arms against the violence of raging foes, and by this means he vanquished in battle the sovereignty of many tribes, his enemies. That was the first time that the God of the heavenly hosts spoke words to him, when he told him many marvellous truths – how the wise Lord created this world, the earth's ambit and the sky above, and established the victorious nation, and his own name which formerly the sons of men, the wise stock of the patriarchs, did not know, though they knew much.

30   Thereafter, he strengthened and distinguished with authentic powers this elder of the multitude, Pharaoh's foe, in the exodus, when a most enormous number of people, of treasure-hoarders, was utterly tormented to death and destruction by momentous punishments. The lamentation was incessant; the pleasures of hall-life, plundered of wealth, languished. At midnight he fiercely struck down the wicked oppressors, the many firstborn sons, and brought the city-dwellers to submission. A slayer stalked abroad, an implacable public foe; the land reeked with the corpses of the dead – and the fellowship set forth. There was weeping abroad and little

worldly delight; the hands of the deriders were stayed – and the people, the migrant nation, were allowed to start the resented journey. The demon was despoiled, and his hellish hordes – there heaven approached, and the idols toppled; it was a day renowned throughout the earth when that multitude set out – according as the Egyptian people, accursed of old, endured captivity for many seasons because they thought to prevent the compatriots of Moses, if the ordaining Lord had allowed them, in their longstanding desire for the cherished journey.

54   The army was filled with anticipation, and intrepid was the one who led their nation, a courageous mentor. With that folk he traversed many regions difficult of access, the land and habitation of hostile people, narrow defiles, an unfamiliar route, until they came bearing arms among warlike blacks – their lands were shrouded with a covering of cloud. Past wasteland abodes on mountain slopes and many obstacles Moses led the army.

XLIII

63   Then two days after they had escaped from their enemies the man of assured glory gave orders to encamp with the strident throng of the army and with the whole train, a most enormous force, about the city of Etham in the border regions of the desert. Dangers had forced them on northward routes; they knew that to the south of them was the land of the Ethiopians, burnt-up mountain heights and people brown from the scorching coals of the sun. There holy God shielded the folk against the intense blaze; he overspread the scorching heaven with a ceiling and the burning sky with a holy veil. A cloud with its broad expanses quite separated earth and sky; it guided the multitude of the people and smothered the flaming fire, scorchingly bright in the heaven. The people looked on in amaze, the gladdest of throngs. The shelter of a shade by day moved across the skies; wise God had screened the sun's course with a sail in such a way that earth-dwelling mortals, for all their skill, could not see the rigging and were unable to see the sailyard, nor how

this hugest of tabernacles was tied, when he gloriously honoured those loyal to their Lord. This third encampment then proved to be a comfort to the people. The whole army saw how the divine sails towered up there, a radiant portent aloft; the people, the multitude of the Israelites, recognized that there the Lord was come, the Lord of hosts, to mark out the campsite. Before them proceeded fire and cloud in the bright sky, two pillars, each of which exalted ministers of the Holy Spirit equally shared the journey of those brave-hearted men by day and by night.

98 Then in the morning, I have heard tell, confident of mood they raised up the trumpets with their loud voices, a portentous proclamation. The whole host arose, a force of courageous folk, an army eager to set forth as Moses, the renowned leader, had commanded them, the people of the ordaining Lord. Ahead they saw the guide to their survival mark out the way of life. The sail determined the course; behind it the voyagers travelled the ocean-way. Folk were in high spirits; loud was the hubbub of the army.

XLIIII

107 Each evening a heavenly beacon, the other portent, rose aloft, wondrous in the wake of the sun, whose declining course it occupied, shining with fire above the people, a blazing column. Bright rays gleamed glisteningly above the soldiers – their protective shields shone – shadows melted away; the abysmal shades of night could not keep their hiding-place close concealed. Heaven's candle blazed; it was needful for this novel night-watchman to abide above the multitudes, lest the horror of the desert, the grey terror of the wasteland, should put an end to their life with sudden overwhelming by ocean storms. This vanguard had fiery curls and glistening rays; it threatened the terror of incineration upon the army and scorching flame, and that it would burn up the multitude in the desert unless, keen-hearted, they obeyed Moses. Girded in light it shone, and the shields shimmered. The soldiers kept sight of the proper path

and of the standard above the troops, until at the land's end the stronghold of the sea impeded the throng of the people, eager for the onward way. Camp was pitched and the weary ones recovered themselves; those in charge of provisions offered the spirited folk food, and restored their physical strength. When the trumpet sang out, the seafarers spread their tents along the hills. This was the fourth encampment, the resting-place of the warriors, by the Red Sea.

135   There fearful news arrived among their army, of pursuit from inland. Fears sprang forth, the multitude's terror of death. Fugitive awaited malignant pursuer – that one who had formerly long subjected them, stateless, to oppression and misery heavy with afflictions. The Egyptians had not kept their pledge, even though the elder Pharaoh previously. . .

The earlier Pharaoh had given Joseph authority over the whole of Egypt (Genesis 41: 41) but the new king knew nothing of Joseph and sought to limit the increase of the Israelites (Exodus 1: 8–10). The poet's survey of this betrayal has evidently been shortened either accidentally by a loss from the MS or deliberately by imperfect editing. The break in narrative continuity is minimal. The next section opens with a reference either to the same 'elder Pharaoh' – who came to own all the people and land of Egypt by following Joseph's advice (Genesis 47: 23) – or to Joseph himself (Genesis 41: 43).

XLV

142   Then he became custodian of the patrimony of the native populace, over people's fortunes, so that he very greatly prospered.

144   This the Egyptian nation entirely forgot when they grew furious over being resisted. They then committed violence against his kindred, caused them injury and revoked their pledge. Surges of bellicosity, that violent human passion, beset their hearts; in bad faith they proposed to repay the debt of their survival with treachery, so that the people of Moses would have paid in blood for that day's work – if mighty God

had granted the Egyptians success in their mission of destruction.

154   Then the men's mood grew desperate when they saw Pharaoh's army advancing forward from the routes to the south, bearing boar-javelins, and saw the cavalry shimmering — spears were deployed, battle approached, shields glinted, trumpets sang out — and saw the banners standing out and the throng tramping the shore. Birds of battle greedy for the clash, flecked-feathered, the dark scavenger of carrion, screeched in wheeling flight after the corpses of the armies. Wolves sang hideous vespers in anticipation of feasting; brazen beasts bold at dusk, they awaited in the wake of the antagonists the slaughter of a mighty throng of people. They would howl, these haunters of the hinterland, in the middle of the nights: the doomed soul would flit away and the populace was reduced.

170   At intervals haughty officers from among the army ranged the highways on horseback. There before them, by the banner, rode the bannered king, the ruler over men, with the ensign contingent. The warriors' warlord fastened his visored helmet, the king his cheek-guard, in anticipation of fighting; the ensigns shone forth. He shook his mail-coat and commanded his troop of picked men zealously to hold fast their battle array. With eyes full of hate the friends watched the advance of the landlubbers. About him moved unfearing soldiers, hoary sword-wolves; they welcomed warfare, thirsting for the violence of battle, loyal to their leader. He had picked himself a force of two thousand people, gloriously privileged according to the right of wealth, who were kings and kinsfolk esteemed for their lineage. Each one consequently led out every male, every soldier he could find on that occasion. All the kings, those belonging to that land, were gathered in his retinue. Repeatedly a familiar trumpet made its proclamation among the horde, as to where the young warriors, a belligerent troop of men, should carry their war-gear. Thus they led there a dark army, reinforcements, foe upon foe, a multitude of the nation's might in their thousands: they were eager to get there. They had

resolved, as regards those mighty hordes, to destroy the Israel-
ite people with swords at dawn, out of vengeance for their
brethren. That was why in the encampments the sound of
weeping was raised, hideous vespers; fears loomed whose
deadly meshes hampered them. When the alarm came, brave
speeches fled.

203   The enemy was unrelenting; the army was burnished for
battle – until the mighty angel who guarded the multitude
thrust in front of those haughty people so that the protagonists
could no longer see one another and the advance was inter-
cepted.

208   The fugitives enjoyed a night-long respite, although on both
sides adversaries lay in wait for them – military force or the sea,
they had no further way out. They had given up hoping for the
homeland due to them. They sat about among the hills in
sombre garments anticipating misery. Watchful, the whole
company of kinsfolk assembled together and awaited the
superior military force, until at daybreak Moses commanded
warriors with their brazen trumpets to summon the folk, the
soldiers, to get up, to don their mail-coats, set their minds on
courageous conduct and take up their bright battle-gear; and
by these signals to muster the army close to the shore. Briskly
the defenders attended the battle-call; the host was alerted. The
seafarers – they were obeying the trumpet – hustled with their
tents over the hills; the army was in haste.

224   Then they detailed twelve battalions of brave-minded foot-
soldiers to be in the vanguard against the enemy onslaught:
their vigour was stirred. In each single battalion the flower of
the nation's noble stock was appointed to arms, fifty select
contingents in total. Each contingent of this distinguished host
held ten hundred spear-bearing warriors all told, gloriously
favoured men. It was a warlike host. The army leaders did not
welcome the weakly into that muster of warriors, those who
because of their youth were as yet unfitted to protect by their
fists behind the shield-formation men's mail-coats against the

treacherous enemy, or who had not experienced a grievous
hurt over the shield-rim, the scar of a body-wound and the
spear's vaunting sportiveness; nor could aged and white-haired
warriors be of use in the battle if their physical strength failed
them, though apt of courage. Rather, they picked the fighting-
force according to stature, and how courage combined with
grace plus the power of physical strength, the grip on the
spear-shaft, would endure among the people.

247   So an army of strong-handed men was mustered, eager for
the advance. Aloft soared the standard, brightest of columns.
So far they had all been waiting until that pointer of their path
close by the sea-tides, luminous above their linden shields,
would break through the cloudy portals.

XLVI

252   Then in front of the men the battle-herald leaped up, the bold
summoner to the fray; he raised his shield and charged the
commanders to silence the army while the multitude listened to
a brave man's speech: the shepherd of the nation desired to
address with holy voice the legion of the chosen. With dignity
the leader of the host spoke:

259   'Do not be the more frightened for it even if Pharaoh should
bring vast armies of sword-warriors, a tally untold of men. The
mighty Lord by my hand wills this day to give them all their
deeds' reward, so that they shall be allowed no longer to
survive and scourge the people of Israel with miseries. You will
not fear dead foot-soldiers, dying bodies: the span of their
fleeting life is at an end. God's counsel has been wrenched from
your breasts: I give you better advice, that you worship the
Prince of glory and pray for the grace of the Lord of life upon
you and for the salvation of victories as you set forth. This is the
everlasting God of Abraham, the Lord of things created, who,
valiant and renowned of strength, will guard this army with
that mighty hand.'

276   In front of the troops then the lord of the living raised his loud voice when he spoke to the people:

278   'Behold! now shall you, the most cherished of nations, gaze with your own eyes upon an instant miracle: how I myself and this stronger hand have struck with a living emblem the ocean deep. A wave is mounting upwards; it is swiftly building the water into a rampart. There are dry thoroughfares, grey causeways fit for an army – the sea being opened up – and ancient foundations which never on earth have I heard of men traversing before, and gleaming plains, the sealed floors of the sea, which henceforth into eternal time the waves would have overspread. A south wind has swept away the storming of the main, the ocean is riven; the sea's retreat has disgorged the sands. The truth I clearly perceive: that mighty God has shown mercy upon you, you men glad as of yore. Speed is the best thing, so that you may escape your enemies' clutch, now that the Lord their owner has heaped up the red waters into a protective shield. The retaining walls are fairly piled up to the dome of the heavens, a wondrous highway through the waves.'

299   Upon these words the whole host arose, an army of spirited men. The deep remained motionless. The squadrons of the chosen raised up their shields and their standards on the shore. The wall of the sea soared upwards; upright it stood for the Israelites for a whole day's duration. It was of one mind, that company of men: it clung to the covenant with a fast embrace. They disdained not at all the holy man's advice when, close upon his footsteps, their song of salvation, their harmony and the blending of their psalmody grew stronger.

310   Then the fourth tribe went foremost and advanced into the main, warriors in a throng, across the green sea-floor. A soldier of the house of Judah hastened along the strange road ahead of his kinsmen. Accordingly, mighty God granted him great reward for that day's work when the glory of victorious deeds proved his – that he should have sovereignty over kingdoms and increase of offspring.

XLVII

319   They had as their standard, when they marched into the sea, an emblem raised up above the shield-phalanx within that spear-armed troop, a golden lion – the greatest of peoples, the bravest of beasts. Because of that wayleader in war, they were unwilling long to endure humiliation upon themselves, being alive, when they lifted the spear in battle with any nation. There was an impetus in the vanguard, hard hand-fighting; there were brave young warriors, soldiers undaunted by weapons' carnage, bloody sword-wounds, onslaught of the battle-force and the crushing of visored helmets, where Judah went.

331   Behind that army paraded those mariners, the sons of Reuben. They carried their shields, those sea-rovers, a multitude of people, across the salty fen; the huge contingent advanced intrepid. He had spoiled his sovereignty by his sins so he went further back, in the wake of the favourite. His own brother had taken over from him the firstborn's right in the nation, his wealth and his nobility; nevertheless he was at the ready.

340   Behind them, with the hosts of their folk, came the sons of Simeon and advanced with their troops. This third tribal power – banners waved above the armed expedition – pressed ahead in a battalion with dew-moist spear-shafts. The portent of day appeared over the ocean, one of the beacons of God, the morning, agleam from the sea. The army proceeded onwards.

347   Then there advanced one tribal power after the other in iron-clad squadrons – one man especially guided the mighty hosts, because he was well known – along the onward paths, the people following the cloudy pillar, tribe following tribe. Each one knew the due status of the tribes according as Moses had informed them of the men's lineage. There was one father of them all, a ruler beloved; sage of spirit, beloved of his noble kinsmen, he had received the entitlement to the land. He, one of the patriarchs, begot a progeny of brave men, a holy nation, the

kin of Israel, the fit folk of God, according as old men, those
who have most inquired into family relationships, the origin of
people and each person's paternal ancestry, skilfully recount.

362   Over fresh floods Noah, the illustrious leader, together with
his three sons, sailed − over the deepest inundating floods
which have ever occurred in the world. In his heart he kept the
holy covenant; thus he guided across the ocean-currents the
greatest of treasures, as I have heard tell. Into that sanctuary of
life he had counted by tally from out of the whole earthly
population of the world the surviving remnant, the parent
stock, the father and the mother of each of the procreating
species, more various than people can know. Besides that, the
men took into the ship's hold every kind of seed for which men
have use here below the heavens.

377   According to what wise men declare in their sayings, ninth in
the line of descendants from Noah was the father of Abraham,
that is that Abraham whose name the God of angels devised
anew and besides that entrusted into his keeping far and near
godly communities and government over nations: he spent his
life in exile. After that, on the orders of holy God, he guided
that most favoured of peoples: kinsmen of one stock, they
climbed the uplands into Mount Zion. There they came by a
compact − they witnessed heavenly glory − a holy solemn
covenant, as men have heard tell, where the discerning son of
David, the glorious king, at the sage's instigations afterwards
built a temple for God; the wisest in the world of the kings of
earth built a holy house, the loftiest and the holiest, the most
celebrated among men, the greatest and most splendid of those
which the sons of men, of mortals upon the earth, have
wrought with their hands. To that place of parley Abraham led
his son Isaac. First the executioner lit a fire; he was none the
happier for that. He meant to yield up his heir to the flame, the
best of men into the pyre's blaze, his beloved son as a sacrifice
for victory, his only successor on earth, the consolation of his
life, since he expected henceforth, as a legacy to his people, a
long-abiding cause for hope. He gave witness, when he took

the lad firmly in his hands and when he, the man of popular
renown, pulled out his ancient sword – the edge rasped – that
he did not esteem the days of his life dearer to him than that he
should obey the heaven-King.

411   He arose: this man meant to slay his stripling son, to bloody
his boy with blade-edges, with the sword – if the ordaining
Lord had let him. The radiant Father did not desire to take the
child, the holy sacrifice, from him, but caught him with his
hands. Then a voice from the heavens came restraining him, the
resonance of glory, and thereupon spoke these words:

419   'Do not slay, Abraham, your own child, your son, by the
sword. The truth is witnessed, now that the King of all crea-
tures has tested you, that you have kept covenant and firm faith
with the Ruler; it shall lastingly prove a protection to you
through the days of your life, for ever to eternity unfailing.
How should a son of man need a greater surety of good faith?

427   'Heaven and earth cannot encompass his glorious word
which is more ample and spacious than the world's plains,
earth's ambit and the sky above, the ocean's expanse and this
vast airy space can contain. He, Prince of the angels, Wielder of
the workings of providence and God of the multitudes, the
righteous Lord of victories, will swear you an oath upon his
own being, that of your kin and of your warrior-descendants
men on earth will not be able with all their skill to tell the tally
in sure terms – unless there should be someone so clever of
mind that on his own he can tally all the stones upon the earth,
the stars in the heavens, the sand of the sea-cliffs or the salty
waves – but amid the oceans as far as to the grudge-bearing
nation of Egypt they shall possess the land of Canaan, your
nation, the free-born sons of their father, the most excellent
of peoples.'

*Between pages 164 and 165 of the MS, both of which, being blank,
were presumably reserved for illustrations, an abrupt jump in the
narrative occurs, indicating the loss of a leaf. This probably contained*

a complete section (XLVIII) of sixty to seventy lines of text. When the narrative is resumed, the Israelites have safely negotiated the crossing of the Red Sea, and the walls of water have been commanded to collapse upon the Egyptians who are still in pursuit across the sea-bed.

XLVIIII

447   The people were panic-stricken; horror of the flood came upon their miserable spirits. The deep menaced them with death. The mountainous screes were bedabbled with blood, the sea spewed gore, there was uproar amid the waves, the water was full of weapons, and the reek of carnage rose above. The Egyptians were thrown into retreat; terrified they fled. They had experienced a catastrophe. The cowards wanted to get back to their homes; their boasting had become more pessimistic. The terrible tumbling of the waves brought darkness upon them, and none of the army there came home, but Providence cut them off from behind by the flood. Where paths had previously lain, the ocean raged – the army was inundated – and cataracts appeared. A turbulence rose up high into the skies, a most mighty cry of despair from the army. The aggressors were shrieking – the air darkened above – with dying voices; blood infused the flood.

464   The shielding ramparts were rent apart. The mightiest death-dealing sea lashed the sky – bold men perished, kings in their pomp – the sea's recession finally failed. High above the men the shields gleamed; the ocean rampart, the moody swirl of the sea, towered aloft: their might was trapped fast in death. Sands caused the swamping of the passage ahead, entangled with accoutrements, and of the army's route of attack when the swirling of the waters, the sea ever chill with its salty waves, came from its deviant ways seeking its wonted state, its eternal foundations – a naked portender of distress, a hostile vagrant thing, which stranded the aggressors. The discoloured air was mingled with blood.

478   The bursting ocean had menaced the voyage of the seafarers with horror of a gory death – until the true ordaining Lord by

the hand of Moses gave space to its fury: widely it coursed and scoured with its fatal clutches. The flood foamed, men fell dying, the water encroached upon the land, the air was agitated. The retaining walls gave way, the ramparts burst, the bastions of the sea dissolved when with his holy hand the Mighty One, Guardian Lord of the heavenly kingdom, struck the bulwarks of the ocean. They could not hinder, those haughty people, the course of the saving waters, the sea's fury, but he destroyed their multitudes with a shrieking terror.

490   The ocean grew enraged, drew itself up, and slid upon them. Appalling fears arose; mortal wounds oozed. The handiwork of God, the foamy-bosomed sea, fell from high in the heavens upon the route of attack. The Guardian Lord of the ocean flood struck the unavailing rampart with an ancient sword so that by that death-blow legions perished, the horde of the sinful. Completely surrounded, they lost their souls, that army white with terror at the deluge, when they bowed to the pent-up mass of dark water, a most enormous and violent wave. Their whole force perished when the hosts of the Egyptians were drowned — Pharaoh along with his people.

502   God's adversary quickly found, when he sank into the abyss, that the Guardian Lord of the ocean was the greater in might. Wrathful and terrible, he had meant to determine the battle by the power of the sword: overwhelming was the reward assigned to the Egyptians for that day's work, for of that quite unfathomable army none came back home as a survivor so that he might tell their fate and proclaim through the cities the greatest evil tidings, the fall of their lords, to those men's wives; but death at sea swallowed up those battalions and the tale-tellers likewise. He who possessed the power voided the boast of those men. They had been contending against God.

516   Thereupon Moses, the man of high virtue, with divine utterance declared to the Israelites on the sea-shore enduring precepts and a profound message. The nations still cite the accomplishments of that day, according as even now they find in the

Scriptures each one of those laws which the Lord with his authentic words enjoined upon them during the exodus. If the faculty which interprets life's meaning, the body's tenant, radiant within the breast, has the will to unlock the ample benefits with the keys of the spirit, the mystery will be explained and wisdom will issue forth. It has wise words in its keeping and it earnestly desires to instruct our minds so that we may not be lacking in God's law and the Lord's mercy. He will enlighten us further: for the present, scholars tell us of the better, more lasting joys of heaven. This present happiness is an ephemeral one, corrupted by sins, one afforded to us exiles, a time of waiting for miserable men. Deprived of our homeland, we anxiously inhabit this lodging-house. We grieve in spirit; we are aware of the dungeon fast fixed beneath the earth where fire is and serpent, the everlasting open pit of every sort of evil — just as, for the present, those arch-thieves, senility and premature death, share dominion. The corresponding event is approaching, the most mighty and majestic upon earth, a day marked by accomplishments: the Lord himself will judge the multitudes in the place of parley and then he will lead the souls of those steadfast in the truth, blessed spirits, into heaven on high where there is light and life and the enjoyment of loving-kindnesses. In bliss that company will praise the Lord, the glorious King of hosts, to existence infinite.

549   Thus turning his mind upon wise precepts he spoke, the mildest of men, fortified in his powers, with a loud voice. Silently the army heard out the appointed leader's will; they apprehended a wondrous thing, the man of spirit's spoken prophecy. He said to the multitudes:

554   'Great in this company and strong the Captain, the greatest of supports, who leads this journey. He has conceded to us in Canaan the people, their cities and treasures, a spacious realm. He will now fulfil what he, Lord of the angels, long since promised with the swearing of an oath to your fathers' generation in bygone days — that if you keep his holy precepts you shall henceforth overrun each one of your enemies and occupy

a victorious realm amidst the oceans, and the banquet-halls of warriors. Great shall be your glory.'

565   After these words the army was jubilant. The trumpets of victory sang out in beautiful harmony and banners stood raised. The people were ashore. The heavenly pillar had guided the army, the holy troops, under God's protection. They exulted in being alive now they had extricated their life from their enemies' power, though they had daringly risked it, those men below the crests of the waters – there they had seen the ramparts rising up. The seas appeared to them all bloody, through which they had carried their fighting-gear. They jubilated in battle-song now that they had escaped away homewards. With loud voice the warrior-throngs, the men and the women among the rest, raised up a song of glory: they praised the Lord for that mighty accomplishment. A most enormous multitude of people, they chanted with awe-thrilled voices a battle-lay about the many miracles.

580   It was easy then to find the Egyptian prostrate on the edge of the ocean. Hands picked up necklaces; they were happy; they gazed upon their reward. They had received the spoil of war; their bondage was loosed. The survivors from the sea began to share out between the regiments on the shore ancient treasures, armour and shields. With entitlement they divided up the gold and the purple, Joseph's wealth, the men's glorious possessions. Their custodians were lying in the place of their death, a most enormous company of people.

Daniel

[Oxford, Bodleian Library, Junius 11, pp.173–212]

'Blessed be God's name from age to age, for all wisdom and power are his. He changes seasons and times; he deposes kings and sets them up; he gives wisdom to the wise and all their store of knowledge to the men who know; he reveals deep mysteries; he knows what lies in darkness, and light has its dwelling with him' (Daniel 2:20–22).

Daniel, in the medieval tradition of scriptural exegesis, stands as a symbol of fearless witness to the Lord, to the law and to the covenant, against idolatry and against backsliding in captivity. His story testifies that such witness is favoured by divine intervention which proves that a just Providence, not the will of unrighteous heathens, the citizens of Babylon and their morally monstrous lords, nor a mechanistic force of necessity, governs the world in which mankind makes the choice between good and evil. So St Boniface, in a letter to Hwætberht, abbot of Wearmouth, in 746–7, asked him to pray for the English missionaries in Germany 'that by your Holiness's prayers the fierce heat of the Babylonian fire may be extinguished in us' (*EHD*, p. 759). Such, in part, is the theme of this poem, as it is of *Jud* and, in part, of *Bwf* – as illustrated for example in the device of the sword-hilt brought out from Grendel's den. Daniel, like Joseph and Solomon, is distinguished in medieval tradition for his judgments which, deriving from God, reflect that attribute of the Christian deity, wisdom, that is revered in various AS writings. The *witig drihten*, 'wise Lord', of *Dan* 403 is the same that the *Deo*-poet acknowledges to control the seemingly arbitrary incidence of affliction and happiness in the world, and the same that is declared the source of all human attributes in *GfM*; while the God that 'changes seasons and times' is the same that by grace gives the wise wanderer his wisdom (*Wan*) and supports the spiritual pilgrim with his universe-framing strength (*Sfr* and *And*, 511–25). In this poem, Daniel and the three youths Hananiah, Azariah and Mishael are, like Noah, Abraham and Moses in the preceding poems, righteous men, steadfast in truth as well as wise. Thus a major theme of the whole codex is sustained and indeed conspicuously preferred in the poem to the Old Testament book's emphasis upon Daniel as prophet. The Prayer of Azariah and the Song of the Three both feature in the liturgy of the early Church and were used during Holy Week. In so far as these rhetorical peaks of the poem give character to its whole landscape, *Dan*, like the other poems of Junius 11, could be considered fit reading for Lent and Easter in a religious house.

The text has seemed to some scholars to be, like *Gen*, a conflation of originally independent poems. Within the first 494 lines – which are primarily concerned not with Daniel but with the three youths and their divine preservation in the fiery furnace – is a sequence, the Prayer of Azariah, which corresponds very closely to part of *Aza*, a poem in the Exeter Book; but the correspondence is not of a kind to support a theory of direct copying. The sequence is followed in both *Dan* and *Aza* by the Song of the Three; but the two versions differ considerably and the likelihood of dependence is remote. Too much, perhaps, has been made of stylistic features distinguishing the Prayer, the Song, and their narrative link from the surrounding poetry; where stylistic distinction corresponds with thematic distinction, as here, the aesthetics of rhetoric can provide an explanation as plausible as any theory of interpolation. Finally, there are arguable examples of clumsy pastiche in certain structural weaknesses in the narrative; but these may reflect the structural compositeness of the Old Testament Book of Daniel itself, in the form in which it was accepted by all the early Fathers of the Church – that is, inclusive of the extensions which were not given a place in the canon of the Hebrew Bible. The poem has long been thought incomplete. Certainly the conclusion is abrupt, but thematically the final speech, given appropriately to Daniel, the mouthpiece of God, is an apt ending with its literal and symbolic assertion that for the unrighteous of this world, the adversaries of God, the citizens of the earth's Babylons, the writing is on the wall.

L

I have heard tell of the Hebrews living blest in Jerusalem, sharing a treasury of gold and enjoying sovereignty as befitted them ever since, through the might of the ordaining Lord, an army had been given into the hand of Moses, a large number of soldiers, and they had departed from out of Egypt by a great miracle. That was a mettlesome nation.

8   As long as they were permitted to dispose over the realm and to govern their cities, theirs was a dazzling prosperity. As long

as the people were willing to keep their Father's covenant among them, the Keeper of the heaven-kingdom, the holy Lord, heaven's Ruler, was a good shepherd to them. He, the ordaining Lord of all creatures, gave courage and strength to their number so that often with the helmed men of their army they scathed the life of many nations which were not loyal to him – until at their feasting, pride and drunken thoughts invaded them with devilish deeds. Then they at once abandoned the teachings of the law and the authority of the ordaining Lord: so must a man never divorce his soul's love from God.

22   Then I saw that nation, the people of Israel, straying into error, perpetrating evil and committing sins. It was a thing painful to God. Often the Keeper of the heaven-kingdom sent to those people for their guidance holy spirits who proffered wisdom to the multitude. For a little while they believed in the truth of that sapience – until a longing for the pleasures of the earth cheated them of everlasting profit, so that in the end they abandoned the decrees of the Lord and preferred the deceitfulness of the devil.

33   Then the Prince of power grew angry and disaffected towards the people to whom he had granted possession. He at the start had guided them who, before that, had in the beginning been dearest to God among the human race, dearest of communities, most loved by the Lord; he had shown these men, being strangers, the military road to the lofty city, into the land of their inheritance where Salem stood, fortified by defensive works and dignified by ramparts – until the Chaldean tribe, those sorcerers, advanced against the city where the possessions of Israel were, hidden with fortifications. There the army advanced, a notorious fighting-force, yearning for violence.

46   This deadly malice Nebuchadnezzar, lord of men, prince of Babylon, had conceived in his city out of malicious hate, in that he had searched in the broodings of his mind as to how he could

most easily expel those people from Israel by an onslaught of cruel foes. So from south and north he mustered a savage host and they advanced westwards with an army of heathen kings to the lofty city. The inhabitants of the homeland of the Israelites enjoyed love and prosperity of life as long as the ordaining Lord allowed them.

57 I have heard tell that the tribe of inveterate enemies then devastated the people's festive city. The aggressors did not believe: they despoiled of its red gold, of its treasure and its silver that marvel among buildings, the Temple of Solomon. They plundered riches among the ruined buildings, all of such as those people were supposed to possess, until they had destroyed each one of the strongholds which had stood as sanctuary to the populace. They loaded up as their booty the riches of the wealth-hoarders, the lucre and the lords, such as was found there, and then with these possessions they journeyed back, and also led the people of Israel upon the long journey, along the eastward roads to Babylonia – a countless number of warriors – to consign those men into the subjugation of heathens. Nebuchadnezzar, contrary to all charity, put the children of Israel, the survivors of his weapons, under constraint as slaves. Then he sent a contingent of the host of his soldiers to go west in order to govern for him the land of those people, their desolate homeland, in place of the Hebrews.

79 Then he ordered his officials to seek out among the wretched remnants of the Israelites which of the youth that had been brought there was wisest in books of the law. He wanted the young men to acquire that craft so that he could declare to them the insights in his mind, and not at all because he could or would remember to thank God for the gifts which the Lord had allotted him there to his benefit. Then they found there three exceedingly wise young men, noble and well-grounded in the Scriptures, youthful and virtuous in respect of their godly stock – one was Hananiah, the second Azariah, the third Mishael – men selected by the ordaining Lord. These three came confident and keen-witted before the prince, there where the

heathen sat, a king fond of pomp, in the Chaldean stronghold. Then the Hebrew men were required in their conversations to make known to the proud king their wisdom and profound intellectual skill, by virtue of a pious mind. Then the warrior ruler of Babylon, the headstrong king, commanded his ministers that the officers should see to it, upon their life, that there would be no lack of food or clothing for the three young men for the duration of their lives.

LI

104   At that time the ruler of Babylon was infamous throughout the earth, a notorious man and arrogant, terrifying to the sons of men. He never observed the law but lived presumptuously in every way. To this despot then in his first sleep after the potent prince had gone to bed the portent of a dream came drifting into his consciousness: how the world was miraculously transformed into a new creation unlike the former ages. The truth was made known to him in sleep that there must befall and come about a violent end of every empire and of earth's pleasures. Then the wolf-hearted ruler of Babylon woke up, who until then had been sleeping befuddled with wine. His mind was not easy for a worry had arisen for him – the portent of the dream. What he had dreamed he did not recall.

120   He ordered together those of his people who had carried sorcery furthest and then asked their number what he had dreamed while mortals were at rest. He had been frightened by the terrible experience since he knew neither the words nor the purpose of his dream; nevertheless he ordered them to declare it to him. Then the warlocks – whose power was not sufficient to explain the dream to the king – uneasily answered him:

130   'How, lord, can we get to know things so hidden in your mind, as to how you dreamed or how the decree of the fates proffered knowledge, if you cannot first relate to us its starting-point?'

134   Then the wolf-hearted king ungraciously answered his wizards:

136   'You are not so far increased beyond all men in intelligence as you told me when you said that you understood my destiny, what would befall me hereafter, or what I should later encounter. Now you, those who offer me wisdom in front of the throng, cannot understand my dream. You shall suffer death unless I come to know the judgment of the very dream which my mind recollects.'

145   Then the crowd in the council chamber was unable to work out or interpret anything at all by way of divination since it was withheld from them to explain to the king the dream and the secrets of the fates – until the prophet Daniel came to judgment in the hall, he who was chosen by the Lord, a wise man and righteous. He was the leader of the wretched remnant of those who had to obey the heathens. To him God granted grace from the heavens through the utterance of a holy spirit, so that an angel of God told him everything just as his master had dreamed it.

158   Then Daniel went when day dawned to recount the dream to his lord. Sagely he told him the destiny of nations so that the headstrong king soon understood the beginning and end of what was revealed to him. So Daniel gained great reputation and renown among scholars in Babylon after he had explained to the king the dream which, on account of his sins, the ruler of Babylon had previously been unable to understand in his heart.

168   Nevertheless, Daniel was not able to bring it about that the king would believe in the power of the ordaining Lord, but he set about building an idol in the plains which people called Dura which was in that province which was so called Babylon the mighty. The city's ruler raised up for men, against the approval of the ordaining Lord, a human image, a god of gold, because he was not a discerning man, this impetuous and wisdom-wanting keeper of the kingdom; good. . .

One leaf of the MS is apparently missing here, though the incidents in the biblical narrative thus lost are only minor: the summons to the dignitaries of the realm and the herald's proclamation (Daniel 3: 2–6).

178   . . . there was obedience then on the part of the people when the call came upon the citizens, the voice of the trumpet. Then they sank down on their knees in front of the effigy; the heathen nation bowed to the idol and worshipped an image. They did not know a nobler wisdom. They did wrong, just as did their lord, polluted by sin, grown audacious in mind. The mass of the people did just as their lord did first: they lived up to their unwisdom – for which an evil last reckoning later befell them – and did wrong.

188   There were three in that prince's city, men of Israel, who would never undertake to comply with their prince's ordinance, that they should lift up their supplications to the icon, although the trumpets were blaring among the populace there. These were by lineage sons of Abraham; they were true to the covenant; they knew the Lord, the Everlasting on high, the Almighty. The noble youths made it known that they would not have nor hold that gold as their god, but rather the high King, the Shepherd of souls, who granted them grace. Repeatedly, moreover, they courageously declared that they had no regard whatever for the idol, nor could the heathen leader of that congregation bully them to the supplication so that they would be willing, those men, to go there to the golden idol which he had ordained for himself as a god. His servants told the prince what they of that persuasion were: 'his highness's captives in this lofty city, who are not willing to do this nor to worship this idol which you have wondrously ordained to your glory'.

209   Then, enraged, the ruler of Babylon furiously answered them and fiercely informed the young men and harshly told them that they must forthwith do homage or else suffer great torture, the terrible swirling of fire, unless they, the Hebrew men,

would pray for indemnity to that most evil thing, to the gold
which he had ordained for himself as a god. But the young men
were unwilling in their courage to obey heathen precepts. They
zealously intended that they should fulfil God's law entirely
and not belittle the Lord of hosts; no more should they convert
to paganism nor beg indemnity of the evil thing even though a
cruel death was threatened them.

LII

224   Then the obstinate king grew furious. He ordered a furnace
to be heated for the destruction of the young men's lives
because they challenged his powers. When it had been made as
hot as it could most fiercely be with the fire's terrible flame, he
assembled the people there, the ruler of Babylon, fierce and
murderous, and commanded God's spokesmen to be bound.
Then he commanded his minions to thrust the youths, the
young men, into the blaze of the fire.

232   He was at hand who afforded them help. Although he had
forced them so brutally into the embrace of the fire's flame, yet
the ordaining Lord's mighty guardianship saved their life, as
many have heard tell. He ordained divine help for them there;
from high heaven God, the Protector of men, sent them the
holy spirit. An angel entered into the furnace where they were
undergoing that torment; he enfolded the noble youths in his
arms under the fiery roof. The swirl of the leaping flame could
not even a whit mar their good looks when God the Ruler saved
them.

241   The pagan prince became distraught. He commanded them
to be burned immediately. The fire was absurdly huge; the
furnace was already grown hot; the iron was thoroughly
aglow. Into it the numerous servants there were throwing
wood as had been explicitly commanded them. They carried
logs into the blaze of the glaring fire – the wolf-hearted king
wanted the iron to boil upon the spot about the devout men –
until up rose the flame over the favoured ones and in its

enthusiasm did much more killing than was expedient, since
the flame whirled towards the hateful men, the heathens, away
from the holy ones. The youths survived, cheerful of spirit; the
minions outside were burnt up about the furnace – the fire had
turned to the hurt of the persecutors while the prince of Baby-
lon looked on. The Hebrew men were cheerful; with alacrity
they praised the Lord in joy – they did as best they could inside
the furnace – for their preserved existence. Glad of heart, the
men worshipped God within the embrace of the one by whom
the terrible heat of the fire had been driven off. The noble
youths had been delivered from the flame's attacks, and they did
them no harm there. The roaring fire was no more distressing to
them than the light of the sun nor did the blaze threaten the men
who were under that threat, but the fire erupted fire upon those
who were perpetrating that wicked thing; it turned upon the
heathen slaves away from the holy youths, and lessened the good
looks of the wretches who were enjoying their work.

268   Then the headstrong king, when he came to trust his senses,
saw a miracle, come to pass in the midst of the punishment. It
seemed uncanny to him: the youths were moving about
unscathed in the hot furnace, all three devout men. In addition
to them there was one more to be seen – the Almighty's angel.
There nothing harmed them at all but rather inside there it was
most of all just as when in summer the sun shines and the fallen
dew is dispersed by the breeze at dawn. It was the God of
heaven who saved them from that persecution.

279   Then the holy Azarias gave voice to his inner thoughts from
out of the hot fire; a man zealous in good deeds and devoid of
faults, he praised the Lord and spoke these words: ·

283   'Lord of all creatures, behold! Mightily strong you are to
save men. Your name, comely and glorious, is renowned
throughout the nations of men. Day by day your decrees are
true and endued with strength and secured of their triumph, as
you yourself are too. Your acts of will in things of worldly weal
are just and generous, Ruler of heaven. Aid us in earnest now,

Creator of souls, and graciously help us, holy Lord, now that we, in our afflictions, in our oppressions and in our humility, hemmed in by fire, pray you for mercies. We, living in this temporal existence, have brought this about; and our forefathers, moreover, committed sin: in their arrogance those city-dwellers broke the commandments and despised the calling of a holy way of life. We are exiled throughout the wide earth, scattered in flocks, lacking protection. In many lands our way of life is held in contempt and notoriety by many peoples who have also exiled us as chattels into the power of the worst of earthly kings, into slavery under savage men, and now we suffer the oppression of heathens. For this, thanks be to you, glorious King of hosts, that you have ordained this chastisement for us.

309 'Do not leave us on our own, eternal Lord, for the sake of those mercies which men ascribe to you and the covenants which you, the gloriously steadfast Saviour of mortals, Creator of souls, entered into with Abraham and Isaac and Jacob. By the word of your mouth you promised them that you would, in days yet distant, augment the offspring which would be born in the generations following them, and that this multitudinous people should be renowned; to increase their race as the stars of heaven encompass their wide orbit or as the sand of the ocean-shore, of the shores of the sea, forms the floor of the deep throughout the salty main, so that for a myriad of years there should ever remain of it a countless tally.

325 'Fulfil now your promise, though few of them survive. Embellish in us your edict and your glory; make known the strength and power of which the Chaldeans and those many nations have heard tell who exist here below the heavens as heathens; and that you only are the Lord eternal, Ruler of the hosts and of worldly creatures, the Arbiter of victories, the Lord steadfast in truth.'

333 Thus the holy man went on praising the Lord's mercy and recounted with eloquence the abundance of his powers. Then

from the heavens an angel, utterly dazzling, was sent from
above, a being of beautiful appearance in his celestial garb who
came to them for their comfort and for the preservation of their
life, with love and with grace. Holy and heavenly bright, he
thrust aside the hot flame of the fire; the glare of the flame he
swept back and brushed aside by his very great might so that
their body was not a whit harmed – rather, he flung the fire in
anger upon their adversaries, for their wicked actions.

345   Then when the angel had come it was breezy and pleasant in
the furnace, most like the weather in summertime when a
sprinkling of raindrops is sent during the day, a warm shower
from the clouds. As is the finest weather, so it was in that fire
through the powers of the Lord in aid of the holy men. The hot
flame was driven back and quenched wherever those men of
courageous conduct, Hananiah and Azariah and Mishael,
walked throughout the furnace, and the angel with them,
preserving their lives, who was the fourth one there. There the
courageous-hearted three praised the Prince in their contem-
plations. They urged the children of Israel and all earthly
creatures to bless the everlasting Lord, the Ruler of nations.
Thus spoke the three of them, men brisk of mind, with a
common voice:

LIII

362   'The beauty of the world's handiworks and each thing
wrought, merciful Father, let them bless you. The heavens and
the angels and the clear waters which by lawful decree subsist
in glory above the skies, let them worship you. And all created
things, the planets shining in the sky which keep their courses,
the sun and the moon, let them each one severally in its degree,
Almighty, praise you. And the stars of heaven, the dew and the
heavy rainstorm, let these glorify you. And souls, mighty God,
let them extol you. Burning fire and bright summer, let them
praise the Saviour. Night and day together, and every land, and
light and darkness, let them praise you in their degree, and heat
and cold together; and frosts and snows, the bitter winter

weather and the cloud-rack, let them, mighty Lord, extol you on high. And the lightnings, bright and instant as a blink, let these bless you. The whole face of the earth, eternal Lord, hills and plains and high mountains, the salt waves of the sea, righteous Lord, the streaming of the waves and the rising and watery spouting of springs, let these worship you. Let the whales praise you, those that swim the ocean currents and the waters, and the birds of heaven, flying aloft. And wild beasts and all cattle, let them bless your name. And let the children of men love you with their hearts and let the people of Israel, your servants, praise you, the Maker of riches, in their degree. And the heart's virtues of holy men and the souls and spirits of every righteous man, let them extol you, Lord of life giving to all their reward, the Lord everlasting. Hananiah and Azariah and Mishael, let them glorify you, Lord, in the contemplation of their heart. We bless you, Lord of every nation, the Father almighty, and the true Son of the ordaining Lord, the Saviour of souls and Helper of men; and we worship you, the Holy Ghost, in glory, the sapient Lord. We praise you, holy Lord, and celebrate you in our observances. You are blessed, for ever worshipped above the roof of the world, high King of heaven, in your holy powers, Author of life and light, throughout every land.'

409 Then Nebuchadnezzar, the lord of the nation, deliberated upon this with his closest nobles:

411 'Many of you, my lords, saw it, that we dispatched three men, sentenced to burning, into the scorching glare of the fire. Now I see four men there for sure: my mind does not deceive me.'

416 Then one who was a counsellor of the king, wise and shrewd of speech, said:

417 'It is a miraculous thing which we are looking at there with our own eyes. My lord, consider your proper duty. Understand clearly who has granted that grace to these young companions.

They are praising God, the One, the Everlasting, and wholly upon him they call in earnest with each name. They are thanking him for his majesty with intrepid words; they say that he alone is God almighty, the wise King of glory, of the world and of the heavens. Summon the men out of the furnace, prince of the Chaldeans. It is not at all good that they should remain in that plight longer than you have reason.'

430   Then the king commanded the young men to come to him. The indomitable youths obeyed the behest; the well-born men went as they had been instructed; the young heroes came before the heathen. The ropes which had lain around their limbs, the ill-intended fetters of the people's king, had been burnt away and their bodies spared. Their appearance was not marred nor was there any damage to their clothing nor was their hair singed by fire, but they had walked rejoicing out of that dreadful horror in the Lord's immunity, men of discerning mind, in the spirit's protection.

440   Then the angel, an exalted and trusty minister to the holy Lord, ascended, making his way back to everlasting joys in the high vault of the kingdom of heaven. By that miracle, he had honoured those who had merited it. The youths praised the Lord in the presence of the heathen people; they enlightened them with statements of the truth, and expressed many true proofs to them, until he himself believed that he who had saved them from out of darkness was a wielder of mighty powers; and so the imperious and headstrong ruler of Babylon decreed to his people that he would be capitally culpable who denied it, that he who had delivered them from that violent death was the true and glorious Wielder of mighty powers.

452   Then he gave them back the heirlooms of their nation which had been brought there into the keeping of their old enemies, so that they had due respect. Glory was theirs in Babylon after they had passed through the fire; their reputation became celebrated throughout the nation after they had been obedient to the Lord. Their counsels were influential after the Ruler of

the skies, the holy Guardian Lord of heaven-kingdom had shielded them from that harm.

458   I have heard that the ruler of Babylon, when he recognized the miracle concerning the fiery blaze, sought to articulate in truthful words how the three young men had survived the heat of the furnace, the fearsome terror of the fire. They had walked through its turbulence as though the savage malevolence of the flames, of the fierce fire, did not hurt them, God's evangelists, a whit; but the Lord's immunity shielded their lives against that appalling terror. Then the prince caused an assembly. He summoned his people together at that time and then in the meeting he announced to the throng the happening that had occurred and the miracle of God which had been manifested in the young men:

472   'Consider now the divine strength and the clever miracle of God. We have witnessed that he saved from death those who exalted his praise, the youths in the furnace, in the leaping fire: therefore he alone is the everlasting Lord, the almighty Arbiter, who granted glory to them and surpassing triumph to those who bear his message. For that reason he reveals himself through many a miracle to those holy souls who have chosen his fealty. It is evident that Daniel correctly declared to me the mysterious dream which had previously much baffled many of my people in their mind, because the Almighty sent a more ample spirit and the faculty of discernment into his intellect.'

486   Thus in these words the mentor of the multitude, the lord of Babylon, spoke when he had understood the sign, God's clear token. It made him none the better, for presumptuousness scathed the prince. His thought grew haughtier and the pretension in his heart and in his mind greater than was fitting – until the almighty ordaining Lord put him down by force, as he does many of those who in their presumptuousness clamber upwards.

LIV

495   Then in his sleep a dream was revealed to Nebuchadnezzar; it concerned himself. It seemed to him that there was a beautiful tree standing handsomely in the ground, which was firm in its roots and bright with fruits. It was not like a woodland tree; instead it towered up to the stars of heaven and likewise it embraced the plains of earth, the whole world as far as the waters of ocean, with its branches and boughs. While he looked on, it seemed to him that this tree sheltered the wild creatures and that itself alone contained food for them all; the birds likewise also received vital nourishment among the tree's fruits.

508   It seemed to him that an angel came descending from the heavens above and called out loud with clear voice. He commanded the tree to be hewn down, and the wild creatures to flee away, and the birds as well, since its fall was coming. Then he commanded that the fruits of the tree itself, the branches and the boughs, be stripped off – and yet that a token should survive, that the root-stump of the tree should remain firm in the earth until green shoots should come again when God appoints. He also commanded the great tree to be fettered with brass and iron shackles and to be given over, bound, into torment so that his mind may know that a mightier being than he can resist has the power of punishment.

523   Then the earthly prince – his dream was at its end – awoke from sleep. The fearfulness of it stayed with him, the terror of that phenomenon which God sent there. Then he commanded his people, the chief men of the nation, to come together. The headstrong king asked among them all what that dream signified – not because he expected that they would know it, but he was testing what they would say. Then Daniel was summoned to the judgment, God's evangelist. A holy spirit was given him from heaven which lent strength to his mind. In him the lord king was conscious of a deep and ample thoughtfulness of intellect, the faculty of perception and wise speech.

Often he had expounded for the man's sake many a marvel and the powers of the ordaining Lord. So the haughty-hearted leader of the multitude set about declaring the portent of the dream and the whole fearsome thing which had been shown him. He ordered him to recount what the mystery signified, to summon up and to find in his mind divine words to express in true words what that tree signified which he saw shimmering, and to interpret for him the foregone conclusions of events.

546   Then Daniel fell silent at the judgment, even though he perceived the truth – that his master, the lord of men, was found guilty against God. The shrewd man hesitated; but then this emissary, learned in the law, declared aloud to the prince:

551   'Ruler of the multitude, it is no trivial marvel which you saw happen in your dream – the tree high as heaven and the divine words, wrathful and terrible, which the angel spoke: that that tree, stripped of its boughs, was to topple over which had previously stood fast, and was then to live on forlorn among the wild beasts, to dwell in the wilderness, and its root-stump embedded in the earth to remain undisturbed in its place for a certain time, so the voice declared, to regain its fruitfulness after seven seasons.

562   'So will your glory be prostrated. As the tree grew tall to the heavens so for all men dwelling on the earth you are sole ruler and guide. There is no man on earth your rival, but only the ordaining Lord. He will hew you down from sovereignty and will send you friendless into exile, and then he will transform your heart so that you have no recall of human pastime and know no intelligence but only the intuition of wild beasts; and you will continue for a long time living among the thickets in the tracks of the deer. There will be no food for you but the grass of the moorland and no resting-place afforded you, but the rain showers will rouse you and drive you on like the wild beasts until after seven years you come to believe the truth: that there is one ordaining Lord, wielding authority and power, for all men, who is in heaven. However, such appears to me his

intention, that the root-stump should remain undisturbed in its place, so the voice declared, and after seven seasons should regain fruitfulness. So will your kingdom abide, resting unharmed by men, until you return.

585 'My lord, think upon my firm advice. Give alms, be the refuge of the wretched; supplicate before the Lord, before the time comes when he will topple you from earthly sovereignty. Often the ordaining Lord allows many a nation rooted in sin to make reparation, when they themselves have been willing, before God's sudden stroke with awesome violence crushed the life from them.'

593 Daniel did not speak to his lord so many true words through his faculty of perception that this potentate, the lord of the earth, would ever pay heed to him; instead, his pride mounted up aloft from his heart. He paid cruelly for this.

598 Then the Chaldean king began to brag with much boasting while he was ruling the fortress, and in his affluence looked out upon the city stretching abroad about the plain of Shinar, towering aloft: that he, the warrior king, had built it as a great marvel for the multitude. So he became self-esteeming above all men and headstrong in spirit on account of the special grace God had granted him – sovereignty over men and a world to wield, during his mortal existence:

608 'You are that great and glorious city of mine which I built for my honour by my vast might. In you I mean to enjoy a resting-place, a dwelling and a home.'

612 Then on account of that boasting the lord of men suffered a seizure and went fleeing away, alone in his pride above all men. Thus, under the punishment of God, he travelled in days of tribulation the most melancholy path of such people as, surviving, find their nation once more; thus Nebuchadnezzar, after God's swift attack from the heavens had implacably stricken him.

620 For seven years together he endured torment, this king of the festive city, and the desolate territory of wild beasts. Then the suffering man, the intellectual peer of the wild beasts, looked upwards through the drift of the clouds; then in his mind he remembered that the ordaining Lord, the high King of the heavens, was for the children of men the only and everlasting Spirit. Then he recovered from his lunatic state of mind, whereas before he had carried an aggressive pride close to his heart; then his soul and spirit, in recalling God, turned towards men, once he had acknowledged the ordaining Lord. The wretched man then made his way back to human society, a naked beggar submitting to his affliction, an extraordinary vagrant and lacking clothes, humbler in his thinking than he had been, as ruler of men, in his boasting. The earth, his dwelling and home, survived after the lord and prince seven years together, and the empire did not dwindle away below the skies, until its mentor returned.

640 When the ruler of Babylon was restored to sovereignty, he had a better disposition, a more enlightened belief in the Lord of life – that God bestowed on every man prosperity as well as punishment as he himself willed.

645 Then the people's lord did not dally over the prophets' pronouncements but he preached abroad, wherever he made a proclamation, the might of the ordaining Lord; he recounted to his people his wandering, the widely nomadic trail he had roamed in company with the wild beasts until a reasonable understanding came from the Lord God upon his soul, when he looked to the heavens. Destiny was accomplished, the portent made plain, the dream fulfilled, the penance overcome, the judgment executed just as Daniel had predicted – that the king was to discover the ways of hardship on account of his arrogance. Thus he urgently preached the powers of the ordaining Lord before mankind, after Daniel had for a long while been voicing his precepts and his judgments to the citizens in Babylon.

661   When the comrade and consort of wild beasts, Nebuchad-
nezzar, came back from his nomadic trail and his punishments
he afterwards retained his wide empire and governed the public
treasury and the capital city, an experienced and outstandingly
mighty mentor of the people, king of the Chaldeans, until death
destroyed him, so that no man on earth was his rival until God
willed to take that pre-eminent empire away from him by
death. Afterwards, his successors enjoyed in strength prosper-
ity, wealth, plaited gold and the eminent store of riches there in
the spacious fortress, the city of warriors, when their lord was
dead.

LV

675   Then into that nation was born the third generation after
him. Belshazzar was lord of the cities and wielded human
empire – until pride destroyed him, despicable presumptuous-
ness. It was then the end of the time in which the Chaldeans
held sovereignty when, within a short while, the ordaining
Lord granted dominion to the Medes and Persians and let the
glory of Babylon, which those men should have guarded,
dwindle away. He knew that the elders, those who should have
guided the empire, were involved in iniquitous things. Then the
lord of the Medes, biding his time at home, resolved upon
something which had not been undertaken before – that he
would destroy Babylon, the city of warriors where the princes
enjoyed their wealth within the shelter of its walls. Of the
fortresses folk have inhabited, that one, Babylon, was the best
known to people, the greatest and most glorious – until Bel-
shazzar in his furious boasting provoked God. They would sit
over their wine, protected by the wall and never fearing the
ill-will of enemies – even though a nation of foes had come
advancing in military trappings on the capital city – or that
they could destroy Babylon.

700   The king of the Chaldeans then sat feasting on that final day
with members of his family, when the leader of that power
grew insolent from the mead. He commanded to be put into the

noblemen's hands the treasure of the Israelites, the holy sacrificial vessels, the gold which together with their sovereign might the Chaldean soldiers had once seized wholesale in the city of Jerusalem, when they destroyed the glory of the Jews with their swords' edges, and in process of their clamorous invasion seized the gleaming treasure in battle. When they plundered the temple, Solomon's hall, they greatly boasted.

712   So the lord over cities grew merry and boasted immoderately, to the anger of God. He declared that his armies were greater and more effectual for people's protection than the everlasting Lord of the Israelites. To him as he looked on there came an awesome portent in the presence of the men within the hall, that he had uttered lying words before the people, when awesomely an angel of the Lord caused his hand to appear there in that lofty hall, and then wrote upon the wall enigmas in words, scarlet hieroglyphs, for the city-dwellers.

724   Then the king grew afraid in his mind and dismayed by that awful phenomenon. He saw the angel's hand in the hall, writing the punishment of the Shinarites. A great number of people, the men in the hall, debated what the hand had written to the admonition of the city-dwellers. Multitudes came to look at the prodigy and then searched hard in their mind's thoughts as to what the hand of the holy spirit had written. Not men expert in writing, nor the community of nobles were able to decipher the angel's message – until Daniel, the Lord's elect, wise and steadfast in the truth, came walking into the hall, in whose soul was an abundant faculty from God. The city's keepers, as I have heard tell, eagerly bargained with gifts, that he should decipher and interpret for them what the enigma might foretell.

741   The mouthpiece of God, skilled in the law, answered them, discerning in his deliberation:

743   'I shall not convey to people in return for riches, nor can I to you for profit, the judgments of the Lord; but I will tell you without payment your fate and the enigma of the words which

you are unable to construe. In your arrogance you put the holy
sacrificial vessels into people's hands to hold. You drank to
devils out of those vessels which the Israelites once kept accord-
ing to the law by the ark of God – until boasting, discretion
drunk with wine, betrayed them as shall happen to you. Your
father would never have brought out the gold vessels of God in
boast, nor did he more readily gloat even though war brought
the treasure of the Israelites under the control of his possession;
but the people's lord more often declared to his army in truth-
ful words, after the Guardian Lord of heaven had revealed to
him a miracle, that he alone was Lord and Ruler of all created
things who granted him the glory, the unsullied splendour, of
earthly empire – and now you deny that he exists, who rules in
majesty above the devils.'

Christ and Satan

[Oxford, Bodleian Library, Junius 11, pp. 213–29]

The poem reviews – appropriately, as the final poem in the codex – the
totality of Christ's triumph over Satan, not only within the episode of
the testing in the desert but within the whole historic framework of
God's irresistible purpose. The poet looks back to the expulsion of the
rebel angels from heaven, where he keeps his audience in conscious-
ness of the co-eternality of the Son, Satan's adversary in the battle. He
looks forward to the harrowing of hell, where the corollary of Satan's
defeat, namely the release and loving absolution of Adam and Eve,
movingly concludes a theme central to the cycle of the Junius poems.
And he looks forward to the Resurrection and Christ's appearances to
the disciples, where he speaks implicitly of the body of the faithful and
the righteous left behind after Christ, that is the Church Militant, and
of faith and righteousness as the individual Christian's alternative
choice to Satan's perfidy, in this present life. The theme of the right-
eous man reaches its natural culmination in this poem with Christ's
promise (308 ff.): 'So he himself has said: "Men steadfast in truth
shall like the sun shine forth clothed in beauty in their Father's

kingdom, in the city of refuge" ', and with the scene of Judgment where, after the warfare of the world, the righteous receive Christ's blessing: 'You are welcome guests. Go on into the light of glory, into the realm of the heavens, where you shall have eternal rest for ever and ever' (616 ff.).

The main *topos*, however, is the Lenten theme of the testing in the desert. It is to be remembered that the desert Fathers, like St Anthony who is depicted breaking bread with Paul on the eighth-century stone cross at Ruthwell, expressed their interpretation of life's purpose by withdrawing into the wilderness to struggle, in emulation of Christ, against the devil. In turn, the literary Life of St Anthony became the model for the genre of the Saint's Life, and so the struggle with the devil in a wild and barren retreat appears a mandatory element in many saints' biographies – hence Guthlac's retreat to Crowland in the Fens. The monastic life was also interpreted in these terms, as *Glc* makes clear. *And* shows that the struggle with the devil can take place in the 'wilderness' of a heathen community; so does *Jul*, where the struggle is crowned with martyrdom; while *Sfr* implies that warfare against the devil is an ideal way of life for any faithful Christian, whose withdrawal from the world is perhaps symbolic rather than actual, a state of spiritual alienation from materialism rather than a literal disengagement from society. Again, then, the poetry of this codex asks of its audience a complex (though conventional enough) interpretation of the narrative and a far-reaching application of its message, in response to the synopsis of the divine plan and the sacred history cyclically reviewed in the codex.

LIBER II

I

It has come to be no secret to earth's inhabitants that the ordaining Lord was possessed of power and of strength when he consolidated the plains of the world. Of himself, he established sun and moon, rocks and soil, the tide out upon the ocean and water and cloud, by means of his potency for marvels. The deep compass of ocean the ordaining Lord in his powers clean embraces, and all the earth in its midst. Of himself, God's own Son can survey the seas and the continents within the ocean, and he can reckon the rain-showers, every drop. The final sum of days he himself established by his authentic power. Thus the Creator on high in the heavens through his glorious Spirit conceived and established in six days the regions of earth and the deep main. Who is there that can know to the full his design, except eternal God?

19 He first appointed those happy estates, the heavenly host and human community, Adam and that noble specimen, the original leader of the angels, who later came to grief. To them in their pride it seemed it could be so, that they themselves might be the rulers of heaven, the lords of glory. In that, it turned out the worse for them, when they set up their home in hell, one after the other, in that terrible pit where they were to endure painful wretchedness in the fire's turbulence, not to have ethereal light in the loftily structured heavens, but rather they were to plummet into that deep turbulence down beneath the ground, into the abysmal gulf, those covetous and rapacious beings. God alone knows how he condemned that guilty throng.

34 Then the old one cries from out of hell with monstrous noise, and with weary voice gives vent to wordy effusions:

36 'What has become of the angelic majesty which we were supposed to possess in the heavens? This home is dark, excessively confined by fixed fiery shackles; the floor is seething with burning venom. There is now no distant end of our having to suffer torment together, miseries among the damned, not to have the opulence of glory in the heavens nor the pleasure of exalted thrones. See! once we enjoyed pleasures in the presence of the Lord, and singing in heaven in better times, where now the illustrious stand, heroes, about the everlasting throne and worship the Lord in words and acts, and I must remain in chains under punishment and, because of pride, never expect for myself a better home.'

51   Then the hideous spirits, black and full of sin, answered him,
lamenting in torment:

53   'You convinced us by your lying that we ought not to obey
the Saviour. To you alone it seemed you had control of every-
thing, of heaven and of earth – that you were holy God, the
Creator himself. Now you are one of the criminals securely
chained in a fiery prison. You in your glory, and we angels with
you, believed you owned the world, and governance over all
things. Your appearance is hideous; we have all fared as
wretchedly because of your lies. You told us as a truth that the
ordaining Lord of mankind was your son: now you have all the
more torment.'

65   Thus the sinful beings railed with treacherous words upon
their leader in anxious utterances. Christ had expelled them,
segregated from joys. Because of pride they had surrendered
the Lord's radiance on high: they had as their prospect the
floors of hell and burning noxiousness. Black, deformed, the
demons wandered about; the criminals, wretched monsters,
roamed throughout that hideous pit, on account of the arro-
gance which they had previously maintained.

II

75   The leader of the fiends spoke again, a second time. He was
even now the malefactor, after he had felt the profuseness of
the punishment. He grew blacker as he began to speak in the
fire and the venom. Such is not the pleasant sound of joy as
when he in his punishments burst out in words:

81   'Once I was a holy angel in the heavens, dear to the Lord. I
had a great happiness with God, in the presence of the Lord,
and this multitude likewise. Then in my heart I resolved that I
would overthrow heaven's Luminary and the Son of God the
Saviour, and have the entire government of the cities in my
control – I and this wretched contingent which I have led home
to hell. Believe it, the portent was plain and the malediction,

when I was banished down beneath the ground into the abysmal gulf. I have obtained you all a home now – as captives away from your settled abode. Here is no glorification of the blessed nor wine-hall of the doughty nor pleasure of the world nor throng of angels, nor may we have heaven. This hideous home is ablaze with fire. I am guilty towards God. Forever at the doors of hell dwell dragons with fire at their heart: they cannot be of use to us. This woeful home is filled with punishment. We do not have darkness enough that we might hide ourselves in this abysmal gloom. Here there is the hissing of snakes, and serpents live. This shackle of punishment is bound tight. The fiends are furious, dismal and dark. Here day, the Creator's light, does not illumine, because of the haze of shadow.

106   'Once I had authority over the whole of heaven, before I was constrained to await in this terrible domain what the Lord God means to pronounce as sentence upon me, outlawed in the abyss. For the present, I have come trekking with a multitude of devils to this dismal home. But on occasions, taking wing in flight, I – and more of you, who were responsible for the beginning of this pride – shall have to seek for settled abodes. We need not expect that the King of heaven will ever hand over to us a settled abode, a patrimony for our possession, everlasting governance, as he did before. The Ruler's Son himself has rule over everything, heaven's glory and hell's torments. Therefore I, dejected and miserable, shall have to turn further afield and wander the paths of exile, deprived of heaven and segregated from its blessings, not to have any joy on high among the angels, since I lately declared that I myself was lord of heaven and ruler of its beings – but it turned out the worse for me.'

III

125   So the cursed spirit, criminal in his sins, put into words all his whole misery; the glare of fire persisted throughout that hideous pit, mixed with venom.

129   'I am of such physical stature that I cannot hide away, wounded by sins, in this vast hall. See! here heat and cold sometimes mingle; sometimes I hear hell's subjects, a querulous people, bewail the abysses down below the ground; sometimes people struggle naked among serpents. This windswept hall is all inwardly filled with venom. I shall not be allowed to enjoy a more promising home, neither city nor palace, nor shall I ever more be allowed to gaze with my eyes upon that radiant creation. It is now worse for me that I ever knew celestial light on high amidst the angels, and singing in heaven where all his own children surround the Son of the Lord with song. None of these souls am I allowed to harm, except the ones whom he will disown: those I am allowed to carry off home as captives and bring them to a dwelling-place in this painful abyss.

149   'We are all changed from when once formerly we had beauty and esteem in the heavens, and very often brought celestial harmony to the bosom of the Son of God the Saviour when we, round about him as limbs about the loved one, all raised the strain of songs of praise and addressed them to the Lord. Now I am besmirched by my deeds, wounded by evils; now I have to bear this shackle of torment burning upon my back, heat in hell, dispossessed of hope and wants.'

159   Many more things yet the master of iniquities, the hideous monster, spoke out of hell, weary from his punishments. His speech flew in sparks much like venom when he burst out:

163   'Alas! the majesty of the Lord. Alas! the Protector of the heavenly hosts. Alas! the might of the ordaining Lord. Alas! the middle-earth. Alas! the bright day. Alas! the joy of God. Alas! the throng of the angels. Alas! the heaven on high. Alas! that I am utterly dispossessed of everlasting joy, that I may not reach up my hands to heaven nor may I look upwards with my eyes, nor indeed shall I ever hear with my ears the sound of the clearest trumpet – because I purposed to drive the Lord, the Son of God, from off his throne and have to myself the rule of that joy, of the glory and the bliss. It turned out worse for me

than I might have hoped. Now I am cut off from that radiant company, expelled from the light into this loathsome home. I cannot conceive how I came to be in it, in this abysmal darkness, besmirched with sins of malice, cast out of the world. I now know that he who is minded not to listen to the King of heaven and obey the Lord will be utterly dispossessed of everlasting joys. I am to endure this punishment, the misery, torment and pain, deprived of blessings, besmirched by my former deeds, because I thought to drive the Lord, the Ruler of the hosts, from off his throne. Now, sorrow-stricken, I must travel the ways of exile, far-flung roads.'

IV

189 God's adversary, then, passed to hell when he had been vanquished; so did his covetous and greedy inferiors, when God drove them into that hot abode whose name is hell. Every man must therefore take thought not to provoke the Son of God the Ruler. Let it be as an example to him, how the black fiends all came to grief because of their pride. Let us take as our delight the Lord of the multitudes, the everlasting Joy on high, the Ruler of the angels. He made it known that he had strength and great powers when he drove out that myriad, prisoners, from the high mansion. Let us keep in mind the holy Lord, eternal in glory with the Author of all created things. Let us choose for ourselves an abode in glory with the King of all kings, who is called Christ. Let us bear in our bosoms peaceable thoughts, love and discretion. Let us keep in mind truth and right when we presume to bow before the high throne and pray the one Ruler for mercies.

209 It behoves the man who lives pleasantly here in the world that his brightness shines forth when he seeks back to the other life, to a land more lovely than is this earth. There it is bright and pleasant, and radiant figures shine forth throughout its cities. It is a spacious land there, a home in the heaven-kingdom for men of hope, for those found acceptable to Christ. Let us return thither where the Wielder of victories, the Lord and

Saviour himself, sits in that precious home, and where gleaming troops of angels and of the blessed stand about the high throne, and the holy throngs of heaven praise the Lord in words and in actions. Their light shall shine forth through an aeon of aeons with the King of glory.

V

224 Still more I have heard the fiends to have confessed. Disgrace extremely rigorous was theirs, and punishments; because of their pride they had forsaken the King of glory. Soon they spoke again in another utterance:

228 'It is apparent that we sinned in the habitation above. Because of this, we must now without choice for ever endure strife with the powers of the Lord. Think; we were allowed to dwell in heaven's brightness while we were willing to obey holy God and we should chant song to him in our thousands about the throne. When we were there we dwelt amidst pleasures, we listened to celestial harmony and the voice of the trumpet. Clear-spoken, the Author of the angels would arise and to that Prince the saints would bow themselves; triumphantly splendid, the eternal Lord would arise and would stand over us and would bless the innocent congregation every day – he, the Creator of souls, and his precious Son. God himself was the embrace outstretched to all who arrived there on high and had beforehand believed in him on earth.

245 'Then it irked, that this Prince was strong and unyielding of temper. I alone then stepped forward to the angels and spoke to them all: "I can direct you to long-lasting profit, if you are willing to trust in my power. Let us presume upon this great Protector, the Ruler of the hosts, and have this whole celestial state of being as our own possession. This that we have endured the whole while hitherto is a vain ostentation."

VI

254   'So we agreed that we would thus drive out the Lord from that precious home, the King from his citadel. It is known abroad that we were obliged to inhabit the ways of exile, the cruel abysses: God keeps the kingdom for himself. He is sole King, who grew angry with us, the everlasting Lord, the Ordainer, strong in powers. Now this multitude must lie here according to its crimes; some to flutter aloft and fly above the ground. Fire envelops each one, though he may be on high. He is never allowed to touch those blessed souls which seek upwards there from the earth; but I with my hands am allowed to snatch down to the depths the heathen chaff, God's adversaries. Some are to roam about through the land of men and often stir up strife in the families of men throughout middle-earth. I, here, have to forfeit – and, sick and full of sorrow, bewail the mischief of my bitter malice – each one of the things over which I myself disposed while I held secure a home in the heavens. Will the eternal Lord ever grant us a home in the heaven-kingdom, a patrimony to possess, as he did before?'

279   Thus, burning in hell, God's adversaries lamented. God the Saviour had become enraged against them for their blasphemies. Therefore each living man whose heart has integrity may understand that he should put away from himself wicked thoughts and loathsome vices. Let us constantly remember in our mind the strength of the ordaining Lord. Let us gird ourselves for the living way upwards to the angels, where the almighty God is; and the noble Son of God will embrace us, if we previously set our minds to it while on earth, and trust to the Holy for help. Then he will never desert us but will give us life on high amidst the angels, and blessed joy. The refulgent Lord will teach us to a secure home, to the radiant ramparts. Radiant blessed souls, separated from cares, will shine forth there where for evermore they may frequent the citadel and the sovereign throne. Let us make this plain. Let us take thought beforehand, living on the earth, and by shrewd means unlock

the Ruler's locked-up keep: let us understand this spiritually. A thousand angels will come to meet us if we are allowed to go thither and if we merit this beforehand on the earth.

303   Therefore he will be blessed who is ever willing to despise wickedness, to please the Lord and to stifle sin. So he himself has said: 'Men steadfast in truth shall, like the sun, shine forth, clothed in beauty, in their Father's kingdom, in the city of refuge.' There the Creator himself, the Father of mankind, will enfold them in his protection and graciously exalt them into the heavenly existence where they will be allowed to dwell with the King of glory ever to eternity, and to possess the joy of joys with God the Lord for ever and ever, world without end.

Lines 315–64 (section VII) are here omitted. They contain a further reiteration of the horrors of hell contrasted with the joys of heaven.

VIII

365   That species of angel mentioned before, called Lucifer, the bearer of light, lived in days of old in the kingdom of God. Then he aroused strife in heaven, because he was willing to give way to pride. Then Satan darkly decided to fashion an exalted throne on high in the heavens, alongside the eternal God. He was their lord, the originator of evil. He afterwards rued it, when he was forced to sink down to hell, and his following with him, to slide into humiliation – the Saviour's hostility, and the fact that never to eternity would they be allowed to see the face of the eternal Lord after that time when a terrifying thing befell them, the din caused by the Judge when he broke asunder and crushed the gates in hell. Delight came upon the mortals when they saw the Redeemer's head – more than there was for the hideous being whom we previously named.

383   They were all at that time, abroad throughout that wind-swept habitation, panic-stricken with terror. They complained aloud:

385 'This is hard to withstand, now that this attack has come, a soldier with a battalion, the Prince of the angels. Ahead of him there goes a light more beautiful than we have ever before looked on with our eyes except when we were on high amidst the angels. Now by the strength of his glory he will utterly overthrow our tortures. Now that this terrifying thing is come, the din caused by the Lord, this horde of miserable beings must forthwith suffer horror now. It is the Son of the Ruler himself, the Lord of the angels. He means to lead the souls up and away from here, and we for ever afterwards shall suffer humiliation for that act of his wrath.'

398 The ordaining Lord, then, by means of his might, went to hell to the sons of men; he meant to lead forth the full complement of mortals, many thousands, up to their fatherland. At that time there came the voice of angels, a thunderous sound in the dawning day: the Lord himself had outfought the fiend. His vengeance was made manifest even then in the early morning when that terrifying event took place. Then he let the blessed souls, Adam's kin, ascend – but Eve could not yet look upon heaven before she declared aloud:

408 'Once I provoked you, everlasting Lord, when we two, Adam and I, through the serpent's malice ate of an apple as we should never have done. The repulsive being – he who will now burn for ever in chains – persuaded us that we should have glory, the holy dwelling-place, heaven, at our command. Then we believed the words of the accursed creature: with our hands we took the bright fruit on that holy tree. We were bitterly repaid for this, when we were obliged to pass into this burning pit and afterwards remain in it the full complement of years, many thousands, cruelly scorched.

420 'Now I beseech you, Keeper of the heaven-kingdom, before the following you have led here, the battalions of angels, that I might be allowed and permitted to ascend from here with my family.

424   'Three days ago the Saviour's vassal came home to hell – he is now secure in shackles, cursed with punishments, according as the King of glory grew angry with him for his arrogance – and he told us as a sure fact that God himself would come down home to the tenants of hell. Then each one rose up and propped himself on his arm and leaned on his hands. Though the horror of hell seemed terrible, they all rejoiced at this among their sufferings, that their noble Lord meant to visit hell in their aid.'

435   Then she reached out with her hands to the heaven-King and prayed the ordaining Lord for mercy through the person of Mary.

437   'Lo, Lord, you were born into the world by my daughter, as a succour to mortals. Now it is manifest that you are God himself and the everlasting Author of all created things.'

IX

441   Then the everlasting Lord let them ascend. He had gloriously imposed the bonds of punishment upon the fiends and thrust them, forcibly crushed, deeper into that abysmal darkness where now Satan, wretched monster, and the hideous creatures with him, cursed with punishments, gloomily converse. They are allowed to possess not the light of heaven but the abyss of hell, and never hereafter may they look for change. The Lord God had grown angry with them and assigned to them, those hideous beings, the bond of punishment as their portion and the horror of that appalling thing, the dim and dark shadow of death – the burning abyss of hell and a horror of dying.

455   It was indeed a beautiful occasion when that throng came up into the homeland, and the eternal God, the ordaining Lord of mankind, with them, into the renowned citadel. The holy prophets, Abraham's kin, between them exalted him with their hands, up to the fatherland. The Lord himself had conquered death then and put the fiend to flight: in far-off days the prophets had said that he would do so. This all came about in

the early morning before daybreak, that the thunderous noise occurred, loud from the heavens, when he broke down and crushed the gates of hell – their frames grew feeble when they saw that light so brilliant.

468   Then he sat, God's Son from the beginning, amidst the gathering, and with words of truth he said:

469   'Wise spirits, by my might I made you, first Adam and the noble woman. Then by God's will they begot forty children so that from then on multitudes were born on earth and were allowed to live, those people in their native home, for many years – until it eventually happened that the fiend in his wickedness later caused their exile: he is guilty in every way. In Paradise I had newly established a tree with boughs whose branches bore aloft apples; and then you ate those bright fruits just as the evil minion from hell urged you. Therefore you have tenanted the burning abyss, because you disregarded the Saviour's word and ate of those appalling things. That hideous being was at hand: he foisted evil ideas upon you both.

487   'Then I repented that the work of my hand suffered the bondage of this prison. There was then no human competence, no angelic strength, no achievement of wise men, no mortal wisdom that might help you – but only that God the Saviour, he who beforehand ordained that punishment in vengeance, came into the world from his fatherland above, through the person of a woman, and endured on earth many torments and much insult. Day and night many men conspired about me, as to how they, the pillars of the state, might inflict upon me the pain of death. Then the term of time was past, so that I had been in the world, by tally of winters, thirty years before I suffered.

502   'I kept in remembrance that the multitude in this evil dwelling-place was longing that I should lead them home out of their shackles up to their own land, so that they should enjoy the splendours of the Lord and the glory of the heavenly host.

They shall dwell among joys. They shall have heaven's riches in their thousands. I atoned for you when men pierced me on the tree, with spears on the gallows: there the young man stabbed me, and I once more attained on high everlasting joys from the holy Lord.'

X

512   So the Keeper of heaven, mankind's ordaining Lord, declared by his words early in the morning on which the Lord God arose from death. There was no stone so stoutly fastened, though it were all braced about with iron, that could resist that mighty force, but out he came, Lord of the angels, from that confine and commanded the all-radiant angels to summon the eleven disciples, and especially he commanded them to say to Simon Peter that he would be permitted to look upon God in Galilee as he had done before.

524   I have heard tell that the disciples all then went to Galilee together. They experienced inspiration of the spirit; they recognized God's son, and they also saw where the Son of the ordaining Lord, the everlasting Lord God, ascended then on high in Galilee. The disciples all hastened to the place where the Everlasting was. They fell to the ground and prostrated themselves at his feet; they thanked the Master that it had so transpired that they had looked upon the Creator of the angels.

534   Then forthwith Simon Peter spoke:

535   'Is it you, Lord, decked in majesty? We saw you at that time when the heathens set a vile crown upon you with their hands. May they rue it when they face the final account hereafter.'

540   Some of them were unable to comprehend in their mind that it was the Beloved – one was called Didimus – before he himself touched the Saviour on the side where he shed his blood, and the waters of baptism fell to the ground.

545   A beautiful design it was that the noble Lord our Prince should have suffered. He mounted upon the Cross and poured out his blood, God on the gallows, through the might of his spirit. Therefore men should at all times express thanks to the Lord by deeds and by works because he led us out of our shackles home, up to the fatherland where we are to possess the splendours of the Lord and where we are entitled to dwell among joys. The brilliant radiance of heaven will be revealed to those of us who think aright.

XI

557   Thereafter, the eternal Lord was attended by folk for forty days and was manifested to mankind before he, Ruler of the people of his citadel, willed to betake his holy spirit into that glorious creation, the heaven-kingdom. He ascended into the heavens, Maker and Governor of the multitudes. There came at that time a divine tumult of clouds from the heavens. With it was the hand of God. It enveloped the noble Lord and led him, King of the heavens, forth to the sacred home. About him flew throngs of angels in their thousands. When it so came to pass, the redeeming Christ also declared that one day after that he would fortify the twelve apostles, the disciples, with the gift of his Spirit.

572   God then had restored to life a countless number of souls. Now absent from among them was Judas, he who had previously given the glorious Lord and Saviour to the sacrifice. That act, by which he sold the Son of the Ruler in exchange for a wealth of silver, did not profit him: the wretched demon evilly repaid him for that in hell.

579   Now the Son is seated on the right hand of the Father. Every day the Lord of hosts deals out succour and salvation to the sons of men throughout the earth. It is known to many that he alone is Maker and Ruler of all created things through the might of his glory and he is seated with them in the heavens, the Holy One with his angels, the Ruler with his prophets. The children

of glory keep his throne surrounded with song. Thither he invites us, through his healing power, into the light where we ourselves may sit with the Lord on high among the angels, to possess that same light where now his holy followers live and dwell among delights, where the glorious splendour of heaven is revealed. Let us determine aright that we shall readily obey the Saviour and be pleasing to Christ. There is a life more excellent than we can ever secure upon earth.

XII

597   Now he, the illustrious Prince, almighty God, the Lord himself, has decided to come to us in the Day of Judgment. He will bid the archangels blow the trumpets with a loud sound above the cities' inhabitants throughout the expanses of the world. Then people will awaken from this earth; the dead will arise from the dust through the Lord's might. It will be the longest of days, and the greatest clamour will be loudly heard as the Saviour approaches and the Ruler comes amidst clouds into this world. He will then survey the fair and the foul, the good and the wicked, on his two sides. On his right hand those steadfast in truth will ascend into rest with the Guardian of the heavens. They will then be happy, those who are allowed to enter into the citadel, into God's kingdom, and the King of all beings will bless them with his right hand and he will call out above them all:

616   'You are welcome guests. Go on into the light of glory, into the realm of the heavens where you shall have eternal rest for ever and ever.'

619   Then the criminals will stand forward, those who have sinned; they will be atremble when the Son of God in the efficacy of his actions purposes to judge them. They hope that they will be allowed to proceed into the illustrious citadel, up to the angels, as the others did. But the eternal Lord will address them and declare above them all:

626   'Descend now, you damned, with all dispatch into the place of punishment. I do not know you.'

628   Upon those words accursed spirits, the prisoners of hell, will forthwith come slinking their ways in thousands and will summon them thither into that devils' pit; they will thrust them into the abyss in that oppressive affliction, and never thereafter will they be allowed up from it, but there they must suffer miserable punishments, the shackle and the prison, and endure the chill deep abyss and the devil's taunting, as to how swarthy torturers will frequently heap scorn upon them: he will take vengeance upon them in suffering since they often forgot the Lord God, the one eternal Ruler, him whom they ought to have had as their hope.

642   Ah! let us throughout this world decide to start obeying the Saviour. Let us by God's grace zealously bear in mind the soul's prosperity, and how the blessed sit there aloft with the ethereally radiant Son of God the Saviour. There is the golden gate, adorned and pleasantly decked about with precious stones, for those who are allowed to pass into the light of glory, into God's kingdom; and about the walls angel spirits and blessed souls, those who depart hence from here, beautifully shimmer. There the martyrs bring pleasure to the ordaining Lord and praise the high Father, the King in his stronghold, with holy voices. Thus say they all: 'You are the Helm of mortals and the heavenly Judge and Author of the angels, and you have led the offspring of earth up into this blessed home.'

659   So with their words, ministrants about the Prince, they praise heaven's Guardian. Great majesty is there, and singing at his throne. There is the King himself, Sovereign of all, in that everlasting existence. He is that Lord who suffered death for us, Prince of the angels.

665   He also fasted for forty days, the ordaining Lord of mankind, out of the abundance of his mercy.

667   At that time, it befell the evil one, who had previously been thrown out of the heavens so that he sank down into hell, that he should tempt the King of all created things. He put into his grasp thick stones and urged him for hunger to create loaves 'if you possess so much power'. Then the eternal Lord answered him:

674   'Did you imagine, cursed creature, that it was not written. . .

Though there is no break in the MS, both sense and syntax seem incomplete in this passage. Only two of the three temptations narrated in Matthew 4 and Luke 4 are alluded to here, and only one of the three scriptural quotations from Deuteronomy (8:3 '. . . man cannot live on bread alone but lives by every word that comes from the mouth of the Lord'; 6:16 'You must not challenge the Lord your God'; and 6:13 'You shall fear the Lord your God, serve him alone') which Jesus cited in rebuttal of Satan. It may be speculated, then, that a short section is missing in which the poet conventionally exploited the correspondence between the forty days' testing of Jesus in the desert and the forty years' testing of the Israelites in the wilderness, in order to assert in his poem the Messianic fulfilment in Jesus and to redefine that righteousness of conduct by which fallen man might yet, by the example of Jesus and through Christ alone, reach the promised homeland according to the covenant made with the patriarchs. The passage may have been freely based on the narrative in Matthew, amplified by reference to Moses' charge to the Chosen People in Deuteronomy; to Psalm 91 (tendentiously quoted by Satan but actually containing the promise to mankind (v.14) 'Because his love is set on me, I will deliver him'); and perhaps to Christ's own elaboration upon the theme in John 6:30–40 'I am the bread of life. . . It is my Father's will that everyone who looks upon the Son and puts his faith in him shall possess eternal life.' The text of the poem, as follows, seems to echo this last juxtaposition of condition and promise.

'. . . except me alone; but you, Lord of the victory, Light to the living, have ordained for them a reward without end, holy joys in the kingdom of heaven.'

679   Then in his insolence the hideous creature seized him with his hands and mounted him upon his shoulder, the malignant

spirit of evil, and climbed up into a mountain and set the Lord and Saviour down in a high place.

683   'Now look out really widely over the inhabitants of earth. I will give you the people and the land into your own jurisdiction. Accept into your authority here at my hands the citadel and the spacious dwelling-place of the kingdom of heaven if you are the lawful king of angels and of men, as you have previously thought.'

689   Then the eternal Lord answered him:

690   'Be off with you, cursed being, Satan himself, into the pit of punishment. Certain torment is ready for your reception, not the kingdom of God. But I promise you, by the highest power, that you shall not offer hope to the inhabitants of hell, but rather you may tell them of the greatest of disappointments – that you have encountered the ordaining Lord of all creatures, the King of mankind. Turn tail and realize, you cursed creature, how wide and broad is the dreary vault of hell, and measure it out with your hands. Grope towards the bottom and then go about so until you know the whole circumference; and first measure from above to the bottom, and how broad is the murky air. Then you will realize the more readily that you strove against God, when you have measured with your hands how high and deep hell is inside, that grim cavernous abode. Go to it quickly, so that before two hours have gone, you have measured that bounded abode.'

710   Then misery descended upon the wicked being. Satan, wretched monster, ran away and fell into torment – sometimes with his hands he would measure the pain and the punishment; sometimes the dark fire would catch at the loathsome creature; sometimes he would gaze upon the prisoners lying in hell; sometimes a lamenting cry would go up when they turned their eyes upon the hideous fiend: God's adversaries, they won captivity – the black evil spirit, so that he stood on the bottom.

719   Then it seemed to him that from there to the gate of hell was a hundred thousand miles in distance, according as the mighty Lord had commanded him in his cunning to measure his torment. When he considered that he was standing on the bottom, the deceitful hideous fiend glared with his eyes across that loathsome pit until a horrible feeling of fear mounted up in the multitude of the devils. Out of their torments the damned spirits began to cry aloud and say:

729   'So, may you now remain thus in evil predicament. You had no will for the good before.'

Finit Liber II. Amen

THE
VERCELLI
BOOK

The Vercelli Book

[Vercelli, Biblioteca Capitolare CXVII]

Vercelli lies on a main pilgrim route to Rome and it is possible, though it is no more than a guess, that the AS codex now called the Vercelli Book was part of the luggage of an English traveller – presumably a distinguished ecclesiastic in view of the quality and content of the work – or a gift intended for English clerics living in Rome which never reached its destination. It is held, on palaeographical grounds, to be of similar date to the Exeter Book, that is deriving from the second half of the tenth century, and it is generally regarded as being written in one hand.

This codex too, like the Exeter Book, was probably compiled by one person, perhaps over a period of time, from pre-existing source materials, though it differs from the Exeter Book and the Junius MS in including prose pieces in the collection. Though there is no far-reaching organizational principle, its criteria of selection are fairly clear.

The prose pieces are homilies, but they do not represent a systematic collection relating to the Church's liturgical year as many homiliaries did; rather, they seem chosen to serve the chief purpose of penitential meditation upon themes familiar to AS spirituality – the Lord's death, one's own death, the death of this world, judgment, the punishment of worldly guilt and the joys of heaven.

Firmly set in this thematic context of the homilies are poems expressive of concern for the historic validity and redemptive efficacy of the Cross (*Ele* and *DrR*). The compiler shares with the shaper of the Exeter Book an interest in non-canonical sacred history (homily based on the pseudo-Matthew gospel) and in the ministry and witness of the early Church (*And*, *FAp*). The popularity of the Saint's Life as a genre is perhaps attested by the inclusion of *Ele*; and that of the English saint Guthlac – the subject of two poems in the Exeter Book – by the presence of a homily which is largely a translation of parts of the Latin Life of Guthlac composed by Felix of Crowland. Two poems carrying the runic 'signature' of Cynewulf (*Ele*, *FAp*) testify to the compiler's eye for quality.

The homilies of the Vercelli Book and of such independent AS homiliaries as Ælfric's or the Blickling Homilies can be of great critical value in the interpretation of the poetry, for it seems very likely that the homily, preached in English as part of an otherwise Latin liturgy, served as a major channel through which the great conventional *topoi* of the Christian intellectual tradition – on which the English poets often based their work – were disseminated in a familiar form and a standard vernacular idiom to the preliterate and literate alike who also formed the audience of the religious poet. Stylistically, too, the often highly mannered and sometimes deliberately metrical and even alliterative rhetoric of the homilies merges with the mode of verse to a degree which the labels of prose and poetry inadequately express. Thus the phenomenon of an AS book which anthologizes both prose and poetry mixed by choice is an important prompt to critical inquiry.

The Vercelli Book, then, offering, perhaps to the members of a religious house, resources for both public and private meditation upon the way of the Cross to personal salvation, having affinities with the Exeter Book and yet showing an overall character distinctly different, extends our understanding of the concept of the Anglo-Saxon book.

Andreas

[The Vercelli Book, fol. 29ᵇ–52ᵇ]

And, an account of the ministry of St Andrew, is followed in the MS by a short self-coherent text listing the fates of the apostles which is itself followed by a further discrete thirty-five-line passage featuring runes that spell the name CYNWULF. It would be pleasing to be able to regard all three pieces as parts of one original conception, the work of Cynewulf; but the evidence does not allow any unchallengeable conclusion. It may well have been the compiler of the codex, not a single original poet, who brought these pieces together.

Certainly *And* shares various characterizing traits with the signed poems of Cynewulf, all of which are religious, deal with the legend-history of Christianity, are based on known sources in Latin and Greek, and demonstrate that Cynewulf's prime skill lay in the creative and often boldly imaginative transmutation of the *topoi*, the imagery and the idiom of his Latin material into the traditional alliterative metre, vocabulary, formulas and imagery of Old English secular heroic verse. Thus *And* too has a primary source in a (lost) Latin version of the Greek *Acts of St Andrew and St Matthew* and, in parts at least, affords a distinguished example of the naturalization of Latin Christian material into English poetry. The poem may at any rate be assigned to the *school* of Cynewulf along with *Chr I*, *Chr III*, *DrR*, *Phx* and *Glc*.

It has been commonly held that *And* was heavily indebted to *Bwf* – to the extent of having borrowed from that poem phrases of which the syntax did not actually fit their new context in *And*. The theory has valuable implications as regards AS literary tradition, in its suggestion that there too a great poem might 'tyrannize' over a following generation as *Paradise Lost*, for example, has been deemed to have done. But with greater understanding of the oral-formulaic nature of much OE verse composition, the obvious similarities between the two poems have come to look less singular, and the premises of any theory of strictly literary borrowing have had to be adjusted. Nonetheless, the verbal correspondences continue to invite wider speculation about the affinities between *Bwf* and *And*. For example, the Christian-'moralized' Germanic monsters of *Bwf* and the Germanicized heathen cannibals of *And* may well have belonged, as far as the poets were concerned, in a common context of 'Anthropophagi and men whose heads do grow beneath their shoulders' as represented in *The Marvels of the East* in the *Bwf* MS; and more recent *Bwf*-criticism, interpretatively seeing the poem as one of deeply Christian sentiment, has brought the two works and their heroes closer together than many earlier scholars perceived them to be.

Notable in the artistic realization of the story is the exploitation of the device of the divine navigator, that helmsman whom early scholars in their determined search for AS paganism found to be a barely modified figure of Woden. In a lengthy sequence, the navigator is shown rehearsing Andrew in a kind of catechism concerning Christ as Messiah and Redeemer, and while this placidly continues Andrew forgets his fear of the storming ocean: for the man whose mind is engrossed in Christ, the tempest upon the ocean of this life is effectively stilled. Later, in another long and balancing sequence, we see that Andrew has learned this calm confidence of faith well, when, while his Mermedonian torturers and demonic taunters storm with grotesque fury about him, he bears his sufferings with still nobility. Thus the structure of the poem serves its didactic purpose: here as in *DrR* we witness a fellow-mortal learning from the example of Christ and then applying the lesson in his own life, as a lesson offered to us, the audience.

I

Listen! we have heard tell in distant days of twelve famous heroes here beneath the constellations – the thanes of the Lord. Their glory in the conduct of the fight, when battle-standards came into collision, did not cease even after they split up according as the Lord himself, heaven's high King, prescribed their lot. They were men of renown in the earth, bold leaders of the people and keen for the campaigning life, brave soldiers when shield and hand defended the helmet in the field of conflict, the fateful arena.

11   One of them was Matthew, the one who first among the Jews undertook with miraculous skill to write the gospel in words, whose lot holy God ordained to be abroad on that island, where still at that time no foreigner was able to enjoy the happiness of his homeland, for frequently the hand of murderous men did him violent injury in the field of conflict. That province, the tribal territory of those people, the native land of those men, was utterly enveloped in murder and devilish evil. For the people in that place the food to be enjoyed was not bread, nor the drink water, but throughout the nation they fed upon blood and flesh – upon the bodies of men who had come from far away. Such was their practice, that they turned into food for the hungry each foreigner who visited the island from abroad. Such was the inhospitable characteristic of this folk, the violence of these accursed people, that they, these malevolent men, bloody, grim and homicidal, would destroy the sight of the foreigner's eyes, the jewels of their head, with spear-points. After that, sorcerers, by means of magic, would obnoxiously mix together a monstrous drink for them, which overturned these men's wits and conscience and the heart in their breast; their reason was warped so that, as blood-greedy men, they retained no instinct for human pleasures, but instead, hay and grass were their mortifying resort when weakened for want of meat.

40   Matthew, then, was come to that infamous city, into the stronghold. There was a great hubbub throughout Mer-

medonia, a closing of the ranks of the wicked, a swarming together of degenerates, when the devil's thanes heard of the noble man's mission. Then they advanced against him swiftly behind their shields, furnished with spears; they were not slow, these angry men bearing shafts of ash, into the fray. There they bound and pinioned the saint's hands with the craftiness of the fiend, these men heading for hell, and with the edge of a sword they destroyed his head's sunlike orbs. And yet even then within the heart inside his breast he praised the Guardian Lord of heaven's kingdom, although he accepted the terrible poison-drink. Composed and resolute, he went on zealously worshipping the Prince of glory, the Guardian Lord of heaven's kingdom with his words, with holy voice, from out of prison; the praise of Christ was fast entwined within his bosom.

59   Then, weeping with weary tears, in sorrowful speech and melancholy voice he addressed his Lord, the Lord of victories, the Ruler of men, the bounteous God of the heavenly hosts, and thus spoke aloud:

63   'Alien men, alas, weave spiteful bonds and a cunning snare for me. I have ever been constantly inclined in my heart to do your will in every way; now in painful fashion I am compelled to do things like dumb cattle. You alone, ordaining Lord of mankind, know the minds of all men, the heart in the breast. If it is your will, King of glory, that these miscreants should kill me with the edges of their weapons, with swords, I shall be ready forthwith to suffer what you, my Lord, munificent King of the angels, Author of deeds of the heavenly hosts, will decree.

76   'Give me, almighty God, as a grace, light in this life, lest I, a blinded man within their cities, am forthwith compelled, following their viciousness with the sword, long to suffer derision in the form of the blasphemous utterances of the blood-greedy, loathsome evil-doers of this nation. On you alone, the world's Guardian, I fix my heart and the steadfast love of my spirit, and to you, Father of angels, sublime Bestower of the breath of life,

I will pray, that you, Arbiter over the multitudes, do not apportion to me a death, the worst upon earth, among these wicked persecutors, these accursed workers of iniquity.'

88   Upon these words there came into the prison from out of the heavens a holy token of glory like the bright sun; in this it was made manifest that holy God had afforded his aid. Then the wondrous voice of heaven's King was heard here beneath the skies, the sound of the eloquence of the glorious Lord. In voice sublime he offered his battle-honoured thane healing and comfort in his imprisonment:

97   'To you, Matthew, I grant my peace under heaven. Do not be too fearful in spirit and do not be anxious at heart; I shall remain with you and free you from these shackles and all of the many who with you dwell in the constraints of bondage. To you Paradise, of glories the most sublime, of splendid abodes the loveliest, of homes the most joyful, shall, by powers divine, be opened in its radiance; there you will be able to enjoy for ever the pleasure of your glorification. Suffer the oppression of these people; it will be no great while that these sinful miscreants by their cunning art are allowed to afflict you with tormenting bonds.

110   'I shall quickly send Andrew to your protection and solace in this heathen city; he will free you from this nation's hate. There will be a measure of time, in fact just twenty-seven days all told, until the moment when you will be allowed out of oppression, afflicted with miseries, and, glorified by victory, will pass out of these humiliations into God's keeping.'

118   So the holy Protector of all creatures, Creator of the angels, departed to the fatherland on high. He is King by right, the immutable Governor, in every place.

II

122   Then Matthew was greatly inspired anew. The shrouding night slipped away and quickly vanished. After it came the

light, portent of the dawning day. The multitude assembled,
the heathen warriors thronged in crowds, in frenzied mood
behind their shields; war-coats were jangling, spears clattering.
They wanted to find out whether those who for a time had
occupied shelterless quarters in prison, fastened with chains,
survived alive, and which they could first rob of life, after the
set space, for eating. Greedy after carrion, they had written
down by letter and by figure the men's death-document, as to
when they were to become food for those wanting meat within
that community. Cold-hearted, they raised a hubbub; one gang
jostled another. The cruel leaders had no regard for right, for
the mercy of the ordaining Lord; often at the devil's instiga-
tions their mind entered under a dark shadow when they
trusted in the powers of the wicked.

143 So they found the wise-minded holy hero, the battle-
honoured man, in his dark confine, waiting for what the sub-
lime King, the Creator of the angels, willed to grant him. By
then the period of the original stipulation of allotted time was
past except for three days, according as the murderous wolves
had written it down, when they intended to break his joints,
quickly part body and soul and then share out the doomed
man's corpse to seasoned soldiers and to youthful, as sus-
tenance and agreeable food for the men. They felt no compunc-
tion for his life, those greedy warriors, as to how the journey of
the soul might be ordained after the agony of death. They held
a meeting like this regularly after the passing of thirty days; the
compulsion that they should tear human bodies apart with
bloody jaws for their fodder was great upon them.

161 Then he who established the world by his mighty powers
was mindful of how Matthew remained in misery among alien
people, locked in shackles, who had often exercised his love for
the Hebrews and for the Israelites; also he had sternly opposed
the necromantic practices of the Jews. Then the voice from the
heavens was heard there where the holy man Andrew was, in
Achaia – he was instructing the people in the way of life. Then
the Glory of kings, mankind's ordaining Lord, the Lord God of

the heavenly hosts, unlocked his heart's treasury to the man of
bold free-will, and thus spoke aloud:

174 'You are to go and commit your being to a journey to visit a
place where eaters of their own kind inhabit the country and
rule the land with murderous practices. Such is the custom of
that people, that they will not spare the life of any stranger
within their tribal territory whenever those criminals come
across the wretch in Mermedonia; after that there has to be a
death, pitiful human slaughter. I am aware that your brother in
victory is lying pinioned with shackles among the inhabitants
of that city. There are now three days until, on account of the
physical violence of the heathens, he will be forced at the brunt
of the spear there in that nation to send forth his soul, eager for
another place – unless you get there first.'

189 Swiftly Andrew returned him the answer:

190 'My Lord, how shall I be able to do the journey on a distant
course across the deep waterway as quickly, Creator of the
heavens, Ruler of glory, as you exhort me to by what you say?
Your angel can accomplish that more easily. From the heavens
he knows the ambit of the oceans, the salt sea-streams and the
vast expanse. They are no familiar friends to me, those foreign
men, nor do I know anything of the mentality of the people
there, nor are the highways across the cold water familiar to
me.'

202 Then the eternal Lord answered him:

203 'Alas, Andrew! that you would ever be hesitant about the
journey! It is not a thing difficult for omnipotent God to
accomplish in the world, that the city, the renowned seat of
princes, along with its citizens, be transported hither beneath
the ambit of the sky into this nation, if the Lord of glory says as
much by his word. You cannot be hesitant about the journey,
nor too feeble of conscience, if you honestly mean to keep faith
and true token with your Ruler. Be ready at the proper time:

there can be no delaying of this errand. You are to go this journey and commit your life to the grasp of cruel adversaries, where battle and the martial strength of warriors will be offered you in the belligerent clamour of the heathens. This very morrow, with the first light of day you must forthwith board a ship at the seashore and scud over the ocean path upon the cold water. Have my blessing as you journey through the world.'

225   So the Holy One, the Defender and the Ruler, Author of the angels above, Guardian of mankind, departed to return to the fatherland, the glorious home where the souls of those steadfast in truth may enjoy life after the body's dissolution.

III

230   The errand, then, was announced to the noble soldier in the city. His heart was not timorous but he was single-mindedly set upon the courageous task, tough and brave-minded, not at all a sluggard in the fray but eager for the fight and ready for God's warfare.

235   So in the dawning with the first light of day he went over the sand-dunes to the edge of the sea, bold of will, and his thanes with him, marching on the shingle. The ocean was roaring, the waters of the deep were pounding. The intrepid man was delighted when he found on the shore a broad-beamed ship. Just then the sun, brightest of beacons, came in its morning radiance, a holy thing, hastening out of the darkness across the deep; heaven's candle shone over the waters of ocean. There on the ship he found the crewmen, three splendid thanes, valiant men, sitting ready for a voyage, as though they had come across the sea. It was God himself, the everlasting and omnipotent, Ruler of the heavenly hosts, with two angels of his. In their dress the men were like mariners, like seafarers, when in their ships they are tossing upon the cold water along a distant course in the encircling expanse of the ocean.

254 So Andrew, who was standing on the shingle, eager to set out on the sea, greeted them and, rejoicing, said:

256 'Where have you come from, you mighty men, voyaging under sail in this ship – a peerless vessel? From where has the flowing ocean brought you over the heaving of the waves?'

260 Almighty God then answered him in such a way that the one who awaited the reply did not realize what man among eloquent men this was to whom he talked there on the shore:

264 'We have travelled from far away, from the province of Mermedonia. The high-stemmed ship, the speedy sea-horse, lapped in swiftness, carried us with the tide upon the whale-road until, swept on by the sea, we reached the land of this people according as the wind drove us.'

270 Then Andrew, humble of manner, replied to him:

271 'I should like to entreat you, though I could give you little in the way of rings and precious adornments, to carry us in this tall ship, the lofty beak-prowed vessel, across the whale's domain, into that province. Your reward would be with God for being charitable towards us as regards a passage.'

277 The protecting Lord of princes, Creator of the angels, answered him again from the wave-riding ship:

279 'Travellers abroad cannot stay there nor do foreigners enjoy a place of residence there; instead those from far away who commit their lives in that direction suffer death in that city. And now you want to cross the wide ocean so that you throw your life away amidst this violence?'

285 Then Andrew gave him back the answer:

286 'Longing, dearest lord, great desire of heart, whets us on to that country, to the infamous city, if you will show us your favour upon the surging ocean.'

290 The Lord of the angels, Saviour of men, answered him from the ship's prow:

292 'We are graciously and freely willing to ferry you with us over the fish's swimming place right to that land where longing urges you to visit — when you have paid your fare, the prescribed charges, as the crewmen, the hands aboard ship, will want you to.'

299 Hastily then Andrew, a man in need of friends, spoke these words to him:

301 'I have no beaten gold nor treasure, no wealth, no food, no filigree ornaments, nothing in the way of land nor of rings joined together, that I might whet your longing and worldly desire, as you exhort me to by what you say.'

305 Then the Lord of men, from where he was sitting against the gunnel, spoke to him across the surf of the seashore:

307 'How has it come about, dearest friend, that you, a man devoid of valuables, were determined to make your way to the headlands by the sea, to the limits of the ocean tides, seeking a ship beyond the bleak cliffs. Do you not have the nourishment of bread as a comfort to you upon the ocean road, nor a pure drink for sustenance? His is an arduous lot who ventures for long upon the watery way.'

315 Then Andrew, wise of mind, unlocked his store of words by way of answer:

317 'It is unseemly in you, when the Lord has poured forth wealth and sustenance and worldly success upon you, that in your presumptuousness you seek out a sarcastic remark for an answer. It is better for anyone that he should humbly and kindly acknowledge the man eager to be gone elsewhere, as Christ the illustrious Lord commanded. We his thanes have been chosen as warriors. He is by right King, Ruler and Maker

of heavenly glory, the one eternal God of all created things since he, supreme in his triumphs, by his holy might comprehends all things, heaven and earth, with the strength of one Being. He himself has declared it, the Father of every nation, and he bade us go throughout the wide earth in order to win souls: "Go now throughout all the earth's surfaces even as widely as the water surrounds it or the plains extend a highway. Preach the sublime faith through the cities across the bosom of the earth; I shall keep safe watch over you. You will not need to carry with you on the journey ornate treasures, neither gold nor silver. I shall afford you the grace of every desirable thing after your own assessment."

340 'Now you can considerately judge our journey for yourself. I must know quickly what you are willing to do in our aid.'

343 Then the everlasting Lord answered him:

344 'If you are the thanes of him who set on high his majesty above the earth, as you tell me, and if you have persisted in what the Holy One commanded you, then I will ferry you across the ocean currents with pleasure, as you request.'

349 So they stepped into the ship, bold in spirit and strong in courage. The heart of each man was filled with delight upon the surging ocean.

IV

352 Then upon the heaving of the waves Andrew began to pray the Prince of heaven for his favour upon the seafarers and spoke thus aloud:

355 'May God, the ordaining Lord of mankind, grant you honour, your will in the world and in heaven splendour, according as you have shown me friendship in this voyage.'

359 So the saint seated himself by the skipper, paragon beside paragon. I have never heard of a ship more splendidly laden

with noble treasures: heroes sat in it, majestic lords and handsome thanes. Then the powerful Lord, everlasting and almighty, spoke; he ordered his angel, his glorious minister, to go and give food and afford comfort to the ill-provided men upon the surging of the water so that they could more easily endure their lot upon the heaving of the waves.

369   Then the ocean grew disturbed and agitated; the garfish dashed and darted through the sea and the grey gull wheeled, greedy for carrion. The sun, candle of the firmament, darkened, the winds increased, the waves crashed together, the currents swirled, the ropes and the sodden sails creaked. The menace of the water mounted with the strength of armies; the thanes grew fearful. None imagined that he would reach land alive, of those who with Andrew had sought the vessel on the flowing ocean. It was not yet known to them who was directing the navigation of the ship.

382   Even then above the welter of the waves upon the ocean path Andrew, a thane loyal to his Lord, still spoke his thanks to the capable master, since he had been provided with food:

386   'May the righteous Lord, Author of light and life, Ruler of the heavenly hosts, yield you reward for these victuals and give you sustenance, heavenly bread, as you have shown favour and goodwill towards me upon the mountainous ocean. But now the young soldiers, my thanes, are dismayed; the sea is raging, a rushing flood; the floor of the deep is disturbed, stirred up in its depths. This troop, a party of brave men, is distressed and greatly worried.'

396   From the helm the Creator of men replied to him:

397   'Permit me then to bring the ship, our vessel, to shore beyond the fastness of the water and then let your men, these servants, await on land until such time as you return.'

401   Then those men quickly gave him an answer, those thanes tough in endurance; they would not agree to leave their

beloved teacher at the ship's prow, and prefer the land for
themselves:

405   'Where shall we turn – lordless, melancholy, starved of your
goodness, wounded by sins – if we desert you? In every land we
shall be despicable and contemptible to people when the sons
of mortals, renowned for their courage, hold debate as to
which of them has always best served his lord in the fray when
hand and shield suffered the pinch on the field of battle, ground
down by swords in the to and fro of the fighting.'

415   Then the powerful Lord, the faithful King, forthwith lifted
up his voice and spoke:

417   'If you are the thane of him who dwells in majesty, the King
of heaven, as you assert by your words, expound those mys-
teries by which he taught men here below the sky. It is long, this
journey across the tawny sea: comfort your men in their hearts.
A goodly way is still to go across the ocean stream and the land
extremely far to seek; the sand, the floor of the deep, is churned
up with silt; but God can easily render help to seafaring
soldiers.'

427   So he wisely set about reassuring his followers, those men
abounding in glory, by his words:

429   'When you embarked upon the sea, you contemplated ven-
turing your lives among a nation of adversaries and suffering
death for love of the Lord and yielding up your souls in the
kingdom of the Ethiopians. I myself am aware that the Creator
of the angels, Lord of the heavenly hosts, is shielding us. The
menace of the water, the tossing ocean, rebuked and checked
by the King of might, shall grow more gentle. It happened like
this once before, that we were hazarding the waves beyond the
surf, riding the sea in our boat. The formidable waterways
looked perilous, running tides lashed the seashore, the ocean
resounded, one wave answering another. Sometimes from
the bosom of the ocean the menacing water mounted up above

the wave-riding vessel and into the ship's hold. The Almighty, mankind's ordaining Lord, was resting there, sublime, within the ship. The men were growing fearful at heart; they made entreaty to the glorious Lord for his safekeeping and mercy. When the group on the ship began to cry out, forthwith the King, the munificent Lord of the angels, rose up and stilled the waves and the water's surgings and checked the winds. The sea settled, the limits of the ocean tides grew tranquil. Then our heart exulted when we saw under the sky's expanse winds and waves and the terror of the water grown frightened before the awesomeness of the Lord. Therefore I will tell you truly that never will the living God forsake a man on earth if his courage holds.'

461   So spoke the saintly warrior, considerate in his ways. The blessed soldier persuaded the thanes and reassured the men until sleep forthwith overwhelmed them in their exhaustion beside the mast. The sea had subsided, the onset of the waves had been turned back, and the wild fury of the ocean. Then, after this terrible time, the saint's spirit was gladdened.

V

469   He then started talking, this man of discernment in his deliberations; wise in his understanding, he opened his store of words:

471   'Never have I met a finer, mightier mariner, as it seems to me, a braver seaman, one more discerning in his deliberations or wiser of speech. I wish to beg of you now, as an honourable man, yet one request, although I could give you little in the way of rings, of precious adornments or treasure of beaten gold: I should like to gain your good friendship, illustrious lord, if I might. For this you will win grace, holy joy in heavenly splendour, if you are generous in your counsels to those wearied by seafaring. I should like to find out one skill from you, man of kingly renown – that you should teach me, inasmuch as the King, the Creator of men, has given you the glory and the

power, how you direct the course of the ocean-steed, the wave-riding vessel drenched by the sea. I have by chance been aboard ship sixteen times now and then, freezing cold, plying the ocean, the flowing tides, by manual strength – this is one time more – without ever having seen any man, any steersman upon the stern, like you, mighty son of heroes. The surging water roars and lashes the seashore, but this boat makes full speed; foamy-prowed it forges onwards and glides over the flood most like a bird. I definitely know that I have never seen superior skill in a sailor upon the path over the waves. It is very much as though it is standing still upon the land where storm and wind cannot shake it nor floods of water smash the tall prow, yet it is speeding upon the sea, swift under sail. You yourself, shelterer of warriors, are young, not at all old in years, yet you, a sea-rover, have in your heart the response of a noble man; of every word with regard to this world you know the wise meaning.'

510   The eternal Lord answered him:

511   'It often chances that we are scudding over the seaway on a voyage in our ocean-steeds with the ships in charge of the crewmen, when a storm comes on. Sometimes it goes hard with us among the waves upon the sea, even though we survive and carry through the perilous journey. The ocean-flood's turbulence cannot suddenly impede any man against the consent of the ordaining Lord: he reserves to himself power over life, he who binds the waters and rebukes and checks the brown waves. He must of right have control over men, who with his own hands raised heaven on high and established it, who wrought and sustained that sublime and happy abode and filled it with glory – thus was the home of the angels blessed through the might of him alone. Therefore the plain truth is manifest, known and recognized, that you are the excellent thane of the King dwelling in majesty, because the sea, the ocean's expanse, at once acknowledged you and that you possessed the grace of the Holy Spirit. The sea, the rollers' churning, slackened; the menace, the broad-breasted wave,

was stilled, and the waters subsided when they understood that God, who by his strong powers founded heaven's splendour, had lapped you about with his safekeeping.'

537 Then with holy voice the bold-spirited warrior spoke, he worshipped the King, the Ruler of heaven, and in his words said this:

540 'May you be blessed, Prince of mankind, Lord Saviour. Your glory shall live for ever; both near and far your name is hallowed, emblazoned with glory among the nations, renowned for mercies. There is no person, no one of humankind beneath heaven's vault, that can recount or knows the reckoning of how majestically, Prince of nations, Helpmeet of spirits, you dispense your grace. It is manifest indeed, Saviour of souls, that you have been gracious to this young man and that you have honoured him, while young, with gifts, with wise understanding and speech. I never met with great discernment of mind among those of an equal age.'

555 The Glory of kings, the Beginning and the End, then answered him from the ship and forthrightly asked:

557 'Tell me, as a thane shrewd in your thinking, if you can, how it came about among men that those lacking in piety, the nation of the Jews, with evil intentions promoted blasphemy against the Son of God. Wretched men, hostile and homicidal, they would not believe of their life-giving Lord there that he was God, even though he revealed to the crowds many miracles, clear and manifest. They could not recognize, the sinners, that royal Child who was born to mankind, to all earth's inhabitants, for their protection and solace. In the Prince, word and wisdom flourished, but he, having the choice, never revealed any part of those miracles in front of that perverse people.'

572 Andrew then gave him back the answer:

573   'How in this nation could it be that you, dearest of men, have not heard of the Saviour's power, how he, the Ruler's Son, revealed his grace abroad throughout the world? He gave speech to the dumb, the deaf received hearing, he brought joy to the heart of the lame and the leprous who had long been crippled, miserable, sick, chained in torments; throughout the cities the blind received sight; and also many various persons from among humankind he, while on earth, awakened from the dead with a word. He revealed many miracles besides, in like fashion, this man of royal renown, by the might of his power. In the presence of a great company he consecrated wine from water and for the people's pleasure commanded it to change into the nobler species. Likewise, from two fish and five loaves he fed five thousand mortals. Being on foot, they had sat down, dispirited; weary after the journey, they enjoyed their rest for they received food, the folk on the ground, which was most pleasant for them. Now you can hear, dearest man, how during life the Ruler of heaven has shown love to us in words and in deeds, and through his teaching has drawn us on towards that pleasant joy where, happy and blessed among the angels, they may keep their dwelling-place, who after death come to the Lord.'

VI

601   Once more the Sentinel of the sea, the man against the gunnel, unlocked the store of his words and spoke directly:

603   'Can you tell me, so that I may know the truth, whether your Lord revealed the miracles – which he performed on no few occasions for the people's consolation – openly upon the earth, where high priests and scribes and elders held council, conferring together? It looks to me as though out of malice they plotted treachery, because of profound misguidedness. Too readily those imminently doomed men listened to the devil's instigations, to the furious miscreant. This fact betrayed them, deceived and misled them. Now, accursed among the accursed, they must soon suffer punishment, cruel fire, in the grasp of their destroyer '

617   Andrew then gave him back the answer:

618   'I tell you for certain that he very often performed miracle upon miracle in the presence of the people's leaders, in public view, just as he, the people's Lord, performed the public good in private, since he was bent upon peace.'

623   The Defender of princes answered him:

624   'Can you, a wise man and a person noble of mind, put into words the power that he, forthright in private, revealed when you often held secret conversation with the Lord, the Arbiter of the heavens?'

628   Andrew then gave him back the answer:

629   'Dearest lord, why do you ask me curious questions and yet because of the strength of your wisdom you know the truth of each fact?'

632   Still the Sentinel of the sea went on talking with him:

633   'I am not questioning you, here on the whale-ridden ocean, either for reproach or as a means to slander you; rather, my heart rejoices and swells with happiness because of your eloquence richly endowed with noble virtues. Nor am I alone in this, but the heart is hopeful and the spirit comforted in every man who far or near recalls in his heart what this man, the divine Child, performed on earth. Eager for their departure, souls went and sought the joys of heaven, the home of the angels, by virtue of that noble power.'

643   Quickly Andrew gave him back the answer:

644   'Since in your person I recognize truth and understanding of wisdom, a competence granted by miraculous strength – by wisdom the breast blossoms within with sublime joy – I will now tell you the beginning and the end since I was for ever

hearing amid a gathering of people the words and the wisdom of that Prince, out of his own mouth. Often large crowds, a countless multitude, would gather in honour of the Lord at which time they would hearken to the teaching of the Holy One. Then after that the Defender of princes, the sublime Bestower of splendour, would go off into some other dwelling, where many would come to him at the meeting-place, wise hall-counsellors praising God; always people rejoiced, blithe of heart, at the coming of the Guardian Lord of the city.

661   'It once so happened that the triumphant Judge, the mighty Lord, went travelling. On the journey there was no greater number of people from his nation than the eleven warriors esteemed gloriously fortunate; he himself was the twelfth. Then we came to the royal city where the temple of the Lord was built, high and wide-gabled, renowned among men, wondrously beautified. Out of evil intent the chief priest began insultingly to mock with derisive talk; he opened his word-store and fabricated slander. He knew in his conscience that we followed the path of the Righteous One and fulfilled his teaching; forthwith he raised a voice hostile and mingled with malaise: "See! you are to be pitied above all men! You trudge far-flung ways, you endure a multitude of misfortunes; now you obey the teachings of an alien outside of the law, unendowed with wealth, you proclaim a prince and declare for certain that you live daily with the son of the ordaining Lord. It is well known to people from where that lord's noble qualities sprang; he was brought up, an infant born among his kinsmen, in this land. Mary and Joseph, so his father and mother remaining at home are called, according to what we have heard through recollections. Two other men have been born in their family in blood brotherhood, Simon and Jacob, the sons of Joseph."

692   'Thus spoke the people's leaders, the nobility studious of their reputation, and thought to conceal the might of the ordaining Lord. The falsehood, the unending evil, rebounded where it had first arisen.

VII

696   'The Prince, Lord of the multitudes, then went from the
meeting-place with his company of thanes, strengthened by his
powers, to seek an obscure region. By a host of miracles and
mighty deeds in that desert place he revealed that he, strength-
ened by his might, was of right King over the earth, Ruler and
Maker of heavenly glory, one eternal God of all created things.
He revealed besides a countless number of other miraculous
works in public view.

706   'Later, the Lord of heaven went back a second time with a
great array and was standing in the temple. A babble of talking
was rising up throughout the lofty building; sinful men had not
taken in the Holy One's teaching, even though he had revealed
so many true tokens where they were looking on. Thus he,
Lord of victories, saw marvellous objects wondrously sculpted,
images of his angels, on the walls of the hall on two sides,
splendidly decorated and beautifully wrought. Aloud he
declared: "This is an image of the most glorious of the species
of angels that there is among the inhabitants of that city: these
are called Cherubim and Seraphim amid the joys of heaven.
They stand unflinching before the face of the eternal Lord; with
their voices they extol in holy tones the majesty of the heaven-
King and the tutelage of the ordaining Lord. Here, by dexterity
of hand, is depicted the beauty of holy beings and carved on the
wall are the thanes of heaven."

727   'Then again the Lord of hosts, the celestially holy Spirit,
declared aloud before that great company: "Now I shall com-
mand a sign to appear, a miracle to take place in the people's
midst – that this beautiful image come down from the wall on
to the ground and speak words and tell in declarations of the
truth, whereby men shall come to believe in my parentage,
what my lineage is."

735   'Then the marvellous thing did not dare to disregard the
Saviour's command in front of the crowds, but it sprang from

the wall, the ancient work of antiquity, stone from stone, so that it stood on the floor. Thereupon a loud voice came out of the hard stone; the sound resonated; by its words – the stone's behaviour seemed extraordinary to the obstinate people – it cajoled and lectured the priests by clear tokens; being possessed of intelligence, it held them in thrall and declared aloud: "You are renegades, seduced into the snares of despicable ideas, or else, being confused in mind, you do not know better. You call the everlasting Son of God a man, him who described with his own hands land and ocean, heaven and earth and the rough waves, the salt sea-streams and the sky above. This is the same all-ruling God whom the patriarchs knew in days of old; he bestowed grace upon Abraham and Isaac and Jacob, he honoured them with riches and openly declared to Abraham in the first place the noble man's destiny – that from his stock should be born the God of glory. This fact is plain and manifest in your midst; with your eyes you may now look upon the God of victory, heaven's Lord."

761   'During these words the crowd throughout the spacious hall was listening; all were silent. Then the most senior ones, full of sin – they did not acknowledge the truth – began after that to say that it had been contrived by sorcery, by tricks of illusion, that the beautiful stone talked in front of people. Wickedness flourished in the men's breasts, hatred hot as fire welled in their consciousness, the worm hostile to happiness, a deadly venom. There the sceptical mind, the men's wrongheadedness, hemmed about by mortal sin, was revealed through their blasphemous talk.

773   'Then the Prince commanded the splendid artefact, the stone, to go from that place into the street and to set out to walk the earth and its green plains, to carry God's news by preaching into the land of the Canaanites, and by word of the King to command Abraham with his two descendants first to come forth out of the grave, to leave their earthly resting-place, to gather their limbs and receive their spirit and their youth, and, wise witnesses from long ago alive once more, to make known

to the people what God they had acknowledged for his powers. So it went journeying along the roads of that land, just as the mighty Lord, the Creator of men, had dictated to it until it reached Mamre, gleaming bright, as the ordaining Lord commanded it, where the bodies, the corpses of the patriarchs, had for a long time been concealed. Then quickly it commanded Abraham and Isaac and Jacob, the third noble man, to rise up briskly from the dust out of that heavy sleep, at God's behest; it commanded them to prepare for the journey, and to set out at the Lord's decreeing. They were to reveal to the people exactly who at the creation framed the earth all-verdant and heaven on high where the Ruler was, who established that work. After that they did not dare to leave unfulfilled any longer the word of the heavenly King; so the three intrepid witnesses went walking through the land; they left the sepulchre and their graves standing open. They wanted speedily to testify to the Father of first created things.

804   'Then the people were seized with terror when those noble men honoured the Prince of heaven with their words. After that, to their happiness, the Guardian of the kingdom immediately commanded them to seek in peace once more the joys of heaven and to enjoy it at will for ever.

811   'Now, most cherished young man, you can hear how he revealed by his words a multitude of wonders, although men blind at heart did not believe his teachings. I know many a long and glorious account besides, which this man, the Arbiter of the heavens, occasioned – ones which you, a wise man in your thinking, are not able to ponder or contain within your breast.'

818   Thus all day long Andrew eloquently praised the teaching of the Holy One until suddenly sleep overwhelmed him on the whale-ridden ocean, at the side of the heaven-King.

VIII

822   Then the Lord and Giver of life commanded his angels to transport Andrew above the jostling of the waves, with loving

care to carry in their arms the cherished one under the Father's protection across the fastness of the water, until which time sleep overwhelmed the sea-wearied men. Through the gusty air he came to land, to the city which the King of angels had earlier revealed to him in Achaia. After that, those ministrants departed to journey, blessed, on the upward way, heading for their homeland. They left the saint sleeping in peace under the lee of heaven beside the highway, content to spend a night's duration close to the city wall and his enemies, until the Lord let the day-candle brightly shine. Shadows, dark beneath the clouds, melted away. Then came the cresset of the sky, the clear lamp of the heavens, shimmering above the houses.

839 The man awoke then, unrelenting in the fight, and surveyed the landscape. In front of the city gates steep slopes and cliffs rose up; round about the grey rock stood tile-adorned buildings, towers, windy walls. Then the wise man recognized that in his journeying he had reached the province of Mermedonia as the Father of mankind himself had bidden him, when he had earlier assigned him the task. Then on the ground he saw his followers, brave men in the battle, reposing close by him asleep. At once he set about waking the warriors up and declared aloud:

851 'I can tell you an obvious truth, that yesterday on the ocean tide a Prince ferried us across the abounding waters; in that ship was the Glory of kings, the Ruler of humanity. I recognized his speaking, though he had disguised his form.'

857 Then the young noble men, in their replies, answered him with spiritual mysteries:

859 'We willingly reveal our experience to you, Andrew, so that you yourself may wisely assess it in your soul's thoughts. Sleep overwhelmed us, being wearied by the sea. Then over the surging of the waves eagles came flying, exulting in their wings; they plucked out the souls from us as we slept and joyously ferried them aloft in flight, noisily happy. Magnificent and

mild, they lovingly adored and were constant in their praise, there where there was song unceasing and the oblation of music, a shining throng of celestial hosts and the multitude of heaven. Round about the Prince angels were standing, thanes around their Master, in their thousands; with holy voice they praised him in the heights, the Lord of lords: the joyful sound was exultant.

875   'There we recognized the holy patriarchs and a great army of martyrs; a company eager for good renown, they sang praise firm founded in truth to the victorious Lord. David was there among them, the blessed champion, Jesse's son, king of the Israelites, come into the presence of the Christ. Also in the presence of the Lord's Son, we saw you standing, richly endowed with noble virtues, twelve of you all told, men blessed with glory; holy archangels dwelling in majesty ministered to you.

885   'It will be well for the men who are allowed to enjoy those delights: the joy of heaven was there, the splendour and the noble disposition of the warriors; no dissension was there. Banishment will be ordained and torment opened up for those who shall become estranged from those pleasures and depart in misery when they go hence.'

892   Then the saint's heart was greatly delighted in his breast, when he heard the disciple's speech, that God was willing to esteem them so much above all men, and the warriors' protective lord declared these words:

897   'Lord God, now that I have realized that you, the Glory of kings, were not far away on the ocean road when I embarked aboard ship, although I could not recognize you on the sea-voyage, Prince of the angels, Helpmeet of spirits, be merciful to me now, almighty Lord; be kindly, sublime King. On the ocean tide I spoke a lot of words; now afterwards I know who was ferrying me to my honour across the waters in the wooden ship. He is the Holy Ghost, the Comforter of mankind. Help and

mercy are ready there at the hands of that glorious Being, and the power to prevail is granted to everyone who looks to him.'

910 Then in that same moment before his eyes the Prince, King of every living thing, was revealed to view in the form of a youth; then he, heaven's Lord, declared aloud:

914 'Hail to you, Andrew, with this willing company, exultant at heart. I shall keep safe watch over you so that wicked enemies and cruel contrivers of evil may not harm your soul.'

918 The wise man fell to the ground then and supplicated in words for peace and asked his friend and Lord:

920 'Ruler of men, Saviour of souls, by what means, sinning against your person, did I bring it about that I was unable to recognize you, one so good, on the sea-voyage – where I spoke more words of mine in the presence of the ordaining Lord than I should have done?'

925 Omnipotent God answered him:

926 'You never sinned so much as when you made protest in Achaia – that you knew nothing of travelling in distant parts and could not get to the city and accomplish the matter within the welter of the waves. Now you are the more thoroughly aware that I can easily support and advance any one of my friends in any land, wherever it most pleases me.

936 'Now, rise quickly up, and consider fully my plan, blessed man – blessed in that the sublime Father will honour you with miraculous gifts, with skill and with might throughout your life. Go into the city, down into the stronghold where your brother is. I am aware that by the hand of the wicked, your close kinsman Matthew has been inflicted with bloody wounds and entangled in cunning meshes. You are to seek him out and free the cherished man from the hatred of his enemies, and all the humankind that languishes with him evilly shackled with

the foreigners' spiteful bonds. To him shall soon come relief in this world and reward in heaven, as I have earlier been telling Matthew himself.

IX

950 'Now, Andrew, you must forthwith venture into the enemies' grasp. A struggle is ordained for you; your body is to be dealt hard sword-strokes and wounds, and your blood is to course in a stream just like water. They will not be able to deal your life the death-blow, even though you will suffer a buffeting and a beating from those sinners. Bear with the pain; do not let the might of the heathens and grim opposition from spears repulse you so that you desert God, your Lord. Be ever eager for good renown. Let it remain in your thoughts how it has come to be known to many men throughout many lands that unblessed men reviled me, tight bound in bonds; they taunted me with words, they buffeted me and flogged me: the sinners could not prove the truth by sarcasm. Then in the sight of the Jews I overspread the gallows-cross and the rood was upreared, where one of the men spilt blood from my side, gore, on to the ground. I put up with many miseries on earth; in this I wanted out of kindly intention to set you an example such as will be demonstrated in this foreign nation. There are many in this notorious city whom you will turn towards the light of heaven by my name, although in days of old they have committed many mortal sins.'

977 Then the Holy One, the King of all kings, in his humility ascended to return to the heavens, to that pure home where grace is to be had by any man who can find it.

981 After that he was thoughtful and long-suffering, a man unrelenting in the fight. Briskly the single-minded champion entered the city, sustained by his courage; a man brave in heart, faithful to God the Disposer, he advanced along the street – the path pointed his way – so that none of those sinful men might notice or observe him. The Lord of victories through his love had cloaked the beloved leader of his people with protection

inside that place. By now the noble man, the soldier of Christ, had pressed on nearly to the prison. He observed a gang of heathens, the guards, standing together in front of the door of the gaol, seven in a group. Death carried all of them off. They died without honour; death's onslaught surprised the blood-soaked men. Then the saint prayed to the gracious Father and in his heart's thoughts he praised the heaven-King's goodness and his lordly power. The door yielded at once at the touch of the saintly soul and he went in by it, regardful of courage, a man brave in strife. The heathens were sleeping, drunk with blood; they had stained red that place of death.

1004   He caught sight of Matthew within the prison, a brave-minded man down in the darkness of his confinement, speaking praise to the Lord and homage to the Prince of the angels. There he sat alone and melancholy over his troubles within that dismal building; then he saw, there beneath the sky, his beloved comrade: saint saw saint, and hope was renewed. He got up to meet him then and thanked God that they had ever been allowed here beneath the sun to see each other unharmed. Happiness was mutual between the two brothers; joy was restored. Each put his arm about the other; they kissed and embraced. Both were cherished at heart by Christ; light shone about them, holy and celestially bright, and their breast was joyfully thrown into commotion within.

1019   Then Andrew spoke first and by his speech greeted his noble God-fearing comrade in the prison-cell; he told him of the outcome of the aggression and of the strivings of those criminal men:

1023   'These people are now eager; men hither on . . .'

A whole leaf is missing from the MS at this point, between the present pages 42 and 43. Andrew and Matthew talk together of God's intervention in their lives. Then after prayer together Andrew heals Matthew's blindness and restores sight and senses to all within the prison.

1025 '. . . deed, to return home.'

1026   After these words the thanes of heaven, both of those brothers, bent down in prayer and sent their petitions before the Son of God. The saintly Matthew too addressed himself in that dungeon to his God and asked him, the Saviour, for aid and for help before his corpse fell in the presence of the martial might of the heathens. And then he led out of their shackles, out from that fortress into the safe-keeping of the Lord, two hundred and forty people reckoned by number, rescued from adversity – he left no one behind, tight-bound with bonds, down there in the stronghold – and furthermore, in addition to this multitude, he freed the frightened women there, one short of the fifty. They were delighted at going and they left quickly; they were not waiting any longer for the violent outcome within that dismal building.

1044   Matthew, then, set off, leading the numerous company under God's protection as the saint had asked him to. He covered the throng upon the willing journey with clouds, in case the wicked persecutors, their old enemies, should come with a volley of arrows to do them harm. The brave men, faithful comrades, conferred there between themselves before they went on their two ways; each one of the men confirmed in the other hope of the kingdom of heaven, and by his words warded off the torments of hell. Thus these warriors, brave-minded men, the chosen soldiers, with holy voices together worshipped the King, the Wielder of things to be, to whose glory an end shall never be comprehended by the aeons of time.

X

1058   Andrew, then, went walking cheerful of heart back into the city to where he had learned the assembly of those cruel people was, the tribe of outcasts, until along a path, standing close to the street, he came across a pillar of brass. He then sat down by the side of it; he was possessed of a pure love and an ever-exalted consciousness of the favour of the angels, whence he expected whatever battle-achievements might be granted him down in the stronghold. Then large crowds gathered, the nobles of the nation; the throng of perfidious creatures, the heathen warriors, came with weapons to the fortress where the captives had previously been suffering pain down in the darkness of confinement. They expected and intended, being perverted in their minds, to make a meal out of the foreigners, the prearranged feast. This expectation cheated them when in their pomp the irate spear-carriers found the door of the prison open, the product of hammers unlocked, and the guards dead. Bootless, deprived of their pleasure, they then turned back to bear the ill news; they told the people that they had found not one living being from among the strange-speaking foreigners left behind there in prison, but the guards were lying there soaked with blood, dead on the floor, the bodies of doomed men, robbed of their spirit. Then on account of that calamitous news many a leader of the nation grew afraid, depressed, melancholy in his thoughts, in anticipation of hunger, that pallid guest at table. They did not know any better course than that they should feed off those blood-soaked dead men for their sustenance: within one hour the deathbed of the doorkeepers, of all of them together, was disturbed at the hands of the ruthless mob.

1093   I have heard that the people, those dwelling in the city, were then quickly summoned together. The men came, a multitude of warriors riding on horses, intrepid upon their mounts, conferring together, proud of their spears. When the people were gathered all together at the assembly-place then they let the rod of divination distinguish between them which of them should first forfeit his life as fodder for the others; they gambled with infernal mysteries and superstitiously made the reckoning, turn by turn. Then the rod moved right above one of their senior comrades who was a distinguished adviser of the select body of earls, in the foremost rank of the army. After that he was soon bound fast with fetters, in despair of his life. Then, brave-hearted man, he began to shout in an anxious voice and declared that he would hand over his own son, a young child, to their disposal, to save his life; gratefully, they accepted the offer at once. The people were filled with cravings, pining for meat; for them there was no pleasure in wealth nor joy in hoarded treasures; they were cruelly harassed by hunger, for that harsh ravager of nations reigned supreme. There was many a warrior then, many a man greedy for a fight, excited in his heart over this youth's life. The evil signal to that act of violence was rumoured abroad and proclaimed to many a man throughout the city, that they were seeking the boy's death with a troop of warriors, old and young; they were taking his portion of life for their life's sustenance. To that end, the heathen keepers of the sanctuary assembled the muster of the citizens; the hubbub mounted. Then the youth, enchained in front of the crowd, with plaintive voice began to wail a lament and, being badly off for friends, to plead for a reprieve. The wretch could find no grace, no reprieve at the hands of those people by which they would be willing to spare his life and being. The monsters had determined upon their violent suit: the sword's edge, sharp and tough-tempered, marked with patterns from the forge, must make its demand, out of the enemy's fist, for his life.

1135   That seemed to Andrew then a pitiable and cruel outrage to suffer, that he, guiltless as he was, should suddenly end his life. The people's hatred was shameless and unrelenting; the hordes, the intrepid warriors were trembling in their lust for murder – well known for their valour, they wanted forthwith to smash the boy's head and kill him with spears. Holy God protected him from on high against the heathen people. He commanded the men's weapons to melt completely away in the strife, just like wax, in case the wicked persecutors, those formidable adversaries, might have done damage by the strength of their sword edges. Thus the youth was freed from the people's hatred and from injury. Thanks be wholly to God, the Lord of lords, because he grants justice to every man who in his wisdom looks to him for help: there infinite peace is always to be had by him who can find it.

XI

1155   Then the sound of lamentation was raised up in the cities of those people, the crowd's loud uproar. Criers shouted and announced a famine; enfeebled men stood about, shackled by their hunger. Gabled mansions and festive halls remained deserted; the men had no use for the enjoyment of riches in that bitter time. Clever men sat apart in secret council, contemplating the distress; for them there was no pleasure in their native land.

1163   One man would often ask another then:

1164   'Whoever may have friendly advice and wisdom in his mind, let him not hide it. A time of calamity beyond measure is now come; the need is now great, that we should listen to the words of the wise.'

1168   Then in front of that company the devil appeared, black and unbeautiful; he had the aspect of one accursed. Then the lavish lord of mortal sin, the deformed creature from hell, being perverse, began to denounce the saintly man and spoke these words:

1173   'Here into the city is come along a distant road a certain noble man, some foreigner, whom I have heard named Andrew. He hurt you deeply when he led out from the fortress more men than was reasonable. Now you are easily able to avenge painful deeds on their doers. Let the weapon's slash, the hard-edged iron sword cleave the seat of life, the doomed man's vital treasure-store. Go boldly forth, to vanquish your adversary in fight.'

1184   Then Andrew gave him back an answer:

1185   'How shamelessly you urge the people and encourage them to battle. You know for yourself the torment of the hot fire within hell and you are inciting a crowd, this troop, to a fight. You are hostile towards God, Judge of the multitudes. See, you devil's dart, you are adding to your misery. The Almighty vanquished you in humiliation and thrust you into darkness where the King of kings fettered you about with a chain, and ever since, those who knew how to esteem the law of the Lord have called you Satan.'

1195   Still the perverse creature urged the people with his words, with fiendish deceit, to a fight:

1197   'You are now listening to the enemy of the people, who has done the utmost harm to this throng. This is Andrew who is quarrelling with me in artfully contrived words, before this multitude of men.'

1201   Then a signal was given to the citizens; men emboldened to battle leaped up with the acclaim of the crowd, and warriors, fierce beneath banners, flocked in a great array to the gates and to the combat, with spears and with shields. Then the Lord of the heavenly hosts spoke in words; the ordaining Lord strong in his powers, said to his thane:

1208   'You must do courageous things, Andrew. Do not stay concealed in the face of the multitude, but buttress your spirit against men of violence. The time is not far off when murderous men will fetter you about with tormenting shackles and cold chains. Reveal yourself, harden your resolution, buttress your heart so that in you they may recognize my light. They, culpable in their crimes, will not be able nor allowed against my consent to deal your body the death-blow, though you will suffer a buffeting and evil malicious blows. I shall remain with you.'

1219   After these words there came a countless throng, corrupt agitators swollen with fury, together with an armoured troop. They soon brought him into the open and there tied up the saint's hands, once he, the delight of worthy men, was made visible and they could see the man famed for victory present to their own eyes. There was many a man there in the host of people on that scene of violence, filled with a craving for aggressive action; they little cared what retribution might come upon them afterwards. The cruel oppressors then ordered him to be taken and dragged at intervals across the land in the most savage way they could devise. They hauled the courageous and stubborn-spirited man through mountain gorges and round rocky screes as widely as to where roads stretched, stone-paved highways, the former works of giants, from within the cities. The commotion, the considerable hubbub of the heathen horde, mounted up through the fortress dwellings.

1238   The body of the saint was sodden from wounds, soaked in blood; the frame of his bones was broken; blood welled out in pulses of hot gore. Within himself he was possessed of unquestioning courage; that noble mind was detached from sins, though he had to endure so much pain from deep cutting blows. So all day until evening came, this man, radiant as the sun, was scourged, and pain then pervaded his breast, until the bright sun, radiant as heaven, went gliding to its setting. The people then led their hated enemy to prison; even so, in mind he remained devoted to Christ, and the saintly spirit was light about his heart, his purpose firm.

XII

1253   Then the saint, the man of unyielding courage, was insidiously chained up in darkness for the entire night. Snow bound the earth in wintry blizzards; the winds were freezing with harsh hailstorms; rime and frost too, hoary aggressors, fettered the land of those men and the people's habitations. The land was frozen with cold icicles; the water's torrent shrank in the rivers and ice bridged the dark ocean road. Peaceful at heart, the blameless man, regardful of courage, remained dauntless and long suffering in severe hardships through the wintry cold night; in his conscience he did not cease, frightened in the face of this terror, from what he had earlier begun, in that he continuously and most gloriously praised the Lord and worshipped him by his words, until the jewel of heaven, the sun, appeared, celestially radiant.

1269 Then to the gloomy dungeon came a mob of men, a considerable force, gluttons after carrion, coming on to the clamour of the crowd. They ordered the noble man, the faithful hero, to be led quickly out into the power of his enemies. Then again as before, he was scourged with wounding strokes for the entire day; the blood welled in pulses from out of his frame; it smothered him in gobbets with hot gore. His body, though exhausted by its wounds, paid no heed to the pain.

1278 Then there came an unhappy sound of weeping issuing forth from the man's breast; the coursing stream of tears welled up and he declared aloud:

1281 'Look on my plight now, Lord God, Benefactor of the multitudes. You are aware and know of the misfortunes of each single creature. I trust in you, my Creator, that you, the Saviour of men, eternal, almighty, by reason of your abundant virtues, will never, being merciful of heart, abandon me – provided that while my life on earth lasts I so manage it that I fall little short of your loving precepts, Lord. You are a protector against the enemy's weapons, eternal Source of well-being, for all your people: do not now let the bane of mankind, the first-begotten offspring of evil, mock and with the cunning of the fiend heap vilifications upon those who maintain your praise.'

1296 Then the hideous spirit, the furious miscreant, appeared there; the devil from hell, damned amid torments, exhorted the warriors in front of the crowd and spoke these words:

1300 'Hit him in the mouth, the sinful enemy of the people, for he talks too much.'

1302 Then again strife was stirred up anew and hostility mounted, until the sun went gliding to its setting below the dark earth; dusky night masked and mantled the steep mountains, and the saint was led, brave and eager for good repute, to the prison, into the murky building; so, in confinement for the duration of the night, the faithful man has to occupy that filthy lodging-place.

1311 Then the hideous monster, as one among seven, came stalking into the chamber, applying his mind to evils, the wicked lord of mortal sin, shrouded in darkness, the devil, deadly savage, stripped of magnificence. He then began to speak contemptuous words to the saint:

1316 'What were you intending, Andrew, by your coming here into the power of your enemies? Where is your glory, which you arrogantly flaunted when you humiliated the idols of us gods? Have you now claimed, all for yourself alone, land and people, as did your teacher? He whose name on earth was Christ vaunted his kingly majesty – while he was able to do so. Him Herod robbed of life; the king of the Jews defeated him at combat, stripped him of power and committed him to the Cross, so that he gave up the ghost on the gallows. So now I shall order my children, strong thanes, that they, my followers in the fight, humiliate you.

1330 'Let the point of the spear and the arrow painted with poison sink into the doomed man's vitals. Advance boldly, to abash the boasting of this soldier.'

1334 They were savage: they rushed upon him immediately with greedy clutches. God, the immutable Governor, guarded him through his strong might. When they perceived the Cross of Christ upon his face, the glorious sign, then in the act of seizing him they were terror-stricken, affrighted and appalled, and they took to flight.

1341 Again as before, the old enemy, hell's captive, began to wail a lament:

1343 'What happened to you, my warriors and armed comrades so brave, that you came off so poorly?'

1345   The wretch, the outcast ancient foe, gave him an answer and replied to his father:

1347   'Suddenly we are unable by cunning to inflict injury and death upon him: have a go yourself. You will straightway meet a struggle there, a fierce fight, if you dare to venture your life any further against that lone man.

XIII

1352   'We can with ease, most revered of generals, give you sounder advice in this duel – before you precipitately proffer battle and the terrors of war – in view of what might happen to you in the counterattack. Let us go back so that we may insult him, trussed-up in his bonds, and taunt him with his miserable plight. Have words ready, all worked out, against the monster.'

1360   So with a loud voice he spoke, the creature afflicted with torments, and declared these words:

1362   'You have long applied yourself, Andrew, to monstrous arts. What a multitude of people you have deceived and misled! Now you will not be able to carry on this work any longer: there are punishments appointed for you, severe according to your deserts. Heart-weary, abject, comfortless, you shall suffer pain and bitter death. My men are ready for the sport of battle, who in a short while will quickly crush the life out of you by their valiant deeds. Who on earth of humankind is so mighty that he will free you from your shackles against my consent?'

1375   Then Andrew gave him back an answer:

1376   'Listen! Almighty God can easily free me, the Saviour of men, who long since fastened you in fetters with fiery chains where, ever since, you have suffered in exile, tied up in torment: you forfeited heaven when you disregarded the word of the celestial King. There was evil's origin; the end of your exile will never be. You shall add to your miseries for evermore; your plight will be ever harsher, day by day.'

1386   Thereupon he fled, who once long since perpetrated that fierce feud against God.

1388   Then with the dawn, in the half-gloom, a troop of the heathens came with a crowd of people to find the saint. They ordered the long-suffering thane to be led out for a third time; they wanted by all means to exhaust the brave man's courage. It could not be so. Then hatred was stirred up afresh, harsh and implacable. The holy man, having been expertly bound, was painfully scourged and pierced with wounds while the day gave light. Then, dejected of mood, he cried to God, unyielding, from out of his bondage, with a holy voice; he wept, weary-hearted, and spoke these words:

1401   'Never beneath heaven's vault have I undergone at the Lord's will a harder plight in which I have had to glorify the law of the Lord. My limbs are disjointed, my body painfully torn, my frame stained with blood, my wounds, bloody gashes sinew-deep, are oozing. How dejected you became, Possessor of victories, Lord Saviour, in the space of a day amidst the Jews, when you, the living God, Lord of things created of old, the Glory of kings, cried to the Father from the gallows and spoke thus: "Father of angels, I wish to ask you, Creator of light and life: why do you forsake me?" And I for three days now have had to suffer deadly fierce torment. I pray, God of hosts, that I be allowed to yield up my spirit into the hand of your own Self, the souls' feast Giver. You promised by your holy word, when you set about strengthening us twelve, that the belligerence of bold enemies would not harm us, nor any bit of our body be suddenly severed, nor sinew nor bone be left lying in our trail, nor a lock from our head be lost, if we were willing to fulfil your teaching. Now my sinews are paralysed, my blood has been shed, my locks lie scattered across the countryside, my hair on the ground. Parting with this existence is much more attractive to me than this concern for life.'

1429   Then the voice of the King of glory replied to him, the man of rugged mind, and uttered these words:

1431   'Do not weep for your miserable plight, dearest friend; it is not too severe for you. I am keeping safe watch over you and encompassing you with the strength of my protection. Power over everything throughout the world, and the guerdon of victory are given to me. Many will testify it to be true at the synod on the great day, that it will come to pass that this beautiful creation, heaven and earth, will collapse together, before any word is annulled which I have spoken from my mouth.

1441   'Now, see your trail where through the breaking of your bones and the bruising of your body your blood has shed a gory track. They will not be allowed to do you any more hurt by the shock of their spears, who have perpetrated the most cruel injuries upon you.'

1446   Then the beloved soldier looked back according to the words of the King of glory: he saw flowering groves standing covered with blossoms where he had previously shed his blood.

1450   The protective lord of his soldiers then declared aloud:

1451   'Thanks and praise be to you, Ruler of nations, and glory for evermore in the heavens, because, my victorious Lord, you have not forsaken me in my pain, a stranger and alone.'

1455   Thus this campaigner praised the Lord with a holy voice until the clear gloriously radiant sun went slipping beneath the waves.

1458   For a fourth time then the public leaders, those formidable adversaries, led the noble man to the prison; they wanted to warp the powerful purpose and the mind of the persuader of men in the dark night. Then the Lord God, Glory of men, came into that gaol-building and greeted his friend then and, Father of mankind, the Preceptor of life, spoke comfortingly. He bade him have the use of his whole body: 'No longer shall you suffer pain under the afflictions of armed warriors.'

1469   So, confident in his strength, he rose up healed out of the bondage of severe torments, and said thanks to the providential Lord; his appearance was not blemished nor was there any tatter impetuously torn from his clothing nor a lock from his head, nor a bone broken, nor any bloody wound pertaining to his body nor any measure of injury from a mutilating blow, wet with gore; but through that glorious might he was once again as before, giving praise and sound in his body.

XIV

1478   Listen! for a while now I have been proclaiming in words of poetry the story of the saint, the praise of what he achieved, a matter of revealed fact exceeding my capacity. It is a great task and a time-demanding discipline to tell what he performed in his lifetime, everything from the beginning. It needs a worldling better versed in tradition than I reckon myself, to find it within his intellect to know from the start all the hardships and the grim struggles which he endured with courage. But nevertheless we must narrate a certain amount of poetry more in short episodes.

1489   It is an ancient legend, how he suffered very many torments and harsh conflicts in that heathen city. He observed against a wall under the side of the building, fixed remarkably firmly, some great pillars standing, weatherbeaten columns, the old work of giants. Mighty and bold of mood he communed with one of them and, wise and remarkably percipient, he lifted up his voice for a moment:

1498   'Listen, marble, to the ordinances of the Arbiter before whose face all creatures will grow fearful when they behold the Father of heaven and earth seeking mankind in the world with the greatest of armies. Let streams now spring from your foundation, a brimming river, since the Almighty, the King of heaven, commands you that you swiftly send forth upon this proud people widespreading water, a gushing flood, to men's destruction. How much nobler you are than gold or a gift of

treasure; on you the King himself, the God of heaven, wrote
and instantly revealed in words his mysteries, and, as Arbiter
strong in his powers, expressed his righteous law in ten com-
mands. He gave it to Moses, just as those brave thanes
unshakeable in the truth, Moses' kinsmen, the God-fearing
men Joshua and Tobias, afterwards preserved it. Now you can
perceive that the King of angels adorned you with favours in
days of old much further than the whole family of precious
stones. At his holy bidding you must swiftly show whether you
have understood anything of this.'

1522   Then there was not a whit more time wasted in talking
before the stone split apart. A stream welled out and flowed
along the ground; by dawn, foamy billows covered the earth,
and the deluge was increasing. After the day of feasting came
the bitter dregs of the mead; the warriors shook off sleep. A sea,
disturbed to its depths, was encroaching upon the land. The
people were panic-stricken by the sudden peril of the deluge;
doomed, they died. Because of the man's voice, a battle-charge
swept off the young men, in the form of the flood. It was a
brewing of sorrow, a bitter beer-drinking: cup-bearers and
serving-men did not dally, and right from the start of the day
there was drink enough to hand for everyone. The force of
water grew greater. Men, old spear-bearing soldiers, lamented.
Their inclination was to flee away from the tawny torrent; they
wanted to save their life, to seek survival in the mountain
gorges, a refuge on land. An angel prevented them in this, who
overspread the city with bright fire, with a hot and hostile
turbulence. Inside, the pounding sea was raging, and the troop
of men was unable to succeed in fleeing from the fortress. The
waves grew greater, the breakers boomed, sparks of fire were
flying, the flood was aswell with surges. There within the city it
was easy to find a dirge being uttered. Many a person, filled
with fear, bemoaned his grief; they were wailing the song of
those about to die. The terrifying conflagration grew obvious
to see, the devastation severe, the noise horrible. Through the
whirlwind, gusts of flame enveloped the walls; the waters
increased.

1554   There the noise of people weeping was heard abroad, the miserable outcry of mortals. Then one person there, a poor man, began to gather the people; abject, melancholy and lamenting, he spoke:

1558   'Now you can perceive the truth for yourselves, that we wrongfully shackled the stranger with chains and tormenting fetters in prison. Fate, harsh and malignant, is crushing us — that is thus evident here. It is much better, according to what I reckon the truth to be, that we all of us unanimously release him from fetters — haste is the best policy — and entreat the holy man for help, aid and relief. Peace after sorrow will be ours at once if we look to him.'

1569   Then the people's disposition was revealed to Andrew in his heart there, that the strength of the obstinate men, the power of the warriors, was humbled there. The waters were spreading, the torrent flowed on, the flood was voracious, until the rising sea crept above people's chests and up to their shoulders. Then the noble man commanded the running of the stream to be stilled and the storms about the stony piles to abate. Confident and elated in spirit, he walked quickly out and quitted the prison, a man of perspicacity, one dear to God. At once a highway was ready cleared for him through the coursing stream. The scene of his victory was calm; wherever his foot stepped, the ground was dry from flooding.

1583   The citizens were joyful in their mood, exultant in spirit, since aid had been forthcoming after misfortune. By ordinance of the saint the sea subsided, the tempest gave heed and the water's expanse settled down. Then the man caused to open up an awesome fissure in the earth and in it he let the flood, the tawny waves, the gushing turmoil, be engulfed; the abyss swallowed everything. Not only did he make the water sink into it, but in the midst of the waves the worst of the crowd went too, fourteen criminal enemies of the people, hastening into perdition down in the depths of the earth. Then many a one among the people left behind grew afraid and intimidated;

they were expecting a slaughter of women and of men and an even more miserable time of harsh circumstances, when the warriors, sin-soiled and guilty of murder, perished down in the abyss.

1601   Then, unanimous, they all declared:

1602   'It is evident now that the true Arbiter, King of all creatures, prevails in strength, who sent this envoy to the nation's aid. Now it greatly behoves us readily to obey the excellent man.'

XV

1607   Then the saint set about cheering the men and comforting the throng of warriors with his words:

1609   'Do not be too fearful, although that tribe of sinners elected for destruction. They suffered death and torments according to their deeds; for you the radiant light of heaven is revealed, if you mean well.'

1613   Then he sent his petition before the Son of God and prayed the Holy One to render help to the young men who had lately yielded up their life in the sea through the flood's embrace, so that their souls should not be conveyed, starved of goodness, in a perdition of torments, cut off from heaven, into the fiends' power. When this intercession had been respectfully voiced to all-ruling God, the guiding Lord of the nations, through the eloquence of the saintly soul, then he commanded all the young men to rise up unharmed from the ground, whom the sea had lately killed.

1625   Then, as I have heard, there in the assembly those numerous callow youngsters hastily rose up; corporeal and spiritual, all was then united although they had lately and instantly lost their life through the sudden onslaught of the flood. They received baptism and the pledge of safe-keeping, the promise of glory freed from torments, and the Lord's protection.

1632   Then the spirited man, the King's craftsman, commanded them to build a church, to prepare God's temple, there where the band of young men rose up through the Father's sacrament of baptism and where the flood sprang out. Men then gathered in a throng of people from far and wide throughout the festive city, single-minded men, and their womenfolk with them; they declared that they would faithfully obey, boldly accept the immersion of baptism at the Lord's will and abandon idolatry and the ancient temples. So among that nation, among those men, the glorious sacrament of baptism was instituted, and God's just law and his ordinance exalted in the land among its citizens, and the church was consecrated. There the envoy of God ordained a particular man, sagacious and wise in his talk, as bishop to the people in that noble city, and in apostolic manner he consecrated the man, called Platan, before the congregation for the people in their need, and he boldly charged them readily to fulfil his teaching and achieve salvation. He said that his mind was eager for him to be gone, that he wanted to quit the rich city, the conviviality of people in the hall and the wealth, and the noble hall for the giving of rings, and he would seek a ship for himself at the sea-shore.

1659   It was a hard thing for the multitude to suffer, that the people's leader would not stay any longer with them. Then the God of glory, the Lord of the heavenly hosts, himself appeared to him on the journey and said these words:

1664   'Because of their sufferings, the folk – their heart is sad – go about grieving; they complain of their anxiety, men and women together. Their weeping, their mourning mood, has come hastening into my presence. You must not abandon that flock in so new a state of joy, rather build my name securely in their breasts. Protector of warriors, remain in the festive city, in the treasure-decked halls, for the duration of seven days; after that you will set out with my favour.'

1675   So back he went one more time, courageous and confident in his strength, to visit the fortress of Mermedonia. The speech and the wisdom of the Christians flourished after they had set eyes on heaven's thane, the envoy of the royal King. He instructed the people then in the way of the faith and splendidly confirmed them; a multitude beyond measure of the blessed he conditioned for glory, for the holy home of the kingdom of heaven, where Father and Son and Comforter-Spirit within the majesty of the Trinity reign in an aeon of aeons over the celestial dwellings. The saint moreover attacked the heathen temples, drove away idolatory and overthrew error. It was a painful thing for Satan to suffer, a great sorrow of the heart, that he saw the masses, through the loving instruction of Andrew, turn blithe of purpose from the temples of hell to that lovely state of joy in the land where there shall never be any attack of fiend and malevolent spirit.

1695   Then the days were fulfilled in number, according to the Lord's decree, in which God had required of him that he should remain in the foreign city. So, blissfully exultant, he set about preparing himself and getting ready for the sea; he wanted to visit Achaia one more time by ship, where he expected the parting of his soul and death in action. It did not turn out a matter for merriment to his slayer, who rather set his course into the jaws of hell and afterwards, an outcast without friends, enjoyed no consolation.

1706   Then I have heard that melancholy men escorted the beloved teacher with a crowd of people to the ship's prow; in many there emotion was surging hot about their heart. So they brought the enterprising soldier to the boat at a headland of the ocean. Then they stood on the shore weeping after him as long as they could see him, the delight of worthy men, among the waves along the seal's paths; and then they worshipped the Lord of heaven. In chorus they cried out to him and thus declared:

1717   'One only is he, the everlasting God of all created things. His right and his power are gloriously blessed throughout the world, and over all in celestial majesty his splendour shines upon the saints, radiantly in glory, for ever and ever eternally among the angels. He is a noble King.'

The Fates of the Apostles

[The Vercelli Book, fol.52ᵇ–54ᵃ]

The poem has its interest as a brief versified martyrology in English. Its core may reasonably be regarded as a mnemonic list of the fates of the apostles, intended as an aid to meditation upon exemplary Christian witness, faithful unto death. But its strength surely lies in the quite intense personal application made of this commonplace material from Christian legendary-historical tradition, especially if the I-persona of the opening lines is identified with the persona of 'Cynewulf' (see the introduction to *Chr II*) by admission of the runic verses (which are formally discrete in the MS) to the text of the poem, as it is indeed conventional to do. The poet, fearful of facing death, finds courage in devising a song which contemplates the deaths joyously faced by the twelve apostles. At the same time as he speaks with personal reference, the poet expresses advice and consolation for everyman. It is not without point to compare the inventive principle of this poem with that of *Deo* where, for a similar purpose, the poet draws not upon Mediterranean-Christian but upon Germanic pre-Christian legend-history. In both poems the persona is that of a poet finding solace within the resources of his own art.

Cynewulf's signature is here deliberately presented as a riddle, of which the theme is relevant to the penitential mood of the opening and closing of the poem. Whoever recites the lay is challenged to find the right meaning for each rune so as to make sense of the passage, and to put the scattered runes (F, W, U, L, C, Y, N) into the right order. Cynewulf must have believed his riddle would be easily solved, for otherwise his purpose of being named in the prayers of his audience would be frustrated. For us, regrettably, the interpretation of the runes remains a subject of unsettled scholarly dispute.

Listen! morbid over dying, I devised this song in my sick spirit. I gleaned it abroad, how these noble men, illustrious and glorious, gave witness of their courage.

4   They were twelve, assured of fame for their accomplishments, men chosen by the Lord and acceptable to him in their life. The repute, the power and the glory of the Prince's servants

spread abroad across the earth, and their more than modest might. Their ordained lot directed the holy flock as to where they were to glorify the law of the Lord and expound it in front of the people.

11   Some, valiant and brave as soldiers, yielded up their lives in the city of Rome through the intransigent treachery of Nero: Peter and Paul. That apostolic dignity is honoured abroad through the nations.

16   Andrew also risked his life before Ægeas in Achaia. He did not vacillate before the might of any king upon earth but he chose for himself eternal and enduring life and unephemeral light when, unflinching in the fight, to the clamour of the mob, after warlike strife he straddled the cross.

23   Listen! we have also heard men versed in the Scriptures tell about John, of his family. Because of his kindred he was among mortals the one dearest to Christ of the male sex once the King of heaven, Creator of the angels and Father of mankind, had sought out the earth through a woman's womb. All the time in Ephesus he instructed the people; from there he sought in death the way of life, celestial joys and the bright paradisal dwelling.

33   Nor was his brother slow or cowardly in dying, but among the Jews James was compelled on Herod's account to depart by the sword's bite from life, his being from his body.

37   Philip was with the people of Asia; from there he shortly sought eternal life by death upon the cross when he was hanged by a hostile throng on the gallows in Hierapolis.

42   Certainly it has been no secret fact abroad that Bartholomew, a soldier strong in the strife, went to live among the people of India. Him the heathen and spiritually blind Astrages ordered to be decapitated at Albanopolis, because he would not obey superstition and do reverence to an idol. His was the joy of heaven and a bounteousness of life more precious than these borrowed benefits.

50   So too Thomas bravely ventured to other parts in India, where the heart was illumined and the purpose strengthened in many people through his holy word. Then this man of exalted spirit by miraculous power, through the might of the Lord, revived the king's brother in front of the multitudes so that he rose up from the dead, a young man and brave in battle, and his name was Gad; and then in the strife Thomas gave up his life to the people. A sword-assault by a heathen hand dispatched him where the saint fell wounded in front of the multitudes. From there his soul sought out the light of heaven in reward for his victory.

63   Listen! we have heard it from sacred books that the truth was witnessed among the Ethiopians, the lordly supremacy of God. The springing of the day dawned, of the light of the faith, and the land was purged through the glorious teaching of Matthew. Him Irtacus, the deadly cruel king, with wrathful purpose ordered to be killed with weapons.

70   We have heard that James suffered death in Jerusalem in front of the priests. Stout-hearted he sank down through being cudgelled with a club, happy in despite of their hatred. Now he has eternal life with the King of glory in reward for his warfaring.

75   These two were not tardy to the battle, to the armed conflict; energetic travellers, they visited the land of the Persians: Simeon and Thaddeus, soldiers strong in the strife. The one final day befell them both together. These noble men were to suffer pain from weapon-wielding hate and to seek the reward of victory and true happiness, joy after death, when life was severed from body and they quitted all these borrowed acquisitions and worthless riches.

85   Thus these nobles delivered up their ending, twelve good-hearted men. These servants of heaven sustained in their consciousness a glory unbreachable.

88   Now then I pray the person who may be pleased by the rendering of this poem that he should pray to that holy flock for help, for sanctuary and support for my morbid self. I shall indeed need friends, and kindly ones, upon that journey, when I am constrained alone to seek my long home and the unknown abode, and to leave behind me my body, this quantity of earth, this mortal spoil, to remain at the pleasure of worms.

96   Here the person clever at deduction, and who takes pleasure in the recitation of lays, can find out who composed this poem:

98   Wealth (F) shall be at its end there. Men enjoy this on earth, but not for ever will they be allowed to remain together abiding in the world. The pleasure (W) which is ours (U) in this native place will fail and then the body's borrowed fineries will crumble away, even as the sea (L) will vanish away when fire (C) and trumpet (Y) exercise their strength in the straits of the night; coercion (N) will lie upon them – their thraldom to the King.

105   Now you can understand who has been revealed to people in these words.

107   May he stay mindful of this, the man who may be pleased by the rendering of this song, that he should seek succour for me and solace. I have to be gone far away from here, onward alone to another place, seeking an abode and setting my course, myself not knowing where, out of this world. The destinations, the land and the home, are unknown – as they are to everyone unless he possesses a god-like spirit.

115   But let us the more eagerly call upon God and send our petitions up to that radiant creation, that we be allowed to possess that dwelling-place, that home in the heights where is the supreme happiness, where the King of angels pays to the pure an enduring reward. Now and for ever his glory shall stand, great and sublime, and his might shall remain, eternal and ever renewed through all creation. Finit.

The Dream of the Rood

[The Vercelli Book, fol.104b–106a]

The poem's dynamic consists in the depiction of a process of experience and of reflection upon experience, leading to enlightenment; and its artistry is designed to engage the audience in vicarious participation in this experiencing and enlightenment (cp. *FAp, Deo, Wan, Sfr*). The AS poets, like the illuminators of the later AS psalters, missals and benedictionals, and like the Benedictine reformers who introduced ritual drama into the liturgy of the Church, surely understood a clear theory of that empathy which they could generate in those who heard or viewed their various imitations of reality. The Latin word for this empathy was *compunctio*, 'compunction'. It was defined, of course, not in the language of psychology and aesthetics but in terms spiritual and mystical. Certain liturgical rituals prescribed by the compilers of the *Regularis Concordia* (the Benedictine monastic code drafted in Winchester about 970, ed., tr. Dom Thomas Symons, London 1953) are performed, they explain, 'in imitation' of scriptural events and thus 'compunction of the soul is aroused by means of the outward representation of that which is spiritual' (37,4). Thus compunction involves an emotional response to the imitation of reality not unlike Aristotle's *catharsis*. The AS poet needed access to one popular work alone, Defensor's *Liber Scintillarum* to read (ch.6) an anthology of utterances by weighty authorities concerning compunction (translated in the OE glosses in *LSc* as *onbryrdnes*, which is also the word used in the OE translation of Bede's story of Cædmon for the God-given quality which made Cædmon's poetry an instrument of conversion and reform). 'No less commendable is the man strong in compunction than the man strong in battle' (Jerome). 'Compunction of the heart is humility of the mind arising in tears out of the remembering of sin and the fear of judgment' (Isidore). 'When compunction is poured forth . . . a way appears in our heart through which we come at last to the Saviour' (Gregory). 'For blessed he is and thrice blessed who has compunction in accord with God. Compunction is the soul's health. Compunction is the soul's enlightening. Compunction is the remission of sins. Compunction attracts to itself the Holy Spirit. Compunction causes Christ the only-begotten to dwell within it' (Ephraim of Syria).

The *DrR*- poet is a master of compunction. In the very process of depicting redemptive compunction being stirred in the Cross by Christ and in the dreamer by the Cross, the poet bids through his art to move his audience to the same virtuous state. The form of his poem – the structure of its plot, the tripartite parallelisms of situation (relating Christ, Cross, Dreamer) and the verbal formulas expressing them, the conceptual juxtapositions within the individual line, exploiting the dynamic of metre and alliteration, the rhetorical lyricism – is regularly an aspect of, not merely a vehicle for, its meaning. The compunction-arousing immediacy of the experiencing that goes on in the poem is achieved by use of the first-person narrator and by prosopopoeia – assigning to an inanimate object, the Cross, a persona and a voice (see *Rdl 30a*) – so that the poem becomes a systematic spiritual exercise comparable in its intensity of Christian contemplation with any lyric of the later Middle Ages or with the best meditational poetry of Herbert or Vaughan.

DrR, then, superbly illustrates what substance and efficacy an AS artist could give to an abstract thesis of the process of spiritual enlightenment, such as was stated by Gregory the Great: 'The penitent thirsting for God feels the compunction of fear at first; later on, he experiences the compunction of love. When he considers his sins he is overcome with weeping because he fears eternal punishment. Then when this fear subsides through prolonged sorrow and penance, a feeling of security emerges from an assurance of forgiveness, and the soul begins to burn with a love for heavenly joys. Now the same person, who wept out of fear of punishment, sheds abundant tears because his entrance into the kingdom of heaven is being delayed. Once we envision the choirs of angels, and fix our gaze on the company of the saints and the majesty of an endless vision of God, the thought of having no part in these joys makes us weep more bitterly than the fear of hell and the prospect of eternal misery did before. Thus the compunction of fear, when perfect, leads the soul to the compunction of love.' (*Dialogues*, tr. O. J. Zimmerman in *The Fathers of the Church*, New York 1959, vol. XXXIX, pp. 173–4.)

The verses carved in runes upon the much older Ruthwell Cross are unlikely to be a quotation from a prototype version of *DrR*. More probably the *DrR*-poet, as he elevates the dreamer to the sublimest level of his vision, to visualization of the historical crucifixion, deliberately borrows from the traditional verses a kind of authentication and the reverential aura belonging to familiar antiquity, in order to communicate both the reality and the charismatic nature of the experience.

Stylistically, the poem is argued to be of the Cynewulfian school rather than of the Cynewulf canon; it is therefore likely to date from the mid-ninth century or later. It is hardly necessary to postulate a specific occasion for its composition, such as King Alfred's receipt of a fragment of the True Cross from Pope Marinus (*Anglo-Saxon Chronicle*, annal 885). The poem's verbal iconography and compunction-arousing emotionalism have close parallels in the pictorial art of the Benedictine renaissance in the late tenth and early eleventh century.

Listen! I want to recount the most excellent of visions, and what I dreamed in the middle of the night when vociferous mortals lay abed.

4   It seemed to me that I saw a wondrous tree spreading aloft spun about with light, a most magnificent timber. The portent was all covered with gold; beautiful gems appeared at the corners of the earth and there were also five upon the crossbeam. All the beautiful angels of the Lord throughout the universe gazed thereon; certainly it was not the gallows of a criminal there, but holy spirits gazed thereon, men across the earth and all this glorious creation.

13   Magnificent was the cross of victory and I was stained with sins, wounded by evil deeds. I observed that the tree of glory, enriched by its coverings, decked with gold, shone delightfully. Gems had becomingly covered the Ruler's tree. However, through the gold I could discern the earlier aggression of wretched men, in that it had once bled on the right side. I was altogether oppressed with anxieties; I was fearful in the presence of that beautiful sight. I observed the urgent portent shift its coverings and its hues; at times it was soaked with wetness, drenched by the coursing of blood, at times adorned with treasure. Nevertheless, lying there a long while, I gazed, troubled, upon the Saviour's cross – until I heard that it was talking. Then that most noble tree spoke these words:

28   'Years ago it was – I still recall it – that I was cut down at the forest edge, removed from my root. Strong enemies seized me there, fashioned me as a spectacle for themselves and required me to hoist up their felons. There men carried me upon their shoulders until they set me up on a hill. Abundant enemies secured me there.

33   'Then I saw the Lord of mankind hasten with much fortitude, for he meant to climb upon me. I did not dare then, against the word of the Lord, to give way there or to break when I saw the earth's surfaces quake. All the enemies I could have felled; nonetheless I stood firm. The young man, who was almighty God, stripped himself, strong and unflinching. He climbed upon the despised gallows, courageous under the scrutiny of many, since he willed to redeem mankind. I quaked then, when the man embraced me; nonetheless I did not dare to collapse to the ground and fall to the surfaces of the earth, but I had to stand fast. I was reared up as a cross; I raised up the powerful King, Lord of the heavens. I did not dare to topple over. They pierced me with dark nails: the wounds are visible upon me, gaping malicious gashes. I did not dare to harm any of them. They humiliated us both together. I was all soaked with blood issuing from the man's side after he had sent forth his spirit. Many cruel happenings I have experienced on that hill. I saw the God of hosts violently racked. Darkness with its clouds had covered the corpse of the Ruler; a gloom, murky beneath the clouds, overwhelmed its pure splendour. All creation wept; they lamented the King's death: Christ was on the Cross.

57   'However, urgent people from afar came there to the Prince: all this I witnessed. I was sorely oppressed with anxieties; nonetheless I bowed to the hands of those men, obedient with much fortitude. There they took hold of almighty God and lifted him out of that grievous torment. Me those valiant men left to stand covered with blood; I was thoroughly wounded by sharp points. There they laid down the man weary of limb; they stood at his body's head. There they gazed upon the Lord of

heaven and he rested himself there for a while, worn out after the great struggle. Then in the sight of the instrument of his death they made him a tomb; they carved it out of the gleaming rock and therein they placed the Lord of victories. Then, pitiful, they sang a song of mourning for him in the evening hour when they were about to depart, worn out, from the glorious Prince. He remained there with little company. But we were standing in position, weeping, for a good while after the sound of the valiant men had ceased. The corpse, the beautiful lodging place of life, grew cold. Then we were all felled to the ground: that was a terrible experience. We were dug down into a deep pit. However, the Lord's servants, friends, found out I was there and adorned me with gold and with silver.

78   'Now, my beloved man, you can hear that I have experienced the pain caused by men of evil, the grievous anxieties. Now a time has come when people far and wide throughout the earth, and all this glorious creation honour me and worship this sign. On me the Son of God suffered for a time; for that cause I now tower up secure in majesty beneath the heavens and I am enabled to heal everyone who holds me in awe. Once I was made the cruellest of tortures, utterly loathsome to people – until I cleared for them, for mortals, the true path of life. You see! the Lord of glory, Guardian of heaven-kingdom, then honoured me above the trees of the forest, just as he, the almighty God, in the sight of all men, also honoured his mother, Mary herself, above all womankind.

95   'Now, my beloved man, I enjoin you to declare this vision to people; make it plain by your words that it is the tree of glory on which almighty God suffered for the many sins of mankind and for the old deeds of Adam. There he tasted death, but still the Lord rose again with his mighty power, to the benefit of men. He then ascended into the heavens. He will make the journey back here to earth, the Lord himself, the almighty God, and his angels with him, to seek out mankind on the day of judgment because he who has monopoly of judgment will at that time judge each one according as he previously merits here

in this transitory life. No one there can be unafraid in the face of the word which the Ruler will speak: he will ask in the presence of the many, where is that man who for the Lord's name would be willing to taste bitter death as he once did upon the tree. Rather, they will be fearful then, and will have little idea as to what they may begin to say to Christ. No one there at that time need be frightened who beforehand carries in his bosom the noblest of signs, but through that Cross every soul which purposes to dwell with the Ruler shall find its way from the earthly path into the kingdom.'

122   Then, in happy spirit and with much fortitude I worshipped that tree there where I was, alone with little company. My spirit was aroused to the onward way and experienced many longings. It is now my hope of life that I be allowed to approach the tree of victory alone more often than all other people, and honour it abundantly. Determination for that is great in my mind and my support is directly in the Cross. I do not have many powerful friends on earth, but they have passed on from here out of the joys of the world, and found their way to the King of glory. Now they live in heaven with the high Father and dwell in glory – and I hope each day for the time when the Cross of the Lord, which I once gazed upon here on earth, will fetch me from this transitory life and then bring me to where there is great happiness, joy in heaven, where the Lord's people are placed at the banquet, where there is unceasing happiness; and will then place me where I may afterwards dwell in glory and fully partake of joy with the saints.

144   May the Lord be a friend to me, who here on earth once suffered on the gallows-tree for the sins of men. He redeemed us and gave us life, and a heavenly home. Hope was renewed with dignity and with happiness for those who had once suffered burning. The Son was victorious in that undertaking, powerful and successful, when he came with a multitude, the company of souls, into God's kingdom, the one almighty Ruler, to the delight of the angels and of all the saints who had previously dwelt in glory in the heavens, when their Ruler, almighty God, came where his home was.

Elene

[The Vercelli Book, fol.121ᵃ–133ᵇ]

Ele, by far the longest of the four poems signed by Cynewulf (see the introduction to *Chr II*), evinces a thoroughgoing self-identification of ninth-century AS poesy with Mediterranean-Christian tradition. Cynewulf's source is literary not oral, Latin not vernacular, and hagiographical with strong liturgical associations rather than secular-heroic: it is the Syriac-Greek *Acta Cyriaci* or Life of St Judas Cyriacus, in a Latin recension. The anachronistic historical setting of the action is amid those fourth-century wars between the Romans, the Huns and the Germanic nations – Cynewulf's ancient kith and kin – which signalized the beginning of the end of the Roman Empire. These wars generated for Germanic legendary tradition heroes of *Wds* and *Deo* and of the earliest German and Scandinavian heroic poetry; but Cynewulf's chosen viewpoint is that of the Roman-Christian world. From the same circumstances was drawn part of the legend of the great cult-symbol of Christianity – the Invention (discovery) of the True Cross in 326 – with Rome and Jerusalem as its poles of action and the convergence of Hebrew and Roman history in post-scriptural time as its perspective: it is the Cross, its omnitemporal significance overriding historical chronology and transcending wars, empires and nationality, that commands Cynewulf's devotion, as his Epilogue makes finally clear. Yet over this adoptive matter Cynewulf, the English poet, presides with assured epic skill, choosing his idiom among the traditional formulas of vernacular poetry, exploiting the dynamics of his native metrical-alliterative scheme, imposing his own organization and proportion upon the narrative structure and dialectic oratory, and adding to his source-material the spirited battle-scene and sea-crossing and the Epilogue. The Latin *De S. Juda Quiriaco Episcopo Martyre Hierosolymis* in the *Acta Sanctorum* (ed. Bollandists, Paris 1863–75) for 4 May (the day after the Feast of the Invention of the Cross in the Roman liturgical calendar) shows the story as Cynewulf probably found it – a narrative unadorned with circumstantial detail and lacking that complex suggestiveness that a poetic mode of statement especially permits. Cynewulf's systematic imagery of light and darkness, for example, often gives actual embodiment in the form of the verse to the cosmic antithesis between good and evil which Cynewulf's (and the *Bwf*-poet's) philosophy comprehends. In accord with the Saint's Life genre, Cynewulf also develops the imagery of the *miles Christi*, the drama of the struggle with the devil and the glamour of miracles and acts of divine grace; but with the principal heroes – Constantine, Helen and Judas Cyriacus – the focus of the saint-ideology is diffused. The portrait of the formidable Helen places her in that quite large gallery of women, literary and historical, recognized by the Anglo-Saxons as being in virtue, intellectual strength, vision, purpose and practical efficacy the peers or superiors of men.

The Epilogue, embodying Cynewulf's name in runes, expressly links the historical Invention of the Cross with the present well-being of the individual journeying towards death and judgment. The narrator – whose persona is probably determined by literary and aesthetic requirements and not by any purpose of self-portraiture – undergoes an experience strikingly like that which transforms the narrator of *DrR*. Both are watchers in the night who, by grace, make their personal discovery of the truth of the Cross. To both, recognition of the Cross affords immediate freedom from the oppression of their sins and a conviction which counters the world's testimony to transience, promising to lead them through death and judgment to heaven. Both are, directly and implicitly, charged with making known to others what has been revealed to them. In this poem the release of a poetic faculty is one with the access of divine intuition, and the whole retelling of the Invention story, as well as the intense sequence upon the world's decline and end and the judgment of its peoples, is the poet's grateful response.

I

When, with the passing of the years, two hundred and three winters, tallied by number, and thirty more, chronologically counted, had gone by in worldly terms since God the Ruler, the Glory of kings, was born upon earth in human form, the Light of those steadfast in truth, it was then the sixth year of the imperial reign of Constantine, after he, a war-leader, had been elevated to military ruler in the Roman empire.

11   This public-spirited warrior-protector was good to his men; the prince's empire increased beneath the skies. He was a just king, his people's defence in war. In excellences and abilities

God made him strong so that throughout the earth he was to many men a consolation, to many nations a scourge, when he took up arms against his enemies.

18   Upon him battle had been declared, the clamour of war. The Hunnish nation and the Hrethgoths gathered their forces and the militant Franks and Hugas advanced. Keen men they were, prepared for the fray; their spears gleamed, and their woven mail-coats. To acclamations by voice and by shield they raised their battle-standard; these stubborn people were then clearly united and fully in alliance.

27   The confederation of tribes advanced. The wolf in the forest howled a battlesong; he did not hide his gruesome broodings. The eagle with dew-speckled wings sent up its song in the enemies' wake. Swiftly over the massive mountain-fortress swept with their battalions to war the hugest military force that the king of the Huns could anywhere muster for battle among the garrisoned soldiers situated round about.

35   This greatest of armies advanced – they formed phalanxes by squadrons – until amongst a foreign people the headstrong spearmen encamped on the Danube shore by the swirling river, with the hubbub of an army. They intended to overrun the empire of the Romans and plunder it with their battalions.

41   Then the approach of the Huns became evident to the citizens. The emperor then ordered soldiers to be mustered with great haste in the face of the assault, to battle against the savage foes, and warriors to be brought to the attack under the open skies. The Romans, men renowned for their victories, were soon equipped with weapons for warfare, though they had a smaller army for the fight than the king of the Huns. About the man of renown they rode: then shield made its clang and battle-targe rang and the king advanced with his host, with his battalion to the fight. The raven shrieked above, black and greedy for carrion. The army was on the march: the trumpeters bounded forward, the heralds sounded their cry, the horse pawed the ground, swiftly the force gathered for the conflict.

56   The king was daunted and dismayed by fear when he viewed the foreign horde of the Huns and the Hrethgoths, because they had assembled by the shore of the river on the boundary of the Roman kingdom an army, a force untold. The king of the Romans nursed a heartfelt anxiety. He had no hope for the kingdom because of the shortage of troops; he had too few soldiers, close companions against the superior power or brave men for the battle.

65   The host encamped – the warriors surrounding the prince – in the immediate vicinity of the river, for the duration of the night after they had first observed the movement of their enemies. Then to the emperor himself there was revealed in sleep as he slumbered among his retinue, by the man renowned for his victories was seen, the portent of a dream. It seemed to him a handsome being in human form, some unknown man, radiant and bright-gleaming, appeared, more singular than he had seen, early or late, under the sun. He started up from his sleep, canopied by the boar-adorned standard. Immediately the messenger, heaven's handsome envoy, addressed him and called him by his name. The darkness of night slipped away.

79   'Constantine! the King of the angels, Ruler of destinies, the Lord of hosts, has commanded his safe-keeping to be offered you. Have no dread though aliens may threaten you with terror and with fierce fighting. Look to the heavens upon the glorious Protector: there you will find help, a symbol of victory.'

85   He was at once alert in accordance with the holy one's command; he laid open his heart and looked up as the messenger, the trusty peace-weaver, had bidden him. He saw, brilliant with ornate treasures, the beautiful tree of glory in the vault of the skies, decorated with gold, gleaming with jewels. The shining tree was brilliantly and radiantly inscribed with letters: 'With this emblem you will overpower the enemy in the perilous offensive; you will halt hostile armies.' Then the radiance vanished; it went up, and the messenger with it, into the company of the pure. The king, the lord of men, was the happier, the less anxious at heart, for the lovely vision.

II

99   Then the protector of princes, the warriors' ring-giver, Constantine, the fame-blessed king, commanded a symbol in the likeness of Christ's cross – just as he, battle-leader of armies, saw that emblem which was lately revealed to him in the heavens – to be made with great urgency. Then at dawn, with the first daylight, he commanded the warriors to be roused and the standard to be upraised for the armed onslaught, and that holy tree to be carried before them, the emblem of God to be borne into the enemies' midst. Trumpets sang out loudly before the armies, the raven exulted in the action, the moist-feathered eagle watched the advance and the warring of brutal men. The wolf, denizen of the wood, sent up its song. The horror of battle materialized. There was cracking of shields, attacking of warriors, cruel sword-chopping and troops dropping when first they faced the volley of arrows. Into that doomed crowd, over the yellow targe and into their enemies' midst, the fierce and bloody antagonists launched showers of darts, spears, the serpents of battle, by the strength of their fingers. Relentless of purpose onwards they trod; eagerly they advanced. They broke down the shield barrier, drove in their swords and thrust onwards, hardened to battle.

123   Then the standard, that emblem, was raised up in front of the troops, and a song of victory was chanted. Golden helmets and spears gleamed in the battlefield. The heathens were dropping and falling, denied quarter. Straight away they took flight, the Hunnish peoples, the aggressors, as the king of the Romans ordered the holy tree to be raised aloft.

130   They were scattered abroad, those stubborn people: some battle took off, some narrowly saved their life in that campaign. Some, half alive, fled into refuge and saved their life behind rocky cliffs and occupied a site near the Danube; some drowning in the river carried off at their life's end. The force of courageous Romans was in cheerful mood, then. They pursued the foreigners from the start of the day through until evening.

Ash-wood spears, the serpents of battle, flew. The confedera-
tion and shield-furbished army of the enemy was shattered.
Few of the Hunnish horde arrived back home from there. It
was apparent then that in that day's action the almighty King
had granted Constantine victory, glory and power here
beneath the skies, through his rood-tree.

148   So when the battle had been decided, the protecting lord of
the armies returned home from there, jubilant over his spoils,
having won distinction in battle. So the guardian lord of war-
riors, the campaign-renowned king, came with a contingent of
soldiers – their mighty shields reverberated – making his way
back to his cities.

153   Then the lord defender of warriors urgently summoned into
conclave the wisest men, those who had acquired a knowledge
of wisdom from ancient writings and who preserved men's
counsels in their memories. Then the people's lord, the king
renowned for victory, began asking among the extensive
assembly if there was anyone there, young or old, who could
tell him for certain and by their divinations inform him, patron
of the palace, what god this might be 'whose emblem this was,
the most radiant of symbols, which appeared to me, so lus-
trous, and saved my people and gave me triumph and success in
war against my enemies, through that handsome tree.' They
could not return him any answer nor could they very readily
speak precisely about that emblem of victory.

169   Then the wisest ones declared aloud in front of the crowd
that it was the symbol of the King of heaven and of this there
was no doubt. When those who had been instructed in baptism
heard this, though there were few of them their heart was light,
their spirit glad, that they might reveal to the emperor the grace
of the gospel, how the Protector of souls, honoured in the
majesty of the Trinity, was born, the Paragon of kings; and
how he, God's own Son, was hung with cruel tortures upon the
Cross in front of the crowds, delivered the sons of men and
their mournful souls from the devil's stronghold and granted

them grace through that same artefact which was revealed to Constantine himself in his vision, the symbol of victory against the tribes' onslaught; and how on the third day the Paragon of men, Lord of all mankind, arose from death from out of the tomb and ascended into heaven.

189   Thus wisely they told the man renowned for victory of spiritual mysteries as they had been taught by Silvester. At their hands the people's lord received baptism and kept to it from then on during the span of his days, in accordance with the Lord's will.

III

194   Then the treasure-giver, the king toughened by war, was glad; a new joy had entered his spirit. His greatest consolation and nearest hope was heaven's Guardian. Then day and night by grace of the Spirit he confessed the gospel of the Lord, and the gold-giving lord of men, renowned for combat with the spear, sincerely devoted himself, unflagging, to the service of God.

202   Then the prince, the people's surety, hardy in battle and daring with the spear, learned from God's Scriptures, through his teachers' help, where the Ruler of the heavens had been spitefully hanged on the rood-tree to the multitude's acclaim – through guile, in that the ancient enemy with his deceitful wiles seduced the Jewish nation and led the people astray so that they hanged God himself, the multitudes' Creator. For this they must needs suffer damnation amid humiliations throughout an infinite existence.

212   From then on, the praise of Christ kept the emperor conscious in spirit of that glorious tree, and so he bade his mother to travel the road to the land of the Jews, zealously to search out with a retinue of soldiers where the tree of glory, the holy cross of the noble King, might be concealed under the earth. Helen had no wish to prove reluctant over this expedition nor

to treat lightly the word of the generous lord, her own son, but the woman was soon ready for the willing journey as the lord of armies and of armoured soldiers had commanded her.

225   A throng of men, then, quickly hastened down to the sea. Ships, the horses of ocean, lay ready along the seashore, sea-steeds moored afloat upon the sound. The woman's expedition had then become common knowledge, when she came with her company to the ocean: many a high-mettled man stood on the shore there by the Mediterranean Sea. Eagerly along the coast-roads advanced one troop after another, and then loaded the ships, wavehorses, with battle-coats, with shields and with spears, with armoured soldiers, with men and with women. Then they let the tall ships slip spuming over the ocean wave. Many times in the surging of the sea the ship's side caught the waves' buffets; the sea resounded. Neither before nor since have I heard of a woman leading a finer looking force on the ocean tide on the sea-road. There he who watched the voyage could have seen, scudding over the waterway, the timbered vessel sweeping along under swelling sails, the sea-steed racing, the wave-skimming ship forging onwards.

246   The soldiers were happy and in high spirits, and the queen was pleased with the voyage when the ring-prowed ships had completed the crossing over the ocean waste to a harbour in the land of the Greeks. They left the ships at the sea-shore whipped with sand, the ancient vessels secure at their anchors, to await on the surf the warrior's fate, until the warlike queen with her company of men returned to them along the roads from the east. There the linked corslet was conspicuous on a man, and the proved sword, the magnificent battle-dress, many a masked helmet and the matchless boar-effigy.

259   The spear-soldiers, the men surrounding the triumphant queen, were keyed up for the expedition; the intrepid fighting men, envoys of the emperor, soldiers clad in their accoutre-ments, set out with a will into Greece. There the precious jewel in its setting was conspicuous among the contingent, a gift of

their lord. The blessed Helen, courageous of thought, zealous of spirit, had in mind her prince's wish, that she with her proved troop of soldiers, her contingent of men, should get to the land of the Jews over fields of battle. So it came about then, within a short space of time, that that pick of the nation, heroes famous in warfare, entered the city of Jerusalem with the greatest of retinues, men renowned for combat with the spear, together with the noble queen.

IV

276   She then commanded it to be proclaimed to the most knowledgeable citizens far and wide among the Jews, to every man of them, that those who could most deeply expound the Lord's mysteries according to orthodox law should come as counsellors to a synod. Then from far-flung parts was gathered together a large assembly who were able to expound the law of Moses. Three thousand men of that nation in all were selected to give advice there. Then the admirable woman addressed her words to the Hebrew men:

288   'I have clearly understood through the mystic sayings of the prophets in the books of God that in former days you were esteemed by the King of glory, dear to the Lord and zealous in his work. But alas! you foolishly spurned that wisdom in your fury, when you cursed him who thought to redeem you from your curse, through the power of his glory, from fiery torment and from bondage. Filthily you spat into the face of him who by his precious spittle cured as new from blindness the light of your eyes and often saved you from the unclean spirits of devils. Him you condemned to death who himself awakened the world from death among the multitude of the people during the earlier life of your nation. Thus spiritually blind, you confused falsehood with truth, light with darkness, malice with mercy; guilefully you fabricated a false accusation – therefore this curse will crush you, the guilty ones. You condemned the light-giving power and have lived in delusion with your dark thoughts to this day.

313   'Go quickly now and think prudently of men of assured
wisdom qualified in speaking, men qualified by their virtues,
who hold your law foremost in their hearts and who can
truthfully tell and make known to me on your behalf the
answer to each one of the proofs which I seek from them.'

320   In sorry mood they went away then, those men learned in the
law, harrassed by fear, miserable with anxieties, and searched
assiduously for the wisest mystic sayings so that they could
answer the queen, whether for good or for ill, as she required of
them. Then they found a thousand men of discerning mind in a
throng such as were most completely familiar with ancient
tradition among the Jews; then they crowded in a throng to
where the emperor's kinswoman waited in majesty upon a
throne, a magnificent warlike queen clad in gold. Helen held
forth and spoke before the men:

333   'Listen, you of discerning mind, to the divine mystery, the
word and the wisdom. Now, you have received the teaching of
the prophets, how the Author of life was born in the form of a
child, the mighty Ruler, of whom Moses, defender of the
Israelites, sang and said these words: "To you shall be born in
obscurity a boy renowned for his powers, whose mother shall
not grow pregnant with offspring through a man's love-
making." Of him King David, the wise prophet, Solomon's
father, sang a noble song and the warriors' lord declared these
words: "I have kept before my gaze the God of creation and
Lord of victories. He, Ruler of the hosts, has been in my sight,
and the glorious shepherd has been at my right hand; from him
shall I not turn my face ever to eternity."

350   'Likewise the prophet Isaiah, concerning yourselves, later
declared in his utterances before the congregations, profoundly
percipient through the spirit of the Lord: "I have reared a
young son and begotten children to whom I granted prosperity
and holy solace of mind, but they have despised me and hated
me with enmity; they have had no understanding of foresight
nor of wisdom. And the weary oxen which every day are

goaded and thrashed, they recognize their benefactors, they do not vindictively hate their friend who gives them fodder; yet never have the people of Israel been willing to acknowledge me, though during my days on earth I worked many miracles on their behalf."

V

364   'Now, we have heard through holy books that the Lord, the Ordainer, granted you glory unblemished, a wealth of virtues, and told Moses how you were to obey the King of heaven and fulfil his precepts. This soon became irksome to you and you have grumbled against that duty, rejected the radiant Maker of all things, the Lord of lords, and, contrary to God's due, followed after heresy.

372   'Now go quickly and again find out those who by virtue of their wisdom best know the ancient Scriptures and your law, so that out of their ample understanding they can answer to me.'

377   So away they went along with the multitude, proud-spirited people miserable in mind, as the queen had commanded them. Then they found five hundred men pre-eminently wise, picked them from their fellow countrymen, who because of their intelligence possessed in the wisdom of their understanding the greatest scholarship. Within a short time they were summoned back to the royal residence, these defendants of the city.

384   The queen addressed her words to them as she scanned across them all:

386   'Often have you done the foolish deed, you wretched outcasts, and despised the Scriptures, the teachings of your fathers – never more so than now when you rejected the cure for your blindness and denied truth and verity: that in Bethlehem was born the Son of the Ruler, the only-begotten King, Prince of princes. Although you knew the covenant, and the sayings of the prophets, you sinners would still not recognize the truth.'

396   In unanimity they then replied:

397   'But we have learned the Hebrew law which in days long since our fathers knew at the ark of God, and we do not readily understand why you, lady, have been so sternly angry with us. We are not aware of the wrong nor of the great offences which we in this nation have ever committed against you.'

404   Helen held forth, and spoke before the men; clearly and loudly the woman's voice rang out before the crowds:

406   'Go quickly now, seek out individually those among you who possess greatest wisdom, strength and skill of mind, so that they may boldly and honestly explain to me each one of the issues on which I shall consult them.'

411   So they went from the council as the powerful queen, strong within her cities, had commanded. In sorry mood, they earnestly considered and deviously inquired what that sin might be which they in that nation had committed against the emperor, and of which the queen had accused them. Then, in the presence of the men there, one spoke up, one very shrewd in his sayings and expert with words, whose name was Judas:

419   'I am well aware that she wants to search for that tree of victory on which suffered the Ruler of nations, free from all evils, God's own Son whom, guiltless of every crime, our fathers in days long since hanged out of hatred upon the high tree. That was a calamitous idea. The great need now is that we should brace our spirits so that we do not become informants of that execution, or as to where that holy tree was hidden after the aggression and the violence, in case the wise writings of old should be overturned and the precepts of our fathers forsaken. Not for long after that would it obtain, that the lineage of Israel and the religion of this people would be capable of dominating any more over the earth, if this should become known.

436   'Just as my gloriously renowned grandfather, a wise prophetic man whose name was Zachaeus, once long ago told that

self-same thing to my father, so my father told me, his son. He was departing the world and he spoke these words: "If in your lifetime it should happen to you that you hear wise men inquiring about that holy tree and raising a controversy about the tree of victory on which the true King, heaven's Guardian, was hanged, then, my dear son, quickly profess the Child of all concord before death seizes you. Never after that shall the Hebrew people be able to hold sway, determining policies, or to govern the multitudes, but in an aeon of aeons filled with joys, the dominion and the dignity shall live on of those who praise and laud that crucified king."

VI

454   'Then I boldly gave reply to my father, the old man learned in the law: "How on earth would it come about that our fathers in cruel consciousness laid hands upon that holy man so far as to execute him, if they already knew that he was the Christ, King in heaven, true Son of the ordaining Lord, the Redeemer of souls?"

462   'Then my parent replied to me, my wise-minded father declared: "Observe, young man, the transcendent might of God, the name of the Redeemer which is inexpressible to any mortal man, and which one cannot fathom by oneself here on earth. At no time did I want to go along with the scheming upon which this people embarked, but I always kept myself clear of those guilty deeds and caused my soul no shame. Often I sincerely opposed them for their injustice, when the elders held conference and searched in their minds as to how they might hang the Son of the ordaining Lord, the Defender of men, Lord of all angels and mortals, noblest of children.

477   ' "Such stupid and unblessed men, they could not inflict death upon him as they had once thought, nor impose it upon him by torments, though for a certain time upon the Cross he did send forth his spirit, God's victorious Son, then afterwards was taken down, Ruler of the skies, the Majesty of all majes-

ties, from the Cross. For three days afterwards he was waiting in the tomb down in a dark confine: and then on the third day the Light of all light rose up alive, the Prince of Angels, and revealed himself, true Lord of victories, shining in splendour, to his disciples.

489   ' "Then after a while your brother received purification by baptism, and the shining faith. Then for his love of the Lord, Stephen was pelted with stones. He did not return evil for evil, but, forbearing, interceded for his old enemies and prayed the King of glory that he should not bring them to retribution for that evil action, that out of malice they deprived of life an innocent sinless man at the instigations of Saul, just as he in his hostility condemned many of Christ's people to execution and death. Yet the Lord later showed him mercy so that he became a consolation to many people, after the God of new beginnings, the Redeemer of men, changed his name, and he was thereafter called by the name Saint Paul; and never has there since been another law-teacher better than he beneath the canopy of the sky among those whom woman or man brought forth to the world, although he ordered your brother Stephen to be killed with stones on the hill.

511   ' "Now you can hear, my dear young man, how merciful is the Ruler of all – though we may often commit an offence against him through the wound of our sins – if we immediately afterwards make amends for wicked deeds and thereafter cease from wrongdoing. For this reason I and my beloved father afterwards truly believed that the God of all glories, the Lord of life, suffered vile torture because of mankind's great need. Therefore, dearest son, I exhort you by this recitation of secrets never to commit scoffing, malice, blasphemy nor surly railing against the Son of God: then you will deserve to have eternal life, the best of rewards for victory, granted you in heaven."

528   'So, in days long since, my father taught me as a youth by his words, instructed me with sayings of truth – his name was Symon, a man made wise by his griefs. Now you will clearly

know what to your mind it seems best to reveal about it, if this queen interrogates us about that tree, now that you know my mind and my thinking.'

536   Then the most discerning in the gathering of men spoke to him these words:

538   'Never have we heard any man within this nation, except you just now, nor any other person of standing speak out in this way on an event so secret. Do as you think, as one versed in ancient lore, if you should be questioned within the assembly of men. He will have need of wisdom, circumspect words and the shrewdness of a sage, who has to deliver an answer to the noble lady in front of such a gathering in conclave.'

VII

547   They grew profuse in their speeches; men deliberated on every side, some this way, some that; they pondered and they ruminated. Then a group of officials came to the assembly, and heralds, messengers of the emperor, shouted:

551   'The queen summons you men to the court so that you may duly recount the findings of your council. Advice is required of you and the wisdom of your mind in the assembly place.'

555   They were prepared, those melancholy sureties for their nation, when they were summoned by stern proclamation. They went to the court and displayed the strength of their cunning when the queen began to address her words to the Hebrews, to question the soul-weary men as to the ancient Scriptures, how in an age previously the prophets, pious men, sang of the Son of God, and as to where the Prince, the true Son of the ordaining Lord, suffered out of love of men's souls. They were stubborn, harder than stone; they would not duly reveal that secret, nor would they, as her bitter enemies, give her any answer on that which she sought from them but, unbudging of heart, they made repulse of every question that she asked of

them, and said that never in their life, neither early nor late, had they heard of any such thing.

573   Helen spoke up and, angry, said to them:

574   'I mean to tell you plainly – and upon my life it shall not prove a lie – that if you who stand before me continue in this deceit for long with your fraudulent lying, a blaze of hottest billowing ferocity will do away with you upon the hill and leaping flames destroy your corpses, for that deceit shall be deemed in you a matter for death. Even though you may not affirm those sayings – which you have for some time now wrongfully cloaked beneath the garments of your shameful deeds – you will not be able to conceal the event nor keep secret that profound miracle.'

584   Then they were under the prospect of death, of fire and their life's end, and there and then they pointed out the one ready-versed in the traditional accounts, to whom the name Judas had been given among his kinsmen. Him they handed over to the queen, and said he was outstandingly clever:

588   'He can reveal the truth to you and discover the secret of events and the law from the beginning through to the end, according to the questions you put to him. He is a man of distinguished parentage in the world, skilled in the art of speaking, and a prophet's son, confident in debate; it is a born gift in him that he has in his heart wise answers, talent. He, instead of a crowd of men, will by his great power display for you the gift of wisdom as your heart desires.'

598   She let each one go in peace to his own home and kept the one man, Judas, as hostage; and then she eagerly asked that he should teach her the truth about the Cross which hitherto had long been hidden in its burial-place, and she took him aside on his own. Helen, the queen blessed with glory, addressed the solitary man:

605   'Two things are open to you: either life or death, just as it
better suits you to choose. Now say quickly what you will
assent to in this matter.'

609   Judas – he could not escape that anguish nor fend off his
regal adversary: he was in the queen's power – responded to
her:

611   'With someone who is trudging the mountain wastes in a
desert, exhausted and without food, obsessed with hunger, and
a loaf and a stone, one hard, one soft, both come into view
together, how could it be that he should pick up the stone for
the relief of his hunger and not bother about the loaf, return to
want and forgo the food, reject the better thing, when he had
both things available?'

VIII

619   Then the blessed Helen answered him plainly in the presence
of the men:

621   'If you want to have an abode with the angels in the celestial
kingdom, a reward for victory in heaven, and on earth your
life, tell me promptly where the Cross of the King of heaven
rests, sacred beneath the soil, which for some time now you
have hidden from people because of the wickedness of that
murder.'

627   Judas spoke; within him was a spirit gloomy and feverish
about his heart, and distress at both threats, that for him the
radiance of the kingdom of heaven should fade away, and that
he should relinquish this present realm beneath the skies, if he
did not locate the Cross:

632   'How can I find something which has become so distant in
the course of years? A long time has gone by now, tallying two
hundred years or more in number; I cannot say, since I do not
know that number. Many men of insight, wise and good, have

since then passed away who lived before us. I came into my youth in after days, as a young boy born later. I cannot find in my heart that which I do not know, that which happened so long ago.'

642   Helen spoke out in reply to him:

643   'How has it come about in this nation that you are so copiously aware in your memory of each single one of all the remarkable things that the Trojans achieved in war? That famous ancient struggle was much longer ago in the course of years than this glorious event. If you can readily and promptly recount that – what slaughter there was altogether in terms of the total of men, of javelin-wielding soldiers fallen dead behind the shield-wall – you will have committed to written records the tomb beneath the rocky slopes and the location likewise and the number of years.'

655   Judas – he was undergoing miserable anguish – declared:

656   'My lady, of course we recall with immediacy that warfare and we have committed to records the battle-campaign and the nations' conduct. But this matter we have never heard from anybody's mouth to have been revealed to men except here and now.'

662   The noble queen replied to him:

663   'You deny too strenuously the truth and the verity about the tree of life, and yet a little while ago you were speaking truthfully to your fellow-countrymen about the tree of victory – and now you revert to lying.'

667   Judas replied to her and declared that he had said that very much under stress and confusion: he had been expecting humiliating punishment for himself.

669   Promptly the emperor's mother said to him:

670 'Listen; we have heard it revealed to men through sacred books that the noble Son of the King, God's spiritual Son, was hanged upon Calvary. You must fully disclose the knowledge, according to what the Scriptures say, concerning the location, as to where the place is on Calvary, before execution does away with you, death for your sins, so that I may then purify it according to Christ's will as a succour to men, so that holy God, the mighty Lord, the glorious Provider to multitudes, the Help of souls, may fulfil for me the purpose of my life and my desire.'

682 To her the stubborn Judas said:

683 'I do not know the place nor anything of the site nor do I know the circumstances.'

685 Helen spoke in impassioned mood:

686 'I swear it by the Son of the ordaining Lord, by the crucified God, that you shall be put to death by starvation in front of your kinsmen unless you cease these lies and plainly reveal to me the truth.'

691 Accordingly, then, she commanded him to be taken away by a squad and the guilty man to be thrust — and the servants did not dawdle — into a dry well where, without company, he remained in his sufferings for the duration of seven days, tormented by hunger within his prison and wrapped about with chains. And then on the seventh day, exhausted by his afflictions, spent and starving — his strength was enfeebled — he began to cry out:

699 'I implore you by the God of the heavens to let me up from out of these sufferings, prostrate from fierceness of hunger. I shall gladly reveal the holy tree now that I can no longer conceal it for hunger. This imprisonment is so harsh, the coercion so cruel and this torment so severe with the passing of the days, I cannot hold out nor keep the secret of the tree of life

longer, although I was earlier imbued with folly and myself recognized the truth too tardily.'

IX

710   When she who dictated to the people there heard the man's attitude, she quickly ordered that he should be let up from out of confinement and from out of prison, from the narrow dungeon. This they speedily did forthwith and mercifully brought him up out of prison as the queen ordered them. Then, firmly purposeful, they walked to the place up on the hill where the Lord, heaven-kingdom's Guardian, was once hanged, the Son of God on the gallows. And yet, reduced by starvation, he did not know exactly where the holy Cross, buried in the earth by devious trickery, long unmoved in its resting-place, secreted from the people, lay in its grave. At once, conscious of courage, he sent up these words and said in Hebrew:

725   'Lord, Saviour, you who have power to effect your ordinances, and who through the might of your glory created heaven and earth and the onward surge of the ocean and the sea's wide circuit, along with all creation; and you who measured out with your hands the whole world-circle and the sky on high, and yourself sit, the Lord presiding over victories, in great majesty of might, above the noblest order of angels who range the air encompassed in light – nor may humankind journey there in the body, up from the paths of earth amidst that radiant company, the messengers of heaven. You, holy and heavenly, fashioned them and set them to your ministry, of whose rank six are named as being in ceaseless bliss – these are also enfolded and adorned with six wings. There are four of these who, always in flight, perform in splendour their ministry before the face of the everlasting Judge and with clear voices sing unceasingly in glory the praise of the heaven-King, the most beautiful of songs, and who – their name is Cherubim – speak with pure voices these words: "Holy is the holy God of the archangels, the Ruler of the hosts; heaven and earth are full of his glory and all his sublime might is illustriously

witnessed." And there are two among them, the paramount species in heaven, who are called by the name of Seraphim. A Seraph has to keep sacred the garden of Paradise and the tree of life with his flaming sword: the sharp edge quivers and the patterned blade shimmers and shifts its hues, menacingly firm in his grasp.

759 'This you shall govern eternally, Lord God. And you cast down the sinful, the evil-working rash wreckers from the skies; then that accursed crew was compelled to tumble down into dark dwelling-places, into a perdition of punishments where even now in that welter they are undergoing the agonies of death in the dragon's grasp, smothered in darkness. He rebelled against your sovereignty: for that, full of every foulness, outlawed, he must suffer miseries and endure subjugation. There he is not able to reject your word: he, the author of all sin, is bound fast in punishments and in torture.

772 'If it is your will, Ruler of angels, that he should reign who was on the Cross and was born of Mary into the world, Prince of the angels in form of a child — if he were not your Son, free from sins, he would never have worked so many true miracles in the space of his days in the worldly kingdom; nor would you, ruler of the nations, have awakened him so gloriously from death in the sight of the multitudes if he were not your Child in glory by that pure woman — show forth your emblem now, Father of the angels. Just as you hearkened to the holy man Moses in his pleading when you, mighty God, on that glorious occasion revealed to that worthy the bones of Joseph beneath the pile of his burial-place, so I will entreat you, the Rejoicer of the multitudes, by that pure woman, if it is your will, to open to me, Creator of souls, the treasure-store which has been long hidden from men.

792 'Author of life! let a pleasant smoke now rise up from the spot, drifting on the air beneath the sky's expanse. I shall the better believe and the more firmly found my spirit and my undoubting hope upon the crucified Christ, that he is truly the

Saviour of souls, eternal, almighty King of Israel and shall everlastingly command the eternal abodes of glory in the heavens, for ever without end.'

X

802   Then from the place rose up a vapour-like smoke beneath the skies, whereupon the man's heart was elated. Blessed and clear-sighted in faith, he clapped both his hands on high. Judas spoke, clear-sighted in his thinking:

807   'Now I have truly ascertained for myself in my obstinate mind that you are the Saviour of the world. Thanks without end be to you, God of the heavenly hosts, enthroned in majesty, because you in your glory have disclosed to one so wretched and so sinful as I the mystery of the workings of Providence. Now I will entreat you, Son of God, Benefactor of the multitudes, now that I know you are the proclaimed and incarnate Majesty above all kings, that you, the Measurer, will be mindful no more of those guilts of mine which I have committed on no few occasions. Give me leave, mighty God, to dwell among the number of your kingdom, together with the congregation of the saints in the shining city where my brother is honoured in glory because he, Stephen, was faithful to you, though he was done to death by stoning. He has the reward of the struggle, splendour without cease: the wonders which he achieved are celebrated in books, in written records.'

827   Eager of will, then, and resolute of courage, he began to dig in the earth for the tree of glory beneath the covering of turf until, within a distance of twenty paces, he found concealed, hidden down in a deep pit, in a dark chamber, and came upon, there in that gloomy lodging-place, three crosses together, buried in soil just as the gang of obdurates, the Jews, had covered them with earth in days long since. They had set up such hostility against God's Son as they would not have done, had they not listened to the promptings of the author of sins.

839   Then his mind was greatly gladdened, his purpose fortified and his heart inspired by the holy tree, when he saw the holy emblem in the ground. With his hands he took hold of the joyous tree of glory and together with the crowd heaved it from its earthly grave. Garrisoned foot-soldiers, men of nobility, processed into the city.

846   Of single purpose, then, and elated in spirit those earls set down the three trees of victory within her view at Helen's feet. The queen rejoiced in spirit at their work and then she asked on which of the trees the Son of the Ruler, men's Giver of hope, was hanged:

852   'Listen! we have heard it plainly proclaimed by sacred books that two suffered with him and that he himself made the third on the rood-tree. The sky entirely darkened in that cruel hour. Say if you can on which of these three the Prince of angels, Shepherd of that host, suffered.'

859   Judas could not definitely inform her, for he did not know for certain, as to the tree of victory on which the Saviour, God's victorious Son, was raised up – until he recommended them to set the trees down amid the tumult in the centre of that famous city and there wait until the almighty King showed them in the presence of the crowds a miracle relating to the tree of glory. The arbitrators, men of victorious renown, sat and raised aloft their singing around the three crosses, until the ninth hour: they had gloriously discovered a new happiness.

870   Then a throng arrived there, a great crowd of people, and they brought a dead person upon a bier with a bevy of people in close attendance – it was the ninth hour – a young man less his soul. Then Judas was much exhilarated in his heart. He then ordered them to set down the soulless corpse of the deceased man bereft of life upon the ground, and he, expositor of truth, discerning of spirit, meditating deeply, raised up two of the crosses in his embrace above the doomed carcass. It remained dead as before, the corpse, unmoving on the bed; the limbs were growing cold, overspread by inexorable affliction.

883   Then the third one was lifted up in its holiness. The corpse was in waiting until the Prince's cross was reared above him, the tree of the heaven-King, the true emblem of victory. At once he rose up, furnished with his spirit, body and soul both together. There was seemly praise exalted among the people; they honoured the Father and extolled aloud the true Son of the Ruler:

892   'To him be glory and the thanks of all creatures for ever without end.'

XI

894   Then within the heart of the people remained present to their consciousness, as they always must be, those miracles which the Lord of the multitudes, the Guide of life, accomplished for the salvation of mankind.

898   Then the deceitful demon rose up there, hovering on the air. The devil of hell, a repulsive monstrosity intent upon evil doings, began then to shout:

902   'See here! what man is this who is destroying my following anew in pursuit of an ancient feud and is adding to old strife and plundering my possessions? This is persecution without end: evil-perpetrating souls are no longer allowed to remain in my possession. Now a man from the other world has come, one whom I had previously reckoned rooted in his crimes, and he has robbed me of every one of my dues and my riches. This is not fair behaviour.

911   'Many injuries and cruel acts of malice the Saviour, he who was nurtured in Nazareth, has done me; indeed, ever since he grew out of childhood he was always making over to himself my possessions. Now I am not allowed to profit from any due of mine. His realm is spread abroad throughout the earth: my authority here beneath the skies has dwindled away. No cause have I to extol the Cross with exultation: indeed! me this

Saviour has repeatedly shut away in that constricting dwelling-place, to the grief of us wretches.

921 'Through a Judas I was once filled with hope – and now I am humiliated, deprived of my goods, outlawed and friendless, once more through a Judas. But yet from out of the dwellings of the damned I shall be able by subterfuges to find retaliation against this. I shall stir up against you another king who will persecute you, and he will abandon your teaching and follow in my wicked ways, and then he will deliver you up to the blackest and vilest horrors of torture so that, probed with pains, you will quickly renounce the crucified King whom once you obeyed.'

934 Then the shrewd-minded Judas, emboldened to the fight – for the Holy Spirit was firmly bestowed upon him, love ardent as fire and an ebullient intelligence – answered him with a soldier's cleverness and, filled with wisdom, spoke these words:

939 'You need not, obsessed with sins, so strenuously renew the pain and resume the persecution, wicked lord of deadly evil. The mighty King will thrust you, a sin-devising disreputable creature, down into the gulf, into an abyss of torments – he who by his word awakened many of the dead. May you recognize the more clearly that you have imprudently lost the most sublime of existences and the love of the Lord, that joyous delight, and ever since have languished upon the fiery lake encompassed in torments, scorched by flame; and there in your perversity of mind you shall for ever suffer damnation and misery without end.'

952 Helen heard how the enemy and the ally raised their wrangle, the beatified and the evil on two sides, the sinner and the blessed. Her heart was the happier because she heard the man overpowering the ravager from hell, the dispenser of sins; and she marvelled then at the man's cleverness, how he had ever become so full of faith in so short a time, and so informed

and imbued with insight. She thanked God the glorious King because her desire had been fulfilled through God's Son in each of two respects: at the sight of the tree of victory and in the faith which she so clearly recognized, the heaven-rooted grace in the man's breast.

XII

967   Then the next day's remarkable news was reported among the populace and widely spread throughout the nation – to the alarm of those many who would keep the Lord's law secret – and proclaimed through the cities which the ocean encircles and in every town: that the Cross of Christ, long since buried in the earth, had been found, the noblest of those emblems of victory which late or early were upraised in holiness here below the heavens; and to those unhappy people, the Jews, the greatest of griefs, the most detestable lot – since they could not change it for the world – was the joy of the Christians.

979   Then the queen gave order throughout the troop of her men for envoys speedily to prepare for a journey; they were to go to the lord of the Romans across the deep ocean and to tell the warrior in person the most welcome news, that by grace of the ordaining Lord the victory-emblem had been discovered and found in the earth, which many years before had been hidden, to the vexation of pious Christian folk.

988   Then was the king's heart exhilarated by these glorious words and his spirit exultant. Of questioners in apparel of gold, transported from afar, there was no shortage in the palace buildings; to them befell the greatest consolation in the world and a jubilant mind at the welcome news which the envoys, chiefs in the army, had brought them along roads from the east – how salutary a journey the men had made with the triumphant queen across the swan's road into Palestine.

998   The emperor commanded them to prepare themselves in great haste for the journey back. The men did not dawdle when

once they had heard his response, the word of the prince. He commanded the renowned soldiers to bid Helen greeting, if they survived the ocean and could make a safe journey, mettlesome men, to the holy city. Constantine commanded the envoys furthermore to bid her to build a church there on the hillside for the benefit of them both, a temple of the Lord on Calvary as a pleasure to Christ and a succour to men, where the holy Cross was found, the most celebrated of the trees of which earth's inhabitants have ever heard on their way through the world. She acted accordingly when her kindred friends brought from the west across the watery fastness many a loving message.

1017   The queen then ordered men trained in their crafts to be severally sought, the best ones, those who knew how to build most exquisitely in stone-bondings, in order to prepare God's temple upon that spot, according as the Keeper of souls directed her from the skies. Then she commanded that the Cross be encased in gold and intricately set with gems, with the noblest precious stones, and then enclosed with locks in a silver casket. There the tree of life, the most excellent tree of victory, has ever since remained, unimpeachable as to its origin. There, ever ready, is a support to the infirm in every torment, trial and sorrow. There, through that holy artefact, they shall at once find aid and grace divine.

1032   Likewise Judas, after due time, received the immersion of baptism and, being faithful to Christ and dear to the Lord of life, was purified. His belief grew rooted in his soul when the Holy Ghost and Comforter occupied a dwelling in the man's breast and moved him to penitence. He chose the better part, the joy of heaven, and strove against the worser and put down idolatries and heresy and false religion. To him the everlasting King, God the ordaining Lord, the Wielder of mighty powers, was gracious.

XIII

1043   So he who many times before had assiduously ignored the light, underwent the cleansing of baptism; his heart was inspired with the better life and directed towards heaven. Surely Providence had decreed that he should come to be so full of faith and so loved by God on earth and so pleasing to Christ. This was made apparent when Helen commanded Eusebius, bishop in Rome, a very wise man, to be brought to the holy city for advice and help in the people's deliberations, in that he appointed Judas to the priesthood in Jerusalem as bishop to the populace within the city, by grace of the Spirit elected for his virtues to the temple of God; and upon wise consideration he named him anew Cyriacus. The man's name was henceforth changed in the city to the better one: 'the Saviour's revelation'.

1062   But Helen's mind was still very much preoccupied over that glorious event on account of the nails which pierced the Saviour's feet and likewise his hands with which the Ruler of the skies, the mighty Lord, was fastened on the Cross. Concerning these, the queen of the Christians began to inquire. She asked Cyriacus once again through the powers of the spirit to fulfil her desire regarding their wondrous fate, and by his glorious gifts to discover it; and she said these words to the bishop and spoke out, confident:

1073   'Refuge of the people, you have duly revealed to me the noble tree, the Cross of the King of heaven, on which the Help of souls, God's own Son, the Saviour of men, was hanged by heathen hands; yet still a yearning in my spirit reminds me of the nails. I would like you to find them, still buried deep in the ground as they are, secreted and hidden in darkness. My mind will always be pining; mournful it will grieve and never rest until the almighty Father, Ruler of the multitudes, the Saviour of mortals, the Holy One from the heights, fulfils for me my desire through the appearance of those nails.

1086   'Quickly now, most excellent apostle, in all humility send up your prayer into that radiant creation, into the joy of heaven, and beseech the majestic Lord of his soldiers that he, the King almighty, reveal to you the treasure beneath the earth which yet remains hidden, secret and concealed from the people.'

1093   Then the people's holy bishop, inspired within his breast, made up his mind. Kindly of heart, he set out with a throng of persons praising God; and when on Calvary Cyriacus diligently bowed down his face, he did not hide secret thoughts but by the powers of the spirit he called upon God in all humility and prayed the Guardian of the angels to disclose to him in this new dilemma the unknown fact – where in that locality he had strongest grounds to expect the nails.

1104   Then as they looked on, the Father, the Holy Ghost and Comforter, caused a sign in the form of fire to rise up from where, by men's conspiracies and out of close cunning, those most noble nails were hidden in the earth. There suddenly appeared then a hovering flame brighter than the sun. The people saw their benefactor reveal a miracle, when from out of the darkness there, like the stars of heaven or fine gems, near the bottom of the pit, the nails, shining from out of their confinement below, gleamed with light.

1115   The people rejoiced, a multitude jubilantly pleased; they all with one accord uttered glory to God, though before, through the devil's havoc, they had long remained in error, having turned aside from Christ. They spoke thus:

1120   'Now we see for ourselves the sign of victory, a true miracle of God, although we once denied it with our falsehoods. Now the course of events is come into the light and revealed. For this let the God of heaven-kingdom have glory on high.'

1125   Then the bishop of those people, he who had turned to penitence through the Son of God, was exhilarated anew. Set trembling by awe, he took up the nails and brought them to the venerable queen. Cyriacus had fulfilled the woman's whole desire according as the noble lady had bidden him. Then there was the sound of weeping, and a passionate flood poured forth upon the cheek, but not because of grief did tears fall upon filigree clasp: the queen's purpose was replete with glory. She knelt, radiant with faith, and, blissfully exultant, worshipped the gift which had been brought to her as a solace for sorrows. She thanked God, the Lord of victories, because she knew at first hand the truth which had often been proclaimed long previously, from the beginning of the world, as a comfort to the people. She was filled with the gift of wisdom, and the holy heavenly Spirit occupied that dwelling and took custody of her mind and noble heart. Thus the almighty and victorious Son of God henceforth protected her.

XIV

1147   Eagerly then she began by spiritual contemplations to search in her understanding for righteousness and the path to glory; and indeed the God of the multitudes, the Father in the skies, the almighty King, supported her so that the queen realized her desire in the world. This prediction had been sung beforehand by the prophets, from start to finish as it afterwards turned out in every respect.

1155   The people's queen began by grace of the Spirit eagerly and very meticulously to seek a use to which she might best and most worthily put the nails for the benefit of the multitudes, and what the Lord's will in this might be. So she commanded a man of pre-eminent wisdom to be quickly fetched for consultation, one prudent in intellect who by the power of his insight would be well capable of advice, and him she asked what to his mind it seemed best to do about this, and she accepted his guidance according to proper form. He confidently replied to her:

1167   'It is fitting that you hold in mind the word of the Lord, the holy Scriptures, most excellent queen, and diligently carry out the King's bidding, now that God, men's Saviour, has granted you the success of your soul's victory and the virtue of wisdom. Bid the noblest of earthly kings and of rulers of cities to put these nails on his bridle as a bit for his horse. It will come to be renowned among many throughout the earth, since with this he will be able to overpower every enemy in combat when brave soldiers, sword-wielding warriors, advance to battle on two sides, when they aspire to victory, foe against foe. He shall have success in war, victory in combat and everywhere immunity and protection in the fighting, who bears this emblem, the bridle, upon a steed, when renowned warriors, proved men, carry shield and javelin into the storm of spears. This shall be to every man that unvanquished weapon in warfare against oppression concerning which the prophet sang, wise in the complexity of his thoughts – his understanding, the faculty of his wisdom, penetrated deep and he spoke these words: "It will come to be known that the horse of the king shall be distinguished among the brave by its bit and its bridling-chains. That ensign shall be called 'Holy unto God', and the favoured warrior whom that horse bears, he shall be distinguished in war." '

1196   Then all that Helen speedily carried out in her men's presence; she commanded a bridle for the prince, the ring-giving lord of warriors, to be embellished and she sent the flawless gift over the ocean tide as an offering to her own son.

1201   Then she commanded those among the Jews whom she knew to be the finest of men and of humankind to come together to the holy city, into the fortress. Then the queen enjoined the assembly of dear friends that they should steadfastly maintain their love of the Lord and likewise peace and friendship among themselves, sinless during their lifetime, and that they should obey the teachings of their preceptor, those Christian usages which Cyriacus, learned in books, would decree for them. His standing as bishop was well established; often there came to him from afar the lame, the paralysed, the maimed, the halt, the mortally sick, the leprous and the blind, the wretched and the miserable: there at the bishop's hands they always found healing and a cure lasting for ever. Furthermore, Helen gave him costly tokens of esteem when she was ready for the journey to her homeland. And then she called upon all those worshipping God upon the earth, men and women, to honour with mind and main strength, with the heart's contemplation, the glorious day on which the holy rood was found, the most glorious of trees which have grown up from the earth, burgeoning beneath their leaves. Spring had by then progressed into the month of May, only six days before the arrival of summer.

1228   May the gate of hell be closed and heaven's unlocked and the realm of the angels opened everlastingly, may their joy be eternal and their portion assigned them with Mary, for everyone who holds in remembrance the festival of the most precious rood beneath the skies which the most mighty, the sovereign Lord of all, overspread with his arms. Finit.

1236   Thus miraculously have I, being old and ready to go because of this fickle carcass, gleaned and woven the craft of words and for long periods pondered and winnowed my thoughts painstakingly by night. I was not entirely aware of the truth about this thing before wisdom, through the sublime Might, discovered to me in the thinking of my mind an ampler understanding. I was soiled by my deeds, shackled by my sins, harassed by cares, and bound and oppressed by bitter worries before the mighty King granted me knowledge in lucid form as solace to an old man, meted out his flawless grace and instilled it in my mind, revealed its radiance, at times augmented it, unshackled my body, laid open my heart – and unlocked the art of poesy, which I have used joyously and with a will in the world.

1251   Not once but often I made inward remembrance of the tree of glory before I discovered the miracle concerning that illustrious timber, according to what, in the course of events, I found in books, related in writings, about the symbol of victory.

1256   Until then, the man had always been a sinking flame (C) buffeted by surges of anxiety even though in the mead-hall he received precious gifts. The horn (Y), his comrade in duress (N), would mourn, and he would suffer oppressive grief, a confined secret, while his spirited horse (E) measured and galloped the mile-stoned highways, proudly adorned with filigree. Pleasure (W) has dwindled, and sportiveness, with the years; youth is transmuted, and the old pomp. Ours (U) was once the beauty of youth; now, after the appointed span, the days of old are passed away and the pleasures of living are gone even as the sea (L), the driven tides, will vanish away. Wealth (F) is an ephemeral thing for everyone below heaven; the fineries of the earth will be gone beneath the skies most like the wind when it gets up loud in front of men and scuds through the skies, rushes raging onwards, and then suddenly grows silent, closely confined in its prison, forcibly suppressed.

1277 Thus this whole world shall vanish; and those likewise who were begotten in it destructive fire will carry off when the Lord himself comes to judgment with his host of angels. Each man there shall hear the truth about each one of his deeds and likewise of his words from the Judge's mouth, and will pay the penalty for all things formerly spoken in folly and for all shameless thoughts.

1286 Then he will divide into three, in the clutches of the fire, each single nation of those that have ever existed upon the wide earth. Those steadfast in truth will be uppermost in the fire, the company of the blessed, an aristocracy of those eager for good repute: thus they will be able to hold out without difficulty and easily endure, an army of the brave. For them he will moderate the full glare of the fire, as it is best pleasing to him and most bearable for them. The sinful, those polluted with wickedness, will be punished, melancholy people, in its midst, in the hot eruption, smothered with smoke. The third part, accursed evildoers and deceitful persecutors, will be consigned to the fire, into the depths of the eruption on account of their former deeds, a rabble of pitiless creatures, into the grip of the flames. Never again will they come into the remembrance of God the King of glory from out of that place of torment; rather, they will be toppled from out of that violent eruption into the abyss of hell, his bitter enemies.

1306   For the other two parts it will be different. They will be allowed to see the Lord of the angels, the God of victories. They will be smelted, sundered from their sins, as pure gold which in the eruption is wholly purged of every impurity by the fire of the furnace, and refined and melted. Just so, each of those men will be parted and separated from each of their guilts and deep crimes by the fire of judgment. Then they will be allowed to enjoy peace thereafter, and everlasting prosperity. The Guardian Lord of the angels will be gentle and kindly to them, because they despised every wickedness and the commission of sins, and called aloud upon the Son of the ordaining Lord. Therefore they now shine forth in beauty like the angels and enjoy the heritage of the King of glory through existence infinite. Amen.

THE
EXETER
BOOK

The Exeter Book

[Exeter, Cathedral 3501, fol.8–130]

The very strong likelihood has never been seriously disputed that the 'large English book about various matters treated in verse' which Leofric, first bishop of Exeter (died *c*. 1072), is anciently recorded as having given to his cathedral, is to be identified with the codex of AS poetry now called the Exeter Book. Though damaged in various ways the book remains substantially as it was known to the Anglo-Saxons. The plain but handsome MS, which appears to have been wholly written in one hand, is palaeographically dated to the second half of the tenth century. This is well before the episcopal seat was established in Exeter in 1050. Probably, then, Leofric came by the MS as a ready-made codex and cannot definitely be credited with the selection of poems it contains.

The codex opens with what might be regarded as a conspectus of the mystical and historic truths at the heart of the Christian faith and of Christian living: three related poems (*Chr I*, which is itself a gathering of short lyrics, *Chr II* and *Chr III*) inviting meditation upon three aspects of Christ, as Messiah, as Redeemer and as Judge.

Episodes in sacred history are treated in *Phr*, *Aza* and *DHl*; while the saints' lives (*Jul*, *Glc*) sample the history of witness to Christ. Accounts of the (anthropocentric) meaning of the created world and of the nature and destiny of man appear in *OrW*, *Pnt*, *Whl*, *Ptg*, *GfM* and *FtM*. The themes of Judgment, Heaven and Hell raised in *Chr* are continued in *SlB II* and *Phx* and there are many prescriptions for living in the world in such a way as to prepare for Judgment (*Wan*, *Sfr*, *Prc*, *Mxm*, *Rsg* and *Alm*).

Thus the codex at large sustains the address made in the opening poems to the essentials of Christian faith and Christian living. Such a classification based upon subject-matter is not the only one which could be made – though perhaps the remarkable conservatism of form in AS poetry indicates that subject-matter concerned the poets more than stylistic experiment and the innovation of many distinct genres; and the fact that the two 'signed' poems of Cynewulf (*Jul* and *Chr II*) are randomly separated may suggest that systematic presentation of a single poet's work was no guiding objective either. Nor are the poems within one subject-matter group illustrative of that group alone; nor indeed are the poems physically ordered into such groups within the codex; and of course not all the poems are accounted for in this classification.

Of the rest, *WfL* and *HbM* may well be metaphorical treatments of Christian concepts; and it may yet be proved that even the aggressively secular-seeming *WlE* had an acceptable didactic application. The *Riddles*, sometimes jauntily indecent, may be accounted for by the popular respectability of the genre among learned ecclesiastics, especially in Latin, over the centuries. And neither *Wds* nor *Deo* can be regarded as unequivocally secular, for all their evocative Germanic legendary content.

The choice of the unknown compiler, who seems to have used the MS as a kind of poetic commonplace-book into which he entered appealing poetry as he came across it, is, then, broadly coherent and intelligible. The prevailing mood is penitential; the prevailing purpose is to induce in an audience that state of compunction held precious by contemporary commentators, in which the soul is opened to the access of grace. Yet the Exeter Book is far from being organized with the firm sense of purpose we may discern in the Junius MS. Had more collections survived, we should be able to say more about AS poetic taste. All too little can be deduced from the extremely sparse indicators of what was popular. But we may note that a very few poems in the Exeter Book are known in related versions elsewhere; and that, according to John of Glastonbury, there once existed in the monastery there a codex containing the Life of Saint Guthlac, a collection of maxims, poems concerning the souls of the dead and the final resurrection, and many riddles – a content strikingly like that of the Exeter Book.

Not only for its unique position in English literary history but also for the absolute quality of much of the poetry it contains, the Exeter Book must be accorded a place of highest priority among English books.

Where in the following pages poems that appear in the codex have been omitted from translation, their position, title and topic are noted so as to provide a full record of the poetic contents of the MS.

Sectional divisions in the MS, which are not numbered there, are here marked with roman numerals as in *ASPR III*.

Christ I (The Advent Lyrics)

[The Exeter Book, fol.8ᵃ–14ᵃ]

At their story-level, the three poems comprising the cyclical *Christ* not only feature three great phases of the dealings of Christ with humankind – the Advent, the Ascension and the Judgment – but by extension subsume the whole Scripture-based account of human history from Creation through present time and future Judgment into eternity. As these poems make clear, this account is to be understood according to a Christian philosophy of history which accepts the premise that earthly reality, including time itself, is a transient construct subordinate to the creating Deity's purpose. 'In Christ he chose us before the world was founded. . . Therein lies the richness of God's free grace lavished upon us, imparting full wisdom and insight. He has made known to us his hidden purpose . . . to be put into effect when the time was ripe: namely, that the universe, all in heaven and on earth, might be brought into a unity in Christ. In Christ indeed we have been given our share in the heritage, as was decreed in his design whose purpose is everywhere at work.' (Ephesians 1:4–11.) Within this philosophy, any parallel discerned between the cycle of history and the life of the individual Christian is seen not as a fortuitous analogy but as a true replication belonging to an order of reality above the reality of finite historical events and of the chronology of the temporal world. Thus, for example, the individual's personal discovery of the truth of the Cross through his devotions (*DrR*, epilogue to *Ele*) is a mystical replication of the singular historical event of the Invention of the Cross. And the same Cross, discovered by St Helen in past history, and mystically discovered afresh and repeatedly by individuals in subsequent time, will be encountered again by all, as advocate or prosecutor, in the future Judgment (*DrR*, *Chr III*): this is part of that hidden purpose 'made known to us'. So too, in the meaning of *Chr I*, compunction generated now in the individual who contemplates the already revealed events of the Judgment to come prepares a mystical replication of Christ's Advent within this individual's heart, and this will prove efficacious against that future Day of Doom. Thus the temporally lodged soul, though constrained to progress through sequential time to Judgment, is presently offered a way to eternal salvation by the intervention of replications and anticipations, which transcend the limits of temporality.

Chr I is comprised of five groups of separately conceived lyric poems, twelve in total, all beginning with the exclamation *Eala!* except the first which, by loss of one or more folios probably containing one or two further lyrics, lacks its opening. Like the Benedictine Office poems (see the headnotes to *LPr III*), these lyrics are in effect meditations upon the words of the liturgy. Most of them are based upon Latin antiphons of the liturgy for Advent (except *Lyric 11* which is probably inspired by the Common Preface to the Sanctus of the Mass), though the Latin texts provided in this translation (see J. J. Campbell, *The Advent Lyrics of the Exeter Book*, Princeton 1959, and M. J. B. Allen and D. G. Calder, *Sources and Analogues of OE Poetry*, Cambridge and Totowa N. J., 1976) do not appear in the Exeter Book. The poems are a tissue of allusions and internal cross-allusions to Messianic lore which sees the Advent as fulfilment of the Old Testament. But their purpose goes beyond simple assertion of the credentials of Emmanuel; they seek to impress the fuller and abiding implications of 'God with us'. With intense concentration of rhetoric they supplicate that the Advent be repeated year by year in the hearts of successive generations living centuries on from the singular historical moment of the revelation of the Incarnation.

Of special stylistic interest, in view of the poet's sense of the relationship between the reality of historical event and the *mystical* 'reality' attainable through liturgical or literary imitation of the historical event, is *Lyric 7*. Apart from one line of narrative, the poem is purely dialogue (though the MS does not indicate, and editors disagree, how speeches are to be assigned). The narrator intervenes so little between audience and action imitated that the poem comes close to the mode of drama. The plot, indeed, hinges about a discovery leading to a reversal of mood – which Aristotle might have recognized as the dramatic device of *peripeteia*. Inevitably, the critic is reminded of the similarly structured *Quem quaeritis?* liturgical drama, formulated in the tenth-century *Regularis Concordia* by the Benedictine reformers, Æthelwold of Winchester and Dunstan of Canterbury. Thus the poet of *Lyric 7* merits at least a footnote in the history of the first emergence of medieval religious drama in England.

By such distinguished exercise of his craft, then, the poet bids to move his audience to a state of compunction (see the headnote to *DrR*) with its ensuing spiritual benefits. The whole tendency of these lyrics, in contrast to such morbid poems as *SlB*, is to rejoice in the worthiness of that humanity whose form the Godhead willingly assumed in order to redeem. Writ large through them is the sentiment vividly expressed by St Augustine (*The Christian Combat*, ch.11, tr. R. P. Russell in *Writings of Saint Augustine*, vol.IV, *The Fathers of the Church*, vol.II, 2nd edition, New York, 1950, p.329): 'Let the human race take hope and rediscover its own nature. Let it see what an important place it occupies among the works of God. Men! do not despise yourselves – the Son of God assumed manhood. Women! do not despise yourselves – the Son of God was born of a woman.' The lyric poetry of *Chr I* – on various occasions urgently incantatory or meditatively tranquil, stately or conversational, austere or fulsome, penitential or ecstatically joyful, always carefully crafted – may be Cynewulf's. If not, it surely testifies that there was another master-poet in the Cynewulfian school, one whose vigorous intellect and didactic purpose are happily matched by his aesthetic judgment and command of poetic form.

I

1 O *King of the nations and object of their longing and the cornerstone which makes both parts one: come and save man, whom you formed out of clay.*

. . . to the King. You are the wall-stone which the builders once rejected from the building. Well it befits you that you are the headstone of the glorious hall and that you conjoin the wide walls, the intact flint, with a firm-fixed bond, so that throughout earth's cities all men may, by their own eyes' seeing, for ever marvel at the Lord of glory. Now, steadfast in truth, sublimely triumphant, make demonstration of your own workmanship in skilful fashion and forthwith leave wall conjunct with wall. Now the building is in need of it, that the Craftsman and the King should come himself and so make good, now it is reduced to ruin, the house beneath its roof. He created the body and the limbs of clay. Now he, the Lord of life, shall save this wearied multitude from its enemies and wretched men from terror, as he has often done.

2 O *key of David and sceptre of the house of Israel, you who open and no one closes: you who close and no one opens: come and lead out of the prison-house the captive who sits in darkness and the shadow of death.*

18   O Judge and just King, you who guard the locks and lay open life and the blessed ways on high, and to another deny the lovely longed-for road if his attainment does not suffice: out of necessity indeed we speak these words and entreat him who created man not be slow . . . [*slight damage to MS*] . . . the cause of those fraught with care, for we sit sorrowing in prison. We look forward to the sun, when the Lord of life will disclose to us the light, and become to us in spirit a source of security, and enfold our feeble consciousness in glory and make us thus worthy, that he should admit into heaven us who have had to come miserably into this confining world, cut off from the homeland. He who speaks the truth may thus say that he saved the human race when it had been led astray.

35   It was a young virgin, a girl free of sin, whom he chose as his mother. It was accomplished without a man's caresses that the bride became pregnant in the bearing of a child. No woman's guerdon comparable to that has come about in the world, before nor since: it was a mystery, the Lord's secret. Spiritual grace entirely over-spread the face of the earth; there a host of things, the long-standing lore and the eloquent singing of the prophets, which before lay concealed under darkness, were illumined through the Author of life, when the Ruler came who amplifies the secret sense of every utterance of those who earnestly desire in ready manner to praise the name of the Creator.

3   *O Jerusalem, city of the most exalted God: raise your eyes round about and see your Lord, for now he is coming to loose you from chains.*

50   O vision of peace, holy Jerusalem, unparagoned among royal thrones, city and realm of Christ, the angels' patrimonial seat: the souls of those steadfast in truth, and they alone, shall rest in you for ever, gloriously jubilant. Never shall any sign of a sin be revealed in that abode; rather, each wicked thing, evil and strife, will be turned away from you. You are gloriously

filled with holy joy, in keeping with what you are called. See now for yourself, spaciously scanning on every side of you, beyond this vast creation and the vault of the sky too, how in his advent the King of heaven seeks for you and how he himself is coming. He will take up his abode in you, just as wise prophets long ago declared in their sayings. They proclaimed the birth of Christ and spoke comfort to you, most excellent of cities. Now that child is come, born as relief to the sufferings of the Hebrews. He brings you bliss; he unlooses the bonds evilly forced upon you. He understands the harsh necessity, how the wretched must wait upon grace.

II

4 *O Virgin of virgins, how shall this be done? for you are seen to have no like, neither before nor after. Daughters of Jerusalem, why do you wonder at me? This is a divine mystery which you behold.*

71 'O delight among women throughout the glory of heaven, noblest virgin across the whole face of the earth of whom the sea-encircled world's inhabitants ever heard tell: expound to us the mystery which came to you from the heavens, how you ever conceived your pregnancy in the bearing of a child and did not know cohabitation according to mortal mind. Truly we have not heard of such a thing ever occurring in former days, as that you thus conceived in a special act of grace, nor need we look for that happening forward in time. Trust has indeed dwelt with distinction in you, now that you have carried the Majesty of heaven in your womb and your great virginity was not corrupted. Just as all sons of mortals sow in sorrows, so do they afterwards reap: they procreate as a torment.'

87 The blessed Virgin spoke, holy Mary, forever abounding in triumph:

89 'What is this wonderment, you son of Salem and you as well, its daughter, whereby you are amazed and, complaining,

bemoan your cares? You ask out of curiosity how I have kept my virgin state and my integrity and also become the mother of the glorious Son of the Lord. That, however, is not a mystery made plain to men; but Christ did reveal in David's dear kinswoman that the sin of Eve is entirely set aside and the curse averted, and the lowlier sex is glorified. Hope is conceived that a blessing may now and always rest upon both alike, men and women, henceforth to eternity in the heavenly joy of the angels with the Father of truth.'

5 *O Dayspring, Refulgence of eternal light and Sun of righteousness: come and illumine those who dwell in darkness and in the shadow of death.*

104   O Dayspring, brightest of angels sent to men upon middle-earth, and the sun's righteous radiance, of a brilliance exceeding the stars; you by your own self continually illumine every hour. If you, God long since begotten of God, Son of the true Father, ever existed without beginning in the glory of heaven, then with confidence your own creation prays to you now on account of its needs, that you send us that bright sun, and yourself come so that you may illumine those who, shrouded in murk and in darkness, have already long continued here in endless night; enveloped in sins they have had to endure the dark shadow of death. Full of hope now, we trust to the salvation brought to the multitudes through that Word of God which in the beginning was with the almighty Father, coeternal with God, and has now subsequently become flesh devoid of transgressions which the Virgin bore as a support to those in sorrow. God was with us, seen to be without sins; together they dwelt united, mighty Child of the Lord and Son of man, among men. We may address our thanks continually to the triumphant Lord according to his deeds, because he willed to send us himself.

6 *O Emmanuel, our King and Lawgiver, Hope of the nations and their Saviour: come to save us, Lord our God.*

130 O God of spirits, how discerningly you were rightly named by the name Emmanuel, as the angel first pronounced it in Hebrew; that is, being freely interpreted according to its hidden sense, 'Now the Guardian Lord of the heavens, God himself, is with us.' Thus men of old long ago truly predicted the King of all kings and the pure Priest too; and thus the renowned Melchisedech, discerning in spirit, once revealed the divine majesty of the eternal Ruler of all. He was the bringer of law, the deliverer of precepts, to those who long had hoped for his advent according as it had been promised them that the Lord's Son himself would purge the people of earth and likewise by the power of his spirit also make a journey to visit the depths. Mildly now they waited in fetters until the Child of God should come to those in grief; and therefore, wasted by their sufferings, they spoke thus:

149 'Come now, high King of heaven, in your own person. Bring salvation, life, to us weary thralls to torment, overcome by weeping, by bitter salt tears. The cure for our excessive hardships belongs wholly with you alone. Seek out us melancholy captives here, and when you return hence do not leave behind you a multitude so great, but in kingly manner show mercy upon us, Saviour Christ, Prince of heaven, and do not let accursed devils have dominion over us. Impart to us the everlasting joy of your glory so that those may worship you, glorious King of the heavenly hosts, whom once you fashioned with your hands. In the heights you will for ever remain with the Ruler and Father.'

III

7 *O Joseph, why did you believe what before you feared? Why indeed? The One whom Gabriel announced would be the coming Christ is begotten in her by the Holy Spirit.*

164 'O my Joseph, Jacob's son, kinsman of David the renowned king, you now feel bound to put quite asunder my love, to disown my devotion?'

167   'I am suddenly scandalized deeply and robbed of repute, because I have listened to many words of insult on your account, many greatly distressing things and hurtful remarks, and they speak ridicule to me and many painful words. Despondent in mind, I must shed tears. God can easily heal the feeling of sorrow in my heart, and console a man of few recourses. O my young bride, Mary, virgin!'

176   'Why do you grieve and cry out as one in anguish?'

177   'Never have I found a fault in you nor any suspicion of your having done defiling things; and you utter those words although you are filled with every sin and evil.'

181   'I have come by too many mischievous hurts from this pregnancy.'

183   'How can I refute the unfriendly talk or find any answer against the ill-willed? It is widely known that I freely accepted from the glorious temple of the Lord a virgin pure and without defilements, and that now she is changed because of some person unknown. Neither will benefit me, that I speak nor that I keep silent. If I tell the truth, then the daughter of David must die, killed with stones. It is still worse that I should cover up a crime: the perjurer must thereafter live loathed by every man, abominated by the people.'

196   Then the Virgin unfolded the authentic mystery and spoke thus:

197   'I will tell the truth by the son of the Lord, the Helper of souls – that I know no man by way of intercourse anywhere upon earth; but to me, a young woman at home, it was granted that Gabriel, heaven's archangel, hailed me with a greeting, and truthfully told that the celestial Spirit would irradiate me with light: I was to give birth to the Life-force, the sublime Son, the mighty Child of God, the illustrious King of glory. Now I am made his immaculate temple; in me the Comforter Spirit has

dwelt. Now give up all bitter grieving. Say everlasting thanks to the Lord's excellent Son that I have become his mother though remaining a virgin, and that you, according to supposition, have come to be called his earthly father. Prophecy had to be truly fulfilled in his own person.'

8   *O King of peace, born before the ages; come forth through the golden gate, visit your redeemed ones and fetch them back to the place whence, through sin, they fell.*

214   O true and peace-loving King of all kings, almighty Christ: before all the world's multitudes you were in being with your heavenly Father, begotten as his Son through his power and his might. There is presently no man under the sky, no subtle-thinking person, so exceedingly discerning that he can inform the sea-encircled world's inhabitants, expound to them with authenticity, how the Guardian Lord of the heavens in the beginning comprehended you as his noble Son. Of those things of which humankind have heard tell here among people, what first came to pass beneath the clouds in the beginning was that the wise God, the Origin of life, parted the light and the darkness in lordly manner, and the power of the fiat lay with him and the Lord of the heavenly hosts proclaimed this directive: 'Let there be light now and henceforth for ever to eternity, a radiant joy to all living creatures which may be born in their generations.' And then immediately it happened, since it had to be so: a luminary lighted the families of man, brilliant among the stars, throughout the passing of the hours. He himself ordained that you, the Son, were co-dwelling with your one Lord before anything of this was even accomplished; you are the intelligence who, with the Ruler, wrought this whole wide creation. Therefore there is no one so wise nor so skilful of thought that he can plainly prove your origin to the children of mortal men.

243   Come now, Lord of victory, Arbiter of mankind, and, being gracious, reveal your mercy here. There is in all of us a longing that we be allowed to know that true mystery, your maternal

lineage, since we cannot at all further explain your paternal lineage. Mercifully gladden this world through your advent, Saviour Christ, and bid those golden gates be opened which in days of old once stood a very long time locked, high Lord of the heavens, and seek us then by coming to earth in your own gentle person. We need your favours: the accursed wolf, the beast and agent of darkness, has scattered your flock, Lord, and driven it widely asunder; that flock which you, the Ruler, once bought with blood, the baleful foe violently injures and carries off into captivity for himself, against the yearning of our desires. Therefore, Redeemer, we earnestly pray you in the thoughts of our breasts that you swiftly afford us weary exiles help, so that the tormenting slayer may fall abject into the abyss of hell, and the work of your hand, Creator of men, may rise up and come as of right to that celestial noble kingdom, whence the swarthy spirit once seduced and misled us in our lust for things sinful, so that we, bereft of glory, will have to suffer misery for ever without end – unless you, everlasting Lord, the living God, Protector of all creatures, are willing to be the more swift to save us from the people's foe.

IV

9 O Lady of the world, born from royal seed, from your womb Christ has now come forth like a bridegroom from the bedchamber; here in the manger lies he who also has dominion over the stars.

275   O splendour of the world, the purest woman on earth of those that have ever been: how rightly all people possessed of speech, men throughout the earth, joyful in mood, name you and say that you are the bride of the most excellent Lord of heaven. Likewise, those servants of Christ most exalted in the heavens also proclaim and sing, that you with your holy virtues are Lady of the heavenly host and of the earthly orders below the heavens and of the dwellers in hell. For you alone among all people, having the courage of your persuasions, gloriously determined that you would offer your maidenhood to the

ordaining Lord and grant it to him without sin. None compar-
able has come, no other above all mortals, a ring-adorned bride
who, with pure heart, then sent the sublime offering to the
heavenly home. On this account, the Lord of victory com-
manded his exalted messenger out of his mighty throng to fly
hither and swiftly reveal to you the abundance of his powers:
that in a chaste birth you were to bring forth the Son of the
Lord God as an act of mercy towards men; and yet thenceforth
keep yourself, Mary, ever immaculate.

301   We have also heard what a certain righteous prophet, Isaiah,
said about you long ago in days of old: that he was transported,
so that he surveyed the entire abode of life in that eternal home.
The wise prophet, then, thus gazed over the peopled land until
he fixed his view where a noble entrance was established. The
huge door was all adorned with precious treasure and bound
about with marvellous bands. He very much despaired that any
mortal man would ever in eternity be able to heave up bars so
secure or undo the fastening of that city gate, before God's
angel with gracious intention explained the matter and spoke
these words: 'I can tell you' – it came true – 'that God himself,
the almighty Father, by the power of the Spirit, will at a certain
time hereafter sanctify those golden gates and visit the earth by
way of these secure locks, and then they will remain perpetu-
ally and everlastingly closed thus behind him, so that no other,
excepting God the Saviour, will ever unlock them again.' Now
that which the sage then gazed upon there with his own eyes is
fulfilled: you are that gateway in the ramparts through which
the Ruler and Lord on that one occasion journeyed forth into
this earth; and in the very same way the almighty Christ found
you, adorned with virtues, chaste and singled out for excel-
lence. In the same way the Prince of the angels, Giver of life,
locked you behind him with a physical key, unmarked by
anything afterwards.

335   Now show towards us that grace which the angel, God's
messenger, brought to you. Especially, we citizens of earth pray
for this: that you will reveal to the folk that consolation, your

own Son. Then we may all with one accord rejoice when we gaze upon the Child at your breasts. Plead for us now with brave words, that he will no longer leave us in this vale of death to listen to the deceiver, but that he will conduct us into the Father's kingdom where, free from sorrow, we may afterwards dwell in glory with the God of the heavenly hosts.

10 *O Lord of the heavens, you who are eternal with the Father, and one with the Holy Spirit, hear your servants; come to save them now; do not delay.*

348   O holy Lord of the heavens, you were of old in equal being with your Father in the noble home. No angel was then yet come into existence, none of that great and mighty throng which, up in the skies, oversees the kingdom, the Prince's splendid dwelling and his ministrations, when first you established, yourself with the everlasting Lord, this vast creation and its broad, spacious foundations. In mutual germaneness to you both is the protective Holy Ghost. To you, Saviour Christ, we all pray in humility that you hear the voice of us captives, your servants, redeeming God, how we are afflicted because of our own desires. Damned spirits, malignant foes from hell have cruelly constrained us exiles and bound us with painful fetters. The cure belongs wholly with you alone, everlasting Lord. Help us in our sorrow, so that your advent may console us paupers, although we have waged a feud against you in our lust for things sinful. Have mercy now upon your servants and think upon our miseries, how we stumble along faint of heart and wander about in abjection. Come now, King of men: do not delay too long. We are in need of your loving favours, that you rescue us and that you, being true and steadfast, grant us salvation, so that henceforth we may in fellowship ever hereafter do better things – your will.

V

11 *O beatific and blessed and glorious Trinity, Father and Son and Holy Spirit; rightly all your creatures praise you, adore you, glorify you, O beatific Trinity.*

378   O beautiful, celestial Trinity, replete with glories, exalted
and holy, blessed abroad throughout the spacious plains,
whom people possessed of speech, miserable earth-dwellers,
must by right praise highly with all their might, now that God,
true to his covenant, has revealed to us the Saviour, so that we
may know him. On this account those industrious beings
endued with splendour, the true and steadfast species of the
seraphim, ever giving praise, and the angels on high, with
untiring strength sing in a loud voice most exaltedly and
sweetly, far and near. They hold the most favoured office with
the King: Christ granted it to them that they, ethereally
arrayed, be always allowed unceasingly to enjoy his presence
with their own eyes and to worship the Ruler far and wide; and
with their wings they watch over the person of the almighty
Lord, the everlasting God, and eagerly throng about the
princely throne, whichever of them in his flight can flit nearest
to our Saviour in those courts of peace. They laud the Beloved
and declare these words to him in heaven and glorify the noble
Author of all created things:

403   'You are holy, holy, King of archangels, true Lord of victory;
you are for ever holy, Lord of lords. Your earthly dignity will
always remain among mortals, honoured abroad in every age.
You are the God of the multitudes, for you have filled earth and
skies with your glory, Defender of those fighting the fight,
Protector of all creatures. To you be everlasting salutation in
the heights, and on earth praise sublime among men. Live on
blessed, you who came in the name of the Lord to the masses as
solace to the lowly. To you in the heights be ever without end
eternal benediction.'

12   O *wondrous exchange: the Creator of mankind, assuming
an animate body, has deigned to be born of a virgin and,
without seed, becoming man has bestowed upon us his
divinity.*

416   O behold, this is a wondrous exchange in the way of life of
men, that mankind's merciful Creator has received from a

virgin immaculate flesh, and she has known nothing of a man's love nor did the transcendent Lord come by means of the seed of any man on earth; but it was a greater work of ingenuity than all earth's inhabitants could understand because of its mysteriousness, how he, the Glory of the skies, the exalted Lord of the heavens, afforded help to mankind through the womb of his mother; and proceeding onwards thus the people's Saviour, Lord of the multitudes, every day dispenses his remission as a help to men. Therefore let us, eager for good repute, faithfully praise him in deeds and in words. It is high wisdom in every person who has recall, that he should always most frequently, most heartily and most eagerly worship God. He, the hallowed Saviour himself, will give him the reward of this love, even in that homeland where he had not come before, in the bliss of the land of the living, where he will afterwards live blessed and remain to all eternity without end. Amen.

Christ II (The Ascension)

[The Exeter Book, fol.14ᵃ–20ᵇ]

Chr I is centrally concerned with the Advent; *Chr II* reaches its main topic, the Ascension, by way of a comparison between the circumstances of Christ's coming into the world in Bethlehem and his departure from it at Bethany. Thus – by design of author or editor – the allusion to the Nativity in the opening of *Chr II* effects a thematic continuity between the two poems. The continuity consists in more than the chronological, historical symmetry between the opening and the closing of the Messiah's incarnate ministry. For the poet of *Chr II* takes an interpretative and homiletic approach to his topic of the Ascension, which amounts to a continued exposition of the relevance of sacred history to the present life of the individual Christian, as launched in *Chr I*. Thus he makes an opportunity to declare that God's descent to earth in human form witnessed to the divinely given potential of each individual man made in God's image, for which gift of worthiness, the poet here says with the poet of *Sfr*, men must repay God with praise and with holy works, valiant deeds in the struggle against the devil. Furthermore, by dwelling upon the examples set by the loyal angel throngs, by the great retinue of souls freed from hell who returned triumphantly home with Christ, and above all by the apostolic fellowship left sorrowing but faithful to continue Christ's ministry on earth, the poet is able to develop a major theme concerning the Church, and the charges and promises made to it by Christ in the hour of his Ascension. Thus the audience that has been induced in *Chr I* to open its heart to the advent of Christ the Redeemer is now exhorted out of gratitude and true discipleship to grow towards full realization of spiritual potential in the militant Christian life, within the fellowship of the faithful, the apostolic Church, the ark piloted by Christ in which alone righteous souls may safely navigate the ocean-flood of this world and reach the haven prepared. Finally, in its closing sequence, the poem makes allusion – all the more pointed because it embodies the poet's signature – to the Day of Judgment, and thus logically, again by design of author or editor, anticipates the chief theme of *Chr III*.

The compiler of the Exeter Book no doubt recognized the authoritative source – a homily by Gregory the Great – of the poet's theme of Christ's 'leaps', and further valued the poem for its highly prescriptive content, the topics, interpretations and idiom it shares with other pieces of the compiler's choosing such as *GfM*, *DHl* and *Sfr*.

The poem is one of four (with *Jul* in the Exeter Book and *Ele* and *FAp* in the Vercelli Book) which weave into their text the name of Cynewulf written in runes. Attempts to construct a biography of this Cynewulf by identifying him with documented personages and deducing personal detail from the poems have not commanded wide support, though textual studies have resulted in some agreement that he was a Mercian poet working in the earlier part of the ninth century and probably, to judge by his education and his religious preoccupation, a man in holy orders. Though other surviving OE poems show a close affinity with the signed poems of Cynewulf in subject-matter, didactic treatment and style, none can unchallengeably be added to the Cynewulf canon; and it may be that Cynewulf was only one of a school of poets sharing these hallmarks. While it is clear that he was master of the old compositional techniques associated with a purely oral process of making and transmitting poetry, Cynewulf, in building his name so carefully into his poems, seemingly expected them to retain the precise form he had given them rather than to undergo the mutations which characterized the wholly oral process of transmission. There is a natural plausibility in the idea that Cynewulf, perhaps first among poets of the English language, composed in writing, not strictly orally, and relied upon a written text of his poetry to preserve the authorial form of it and thus to achieve that identity between a poet's name and the stable corpus of his works that the Latin poets were seen to enjoy.

If the opening apostrophe to an 'illustrious man' is addressed to a specific (though unidentified) patron, it implies in Cynewulf a confidence in the stability of his text which a written version would justify. If addressed to the general reader – any one of those 'dear friends' he says he aspires to enlighten – its privacy of tone, in contrast with the public tone of the standard homily formula, 'Beloved people', may still suggest that Cynewulf was assuming that intimate treaty with a single person which only a written text could have afforded.

Runes, the letters of the ancient Germanic alphabet used by the Anglo-Saxons before they adopted the Roman alphabet, possessed names, and so a rune can stand either as the letter that it is or as a substitute for the word that is its name. Cynewulf builds into his text the words which are the names of the runes constituting his name, but he writes them down as runes, not as words; thus his name spelt in runes appears on the MS page. The standard nouns for the runes in 'Cynewulf' are *cen*, 'torch'; *yr*, 'bow'; *nyd*, 'necessity'; *eoh*, 'horse'; *wynn*, 'happiness'; *ur*, 'ox, bison' or possibly 'male strength, man'; *lagu*, 'sea' and *feoh*, 'wealth'. Unfortunately these words do not always make good sense when mechanically applied in Cynewulf's signatures, and so the possibility must be considered that a given rune may be used for any word beginning with that letter which is appropriate in the given context of sense and metre. Thus the challenge of finding the right word becomes a riddle of the kind much favoured in AS poetry (cp. *Rdl 42*). The interpretation of Cynewulf's runic signatures continues to be a subject of scholarly dispute. The solutions adopted here somewhat arbitrarily illustrate various approaches that may be made.

VI

440   Now, illustrious man, with strength of mind and sagacity of
spirit, seek earnestly into spiritual mysteries so that you may
know the truth as to how it came about, when the Almighty
was born out of a state of chastity after he had chosen the
sanctuary of Mary, the flower of maidens, the illustrious Vir-
gin, that there did not appear angels clothed in shining gar-
ments when that Prince and Hero came to Bethlehem. Heralds
were in readiness, who revealed and declared to the shepherds
in proclamations the real joy, that the son of the ordaining
God was born into the world in Bethlehem. However, it does
not say in books that they appeared there in shining garments
in that glorious hour, as they afterwards did, when the illustri-
ous Lord, the majestic Prince, summoned his band of thanes,
the beloved company, to Bethany. They did not, on that
longed-for day, despise the word of the Master, their Dispenser
of treasure. They were ready to go at once, heroes with their
Lord, to that holy city where the Bestower of glory, heaven's
Protector, revealed to them many tokens in parables before he
ascended, the only-begotten Son, the Child co-eternal with his
own Father, after forty days in number since he had previously
arisen out of the ground from death: he had then fulfilled
through his sufferings the words of the prophets, just as they
had once sung in the past throughout the ages. The thanes
praised and lovingly extolled the Lord of life, Father of things
created. He gave his beloved companions handsome reward
for that thereafter and, Ruler of the angels, the mighty God set
to go to his Father's kingdom, he spoke these words:

476   'Rejoice in spirit! I shall never leave you, but I shall always
continue in love towards you and give you power and remain
with you for ever and ever so that by my grace you will never be
wanting in virtue. Go forth now throughout the whole wide
world, along far-flung ways; make known to the masses,
preach and proclaim to them the glorious creed, and baptize
the people here below the skies and divert them to the heavens.
Demolish idols, fell them and treat them with contempt; wipe

out enmity, sow peace in men's hearts through the abundance of your powers. I shall remain with you henceforth as a comfort and preserve you in peace with a steadfast strength in any place whatsoever.'

491   Then suddenly loud harmony was heard aloft. A squadron of angels, a shining throng, heaven's heralds, came crowding. Our King passed through the roof of the temple whilst they gazed on, they who in that meeting-place still followed in the footsteps of the Beloved, chosen servants. They witnessed the Lord, the Son of God ascend to the heights out of the depths. Their spirit was sad, smouldering about their heart; their mind was mournful because they would no longer be able, here below heaven, to see him held so dear. The celestial heralds raised up a song; they praised the Prince, they extolled the Author of Life, they rejoiced in the light which radiated from the Saviour's head. They saw two resplendent angels beautifully gleaming with adornments about the first-born Child, the Glory of kings. With clear voice they called out from the heights over the crowd of people in wondrous words:

510   'People of Galilee, why do you stand waiting in a circle? You clearly see the true Lord, Possessor of the victory, passing into heaven. He, the Sovereign of princes, together with this company of angels, will ascend from here up to his dwelling-place, the Author of all peoples up to the royal seat of his Father.

VII

517   'We, together with a squadron like this, will carry the Lord, that best and noblest of all victorious sons, beyond the canopies of the heavens to that radiant city, together with this happy company which you gaze on here and see gleaming with adornments in their joy. However, he himself with a great legion will visit again the nations of the earth and at that time judge every deed which people have committed here below the skies.'

527   Then the Protector of heaven, King of the archangels, Guardian of the saints, was enveloped in clouds beyond the vaults on high. Joy was renewed, and bliss in the cities, by the Hero's coming. Exultant in victory, the everlasting Author of happiness took his seat on the right hand of his own Father.

533   Then the brave-spirited men went, sad of mood, from where they had just now witnessed with their eyes God, their generous Benefactor, ascending. The sound of weeping was there; that faithful love, hot about their heart, was overcast by grief. Their bosom was agitated within, their emotions smouldered. There the heroic servants all waited a further ten days in that splendid city for the Prince's promise, as the Lord of heaven himself commanded them, before, Ruler of all, he ascended into the refuge of the heavens. Shining angels came to meet men's Giver of happiness. Well is it declared, as the Scriptures say, that in that holy hour resplendent angels came in throngs to meet him, descending in the sky. Then there was the greatest celebration in heaven. Well it befits that his servants came into that bliss in the city of the Prince, radiantly clad, a shining throng. Welcome guests, they saw in his trappings on the high throne heaven's Ruler, the Life-giver of nations, Ruler of all the world and of all the heavenly host.

558   'Now has the Holy One robbed hell of all the spoil which it wrongfully swallowed up during the strife in days of old. Now the devils' champions are overcome and humiliated and enchained in living torment, stripped of blessings in the abyss of hell. His adversaries could not succeed in war, in the hurling of weapons, after the King of glory, Protector of the heaven-kingdom, did battle against his ancient enemies with the resources of the one God. There from the fortress of the fiends he delivered out of bondage the most enormous booty, a countless tally of people – this same throng on which you are gazing here. Now after the strife the Saviour of souls, God's own Child, will seek the throne of spirits. Now you know well enough what this Lord is who is leading this legion. Go now, glad of mood, boldly to meet with friends. Open up, you gates!

The Ruler of all desires to enter into you, the King into the city with no little crowd, the Author of things long since created, leading into the joy of joys the folk whom he seized from the devils by virtue of his personal victory. Henceforth for ever there shall be eternally peace between angels and mortals. There will be a covenant between God and men, a sacred pledge, love, the joy of life and the pleasure of the whole of heaven.'

586   So, now we have heard how the Child of salvation by his coming hither gave back health, and freed and defended folk here below the skies, illustrious Son of the ordaining Lord, so that every man alive, whilst he is dwelling here may choose as well the humiliation of hell as the glory of heaven, as well the radiant radiance as the loathsome night, as well the thronging of the heavenly multitude as the exiled state of darkness, as well joy with the Lord as sorrow with the devils, as well torment among evil beings as glory among the angels, as well life as death, according as he prefers to act whilst body and soul dwell in the world. For this may the Majesty of the Trinity have glory and gratitude without end.

VIII

600   It is fitting that the peoples should speak their gratitude to the Lord for each one of the benefits which he, in the mystery of his manifold powers, has always achieved for us late and early. He gives us food and the prosperity of possessions, wealth across the wide earth and mild weather beneath the shelter of the sky. Sun and moon, noblest of the heavenly bodies, the candles of heaven, shine upon all the men on earth. Dew comes down, and rain; they call forth blessings for the nourishment of humankind; they augment the earth's wealth. For all of this we should speak gratitude and praise to our Prince, and especially for that salvation which he granted as our hope, when at his ascension he turned aside again the misery which we previously suffered and, only begotten King, made atonement on mortal men's behalf with the beloved Father, for the greatest of feuds.

For the peace of souls he reversed again the pronouncement which had once been uttered with angry intent to the grief of men: 'Out of earth I made you; on it you shall live in misery, dwell in strife, suffer pain and chant the song of imminent death, to the pleasure of the fiends, and into the same you shall turn again, to swarm with worms, whence you shall thereafter go, out of the earth, to find the fire of punishment.'

627   See! this the Prince mitigated for us, the progeny of man, when he took limbs and body. When, in that holy hour, the Ordainer's Son, the God of hosts, desired to ascend into the home of the angels, that desire came as a help to us in our wretchedness. Concerning that, Job, as he was well able to, recited a poem: he praised men's Protector, extolled the Saviour, and with the sympathy of love devised a name for the Ruler's Son and called him a bird whom the Jews could not understand in the strength of his divine spirit. The flight of this bird was concealed and hidden from those enemies on earth who had dim perception of mind and a stony heart. They were unwilling to recognize the splendid miracles which the noble Son of God performed before them, many and various, throughout the world.

645   So the beloved bird ventured into flight. Sometimes, brave, strong in his powers, he would attain to the dwelling of the angels, that illustrious home; sometimes he would dive back to earth, reached the ground, by grace of the Spirit, and returned into the world. Concerning this the prophet sang: 'He was lifted up in the arms of angels in the great abundance of his powers, exalted and holy, above the splendour of the heavens.' They could not have known of the flight of the bird, those who made denial of the Ascension and did not believe that the holy Author of life had been raised up in form of man, above the glory of the heavenly hosts. He dignified us at that time – he who created this world, the spiritual Son of God – and gave us gifts, everlasting mansions among the angels on high; and also he sowed and planted abundantly throughout men's minds wisdom of intellect.

664 To one he sends wise eloquence through the breath of his mouth into his mind's consciousness, and fine perception. He in whose spirit the virtue of wisdom is invested is able to sing and narrate very many things. One is enabled to play the harp well with his fingers, loud in men's presence, to handle the mirth-making instrument. One is enabled to recite the true divine law. One is enabled to tell the course of the stars, the vast creation. One is enabled skilfully to write down language. To one he grants martial success in battle when bowmen send flying barbed missiles at the armed contingent above the shield-phalanx. One is enabled daringly to drive the ship over the salt sea, to churn the restlessness of the ocean. One is enabled to climb the lofty upright tree. One knows the expanse of earth's plains and far-flung ways. Thus the Ruler, the Son of God, dispenses his gifts to us on earth. He is not willing to give to any one man entire wisdom of spirit, in case pride over the excellence of himself alone, prominent beyond others, should harm him.

IX

686 Thus mighty God, King of all creatures, by unstinted gifts dignifies with skills the offspring of earth. In like manner he bestows splendour upon the blessed in heaven. He will establish peace for ever and ever, for angels and for mortals. Thus he dignifies his handiwork. Concerning this, the prophet said that holy jewels, the bright stars of heaven, the sun and the moon, were raised up on high. What are those jewels so brilliant but God himself? He is the true light of the sun, a noble radiance for angels and for earth's inhabitants. Over the world the moon shines, the holy star – so the church of God gleams brightly in the union of truth and right, as it says in books, after the Son of God, King of every pure being, ascended from the earth. Then the church of the practitioners of the faith here met with oppression under the governments of pagan rulers. Those sinful vandals did not cherish truth there, nor the soul's need, but they smashed and burned God's temple, caused bloodshed, persecuted and killed.

709   However, by grace of the Spirit, the glory of the servants of God emerged after the ascension of the eternal Lord. Concerning this, Solomon, son of David, a man most accomplished in poems, a ruler of nations, sang in spiritual enigmas and spoke these words: 'It shall be made known that the King of the angels, the Lord strong in his powers, will come springing upon the mountain, and leaping upon the high uplands; he will garland the hills and heights with his glory; he will redeem the world, all earth's inhabitants, by that glorious spring.'

720   The first leap was when he descended into a virgin, a maiden unblemished, and there assumed human form, free from sins, which came to be a comfort to all earth's inhabitants. The second spring was the birth of the Child when he was in the manger, wrapped up in garments in the form of a baby, the Majesty of all majesties. The third leap was the heavenly King's bound when he, the Father, the comforting Spirit, mounted upon the Cross. The fourth spring was into the tomb, secure in the sepulchre, when he quitted the tree. The fifth leap was when he humiliated the gang of hell's inhabitants in living torment and enchained the King within, the malignant mouthpiece of the fiends, in fiery fetters, where he still lies, fastened with shackles in prison, pinioned by his sins. The sixth leap was the Holy One's hope-giving move when he ascended to the heavens into his home of old. Then in that holy hour the throng of angels became enraptured with happy jubilation. They witnessed heaven's Majesty, the Sovereign of princes, reach his home, the gleaming mansions. The Prince's flittings to and fro became thereafter a perpetual delight to the blessed inhabitants of that city.

744   Thus here on earth God's eternal Son sprang in leaps over the high hillsides, courageous across the mountains. So must we men spring in leaps in the thoughts of our heart from strength to strength and strive after glorious things, so that we may ascend by holy works to the highest heaven where there is joy and bliss and the virtuous company of God's servants. It greatly behoves us that we should seek salvation with our

heart, when we readily believe with our spirit that the Son and Saviour, the living God, will ascend from here with our bodily form. Therefore we must always despise vain desires, and delight in the better part. We have as our help the almighty Father in the skies. He sends thence his holy messengers here from the heights, who shield us against the grievous arrow-attacks of adversaries, lest the fiends should cause wounds when the lord of sin dispatches a cruel dart from his crafty bow. Therefore we must continually keep guard steadfastly and watchfully against a sudden shot, lest the poisoned point, the cruel arrow, the sudden device of the fiends, should penetrate the body. That is a dangerous wound, the most livid of gashes. Let us then protect ourselves whilst we occupy a dwelling on earth. Let us beseech the Father for sanctuary and pray the Son of God and the gracious Spirit that he should shield us against the weapons of adversaries, the lying devices of enemies, he who gave us life, limbs, body and spirit. Praise be to him for ever, glory in the heavens, world without end.

X

779   None of mortal kind on earth need fear the devil's darts, the spear-assault of fierce foes, if God is shielding him, the Lord of the heavenly hosts. It is close to that judgment at which we shall obtain commensurate rewards, according as we have laid up for ourselves by our works over the span of our life throughout the wide world. Books tell us how at the first that Treasury of virtues, God's noble Son, the Holy One, descended in humility from the heights into the earth, into the Virgin's womb. I truly expect for myself, and I dread too, when the Prince of angels comes again, a judgment all the harsher because I have not kept well that which my Saviour commanded me in those books. Because of this I shall have to look upon terror, the punishment for sin — according to what I reckon as a certainty — where many will be led in assembly before the face of the eternal Judge.

797   Then the bold man (C; 'Cynewulf'?) will tremble. He will hear the King, the Arbiter of the heavens, pronounce and utter

harsh words to those who had harkened to him feebly in the world before, while they could most easily have found solace from the trumpet (Y) and the duress (N). Many a frightened man will have to await there, accursed, in that arena, what horrible punishments he will adjudge to him according to his deeds. Fled will be the pleasure (W) of earth's fineries. Long has our (U) share of the pleasures of life been hemmed about by the waters of ocean (L), and our wealth (F) on the earth; but then, those fineries shall burn in the conflagration. Bright the quick red fire will rage; swift it will race abroad through the world. The plains will sink under; cities will be shattered. The flame will be on the move; remorselessly the greediest of spirits will consume ancient treasures which men once hoarded, while pomp was theirs on earth.

815   I want, therefore, to teach every one of my dear friends that he should neither neglect nor overwhelm in ostentation the soul's need, as long as God wills that he may dwell here in the world and his soul in his body, within its guest-hall, travel together. Each man should earnestly reflect during the days of his lifetime that on that first occasion the Wielder of mighty powers came to us meekly through the angel's word; now, when he comes again, he will be rigorous, angry and righteous. The sky will be thrown into turmoil and the great expanses of the world will lament when the radiant King rewards them for having lived on earth in slothful deeds, stained with vices. For that they shall protractedly undergo, exhausted in spirit in a sea of fire, afflicted by its billows, a bitter retribution.

832   When the King of hosts, that greatest of majesties, comes to that concourse, the loud terror of the people will be heard along with the trumpeting from the heavens, the cry of the mourners. Anxiously they will weep before the face of the eternal Judge, those who have feeble faith in their achievements. Greater terror will be disclosed there than ever was heard tell of upon earth from its first creation. To every one of the evil-doers there in that imminent hour, much more desirable than this whole ephemeral creation will be somewhere

that he may hide himself in that triumphant crush, when the Lord of hosts, Paragon of princes, will adjudge to all, to the loved and the loathed, reward according to right for every person. A great need is ours: that we earnestly reflect upon our soul's appearance during this barren time before that appalling event.

850   It is at present very much like this: as though we are sailing across chill water upon the ocean-flood in ships, over the wide sea in steeds of the deeps, and navigating ocean-going boats of wood. The streaming sea is hazardous, inordinate the waves in which we pitch about through this frail world, and squally the oceans along the deep water-way. Our plight would have been severe before we had voyaged to a landfall across the stormy horizon. Then help came to us, that piloted us to salvation in port, God's Spirit-Son, and granted us grace that we might know a place where we shall secure our steeds of the deeps, our old horses of the waves, securely with anchors over the ship's side.

864   Let us found our hopeful expectation upon that port which the Ruler of the skies, the Holy One in the heights, laid open to us when he ascended into the heavens.

Christ III (The Judgment)

[The Exeter Book, fol.20ᵇ–32ᵃ]

The poem completes the 'plot' of the cyclical *Christ* by treating of the third pivotal point in the history of Christ the Redeemer, namely the Second Coming and the Judgment. The suprachronological rationale of *Chr I* (see introduction to *Chr I*) provides the logic which validates *Chr III* as a penitential contemplation of Doomsday. Doomsday will be the culmination of the world's chronology; it will be the final consummation of God's redemptive purpose through human time; it will be the hour of reckoning for every individual soul in the poem's audience and in the world; it cannot be averted – but it can be beneficially anticipated, and is anticipated, dramatically and methodically, here in the poem. The poet's vivid realization of the Judgment, above all the direct voice of Christ reviewing his incarnate ministry, appeals powerfully to the emotions and to the visual imagination. The charge that all humankind will have to answer then for the crime historically committed by a few of them at the Crucifixion, as well as for the personal crimes of their present life by which Christ is repeatedly crucified anew, challenges the intellect. Emotionally, imaginatively and intellectually the poet bids to move his audience to compunction now, and to an abundance of penitential tears; for, according to Ephraim of Syria (*De Indicio et Compunctione*, 'Concerning Judgment and Compunction', cited in *LSc*, p.29), 'Compunction is the remission of sins' since 'where tears are in abundance, there foul thoughts come not near.'

The imagery of the poem is expressed in bold, often majestic rhetoric. The poetry of Christ's reproaches is not excelled in any of the later treatments of this popular theme in Middle English lyric, narrative and drama. The poet's sources are in the Bible (the Revelation of John) and the writings of the Fathers and other received authorities of the Church. Part-analogues are many in OE writings; they include the *JgD* poems, the *SlB* poems and *Rsg*, and homilies in the Vercelli Book, the Blickling collection and the homiliaries of Ælfric and Wulfstan. Though the balance of scholarly opinion rejects *Chr III* from the Cynewulf canon, there has been a substantial body of opposition which doubts the unimpeachability of arguments based on the technical features of composition and vocabulary, and which counter-stresses the thematic coherence of the three *Christ* poems, one of which (*Chr II*) is signed by Cynewulf. Most agree at least that the poem is close to Cynewulf.

XI

867   Then with sudden swiftness upon the midnight, round about earth's inhabitants and this shining universe will mightily blare the great day of the puissant Lord; just as an insidious vandal, an audacious thief who goes abroad in the dark, in the black night, will often suddenly take careless, sleep-bound men by

surprise, it will painfully cast down those people unprepared. Likewise up into Sion mountain there will come together a great throng of people faithful to the ordaining Lord, radiant and joyful: to them shall glory be granted.

878   At that time from the world's four regions, from the uttermost regions of the kingdom of earth, angels all radiant will clangorously blow in unison upon trumpets: middle-earth, the ground beneath men's feet, will shudder. Firm and clear they will sound together towards the orbit of the stars; they will sing and ring out from the south and from the north, from the east and from the west, over all the universe. They will awaken from the dead the children of the fellowship of man, all humankind, fearful from out of the ancient earth, to their inexorable destiny; they will command them at once to stand up from out of that heavy sleep. There it will be possible to hear folk grieving, morbid of mind and sorely agitated, miserably bewailing their deeds while alive, and terrified with fear. That will be the greatest portent that was ever revealed to men, early or late. Mingled together there will be the entire hosts of the angels and of the devils, of the bright and of the black. There will be an appearance of both the white and the swarthy, according as a different home has been ordained for them, for angels and for devils.

899   Then suddenly on Sion mountain from the south-east the incandescence of the sun will come shining from the Creator, more luminous than men in their minds can imagine it, gleaming bright when the Son of God reveals himself hither through the canopies of the heavens. Christ's wondrous figure, the form of the noble King, will come from the east from out of the skies, sweet to the minds of his own folk, bitter to those steeped in sin, strangely diverse and different towards the blessed and the wretched.

910   To the good he will be gracious in appearance, beautiful and delightsome to that holy throng, attractive in his joy, affectionate and loving; agreeable and sweet it will be for his cherished

people to look upon that shining form, to look with pleasure upon the mild coming of the Ruler, the mighty King, for those who had earlier pleased him well in his heart with words and with works.

918   To the evil he will be fearsome and terrible to see, to those sinful people who come forth there condemned by their crimes. It may serve as a warning of punishment to one who is possessed of the wise realization, that he indeed dreads nothing at all who will not grow terrified in spirit with fear for that figure, when he sees the actual Lord of all created things journeying amid mighty marvels to judgment of the many, and round about him on every side journey squadrons of celestial angels, flocks of radiant beings, armies of saints, teeming in throngs.

930   The deep universe will reverberate, and ahead of the Lord the most enormous billowing fire will sweep across the spacious earth; scorching flame will roar, the heavens will split asunder and the stars, fixed and shining, will fall. Then the sun which brightly shone above the earlier world on the children of men will be made dusky with the colour of blood; likewise the moon which once illumined humankind by night will fall down, and so too the stars will be scattered from heaven, lashed by storms through the violent air.

941   The Omnipotent with his company of angels, the ordaining Lord of mighty kings will come to the conclave, a Prince secure in majesty. There too will be the throng of his thanes, blessed with victory: those saintly souls will journey with their Lord when he, the Protector of his peoples, himself visits the nations of earth with throes of terror. Across the broad earth the heavenly trumpet's loud voice will be heard and on seven sides the winds will howl; they will blow, blustering, with the mightiest uproar, and enfeeble and reduce the world by storm and fill with fear earth's creatures. Then a jarring crash will be signalled, loud beyond measure, painful and immense, a most enormous noise, appalling to mortals, whereupon the sad hordes of humankind will pass in their multitudes into the

far-flung flame, some upwards, some downwards, turgid with fire, when the destroying blaze meets with the living. Then without a doubt it will be so, that the kin of Adam, turgid with griefs, will lament sorely pained, a people in mourning not for trivialities but for the most enormous and acute miseries. Then simultaneously the fire's dark billowing, the sooty flame will far and wide catch all three things together, the seas with their fishes, the earth with its mountains and the shining heaven on high with its stars: the destructive flame will forcibly and fiercely burn the three together all at once. Sorely pained, all middle-earth will mourn in that notorious hour.

XII

972   Thus the ravening visitant will scour earth's plains; the ravaging flame will raze tall buildings to the ground by the terror of fire, and the holocaust, notorious afar, hot and ravening for gore will raze the world withal. The shattered walls of cities will collapse outright. Mountains will melt and lofty cliffs, which once securely shielded the land against the main and against its tides, firm and stable, bastions against the breaker and the leaping water. The deadly flame will catch every creature then, beast and bird; the fiery sooty flame, a turbulent warrior, will travel across the land. Whereas waters flowed before and driven tides, then the fishes of ocean will scorch in a sea of fire, stopped from swimming; every beast of the wave will perish in misery; the water will burn like wax. There will be more prodigies than anyone can imagine in his mind, as to how that crash and the storm and the violent air will broadly breach the universe. Men will cry; they will weep, wailing with weary voices, wretched, morbid of mind and tormented with regrets. The sooty flame will smelt the sins in those corrupted, and embers swallow up ornaments of gold, all the one-time wealth of hereditary kings. There will be uproar and anxiety and turmoil of the living, regret and loud weeping at the tumult from heaven, a wretched welter of mortal men. No one marked by wicked deeds will be able to gain a refuge thence, nor anywhere in the land escape the conflagration; for the fire will take hold throughout whatever country, and

fiercely delve and zealously scour earth's regions inside and out, until the fiery incandescence has burned up in its billowing all the pollution of worldly filth.

1007   Then mighty God will come, King of heaven's angels, into that famed mountain; holy, glorious, he will shine out above the hosts, the reigning God, and round about him that supreme and noble multitude, the holy warrior-bands will shimmer clear, the blessed company of the angels. In their inner thoughts they will be trembling, fearful in the presence of the Father's wrath. It is no wonder, then, that the impure species of worldly men, anxiously grieving, should dread it acutely when this holy species, white and heavenly-bright, the army of archangels, are afraid with fear for that figure, and his bright creatures await in trembling the judgment of the Lord. It will prove to be the most appalling day in the world when the King of glory in his majesty punishes every people and commands humanity to arise from out of their graves in the ground and each single person, each member of mankind, to come to the conclave. Then promptly all the kin of Adam will take on flesh; it will have come to the end of its earthly rest and habitation. Each one shall then rise up alive in the face of Christ's coming and take on limbs and body and be young anew; upon him he will have everything of virtue or of folly which in past days on earth he laid upon his spirit with the passing of the years; he will have both body and soul conjoined. The display of his works and the remembrance of his words and the intentions of his heart must come into the light before the King of the heavens.

1039   At that time mankind will be replenished and reconstituted by the ordaining Lord. The great human multitude will rise up to judgment when the Lord of life looses the bonds of death. The sky will burn, the stars of heaven will fall, the ravening flames will ravage abroad and spirits will pass into an everlasting habitation. Throughout middle-earth, people's deeds will be exposed. Not in the least will men be able to conceal that store, the thoughts of their heart, in the Ruler's presence. Not to him will their deeds be secret, for there in that momentous day it will be known to the Lord how each person has previously merited the life everlasting, and everything will be present that early or late they accomplished in the world. Not a whit of people's intentions will be hidden there but the notorious day will reveal all the store of their bosoms' vaults, the thoughts of their heart. Whoever is determined to bring to God a clear countenance when the blaze, scorching and gorily ravenous, assays before the triumphant Judge how souls have been cherished against sins, he must reflect beforehand upon his spirit's needs.

1061 Then the voice of the trumpet and the bright symbol and the scorching fire and the exalted multitude and the host of angels and the threat of terror and the harsh day and the high Cross reared upright as a symbol of power, will summon into his presence the human throng, each one of the souls which late or early received limbs in the flesh. Then this, the hugest of hordes, eternal and young anew, will proceed into the Ruler's presence by desire or by compulsion. Summoned by name, they will carry before the Son of God their breasts' hoard, the trappings of their existence. The Father will consider how sound are the souls his sons bring back from the land in which they lived. The bold ones then will be those who bring a bright countenance to the Lord. Their power and their joy will be exceedingly blessed as a reward to their souls, a glorious repayment for their works. It will be well for those who in that grim hour may please God.

XIII

1081 There sin-stained people, grieving in spirit, will themselves behold him with the utmost distress. It will be no consolation to them that there in front of those other-worldly peoples the Cross of our Lord will stand present, the brightest of portents, moistened with blood, with the pure blood of the King of heaven, besprinkled with gore, which will shine out clearly across the broad creation. The shadows will be repressed where that radiant tree illumines the peoples; yet it will prove a reproach and a threat to those people who, being evil-doers, acknowledged no thanks to God for his torments whereby he was hanged on that holy tree for the wicked misdeeds of mankind. There he, the Prince, lovingly bought life for mankind on that day at that price – he whose body never did itself the blemish of vicious transgressions – through which he redeemed us. For all this he will sternly demand repayment when the crimson cross shines brilliantly over all, instead of the sun. On it those seduced by sins, dark evil-doers, will fearfully stare in distress; they will see as their ruin that which would have best befitted them, had they been willing to understand it for the good. And also the ancient wounds and the gaping gash upon their Lord they will behold, desolate in spirit, according as men of malicious purpose pierced with nails those white hands and those holy feet and likewise set flowing the blood from his side, whence blood and water both came running out together in front of the men and in the sight of their eyes, when he was on the Cross.

1115   At this they themselves will be able to see then, plain and manifest, that for the love of men, of evil-doers, he suffered much. The children of men will be able clearly to perceive how, lacking faith, they denied him in their thoughts, mocked him with insults and also voided their spittle in his face. They voiced their scorn upon him, and hell-bent men likewise struck the blessed face with their hands, with claws outstretched and with fists too, and about his head they twisted a cruel thorny crown – men blind in their thoughts, stupid and misguided. They saw the voiceless universe, the all-verdant earth and the sky, fearfully sense the sufferings of the Lord, and though they were not living things they mourned in sorrows when those ruffians seized their Creator with sinning hands. The sun was extinguished, stifled by pangs; while in Jerusalem the people were looking at the fine cloth of highest quality which formerly the congregation was supposed to gaze upon as an ornament of the holy house: it all ripped apart from above, so that it lay on the earth in two pieces. The veil of the temple, made in wonderful hues to the splendour of the house, tore itself in two as though a sharp sword-edge had sliced through it. Many gleaming walls and stones shattered to the ground and the earth too, disturbed by fear, trembled upon the instant, and the spacious sea revealed the might of its strength and broke away from its constraint up in anger on to the surface of the land; and in their shining fixedness the stars lost their familiar beauty. In that same hour heaven recognized him who sublimely arrayed it in its brilliance with starry gems, for it had sent his herald when the shining King of created things was first born. Behold too, those guilty men surely observed a great prodigy on the same day on which he suffered, that earth rendered up those who lay in it. Alive once more, they whom formerly it had tightly clasped rose up – the buried dead who had kept the Lord's commandment in their breast. Hell too, instigator of sin, recognized that the Creator, the reigning God, had come, when it rendered up the throng, its booty, from its hot bosom. Within that multitude, hearts were enraptured and sorrows slipped away from their souls. Behold too, the sea confessed who had established it within its spacious bed, the King gloriously mighty, for it had made itself firm to tread upon when God willed to walk upon its waves: the watery current did not dare to swamp its Lord's feet in its flood. And trees too, not just a few, but many, proclaimed who had fashioned them with their foliage, when mighty God mounted upon one of them there where he suffered torments for humanity's need, and a loathsome death for the relief of the peoples. Many a tree beneath its bark was then streaked with bloody tears, red and viscous: the sap was turned to blood. By no wise awareness can earthdwellers tell how much those inanimate forms of creation which cannot feel, experienced the suffering of the Lord. Those which are the noblest of earth's species and the lofty structure of heaven too, all on account of that lone man, were grieved and gripped with fear. Though of their natures they knew no spiritual awareness, even so they miraculously sensed when their Ruler departed from the body. People, men blind of heart, harder than flints, could not confess the Ordainer, nor that the Lord, all-wielding God, by his holy powers had saved them from the torment of hell. This, at the very first, from the world's beginning, men of forethought, prophets of the Lord, holy men discerning of mind, out of their wise awareness have told people not once but often about the noble Child – that he, the precious Stone, should come into the world as refuge and solace to all mankind, heaven's Lord and the Author of happiness, by that noble woman.

XIV

1199   What does he expect who is unwilling to remember in his conscience the gentle precepts of the ordaining Lord and all the sufferings he underwent on men's behalf, because he wished that we might own the abode of heaven in everlastingness? So it will be a sad thing on that grim day of the great judgment for him who, seduced by sins, has to gaze upon the Lord's scars, the woundings and the torture. In their wicked spirits they will see the greatest of griefs – how that same King out of his gentle heart loosed them from sins with his body, so that they might live free from evil deeds and own the everlasting splendour of glory. For this patrimony they expressed thanks to their Ruler not at all: to their reproach therefore, unhappy people, they will behold those conspicuous marks upon God, when Christ sits upon his royal throne, upon the high seat, God of the heavenly hosts, Father almighty. To each one of the people the radiant Creator, Ruler of the skies, will prescribe according to his deeds, all according to justice.

1221   Then on the right hand of Christ himself will be gathered those pure people, chosen according to their virtues, who had previously, during the days of their life, fulfilled his decree with zeal and with delight; and there before the Creator evil-wreakers will be assigned into the inferior portion; them the veritable King of victories will command to depart upon his left hand, the multitude of the sinful. There, having been exposed, they will weep and tremble, terrified, before the Lord, an unclean people as foul as goats; they will not expect mercies.

1232   Then the judgment of souls before God will be determined upon the generations of men according as they had previously deserved. Readily conspicuous in the blessed there will be three marks together, because they kept well the will of their Prince in words and in deeds. The first one manifest there will be that they gleam with light before the people, with splendour and with brightness beyond the mansions of cities. Their former achievements will shine in each one of them brighter than the sun. The second one moreover will be just as recognizable – that in glory they will know for themselves the Ruler's grace and will perceive to their eyes' delight that they, the blessed amidst the angels, are allowed to enjoy pure pleasures in the kingdom of heaven. Then there will be the third one – how that happy throng will see the abandoned throng suffer pain in the malignancy of darkness as punishment of their sins, and the billowing flame and the bite of serpents with stinging jaws, the horde of burning people. From this a pleasant joy will burgeon within them, when they see others undergo that misery which they by the Lord's mercy have escaped. They will thank God the more earnestly then for the splendour and the ecstasies, because they perceive both things – that he saved them from violent torment and also granted them joys everlasting; to them hell is closed and the kingdom of heaven vouchsafed. Thus shall the bargain be honoured towards those who through heartfelt love formerly kept well the will of the Lord.

1262   For the others at that time their will shall be realized with a difference. They will be able to see the superfluity of evils in themselves, their abundant sins and the atrocious and unfortunate things once committed. To them, sorrowing there, pain will attach, a general tormenting malignancy, in three respects. The one of them shall be that they will see on hand an excess of miseries and the fierce fire of hell ready as a torture in which, undergoing banishment, they will have for ever to endure their condemnation. Then there will be a second misfortune likewise, to the ignominy of those found culpable, that there, brought to ruin, they will endure the utmost humiliation. In them the Lord will discern each loathsome and outrageous evil, far from few; and the all-radiant array of heavenly angels too, and the children of mortals, all earth's inhabitants, and the hideous devil will be scrutinizing their sinister strength; every guilty blemish, their vicious transgressions, they will be able to see in those souls, through their bodies. Their sinful flesh will be ignominiously pierced through like the clear glass that can be completely seen through with the greatest ease. Then there will be the third cause for sorrow in those destitutes, the plaintive anguish that they see in the innocent, how gladly they rejoice because of those good works which they, unhappy and weeping sorely over their works because they had freely done wrong before, had formerly disdained to do while their days lasted. They will see their betters shine in splendour. Not only will their own miseries be as a torment to them but the felicity of the others will be to their grief, since in days past they renounced such pleasant and peerless joys for the fickle delights of the body and the vain lust of the wretched fleshly frame. There, ashamed and tormented by the ignominy, they will be wandering about in a daze; they will be bearing the burden of sin, their wicked works, and the multitude will see it. It would have been better for them then that they had shown shame for their outrageous deeds, for every wrong and for their wretched works earlier, before a single mortal, and had told a minister of God that they knew to their sorrow of the wicked deeds upon them. The confessor cannot see through the flesh into the soul, whether a man is telling him the truth or a lie about himself, when he confesses sins then. Even so a man may cure every vice and unclean evil if he tells it to one single person; and no one will be able to hide a blemish unatoned on that harsh day, where the multitude will see it.

1312   Alas! were we now able to see in our souls the grievous crimes, the wounds of sins, and in the flesh the vicious broodings, and with our eyes the unclean inward thoughts; no man can tell another with what great zeal each would want fearfully to strive by every device for life and for being, to hold out longer, in order to salve the canker of sin, and correct himself and heal the blemish of his earlier wound in the little span there is of existence here; so that, being unashamed before the eyes of earth's inhabitants, free from reproach he may enjoy his home among mortals as long as body and soul are allowed to live, the two together.

XV

1327   Zealously now we must keenly penetrate our breasts and the wickedness within with the eyes of the heart. With those other eyes, the head's jewels, we cannot in any circumstances scrutinize the spirit of the mind's thought, whether evil or good resides beneath it, so that he may approve it well in that grim hour when he, above each of the multitudes, will shine in glory from his high throne with a pure flame.

1336   There in the presence of the angels and of the peoples of the other world he, high King of the heavens, will speak first to the most blessed, and lovingly he will bid them peace; with holy voice he will gently comfort them, and he will offer them refuge and bid them pass whole and hallowed into the homeland of angelic bliss and pleasantly enjoy it into infinite existence.

1344   'Now amidst friends receive the kingdom of my Father which was joyfully made ready for you before the ages — splendour amid ecstasies, the radiant beauty of your homeland — for when you would be permitted to see the riches of life amid those most loved, and sweet celestial pleasures. This you merited when you willingly received in charitable spirit poor men and those in worldly need. When they, the humble, begged mercies of you in my name, then you helped them and gave them shelter, to the hungry bread, and clothing to the naked, and those who lay sick in pain and suffered hard, shackled by disease, devoutly you strengthened their courage with your heart's love. All that you did to me when you approached them with kindnesses and in mercy fortified thenceforth their spirits. For this you shall long and happily enjoy the reward amid my beloved.'

1362   Then to the evil in a manner different, to those who are on his left hand, omnipotent God will begin to speak words by way of an awful threat. They need not expect mercy of the Lord then, nor life nor kindnesses; but there rewards come to mortal men according to their accomplishments of words and of deeds: they will have to endure the only just judgment, one replete with terror. There the great mercy of the Almighty will be far removed from those occupying that position on the day when he wrathfully imputes their wickedness to that perverse people with hostile words and bids them show the current reckoning of that life of theirs which he once granted them, the sinners, for their happiness.

1376   He himself, the Lord almighty, will begin to speak as if he were talking to a single one, and yet he means them all, the inordinately sinful multitude:

1379   'Behold, I first made you, man, with my hands and gave you intelligence. Of clay I formed limbs for you. I gave you a living soul. I honoured you above all creatures. I brought it about that you had a figure and form resembling myself. I gave you too an abundance of powers and prosperity throughout each spacious continent. You knew no share of sorrow or of gloom that you had to suffer – nor did you know gratitude for this. When I had created you so beautiful and made you so pleasing and had granted you prosperity so that you might rule over the creatures in the world and when I set you upon the lovely earth to enjoy the radiant luxuriance of Paradise agleam with colours, then you were unwilling to abide by the word of life, but rather you broke my behest at the word of your slayer. To that treacherous fiend, that destructive destroyer, you listened more than to your Creator. Here I will leave out that old account of how in the first place you resolved upon evil and by your wicked actions lost what I had granted you to your advantage. When I had vouchsafed you so many benefits and there seemed to you in your heart too little happiness in all these things if you might not possess an abundance of power commensurate with God, then to the devils' satisfaction you were cast out from that state of joy far afield, a stranger. The beauty of Paradise, the homeland of your spirits, you had perforce to forgo, wretched, miserable, parted from all privileges and pleasures; and then you were driven into this gloomy world where you have since suffered physical afflictions for a long time, pain and heavy toil and dark death, and after your going hence you were constrained to sink abject into hell, devoid of helpers.

1414 'When I repented that the work of my hands should pass into the power of devils, that the issue of mankind should see mortality and be constrained to venture upon an unknown dwelling-place and painful experiences, then I myself came down as a child into a mother, though her virginity remained wholly intact, and I was born, I alone, as a comfort to the people. By human hands I was wrapped and clad in a pauper's coverings, and then I was laid in the darkness wrapped in drab clothes. See! this I suffered for the world's sake. Little I seemed to the sons of men; I lay on the hard rock, an infant in its crib. By this I meant to put far from you death and the scorching noxiousness of hell, so that you might shine holy and blessed in the life everlasting, because I suffered the hardship.

XVI

1428 'It was not because of pride in me, but rather I endured misery and pitiless bodily pain in my young manhood so that through it I might be like you, and you might come to be like my image, detached from wickedness. And for the love of men my head suffered insulting blows; often my cheek endured and my face caught from their mouth the spittle of ruthless malefactors. Likewise they mixed together for me a drink, sour in its bitterness, of vinegar and gall. Then in front of the people I underwent the spitefulness of my foes; they harrassed me with torments; they had no qualms about violence and they flogged me with whips. All that pain I suffered in humility for you, the mockery and the harsh talk. Then they wreathed a hard sharp crown about my head and abusively they crushed it on: it was made of thorns. Then I was hung on a high tree, fastened to a cross; then with a spear they forthwith shed gore, the blood from out of my side, to the ground, so that by this you might be rescued from the tyranny of the devil. Then I, a man without sins, suffered punishment and evil afflictions until I released from my body my solely surviving spirit.

1454 'See now the mortal wounds which you once made in my hands and in my feet the same, by which I hung cruelly fastened. Here too, visible even now, you may see in my side the bloody wound. It was indeed an inequable reckoning between the two of us there. I took on your pain so that you might enjoy my kingdom, happy and blessed; and with my death I dearly bought you lasting life, so that you might thereafter dwell in light, radiant and free from sins. My body, which harmed no one, lay buried in earth, hidden down in the tomb, so that you might be bright above in the skies, ranking among the angels.

1469 'Why did you forgo the lustrous life that for love I faithfully purchased with my body in aid of you, being abject, and why did you grow so witless that you knew no gratitude to the Ruler for your redemption? I ask nothing now for that bitter death of mine which I underwent on your behalf; but pay me for your life, since I once gave you mine as a ransom in worldly torment. I claim the life which you have sinfully destroyed with vices, to your own shame.

1480 'Why did you of your own free will, through wicked lusts and foul sins, filthily pollute the lodging-place, the cherished house I hallowed within you for my delight; and why did you shamefully blemish by evil-doing the body which I freed for myself from the fiends' grasp and then forbade it sin? Why do you more grievously hang me on the cross of your hands than I hung before? for indeed this seems to me more painful. The cross of your sins on which I am unwillingly fastened is presently more oppressive to me than was the other, which once I mounted of my own free will when your woeful state most moved me at heart, so that I led you out of hell on condition that you yourself would keep it so thereafter.

1495   'I was a beggar in the world, so that you should be prosperous in heaven; I was destitute in your country so that you should be blessed in mine. For all this you knew then in your heart no gratitude to your Saviour.

1499   'I commended you to comfort well my brothers in the worldly realm from among those possessions which I gave you on earth, and to help the destitute. Feebly have you fulfilled that; you denied it to the needy that they might enter under your roof, and in your hardheartedness you completely withheld clothing from the naked and sustenance from those without food. Though in my name the weary and the sick begged water for themselves in torment for a drink, devoid of means and consumed with thirst, you shamelessly withheld it from them. You did not visit those in grief nor speak to them a friendly word of consolation, so that they might attain in heart to a happier state of mind. All that you did to me, the King of heaven, by way of slight; for which you shall cruelly endure torment to existence infinite, and suffer banishment with the devils.'

1515   Then over all those there, over that doomed people, the Governor of victories himself will issue forth the appalling sentence fraught with pain; to the legion of those sinful souls he will say:

1519   'Depart now, damned, divorced of your own volition from the bliss of angels, into the everlasting fire that was prepared for Satan and his comrades with him, for the devil and that dark swarm, hot and deadly fierce: into that you are constrained to sink.'

1524   This time they will not be able to slight the commandment of the King of heaven, being bereft of their powers. They will be forced at once to fall into the terrible abyss, who formerly strove against God. The Guardian of the kingdom will be severe then and puissant, angry and awesome. No enemy on this earthly highway will be able to remain present.

XVII

1530 With his right hand he will swing the sword of victory so that the devils will fall into the deep pit, the horde of the sinful into black flame, the doomed spirits below the plain of earth, the swarm of those filled with defilement into the dwelling-place of fiends, those condemned to perdition into the house of punishment, the devil's hall of death. Thereafter they will not come into the Lord's remembrance, nor will they extenuate their sin; there, condemned for their crimes, surrounded by flame they will suffer death. The penalty of sin will be plainly present: it is everlasting torment. Not in eternity, not in existence infinite will the hot pit be able to smelt away the sins of the populace of hell, the blemish from their souls; but there the deep groundless gulf will gorge those prostrate spirits and nurture them in the darkness, and will burn them with the ancient flame and the awful frost; by fierce serpents and with many tortures and by its greedy deadly jaws it will ravage its peoples.

1549 This we can appreciate and declare at once and say in truth, that he has forfeited the Warder of the soul, the Wisdom of life, whoever does not presently care whether his spirit is wretched, or blessed, since after its departure hence it will have to stay eternally tied to its home. Nor does he, this heedless man, regret committing sin, nor does he have a scrap of remorse in his heart that the Holy Ghost is lost to him because of his vices in this transient time. Then he will stand, a dingy malefactor at judgment, afraid before God; and, condemned to death, damned for his defilements, the renegade will be steeped in fire. Unworthy of life, harassed by fear, livid and unlovely in the presence of God, he has the countenance of a criminal, the flawmark of his life. Then the children of iniquities will gush with tears and lament their sins – when the time for this is no more; for they render help to their spirits too late since the Ruler of the multitudes will not care how those evil-doers sorely bemoan the acquisitions of their past in that revelatory hour. That hour of griefs is not granted to people in order that a person might find the medicine there, who has no will to acquire health for his spirit now, while he is living here.

1575   In no good man there will remorse be displayed, and in no evil one well-being, but everyone there present will experience his individual deserving. Therefore he who wants to have life at the Lord's hands must make haste while existence and soul, secure together, are his. May he diligently care for the candour of his soul under God's will and be wary in words and deeds and habits and thoughts as long as this world, wandering on in the darkness, is permitted to shine for him, so that in this transient time he does not forfeit the abundance of his joys, and the tally of his days, and the splendour of his achievement, and the reward of celestial glory that the King of heaven steadfast in truth will give in that sacred time, as rewards of victory to those who diligently obey him in their spirits.

1591   Then heaven and hell will be filled with the children of mortals, with the souls of men. The depths will swallow up God's adversaries; leaping flame will punish men of malignant disposition, the arch-offenders, and never will it let them go in relief to their redemption, but the holocaust will hem in the tightly restricted throng and harass the children of iniquities. It seems to me reckless that mortals possessed of a spirit will not give heed in their heart, when they commit crime, to what the Ruler has ordained as the punishment for them, those evil people, when life and death swallow up souls: the home of torments will be open and revealed for the reception of renegades, and people diligent in wickedness shall fill it with their swarthy souls. Then in punishment of their sins the swarm of those deemed culpable will be dissevered, the despised from the saintly, into painful destruction. There thieves and arch-criminals, deceivers and adulterers shall have no hope of life, and perjurers shall see the reward of crime, harsh and extremely severe. Then hell will receive the multitude of the faithless and the Ruler will resign them to fiends in perdition; being guilty, they will suffer appalling deadly harm. Miserable will be the man who chooses to commit deeds of wickedness so that, being guilty, he shall be dissevered from his Creator at the day of judgment, down into death, in subjection to the brood of hell, in the scorching fire in a dungeon of flame, where they will offer their limbs for binding and burning and scourging in punishment of their sins. Then the Holy Ghost, by the might of God at the word of the King, will lock up hell, that hugest house of torment filled with fire, and the host of his enemies. It will be the extremest anguish for devils and for men. It is a house devoid of joy where no one may ever shed his chill shackles. They violated the word of the King, the divine commandment of the Scriptures; therefore they will have to languish in perpetuity and go on suffering endless pain, being guilty of wicked deeds, such as here rejected the majesty of the kingdom of heaven.

1634   Then the elect will bring their bright treasures before Christ. Their splendour will survive at the day of judgment; they will possess the joy of a gentle life with God, which is granted to each one of the holy in the kingdom of heaven. That is the homeland which will never be brought to an end, but there for ever onwards those free from sins will command happiness; they will praise the Lord, life's cherished Guardian, girded with light, lapped in peace, protected from sorrows, pampered with pleasures, held dear by the Lord. For ever to eternity they will enjoy amid bliss the communion of the angels and, radiant amid tranquillity, love the protective Lord of the people. The Father will have the sovereignty over all and he will preserve the multitude of the holy.

1649   There will be angels' singing and the bliss of the blessed; there will be the precious face of the Lord, lighter to all those happy beings than the sun. There will be the love of dear ones, life without the finality of death, a merry human multitude, youth without age, the majesty of the heavenly hosts, health without sickness, for the workers of righteousness rest without toil, the day of those deemed blessed without darkness, radiant, replete with splendour, bliss without sorrows, peace without rivalries thenceforth between friends happy in heaven, and love without hostility among the holy.

1660   There will be neither hunger nor thirst, nor sleep nor sluggish sickbed, nor sun's scorching nor cold nor care; but there the fellowship of the blessed, of multitudes the most dazzling in beauty, will enjoy for ever the King's gift, glory with the Lord.

Guthlac A

[The Exeter Book, fol.32ᵇ–44ᵇ]

The link between the doctrinal exposition and spiritual exercises of the three poems of *Chr* and the two *Glc* poems which follow them in the Exeter Book is apposite if not particularly dynamic. *Chr* was concerned with humankind's share in the divine purpose of bringing all things into a unity with Christ which St Paul sees as the consummation of the ages (Ephesians 1:4–11); *Glc* is concerned with the example of an individual man's life lived in active consciousness of that purpose. *Chr* ranged among the omnitemporal implications of events, two past and one future, in 'scriptural' history; *Glc* finds localized testimony in eighth-century English history. Both *Glc*-poems have an introduction which places the life and death of the saint in the larger perspective of *Chr*; indeed, the preface to *Glc A* so deliberately carries over the theme and final topic of *Chr III* that the first twenty-nine lines here treated as part of *Glc* have been regarded as belonging to the end of *Chr III* (though the formal division of the MS which marks the opening of these lines makes this view untenable). There is then some sign of thoughtful organization of the codex at this point.

Guthlac, born (673) into a branch of the Mercian royal house, served from his youth as a military commander in Mercia's wars. But according to his eighth-century biographer, Felix of Crowland, reflection upon the unhappy deaths of the ancient Mercian kings, his ancestors, converted Guthlac, soldier of the king, into a soldier of Christ. Aged twenty-four, he became a monk at Repton. Two years later, following the example of monks of old, he withdrew into the wilderness, to Crowland in the Lincolnshire fens. There he passed the remaining fifteen years of his life and there after his death on 11 April 714 he was buried in his oratory. One year later he was confirmed a saint when his body was found incorrupt, and King Æthelbald of

Mercia, whose confessor and counsellor Guthlac had been, caused a shrine and a building to be erected, about which developed the abbey of Crowland dedicated to St Bartholomew who had come to Guthlac's aid. The Latin Life of St Guthlac was probably composed between 730 and 749 when King Ælfwold of E. Anglia, to whom Felix dedicated the work, died. The poems probably date from the late eighth century.

Guthlac did not die for the faith (*FAp*, *Jul*) but he was, in a sense then popular, a martyr, for in the words of St Jerome (*LSc*, p.208): 'It is not the shedding of blood alone that is counted as suffering witness, but the impeccable service of a faithful mind is also a daily martyrdom' (cp. *Sfr*, *Rsg*). He struggled with devils in the wilderness beneath the sign of the Cross: 'For as fire proves gold and silver, so temptation the heart of the monk. Where the Cross of Christ is brought to bear, the malice of the Devil will not prevail' (*Vita Patrum*, *LSc*, p.212). He overcame the devils through faith, God-given courage (that *ellen* which, in *DrR*, the Cross learns from Christ and the narrator from the Cross; and which characterizes Beowulf and Andrew) and direct divine intervention (cp.*Bwf*), for 'He is greater who defends us than he who persecutes' (Eusebius, *LSc*, p.212); and miracles proved his sainthood, for 'Nothing is stronger than he who overcomes devils' (Jerome, *LSc*, p.208). The *Glc*-poems, in short, exemplify, in these and other respects, features (though by no means the full regular format) of the literary Saint's Life of Latin tradition, modelled on the Latin version by Evagrius of the *Life* of St Anthony (who is represented on the Ruthwell Cross). Much of this orthodoxy they have drawn from Felix (though *Glc A* shows less specific dependence on Felix than *Glc B*, omitting material found in Felix, notably the first ninety-two lines and the description of nature regenerated when the devils abandon Crowland) and Felix is typical of his age and profession in reordering and supplementing the probably untidy and incomplete pattern of Guthlac's *actual* life to fit the model. Since, as the poems record, there were those still living who were witnesses of these miraculous things and could challenge the facts if they thought them misrepresentations, Felix must have been regarded not as inventing fictions but as documenting the already established efficacy of Guthlac's sainthood by organizing and interpreting his life-record in categories long since devised for the exposition of what is typically true about the whole communion of saints. On the other hand, a motive for special pleading is not far to seek: the poem, if not blatantly propagandist, directly voices through a collective 'we-persona' the *amour propre* of the monks of Crowland towards their calling, their own saint, their community and the sanctified site in their custody.

In *Glc A* the rhetoric and vocabulary of secular heroics are used with modest success to prompt audience recognition of the largely passive Guthlac as a belligerent *miles Christi* (soldier of Christ). We are entitled to think that the same audience may well have listened on other occasions to the (perhaps) contemporary poem *Bwf*; and we might then ask whether concepts common to the religious-historical *Glc* and the secular-legendary *Bwf*, and expressed in the same words, were kept apart or correlated in the mind of the audience – for example, the concept of the *soðfæste*, 'those steadfast in truth', among which both Beowulf and Guthlac are counted, and whose qualities and rewards are fulsomely described in the final lines of *Glc A*.

I

The loveliest of delights it is when first they meet, the angel and the blessed soul. It resigns these pleasures of the earth, lets go of these transient joys and parts from the body. Then the angel speaks (he has the higher degree); the one spirit welcomes the other and proclaims to it God's message:

6   'Now you may journey to the place you have been striving towards long and often. I shall lead you; for you the ways will be smooth, and the light of heaven radiantly revealed. You are now a timely traveller to the sacred home, where sorrow never comes nor beggary owing to afflictions, but where there is the joyful sound of the angels, peace and happiness and souls' rest, and where for ever to eternity those who fulfil his ordinances here on earth may exult and rejoice with the Lord. For them he keeps an everlasting reward in the heavens where the highest King of all kings rules over the cities. Those are edifices which never decay nor for those who dwell therein does life dwindle away on account of afflictions but for them it grows better the longer it goes on; they enjoy youth and God's favours.

22   'There the souls of those steadfast in truth will be allowed to come after death, those who here teach and practise Christ's law and exalt his praise; they will overcome the accursed spirits and gain for themselves the repose of heaven, to which, early or late, a man's heart must aspire when he nurtures his unique soul here, so that he may come, clean from defilements, into the power of God.'

30   Many conditions of men there are throughout the world beneath the heavens which belong in the number of the saints, and accordingly we may duly serve in any one of them, if we are willing to keep the holy commandments. The wise man may use the opportunity of good times now and aspire to the journey onwards for his soul. The world is embroiled; love for Christ cools; many are the tribulations arisen throughout the world, just as God's spokesmen declared in their sayings long since, and spelt out in prophecy everything just as it is now happening. Earth's vitality is aging in each of its noble qualities and the species of its offspring tend away from beauty; this latter season of each fruit is feebler in vigour. Therefore this man need not look to this world for an improvement, that it will bring us pleasant happiness beyond the afflictions which we presently endure, before all creatures, great and small, which he established in six days and which presently bring forth their families beneath the heavens, come to an end. This world is divided in parts. The Lord looks to see where those dwell who keep his law, but every day he sees dwindle and diverge from worldly law those ordinances which he established by his own word. He will meet with many but few will be chosen.

60   Some people aspire in their words to wear the glory of this status and do not carry out the actions. To them earthly wealth, more than the life eternal, is the highest of their hopes – that which is bound to be sequestrated from every dweller on earth – and therefore they now deride the courage of those saints who make steadfast their thought upon heaven, who know that that homeland will last eternally for all the multitude who serve the Lord throughout the world and by their works aspire

to that precious home. So these worldly treasures will be exchanged for those glorious benefits when those over whose heads impends the fear of God yearn for it. They are corrected by that most exalted majesty; according to his commandments they make use of this life and wish for and look forward to the better one hereafter. They purchase heavenly glory: they give alms; they comfort the poor; they are generous of heart with their lawful possessions; with gifts they show love towards those who own less; daily they serve the Lord and he observes their deeds.

81 Some dwell in desolate places and of their own volition seek out and settle homes in shadowy retreats; they await the heavenly abode. Often he who begrudges them life aims at them some evil prodigy – sometimes he displays to them a terrifying thing, sometimes a worthless splendour (for the crafty killer has skill in both) – and persecutes these anchorites. Before them stand angels, ready with the weapons of spirits; they have their safety in mind; they guard the saints' life; they know their trust is with the Lord. These are the tried warriors who serve a king who never witholds the reward from those who persist in loving him.

II

93 Now we can tell what has been recently made known to us in holy manner: how Guthlac held out his heart to the will of God, renounced all wickedness and earthly pre-eminence and set his mind on high, on the home in the heavens. In this was his trust, once he who prepares the pathway of life for souls had illumined him and given him angelic grace, so that he started inhabiting, alone, a hilly dwelling-place and in humility gave to God his entire wealth which in his youth he is supposed to have applied to worldly pleasures. A holy guardian from the heavens watched over him, who eagerly encouraged that pure heart in virtuousness of spirit.

108 Now we have often heard that in the earliest periods of his life the saintly man loved many perilous things. However, the

time was within the discretion of God at which he would assign an angel to Guthlac in his conscience so that the cravings for sinful things subsided within him. The hour was at hand; two guardians watched about him who kept up a struggle – the angel of the Lord and the terrible demon. On many occasions they put to him in the thoughts of his heart promptings by no means alike. The one told him this whole earth beneath the sky was ephemeral and praised those lasting benefits in the heavens where souls of saints possess the joys of the Lord in triumphant glory; gladly he yields them reward for their deeds, those who are willing gratefully to receive his grace and more utterly to let this world escape them than the life everlasting. The other urged him that he should seek out the society of criminals by night and in reckless fashion strive after worldly gain, as fugitive wretches do, who have no compunction for the life of a man who brings loot into their hands if only they may thus get possession of the pickings.

133   So they incited him on both sides until the Lord of the heavenly multitudes made an end of the strife, in favour of the angel. The fiend was routed; thereafter the comforter-spirit continued in support of Guthlac, showed him love and guided him ever more earnestly so that the pleasure of the countryside and his dwelling-place on the hill grew dear to him.

140   There terror often came, appalling and grotesque, the ancient adversaries' malice, inexorable in its crafty wiles. They flaunted their own aspect before him; and they had previously established many lairs there, whence, flitting through the air, they would make their way in far-flung wandering, having been cut off from heavenly glory. This rural locality had been hidden from people until the ordaining Lord revealed the hill within a wood when that builder turned up who erected a saintly retreat there – not out of greed, because he bothered about the ephemeral benefit of material riches, but so that he might justly keep watch over that region for God, once he, the soldier of Christ, had outvied the devil. He was tempted within the lifetimes of people who can remember, who even now, on

account of his wondrous spiritual works, honour and cherish the fame of his wisdom which the saintly servant gained by his courage when he settled the secret place alone. There he professed and exalted the Lord's praise, and often he would verbally declare God's messages to those who loved the ways of the martyrs, when the Spirit had revealed to him a prudent understanding of the mortal existence, so that he denied his body pleasures and worldly delights, comfortable residences and days of feasting, likewise too the eyes' vain pleasures and ostentatious dress. The fear of God was too great in his thoughts for him to want to pander to human glory for his gratification.

III

170   Guthlac was good. In his soul he carried celestial hope; he attained the salvation of eternal life. Close by him was an angel, a trusty guardian to him who, as one of the few, settled the wasteland. There he came to be an example to many in Britain when he climbed the hill, a blessed warrior, tough in resistance. Zealously he equipped himself with spiritual weapons and vestments; he sanctified the place and as his rallying-point he first raised up the Cross of Christ. Where this soldier outvied a host of perils, many of God's martyrs became active. Guthlac's precious part in this we attribute to God; he gave him the victory and the strength of prudence, the protection of mighty powers, when with sudden volleys a multitude of devils came to begin feuding. In their malice they were incapable of leaving him alone and they brought many temptations to Guthlac's spirit. Help was close by him; the angel fortified him with courage when they furiously menaced him with the greedy turbulence of fire, and appeared to him in troops and said that he was going to burn on that hill and flame engulf his body so that his suffering would absolutely entail misery for his kinsmen — if he was not willing himself to turn from that contest back to human conviviality, and to attend with a will and with greater industry to his familial duty in the midst of mankind, and let the feuding rest.

200   So the one who spoke for the whole multitude of devils raged at him. Guthlac's spirit was none the more intimidated for that; rather, God gave him courage against that fearsome being so that the ancient adversary's hordes of criminals suffered a humiliation. The engineers of evil were filled with mortification and said that, besides God himself, Guthlac on his own had perpetrated the greatest affliction upon them when, for the sake of bravado in the wilderness, he violated the hills where they, wretched antagonists, had formerly been allowed at times a lodging-place after their punishments, when they came weary from their wanderings to rest for a while, and enjoyed the quiet; this had been conceded them for a little time.

215   This secret place stayed prominent in the Lord's conscious-ness; empty and desolate, remote from hereditary jurisdiction, it awaited the counter-claim of a better tenant. From this the ancient adversaries took alarm, according as they do inces-santly suffer anxiety. They are not permitted to enjoy a habi-tation on the ground, nor does the air lull them into repose of their limbs; instead, shelterless, they lack homes and amid their sorrows they lament and wish for extinction and yearn for the Lord to concede, through the extinction of death, an end of their miseries.

226   They were not permitted to harm Guthlac's spirit nor with wounding stroke to sever soul from body, but by mendacious ploys they set up harassments. They ceased from laughter and sighed in sorrow when the more powerful possessor van-quished them in the field; grumbling, fugitive wretches, they would have to quit the green hills. Meanwhile, however, God's opponents spoke wounding things and emphatically vowed that he would have to suffer death's disseverance if he waited longer for the more hostile encounter when they would come with a greater throng, who would care little for his life.

233   Guthlac talked back at them and said that they need not brag of their deeds against the powers of the Lord.

240 'Though you vow death to me, he will preserve me against those acts of spite, who wields the constraints upon you. God alone is almighty; he can shield me with ease and he will protect my life. I want to tell you a number of truths. Alone against you I can extort possession of this seat without difficulties. I am not so destitute as I appear before you, destitute of any company of men, but a greater contingent dwells and increases in the divine thoughts of my spirit, which will afford me support: here I shall easily build for myself alone a house and shelter. The promptings within me are in harmony with the heavens, so I little doubt that an angel will convey to me completely availing success in words and in deeds. Now be gone, damned and demoralized beings, from this site on which you are standing here; flee on your far-flung way. I mean to supplicate to God for refuge; my soul shall not commit error with you, but the Lord's hand will guard me with its might. Here shall my earthly dwelling-place be, yours no longer.'

IV

262 Then there was a clamour raised. Fugitive wretches surrounded the hill in clusters. The din mounted up, the hubbub of beings filled with anxiety. Many, the devils' spokesmen, shouted out and bragged outrageously:

266 'Often within the ambit of the oceans we have observed peoples' dispositions and the bombast of headstrong men who have persevered with life amid vicissitude. Not in a single man throughout the earth have we met with greater arrogance. You vow that you mean to wrest a home from us, you who are one of God's indigents. On what will you live even if you do own the ground? No one will supply you here with food; hunger and thirst will be stern foes to you, if you go off alone, like the wild beasts, from your native place. That is not at all a good scheme. Abandon this seat. No one can give you better advice than all this multitude. We shall be friendly to you if you will listen to us; otherwise we shall seek you out again, unprepared, with a bigger force, in such a way that it will not be necessary to lay hands upon you nor for your corpse to fall from the wounds

of weapons. With our feet we can raze this dwelling-place; the throng will come trampling in with troops of horses and with armies. Then they will be enraged; then they will knock you down and tread on you and harass you and wreak their anger upon you and scatter you in bloody remnants. If you presume to face us out we shall attack you with afflictions. Start wishing yourself a refuge; go where you have hope of friends if you are concerned for your life.'

292   Guthlac was prepared – God made him strong – in answer and in courage. He did not hesitate for speech but said things painful to his opponents and expressed to them the abundant truth:

296   'Wide is this wilderness and the multitude of fugitive settlements and the secret dwellings of wretched spirits, and those who inhabit these lodging-places are devils; but even if you summon out all those and work yourselves up for strife more widely still, you will be taking on a profitless venture here in these acts of vengeful bitterness. I do not intend to carry against you a sword, a weapon of the world, with hand enraged, nor shall this site be colonized for God through the shedding of blood, but I intend to please my Christ with a gift more acceptable. Since I came up into this region you have, with vain words, recommended many dwelling-places to me. My heart is neither frightened nor faint, but he who controls the workings of every mighty force keeps watch over me above mankind. Not a thing agreeable to me is dependent upon you, and you may do nothing disagreeable to me. I am the servant of the Lord; through an angel he often comforts me. Cravings therefore affect me little, and anxieties seldom, now that a spiritual guardian looks after me. My hope is with God; I care nothing at all for earthly well-being, nor do I yearn in my heart after much for myself, but every day the Lord provides me with my wants by the hand of man.'

323   Thus bravely he behaved, who stood against the many – a soldier of glory, deservedly supported by the strength of angels.

The whole multitude of fiends withdrew from there: the respite was not great which they intended to grant Guthlac.

328   He continued in courage and in humility and remained on the hill – he was pleased with his dwelling – and eschewed cravings after ephemeral joys. He did not disengage himself from compassion towards men but prayed for the salvation of every soul whenever he bowed down his face to the ground in that lonely wilderness. From heaven his heart was inspired with a glad spirit. He was constantly vigilant – the angel was near him – as to how needful it was for him to take least enjoyment with his body in the pleasures of this world. His faith did not falter before the terror of wretched spirits, nor did he delay the time at which he was supposed to be busy on his Lord's behalf, so that the oblivion of his slumbers or a sluggardly mind robbed him of zeal for rising up. A warrior must always so fight for God in his heart and constantly dispose his spirit to enmity against him who will be vigilant over every soul, as to when he may ensnare it.

348   They found Guthlac continuingly confident in the will of God when, wild and on the wing, they, who inhabited secret dwellings, came seeking through the darkness of the nights whether his delight in that place was dwindling. They wished that a pining for human love would go to his heart so that he would set his course home again. Such was not his intent once the angel had most eagerly greeted him in that lonely wilderness and had granted him grace so that no craving could hinder him from the will of the ordaining Lord, but he remained in his counsellor's keeping. Often he would declare aloud:

361   'It befits him indeed whose will the Holy Spirit guides and whose work he reinforces and whom he summons with sweet words and promises him rest after life, that he listens to this leader's precepts and does not let the ancient foe turn back his heart from his ordaining Lord. How shall my spirit come to safety unless I yield to God a listening mind so that to him the heart's thoughts. . .'

Between the present folios 37 and 38 one leaf has evidently been lost in which, apparently, the devils make or threaten another assault upon Guthlac.

V

369 '. . . early or late there will be an end of your ability to torment me prodigiously? My body cannot, in despite of this ephemeral condition, set death aside, but it must suffer it like this whole earth in which I here stand. Though, being malignant, you may assail my fleshly veneer with fire's turbulence and with greedy flame, you will never budge me from these words as long as my wit shall serve me. Though you may make assault upon it with painful afflictions you will not be allowed to touch my soul; rather, you will induce it to a nobler state. I will therefore await what my Lord decrees me. For me there is no anxiety over dying. Though my bones and blood moreover both turn to dust, my immortal part will pass into bliss where it will enjoy a beautiful abode. The dwelling-place of this hill is not more modest nor greater than will suffice for a man who in his sufferings daily fulfils the Ruler's will. The servant of the Lord must not cherish in his heart more of earth's goods than a sufficiency for himself alone, so that he has sustenance of his body.'

390 Then again just as before the malice and anger of the ancient foes were brought to the boil. A din resounded for a second brief while, when the hubbub of the anguished visitants rose into the air. In Guthlac's noble heart the praise of Christ steadily increased and remained, and the God of hosts protected him on earth, as he keeps every life in safety where the superior spirit excels in virtues. He was one of them; he did not strive after the world but he exalted the joys of his heart into glory. Who was greater than he? This lone warrior and soldier reveals in our own times that for his sake Christ has revealed further worldly miracles.

VI

404 He shielded him against the loathsome onslaughts of the harm-dealing wretched spirits; they were fierce in attacking

with greedy clutches. God was not willing that the soul within his body should suffer pain by this; however, he allowed that they might lay hold of him with their hands, and that immunity be safeguarded towards his soul.

412   Then they lifted him up high in the air and gave him powers exceeding humankind so that before his eyes he saw all the actions of such men in monasteries, under the rule of holy pastors, as were enjoying their life according to their appetite for worthless possessions and superfluous vanities and ostentatious adornments, such as is the custom of youth, when fear of the Lord is no guide. They need not have exulted, those fiends there, for too soon they had squandered the flush of success that was allowed them for a little while, so no longer were they enabled to do his body violence by their torments, nor did anything of what they had put him through with malicious intent harm him.

427   So they led him from aloft to that most cherished dwellingplace on the ground, so that once again he ascended the hill up to the grove. The murderous demons were grumbling and mournfully bemoaning that a son of man should outdo them in threats and should arrive thus indigent, alone, to their affliction – if they could not pay him retribution with greater pains.

434   Guthlac rested his hope in the heavens and trusted in his salvation. He had escaped the clutch of the fiends with his life; the first testing by the wretched spirits had been overcome. The soldier remained peacefully on the hill; his success was through God. In his heart he felt that the blessed man among humankind was the one who here safeguarded his unique spirit so that at the utmost end the fiend's hand would not harm him when the Lord's decree brought him to the final inevitable dissolution. But now yet again, conscious of their frustrations, the slanderers were promising him miseries in bitter and angry outbursts. His trust was acknowledged, in that God rewarded the courage in Guthlac – that he strove alone – with grace.

451 To him the damned spirit spoke with these words:

452 'We should not have needed to harass you this hard if you
had been willing promptly to listen to the opinions of friends
when you first entered, lowly and destitute, into this fight,
when you promised that a holy spirit would easily shield you
against afflictions for the sake of the badge which by its virtues
turned human hand aside from your face. In that guise there
are many men living, indulgent in sins; they profit God not at
all, but for love of their body they gratify it with the pleasures
of banquetings. Thus you men pay respects to the Lord in a
foolish smugness. In front of mortals you conceal much of
what you are contemplating in your heart; but though you
practise them in secrecy, your deeds are not undiscovered. We
led you aloft and deprived you of the pleasures of the firm earth
because we desired that you should see for yourself that we
have charged you with the truth. For all this you have endured
torment, because you were not able to controvert it.'

470 Now the time was advanced when God would render him
regard after his sufferings because he cherished with courage
the rank of martyr; he gave him wisdom in his heart's thoughts
and a resolute mind. Against the numbers of ancient foes he
stood, confirmed in valour, and told them to their distress that
they would have to concede that green expanse, defeated:

478 'You are utterly estranged; guilt remains upon you. You
cannot pray to the Lord for salvation nor in humility seek for
grace even if he did give you leave for a little while that you
might have mastery over me; nor would you accept that with
restraint, but led me irately upwards so that I could see from
the air the lands' buildings. The radiant light of the firmament
was displayed to me even if I endured suffering. You put me to
reproach because I readily tolerated the loose rules and
impetuous temperaments of young men in the churches of
God. You wanted thus to besmirch the repute of holy men; you
looked for the worse ones, and the better ones you did not
esteem according to their deeds – and yet these are no secret. I,

on the other hand, will tell the truth to you: God created young people and human happiness. They cannot bring forth maturity and fruit at the very first, but they take pleasure in the world's joys, until a term of years passes away in youthfulness so that the spirit favours the aspect and essence of a maturer status, which many men throughout the earth fittingly serve in their customary ways. These men make their wisdom evident to people, they shed their vanity, once their spirit flees from the folly of youth. This you do not admit; instead you tell of the sins of the guilty and you are never willing to proclaim the courage and the virtue of those steadfast in truth. You rejoice in transgressions; you have no hope of grace so that you might experience relief from your exiled wanderings. Repeatedly you persist in your allegations; accordingly, punishment comes from heaven. He therefore sends me, he who is able to arbitrate between us, and who governs the length of every life.'

513   So spoke the saintly warrior; he was a martyr dissevered from humanity's sins. He was still to suffer a deal of pain although the Lord controlled his torments. Now, it has seemed a remarkable thing to people that he was willing to allow those miserable spirits with their sharp clutches to touch him further, and yet it came about. A still greater thing it was that he himself visited the world and poured out his blood at the hands of murderers; he had dominion over both life and death when, humble, he gladly endured the malice of persecutors on earth. Therefore it is now proper that we should esteem the deeds of those steadfast in faith and declare praise to the Lord for all those examples by which for our sake the Scriptures show forth wisdom through his working of wonders.

VII

530   Grace found in godly strength was with Guthlac. It is a major task to tell from the beginning everything that he endured in fortitude − for the almighty Father himself appointed this his delegate against life's furtive adversaries − when his soul was purified and assayed. Widely throughout the

world it is acknowledged that his courage flourished in the will
of God; and yet there is much still to be told of what he endured
under the oppressive constraints of those malicious spirits.
Suffering, then, and the soul's eventual destruction he dis-
counted by virtue of the helpmeet who upheld his courage, so
that the faith in his breast caused him no doubt, nor did regrets
disturb his spirit; but this staunch heart remained holy until he
had outlasted those tribulations. Their threats were violent, the
perpetrators savage; they all vowed an end to his existence. But
they, sins' drovers, were not allowed to condemn him to death,
and his soul bided a more pleasant occasion within his body.

552   Clearly they realized that God had willed to save him from
their malicious deeds and thoroughly to condemn their per-
secution. Thus is the Lord, the one Almighty, easily able to
shield each blessed person from afflictions. Even so, infuriated,
the irate fugitive wretches conducted him, heaven's champion,
saintly child of the eucharist, to the portal of hell where, after
death's agony, doomed spirits of the sinful first seek entry into
that hideous dwelling-place, into the precipitous abysses down
beneath the ground. They terrorized him and mercilessly prof-
fered him strife, horror and injury and a rough passage, as is the
practice of devils when they want to subvert through sins and
treacherous ploys the souls of those steadfast in truth. Cruel-
hearted, they tormented God's warrior in his mind and strenu-
ously vowed that he must enter into that grim horror and,
being condemned, go down to the denizens of hell and there in
shackles suffer burning. The wretched monsters wanted by
these hurtful statements to bring into despair the soldier of the
ordaining Lord. It was not possible to do so.

577   Filled with distress, hateful to Christ, they addressed
Guthlac with ferocity:

579   'You are not worthy, no servant of the Lord purely assayed,
no virtuous soldier well known for words and for deeds, holy in
heart. Now you shall sink deep into hell and not possess the
light of the Lord in the heavens, the mansions aloft and a

throne in the sky, because you have committed too many sins and evils in the flesh. Now we will pay the reward for each one of your crimes where it will be most loathsome for you, in the fiercest spiritual suffering.'

590   The blessed man Guthlac answered them in spirit, with the strength of God:

592   'Do so indeed – if the Lord Christ, Author of light and of life, Ruler of the heavenly hosts, will give you leave that you might lead his dependant into the loathsome fire. That is under the control of the heaven-King, the Saviour Christ, who condemned you and drove you into captivity under strict bondage. I am his humble and dutiful minister, a patient servant. I shall submit entirely to his sole jurisdiction in all places, and will at all times be completely subject to him in my thoughts, and loyally obey my Redeemer in things of personal conduct and of public calling, and thank him for all those gifts which God first created for the angels and for the inhabitants of earth; and I bless the Author of light and of life with a happy heart, and with befitting honour I sing his praise by day and by night, and I laud in my heart the Guardian of the celestial kingdom. Never from on high will it be granted to you in the tranquil joys of heaven that you may speak to the Lord praise; rather, in death, in weeping, you shall sing your surging grief; mourning in hell you shall have, not holy laud of the heaven-King.

VIII

618   'Throughout my days I will honour the Judge in words and in works and will love him during my life, according as his guidance and grace are brought into effectual utterance in those who in doing his works perform his will. You are betrayers of trust: accordingly you have long lived in exile, inundated with flame, having been miserably deceived, deprived of heaven, despoiled of happiness, delivered up to death, ensnared by sins, without hope of life, that you would find a cure for blindness. In ancient days you renounced this lovely crea-

tion and spiritual happiness in God when you rejected the holy
Lord. You could not be allowed to go on living for ever in days
of content, but in contumely for your crimes you were thrust,
because of your presumptuous thoughts, into everlasting fire
where you shall endure death and darkness, and lamentation
into boundless eternity: never will you experience relief from it.

637   'And I believe this of the Author of life, the everlasting Ruler
of all created things, that he, men's Saviour, on account of his
mercies and abundant virtues, will never desert me in the
valiant action in which I have fought long for God, in body and
in my soul, by means of the mysterious workings of manifold
virtues. I trust therefore in the most glorious power of the
Trinity, who heedfully holds heaven and earth in his hands,
that you with your acts of malice will never be permitted,
cruel-minded, to drag me into torment – you, evil murderers,
criminal ravagers, swarthy and cheated of victory. Truly, I am
fairly filled in my heart with the light of faith and with love of
the Lord, inspired in my breast towards that better home and
radiantly illumined towards that most beloved everlasting
abode where the homeland is, beautiful and pleasant, in the
glory of the Father. There in the Saviour's presence never will
the radiance of light nor the hope of life in God's realm be
granted to you, because of those presumptuous thoughts which
quite excessively uprose in your mind through vain boasting.
You, being perversely-minded, imagined and desired that you
should become like the Creator in glory. It turned out the
worse for you when the Ruler angrily plunged you into that
dark torture where fire was then kindled for you, mingled with
venom, and where, by solemn sentence, happiness and the
companionship of the angels were taken away from you. Now
and forever, it will always be so, that you have the burning
welter of damnation, and no blessings at all. You need not
imagine, you being divorced from glory, that your sin-filled
selves with your ingenious tricks can ignominiously thrust me
into darkness or throw me downwards into blazing confla-
gration in the house of hell where a home has been made for
you, black perpetual night, affliction without end, painful

destruction of the soul. There, lamenting, you shall endure death, and I shall have the bliss of pleasures among the angels in the sublime kingdom of the heavens where the true King is, the succour and salvation of mankind, and company and community.'

684   Then from the heavens came a holy messenger of the Lord who by word of mouth proclaimed supernal terror upon the miserable spirits, and commanded them speedily to bring heaven's champion back, sound of limb, from that wretched expedition, so that his most cherished spirit, being prepared, might journey in joy into the keeping of God. Then the throng of the devils grew dismayed in the face of that terror. The superior being, the Lord's beloved servant, spoke; he shone with the brightness of day. Guthlac's spirit he held in his protection, this bold bringer of aid, abundant in his powers; the servants of darkness he peremptorily bound, placed constraint upon them and charged them outright:

698   'Let there be no bone-breaking, nor bloody wounding, bruising of his body, nor any whit of injury from what you can do to his hurt; but you will set him down unharmed there where you seized him. He is to exercise authority in that place; you cannot defend this dwelling-place against him.

703   'I am the judge; the Lord commanded me to say at once that you should heal each one of his hurts with your own hands and thereafter be obedient to him at his own discretion. I shall not conceal my aspect in front of the multitude of you. I am servant of the ordaining Lord. I am one of the twelve whom he, in human form, loved in his heart as most trusty. He sent me here from the heavens. He saw that on earth you were inflicting torments on his dependant, out of envy. He is my brother; his tribulation distressed me. I shall see to it that when this friend – with whom, now I am allowed to succour him, I want to keep up this friendship – is living in that sanctuary, you will often see my face. I want to visit him often now. I shall bring his words and works to the Lord in witness; he will know his doings.'

IX

722   Guthlac's spirit was filled with bliss then, once Bartholomew had proclaimed the message of God. The compliant captives, who did not lightly disregard the words of the saint, stood ready. So, blessed with favourable judgment, the soldier of the Lord set out on the grateful journey to that coveted portion of the earth. They carried him and kept him from injury; in their hands they lifted him up and prevented him from falling – for fear of God their movements were smooth and comfortable. Triumphant, the founder came to the hill. The many species and families of tree-habiting birds blessed him with strenuous voices and by these tokens acknowledged the blessed man's return – often he would hold out food for them and then, hungry, they would fly about his hand, greedily eager, and were glad of his help. Thus that gentle heart cut itself off from the pleasures of mankind and served the Lord and he found his delight in wild creatures, once he had rejected this world. The site of his triumph and his lodgings were peaceful anew, the singing of the birds was lovely, the countryside was sprung into blossom and cuckoos heralded the year. Guthlac, blessed and resolute, could enjoy his dwelling-place. The green site stood under God's protection; the defender who came from the heavens had driven the devils away. What lovelier desire has been realized in men's life, among those which our elders remembered or which we ourselves have come to know since?

752   Now we are witnesses of these miraculous things – they all took place within the period of our lifetimes – therefore no mortal man on earth has cause to doubt this; rather, God effects such things for the strengthening of the vitality of souls, lest those faint hearts be constrained to set aside the evidence, when they have the truth in plain view. The Almighty so loves all creatures in corporeal form under heaven, and all the races of men throughout the earth, that he, the Ruler, wants us always prudently to imbibe wisdom, so that through us his truth may come to prevail as a return upon those gifts of his which he grants and sends to our honour and for our understanding; he clears for souls pleasant paths through life,

reaching to the light. Certainly it is not the least of what that love performs, when it erects spiritual grace in a person's heart. Thus he exalted the days and the deeds of Guthlac, by his decree. The founding father was steadfast in his enmity with the fiends and entrenched against sins, since he did not lightly skimp his pledge; often in humility he would send up his words to God and caused his prayer to enter into that sublime world, and thanked the king that he could remain under afflictions until by the will of God a better life should be granted him.

781   So Guthlac's soul was brought into heaven in the arms of angels; lovingly they led him before the face of the eternal Judge. Need was granted him, a throne in heaven where he could always to eternity live for ever secure of tenure and dwell in bliss. The Son of God, the mighty Lord, the holy Shepherd, heaven-kingdom's Keeper is his gracious advocate. Thus the souls of those steadfast in truth will be able to ascend into an everlasting abode in the kingdom of the skies, those who here carry through in words and in works the abiding precepts of the King of glory, and in their lifetime earn on earth eternal life and a home in the heights. These are men of the sacrament, the chosen warriors dear to Christ; in their breasts they bear shining faith and divine hope; pure in heart, they worship the Ruler. They have a wise and impetuous sense of purpose towards the way ahead to the Father's paternal homeland. They equip the house of the soul and with diligence outfight the fiend and abstain from wicked desires in their breasts. Brotherly love they eagerly profess; they put themselves to trouble in the will of God; they beautify their souls with holy thoughts and fulfil on earth the heavenly King's command. They delight in fasting, avoid wickedness and turn to prayer; they struggle against sins and uphold truth and right. They do not regret it after their departure hence, when they pass over into the holy city and journey straight to Jerusalem, where they may for ever rapturously and eagerly gaze upon the face of God and upon the peace and the prospect of Jerusalem, there where she will surely abide, beautiful and glorious, for all eternity, in the bliss of the land of the living.

Guthlac B

[The Exeter Book, fol.44^b–52^b]

The death-legend is an important part of any Saint's Life. Here Guthlac's death is made the subject of a poem separate from the one covering his strife with the devil and very likely by a different poet. The loss of Paradise and the coming of death into the world through Man's first disobedience are the topics which open the poem; the exemplary death of an individual man of saintly obedience by which he gains Paradise is the theme of the narrative which follows. The essence of Guthlac's worthiness is that with the aid of grace he has remained *soðfæst*, 'righteous, steadfast in truth' in his struggle with the devil; the tokens of his sainthood are the portents upon earth at his passing and the rejoicing in heaven. These are the universal aspects of the narrative and they link the poem's theme of the man found righteous with the same theme in other OE poems, notably those of the Junius MS. Another, more parochial concern is discernible: to lend charisma to the cult of Guthlac at Crowland. Though the poem accommodates no first-person witness of the latter-day monks as *Glc A* seems to do, it cites what 'books tell us' of Guthlac's powers to heal the sick, the self-disgusted and distressed who came as pilgrims to the saint while he lived, there in the very place of his victory over the devil, just as the hungry birds would fly fearlessly to his hands for sustenance and honour him afterwards with song. His disciple is not only the mandatory witness to the saintliness of his death, such as Brother Heribert was to Cuthbert's, but he is also recipient, as it were on behalf of the monks of Crowland and all who make themselves Guthlac's disciples, of the promise: 'I will not leave you for ever after my death – I will always keep friendship with you.' Finally, the poem asserts Crowland's possession of Guthlac's body in fulfilment of his own will. All this adds up to a strong assertion of the efficacy of Guthlac's intercession for those who pay homage to his shrine at Crowland.

Glc B is more clearly dependent on the Latin Life by Felix than is *Glc A*, though it is indebted for subject-matter rather than for idiom and even in subject-matter it is not very strictly constrained by its source. The poem's successful fusion of matter and idiom from English native poetic tradition with subject-matter drawn from a Latin-Christian model has encouraged the view that *Glc B* may belong to the canon of Cynewulf's work. That it is not signed by Cynewulf is possibly accidental, for the ending of the poem is missing where the MS has been damaged.

X

819   It is universally manifest to the races of men and celebrated among the peoples that the God of the elements, the almighty King, fashioned the first one of the species of men out of the purest earth, whereupon a new creation existed, that of the human stock – a happy order, beautiful and pleasing.

825   Adam the father was first brought forth, by the bounty of God, into Paradise, where for him there was lack of nothing desirable, no withering of prosperity, nor loss of life, nor decay of body, nor decline of happiness, nor visitation of death; rather, he might have lived in that land free from all flaws, long to enjoy those new-found pleasures. There in that radiant home he had no cause to expect an end of life and of joys through the span of the ages, but after a time he might have passed into the loveliest delight of the heaven-kingdom, limbs, body and living soul together, and there he might ever afterwards have dwelt to an infinite existence among endless joys in the sight of the Lord, free from death in perpetuity – if they had been willing to keep the Holy One's words shining in their hearts and to follow and fulfil his commandments in their native place. Too soon they tired of following the Ruler's will; instead his wife took the forbidden fruit at the serpent's promptings and plucked from the tree the prohibited crop against the word of God, the King of glory, and gave the mortality-bringing food to her husband through the guile of the devil, so that he lured the married pair to their death.

852   Thereafter this homeland grew inaccessible to Adam and Eve; this radiant and most excellent of dwelling-places was snatched from them and from their children alike and their offspring after them, when, hurrying in shame, they were

thrust into an alien land, into a world of toil. For the action of the profound sins which rashly they had formerly committed, they paid in the anguish of death. From then on, in the punishment of wickedness, women and men, guilty before God, would have to pay for their crime the penalty of their profound sins, through the soul's disseverance: death invaded humankind and the devil reigned throughout the world. Ever afterwards, there was no man from that distinguished stock so zealous in the will of God or so amply instructed that he may avoid the bitter drink which Eve the young bride gave and served up to Adam of old: it harmed them both within that precious home.

871   Death has reigned over earth-dwellers – and yet there has been a great number of those saintly of spirit where, in various foundations of men throughout the dwelling-places of earth's plains, they have done God's will; some early, some late, some, according to date, within the memories of our own times, they have sought the reward for having overcome.

878   Books tell us how, through God's will, Guthlac achieved perfection among the English. He chose for himself eternal strength and support. His working of miracles became famous far and wide, renowned through cities throughout Britain – how, through the might of God, he often healed many unhappy people of serious afflictions, anxious, sad people who, shackled by disease, with difficulty came seeking him from far-flung ways. Always they found comfort there at hand, help and healing from the soldier of God. There is no man who can recount or who knows the tally of all those miracles which, through the Lord's grace, he achieved for the people here in the world.

XI

894   Often multitudes of devils, lethal troops shorn of privileges, would come in throngs to invade the dwelling-places where this saintly servant, single-minded in courage, kept his abode.

There in that wilderness, robbed of their beauty, despoiled of their pleasures, they would randomly raise a hubbub with their many voices, a loud warlike clamour. The Lord's soldier, the energetic leader of men, would sturdily withstand the devils' harassments. The hour of those miserable spirits was not slow nor the waiting-time long before those workers of iniquity would raise up lamentation and howl, bereft of victory, and join their loud cries together. Sometimes raging like wild beasts they would clamour in chorus, sometimes the evil and wicked ravagers would turn back into human form with the utmost din, sometimes the damned faith-breakers would be transformed again into the shape of a dragon and the fire-crippled wretches would spew forth venom. Always they found Guthlac prepared, shrewd of thought. Patiently he would endure, even though the throng of devils threatened the extinction of his life.

916   Sometimes a family of birds, urged by hunger, would fly to his hands where they would find sustenance of life provided, and with strenuous voices they would honour him. Sometimes again human messengers would humbly visit him and there on the scene of his victory energetic pilgrims would meet with help from the saintly servant, and comfort of the spirit. There was not even one who departed again conscious of his stigma, despised and hopeless; but every one of those persons, unhappy people, who, tormented, sought him out in their need, this saintly man would heal through his special power, both in body and in soul, as long as life's Guardian, the everlasting Almighty, was pleased to grant that he might enjoy the breath of life here in the world.

932   The day of the ending of warfare and austerities as to the world, through death's inevitable disseverance, was now near advanced – fifteen years after he had chosen a dwelling-place in the wilderness. Then the Holy Ghost from the heights, the Comforter, was sent from above to the blessed evangelist. His breast was afire within, inspired with yearning for the onward path. Suddenly a sickness invaded him, but even so with courage he waited unafraid for the sublime things promised, cheer-

ful in those places of refuge. During the gloom of the nights his bone-framed body was hard oppressed, and his heart enfeebled; his cheerful spirit was eager for the onward way.

945   The Father of the angels was not willing to let linger for a long time after that, in this unhappy world's existence, a man devoid of sins who with prompt courage had pleased him by his deeds and in his achievements here during the span of his days. So the Almighty caused his hand to visit where the saintly servant, blessed with favourable judgment, was waiting in his retreat, brave of heart, staunch and stout of purpose. Hope and ecstasy were made new again in his breast. His bony frame was being consumed by disease; the treasury of his body, secured by bonds within, was unlocked. His limbs grew heavy, probed by pains; he knew the truth, that the Almighty, the ordaining Lord, in his mercy had visited him from above. Securely he fortified his spirit against the encompassing danger of the devils' attacks, and yet he was not afraid, nor was the violence of the disease nor the severance of death appalling to his mind; but praise of the Lord burned in his breast and love triumphant, hot as a brand, in his spirit, which steadily transcended his every pain. In him there was no misgiving about this borrowed time even though his body and soul, two spouses, should sunder their cherished life together.

969   The days slipped away, and the darkness of the canopy of the nights. The time was near when he would have to satisfy the ancient transgression and to take his chance at judgment through the coming of death — of that very death which our sinful parents received of old according as those first parents of the human race earned it before them.

XII

976   Then during this bleak time Guthlac's strength was exhausted; but his mood was quite unyielding, single-minded in courage. The disease was virulent, feverish and deadly fierce. His breast was inwardly fervid, his bone-framed body was on fire. The brew was in the making which Eve fermented for

Adam at the world's beginning. First the fiend served it to the woman and she then poured the bitter cup for Adam, her dear husband. From that time onwards, because of that ancient transgression, the children have painfully paid the forfeit, so that there has been not one of the human race, not a man on earth from the beginning onwards, that has been able to escape and avoid that grievous drink from the deep cup of death, but the door into that hard time soon opens itself to them and reveals the way in. No one conceived in the flesh, powerful or humble, can prevail against it with his life, but it will rush upon him with greedy clutches. Just so had the cruel companionless thing, a warrior greedy for slaughter, approached closely, right up to Guthlac now, through the darkness of the night.

999   There was remaining with him one attendant who visited him every day. He, then, a deeply considerate, prudent-minded man, set off for the church of God within which he knew the herald of the heavenly home, the most beloved and precious teacher, would be, and went in then for a talk with the blessed man; he wanted to hear the saint's teachings, the kindly man's discourses. Then he found his master exhausted from sickness; that attacked him sorely at the heart and he suffered mental grief and great anxiety of mood. Then his servant asked:

1011   'How has your spirit come to be so afflicted, my friend and master, father, refuge of your friends, and so severely assailed? I have never found you like this before, dearest lord, so exhausted. Are you able to command words for converse? In my opinion it seems that during this last night a feebleness from the inroads of the disease has afflicted you, probed by wounding pains. It will be the most fervent anxiety in my heart until you comfort my mind and spirit: do you know, noble master, how in the end this bone-disease is to abate?'

1023   Then a while later he answered him – he was unable to muster the breath immediately – when the painful and deadly sickness had subsided in him. Confident, blessed in his courage, he spoke and returned the answer:

1027 'I will say this, that during this dark night pain laid hold of me, agony pervaded me and unlocked the treasury of my body. My limbs, probed by pains, are growing heavy. This house of the soul, my dying carcass, must be covered over by an earthy vault and my limbs by a roof of loam, to languish in its mortal resting-place, fast in the grave. The warrior is approaching near, not slow to the fray. Remission of the soul's disseverance will last no longer than seven nights of respite, so that my life will arrive at its end on the eighth night from now, as day is approaching. Then my days in the earthly journey will have slipped away, my sorrow will be assuaged and then I shall be allowed to get rewards of fresh gifts before the knees of the dispensing Lord and follow continuously the Lamb of God for ever after amid unceasing joys: my spirit is already yearning to be gone and eager for the journey there. Now you have ready knowledge of my limbs' disseverance from life. It is a long wait, this of the worldly existence.'

1047 It was a time of weeping and mourning, of bleak mood and grieving mind for the young man when he heard that the saint was yearning for the onward journey. Because of the unexpected news, he sustained a heavy sorrow at heart on his master's behalf. His spirit, his anxious mind, grew dark because he saw his lord yearning to be gone elsewhere. He could not keep his forbearance over it but, allowing his grief, he let the passionate tears flow and the streaming droplets spring; but fate could not constrain that precious treasure, the spirit, in a dying man longer than had been ordained for him.

XIII

1060 The saintly soul understood the grieving man's faltering mind, and so the refuge of his followers, cheerful of mood and dear to God, set about comforting the young man, and to his most cherished friend he spoke these words:

1064 'Do not be sad, although this disease is consuming me within. To me it is not a hardship to suffer the will of the Prince, my Lord; and in this time of trouble I have no anxiety of mood over dying, nor do I much fear the plundering horde of hell's vassals, nor will the original offspring of iniquity be able to establish in me sin or transgression or fleshly flaw; in fire they must rather bemoan their pain, stewed in the seethings of their misery, and beweep their exile, severed from pleasures in that abode of death, and from every privilege and act of love and gesture of forgiveness.

1076 'My beloved son, do not be too troubled in mind. I am full of yearning for the journey in order to receive a dwelling-place above, and eager for the rewards, in eternal joy, of my former deeds, and to gaze upon the Lord of victories. My dear son, to me it is no distress or trouble that I seek the God of glory, King of heaven, where there is peace and bliss, the happiness of those steadfast in his ordinance, where the Lord is present to whom I have been eagerly obedient in the secret thoughts of my soul and in my deeds, in mood and in might, during this drear time. I know that reward to be without flaw, a meed not transitory but divine in the heights. There my hope is minded to seek; my soul goes questing from its corporeal vessel to that lasting joy in happy prosperity. To me this homeland will be neither pain nor sorrow. I know that after the body's downfall there will be for me a meed not transitory.'

1094 Then this man of heavenly glory, the brave witness to mysteries, stilled his words; he had need of rest, being weary.

1096 The firmament rolled on above the children of men and a number of dark nights went gliding by over the multitudes. Then that day arrived on which the living Lord, everlasting and almighty, amid joy accomplished resurrection in the body when he arose, sovereign, from death, from out of the earth, in that Easter-tide, Majesty of all majesties, and raised to the heavens the greatest of throngs when he ascended from out of hell. So in that glorious festal-tide the blessed man, blissfully exultant upon that radiant day, meek and steadfast in what was meet, not easily sustained his strength by courage. The people's joy, then, austere and prudent of thought, got up as briskly as he could, being exhausted on account of the great afflictions. Then he confirmed his mind in the pure faith and offered the sacrifice, as a thing pleasing to the Lord, deeply meditating in the secret thoughts of his soul within God's temple and, as befitted a master, preached the gospel to his follower through grace of spirit and told about the proofs of the victory and wondrously convinced his mind as to the glory and the happy prosperity in that beautiful existence, so that never in his life, neither before nor after in this ephemeral span, did he hear other teaching like it, nor the mystery of the Lord so deeply expounded in breadth of understanding out of human mouth. The truer idea came to him that it was the word of a celestial angel from out of the joys of heaven, of a mighty minister, much rather than the teaching of any man among mortals throughout the earth. The thing witnessed seemed to him the greatest of miracles, that such skill of perception inhabited the breast of any person here, of any of the children of men, so profound was his every word, and his wisdom and the man's disposition, the bravery and the physical strength which the ordaining Lord of the angels, the Helpmeet of souls, had granted him.

XIV

1134   Four days in succession were since passed away which the Lord's servant endured in courage, afflicted by the disease and tormented by pains. He nursed no anxiety, no gloomy spirit nor morbid mind over the dissevering of his spirit. Death was drawing near; with stealthy steps it advanced, and, strong and cruel, it sought out the house of the soul.

1141   The seventh day came into existence for mortals since the flying volley of arrows in belligerent showers sank into him, burning, close to his heart, and unlocked the treasury of his spirit, it having been probed with cunning keys. The prudent youth, the servant and attendant, went at that time to visit the noble man in the holy sanctuary, when he found, prostrate and ready to depart on the onward journey, his lord, past hope, the man saintly of soul in God's temple, overwhelmed by the surges of pain.

1150   It was the sixth hour, upon the midday; for his lord the last day was now at hand – severely assailed by resistless tribulations, pierced by deadly arrows, he could barely muster breath or lift up his voice and valiant speech. Melancholy, chilled and weary of spirit, then, he greeted the dying and exhausted yet cheerful-hearted man, and he prayed him by the Maker of miracles, if he could command his verbal faculties, to summon up speech so that in his accounts he would indicate to him and explain to him in the course of his words how far he might trust in his circumstances and his condition in that dismal illness before it should be that death laid him prostrate. The blessed man gave back an answer to him, beloved man to beloved man, even though the sternly courageous warrior could only slowly draw breath.

1166   'My dear son, it is not very far from the utmost and final day of the inevitable parting, so that not long after this you must listen to the last guidance by words of mine – never devoid of things profitable – in this worldly existence. Acquit well all the concord and the friendship and the words, dearest of men, we two have spoken together.'

1173   'Master, never shall I let the kinship of love grow sluggish in your time of need.'

1175   'Be prepared for a journey once my body and limbs and the breath of life sunder their union in the severance of the spirit; after that, hasten to tell my most cherished sister of my journey onward upon the long road to that lovely joy in the everlasting abode, and let her know, too, by my words that I have all the time denied myself her presence in this worldly life because I desired that we might see each other again in that everlasting joy in heavenly glory, free from imperfections, before the presence of the everlasting Judge. There our love will be abiding,

1348   'Courage is the best thing for the man who must very often endure deadly harm done his lord and deeply brood upon the agony of separation from his master when the time devised by the instruments of Providence arrives. He who has to wander wounded in spirit knows this; he knows his gracious wealth-bestowing lord lies buried. Thence he must go roaming, downcast and miserable. There is a dearth of distraction for him who most often endures hardships in his wounded spirit.

1356   'Certainly I do not have very much cause to exult over his passing. My lord, leader of men, and your brother, the best man amid the encircling oceans of those of whom we have ever heard born in childhood of humankind among the English, prop of the weary, delight of his loving kinsmen, shelterer of his friends – he has gone to God's judgment from out of the pleasures of the world into the splendour of heaven, to seek the dwellings of an abode on high. The earthly part, the shattered lodging-place of bone, rests on its deathbed inside the buildings, and the heavenly part has gone out of the bodily vessel to seek the reward of victory in God's light; and he bade me tell you that you two will for ever be allowed to take up an abode together, the heavenly reward for your deeds, amid that loving company in everlasting happiness, and pleasantly enjoy the splendour and the ecstasies. My victorious master also bade me charge you, when he was about to set out on the journey, most cherished virgin, that you should cover his corpse with earth.

1377   'Now you are fully acquainted with my mission. I shall go away, wounded in spirit, downcast of mood; my languishing thought. . .'

A few lines, perhaps comprising the ending of the poem, have been lost through trimming of the MS at the top of fol.53.

Azarias

[The Exeter Book, fol.53ᵃ–55ᵇ]

191 verse lines. A portion is lost of this poem featuring the prayer of Azariah and the song of the three youths, Hananiah, Azariah and Mishael, in Nebuchadnezzar's furnace. It is related in subject-matter to *Dan* (see the headnotes to *Dan*) but is most probably an independent version. The codex-compiler perhaps owes his interest in this subject matter to its prominent place in the liturgy of Holy Week (see the headnotes to Junius 11 and to *Dan*).

The Phoenix

[The Exeter Book, fol.55ᵇ–65ᵇ]

This optimistic, consolatory poem, whose minimal stress upon human guilt and punishment contrasts starkly with such poems as *Chr III* and *JgD*, is founded (lines 1–380) upon a free reworking of the fourth-century Latin *Carmen de Ave Phoenice* ('Song Concerning the Bird Phoenix') usually attributed to Lactantius. This Roman convert to Christianity spent the notable part of his life in the Roman province of Africa where, presumably, he culled the Egyptian (Arabian) legend of the phoenix. While there is no need to seek beyond the ordinary channels of Mediterranean cultural influence upon the North in accounting for the transmission of the *Carmen* to England, it is worth noting that the Anglo-Saxons were brought into touch with the Christianized scholarship of Athens and the African centres of learning as early as 669 when Theodore of Tarsus arrived in Canterbury to begin his reign of twenty-one years as archbishop. He had himself been educated in Tarsus and in Athens, and had studied secular and sacred literature in Greek and in Latin; and he brought with him the African scholar Hadrian, who became abbot of the monastery at Canterbury. The immense spiritual and secular benefits of their teaching are described by Bede (*HE*, Bk.IV, ch.2).

Lactantius had retold the phoenix-legend in distinguished verse composed according to the rules of the classical schools of Latin rhetoric: as a result, some elegant description of nature, different from the sombre landscapes of native tradition, was transposed into English poetry when the *Carmen* was paraphrased. And though the English poet – a disciple of the poetry of Cynewulf perhaps, but probably not Cynewulf himself – drew with creative skill upon the compositional formulas of traditional vernacular poetry and thus thoroughly naturalized the eastern legend, he also experimented creatively under the influence of the classical Latin rhetoric of Lactantius, and to his repertory of English rhetorical devices added occasional internal rhyme and assonance and concluded his poem with ten lines of macaronic (mixed Latin and vernacular) verse.

The English poet's chief addition to the *Carmen* is, of course, his exposition of the 'true' significance which Christian scholars saw in the phenomenon of this unique bird. His immediate source would have been a biblical commentary on Job 29 especially v.18: 'Then I said: "I shall die with my nest, And I shall multiply my days as the phoenix" ' (*The Holy Scriptures according to the Masoretic Text: A New Translation*, Cambridge, 1917) – where the reading 'phoenix' has Hebrew authority behind it, and the weight of having been preferred in the Septuagint (Greek) version of the Old Testament, though modern Christian Bibles have generally adopted the alternative readings 'sand' or 'palm-tree'. The text is exegetically paraphrased in the poem (546–69) in such a way that it becomes a prophecy of the bodily resurrection not only of Christ but of all mortals steadfast in truth – whose righteousness (a major theme of so many other AS poems) is here partially defined in terms of the righteousness of Job (e.g. 29:14–17). Fire, so prominently featured in *Chr III* and *JgD* for its destructive voracity, is here a cleansing power, purifying the souls of such as are attired in their good works like the phoenix within its nest of sweet herbs. Regenerate humanity thus regains the lost paradise, in heaven. Every righteous soul is a phoenix, the poet implies; every righteous man and woman in the mass of humankind is singular in the esteem of the Redeemer, as in *DrR* the tree of the Cross is singular among the trees of the forest, Mary among womankind and the dreamer among humanity: this is the valuable philosophy of individual worth which Christianity advanced among the Anglo-Saxons.

I

I have heard that far away from here in the regions of the east exists the noblest of lands renowned among men. This expanse of earth is not accessible to many of the potentates across the world, for through the might of the ordaining Lord it is far removed from evil-doers. The whole plateau is beautiful, delightfully endowed with earth's loveliest perfumes. Unparalleled is that land of rivers and noble the Maker, magnanimous, abounding in powers, who formed that land. There heaven-kingdom's portal is often open and the delightfulness of singing voices revealed to the blessed. It is a delightsome plateau. There the green woodlands, spacious beneath the skies, not rain nor snow, nor breath of frost nor scorch of fire, nor falling of hail nor drizzle of rime, nor heat of the sun nor incessant cold, nor torrid weather nor wintry shower may spoil a whit, but the plateau remains perfect and unmarred. That noble land is abloom with blossoms. There stand no mountains nor steep hills there, nor do rocky cliffs rear aloft as here with us, no valleys nor dales nor ravines, hillocks nor dunes, and there lies there never a scrap of rough ground, but this noble plateau burgeons beneath the heavens, abloom with delights.

28   That radiant land, that region, is higher by twelve fathoms — so in their wisdom sages knowledgeable from their studies inform us in their writings — than any of the mountains which rear aloft, luminous beneath the constellations, here with us.

33   It is serene, that transcendent plateau. The grove of the sun shimmers, a delightsome wood; the foliage, the luminous leaves, do not fall, but the trees stand ever green as God commanded them. Winter and summer alike, the wood is festooned with leaves; never a leaf will wither under the sky nor fire ever to the fullness of time cause them harm, before the transformation comes upon the world. When of old the water's torrent, the flood, covered the whole world, the earth's ambit, then this noble plateau, in every way unmarred, stood secured against the rough waves' watery encroachment, blessed, unsul-

lied, by the grace of God: so it will remain, abloom, until the coming of the conflagration and the judgment of the Lord, when the vaults of death, the gloomy tombs of mortals are opened.

50   There in that land is no loathsome foe, not weeping nor anguish, no sign of woe, not senility nor disease nor painful death nor losing of life, no onset of the abhorrent, neither sin nor strife nor wounding anguish, neither poverty's struggle nor want of wealth, not sorrow nor sleep nor grievous illness, not wintry squalls nor the flurry of tempests and stormy weather beneath the heavens, nor does harsh frost oppress anyone with its freezing icicles. Neither hail nor rime is there, falling to the earth, nor wind-blown cloud, nor does the water there, agitated by the breeze, fall downwards, but there wonderfully ornamental streams and wells spout forth in lovely springs. Delightful waters from out of the midst of the wood irrigate the earth, which every month gush cold as the sea from the turf of the ground and at these seasons percolate the whole grove in spate. It is the Prince's bidding that twelve times the delightfulness of fluent streams should ripple throughout that glorious land. The groves are festooned with leaves, with beautiful fruits. There the wood's adornments, sanctified though below the heavens, never fade, nor do the blossoms, the beauty of the trees, fall brown to the ground, but there on those trees, perpetually, like a work of art, the laden branches continue green on the grassy plain, and the fruit fresh through all time, and that most dazzling of groves pleasantly bedecked by the powers of holy God. Never does the wood come to be marred in its appearance; the sanctified perfume there lingers throughout that land of delight. Never to the fullness of time will this be changed before the wise God who shaped it in the first place brings to an end his ancient work.

II

85   That wood a bird inhabits, wonderfully handsome, strong of wings, which is called Phoenix. There this creature unparalleled

keeps his dwelling and, courageous of heart, his way of life; never shall death harm him in that pleasant plateau while the world remains. He is accustomed to observe the sun's course and to address himself towards God's candle, the brilliant gem, and eagerly to watch for when the noblest of stars comes up over the billowy sea, gleaming from the east, the ancient work of the Father ornately glinting, God's radiant token. The stars are hidden, gone below the ocean in the western regions, obscured in the dawning, and the dark gloomy night departs. Then the bird, powerful in flight, exultant in his wings, gazes eagerly upon the main beneath the sky, across the water, until the lamp of the firmament comes gliding up from the east above the broad sea. As the noble bird, unchangingly handsome, frequents the welling streams at the fountain-head, there the glory-blessed creature laves himself in the brook twelve times before the advent of the beacon, the candle of the firmament, and ever as often at each laving sips water cold as the sea from the pleasant well-springs. Then after splashing in the water, exalted in mood he betakes himself up into a tall tree from where he may most easily observe the journey on the eastern paths, when the taper of the firmament, a lamp of light, brightly glints over the tossing of the deep. The land is embellished, the world beautified, when across the expanse of the ocean the gem of heaven, of stars the most glorious, illumines the earth throughout the world.

120   As soon as the sun high overtops the salt streams then this shining grey bird goes from the tree, out of the grove, and swift on his wings he takes flight upon the air and makes melody and sings towards the firmament. Then so lovely is the bird's articulation, so inspired his heart, ecstatically jubilant, he modulates his singing more wondrously, with clear voice, than ever a son of man heard below the heavens since the exalted King, Creator of glory, founded the world, the heaven and the earth. The harmony of the song is sweeter and more beautiful than all musical instruments and more delightsome than every melody. Not trumpets, nor horns, nor the sound of the harp, nor the voice of any man on earth, nor the strain of the organ's melody,

nor the wings of the swan, nor any of the joys which the Lord created for men's mirth in this mournful world may match that effusion. So he sings and makes melody, joyously enraptured, until the sun has sunk in the southern sky; then he falls silent and takes to listening. Intrepid, discerning in his contemplation, he upturns his head, and three times beats his swift-flighted wings; then the bird is silenced. Always, twelve times by day and by night, he marks the hours.

147   Thus it is ordained to the grove's denizen that there amidst its pleasures he may make use of the plateau and enjoy well-being, life, the joys of peace and the land's ornate beauties until this custodian of the woodland grove will have bided a thousand years of this existence.

153   When he is grown weak, the grey-feathered bird, aged and old in years, from the verdant earth and the luxuriant land he flies away, the finest among fowls, and then seeks out a spacious realm in earth, a dwelling and a domain where no people live. There he accepts supreme sovereignty over the family of birds, a paragon among his people, and for a while he dwells with them in the desert. Then resolute in his objectives, burdened with years, he goes flying westwards with fleet wings. Birds throng about the prince – each wants to be vassal and servant to the glorious lord – until they arrive, in greatest multitude, in the land of the Syrians. There the chaste bird quickly hastens away from them in order to occupy a deserted place in obscurity within a grove of trees, concealed and hidden from numbers of mortals. There in the wood he inhabits and occupies a lofty tree, secure upon its roots beneath the vault of heaven, which people on earth call Phoenix, from the name of the bird. To this tree the King potent in glory, the ordaining Lord of mankind, has granted it, I have heard, that this one of all the upward-spreading trees on earth is most resplendently luxuriant. No violent thing can wickedly harm it, but it will continue for ever shielded and inviolate while the world remains.

III

182   When the wind lies low and the weather is fair and the holy
clear gem of heaven shines, when the clouds are cleared away
and the torrent of the waters remains stilled and every storm is
lulled beneath the firmament, when from the south the warm
ethereal candle sweetly sheds its light, then he begins to build in
the branches, to prepare a nest. A great compulsion is upon
him, through an upsurge of awareness, that he must urgently
turn that senility to life and take on a new being. Then far and
near he garners and gathers in to that dwelling-place the most
fragrant and delightsome herbs and woodland flowers, every
noble perfume of delightsome herbs that the King of glory,
Father of each created thing, created to the honour of mankind,
the most fragrant beneath the firmament. There he himself
bears the splendid treasure into the tree where in the wasteland
the wild bird builds a house at the top of the tall tree, lovely
and delightsome, and there in that solarium he installs himself
and in that leafy obscurity surrounds himself body and wings
on every side with sanctifying odours and the noblest flowers of
the earth. He settles down, eagerly anticipating his destiny.

208   When in the season of summer the sun at its hottest, gem of
the firmament, shines upon the gloom and fulfils its appointed
task and scans the world, then his house becomes heated by
virtue of the clear firmament. The herbs grow warm; the abode
of his choosing exhales fragrant odours. Then in the heat the
bird burns along with his nest in the grip of the fire.

216   The pyre is kindled. Then flame engulfs the house of the
bloodied creature; fierce, it races on; yellow flame devours and
burns the phoenix, old with years long gone. Then fire devours
the ephemeral body; the life, the spirit of the dying bird is on its
way when the flame of the funeral pyre incinerates flesh and
bone.

222   Yet after a space of time, life returns to him anew, when the
cinders, congealed into a ball, begin to join together again after

the fury of the flame. When that most resplendent of nests, the brave bird's dwelling, is clean reduced by the blaze, and the corpse, the fragmented bone-frame, is grown cool and the conflagration subsides, then out of the pyre, among the ashes, the likeness of an apple is afterwards discovered, from which a worm develops, wonderfully handsome, as though it had hatched out of eggs, gleaming out of the shell. Then in a shady place he develops, so that he becomes like an eagle's chick, a handsome fledgling. Still further then he blissfully burgeons until he is alike in features to an adult eagle, and after this he is adorned with feathers just as he was in the beginning, brought radiantly to fulfilment. At that time the flesh is born again, wholly renewed and dissevered from sins.

242 In somewhat the same way as people carry home for food the fruits of the earth, pleasant nourishment, in autumn at reaping-time, before winter's advent, lest the pelting of rain destroy them below the clouds, wherein they find sustenance, the joy of eating, when frost and snow with overwhelming might bedeck the earth in wintry vestments, from which fruits the abundant prosperity of men shall sprout forth again according to the nature of the corn which is first sown as pure seed, when the gleam of the sun, the sign of life, in spring brings forth the world's wealth, so that according to their proper nature these fruits are born again, the adornments of the earth; so this bird, old according to his years, is young and clothed in flesh anew. No provender does he eat, no food on earth, except he tastes a portion of the honey-dew which often distils upon the midnight, by which the courageous bird nurtures his being until he seeks again his ancient dwelling, his own homeland.

IV

265 When in amongst the herbs he is grown into a bird exultant in his wings – his life is renewed – young and full of grace, then out of the dust he gathers up his body strong of limb which fire once disfigured, the residue of cremation, meticulously assembles the bones fragmented as a consequence of the fury of

the blaze and then brings bones and cinders, the residue of the funeral pyre, together again, and then rolls up that plunder from the slain, handsomely adorned, in herbs. Then he is impelled to seek again his own homeland.

276 Then in his feet he grips the fire's residue and clasps it in his claws and seeks again in ecstasies his home, a dwelling radiant with sunlight, his blessed native land. The whole of him, vital being and feather coat, is made new just as he was at the beginning when God, the immutably triumphant, first established him upon that noble plateau. There he brings his own bones which once the billowing of fire engulfed with flame upon the funeral mound, and the ashes too. Then the bird strong in adversity buries bones and cinders all together in that land of rivers. The symbol of the sun is his anew when the sky's luminary, of jewels the most brilliant, paragon among the noble stars, gleams out from the east up over the ocean.

291 The bird is handsome of colouring at the front, tinted with shimmering hues in his forepart about the breast. His head is green behind, exquisitely variegated and shot with purple. Then the tail is handsomely pied, part burnished, part purple, part intricately set about with glittering spots. The wings are white to the rearward, and the throat, downward and upward, green, and the bill, the beautiful beak, inside and out, gleams like glass or a gem. The mien of his eye is unflinching, in aspect most like a stone, a brilliant gem, when by the ingenuity of the craftsmen it is set in a foil of gold. About the neck, like a circlet of sunlight, there is a most resplendent ring woven from feathers. The belly below is exquisite, wondrously handsome, bright and beautiful. The shield above, across the bird's back, is ornately yoked. The shanks and the tawny feet are grown over with scales.

311 This bird is in every way unique of appearance, nearest in likeness to the peacock, blissfully mature, of which writings speak. He is not laggard nor slothful of purpose, lethargic nor ponderous, like certain birds which flap slowly on their wings

through the air, but he is brisk and swift and extremely lightsome, lovely and pleasant, marked out for heaven. Everlasting is the Prince who bestows on it that bounty.

320   When he sets out from this earth to seek the expanses of his ancient dwelling-place, as the bird flies he reveals himself to the nations, to the multitudes of men throughout the world. Then they gather from south and north, from east and west, in flocks; from far and near they journey in troops of peoples to where they gaze upon the Creator's beauteous gifts in the bird, according as the true King of victories in the beginning ordained for him a rarer nature and fairer embellishments beyond the family of birds. Then people throughout the earth wonder at his form and stature, and their writings proclaim it and they depict it by hand in marble, when the day and the hour reveal to the nations the ornate beauties of the swift-flighted bird.

335   Then the family of birds throng in flocks on every side; from far-flung ways they draw near. With song they praise and with loud voices glorify the brave one, and in a circle surround the holy bird in his flight aloft; in the midst is the phoenix, thronged about with crowds. The nations gaze on and in amazement marvel how the devoted company, one multitude after another, do homage to the wild bird, vigorously proclaim and glorify as king the cherished lord, and escort in raptures the prince to his dwelling-place, until the lone being flies away, swift upon his wings, so that the jubilant company cannot keep up with him. Then the delight of the peoples departs this earth to seek his homeland.

V

350   So, after a time of death, the blessed one goes back to his ancient home, that lovely land. The birds, mournful of mood, turn from the hero of the ordeal back to their abode; the princely one then remains, youthful, in his habitations. God alone, the King almighty, knows what his gender is, female or male; no one of humankind knows it, only the ordaining Lord

alone, how miraculous are the circumstances, the admirable dispensation of old, concerning this bird's birth.

361 There the blessed creature is allowed to enjoy his abode, the springing streams in the woodlands, and to dwell in the plateau until a thousand years are run. Then comes the ending of his life; the pyre engulfs him with its kindled fire. Yet, wondrously awakened, he miraculously returns to life. Therefore he does not agonize, moping, over death and painful dissolution, for he knows that after the fury of the flame there is renewed existence, life after extinction, when he is regenerated again from ashes in the shape of a bird and grows young afresh beneath heaven's canopy. He is himself both his own son and dear father, and always too the inheritor again of his own old remnants. The mighty Lord of mankind granted him that he should so wondrously become again the same that he was before, clothed about with plumage, though fire carry him off.

381 So each of the blessed chooses for himself, through dark death, that everlasting life after painful exile, so that after his lifetime he may enjoy God's favours among unending joys and ever after dwell in glory as guerdon for his works. The nature of this bird betokens much similitude to those elect servants of Christ in earth's habitations, how through the Father's aid they maintain during this perilous time here below the heavens a radiant happiness, and lay up for themselves sublime prosperity in the celestial homeland.

393 We have learned that the Almighty wrought man and woman through his faculty for wondrous things and established them in the finest of earth's regions, which the sons of men call Paradise. There was not any blessing lacking to them there – while they were willing to keep the word of the Everlasting, the Holy One's dictate – in that new state of happiness. There envy injured them, the spite of the old enemy who proferred them food, the fruit of the tree, so that foolishly they both partook of the apple against the permission of God and tasted the forbidden fruit.

404   Bitter was the misery upon them there and upon their children too after the eating — a meal hurtful to their sons and daughters. Painfully their alacritous teeth were punished according to their guilt; they endured the wrath of God, bitter and baleful sorrow. Ever since, their children have paid for it, because they consumed that food against the word of the Everlasting. Thus, mournful of mood, they had to give up the bliss of their homeland through the serpent's envy, when it artfully seduced our parents in former days, out of its deceitful spirit, so that far away from there in this vale of death they looked for somewhere to live, for dwellings more fraught with care. The worthier existence was hidden from them by obscurity and the hallowed plateau firmly closed through the devil's guile for a great number of years, until the King of glory, mankind's Joy, Comforter of the weary and the one Hope, through his advent opened it again to the holy.

VI

424   Most similar to this, according to what scholars in their pronouncements tell us and writings testify, is the migration of this bird when, old and wise, he forsakes dwelling-place and homeland, and is grown elderly. Weary of mood he sets out, harassed by his years, to where he finds the lofty canopy of the woodland in which, with twigs and with the noblest herbs, he builds a new abode, the nest in the grove. A great longing is upon him that he might receive a fresh existence again through the holocaust of fire, life after death, and be young anew; and that he might seek his ancient home, a dwelling radiant with sunlight, after his fiery bath. Just so, those forebears, our parents, left that lovely plateau and that precious seat of glory behind them and made the long journey into the grasp of malignant beings, where their persecutors, miserable monsters, harmed them often.

443   Yet there were many who served the Lord well below the heavens with holy virtues and praiseworthy deeds so that the Lord, the heavens' high King, was well-disposed towards them

in his heart. This is the lofty tree, in which the holy now keep their habitation, where none of the ancient enemies can harm them at all with their venom, the token of their wickedness, during this perilous time. There the Lord's warrior builds himself with praiseworthy deeds a nest against every malicious attack when he distributes alms to the destitute and to those without means and calls upon the Lord and Father as his help; onwards he hastens; the vices of this ephemeral existence, the dark doings of evil, he stifles; he keeps the law of the ordaining Lord, confident in his bosom and turns to prayer with pure intentions and nobly bows his knee to the earth; he flees every evil and dire sin out of awe for God; joyous of spirit he yearns to accomplish the greatest number of good deeds. To him the Lord, Disposer of victories, generous Benefactor of the multitudes, is a shield. These are the herbs and the fruits of the plants which the wild bird gathers from far and wide below the sky to his lodging-place, where he builds a nest marvellously secure against every malicious attack.

470   Thus, here in these habitations and now, by courage and by main strength, the soldiers of the Lord accomplish his will and strive towards glories. For this the everlasting Almighty will recompense them with a blessed meed. Out of those herbs a habitation shall be founded for them in the heavenly city as reward for their works, because they passionately cherished holy precepts in their heart. With fervent purpose by day and by night they show love to the Lord; with shining faith they choose the Beloved above the world's wealth: not for them is the comfortable expectation that they will inhabit long this ephemeral existence.

482   Thus the blessed man earns by valour joy everlasting and a heavenly home with the high King until an end comes to his tally of days, when death, the warrior gluttonous for carnage, fortified with weapons, snatches the life of each individual man and swiftly dispatches the ephemeral corpses, robbed of their souls, into earth's embrace where they will long remain concealed in the ground until the coming of the fire. Then the

multitude of humanity will be led into congregation: the Father of angels, true King of victories, will hold a synod and the Lord of the elect, with justice, will pass judgment. Then shall all the people in clay achieve resurrection as the mighty King, Ruler of the angels, Saviour of souls, proclaims his summons by the voice of the trumpet across the wide earth. By the Lord's powers that dark state of death shall be ended for the blessed. Those noble beings will depart, in squadrons they will go thronging, when this sin-working world burns in disgrace, kindled with flame. Each single man will grow fearful in spirit when fire destroys the dry land's ephemeral wealth and flame devours all the chattels of the earth, voraciously attacks the coined gold and greedily swallows the treasures of the dry land.

508   Then in that hour of revelation shall come in radiance to men, lovely and delightsome, the portent of this bird, when the divine authority raises up from their tombs and gathers all the bones, limbs and body together, and the spirit of life, before Christ's knee. Majestically from his high throne the King, heaven's comely Gem, will shine upon the saints. It will be well for those who, in that bleak hour, may find favour with God.

VII

518   There the bodies, clean from vices, will walk glad-hearted, and spirits will return to their bony vessels while the holocaust mounts high to the heavens. For many, fearful heat will be kindled when each single being, righteous and sinful, soul with body, proceeds from out of earthen graves to the judgment of the Lord, aghast with fear. Fire will be on the advance; it will set light to wickedness. There the blessed, because of their time in exile, will be attired in their works, their own deeds: these are those noble and delightsome herbs with which the wild bird encompasses his own nest so that it suddenly bursts into fire and burns up beneath the sun and himself with it; and then after the flame he recovers life anew. Just so shall each one of humankind be attired in flesh, peerless and rejuvenated, who through his own will works it here that the mighty King of

heaven is gracious to him at that conclave. Then holy spirits, souls steadfast in truth, will cry aloud and raise up song and, pure and elect, praise the King's majesty, voice upon voice, and ascend into glory handsomely herb-bedecked with their good deeds. The souls of men, then, shall be purified and brightly refined by the holocaust of fire.

546   Let none of mankind imagine that I am composing a lay and writing poetry with lying words. Listen to the wisdom of Job's songs. Inspired in his breast through the breath of the spirit, he gave voice, bold, gloriously exalted; he spoke these words: 'This I do not disdain in my hearts' thoughts, that I, a man weary of body, should settle for a deathbed within my nest and from there set out abject upon the long journey, despondent of my former deeds, covered in clay in the soil's embrace – and then after death, by grace of the Lord, be allowed, just as the phoenix bird, to possess renewed life after resurrection, and pleasures with the Lord where the precious company give praise to their Beloved. Of that life, of the light and the loving kindnesses, I shall not be able, ever to eternity, to experience an end. Though my corpse must grow mouldered in its earthen chamber as a thing desirable to worms, even so the God of the multitudes will set free my soul upon the hour of death and awaken it in glory. The hope of this will never crumble in my heart, for I have secure an enduring joy in the Ruler of the angels.'

570   So the wise man in distant days sang, discerning of mind, God's spokesman of his message, concerning his resurrection into everlasting life, so that we might the more readily understand the glorious significance that the illustrious bird betokens through his burning. The remnants of bones, ashes and cinders, he gathers them all after the cremation; then the bird brings them in his feet to the Lord's habitations, towards the sun. From then on they remain there many years, made new again in form, completely rejuvenated where none in that land may threaten injuries.

583 Now just so after death, through the Lord's might, souls together with body will journey – handsomely adorned, just like the bird, with noble perfumes – into abundant joys where the sun, steadfastly true, glistens radiant above the multitudes in the heavenly city.

VIII

589 Then the redeeming Christ, high above its roofs, will shine upon souls steadfast in truth. Him they will follow, these beautiful birds, radiantly regenerate, blissfully jubilant, spirits elect, into that happy home everlasting to eternity. There the fiend, outcast, importunate, cannot treacherously harm them by his evil, but there they shall live for ever clothed in light, just as the phoenix bird, in the safe-keeping of the Lord, radiant in glory. Each one's achievement will brightly sparkle in that joyous home before the face of the everlasting Lord, perpetually at peace, like the sun. There a bright halo, marvellously braided with precious stones, will rise above the head of each of the blessed. Their heads will glisten, crowned with majesty. The rare and regal diadem of a prince will adorn with light each of the righteous in that existence where enduring joy, everlasting and fresh anew, never wanes; but rather they will dwell in beauty, surrounded with glory, with lovely adornments, together with the Father of the angels.

611 In those habitations there shall be nothing at all to distress them, not strife nor poverty nor days of toil, violent hunger nor cruel thirst, disease nor age. The noble King will grant them every good thing. There the company of spirits will laud the Redeemer and glorify the might of the heaven-King and sing praises to the Lord. In loudest harmony they will carol clearly, a loving company, about the holy high throne of God; blithely the blessed together with the angels will extol the worthiest of rulers thus in unison: 'Peace be with you, true God, and the strength of wisdom; and to you, seated in majesty, be thanks for your fresh gifts and for every good thing. Great, immeasurable strength of might, high and holy! the heavens are fairly

filled, Father almighty, Majesty of all majesties, with your glory, aloft with the angels and on earth as well. Preserve us, Maker of created things. You are the Father almighty on high, Ruler of the heavens.'

632   Thus the righteous, purged of guilt, express themselves in that glorious city: the company of those steadfast in truth proclaim his royal majesty and sing in heaven the praise of the Sovereign to whom alone is everlasting honour henceforth without end. Of his blessedness was never a beginning nor inception. Though he was born into the world here on the earth in form of a child, yet the wealth of his powers remained holy, high above the heavens, supremacy inviolate. Though he was to undergo the pangs of death, cruel torment on the rood-tree, on the third day after his body's decease he received life again by the Father's help. Just so the young phoenix in his lodgings betokens the might of the Son of God, when out of the ashes he wakes again into the life of life, fully developed in his limbs. Just as the Redeemer afforded us aid through his body's severance, life without end, so this bird fills his two wings with sweet and delightsome herbs, with the lovely fruits of the earth, when he is inspired to be gone.

655   These are the words, as writings tell us, and the invocations of the holy whose hearts are inspired to be gone to the heavens, to that merciful God, into the delight of delights, where they will bring the delightsome perfume of words and works, as a gift to the Lord and Ordainer, into that glorious creation, into that luminous existence.

661   To him be laud for ever through an eternity of eternities, and the splendour of glory, honour and power in that celestial kingdom of the skies. He is of right King of the world and of the heavenly host, environed in glory in the beauteous city.

667   The Author of light has granted us that here we may merit and gain by good deeds joys in heaven. There we may seek out realms most broad and sit upon lofty thrones, live in the grace

of light and of peace, obtain abodes of genial delight, enjoy days of prosperity, look upon the Lord of victories, gentle and mild, without cease, and sing him praises in perpetual laud, blessed, amid the angels. Alleluia.

Juliana

[The Exeter Book, fol.65^b–76^a]

This is the second of the signed poems of Cynewulf (see the introduction to *Chr II*) contained in the Exeter Book; his name is spelled out in runes woven into a personal penitential epilogue. Here, as in *Chr II* and in his two signed poems in the Vercelli Book (*Ele*, *FAp*), Cynewulf has sought from Christian legend subject-matter amenable to that heroic treatment at which the OE poets had traditionally excelled. The signed poems further relate to a small group of other OE poetic saints' lives (*Glc A*, *Glc B* and *And*) and to other explicitly religious poetry (*Chr I*, *Chr III*, *DrR* and *Phx*) which is conventionally called Cynewulfian because, though these other poems lack runic signatures, they share together and with the signed poems of Cynewulf a broad similarity of subject-matter, approach and style, which suggests that they might be unsigned work by Cynewulf himself or the work of a school of poets deliberately conforming to a literary standard best exemplified in the poems of Cynewulf.

Early Germanic communities, if the *Germania* of Tacitus is to be trusted on the point, respected the advice of their women. Germanic secular literature has normally afforded a dignified and often instrumental role for women in its (admittedly male-dominated) heroic depictions of society. In reality too, as Bede for one often indicates, women like the abbess Hilda of Whitby could decisively influence ecclesiastical and political life in the land. The AS poets, therefore, may have found no great difficulty in accommodating from Latin Christian example the notion of a story celebrating a woman as its protagonist; but were vernacular narrative techniques and the formulaic elements of composition suited to the poetic rendering of such stories of female heroics? Certainly Cynewulf tackles in a workmanlike way his task of rendering the Latin Life of Juliana (a related text is printed in the Bollandist *Acta Sanctorum*, Februarius, Tom. 2) in the traditional form of OE verse. But he seems barely fired emotionally or imaginatively by his heroine who, compared with Judith, is assigned little charisma. The narrative is elegantly mannered but – despite the grotesque aspects of Eleusius and the discomfiture of the devil being interrogated by Juliana – unenriched by such irony and humour as distinguish *Jud*, and lacking the immediacy in place and time of the *Glc*-poems. There is room for some wincing at the tortures and much enthusiasm over the polemic, but little beyond this to stretch the emotional response of the audience, for martyrdom bringing an instant reward in eternal bliss is a bland and undisturbing end to a plot. Nevertheless, or perhaps because of this, the poem's position as last of the long and weighty works which open the codex pays due deference to this very important genre of the Saint's Life in monastic reading. Juliana is not included among the four dozen virgins celebrated in Aldhelm's prose *De Virginitate* (before 706).

I

Listen! we have heard heroes tell, bold men pass judgment on what happened in the days of Maximian, the ruthless king who launched a persecution throughout the earth, killed Christian people and tore down churches. On the grass-clad ground the pagan war-lord shed the blood of God's worshippers, the saints, the doers of right. Wide, far-reaching and imposing was his rule over the nations of men, over almost all the spacious earth. Through the cities, as he had commanded, went harsh soldiers; often being depraved in their doings, they used violence, those men who in their wickedness hated the Lord's law; they promoted enmity, upraised idols, murdered the pious, killed the learned, burned the elect, and persecuted God's soldiers with spear and with fire.

18   There was a certain wealthy man of aristocratic stock, a powerful governor; he ruled over fortified cities, most often kept residence in the city of Nicomedia, and owned hoarded wealth. Often, against the word of God, he would very dilig-

ently visit some idol, the object of heathen sacrifice. He was called Eleusius; he possessed great and renowned power. Then his heart began to yearn after Juliana, a virgin – desire took him by storm. She in her soul kept saintly faith and firmly intended for the love of Christ to preserve her virginity pure from any sin.

32   Then this virgin, at her father's will, was pledged to the wealthy man; he was not quite aware of the situation, how in her spirit the young girl despised the conjugal state. To her mind the fear of God was greater than all the treasure which lay among the nobleman's possessions. So the wealthy, gold-abounding man yearned in his mind for the marriage, longed for the virgin to be made ready for him as urgently as possible, as a bride for his house. She steadfastly rejected the man's love though he had in store treasures upon earth, a countless quantity of jewels. All that she disregarded and in the midst of the multitude of men she spoke these words:

46   'I can say to you that you need not torment yourself further; if you love and believe in the true God and exalt his praise, if you acknowledge him the Refuge of souls I shall be immediately and unwaveringly at your will. Similarly, I say to you that if in fact you put your trust, by way of devil-worship, in an inferior god, if you invoke the pagan idols, you may neither have me nor coerce me into marriage with you; never, in violent spite, shall you contrive suffering, harsh tortures, so severe that you make me swerve from these words.'

58   Then the nobleman became excited with rage; corrupted by his sinful deeds he listened to the virgin's words; then wild and blinded in his mind he ordered hasty messengers to fetch the saintly girl's father quickly for consultation. The clamour of voices rose up when they, warlike men, leaned spears together. Pagans they both were, father-in-law and son-in-law, cankered with sins. Then, raising his spear, the guardian of the realm addressed the virgin's father in aggressive mood:

68   'Your daughter has shown me disrespect: she tells me out-
right that she does not care for my conjugal love and affection.
To my mind these insults are painful in the extreme, in that she
so grievously assailed me with blasphemy in front of these
people. She called upon me lavishly to honour, to praise aloud
and to laud in my thought an alien god, above the others we
hitherto knew – or else not have her.'

78   Then the headstrong man, the virgin's father, grew furious,
and after this speech swore and disclosed his heart:

80   'I swear it by the true gods – so may I always meet with grace
from them, and from you, my lord, your favour in your luxurious
courts – if these words which you tell me are true, most
esteemed among men, that I shall not spare her but I shall
resign her to destruction, famous lord, at your disposal. Sen-
tence her to death, if you think it fitting, or grant her life as may
be more acceptable to you.'

89   Then, single of purpose and evilly disposed, swollen with
fury, he went forthwith to speak to the virgin, to where he
knew the young girl, cheerful of spirit, was keeping residence.
Then he made this pronouncement:

93   'You are my daughter, the dearest and sweetest to my heart,
you alone in the world, the light of my eyes, Juliana! You, by
your opposition, have foolishly taken a fruitless course against
the advice of sensible people. Too strictly you refuse, upon
your own advice, your bridegroom who is a better person than
you, of higher birth in the world, wealthier in riches. He is good
to have as a friend. Therefore it is worth it for you not to let slip
this man's love, his lasting affection.'

II

105   Then the blessed Juliana – she had steadfastly consecrated
her conjugal state to God – gave him her reply:

110   'Never will I accept a relationship with this lord unless he accepts the worship of the God of hosts more readily than he has done yet, and shows with sacrifices his love for him who created light, heaven and earth, and the ambit of the oceans and the extent of the habitable regions. By no other way may he take me into his house. He with his wealth must seek a bride's love from some other woman; he shall have none here.'

117   Then in his fury her father fiendishly answered her – nor was he making her a promise of trinkets:

119   'I shall see to it, if my life lasts, that if you do not soon stop your foolishness, and if you go on worshipping alien gods and neglect those who are dearer to us and who stand in support of this nation, then before long, being deemed to have forfeited your life, you shall suffer death through savaging by wild animals – if you will not consent to the proposition of union with a magnanimous man. For you to slight our lord is a great and disastrous course of action for such as you.'

130   The blessed Juliana, discerning and dear to God, then answered him:

132   'I will tell you truthfully: as long as I live I will not speak a lie. Never shall I fear your ordeals, nor do the horrors of torture or the terrors of trial trouble me, with which you, furthering evil, ferociously threaten me; nor shall you ever bring it about by your idolatry that you convert me from the worship of Christ.'

140   Then the father was mad with rage, furious and incensed, menacing and savage-minded towards his daughter. He ordered her then to be flogged, to be put under torture, to have torments inflicted upon her, and he spoke these words:

144   'Change your mind and amend the words which you unwisely spoke before when you rejected the worship of our gods.'

147   The undaunted Juliana answered him out of her spiritual insight:

149   'Never shall you teach me to offer oblations to spurious things, to dumb and deaf devil-images, to the soul's enemies, to the worst ministrants of torment, but I honour the glorious Lord of earth and of the heavenly host and in him alone I put my whole trust that he shall be my protector, my helper and my saviour against hell-fiends.'

158   Then in his fury, the virgin's father Africanus handed her over to the disposal of her enemies, to Eleusius. At daybreak, when light had come, he ordered her to be taken to his judgment seat. The court and the people all assembled were fascinated by the virgin's beauty. The nobleman, her bridegroom, then addressed her, with gentle words at first:

166   'Juliana! sweetest incandescence of the sun to me! Look what radiance you have, what abundant endowment of the splendour of youthfulness! If, even now, you propitiate our gods and seek protection from them, they being so merciful, and favour from the holy ones, a countless tally of tortures, cruelly executed, will be averted from you – painful miseries which stand ready for you if you will not sacrifice to the true gods.'

175   The noble girl gave him her answer:

176   'Never shall you intimidate me with your threats, nor shall you prepare so many cruel tortures that I shall come to take pleasure in your companionship unless you abandon these false practices, the honouring of idols, and sensibly acknowledge the glorious God, the Creator of souls, the Lord of mankind, in whose power are all created things for ever and ever.'

184   Then in front of the people, in savage mood, he uttered threats; the people's ruler violently worked himself into a

passion, and in spiteful punishment he ordered the virgin to be stretched out naked and, guilty of no sin, to be flogged with whips. Then the soldier laughed and spoke in mocking words:

190   'Thus is the mastery in our quarrel seized at the start. Still I will spare your life even though you earlier spoke many indiscreet words, too strenuously refused to love the true gods. Horrible tortures will henceforth be your reward, being stubborn, unless you settle with them soon and offer acceptable gifts to them after your mocking remarks, and make peace. Let it rest, the struggle, the distasteful contention. If, after this, you in your rashness persist any longer in perversity, then, constrained by your hostile attitude, I shall be obliged to take vengeance on you for this most terrible impiety and for the vexatious blasphemy in which you slanderously engaged against the best and the most merciful of those beings whom men know, and to whom this nation has long ministered in its midst.'

209   To him that noble fearless soul replied:

210   'I do not fear your judgments, you condemned sinner, nor the hurt of your tortures: I have as my hope the Guardian of heaven, the merciful Protector, the Lord of hosts, who will shield me against your delusion and from the clutches of the demons whom you regard as gods. They are devoid of every virtue, worthless, unprofitable, useless, nor shall anyone encounter there that benefit, true peace, even if he does seek their friendship. He will not find salvation there, amid devils. I shall fix my mind upon the Lord who, as glorious Ruler, for ever disposes over every virtue, every triumph: he is the true King.'

III

225   Then it seemed to the governor ignominious that he could not change the mind and purpose of the virgin. He ordered her to be hung and hauled up on a high gallows by her hair where she, dazzling as the sun, suffered a beating and extremely

savage treatment for six hours of the day: and he, odious oppressor, ordered her to be taken down directly and instructed that she be taken to prison. The worship of Christ was fast enfolded in her heart and in her meek spirit, an indestructible strength. Then the prison door, the work of hammers, was fastened with a bar; the saintly girl lay inside, secure in faith. Constantly she praised the King of glory in her heart, the God of the heaven-kingdom within that place of confinement and the Saviour of men, enveloped in darkness. To her the Holy Ghost was a constant companion.

242   Then all at once into that prison entered the enemy of men, expert in evil: he had an angel's form. An adept in torments, the soul's oppressor and prisoner of hell spoke to the saint:

247   'Why hold out, dearest and most precious to the King of glory, our Lord? This judge has prepared for you the most evil tortures, agony without an end, if you will not, reflecting prudently, do sacrifice and propitiate his gods. Make haste, when he orders you to be taken out from here, to offer a sacrifice as an oblation to their triumph before destruction seizes you, death in front of the people. Thus you shall survive, a maiden exultant in her blessings, the judge's wrath.'

258   Then she, a woman pleasing to Christ, who was not afraid, immediately asked where he had come from. The outcast declared to her:

261   'I am God's angel, his accomplished minister, a holy one sent to you from on high. Heavy tortures, wondrously brutal ones, have been prescribed as capital punishment upon you. God the Son of the Ruler ordered me to command you to spare yourself these.'

267   Then the virgin was appalled with dismay at the abrupt tidings which the demon, heaven's enemy, announced to her by his words. Then the innocent young woman firmly braced her spirit and cried out to God:

272 'Protector of men, eternal, almighty, I wish to beg you now, by that noble creation which you in the beginning founded, Father of the angels, not to cause me to turn aside from the praise of your grace, although this messenger, who stands before me, tells me these terrible abrupt tidings. I wish as well to beg you, merciful Lord, to prove to me, Glory of kings, and Keeper of the heavenly host, who this minister is, hovering on the air, who on your behalf exhorts me upon a harsh road.'

282 A comely voice answered her from the skies and spoke these words:

284 'Seize the perverse creature and hold tightly on to him until he tells you his mission truthfully, all of it from the start, what his origins are.'

287 Then the soul of this woman, blessed in the outcome, was enraptured. She seized the devil. . .

Between the present folios 69 and 70 a leaf has been lost from the MS. The text resumes part way through the devil's confession.

289 '. . . to sell the King of all kings to his death. Furthermore I contrived it that the soldier wounded the Ruler – the crowd was looking on – so that blood and water both together fell on the ground. Furthermore I impelled Herod in his mind to command that John's head should be cut off when that holy man outspokenly opposed his love of the woman and his unlawful marriage. I also cunningly persuaded Simon so that he began his persecution against Christ's chosen servants and in his profound misguidedness blasphemously addressed those holy men and said that they were sorcerers. I engaged in devious schemings when I seduced Nero so that he ordered Christ's servants, Peter and Paul, to be executed. Pilate, by my promptings, previously hung on the Cross the Ruler of the skies, the mighty ordaining Lord. Similarly I also instructed Ægeas so that in his folly he ordered the saintly Andrew to be hung on a high cross, so that he dispatched his spirit from the gallows into

the splendour of heaven. So together with my brothers I have committed many terrible evils, black sins, cruel malign plottings which I cannot relate nor recount at large, and the number of which I cannot know.'

315   The saintly Juliana by grace of the spirit answered him:

317   'Enemy of mankind, you must tell still more about your mission: who sent you to me?'

319   The monster, afraid, pinioned, without hope of truce, gave her back the reply:

321   'Hark then; my father, king of hell's denizens, sent me here on this journey to you from out of that oppressive abode. In that mournful hall he is more assiduous in every evil than I. When he sends us to pervert by evil deception the minds of those steadfast in the truth, and to put them out of the way of salvation, we are miserable in mind and frightened at heart. He is no kindly master to us, that fearsome prince; if we have not done something of evil we dare not afterwards come anywhere into his sight. Then he dispatches his servants from out of the darkness throughout the wide world, and bids them offer force if we are found on earth or discovered far or near, and that they should bind us and scourge us with torments in a welter of fire. If the mind of those steadfast in the truth and the heart of the saintly is not perverted by means of some blemish, we suffer the harshest and severest punishments, through a painful thrashing. Now you may understand for yourself in your own mind the truth that I was forcibly constrained to this audacious deed and persistently harassed to seek you out.'

IV

345   Then again the saintly woman questioned the enemy of men, the agent of evil and author of ancient sins, with these words:

347   'You shall further tell me, enemy of souls, how you, a creature engrossed in evil, most seriously injure those steadfast in truth through a lapse into sins.'

350   The devil, the faithless outcast, answered her and spoke these words:

352   'Blessed virgin, I shall reveal to you the beginning and onwards to the end of each of the evils I have accomplished – and not on just a few occasions – by sins' wounds, so that you may yourself appreciate that this is true, not false. I believed, and in my arrogant thinking counted it certain, that without difficulty and by my sole contriving I could turn you aside from salvation so that you renounced the King of heaven, Lord of victories, and bowed down to a baser being, and sacrificed to the author of sins. Thus I, in a shifting shape, pervert the mind of the man steadfast in truth. Where I find him buttressing up his spirit to the will of God I am instantly ready to induce in him multifarious lustings of the heart, savage thoughts and secret aberrations, by means of a series of delusions. I make delectable to him the pleasures of sinful things, the false infatuations of the heart, so that, addicted to his vices, he is soon obeying my promptings. So greatly do I fire him with sins that, inflamed, he ceases and impetuously walks off from prayer and cannot for long stay steadfast in the place of prayer, because of his infatuation with vices. Thus I bring loathly terror upon the one whose life and the light of whose faith I resent. If he is willing out of his heart's desire to obey my promptings and perpetrate sins, he shall afterwards die barren of pious virtues.

382   'But if I meet with a storm of darts any staunch soldier of the Lord, renowned for courage, who is unwilling to flee away far from the battle but, astute in his thinking, lifts up against me a targe, a holy shield and spiritual armour, and is not willing to fail God, but who, bold in prayer, makes a stand, steadfast amid the infantry, I have to retreat far away from there, humiliated and deprived of my pleasure, to bewail my sorrow in the clutch of smouldering fires because I could not by force of strength prevail in the fray, but, downcast, must seek out another, one less courageous among the ranks of battle, a baser soldier whom I can puff up with my leaven and hinder in the fray. Although he may spiritually attempt some good thing, I

am instantly ready to scrutinize his whole conscience, as to how his spirit is fortified within and its defence constructed. Through some injury I open the gate of the rampart, once the tower is penetrable and access opened, then with a fusillade of arrows I first dispatch embittered thoughts into his mind by use of various desires of the heart, so that it seems to him better to practise vices, the lusts of the flesh, than the praise of God. I am his tutor, eager that he should live by my practices, avowedly lapsed from the law of Christ, his mind gone astray and into my power within the pit of sins. I am more, and more assiduously, concerned for the destruction of the soul, of the spirit, than of the body which, in its grave here in this world, shall become a treat for the worm, buried in the ground.'

417   Then again the virgin spoke:

418   'Tell me, miserable sullied spirit, how you, a dispenser of darkness, enrolled yourself in the company of the unsullied? Long since, you perfidiously strove with Christ, stirred up strife and schemed against Holy God; for you hell pit was dug below, and there, plagued with anguish on account of your pride, you found a dwelling-place. I had expected that you would have been warier and less impetuous over such a contest with one steadfast in truth who, through the King of glory, has often withstood your will.'

429   Then the cursed and miserable monster answered her back:

430   'First tell me how you, emboldened by your deep resolve, became thus daring in battle beyond all womankind, that you have me utterly impotent, bound fast with fetters in this way? You placed your trust in your eternal God sitting in majesty, mankind's ordaining Lord, just as I found my hope upon my father, king of the denizens of hell. When I am sent against a man steadfast in truth, so that I might warp his mind into wicked deeds and his thought away from salvation, sometimes I am thwarted of my will and of my hope by resistance from the saintly man, just as I have come to grief in my mission here. I

came to know that for myself much too late. Now I, being an evil-doer, will long have to suffer humiliation over this. Therefore I beg you by the might of the Lord most high, by the grace of the King of the skies who suffered, Prince of the heavenly host, upon the rood-tree, pity me in my need so that I, miserable being, will not utterly perish, even though, rash and misguided in this way, I sought you out on my mission – in which I certainly did not anticipate for myself such a bad time as this.'

V

454   Then the radiantly beautiful woman, the candle of heaven, spoke words to the deceiver:

456   'You will have to confess more evil deeds, abject spirit of hell, before you may go from here, what great wicked act you have carried out by dark delusions, to the hurt of the children of men.'

460   The devil answered her:

461   'Now from your eloquence I can hear that, forced by these afflictions, I must of necessity declare my mind as you command me, and suffer the pain of punishment. The occasion is extremely violent, the ill-treatment excessive. I must suffer and submit to everything within your jurisdiction and discover every one of those black and evil deeds which I have over long duration contrived.

488   'Repeatedly I have deprived of sight and blinded with wicked thoughts a countless tally of men of the human race, and obscured the light of their eyes with a helm of mist by means of venomous darts in dark showers; and of some I have shattered the feet with vicious snares; and some I have dispatched into the furnace, into the fiery keep, so that the last was seen of their tracks. Some too I have so treated that their bodies spewed blood, so that they relinquished their life suddenly by the bursting of their blood-vessels. Some on a sea-journey were by my powers engulfed in the waters on their way upon

the ocean, beneath the dismal tide. Some I have consigned to the cross, so that they yielded up their life, blood-besmeared on the high gallows; some I have led on by my counsels and brought them into discord, so that suddenly, drunk with beer, they renewed old grievances; I have served them strife from out of the goblet, so that by resorting to swords within the wine hall, being stricken with wounds, they released their souls to flit doomed away from their body. Some, whom I have come across without the mark of God, uncaring and unblessed, I have boldly and cunningly killed by various kinds of death with my own hands. Even if I should sit a summer day's length, I cannot tell all the miseries which I have caused early and late by way of evil, ever since the sky was upraised and the constellations' course, and the earth was established and the first people, Adam and Eve – from whom I wrested life and so tutored them that they threw away the Lord's love, the eternal gift of grace, and their bright paradisal home: that was to become to both of them and to their children likewise for ever a misery, the foulest of criminal deeds.

505 'Why must I further recite my endless evil? I spawned it all; the bitter quarrels among the nations which have always befallen mankind, the people on earth, from the beginning of the world. There was none of them who dared lay hands on me as confidently as you, a saintly woman, now do; nor was there anyone on earth so courageous by virtue of divine power, not one of the patriarchs nor of the prophets. Albeit the God of hosts and King of glory showed them the spirit of wisdom and grace infinite, still I might have access to them. There was none of them who so boldly loaded me with shackles and trod me under with rebukes before now, when you overpowered and clung fast to my great strength which my father, foe of mankind, gave me, when he, my lord, commanded me journey from out of darkness because I had to make sins sweet to you. In this I have come to sorrow and grievous contest. After this painful retribution I shall have no cause to jubilate among my fellows over this mission, when, mournfully anxious, I have to render my account in that dismal home.'

530   Then the governor, rabid-hearted man, commanded Juliana
to be conducted out of the narrow cell, in saintly state of mind,
to a parley with the pagan at his judgment seat. She dragged the
devil along – she inspired within her breast, he fast in fetters;
she holy, he heathen. Then, cruelly anxious, he began to regret
his mission, to whine over his wounds and to lament his lot,
and he spoke these words:

529   'I beg you, my lady Juliana, for the sake of God's peace, not
to do me further insults and disgrace before these men, more
than you have already done when you overpowered the clever-
est one beneath the dungeon's darkness, the king of hell's
denizens in the fortress of the fiends, that is, our father, the evil
prince of mortal sin. Look, you have punished me with a
painful beating. I know for certain that neither early nor late
have I met any woman like you in the worldly kingdom, more
confident of purpose or more stubborn, among womankind. It
is clear to me that you have come to be blameless in every
respect and wise in spirit.'

553   Then the woman released him after his hard time, to go into
darkness in the black abyss, an enemy of souls into a perdition
of punishments. He was the more conscious, that tale-bearer of
evil, that he had to tell his peers, the ministers of torment, how it
had turned out for him on his mission. . .

*Between the present folios 73 and 74 a leaf has been lost from the MS.
The text resumes at the end of what is apparently a prayer spoken by
Juliana.*

VI

559   '. . . zealously once they praised him in the heights and his
holy works, and rightly they said that he alone through all
creation commanded every triumph, and eternal gift of
blessedness.'

563   Then came the angel of God gleaming with adornments and
thrust aside the fire and freed and protected the woman pure

from blemish and devoid of vices, and extinguished the deadly voracious flame where the saintly paragon of virgins was standing unharmed in the midst. That was a dilemma for the wealthy governor to suffer, as to whether for the world he could alter it. Dyed in his sins, he investigated how he might most painfully and by the worst torments devise her death.

573   The devil was not over-slow who prompted him to have wrought, by a strange craft and with belligerent howlings, an earthenware cauldron and to have it stacked about with logs of wood and timber. Then the ruffian directed that the earthenware cauldron should be filled with lead and then he ordered the hugest bonfire to be kindled, a pyre to be set alight. On every side it was surrounded by fire-brands: the bath bubbled with heat. Then he, swollen with fury, ordered her, devoid of vices and without guilt, to be thrust into the welter of the lead.

584   Then the fire was riven and scattered and the lead exploded wide, hot and deadly voracious. People were terrified and fear-stricken in the face of its onrush. Seventy-five in number of the heathen host were scorched up there by the blast of the fire: yet still the saint was standing with beauty unscarred. Not her hem nor her robe, neither hair nor skin were blemished by fire, neither body nor limbs. In the flame she stood, unharmed in any way, and spoke thanks for all to the Lord of lords.

594   Then the judge grew wild and savage-minded and began to tear his robe. He bared his teeth too and ground them. He grew crazed in his wits as a wild beast. Rabid-hearted, he stormed and abused the gods because they with their power could not withstand the will of a woman. The glorious maiden was resolute and unafraid, conscious of her strengths and of God's will. Then, anxious with despair, the judge commanded her, saintly in her purpose, to be killed by slash of the sword and the head to be cut off the elect of Christ. For him, that killing was no gain when he later came to know the consequence.

VII

607   For the saint, hope was renewed then, and the virgin's heart was greatly cheered when she heard the man devise that spiteful counsel, that for her it was to be the end of her days of strife, that her life was to be set free.

612   So he, one full of vices, commanded the pure and elect, the sinless, to be led to execution. Then suddenly an abject spirit from hell arrived and wailed a song of woe, wretched and miserable — the cursed creature whom she had previously snared and scourged with torments; full of anxious incantations, he cried out in front of the crowd:

619   'Now pay her back with evil because she mocked the might of our gods and utterly unmanned me so that I turned talebearer. See to it that she gets her unwelcome deserts through the weapon's wound; beleaguered by sin, take vengeance for old persecution. I remember the anguish, how in one night, secured in shackles, I endured an infinity of tortures and miseries and evil inordinate.'

627   Then the blessed Juliana looked towards the fulminating creature and listened to the hell-fiend crowing abuse. Then mankind's enemy scuttled off in retreat, to return into torments, and he spoke these words:

632   'Alas for me! I am ruined! Now there is a great probability that she will again shame wretched me with evil humiliations, just as she did to me before.'

635   Then she was conducted close to the border of the country and to the place where the cruel-minded people meant in their violent hostility to kill her. She then began to exhort the people and to encourage them from wicked deeds to worship and promised them grace and the way to heaven, and she spoke these words:

641   'Be mindful of him who is the joy of his warriors, the Majesty of heaven, the Hope of the saints and God of the celestial angels. Of this he is worthy, that the nations of men and all angelkind above in the skies should praise him, the Power supreme, where help is at hand everlastingly to eternity for him who shall obtain it. Therefore, dear people, I wish to teach you, in fulfilling the law, to make fast your house in case the winds should wreck it with sudden blasts; a strong wall shall more stoutly withstand the onslaughts of storms, the thoughts, of things vicious. In the tranquillity of love, in the light of faith, being resolute of purpose, make fast a foundation to the living rock. Hold in your hearts true belief and peace among you, and the holy mysteries with devotion of mind. Then the almighty Father will grant you grace when during troubles you have most need of help from the God of strength; for you yourselves are ignorant as to your departing hence and the ending of life. To me it seems prudent that you should maintain your guard, keeping watch against the clamour of battle, in case adversaries deny you the way to the city of heaven. Pray the Son of God that the King of angels, mankind's ordaining Lord and Giver of victories, be merciful to me. Peace be with you and true love for ever.'

669   Then her soul was dispatched from her body into lasting bliss by the stroke of a sword.

671   Then the wicked persecutor Eleusius, the craven-hearted, went to sea by ship with a band of warriors and for a long time tossed upon the flowing ocean along the swan-road. Death destroyed them all, the crew of men and himself along with them, before they had voyaged to land, by way of severe punishment. There the life of thirty of the warrior sort and four besides was exacted by the welter of the wave; deprived of comforts, destitute of hopes, they headed for hell. The thanes in that dark dwelling, the flock of retainers in that deep pit, had no reason to look expectantly to the overlord for the appointed treasures, or that they would receive upon the beer-bench rings and embossed gold in the wine-hall.

688   In different fashion was the body of the saint escorted by a
      great throng to the grave with songs of praise when, a great
      multitude, they brought it inside the city ramparts. Since then,
      with the passing of the years, God's praise has been exalted
      there among that nation with great splendour up to this day.

695   I have a great need, that the saint will afford me help when
      those dearest of all to me part, and the wedlocked pair sever
      their relationship, their great love. My soul must away from
      out of my body upon a journey – to where I myself do not know –
      in ignorance of its settling-place. From this one I must go seeking
      another with my former works and previous deeds.

703   C, Y and N (? mankind ? Cynewulf) will pass sorrowing
      away. The King, Giver of victories, will be wrathful when,
      stained with sins, terrified, E, W and U (? the sheep ? Cynewulf)
      await what he wills to decree them according to their deeds as
      reward for their life. L and F (? the body ? Cynewulf) will
      tremble and temporize, miserably anxious.

709   I remember all the hurt, the wounds of sins, which late or
      early I did myself in the world: this, weeping, I shall bewail
      with tears. Too tardy I was at the proper time in sooner feeling
      shame while spirit and body journeyed together in health upon
      the earth. I shall be in need of favours then, for the saint to
      intercede for me with the supreme King. My distress, my great
      anxiety of mind, forewarns me of this.

718   I pray each person of humankind who recites this poem that,
      diligent and magnanimous, he will remember me by name and
      pray the ordaining Lord that he, the Protector of the heavens,
      will afford me help, the Wielder of powers, upon that great
      day, the Father and the Spirit of consolation, in that perilous
      hour, the Judge of deeds, and the beloved Son, when the
      Trinity, majestically enthroned in oneness, throughout the
      radiant universe shall adjudge to humankind, to each man his
      reward according to his works.

729   Grant us, God of the hosts, Paragon of princes, that we may
find your face merciful in that momentous hour. Amen.

The Wanderer

[The Exeter Book, fol.76ᵇ–78ᵃ]

'It is very profitable for Christians to be often calling to mind the very
beginnings of Grace with their souls,' wrote John Bunyan (Author's
Preface to *Grace Abounding*, 1666). 'My dear children, call to mind
the former days, and years of ancient times: remember also your songs
in the night; and commune with your own hearts. Yea, look diligently,
and leave no corner therein unsearched, for there is treasure hid, even
the treasure of your first and second experience of the Grace of God
towards you.' Often such 'very beginnings' of grace are granted to
wanderers over the face of the earth, says the *Wan*-poet; and he leads
his audience through a retrospective account of the rational process by
which a man whom destiny or volition has set apart (like the dreamer
in *Pearl* or Will in *Piers Plowman*) has come, through grace, and by
empirical evaluation of the world through which he wanders, to a
redeeming insight: that beyond the ephemerality of earth's cities and
communities lie attainable stability and security with God in heaven.
Through grace he has first learned the despair-threatening lesson of
worldly mutability; through grace he has been saved from despair by a
consciousness of God's immutability, and given a sense of direction in
this world.

   Read in these terms, *Wan* is seen to involve a spiritual exercise of
ancient standing. As Bunyan himself notices, the wandering Israelites
were turned back to the Red Sea to remind them of their salvation by
God's grace (Numbers 14:25); and St Paul recalled before his judges
the encounter with grace by which he had been converted, for he
found it supported him to do so (Acts 22 and 24). St Augustine's
Confessions rendered exemplary to the whole Church the salutary
exercise of tracing the workings of grace in one's personal redemp-
tion; and after *Wan* follow many literary examples including major
poetical works such as *Piers Plowman* and *Pearl*, prose works such as
Pilgrim's Progress and *Grace Abounding*, and short lyric statements

such as that of the sinful seafarer turned minister of God, John Newton (1725–1807), whose hymn *Amazing Grace* shows the sentiments and central imagery collocated in *Wan* still holding together more than seven centuries on in English literary tradition.

Interpreting scriptural history in a way typical of the Christian Middle Ages, St Augustine of Hippo finds in the story of Cain and Abel the archetypal pattern of any individual's progress from worldly obsession to spiritual awareness. 'In regard to mankind,' he says (*CG*, Bk.XV, ch.1, p.413), 'I have made a division. On the one side are those who live according to man; on the other, those who live according to God. And I have said that, in a deeper sense, we may speak of two cities or two human societies, the destiny of the one being an eternal kingdom under God while the doom of the other is eternal punishment along with the devil... Now, the first man born of the two parents of the human race was Cain. He belonged to the city of man. The next born was Abel, and he was of the City of God. Notice here a parallel between the individual man and the whole race... As soon as human birth and death began the historical course of the two cities, the first to be born was a citizen of this world and only later came the one who was an alien in the city of men but at home in the City of God, a man predestined by grace and elected by grace. By grace an alien on earth, by grace he was a citizen of heaven... Now, it is recorded of Cain that he built a city, while Abel, as though he were merely a pilgrim on earth, built none. For, the true City of the saints is in heaven, though here on earth it produces citizens in whom it wanders as on a pilgrimage through time looking for the Kingdom of eternity.'

This progress we witness in *Wan*. The superbly voiced yearning for the lost splendour and fellowship of the perished community leaves no doubt of the intensity of the worldly attachment. Here, as in *Sfr*, the literary trappings of heroic society such as is celebrated in *Bwf* are imaginatively used – though not to depict mere nostalgia. Remembrance of the noble past gives temporal form to the inborn yearnings of the speaker's soul, and loss and yearning alike prove beneficial to the speaker, for they define the need of his thinking mind and his feeling heart for that which is – what the world even of heroes is not – immutable. 'Even the desire for the help of grace is itself the beginning of grace,' Augustine wrote (*Admonition and Grace*, tr. J. C. Murray, *Writings of Saint Augustine*, vol.IV, p.246 in *The Fathers of the Church*, vol.II, New York, 1950); and sure enough, by grace, the speaker having thus begun proceeds to a realization that immutability is to be found in the Creator himself, and there alone. Thus, and 'only with great effort', as Augustine remarks (CG, Bk.XI, ch.2, p.188), 'does a mind, which has contemplated both the material and spiritual creation of the universe and discovered the mutability of all things, soar to the unchangeable substance of God'.

In Augustinian thought, such clarification of the minds leads logically to an awareness of the peregrinatory nature of human existence on earth. So in *Wan*; it is clear that the wanderer will not find on earth the lord he needs, and the journey homewards to which his yearnings impel him is finally understood to be the journey of life towards death and eternity beyond – on which journey, in the poem usually taken as a companion piece, the seafarer is already embarked, and for which, in *Rsg*, the exile is preparing. Hearers of the poem, led vicariously through the experiencing of this rational process, are thus tutored – as Bede says Cædmon's audience was tutored by his didactic poetry (*HE*, Bk.IV, ch.24) – to share in its insights and so perhaps gain for themselves that gift of grace for which the exile prays in *Rsg*, for which Conscience cries at the end of *Piers Plowman* when he resolves to be a pilgrim, and in faithful reference to which *Wan* opens and closes.

'Often the man on his own experiences grace, the mercy of the ordaining Lord – even though for a long time, anxious of mind, he has to row laboriously upon the ice-cold sea over the watery way, to travel the paths of exile: fate is inexorable.'

6   A wanderer on earth, remembering hardships, the violent assaults of enemies, the extinction of loving family, spoke thus:

8   'Often I have had to bemoan my anxieties alone at each dawning. There is now not one living being to whom I dare plainly express my heart. I know, to be sure, that it is an excellent virtue in a man that he should bind fast his bosom and lock up the treasury of his thoughts, let him think as he wishes. A weary mind cannot resist fate, nor can rueful thought afford help. For this reason those caring for reputation often bind fast in their breast some sorrowful thing. So I, often wretchedly anxious, separated from my home, far from noble kinsfolk,

have had to fasten my heart with fetters ever since, years ago, the darkness of the earth enfolded my generous and loving lord, and I, despondent, travelled away, oppressed by wintry anxiety, over the ambit of the waves; full of sorrow I was seeking the hall of a treasure-giving lord where, whether far or near, I might find the one who would acknowledge my love in the mead-hall or would comfort me in my friendlessness and win me over with good things.

29   'He who tries it knows how cruel is grief as a companion to him who has few loved bosom friends. Him the paths of exile preoccupy, not coiled gold, the frozen precinct of the heart, not the splendour of the earth; he recalls the men of the hall and the gift-receiving ceremonial, and how in his youth his generous lord entertained him at the banquet. Happiness has perished utterly. He understands, therefore, who has to do without his beloved lord's guiding words for long.

39   'Often, when grief and sleep combined together enchain the wretched solitary man, it seems to him in his imagination that he is embracing and kissing his lord and laying hands and head on his knee, just as at times previously in days of old he enjoyed the gift-throne. Then the friendless man awakes again and sees before him tawny waves, sea-birds bathing, spreading their wings, rime falling and snow, mingled with hail.

49   'Then the heart's lacerations, sore in the wake of the loved ones, are the harder to bear. Sorrow is renewed. When the memory of kinsfolk passes through his imagination, the man greets his comrades with cheerful words, eagerly he watches them: they drift away again. The company of fleeting figures does not bring many familiar exclamations there. Anxiety is renewed in him who oft and again must drive his weary spirit on over the ambit of the waves.

58   'I cannot think, therefore, why in this world my heart does not grow dark, when I thoroughly contemplate the life of men – how swiftly they, brave warrior-thanes, have yielded up the

hall. Just so this middle-earth each and every day declines and decays.

64   'A man may not become wise, therefore, before he has had a deal of years in the world. A wise man must be patient; he must not be too passionate nor too impulsive of speech, nor too weak a warrior nor too reckless, nor too timorous nor too eager, nor too greedy for riches, and never too desirous of making a boast before he is fully aware: a man must wait before he utters a pledge until that person of bold spirit is fully aware which way his mind's thinking wants to turn. A prudent man must recognize how appalling it will be when all the wealth in this world stands waste – as even now randomly throughout this middle-earth walls are standing, wind-blown, rime-covered, the ramparts storm-beaten. The wine-halls are crumbling, the rulers are lying dead, deprived of pleasure, the whole proud company has fallen near the wall; some war snatched away and carried off along the onward road; one a bird bore away over the deep ocean; one the grey wolf dismembered in death; one a sad-faced man buried in a grave in the earth. Thus the Creator of men laid waste this earthly abode until, bereft of the sounds of the citizens' revelry, the ancient gigantic structures stood desolate.

88   'He who has sagely reflected upon this foundation and, wise at heart, deeply contemplates this dark life, often recalls a multitude of violent assaults, and utters these words:

92   ' "Where has gone the steed? Where has gone the man? Where has gone the giver of treasure? Where has gone the place of the banquets? Where are the pleasures of the hall? Alas, the gleaming chalice; alas, the armoured warrior; alas, the majesty of the prince! Truly, that time has passed away, has grown dark under the helm of night as though it had never been. Now there remains among the traces of those dear people a wall, remarkably high, painted with serpentine patterns. The might of ash spears has snatched away the men, the weapon greedy for carnage, notorious fate; and storms beat upon those heaps

of stones. A falling snowstorm fetters the earth, winter's howling. Then darkness comes; the shadow of night spreads gloom and sends from the north fierce hailstorms to the terror of men. The whole kingdom of earth is full of hardship; the dispensation of fate makes mutable the world below the heavens. Here wealth is ephemeral; here a friend is ephemeral; here man is ephemeral; here kinsman is ephemeral; all this foundation of earth will become desolate."

III   .'Thus the wise man spoke in his mind, and sat apart in thought. Worthy is he who retains his faith; a man must never too hastily express his anxieties from his heart, unless the man knows beforehand how to effect the cure with courage. It will be well for him who seeks grace, consolation from the Father in heaven, where for us all the immutable abides.'

The Gifts of Men

[The Exeter Book, fol.78ᵃ–80ᵃ]

'What words can tell,' asks Augustine, 'or what thought can conceive the reward which He will give at the last day, when He already has given so great a measure of His spirit for our consolation in this journey, in order that, in the midst of the adversities of this life, we may have such great trust in Him and love of Him whom we do not yet see? Moreover, He has granted to each of us the special graces [Romans 12:6] requisite for the upbuilding of His Church, so that we will do what He has indicated should be done, not only without complaint, but even with joy.' (CI, Bk.I, ch.15, p.38).

The editorial title of this poem properly stresses the poet's theme of grace abounding: 'It is God's gift, not a reward for work done' (Ephesians 2:9). But it has been persuasively argued (J. E. Cross, 'The OE poetic theme of the gifts of men', Neophilologus 46, 1962) that its topic of human gifts relates the poem to Matthew 25:14–20, the parable of the talents, interpreted in the manner of Gregory's Homilia XIX in Evangelia (PL, Tom. LXXVI) where the talent given to the third servant by the 'man travelling into a far country' (Christ returning to heaven after his ministry) is *intellectus* (see *Chr II*, 659–86). For wasting the talent the 'unprofitable servant' will be cast into outer darkness when the lord returns (Judgment Day). The gospel's unedifying rationale of usury, though well laundered by Gregory, is not the AS poet's concern; rather, the classifying and cataloguing of human talents provide his rationale, and the inevitable reiteration of formulas provides his rhetorical structure. Though not all the talents listed are in fact intellectual in a modern sense, *GfM*, like various other OE poems (*Chr II*, *FtM*, *Mxm*, *Wds*, *Bwf*), shows the Anglo-Saxons drawing from their concept of the Deity endorsement for their high esteem of human intelligence, skills and crafts, which make individuals of humankind and which supply the multifarious needs of human community.

Many and obvious are the fresh acts of grace in the world, which soul-endowed beings experience in their understanding, according as the God of the multitudes, the ordaining Lord strong in his powers, apportions and assigns to people his special grace and distributes abroad his own riches, of which each member of the community may receive a share. There is no one on earth so poorly off nor so ill-fortuned, nor so shallow of purpose nor so lethargic of purpose, that the wise Giver of grace will disendow him entirely of skills of mind or of deeds of strength, in understanding or in spoken utterances – lest he should come to despair of all the things which he had achieved in this worldly existence, and of every act of grace. Never does God decree that anyone should become so wretched. But nor again shall anyone through his strength of wisdom advance in the popular glory of this life to such an extent that the peoples' Guardian by his holy grace will send him here wise thoughts and worldly skills and allow them all to be under one man's control; lest out of arrogance, being replete with heavenly favours, he turns from moderation, an overbearing man in his pride, and thereafter neglects the more ill-fortuned. Instead, he who has the power of decree diversely shares out the skills embodied in humans to earth's inhabitants throughout the world.

30   One he lends possessions here on earth, worldly treasures. One is unsuccessful, an ill-fortuned man, but yet he is skilful in the arts of the mind. One more amply receives physical strength. One is handsome and good-looking in figure. One is a poet gifted with songs. One is ready of speech. One is a hunter in the chasing of mettlesome beasts. One is favourite to a worldly-powerful man. One is hardy in warfare, a man skilled in fighting, when shields resound. One has ability to resolve upon public policy in the council of the wise where many knowledgeable men are in assembly. One has the artistic ability to plan the construction of every sort of lofty building – his hand is trained, experienced and controlled – and to erect a hall; he knows how to truss the spacious edifice securely against sudden collapses.

49   One has ability to play the harp with his hands; he has the art of dexterous flourishes upon the singing wood. One is good at running, one a sharp shooter, one athletic, one swift on land, fleet of foot. One steers a ship on the tawny wave and as fleet's pilot knows the sea-road across the wide ocean, when with brisk vigour intrepid seamen ply their oars by the gunnel. One is good at swimming. One is subtly skilled in gold and gems when a lord over people commands him embellish jewels to be objects of renown for him. One, an ingenious smith, can make many weapons for use in war when he forges helmet or hip-sword for human combat, or battle-corselet, shining blade or shield's disc, and can weld them firm against the spear's flight.

67   One is pious and charitable and virtuous in his morals. One is a servant appointed within the mead-hall. One is discerning over a horse and experienced in equestrian skills. One, self-disciplined, suffers in patience what he needs must. One is competent in giving judgments when men of the community are deliberating a resolution. One is quick with the dice. One is knowledgeable in the tasting of wine, a good keeper of the beer. One is a builder excellent in putting up a house. One is a warlord, a bold leader of armies. One is a public councillor. One is a thane with his prince, braver of purpose at time of

need. One has patience and a persevering spirit. One is a fowler, skilled with the hawk. One is dashing on horseback. One is very agile and has ingenious tricks, a talent for amusing performances in front of people; he is light and supple of limb. One is seductive and has a temperament and speech agreeable to people. One eagerly embraces in his heart the soul's needs here and chooses for himself the loving-kindness of the Lord above all earthly wealth. One is brave-hearted in struggling with the devil; he is ever alert in the fight against sins. One has skill in many of the offices of the church and can loudly extol the Lord of life in songs of praise; he has a high clear voice. One is wise from books and thoroughly competent in his teachings. One is dexterous in writing down words in their literal form.

97   There is now no one man on earth so ingenious of mind nor so enhanced with strength that all these things would ever be furnished for him alone, lest vainglory should harm him, or his heart be puffed up because of the renown if he, alone over all people, has beauty and wisdom and the glory of achievements. But in various ways he restrains mankind from vainglory and grants his grace: to one in virtues, to one in skills, to one in beauty, to one in warfaring; to one man he gives a meek heart and a virtuous mind and one is loyal to a master.

110   Thus worthily the Lord sows abroad his benefits. May he ever have honour for this and lightsome praise, who gives us this life, and proves to men his merciful heart.

Precepts

[The Exeter Book, fol.80ᵃ–81ᵃ]

94 verse lines. The poem begins 'Thus a sage father taught his son' and moves into direct speech comprised of ten formal utterances each embracing a large number of precepts drawn from secular and religious wisdom and morality. The values expressed often interestingly

gloss conduct described in other poems. *Prc* belongs within the substantial body of gnomic and proverbial wisdom-poetry in OE: see headnotes to *Mxm I* and *Mxm II*.

The Seafarer

[The Exeter Book, fol.81ᵇ–83ᵃ]

'A stranger here as all my fathers were/That went before, I wander to and fro./From earth to heaven is my pilgrimage,/A tedious way for flesh and blood to go./O Thou, that art the way, pity the blind,/And teach me how I may thy dwelling find.' (John Amner, *Sacred Hymns*, 1615). Pilgrimage literature in English is extensive and widely varied in form as in date; but among the very earliest lyrical collocations of its characterizing sentiments and images is *Sfr*. If *Wan* portrays the wise man's reasoned rejection of this mutable world, *Sfr* suggests itself as the logical sequel: a positive prescription, though partly in metaphorical terms, of the frame of mind in which a person so enlightened may thereafter safely negotiate this life and reach the immutable. Indeed, though *Sfr* is separated by two poems from *Wan* in the Exeter Book, a justification for linking them, as literary scholarship has habitually done, may be found in the concluding hortatory lines of *Sfr*: 'Let us consider where we have a home, and then think how we may get there.' The first proposition may be regarded as the thesis of *Wan* (see the headnotes to *Wan*), the second as that of *Sfr*.

   An ultimate source of this doctrine of self-alienation from the world is St Paul's accommodation of the patriarchal families of the old covenant within the scheme of salvation: 'All these persons [Abel, Enoch, Noah, Abraham, Isaac, Jacob, Sarah, Moses – see *Gen* and *Exo* and their headnotes] died in faith. They were not yet in possession of the things promised, but had seen them far ahead and hailed them, and confessed themselves no more than strangers [Latin Vulgate: *peregrini*, 'pilgrims'] or passing travellers on earth. Those who use such language show plainly that they are looking for a country of their own. If their hearts had been in the country they had left, they could have found opportunity to return. Instead, we find them longing for a better country – I mean, the heavenly one. That is why God is not

ashamed to be called their God; for he has a city ready for them.'
(Hebrews 11:13–16.)

Perhaps as familiar, at least to educated Anglo-Saxons, was St
Augustine's development of this topic – a development to which this
poem may seem specifically indebted. Discussing man's proper rela-
tionship with the world, Augustine draws a distinction between
'enjoying' and 'using': 'To enjoy anything means to cling to it with
affection for its own sake. To use a thing is to employ what we have
received for our use to obtain what we want, provided that it is right
for us to want it. . . Suppose, then, that we were travellers in a foreign
land, who could not live in contentment except in our own native
country, and if, unhappy because of that travelling abroad and desir-
ous of ending our wretchedness, we planned to return home, it would
be necessary to use some means of transportation, either by land or
sea, to enable us to reach the land we were to enjoy. But, if the
pleasantness of the journey and the very movement of the vehicles
were to delight us and turn us aside to enjoy the things which we
ought, instead, merely to use, and were to confuse us by false pleasure,
we would be unwilling to end our journey quickly and would be
alienated from the land whose pleasantness would make us really
happy. Just so, wanderers from God on the road of this mortal life, if
we wish to return to our native country where we can be happy, we
must use this world, and not enjoy it, so that the "invisible attributes"
of God may be clearly seen, "being understood through the things that
are made," [Augustine echoes Romans 1:20] that is, that through
what is corporeal and temporal we may comprehend the eternal and
spiritual.' (CI, Bk.I, ch.4, pp.29–30.) The two alternatives of enjoying
and using, Augustine elsewhere proposes, are epitomized in Cain and
Abel – and they characterize the two main divisions in humanity ever
since. Furthermore, the two alternatives relate to the two cities – of
men and of God – to which the two divisions of humanity commit
themselves, choosing either to cleave to the city of men into which all
humanity is born, or to make themselves aliens in the city of men and
become members of the City of God in exile. 'It is recorded of Cain
that he built a city [Genesis 4:17], while Abel, as though he were
merely a pilgrim on earth, built none. For the true City of the saints is
in heaven, though here on earth it produces citizens in whom it
wanders as on a pilgrimage through time looking for the Kingdom of
eternity.' (CG, Bk.XV, ch.1, pp.414–15; see also the headnotes to
Wan.)

If this Pauline-Augustinian thought is indeed the philosophical matrix of *Sfr*, the poem takes its place in a substantial body of AS literature, prose and verse, utilizing elements of the topic of the pilgrimage of life and sharing its imagery: they include the tenth Blickling Homily; Ælfric's Sermon on Mid-Lent Sunday; the ending of Cynewulf's *Chr II*; parts of *Exo*; *Glc A*, 790–818; *XSt*, 209–23 and 279–314; *Glc B*, 819–77; *Gen*, 1049 following; *Dan*, 598 following; *Jud*, 15 following; and *Advent Lyric 3* (*Chr I*). The poet's patristic distaste for the city of men and its archetypal citizen, *wlonc and wingal*, 'arrogant and wanton with wine', anticipates Milton's: 'In courts and palaces he [Belial] also reigns/And in luxurious cities, where the noise/Of riot ascends above their loftiest tow'rs,/And injury and outrage; and when night/Darkens the streets, then wander forth the sons/Of Belial, flown with insolence and wine./Witness the streets of Sodom. . .' (*Paradise Lost*, Bk.I, 497–503). Among the *Sfr*-poet's many successors in the literary treatment of the topic of life as a pilgrimage are Langland, Chaucer and Bunyan.

To recognize that the *Sfr*-poet is working within an established Christian metaphor is surely in no way to derogate from the absolute quality and power of the poetry in the seafaring section, which stands among the finest sea-poetry in the language. Rather, recognition of the poet's metaphorical dimension, and the location of his thought within the complex Augustinian rationale of the worldly experience, greatly enhance the *intellectual* suggestiveness of his poem. The homiletic section, regarded by earlier editors as spurious, is in effect a plain exposition of what has first been presented as an enigma – a characteristic AS riddling exercise which challenges the mind by paradox and by signalled ambivalence to seek a correct solution veiled in ambiguous statement, and thus to seek the truth veiled in the metaphor and the spiritual and eternal veiled in the corporeal and temporal. The concept of 'travelling or sailing to our own country' is not literally intended, Augustine reminds his readers (*CI*, Bk.I, ch.10, p.34). It is a metaphor for a process of cleansing the mind, dulled by carnal grossness, 'in order that it may be able to look upon that light [of Truth, God] and cling to it when it has seen it. . . We are not brought any closer to Him who is everywhere by moving from place to place, but by a holy desire and lofty morals.'

The prescriptive coda – amputated by some editors because of textual uncertainties, despite its manifest integrality with the poem's thesis – contains wisdom which seems to be drawn from some collection of maxims such as, in the Scriptures, Ecclesiasticus 2:1–7, upon which the following interpretation is based; but it is worth also noting Augustine's prescriptions to the pilgrim citizens of God on self-discipline and on their duties towards one another, based on such texts as 1 Thessalonians 5:14–15, Ephesians 4:26 and Matthew 18:15 (CG, Bk.XV, ch.6, pp.422–4).

I can tell the true riddle of my own self, and speak of my experiences – how I have often suffered times of hardship in days of toil, how I have endured cruel anxiety at heart and experienced many anxious lodging-places afloat, and the terrible surging of the waves. There the hazardous night-watch has often found me at the ship's prow when it is jostling along the cliffs. My feet were pinched by the cold, shackled by the frost in cold chains, whilst anxieties sighed hot about my heart. Hunger tore from within at the mind of one wearied by the ocean. This that man does not understand who is most agreeably suited on land – how I, wretchedly anxious, have for years lived on the ice-cold sea in the ways of the sojourner, bereft of kinsfolk, hung about by ice-spikes; hail pelted in showers. There I heard nothing but the raging of the sea, the ice-cold wave. Sometimes I would take the song of the swan as my entertainment, the cry of the gannet and the call of the curlew in place of human laughter, the sea-mew's singing in place of the mead-drinking. There storms would pound the rocky cliffs whilst the tern, icy-winged, answered them; very often the sea-eagle would screech, wings dappled with spray. No protective kinsman could comfort the inadequate soul.

27 He, therefore, who has experienced life's pleasure in cities, and few perilous journeys, insolent and flown with wine, little credits how I, weary, have often had to remain on the ocean path. The shadow of night would spread gloom; it would snow from the north, rime-frost would bind the ground; hail, coldest of grains, would fall upon the earth.

33 Now, therefore, the thoughts of my heart are in conflict as to whether I for my part should explore the deep currents and the

surging of the salty waves – my mind's desire time and time again urges the soul to set out, so that I may find my way to the land of strangers far away from here – for there is no one on earth so confident of temperament, nor so generous of his gifts, nor so bold in his youth, nor so courageous in his deeds, nor his lord so gracious to him, that he never worries about his seafaring, as to what the Lord will send him; he will have no thought for the harp, nor for the ring-receiving ceremonial, nor for the pleasure of a woman nor for trust in that which is of the world, nor for anything else, but only for the surging of the waves – and yet he who aspires to the ocean always has the yearning.

48   The woodlands take on blossoms, the cities grow more lovely, the meadows become beautiful, the world hastens onwards: all these urge anyone eager of mind and of spirit, who thus longs to travel far upon the ocean paths, to the journey. The cuckoo too serves warning by its mournful cry; summer's herald sings and foretells cruel distress at heart. That man, the fellow blessed with affluence, does not understand this – what those individuals endure who follow the ways of alienation to their furthest extent.

58   Now, therefore, my thought roams beyond the confines of my heart; my mind roams widely with the ocean tide over the whale's home, over earth's expanses, and comes back to me avid and covetous; the lone flier calls and urges the spirit irresistibly along the whale-path over the waters of oceans, because for me the pleasures of the Lord are more enkindling than this dead life, this ephemeral life on land. I do not believe that material riches will last eternally for him. One of three things will ever become a matter of uncertainty for any man before his last day: ill-health or old age or the sword's hostile violence will crush the life from the doomed man in his heedlessness.

72   For every man, therefore, praise from the living, speaking out afterwards, is the best of epitaphs: that, before he has to be on his way, he accomplishes gains against the malice of fiends,

brave deeds in the devil's despite, so that the sons of men may afterwards extol him, and his praise may endure for ever and ever among the angels, and the splendour of his eternal life and his pleasure endure among the celestial hosts.

80   The days have been slipping away, and all the pomps of the kingdom of earth. There are not now kings nor emperors nor gold-giving lords like those that used once to be, when they performed the greatest deeds of glory among themselves and lived in most noble renown. This whole company has perished; the pleasures have slipped away. The weaker remain and occupy the world; in toil they use it. Splendour had been humbled. Earth's nobility ages and grows sear just as each man now does throughout the middle-earth. Old age advances upon him, his face grows pallid, grey-haired he mourns: he is conscious that his former friends, the sons of princes, have been committed to the earth. Then, when life fails him, his body will be unable to taste sweetness or feel pain or stir a hand or think with the mind. Although a brother may wish to strew the grave with gold for his kinsman, to heap up by the dead man's side various treasures that he would like to go with him, the gold he hides in advance while he lives here cannot be of help to the soul which is full of sins, in the face of God's awesomeness.

103   Great is the awesomeness of the ordaining Lord, for this world will pass away; but he made stable the solid foundations, the earth's surfaces and the sky above. Foolish is he who does not fear his Lord: death will come upon him unpremeditated. Blessed is he who lives in humility: to him will come grace from the heavens. The ordaining Lord will make stable his heart, because he trusts in his might. A man must steer a wilful heart and keep it fixed upon stable points; and, worthy of men's trust and pure in his ways, each man must conduct himself with moderation through happiness and through adversity, in joy and in affliction, even if the Lord wills to prove him, permeated by fire, or assay, smelted in the flame, the friend he has made. Fate is stronger, the ordaining Lord mightier, than the mind of any man.

117   Let us consider where we may have a home, and then think how we may get there and how we may henceforth also strive so that we might arrive in everlasting blessedness, where there is life originating in the Lord's love, and hope, in the heavens.

122   Thanks be to the Holy One, that he has made us worthy, the Prince of glory, everlasting Lord, through all time. Amen.

Vainglory

[The Exeter Book, fol.83ᵃ–84ᵇ]

84 lines. The poem begins 'Lo! a sage counsellor in days long gone, a wise informant, told me many special and remarkable things' (see the note on *OrW*), and develops into a lengthy gloss on the kind of man who stands for what the seafarer rejects (*Sfr*) – the kind of city-dweller who sits arrogant and drunk at his banquet, trusting in his present affluence (see the note on *Rim*), the type of Holofernes (*Jud*), Nebuchadnezzar (*Dan*) and certain figures in *Bwf*, the type of Cain as he is depicted, enthroned, in the illustration on p.57 of Junius 11. This is the antitype of the man who lives in humility and as an exile in this transitory world (*Sfr*, *Rsg*) so as to ensure immutable happiness in eternity, in the City of God.

The illustrations on fol.66ᵇ of the early eleventh-century psalter, London, British Library, Harley 603, furnish images matching these poetically stated concepts (Vulgate Ps.126, *NEB* Ps.127: 'Unless the Lord builds the house, its builders will have toiled in vain.').

Widsith

[The Exeter Book, fol.84^b–87^a]

The songs of the Germanic peoples of his day, Tacitus asserts (*Germania*, ch.3), were their sole species of recorded history; and there can be little doubt that for their descendants, the AS migrants to Britain, *Wds* or poems like it served this important function of preserving in mnemonic form legends enshrining much of their cultural identity and collective ethic. Accordingly, *Wds* is probably one of the longest-lived poems in the AS corpus, originating perhaps as early as the seventh century. It is surely a poets' poem, which may account for its long life and MS preservation. It rehearses a repertory of heroic themes which a professional poet presumably ought to command; it makes high claims for the role and dues of the poet in any civilized society; and the speaker is himself a poet – a symbolic poet who has travelled all the known world and the near and far reaches of history as no real man could have done in one lifespan.

Most of the names are now without signification. But Roman history tells of Eormanric, the fourth-century ruler of the Ostrogoths who is also mentioned in *Deo* and *Bwf*, and of Ætla (Attila), the notorious Hun; and both of these figure elsewhere in Germanic legend, from the Icelandic story of the Volsungs through the *Nibelungenlied* to Wagner's nineteenth-century operatic treatment of this cycle. We may note too the poet's special knowledge of Danish history, shown first in his complimentary association of Alewih the Dane with Offa, ruler of the continental Angles (Danish sources too link the origins of the Danes and the English, who were for centuries neighbours with a common frontier), and then in his allusion to the strife between Hrothgar, Hrothulf and Ingeld which is more amply treated in *Bwf*. The eulogy of Offa as founder of the territorial frontiers of the continental Angles may hint that *Wds* belongs in Mercian tradition, even that it may have been devised in praise of the eighth-century Offa, king of Mercia, descendant of the continental Offa and founder of the great Mercian dyke. The Graeco-Roman and Middle Eastern presence in the lists of nations may be considered in the light of the iconographic programme on the Franks Casket, generally held to be a seventh-century Northumbrian reliquary, now in the British Museum. In this programme, the three great histories known to the Christianized Anglo-Saxons – their own Germanic, and the adoptive Roman and Hebrew – are implied to converge, as Augustine declared universal history to converge, upon the Incarnation (represented on the casket by the Epiphany). So the *Wds* reference to Medes, Persians, Assyrians and Hebrews (who all belong, incidentally, in the story of *Jud*) is more than mere monkish interpolation: it implies acceptance of a Christian view of history such as had been definitively argued by Augustine's contemporary, the fifth-century Orosius, whose *Universal History* was translated into AS and supplemented by king Alfred in the ninth century.

Widsith spoke forth, and unlocked the treasury of his words, he who had travelled through most of the peoples, nations and tribes upon the earth; many a time on the floor of the hall he had received some commemorative treasure. His family were sprung from the Myrgingas, and he had in the first instance gone with Ealhhild, the beloved weaver of peace, from the east out of Anglen to the home of the king of the glorious Goths, Eormanric, the cruel troth-breaker. He began then to say many things.

9   'I have heard tell about many men ruling over nations. Every prince ought to live ethically – one man governing the land in succession to the other – who presumes to receive its princely throne. Hwala was at one time the noblest of these, and Alexander the most powerful of all mankind and he prospered most of those of whom I have heard tell throughout the earth.

18   'Attila ruled the Huns, Eormanric the Goths, Becca the Baningas, Gifica the Burgundians. Caesar ruled the Greeks and Cælic the Finns, Hagena the Holmrygas, and Heoden the Glommas. Witta ruled the Swabians, Wade the Hælsingas, Meaca the Myrgingas, Mearchealf the Hundingas. Theodoric ruled the Franks, Thyle the Rondingas, Breoca the Brondingas, Billing the Wernas. Oswine ruled the Eowan and Gefwolf the Jutes; Finn son of Folcwalda the tribe of the Frisians. Sigehere ruled the Sea-Danes for a very long while, Hnæf the Hocingas, Helm the Wulfingas, Wald the Woingas, Wod the Thuringians,

Sæferth the Secgan, Ongendtheow the Swedes, Sceafthere the Ymbras, Sceafa the Longbeardan, Hun the Hætwere and Holen the Wrosnas. The king of the Herefaran was called Hringweald.

35 'Offa ruled Anglen, Alewih the Danes, who was the most spirited of all those people; he did not, however, accomplish heroic achievements beyond those of Offa, for of these men Offa, being in his youth, first conquered the greatest of king-doms. No one contemporary with him made a greater heroic achievement in battle. With his lone sword he defined a frontier against the Myrgingas at Fifeldor. From then on the Angles and the Swabians maintained it as Offa had conquered it.

45 'Hrothwulf and Hrothgar, nephew and uncle, kept peace together for a very long while, after they had driven off the tribe of the Wicingas and humiliated the vanguard of Ingeld and cut down the host of the Heathobardan at Heorot.

50 'Thus I journeyed through many foreign lands throughout this spacious earth. Good and evil I experienced there; sepa-rated from family, distant from noble kinsmen, I served far and wide. I can sing, therefore, and tell a tale, and mention before the assemblage in the mead-hall how royal benefactors have been generously kind to me.

57 'I have been with the Huns and with the glorious Goths, with the Swedes and with the Geats and with the South-Danes. I have been with the Wendlas and with the Wærnas and with the Wicingas. I have been with the Gefthas and with the Wends and with the Gefflegas. I have been with the Angles and with the Swabians and with the Ænenas. I have been with the Saxons and with the Secgan and with the Sweordweras. I have been with the Hronas and with the Danes and with the Heath-oremas. I have been with the Thuringians and with the Throwendas and with the Burgundians where I received a collar: Guthhere gave me that gleaming treasure in reward for a song. He was no indifferent king.

68   'I have been with the Franks and with the Frisians and with
the Frumtingas. I have been with the Rugas and with the
Glommas and with the Romans. I have also been in Italy with
Ælfwine, son of Eadwine, who, I have heard, had the prompt-
est hand among mankind in achieving praise, and a heart quite
unniggardly in giving out rings and gleaming collars.

75   'I have been with the Saracens and with the Seringas. I have
been with the Greeks and with the Finns and with Caesar who
held sway over festive cities, over riches and desirable things
and over the empire of the Romans.

79   'I have been with the Scots and with the Picts and with the
Scridefinnas. I have been with the Lidwicingas and with the
Leonas and with the Longbeardan, with the Hæthnas and with
the Hælethas and with the Hundingas. I have been with the
Israelites and with the Assyrians, with the Hebrews and with
the Indians and with the Egyptians. I have been with the Medes
and with the Persians and with the Myrgingas and the Mofdin-
gas and the Myrgingas again and with the Amothingas. I have
been with the East-Thuringians and with the Eolas and with
the Iste and the Idumingas.

88   'And I was with Eormanric for quite a while, where the king
of the Goths was graciously kind to me. He, the ruler of the
city-dwellers, gave me a collar in which there was six hundred
coins' worth of pure gold, counted by shillings. This I gave to
Eadgils, my lord and protector, to keep when I arrived home as
a reward to the beloved man because he, the lord of the
Myrgingas, gave me land, the ancestral home of my father. And
then Ealhhild, Eadwine's daughter, the queen of the people,
gave me another. Her praise extended through many lands,
whenever I was to say in song where below the sky I best knew
a queen ornate with gold, bestowing gifts. Whenever Scilling
and I with clear eloquence upraised a song before our victori-
ous lord and my voice rang out melodiously and loud to the
lyre, then many people high-mettled of mind, those who were
well informed, have said they never heard better singing.

109   'From there I travelled throughout the whole land of the Goths. I constantly visited the best of comrades, who were the company of Eormanric's household. I visited Hethca and Beadeca and the Herelingas. I visited Emerca and Fridla and Eastgota the wise and good, father of Unwen. I visited Secca and Becca, Seafola and Theodric, Heathoric and Sifeca, Hlithe and Incgentheow. I visited Eadwine and Elsa, Ægelmund and Hungar and the high-mettled nation of the Withmyrgingas. I visited Wulfhere and Wyrmhere; not very often was there respite from warfare there, when the army of the Goths with tough swords had to defend their ancient ancestral seat near the Vistula Forest against the people of Attila.

123   'I visited Rædhere and Rondhere, Rumstan and Gislhere, Withergield and Freotheric, Wudga and Hama: these were not the worst of comrades even though I should name them last. Very often the singing spear flew whining out of that troop against a hostile nation; there the adventurers Wudga and Hama ruled over men and women with coiled gold.

131   'I have always found it to be so in my journeying, that the man most acceptable to the country's inhabitants is the one to whom God gives the government of the people to uphold for the time that he lives here.'

135   So the people's entertainers go wandering fatedly through many lands; they declare their need and speak words of thanks. Always, whether south or north, they will meet someone discerning of songs and unniggardly of gifts who desires to exalt his repute and sustain his heroic standing until everything passes away, light and life together. This man deserves glory; he will keep his lofty and secure renown here below the heavens.

The Fortunes of Men

[The Exeter Book, fol.87ᵃ–88ᵇ]

Another of the wisdom-poems cataloguing aspects of human experience of life and death (cp. *FAp*, *GfM*, *Mxm*, *Deo*, *Wan*), *FtM* closely matches *GfM* in exalting the grace of God, but lays more emphasis, like *Deo*, on confident resignation, whatever one's lot, to an Ordainer whose wisdom and benevolence are trustworthy. The poem is ennobled by a certain human poignancy, felt for the parents who lovingly nurture their child, wishing for it weal but often sharing at last in its woe. This is the note of human compassion, mitigating the sometimes over-austere and world-contemptuous doctrines of AS Christian poetry, which rings authentically in other OE poems too – for example in the lay of the last survivor (*Bwf* 2233–70), in Hrothgar's parting from Beowulf (1840–87) or his lament for Æschere (1321–9), in *Sfr* and in *WlE* – and which is evident in later AS pictorial and plastic art.

It very often happens through God's powers that man and woman bring forth a child by birth into the world, and clothe him in colours and curb him and teach him until the time comes and it happens with the passing of the years that the young and lively limbs and members are mature. Thus his father and mother lead him along and guide his footsteps and provide for him and clothe him – but only God knows what the years will bring him as he grows up.

10   To one it happens that the concluding letter of his life tragically befalls the unfortunate in his youthful prime. Him the wolf, the grizzled haunter of the wasteland, shall devour; then his mother will mourn his going hence. Such things are not man's to control.

15   Famine shall make one its prey; one wild weather shall sweep away; one the spear shall spill; one warfare shall destroy. One will have to endure a life deprived of his eyes' light and to grope about with his hands; one, lame in a foot, infirm from

lesions of the sinew, will have to bewail his painful affliction and, oppressed in mind, mourn his destiny. From a tall tree in the forest one shall tumble – wingless, and yet he is in flight – and flails in the air until there is no further branch of the tree and then he falls to its foot unconscious; robbed of his soul he tumbles to the ground, and his spirit is on its way.

27   One must needs travel on foot in ways remote and carry his provisions with him and tread the spray-flung track and the dangerous territory of alien peoples. He has few surviving providers; everywhere the friendless man is disliked because of his misfortunes.

33   One shall ride the high gallows and upon his death hang until his soul's treasury, his bloody bone-framed body, disintegrates. There the raven black of plumage will pluck out the sight from his head and shred the soulless corpse – and he cannot fend off with his hands the loathsome bird of prey from its evil intent. His life is fled and, deprived of his senses, beyond hope of survival, he suffers his lot, pallid upon the beam, enveloped in the mist of death. His name is damned.

43   One fire shall do to death on the pyre; greedy flame shall consume the doomed man, red fierce incandescence, where severance from life comes quickly, and the woman weeps who sees the flames engulf her child.

48   From one, an irascible ale-swiller, a man full of wine, a sword's edge will thrust out the life upon the mead-bench; previous to that, his words will be too hasty. One, through the steward's ministration during beer-drinking, shall turn into a man made intemperate by mead; then he will know no moderation, to measure his mouth with his mind, but he shall end his existence quite wretchedly and, shorn of his pleasures, suffer egregious ruin; and men will brand him a suicide and tell yarns of the tippling of the man made intemperate by mead.

58   One, through God's powers, shall expend all his misfortune during his youth, and in his maturity he shall become prosper-

ous again and live out days of happiness and indulge in his wealth, in treasures and the mead-flagon, in his family's midst, as far as any person may keep possession of them continually.

64   Thus for all across earth's face the mighty Lord deals out, decrees, and allots and controls their destinies: to one wealth, to one his share of miseries, to one gladness in youth, to one glory in war and battle mastered, to one skill in throwing or shooting and illustrious fame, to one cunning at the dice-game and deftness at the chequered board. Some become wise scholars. To one amazing talents are furnished as a craftsman in gold; he will be regularly tempering and finely ornamenting the mail-coat of a mighty king and he will bestow broad lands upon him in reward, which he will willingly accept.

76   One shall amuse men at their gathering and cheer those sitting at beer on the benches; there will be great revelry among the drinkers there. One shall sit with a lyre at his lord's feet, receive his fee and smartly pluck the strings and make the picking plectrum — briskly it skips on the soundbox — set free their voice.

85   One shall train the proud wild bird, the hawk, to his hand, until the savage bird becomes a thing of delight. He puts jesses upon it and thus feeds it, whose pride is in its wings, in fetters, and gives the swift flier little scraps to eat until the unfriendly bird becomes subservient to his provider in livery and in actions, and accustomed to the young man's hand.

93   Thus with artistry has the Saviour of the multitudes throughout the world shaped and appointed and guided the destiny of every one of humankind on earth. Therefore let everyone now utter thanks to him for all that he for his mercies' sake ordains for men.

Maxims I

[The Exeter Book, fol.88^b–92^b]

'Discerning people must exchange maxims,' says the poet, and challenges his audience to probe his wisdom with their own intelligence, to bring to bear their own understanding of things, to reflect in their hearts upon his words, and so to reach fullest insight into his meaning. 'Common cause the wise must achieve with the wise.' The context in which the *Mxm* appear in the Exeter Book, in close adjacence to *GfM*, *FtM*, *Wds*, *OrW*, *Physiologus* and the *Rdl*, indicates how attractive to the AS mind was the rehearsal and propagation of received wisdom and knowledge in formulaic utterances, and the exercise of intelligence, often of ingenuity, in probing through the surface form of things to their inner construct and in perceiving in circumstantial detail of events the general precept. Broadly speaking, all this lore is anthropocentric: knowledge – of the phenomena and creatures of the physical world, as of kings and communities of history and the accrued experience of the human condition – is chiefly prized in so far as it forms a pattern according to which the discerning individual may rough-hew the ends of his own life.

Wisdom-poetry of this kind was of course known to the Anglo-Saxons through the Scriptures, both canonical and apocryphal; but it is very probable that the Anglo-Saxons, like the Celtic peoples on their western frontiers and their Germanic kindred in Scandinavia, inherited an independent and ancient tradition of gnomic formulations such as occur in the earlier stages of various world literatures. But AS wisdom-poetry is not, as much folk-wisdom is, cynical, opportunistic, amoral; nor is it cultivatedly esoteric. The AS attitude is well stated in the versified *Instructions for Christians* (Cambridge, University Library MS Ii.I.33, ed. James L. Rosier, *Anglia* LXXXII (1964), pp.4–22): 'Wisdom is a light to be had by everyone here in this world. It has to be kindled by humility. No one can ever light it with any other taper ... because of those acts of presumption which formerly smothered it.' This formulation is a Christian one, and it most likely accords with the view of the redactor of this codex. Whether or not the gnomic habit and some of his specific formulations were Germanic, even pagan, in origin, the redactor probably saw the wisdom of these maxims as evidence of the ineffable superiority of God – as Augustine did. Those who contemplate the mutable phenomenon of life, says

Augustine, logically esteem most highly, above the insentient life of trees and the sentient life of animals, the 'intelligent life' of humankind. 'When they have seen that even this life is still changeable, they are compelled to prefer something unchangeable to it, that very Life, in fact, which is not sometimes foolish and at other times wise, but is rather Wisdom itself. For a wise mind, that is, one that has attained wisdom, was not wise before it attained it; but Wisdom Itself was never unwise, nor can It ever be.' (*CI*, Bk.I, ch.8, p.33).

The prescriptive statements of *Mxm* do indeed cover a wide and broadly coherent range of circumstances: man's relationship to God; the converse of wise men; the necessity of accepting mortality; the pursuit of righteousness through weal and woe; trust in God who sends both affliction and healing; the careful balance of chastisement and encouragement in educating a child; the merit of moderation which brings peace between men and nations; the propriety of station, according to social rank, sex and virtue; the mutual obligations of ruler and subject; and so on. Often verifiable truisms of natural law or human logic are invoked, evidently to lend to less easily verifiable propositions, interspliced among them, an analogous certainty. Throughout, the prescriptions are explicitly or implicitly conducive towards virtue, stability, moderation and harmony in family and in community, within a disordered world made meaningful only by reference to a God who is the source and the consummation of all these human perceptions.

Mxm I may well be three poems with more or less the same elements in each, or a single poem constructed on the principle of threefold reiteration which can be observed in some other AS poems. There are many formulaic echoes of other poems and some valuable glosses upon ideas found elsewhere – for example, the references to the ocean have a bearing on *Sfr*, and the observations concerning Abel echo *Gen* (982–1001) and put the kinship of Grendel (*Bwf*) with Cain in a more dogmatic context.

Three short passages have been omitted from the translation.

I

Sound me out with shrewd words. Let your own intellect not be hidden, nor that of which you have deepest understanding be kept secret. I will not speak my mystery to you if you hide from me the faculty of your reason and the reflections of your heart. Discerning people must exchange maxims.

4 God is first and justly to be praised, our Father, for he in the beginning afforded us life and temporal free will. He wishes to remind us of those loans.

7 The ordaining Lord belongs in glory. Man must be on earth and, being young, grow old. God is ours everlastingly. Events do not change him, the Almighty, nor sickness nor senility at all affect him. He does not age in spirit but he is still as he was, the forbearing Ruler. He grants us rationality, diverse tempers and many tongues. Many an island broadly embraces a profusion of kinds of life – these spacious lands the ordaining Lord, almighty God, established for mankind – and an equal profusion of both peoples and practices.

18 Common cause the wise must achieve with the wise. Their minds will be like. They will always resolve disputes; they will preach peace when discontents have once disturbed it. Counselling belongs with wisdom, justice with the wise; goodness belongs with the good. Two make a match. Woman and man will bring forth children in birth into the world.

25 A tree must needs shed its leaves on the earth; its branches needs must mourn. The would-be voyager must needs set forth; mortal man must needs die and every day take steps with regard to his severance from the world. The ordaining Lord alone knows where death will go when it departs hence out of our ken. New-born complements when disease first takes away; thus there are just as many of the human race in the world, nor would there be a limit to the progeny upon earth if he did not diminish it who established the universe.

35 Foolhardy is the man who does not know his Lord, so often does death come unpremeditated. Wise men will guard their souls: they will maintain their righteousness with rectitude.

Fortunate is the man who prospers in the place of his birth; hapless the one whom his friends betray. Never shall he prosper whose food-supply fails: he must for the while be constrained by need. Happy shall be the heart free from mischief.

39 A blind man must necessarily miss his eyes: their clear vision is taken away and they cannot observe the constellations, ethereally clear, nor sun nor moon. To him this is cruelly painful in his mind while he alone is aware of it and does not expect that any reversal of it will come to him. The Ruler ordained for him this torment: he can grant him relief, the healing of his head's jewels, if he knows the heart to be pure. An ailing man needs the physician.

45 A young man must be taught and encouraged and persuaded in order that he be thoroughly competent, until he has been tamed; let him be given food and clothing until he is brought into a condition of understanding. He must not be decried as a young child before he is able to prove himself; thus he will thrive in the community so that he becomes courageous in his convictions.

50 An impetuous heart has to be steered. Often a storm reduces the sea, the ocean, into raging conditions. Angry tawny waves far out start sweeping towards land trying whether it will stay firm. The cliffs maintain their stand against them; the wind is subdued upon them. Just as the sea is placid when the wind does not rouse it, so nations are amicable when they have negotiated together. They settle down in safe circumstances and then along with their comrades brave men will rule the lawful realm.

58 A king is keen for power: hateful to him the man who demands land, dear the one who offers him more. Majesty must go with pride, the daring with the brave; both must wage war with alacrity. An earl belongs on a charger's back; a mounted troop must ride in regular array, and the foot-soldier stand firm.

63　　Woman belongs at her embroidery; a roving woman gives rise to talk – she is often accused of sordid things; men speak of her insultingly; and often her complexion will decay. A person nursing guilt must needs move about in darkness; the candid person belongs in the light.

67　　The head must influence the hand; treasure must wait in its hoards – and the gift-throne stand prepared – for when men may share it out. Eager for it is he who receives the gold; the man on the high seat has plenty of it. There must needs be a return, if we do not mean to deceive, to the one who afforded us these favours.

II

71　　Frost must needs freeze, fire crumble wood, earth burgeon, ice build bridges – and the water support a canopy – and miraculously lock away earth's seeds. One alone, the God of powers manifold, shall unbind the frost's fetters. He shall drive away the winter; good weather shall come again and summer hot from the sun. The unresting ocean, the deep route of the dead, will longest remain a mystery. Holly has to be burned, and a dead man's legacy divided. Good repute is the best thing.

81　　A king has to procure a queen with a payment, with goblets and with rings. Both must be pre-eminently liberal with gifts. In the man, martial warlike arts must burgeon; and the woman must excel as one cherished among her people, and be buoyant of mood, keep confidences, be open-heartedly generous with horses and with treasures; in deliberation over the mead, in the presence of the troop of companions, she must always and everywhere greet first the chief of those princes and instantly offer the chalice to her lord's hand, and she must know what is prudent for them both as rulers of the hall. The ship must be riveted; the shield, the light linden board, bound together; and cherished by his wife the yearned-for returning Frisian, when his ship docks. His vessel has returned and her husband is home, her own provider, and she leads him in, washes his

wrack-stained clothes and gives him fresh garments and sails
with him to a landfall as his love demands. A woman must keep
her promise to her man. Often they will be accused of shameful
things. There are many constant ones; there are many promis-
cuous ones, and they entertain strange men when the other is
travelling far away... (102)

120   ... God will prevail: it is congruous with God. The mind
must be disciplined, the hand controlled. Seeing is essentially in
the eye, understanding in the heart where a man's thoughts are.

124   Every mouth needs food; meals must come on time. These
fitly belong: gold on a man's sword and as exotic ornament and
jewellery on a woman; a good poet to the people; to menfolk
armed strife, and to defend the civic security against war. A
shield necessarily goes with a soldier, an arrow with a poacher;
a ring necessarily goes with a bride, books with a student, the
eucharist with a holy man, and with a heathen sins.

132   Woden fashioned idols; the Ruler of all fashioned heaven
and the spacious skies. He is the mighty God, the very King of
truth, the Saviour of souls, who gave us all that we live on and
who at the end will again dispose over all mankind. He is
himself the ordaining Lord (137).

III

146   ... The unbefriended man gets wolves as his comrades,
beasts abounding in treachery; very often that comrade will
savage him. For the grey one there has to be dread, and for the
dead man a grave; it will mourn, this grey wolf, out of ravening
and it will wander round the grave, but not with a dirge nor
indeed will it weep for the death and destruction of men but
will always wish for more.

152   For a wound there has to be a bandage, for a hard man
vengeance; for an arrow there has to be a bow and for both
alike there has to be a man as a partner. One rich gift rewards

another: gold is meant for giving. God may grant belongings to prosperous people, and take them away. The hall itself must stand and grow old. A felled timber grows least; trees must necessarily spread themselves, and faith flourish, for it burgeons in the breast of the innocent. The renegade and reckless man, venom-hearted and faithless, over him God will not watch. Many things the ordaining Lord created, and as it was of old he bade that it should so be thenceforth.

165   Wise words are becoming in everyone: to the minstrel his song, to a man sagacity. As many as there are people upon earth so are there intellectual conceptions; each man has his individual intelligence. That man languishes the less who knows a lot of songs or who knows how to ripple the harp with his hands; he has in him his gift of music-making which God gave him. Miserable is the one that has to live alone: Providence has ordained that he should remain unbefriended ... (173).

192   ... Feuding has existed among mankind ever since earth swallowed the blood of Abel. That was no one-day strife: from it the drops of enmity splashed abroad, great wickedness among men and malice-mingled strife among many nations. His brother killed his own; but Cain kept no prerogative over murder. After that it became widely manifest that chronic strife was causing harm among men so that far abroad through the earth its inhabitants suffered a contest of arms, and devised and tempered the destructive sword.

202   The battle-board must be at the ready, the javelin on its shaft, an edge on the sword and a point on the spear. To the hardy man belongs determination, to the bold a helmet, and always to the coward's mind the most meagre store.

The Order of the World

[The Exeter Book, fol.92^b–94^a]

102 verse lines. The poem purports, like *Vgl*, to relay wisdom of implicitly divine origin, derived from a special informant, a prophet or book-learned scholar, who in this case is the first-person speaker, the I-persona, addressing 'you', the audience. The manifestly ordered universe, he says, is evidence of the nature and of the powers of God, and of his purpose for humankind, in knowledge of which mortals should live wisely in this transitory world, so as to achieve at last the 'better kingdom' of heaven. The themes and the idiom in which they are articulated occur frequently in other OE poems, especially within the Cynewulfian group. Ultimately, the poem's thesis relates to the man-centred interpretation of the physical universe which early Christian scholarship formulated out of the legacy of Greek and Roman natural philosophy, and which persisted throughout the Middle Ages. *Homo mundus minor est*, 'man is the world in miniature', the microcosm; therefore, those explanations of the macrocosm are preferred which contribute to the definition of man's moral nature and probationary status in this ephemeral world.

The Rhyming Poem

[The Exeter Book, fol.94^a–95^b]

87 verse lines. A first-person speaker describes in familiar detail his former life of worldly affluence, its inexorable decay, the onset of griefs and old age, the passage to the grave and the body's dissolution, all in parallel with the deterioration of this world itself – the cyclical theme of other OE poems (*Wan*, *SlB I* and *II*, *JgD I* and *II*) and of later medieval poems. The accumulation of detail is lent overpowering weight by the rhyme-scheme. The pairs of half-lines are linked not only by head-rhyme (alliteration) but also by end-rhyme. This latter kind of rhyme was evidently little favoured among AS poets – perhaps this jangling poem shows why – though popular with Norse and Icelandic poets. It has been held that the poem was composed under the direct influence of Scandinavian settlers or visitors at the English

or Norse courts (such as that of Eirik Bloodaxe at York which came to its end in 954, and where Egill Skallagrimsson saved his head by extravagantly flattering Erik, his bitter enemy, in verse) but there is no good evidence of any sort to support this view. The form of the poem has important implications for oral-formulaic theory of composition and transmission, since preservation of the integrity of the rhyme-scheme must rest either upon a definitive written text or upon ver-batim oral transmission from one reciter to the next.

The Panther (Physiologus)

[The Exeter Book, fol.95ᵇ–96ᵇ]

No poetry in the Exeter Book evinces more clearly than the three poems derived from *Physiologus* or the Bestiary the fact that the Anglo-Saxons became through the conversion to Christianity heirs by adoption to the intellectual legacy of Greece and Rome. Originally composed in Greek, later translated into Latin, *Physiologus* was esteemed by early Christian scholars because such quasi-scientific lore concerning the character of beasts and birds aided the interpretation of the Bible where references to the natural world abound. As Augus-tine wrote, 'An imperfect knowledge of things causes figurative pas-sages [of Scripture] to be obscure; for example, when we do not recognize the nature of the animals, minerals, plants, or other things which are very often represented in the Scriptures for the sake of an analogy. It is well known that a serpent exposes its whole body, rather than its head, to those attacking it, and how clearly that explains the Lord's meaning when He directed us to be 'wise as serpents'. We should, therefore, expose our body to persecutors, rather than our head, which is Christ. . . A knowledge of the nature of the serpent, therefore, explains many analogies which Holy Scripture habitually makes from that animal; so a lack of knowledge about other animals to which Scripture no less frequently alludes for comparisons hinders a reader very much.' (*CI*, Bk.II, ch.1, pp.82–3). Christian use of the *Physiologus* rested upon the belief that all things in the created uni-verse offered by design some portion of the truth of God's purpose for mankind, or illumined some truth about man's nature, moral or physical, since man was the sum of the traits of the whole created world (compare *OrW* and the note on it, above). The *Physiologus* enjoyed enormous popularity over many centuries throughout the Western world. In its moralized form it is closely akin to the *Marvels of the East* which occurs in a prose version, with pictorial illustrations, in the *Bwf* codex.

The compiler of the Exeter Book may have chosen symbolically among the many creatures and things available in *Physiologus*. Though the Panther, the Whale and the Partridge occur in successive chapters in the standard text of the original, they also happen to treat, respectively, of the nature of God, of the nature of the devil, and of man's choice between the two. Interestingly, the Exeter Book includes a further example of the compiler's taste for Bestiary material in *Phx*, which treats of a creature uniquely associated with the fourth and last of the elements, fire, and with the destiny of the righteous human soul.

Many are the countless species throughout the world whose noble qualities we cannot rightly recount, whose numbers we cannot know; for as widely scattered are the multitudes of land-going birds and beasts throughout the world as the water which encircles this shining plain, the roaring ocean, the salt waves' surge.

8   Concerning a certain one of these wild creatures we have heard tell of his remarkable nature and that he haunts a habitat very well known to people in far-off lands and makes his home among mountain caves. The animal is called Panther by name, according to what the children of mortals, men reliable in their wisdom, reveal in their writings concerning that singular rover.

15   He is a friend, generous of benefactions, to everyone except the serpent alone: towards him he remains antagonistic for all time because of all the evils which he is able to perpetrate.

19   He is an exquisite animal, wondrously beautiful in every hue. Just as people, pious men, say that Joseph's coat was ashimmer with colours of every tint, each one of which shone more bright and altogether more incomparable than the other

upon the children of men, so this animal's hue, agleam in its every variegation, brighter and more beautiful, shines wondrously so that each one ornately gleams more exquisitely than the other, yet more incomparable and more handsome, ever more exotic.

30   He has a nature apart, mild and meek. He is gentle, loving and lovable, and will do no injury at all to any thing, except to that poisonous predator, his rival of old, about whom I spoke before. Ever glad of his fill when he receives food, after meals he seeks his rest in a secret place inside the mountain caves. There for the space of three days this people's champion slumbers dormant, absorbed in sleep. Then confident in his strength he rises up forthwith from sleep, augmented in might, upon the third day. A sonorous voice, the most gladdening of sounds, come from the wild creature's mouth. After the voice, a fragrance comes out of that place, an exhalation more gladdening, sweeter and stronger than any perfume, than the flowers of herbs, than woodland blossoms, more noble than all the adornments of the earth.

49   Then from cities and regal thrones and from castle halls many troops of warriors travel the country roads, spear-wielding soldiers, with throngs and legions of the peoples, urged speedily on; animals too the same – after the voice, they travel into the fragrance.

55   Just so the Lord God, Master of delights, is ready of heart with every benefaction towards all other creatures except the serpent alone, the fount of poison – that is, the ancient foe whom he chained in the abyss of torments and fettered with fiery bonds and engulfed in the throes of distress; and on the third day he rose from the grave, after he, the Prince of the angels and Giver of victories, had endured death for us for three days. That was a sweet fragrance, beautiful and gladdening, throughout the whole world. Thereafter, people steadfast in truth on every side thronged in crowds to that perfume throughout the whole circle of earth's surfaces.

70   Thus spoke Paul, the wise saint: 'Manifold are the unsparing benefits throughout the world which the almighty Father and the one Hope of all creatures above and below apportions us as a gift and for the preservation of life.' That is a noble fragrance.

The Whale (Physiologus)

[The Exeter Book, fol.96ᵇ–97ᵇ]

Strictly, the creature described is a fictitious beast sometimes called the asp-turtle but it has always been popularly confused with the whale. Milton, using medieval lore to extend his characterization of Satan (*Paradise Lost* I, 200–8), equates this beast with the Leviathan. Doubtless, the compiler of the Exeter Book appreciated a consistency of metaphor between this poem, *Sfr* and the ending of *Chr II*, each with its imagery of the stormy sea symbolizing the vicissitudes encountered by men in their pilgrimage through this life. The message of *Whl* is that Satan offers a tempting but disastrous refuge amid such trials of faith; and it is perhaps the imagery of *Whl* which lies behind the *Bwf*-poet's warning (lines 183–8) to such as the Danes who turn from God to idols in their afflictions under Grendel.

Again now, in a song about the fish species, I will set forth words with poetic skill conforming to my intellect, concerning the great whale.

4   He is often encountered unintentionally, dangerous and savage in his every attack, by all seafaring men. To him, floating creature of the mountainous oceans, the name Fastitocalon is attributed. His appearance is like shaly rock such as crumbles along the water's edge surrounded by sand-dunes, a most enormous reef, so that travellers on the ocean wave imagine that they are looking with their eyes upon some island; and then they tie up the high-prowed ships to the false land with

anchor-ropes, secure the sea-steeds at the ocean's limit and then go bold-hearted up on to the island. The vessels remain fast by the shore eddied about by the current.

19   Then, weary at heart, the seafarers encamp: they are unsuspecting of danger. On the island they kindle a light and light a great fire; the men are happy, weary and longing for rest. When, sly in his trickery, he feels that the travellers are resting secure in him and are keeping to their camp yearning for fair weather, then forthwith into the salt wave down he boldly goes with them, this demon of the ocean, and makes for the bottom, and then in a cavern of death consigns them to drowning, the ships with the men.

31   Just so is the practice of evil spirits, the way of devils – that by hidden strength they trick people associating with them and incite them into the ruination of their good works and seduce them in their wills so that, incensed, they look for consolation to their foes until there with the perjurer they choose permanent lodging. When from out of his living torment the wily and wanton foe perceives that any of the people of humankind are trussed up tight in his noose, then with cruel treachery he becomes a murderer to them, to the proud and to the lowly who here wickedly further his will. Forthwith, covered by the helm of invisibility, the being barren of virtues makes for hell with them, the bottomless ferment beneath a vaporous twilight, just like the great whale who sinks seafaring men and their wave-steeds.

49   He has another characteristic, this proud roamer of the waters, yet more remarkable. When hunger troubles him at sea and provokes the monster with longing for food, then the lord of the ocean opens his mouth, his wide lips. From out of his inwards comes a delightful fragrance so that other kinds of sea-fish are tricked by it, and those swift in swimming swim to where the sweet fragrance is issuing forth. There they enter in an unwary crowd until the wide muzzle is filled; then suddenly the grim jaws gnash together around the prey.

62 Just so it is with any man who very often regards his life unwarily in this ephemeral time and lets himself be tricked by a sweet fragrance, a vain desire, so that he is stained with sins against the King of glory. The accursed devil opens hell towards those, after their departure hence, who have vainly and improvidently promoted the pleasures of the body above the dues of the spirit.

71 When the deceiver, sly in his mischief, has brought into that prison, into that swirling ferment, those who cleave to him encumbered with their crimes, and eagerly attended to his prompting previously in the days of their life, then after the mortal agony he gnashes fast together those grim jaws, the gaol-gates of hell. Never will they have a return nor an escape nor an exit who enter there, any more than the seafaring fish can return out of the whale's clutch.

82 Therefore it is altogether . . . [*No gap in the MS but the sense is incomplete*] . . . the Lord of lords and always strive with words and with deeds against the devils so that we may see the King of glory. Let us ever look to him for love and for salvation in this transitory time, so that in glory with the One so cherished we may to existence infinite enjoy heaven.

The Partridge (Physiologus)

[The Exeter Book, fol.97ᵇ–98ᵃ]

16 verse lines. Most of the text is missing, apparently through the loss of one leaf of the MS. No name or unmistakable characteristic of the bird described survives in the test, so the usually accepted identification with the Partridge rests upon the moral application rather than upon the description proper. According to *Physiologus* the Partridge steals the nest and eggs of other birds but when the kidnapped brood grow independent they choose to fly to their true parent. So men may choose to return to their true Father from out of the unnatural parentage which Satan has wrongfully foisted upon them.

Soul and Body II

[The Exeter Book, fol.98ª–100ª]

'But, the soul of one who does not die to this world and begin to be fashioned according to the image of Truth is drawn, by the death of the body, into a more serious death and will be restored to life, not in order to change to a heavenly home, but to undergo punishment. Faith maintains this principle and we must believe it: Neither the soul nor the human body suffers complete annihilation; the wicked arise again for punishment beyond imagination, while the good rise again for everlasting life.' (*CI*, Bk.I, ch.20, 21, p.40).

The antithesis of the cultivation of the world and the cultivation of the spirit is the subject of various OE poems. The *Wan*-poet rehearses the argument through the review of a wise man's debate with himself on the meaning of worldly experience; the *Sfr*-poet embodies the two alternatives in the personae of the pilgrim-seafarer and the city-dweller, 'arrogant and flown with wine'. Both these poems are austere of tone and ascetic in their advocacy of distrust of the world's bland-ishments, but they are ultimately emphatic of the stability, strength and benign purpose of God. *SlB*, in contrast, is as morbid of spirit as it is of descriptive detail. The Body, unable to make a response because its tongue is torn into ten pieces, is hectored remorselessly by the Soul from dark to cock-crow and Prime, in weekly visitations until the expiry of three hundred years or until Doomsday, whichever is the sooner. Here the dignified asceticism of *Wan* and *Sfr* is displaced by a hysterical revulsion against the bodily frame, an attitude discouraged by Augustine (*CI*, Bk.I, ch.24, pp.44–5), and more characteristic of the later medieval mortality-lyrics which are sometimes said to have been provoked by the horrors of the Black Death. Like *DrR* it is in effect an intense meditation designed to induce spiritual change in its hearers; but if *DrR*, with its themes of grace, altruism and heroic service, and its philosophy of individual redemption, teaches the worth and dignity of man, this poem can only inculcate a despairing sense of man's squalid want of dignity. Yet the poem was evidently popular enough and belonged in an established tradition, for another version of it is collected in the Vercelli Book where there is also a homily on the subject. Its position in the Exeter Book, in a group of poems of wisdom, lore and intellectual conceits, is hardly justified. Such lore as it contains is coarse and near-superstitious: the spirit returns, not like the sons of the Wife of Usher's Well humanely to urge an end to a loved-one's grief which merely wets the winding-sheet of the dead, but solely to exacerbate the Body's grievous distress. The poem offers no wisdom, no true debate, no positive precepts, no sympathetic appreciation of the complex problems of human experience, only macabre emotionalism, threats and unmitigated pessimism. It is arguable that it presents AS Christianity in its least charitable, most unintelligently minatory aspect. Nor does the poem display redeeming distinction of poetic technique. The metre is slack, tension of sound and sense relationships is rarely achieved in the alliteration and the language is largely prosaic and uninventive. The critical lesson here is that didactic verse evidently did not have to be fine poetry to gain admission into the Exeter Book.

Of this, certainly, every man has need: that he should give attention to the fate of his soul and how grave it will be when death comes and cleaves those kinsmen who were before joined together – the body and the soul.

5   It will be long afterwards that the spirit receives from God himself either torment or glory exactly as that earthy vessel previously prepared for it in the world before. This spirit, the soul, must come, strident in its griefs, to find the bodily covering which it once long wore, every seven days for three hundred years – unless the everlasting Lord, almighty God, brings about the end of the world beforehand.

15   At that time the spirit so full of anxiety will cry out with a cold voice and say grimly to that dust:

17   'Listen, dreary dessicated thing! Why have you, a foul thing of earth, afflicted me? You, a semblance of clay, will rot wholly away. Little did you consider to what the fate of your soul might come after it was led forth from the body. What did you have against me, you criminal? Lo, worms' meat! little indeed did you consider how long this will go on. And to you, by an angel from the skies above, the almighty ordaining Lord out of

his power and glory sent a soul through his own hand, and then bought you with that holy blood: and you have bound me with harsh starvation and held me captive in hellish torments.

30 　'I dwelt within you – I could not get out from you, being engrossed in flesh – and your wicked lusts oppressed me so that it very often seemed to me that it would be thirty thousand years to your death-day. See! I reluctantly waited for our severance: now the outcome is none too good. You were extravagant with food and glutted with wine; full of your glory you flaunted yourself and I was thirsty for the body of God and spiritual drink. If you had made up your mind then, during your lifetime here while I was constrained to occupy you in this world, that you would be strictly steered through carnality and through wicked lusts, and stabilized by me, and that I was the spirit in you sent from God, you would never have prepared for me such harsh hellish torments by the lust of your needs. But now you must suffer the shame of my humiliations in that great day when the Only-begotten will muster all mankind.

49 　'Now you are no more desired as a companion by any man among the living, by mother or by father or by any of your kindred, than the black raven, ever since I journeyed out alone from you by the hand of that Being by whom I was first sent. Now no ruby jewels can get you out of here, not gold nor silver, none of your goods, but here your bones must abide, robbed and ripped from their sinews; and I your soul, against my will, must repeatedly seek you out to revile you with my words in accordance with what you have done to me. You are dumb and deaf and your pleasures are come to naught; yet I, afflicted by sins, must needs seek you out by night and go from you again immediately upon the cock-crow, when holy men perform a song of praise to the living God, to seek out those abodes and that dishonourable dwelling-place to which you previously doomed me. And you the many earthworms shall gnaw; they shall rip you from your sinews, black creatures, gluttonous and greedy. Those vanities of yours which you showed off to people here on earth are come to naught; therefore it would have been

very much better for you than if all the riches of the world had been yours – unless you had handed them over to the Lord himself – had you become at your creation a bird or a fish in the sea, or a beast of the soil, a field-trudging ox without understanding, and tilled for food, or the fiercest of wild animals in the wilderness if God so willed, yes, even though you had been the worst kind of snake, than that you ever became a man on earth or should ever have received baptism, since you will have to answer for us both in that great day when to all mortals will be revealed the wounds which sinful mortals perpetrated in the world once long ago.

86   'At that time the Lord himself will want to hear by word of mouth from each of all those people their achievements, their payment in compensation for his wounding: but what will you say to the Lord there in the day of judgment since there is no member matured into a limb so small but that for each one of them separately you will duly have to pay compensation.

92   'At that time the Lord will be wrathful in judgment, but what shall we two do when he has regenerated us for a second time? We shall then have to enjoy together thereafter such miseries as you doomed us to before.'

97   Thus it will revile that fleshy mass; then it will have to journey on its way, to seek not the joys of heaven but the abyss of hell, anguished by those deeds. The dust will remain where it was. It cannot articulate any reply to it nor offer any shelter, help or comfort there to the grieving spirit. The head is cracked apart, the hands are disjointed, the jaws dropped open, the palate ripped apart, the sinews have been sucked away, the neck gnawed through. Rampant worms rob the ribs and grip the corpse in swarms, thirsty for blood. The tongue is torn into ten pieces for the hungry worms' pleasure and therefore it cannot readily exchange words with the damned spirit.

111   The worm is called Gluttony, whose jaws are sharper than a needle, that first of them all sets to within the earthy grave. He

tears the tongue apart and crawls among the teeth and eats
through the eyes down into the head and clears the way to a
surfeit of food, to a banquet, for the other worms.

117   When the vile body, which one long decked with clothes
before, has grown chill, then it will be worm's meat, its food, in
the earth.

121   To every man among the wise this may serve as a reminder.

Deor

[The Exeter Book, fol.100ᵃ–100ᵇ]

What Greek, Roman and Hebrew matter is to later poets, Germanic
matter is to the poet and the presumed audience of *Deo*. The AS
hearer's emotive response, economically generated by mere allusion
to tales of grief pre-established as archetypal by their currency in other
legendary lays, is stored up in the riddling 'this' of the refrain, until – a
philosophical context for its resolution having been prepared in
strophe VI – 'this' is at last explained as being the poet's own condi-
tion of grief. Here, as in *FAp*, is a striking example of a poet finding
solace for his personal affliction within the resources of his own art.

The strophic form of *Deo* and its use of refrain make it a rhetorical
enterprise extremely rare in the surviving AS poetic corpus. To judge
by the extant poetry, the AS poets vastly preferred to be free from the
exigencies of strophe and end-rhyme (see the note on *Rim*) – though
the strophic form of *Deo*, while it certainly gives an enhanced struc-
ture to the exposition of the thought of the poem and contributes
significantly to its intellectual and emotional dynamics, is not so
regular and rigorous that it severely tests (as does the medieval
Icelandic strophic form, for example, or the later sonnet form) the
poet's capacity to achieve predetermined *form* without compromising
meaning.

The poem's allusive treatment of Germanic legend, all too little of
which remains meaningful, has suggested to some critics a very early
date; but argument as to the time-span over which intimate know-
ledge of traditional legend died out in AS England can be no better

than speculative. Relevant facts are few, but one of them is that King Alfred, as late as the last quarter of the ninth century, could assume in his translation of Boethius' *Consolation of Philosophy* that his people still rated Weland a memorable hero, for he substituted the name of Weland 'the goldsmith who was once most renowned' (*The Metres of Boethius*, ASPR V, p.166) for that of the renowned Roman consul and general Fabricius, in the question posed by Boethius to prove the ephemeral nature of worldly glory: 'Where now rest the bones of the faithful Fabricius?' (Bk2, Metrum 7). The figure of Weland in his smithy, and possibly that of Beadohild too, appears on a panel of the Franks Casket, the AS whalebone box in the British Museum commonly held to be of eighth-century date. This fact illustrates the important relationship of AS pictorial and verbal iconography; but it does little to establish a date for *Deo*.

The poem has been classed in the genre of begging-poems better known from later medieval examples; but its purpose is surely more generous, more didactic and universal: it is to offer a philosophical consolation to everyman. The poet speaks with Boethian wisdom of transcending the incidence of worldly adversity by rational resignation to the providence of the wise Lord (see the headnotes to *Wan*). Philosophy teaches Boethius (Bk.IV, Prosa 6; *Boethius: The Consolation of Philosophy with the English Translation of 'I.T'* (1609), revised H. F. Stewart, London, 1918 and reprints, pp.41–3): 'The generation of all things, and all the proceedings of *mutable* natures, and whatsoever is moved in any sort, take their causes, order and forms from the *stability* of the Divine mind.' The divine disposition over things is properly called Providence: 'Providence is the very Divine reason itself . . . which disposeth all things.' But the manifestation of this disposition in the events of the mutable world is popularly called Fate: 'Fate is a disposition inherent in changeable things.' Thus, 'Providence is an immoveable and simple form of those things which are to be done, and Fate a moveable connexion and temporal order of those things which the Divine simplicity hath disposed to be done. So all that is under Fate is also subject to Providence, to which also Fate itself obeyeth.' It may be argued, then, that Deor, at first overwhelmed by the arbitrariness of Fate, learns from history that both glory and grief pass away, that the incidence of Fate, whether malign or benign in effect, is subordinate to the disposition or providence of a wise Godhead; and thus, by moving nearer the stable centre, which is God, Deor is the freer from the effects of Fate, for 'that which departeth farthest from the first mind (God) is involved more deeply in the meshes of Fate, and everything is so much the freer from Fate, by how much it draweth nigh to the hinge of all things. And if it sticketh to the stability of the Sovereign mind, free from motion, it surpasseth also the necessity of Fate.' This Boethian thesis accommodating the concept of Fate by defining it as the worldly-operative aspect of divine Providence is relevant to any context in AS poetry where determinist sentiment is expressed: see, for example, *FtM*, *GfM*, *Sfr*, *Wan*, *Mxm* and *Bwf*, *passim*.

I

Weland, by way of the trammels upon him, knew persecution. Single-minded man, he suffered miseries. He had as his companion sorrow and yearning, wintry-cold suffering; often he met with misfortune once Nithhad had laid constraints upon him, pliant sinew-fetters upon a worthier man.
— That passed away: so may this.

II

8   To Beadohild her brothers' death was not so sore upon her spirit as her own situation, in that she had clearly realized that she was pregnant. Never could she confidently consider what must needs become of that.
— That passed away: so may this.

III

14   About Maethhild many of us have heard tell that the affections of the Geat grew fathomless so that this tragic love reft them of all sleep.
— That passed away: so may this.

IV

18   Theodoric ruled for thirty years the city-fortress of the Merovingians: this was well-known to many.
— That passed away: so may this.

V

21   We have learned of the wolfish mentality of Eormanric. Far and wide he ruled the people of the Gothic kingdom. That was a cruel king. Many a man would sit shackled with sorrows, in expectation of misfortune, and frequently wish that the kingdom might be defeated.
— That passed away: so may this.

VI

28   The sorrowing anxious man sits, severed from prosperity, and grows dark in spirit: it seems to him that his share of miseries is without ending. He may then consider that throughout this world the wise Lord frequently causes change: to many a man he shows grace and certain success, to some a share of misfortunes.

35   I want to say this about myself, that for a time I was the poet of the Heodeningas, dear to my lord: Deor was my name. For many years I had a good standing and a loyal lord – until now Heorrenda, a man expert in poesy, has received the entitlement to land which the men's protector formerly granted me.
— That passed away: so may this.

Wulf and Eadwacer

[The Exeter Book, fol.100ᵇ–101ᵃ]

Because religious poetry so largely predominates in the Exeter Book, it is tempting to seek a Christian metaphor even in those poems which are aggressively secular on their literal level; but it is a temerarious critic who does not qualify with the utmost caution his patristic interpretation of this poem. Its articulation of an apparently adulterous sexual passion is startlingly vivid, and in its seemingly frank distinction between the union of bodies and the union of hearts and minds it is psychologically plausible; yet it is impossible to be certain of the relationships about which the poem centres, and any translation must be to some extent an arbitrary assertion of readings. The poem seems very carefully composed. Its form finely embodies its motifs of like and unlike, oneness and separateness; yet it is as allusive and cryptic of meaning as a riddle – and indeed the fact that a long series of riddles follows it in the MS has prompted the ingenious suggestion that it is itself a prefatory riddle with the solution 'A riddle' or 'Cynewulf'. At least the topic of exile and the elegiac tone are familiar from more overtly religious poems such as *Wan* and *Sfr* – poems which also demonstrate that the poets felt free to develop the concrete and secular imagery of their Christian message boldly and far. Perhaps in patristic commentaries on *The Song of Songs* there was sufficient example to an AS poet of the way in which the metaphor of sexual passion might permissibly express truths about divine love, as between the Church and Christ; certainly later medieval writers such as Richard Rolle exploited the equation. But some critics have reasonably looked to completely secular sources in pre-Conversion Germanic heroic legend. Either way, we have here evidence that the AS poets' perception of, and licence to treat of, human passions was not confined to the austere range conventional in heroic poetry and saints' lives.

To my people it is as though one might present them with a sacrifice: they want to destroy him if he comes under subjugation.

3   A difference exists between us.

4   Wulf is on one island; I am on another. That island is secure, surrounded by fen. There are deadly cruel men on the island; they want to destroy him if he comes under subjugation.

8   A difference exists between us.

9   In hopes I have endured the remoteness of the footsteps of my Wulf, when it was rainy weather and I sat weeping, and when the intrepid warrior pinioned me in his arms – there was pleasure for me in that, but it was loathsome to me too.

13   Wulf, my Wulf! my hopes in you have made me sick, the
       rareness of your visits, my grieving mind; not want of food.

16   Are you listening, Eadwacer? Our wretched whelp Wulf will
       carry off to the wood. One easily divorces what was never
       united – the riddle of us two together.

Riddles 1–59

[The Exeter Book, fol.101ª–115ª]

Riddles are in origin a folk-art, ancient and worldwide. Their status in
the AS literary conspectus is evidently high since the Exeter Book
compiler assigns them approximately as much codex space as, for
example, the whole of *Glc*; while they comprise more than one-third
of the shorter poems in the codex. The Exeter Book riddles, however,
are developed well beyond any origin in folk-art. *Rdl 90*, in Latin, is a
symbolic reminder in this English book that alongside the traditional
and insular art of vernacular poetic composition the Anglo-Saxons
cultivated a Latin *ars poetica* which was borrowed, cosmopolitan and
sophisticated, and to which the OE riddles are plainly indebted. No
doubt there were many AS poets skilled in the poesy of both lan-
guages, as was Aldhelm (*c*. 640–709), bishop of Sherborne and abbot
of Malmesbury. He vies with Cædmon for the title of first Christian
poet in the English vernacular, and he was, by his own claim, the first
Anglo-Saxon to write about and exemplify in original compositions
the metrics of Latin poetry. It was for his study *De Metris* that
Aldhelm composed his hundred riddles (*aenigmata*): not, since he
headed them with the solutions, so much for puzzlement as for illus-
tration of the Latin hexameter – though his taste for involved diction
and allegorical exposition set a fashion in literary codes and their
decipherment to which the vernacular riddles in some degree belong.
    Literary precedents existed by the time of the Exeter Book's com-
pilation for riddle collections comprising a round one hundred poems:
the popular collection of three-line *aenigmata* by Symphosius, a
Latin poet of uncertain dates and nationality; the riddles of Aldhelm,
which were soon being copied separately from the *De Metris*; and the

combined collection of eighth-century riddles, forty composed by Tatwine, archbishop of Canterbury, and sixty by 'Eusebius' who was most likely Hwætberht, abbot of Jarrow and friend of Bede. In the three groupings of riddles in the Exeter Book only ninety-five riddles are normally reckoned. The loss of a folio between the present *Rdl* 20 and 21, and of another between the present *Rdl* 40 and 41 may have reduced the original tally. But it may also be justifiably asked whether the compiler counted as *aenigmata* any of the shorter poems surrounding the texts usually designated riddles. Certain at least is his taste for poems which adopt an enigmatic technique if not the formal cast of the riddle-genre. The simple addition of the riddling question – 'Say what this is' or 'Say what (or who) I am' – would have made explicit the implicit enigma-posing of *Deo*, *WlE*, *WfL*, *HbM* and even *Rui*.

The riddles, therefore, enjoyable for their wit and its poetic expression, are also of critical importance for the insight they afford into the intellectual structure of the AS literary mind. The mentality which can simultaneously engage with the sense of the *literal* statement and with the *implicit* and 'truer' import of the concealed meaning is a mentality alert to symbolism and allegory; and not surprisingly techniques of the riddle may be traced in poetry of other genres where ambiguity and systematic symbolism or allegory are deliberately cultivated as in *Sfr*. In many riddles one particular device for concealing the true solution is the I-persona, by which convention an inanimate or non-human subject speaks with its own voice – the device called, in Latin rhetoric, *prosopopoeia*, which Aldhelm introduced into his riddles not in imitation, he says, of classical literary practice but upon the example of the Bible. Here is a device of major literary potential, inviting the poet to dramatization of the self and towards the realistic representation of fictive identity. Its use in *DrR* is fundamental to the working of that remarkable poem.

Several of the *Rdl* are plainly based upon known Latin originals by Symphosius and Aldhelm. Of the rest, the originality, the homogeneity and the authorship have long been disputed, without resolution. The first three (wind) conspicuously call for the naming not only of the thing itself but also of him who controls it – God. Thereafter, overtly Christian topics are few (creation, the family of Lot, the Cross, a Gospels book, paten, chalice, soul and body), and the subject-matter, whose range corresponds broadly with that of Aldhelm's *aenigmata* and like them inclines to the concrete rather than to the abstract topics favoured by Tatwine and Eusebius, helps little to define a specific social milieu for the poems. Perhaps something of their popular origin is retained in the elemental topics of some (sun, moon, ore, wind, fire, water); and in the sexual suggestiveness of others (cock and hen, onion, poker, key, shirt). Many more refer to the natural world – to birds such as jay and cuckoo, to land-animals such as badger, and to water-creatures such as oyster and fish. A large number deals with artefacts of daily life (plough, loom, rake, bellows); and a few with warfare (sword, lance, battering ram) and courtly leisure (book, harp).

The following is a list of the riddles not included in the present translation. The solutions offered are those given most weight in *ASPR III*. The number of verse lines indicated is based on the same edition.

1 Storm [15 lines]; 2 Storm? submarine earthquake? [15]; 4 Bell [12]; 6 Sun (with runic clue) [10]; 7 Swan (with runic clue) [9]; 8 Jay [11]; 10 Barnacle goose [11]; 11 Wine [10]; 12 Oxhide [15]; 13 Ten chickens [11]; 14 Horn [19]; 15 Badger [29]; 16 Anchor [10]; 17 Ballista? [11]; 18 Leather bottle? (imperfect) [4]; 19 Wildfowler on horseback? (with runic anagrams) [9]; 20 Sword (imperfect) [35]; 21 Plough [15]; 22 Month? bridge? [21]; 23 Bow (with anagram clue) [16]; 24 Magpie (with runic anagram) [10]; 27 Mead [17]; 28 Beer (John Barleycorn) [13]; 31 Bagpipe [24]; 32 Ship [14]; 33 Iceberg [13]; 34 Rake [9]; 36 Ship? (with perplexing code language) [14]; 37 Bellows [8]; 39 Day? [29]; 40 Created things (incomplete) [108]; 41 Earth? water? (imperfect) [9]; 49 Bookcase? oven? [11]; 50 Fire [10]; 51 Pen and three fingers [7]; 52 Flail [7]; 54 Churn? baker's boy and oven? [12]; 55 Sword-rack? [16]; 56 Loom [12]; 57 Swallows? jackdaws? crows? [6]; 58 Well? [15]; 59 Chalice [18].

62 Poker [9]; 63 Beaker [15]; 64 Wildfowler on horseback (with runic clues) [6]; 65 Onion [6]; 67 Bible? (imperfect) [16]; 68 (Uncertain) [2]; 70 Shepherd's pipe [6]; 71 Iron weapon [10]; 72 Ox [18]; 73 Lance [29]; 74 Cuttlefish? swan? siren? [5]; 75 The Saviour? [1 line and four runes]; 77 Oyster [8]; 78 Oyster? (imperfect) [8]; 79 (Variant opening to *Rdl 81*?) [1]; 80 Falcon? horn? [11]; 81

Weathercock? [12]; 82 Crab? (imperfect) [6]; 83 Ore? money? [14]; 84 Water [56]; 85 Fish and river [7]; 87 Bellows? (imperfect) [8]; 88 Antler [32]; 89 (Uncertain, imperfect) [10]; 90 (Latin, uncertain) [5]; 91 Key [11]; 92 Beech-book (imperfect) [7]; 93 Antler-inkhorn [35]; 94 Creation? [6]; 95 Wandering singer? moon? [13].

Riddle 3 (Wind)

[The Exeter Book, fol.101^b–102^b]

Whether this truly is the third of three thematically related riddles or part of a single riddle of great length is not clear from the codex layout. There is some fine poetry of nature here, rarely matched in the surviving corpus. The poet holds the ancient and medieval belief that earthquakes were caused by wind pent up in subterranean caverns.

Sometimes my lord confines me fast; he sends me below ground then, below its broad bosom, and banishes me into waiting and forcibly restrains me, one among the great forces, in darkness and cramped constraint. There the earth sits hard upon my back. I have no escape-route from out of that oppression: instead I stir the established abode of men. Gabled halls, men's habitations, shudder; walls tremble, towering above the occupants. Still seems the air above the land and the sea silent — until I go thrusting forth from my cramped constraint according as he instructs me who in the first place previously laid fetters upon me, bonds and shackles, so that I might not elude the control of him who signposts my paths.

17   Sometimes, up above, I have to work up the waves and arouse the streaming tides and drive to shore the flint-grey flood. Foamy, the breaker battles with the cliff; dim rises the mountain of water above the deep; dark in its wake another is moving, mingled with mud, so that they reach the high ridges by the boundary of the land.

24   There is a creaking ship and the clamour of mariners. Quietly the steep slopes of the rocks bide the streaming ocean's tumult, the impact of the waves when their towering press crowds upon the cliffs — where there is likelihood of a savage struggle for the vessel if the sea carries it away, full of souls, in that grim hour, so that it comes to be stripped of its steerage, defeated in the fight for survival, and must ride, foamy, on the backs of the waves. There, flaunted before men, is one of those terrors which I have to serve, resolute upon my unrelenting way. Who will still it?

36   Sometimes I storm through what rides upon my back, and I thrust far asunder the dark water-vessels plump with the streams of ocean. Sometimes I cause them to slide back together. That makes a most mighty noise and clamour above the cities, and an extremely loud crash. Then one sharp shoe comes up against another, edge against edge. Dusky creatures, straining forward above the peoples, sweat fire and flashing flame, and the crashes travel dark above the multitudes with great din. Fighting they advance, and let fall a murky pattering rain from their bosom and wet from their belly. Skirmishing, this terrible cavalry advances. A sense of panic arises, great anguish of mind among humanity, a feeling of horror when the black stalking phantoms shoot off their sharp weapons. The fool does not dread these spears of death — but yet he will perish if the true ordaining Lord from out of the whirlwind lets fly a bolt, a speeding arrow, straight at him through the rain from above. Few survive it of those whom the fleet foe's weapon strikes.

61   I set in motion the start of this strife; then I withdraw from the aerial conflict to thrust tumultuously with great force across the bosom of the ocean while the throng of troops above loudly reverberates. Then I sink down again below the vault of the sky close to the ground and on my back I load that which I have to bear, admonished by the powers of my lord.

69   Thus I, majestic minister, sometimes struggle in paroxysms beneath the earth; sometimes I have to sink low under the

waves; sometimes from on high I stir up the ocean and its currents; sometimes I mount aloft and excite the scudding of the clouds, and travel abroad, swift and exceedingly strong.

74   Say what I am called, or who raises me up when I may not rest, or who steadies me when I am still.

Riddle 5 (Shield)

[The Exeter Book, fol.102ᵇ]

I am one on my own, wounded by weapon of iron, scarred by sword, wearied from the actions of the fray, exhausted from the edges of the blade, Often I see battle and fight the foe. The consolation that relief from the toil of war shall come to me before I am completely done for amongst men, I do not expect; instead, the products of hammers, the hard-edged blade, bloodily sharp, the handiwork of the smiths, buffet and bite me within the strongholds. I must continue to await encounters yet more hostile. Never have I been able to find in town the kind of physician that has healed with herbs my wounds; instead, the sword-gashes upon me grow bigger through mortal blows by day and by night.

Riddle 9 (Cuckoo)

[The Exeter Book, fol.103ᵃ–103ᵇ]

My father and mother abandoned me in this world while I was dead: there was as yet no life, no being in me. Then a very kindly wife covered me with clothes, kept me and cherished me and canopied me with a protective covering, as fittingly as her own child – until under that sheet, as were my innate qualities,

I became to my unrelated kindred inordinate of spirit. This beautiful wife continued to feed me until I grew mature and could set my paths further afield. She had the fewer beloved sons and daughters because she did so.

Riddle 25 (Onion)

[The Exeter Book, fol.106^b–107^a]

The abiding popularity of penis-riddles in the English tradition of literary ribaldry is attested, for example, by their presence in the great eighteenth-century song-collection *Pills to Purge Melancholy* edited by Thoms D'Urfey in 1719–20: see among others, *Pills* (reprint of 1876 reprint, ed. C. L. Day, New York, 1959), vol.IV, no.71, 'The Riddle', and no.195, 'A Song' ('The Lusty Young Smith'), and vol.VI, no.91, 'The Jolly Trades-Men', all edited in S. A. J. Bradley, *Sixty Ribald Songs from Pills to Purge Melancholy* (London, 1968). A chief difference, however, is that the later songs often titillate their audience by treating an indecent topic disingenuously in innocuous metaphor, while these riddles tease their audience by treating an innocuous topic with a pretended disingenuousness of description. All the same, the images which the monks of Exeter are invited to contemplate on their way to the solution sort incongruously with the religious didacticism of the rest of the codex.

I am a wondrous creature: to women a thing of joyful expectancy, to close-lying companions serviceable. I harm no city-dweller excepting my slayer alone. My stem is erect and tall – I stand up in bed – and whiskery somewhere down below. Sometimes a countryman's quite comely daughter will venture, bumptious girl, to get a grip on me. She assaults my red self and seizes my head and clenches me in a cramped place. She will soon feel the effect of her encounter with me, this curly-locked woman who squeezes me. Her eye will be wet.

Riddle 26 (Gospel-book)

[The Exeter Book, fol.107ᵃ–107ᵇ]

There is a substantial group of AS riddles in Latin which deal with the making of a book or with writing on vellum.

A certain enemy robbed me of life, took from me my mortal powers, then doused me and immersed me in water, took me out again, and set me in the sun where I was violently despoiled of the hairs that I had. Then a hard knife's edge dissected me, buffed clean of blemishes. Fingers folded me and the bird's delight repeatedly made tracks across me with lucky droppings. Across the burnished rim it would drink down dye from the tree, a measure of liquid, and step back on to me and travel its black trail.

11   Then a man clad me in protective boards and covered me with hide and decked me with gold. Forthwith the smiths' exquisite artefacts enhanced me, encased in filigree.

15   Now those embellishments and the red dye and their splendid settings proclaim abroad the protector of nations, and the punishment of folly no less. If the children of men are willing to make use of me, they will be the healthier and the surer of victory, the bolder in their hearts and the blither of mind and the wiser in spirit. They will have the more friends, dear ones and close, true and virtuous, good and faithful, who will liberally augment their fame and fortune and graciously surround them with kindnesses and clasp them tight in the embrace of love.

26   Inquire what I am called, a thing of advantage to people. My name is renowned, and I myself am bountiful to men, and holy.

Riddle 29 (New Moon and Sun)

[The Exeter Book, fol.107ᵇ–108ᵃ]

The solution 'Bird and wind' has also been offered.

I saw a creature wondrously carrying plunder between his horns, an airy lantern artfully adorned, plunder from a raiding foray, to his home. He meant to build and expertly erect for it a bower within the fortress, could it have been so.

7   Then a wondrous creature came over the roof of the rampart, who is familiar to all dwellers on earth. Then she rescued the plunder and drove the wretch home against his will. From there she set out to journey westwards from her feudings. Onwards she hastened; dust rose swiftly to the heavens and dew fell on the earth. Night passed away. After that, no one knew where the creature went.

Riddle 30a (Timber-Cross)

[The Exeter Book, fol.108ᵃ]

This is a poem of remarkable economy yet of rich didactic suggestiveness, not much of which survives translation since it rests so extensively on ambivalence of terminology and the use of formulas with pre-established special implications: these are no doubt the clues which the poet's AS audience would have readily discerned. The I-subject is a thing of fire and air, a living thing, a tormented and perishable thing, rooted in the earth yet free and eager to be gone hence, submissive yet worshipped, self-exalting and desiring to exalt others; a tree for burning, for building a ship for the onward voyage, for fashioning a rood, the Cross. The riddle is most usefully explored alongside *DrR*, where a similar dynamic correlation is developed between humanity, the Cross and Christ, using similar concepts, images and language. The text is, significantly, recorded twice in the codex.

I am concerned with fire, at play with the wind, spun about with glory, made one with the firmament, eager for the onward way, afflicted by burning, blossoming in the coppice, a burning ember. Very often comrades lay me across their hands so that proud men and women may kiss me. Then I raise myself up and they bow down to me in their multitudes with joy, since I shall increase for these people the fount of blessedness.

Riddle 35 (Mail-coat)

[The Exeter Book, fol.109ᵃ–109ᵇ]

Another version of this riddle survives in a Northumbrian dialect, in the Leiden MS University Library Cod. Voss. 106, fol.25b at the end of a collection of the Latin riddles of Aldhelm. The AS poem is in fact a translation of a Latin riddle with the solution '*Lorica*' ('Breast-plate, corselet') by Aldhelm.

Me the moist earth amazingly chill first brought forth from its interior. I know myself, in my mind's deliberations, not to be made with wool from fleeces, not, by outstanding craftsmanship, with hairs. There are not woofs woven about me; nor do I have warps; nor does thread thrum in me under the strain of the pressures upon it; nor does shuttle slide rasping at me; nor is it necessary for loom-sley to thump me anywhere. Those worms which decoratively embroider the yellow silk did not spin me with the skills of the Fates. Yet even so abroad across the earth people are pleased to call me, in the presence of worthies, a confidence-inspiring garment.

13   Man of insight with your ingenious deductions, wise in your words, say in precise terms what garment this is.

Riddle 38 (Bullock)

[The Exeter Book, fol.109^b]

The bullock is suckled by the cow. If it lives it will be yoked to the plough. If it dies and is butchered, the hide will be made into thongs.

I saw this creature of the weapon-equipped sort, greedy in the exuberance of his youth. As his due, his life-guardian set running four springs, white fountains, as his portion. A man spoke, who said to me: 'This creature, if he thrives, will break up the downs; if he goes to pieces, he will bind the living.'

Riddle 42 (Cock and Hen)

[The Exeter Book, fol.112^a]

With its inbuilt solution in the form of runes which the speaker is called upon to scratch in the dust on the floor, and its teasing challenge for anyone who has solved it to put up his hand, the poem offers scope for a delightfully entertaining performance by its teller. The runes spell the AS words *hana* 'cock' and *hæn* 'hen'.

I saw two curious creatures blatantly frolicking out of doors, in copulation. The fair-locked, cocky woman would get her fill beneath her clothes if the job proved successful.

5   To those men who understand books, I can tell by runic staves upon the floor both the names together of those creatures.

8   Need (N) must be there, and the second of a pair (N), and the splendid ash-tree (Æ), one in a row, two oaks (A, A) and just the same number of hailstones (H, H).

11   Which man has unlocked, by virtue of this key, the fetters of the treasury-door that resolutely guards the riddle, its heart protected by ingenious chains against the adepts? It is now no secret to folk at their wine that those two vulgar-minded creatures are called among us.

Riddle 43 (Soul and Body)

[The Exeter Book, fol.112ᵃ–112ᵇ]

The clues here lie in topics and terminology made familiar by convention in poetry of other genres. Various AS poems survive, including *SlB*, in which the Christian view of the soul's transient but all-critical habitation of the earthly body, is expressed in similar terms.

I know an excellent guest, one cherished for his noble virtues in the courts, whom fierce famine cannot scathe nor parching thirst nor old age nor disease. If the man who is supposed to do so ministers honourably to him upon their journey, they will assuredly find, safe at their destination, sustenance and merriment and a countless host of their kin – care, though, if the man ill obeys his lord and master upon the way, and if the one brother is unwilling to remain in awe of the other. That will scathe them both when they both pass on, impetuous for another place, from the bosom of their sole kinswoman, their mother and their sister.

14   Let the man who will, declare in fitting words what the visitor is called, or the man, of whom I here speak.

Riddle 44 (Key)

[The Exeter Book, fol.112ᵇ]

The *double-entendre* of key-penis continues to be exploited in ribald song into the seventeenth and eighteenth centuries and beyond. An alternative solution 'Sheath of a dagger' has been offered.

A curiosity hangs by the thigh of a man, under its master's cloak. It is pierced through in the front; it is stiff and hard and it has a good standing-place. When the man pulls up his own robe above his knee, he means to poke with the head of his hanging thing that familiar hole of matching length which he has often filled before.

Riddle 45 (Dough)

[The Exeter Book, fol.112ᵇ]

I have heard of a something-or-other, growing in its nook, swelling and rising, pushing up its covering. Upon that bone-less thing a cocky-minded young woman took a grip with her hands; with her apron a lord's daughter covered the tumescent thing.

Riddle 46 (The Family of Lot)

[The Exeter Book, fol.112ᵇ]

Clearly incest is necessary to achieve the equations of the riddle. There has been general agreement on the source in Genesis 19:30–38.

A man was sitting at wine with his two wives and his two sons and his two daughters, gracious sisters, and their two sons, freeborn and firstborn children. The father of each of these noble youths was in there with them, uncle and nephew. There were in all five men and women sitting within.

Riddle 47 (Bookworm)

[The Exeter Book, fol.112ᵇ–113ᵃ]

A riddle by Symphosius with the solution 'Tinea' 'Moth, bookworm' is generally agreed to be the source.

A moth ate words. That seemed to me a curious occurrence when I heard of that marvel, that this worm gulped down the utterance of a certain man, this thief in the dark his illustrious discourse and its tough foundation. The pilfering visitor was not a whit the wiser because he had gulped in those words.

Riddle 48 (Paten or Chalice)

[The Exeter Book, fol.113ᵃ]

I have heard tell of a circlet that spoke in front of people –
beautiful, but without a tongue, a profitable thing though it did
not cry out with a loud voice. With powerful words this treas-
ure, keeping silence, said in front of the people: Save me,
Helper of souls.

6   May men understand the secret of the red gold and its occult
utterance. May the discerning entrust their salvation to God, as
this circlet has said.

Riddle 53 (Battering Ram)

[The Exeter Book, fol.113ᵇ]

I saw in a wood a tree towering up, splendid in his branches.
The tree was happy as a growing timber. Water and earth fed
him well until, old of days, he came into a different, distressing
state – deeply scarred, dumb in fetters, trussed over his
wounds, covered to the front with dark ornaments. Now, by
the main strength of his head, he clears the way for another, the
treacherous warmonger. Often in a siege they have plundered
the treasury together. Swift and unsluggish it was, this hinder
one: if the one in front gained no headway in a tight spot, he
would have to make the assay.

The Wife's Lament

[The Exeter Book, fol.115ᵃ–115ᵇ]

The poem well exemplifies the problems besetting the critic of OE poetry. It follows a series of riddles and, like many of them, takes the form of a first-person narrative and is mystifyingly allusive in its plot. Perhaps the poet meant deliberately to challenge his audience's intellect by assigning a human persona and dramatic action to what might well be things, concepts, conditions or situations, in riddle-fashion.

Outwardly, it is a wholly secular poem dealing, like *HbM* and *WlE*, with passionate relationships between the sexes; and so, despite the example of *The Song of Songs*, critics have generally shied from a religious interpretation. Yet no Germanic legend convincingly matches the plot circumstances, and efforts merely to explain the literal circumstances of the narrative have proved as arbitrary as symbolic expositions; while mood, language, imagery and theme undeniably invite association with other, more overtly Christian poetry (*Wan*, *Sfr*, *Rui*, *Rsg*, *SlB II*, *JgD II*).

The poem is a lamentation; the speaker is in friendless exile, left behind by a lord, betrayed by an intimate companion, tormented by an unfulfilled longing; there is imagery of the deserted, decaying city in an aged world, of death and of the grave, of weeping and of retribution: the language and whole mood of the poem may signal a penitential interpretation. Some of its motifs are available in the Scriptures and apt for this purpose. The oak (usually *quercus* in the Latin Vulgate Bible) is confined mainly to the Old Testament, where it is regularly associated with sanctuaries, altars and graves, or symbolizes worldly splendour humbled in the day of the Lord's retribution. The poem's double theme of penitential suffering and imprecation against the unrighteous persecutor is well matched in the Psalms such as Ps.69 with its Messianic plea: 'Come near to me and redeem me; ransom me, for I have many enemies' (v.18). The type of the treacherous friend recurs often in the Old Testament: 'Even the friend whom I trusted, who ate at my table, exults over my misfortune' (Ps.41:9); 'It was you, a man of my own sort, my comrade, my own dear friend, with whom I kept pleasant company in the household of God' (Ps. 55:13–14); and 'All her friends turned traitor and became her enemies' (Lamentations 1:2). The female persona in this last citation is Jerusalem, the captive Zion – once full of people, now solitary; once great, now a widow;

once a queen, now a slave (v.1); bitterly she weeps in the night, comfortless because her friends have turned traitor (v.2). She and her people are in mutual exile (v.3); her Lord has punished her for her many misdeeds (v.5). In her association of remorse and imprecation against her persecutors, Jerusalem is a counterpart of the psalmist.

An AS Christian poet dealing with these themes would almost certainly understand them not in a restricted historical sense but rather according to the interpretative criteria of the Fathers in their commentaries, proving the supra-chronological concordance of the Old and New Testaments, as the poet might learn them from scriptural-patristic anthologies or from the liturgy of the Church, especially the antiphons and the homilies.

In such interpretations, the concept 'Jerusalem' may be taken as signifying the earthly city of the Hebrews, the Church of Christ, the heavenly City and the human soul (for a lengthy exposition of this interpretation, see *CG*, Bk.XV, ch.2, pp.415–17). As for the betrayer, the Fathers followed Peter in declaring that the prophecy made by David (Ps. 69:25) was fulfilled in Judas Iscariot. The theme of betrayal and the lamentation of Zion come together in the Roman liturgy of Holy Week, when readings from this chapter of Lamentations are interspersed with verses including: 'My friend betrayed me by the token of a kiss. . . It were well for him if this man had not been born' and 'Jerusalem, Jerusalem, turn back to the Lord your God'.

If this complex of scriptural associations and their orthodox interpretation already existed, *WfL* could conceivably be a riddle with the solution 'Zion, the soul'. The woman's exile and betrayal would then suggest historically the alienated state of mankind before the Messiah's advent, and symbolically the soul of everyman before the realization of personal redemption (cp. *DrR*); the woman's longing and her imprecations would suggest Zion's and the soul's intuition of a saviour and a judge to come.

Alternatively a solution in similar terms could be *Cirice*, 'Church', a feminine noun applied in OE not only to the post-Messianic Church but to the congregation of the Old Testament of which Gregory, Apostle to the English, wrote: 'The saints of the Old Testament . . . were saved by their faith in the future passion and resurrection of Christ, as we by the same passion and resurrection that are now past. They loved and believed in Christ before He came; we after His coming' (*Homilia in Ezechiel*, tr. F. Homes Dudden, *Gregory the Great* (London, 1905), vol.II, p.407).

An attractive result of either of these interpretations is that a plausible relationship with *HbM* is established – the message being a token that love has at last come out of longing and the just judgment is at hand. Isaiah 54:1–8, especially 5 and 6, may seem relevant to this argument. But many other interpretations have been argued for *WfL* and it may well be that any such claims of complex religious suggestiveness for this ostensibly quite secular poem are misplaced. See the headnotes to *HbM*.

In the following partly speculative translation the woman whose lord has gone away is ever tormented by anxiety and longing for him, especially as his own kindred are plotting to make the separation permanent. She has few friends still living: it is therefore especially painful that one of them, a man she had treated as her equal and much loved, proves to have concealed murderous intentions beneath a benign demeanour. Her sense of longing for her lord is all the more acute now that she is betrayed and utterly abandoned in her grave-like den beneath the oak. She wishes upon her false friend such misery as she herself suffers: then he will understand what she has learned from her own experience – the pain of waiting for longing to be relieved by love restored.

This riddle, my personal experiencing, I put, about my most melancholy self. I can tell what tribulations I have endured recently or of old since I grew up, and never more than now. I have suffered perpetually the misery of my exile's paths.

6   In the beginning my lord went hence away from his people beyond the jostling of the waves. I knew anxiety with the dawn as to where upon earth my prince might be. When on account of my woeful plight I went wandering, a friendless exile, to find a following, the man's kindred plotted with secret purpose to sunder us two so that we should live most abhorrently, utterly apart, in the kingdom of the world – and I pined.

15   My lord commanded me to take up my dwelling in this sanctuary. I owned few loved and loyal friends in this earthly place. Therefore my mind is melancholy since I found out that a man treated fully as my peer was ill-starred, melancholy-

minded, dissembling his heart, scheming murder with demeanour benign. Full often we two would vow that nothing other than death alone should come between us: that has been repudiated. Now it is as though our friendship had never been. Far and near I have to endure the enmity of my much-loved one.

27   I was bidden to dwell among a thicket of trees under an oak-tree in this earthen dug-out. Ancient is this earthen abode – I am quite consumed by longing – the dales are dark, the hills high, the bastioned towns grievously overgrown with briars, their habitations void of pleasures. Here full often my lord's departure has bitterly obsessed me. My friends, loved while they lived, are in earth; they keep their rest while I in the dawning pace alone under the oak-tree around this earthen dug-out. There I must sit the summer-long day. There I may weep for the ways of my exile, my many hardships; for never shall I be able to soothe this my anxiousness of mind nor all the longing which has obsessed me in this life.

42   For ever that youth shall remain melancholy of mind, and painful the brooding of his heart. He shall sustain, as well as his benign demeanour, anxiety too in his breast and the welter of incessant griefs. Let his whole pleasure in the world lie with his own self; let him be an outcast far afield in a distant land, so that my friend may sit under a stony pile, rime-encrusted by the storm, my evil-minded comrade, drenched in water in a drear dwelling. This comrade of mine will endure great anxiousness of mind; too often he will think upon a more agreeable habitation.

52   Woe is to the one who must wait for love to come out of longing.

Judgment Day I

[The Exeter Book, fol.115^b–117^b]

119 verse lines. Another homiletic, hortatory poem in which a first-person speaker appeals directly to the audience, here on the matter of Doomsday. With the unpenning of the waters divided by God at the Creation, briefly released in judgment upon humankind in Noah's Flood, and serving similarly to set God's chosen people apart from their enemies in the crossing of the Red Sea (which itself prefigures the sacrament of Baptism), the Day of Judgment will begin; but the poem is less concerned with an epic narrative (compare *Chr III*) than with the impressionistic anticipation of how individual souls will perceive their condition on that day, according to the burden of guilt they are accruing here and now in this world. It is a major contribution to the penitential content of the codex. See the headnotes to *JgD II*.

Resignation

[The Exeter Book, fol.117^b–119^b]

'Sine ferro martyres esse possumus. *Buton ysene martiras beon we magon* (We can be martyrs without [suffering] the sword)', wrote Defensor (*LSc*, *De Patientia*, p.10), citing Gregory, who meant that Christian patience and humility under the afflictions of this world would be rewarded with a crown in the next. St Basil said so explicitly: 'He who endures evils patiently will merit being crowned in the world to come' (*LSc*, p.11). This poem, which is a prayer for patience and humility, adopts as a major theme the condition of exile, which is a martyrdom to the speaker. Superficially, it is exile from family, friends and birthplace; but the true poles of this exile are the present world and the heavenly homeland. The way between is a storm-threatened journey, calling for endurance of human contempt, devilish temptation and the trials of poverty and loneliness ordained by God – the three tests of patience defined by St Ambrose (*LSc*, p.9) – and ultimately death. A safe landfall is not to be secured by merit, for the traveller knows he has none of his own to plead; and vainglory, as the companion-poem of that title declares, is no way to the heavenly home.

The consequent anguish, though less poignantly analysed here than in *Sfr*, is plain: the *mod* is *morgenseoc* (line 96, 'his heart [is] sick at the break of day'). But this condition might be called, without facetious intent, the morning-sickness of the pregnant soul – for it is a sickness that comes only to the person in whom an inescapable awareness of spiritual truth has been seeded. The arrogant city-dweller of *Sfr* feels no such discomfort, for no spiritual life quickens within him. By humility alone is wisdom kindled, says the *Instructions for Christians* (Cambridge, University Library MS Ii.I.33, ed. J.L. Rosier, *Anglia* LXXXII (1964), pp.4–22). Trust in the divine helmsman, hope in the unmerited grace of God, and voluntary resignation to the will of the God with whom alone the world's remedy lies, beyond this life: these are the prescriptions of this poem and this is the wisdom kindled by humility, expressed in an idiom echoed in other OE Christian poetry. Here is a full description of that state of *conpunctio* (*onbryrdnes*) which the religious art and literature of the Anglo-Saxons sought to inspire, and of which Ephraim wrote (*LSc*, p.29): 'Compunction is the soul's health . . . the soul's illumination . . . the remission of sins; compunction draws to itself the Holy Spirit; compunction causes the only-begotten Christ to dwell in it.'

Defensor (*LSc*, p.21) quotes Isidore's dictum: 'Summa monachi virtus est humilitas. *Healic munuces mægen ys eadmodnyss* (The highest virtue of a monk is humility).' Perhaps in the context of the Exeter Book this poem had its special application: the monastic life was held to be both exile and martyrdom (see the headnote to *Glc*). But *all* souls on earth, Augustine argued (see the headnote to *Sfr*), are in exile; and St Jerome declared (*LSc*, p.208) that 'Not only the shedding of one's blood is counted in witness, but the immaculate service of a faithful mind is indeed a daily martyrdom.' Whether addressed to monks or to Christian layfolk, the poem is hardly a work of individualistic self-articulation as an end in itself, but rather a spiritual exercise for others to practise. The dramatic I-persona is doubtless chosen for the intensity of realization it helps the audience to achieve.

Deliver me, almighty God; help me, holy Lord. You fashioned heaven and earth and all the great and manifold wonders, my wondrous King, eternal Lord, which are therein. To you, God sublime, I offer my soul and my bodily self and my words and my works, wise Lord, and all my limbs, Custodian of light, and these manifold thoughts of mine. Signify to me, Custodian of the constellations, where it is best for my soul to observe the ordaining Lord's will so that I may serve you in everything and, King steadfastly true, elevate within myself your ordinance. Do not let the blatant thief do me harm in the darkness although I have more feebly listened to the creative King of glory, to the mighty Lord, than would have been my benefit. Forgive me, as a loving kindness, living God, my virulent sins; I am mindful of the remedy, Glory of kings: may I attain to it, if I am allowed.

22   Vouchsafe me, my Lord, respite and understanding and patience and purpose in each of the things which you, King steadfastly true, will to send to my testing. You know the many deeds of wickedness in me now, but yet, Lord, for your compassion's sake receive me even though I have done more dire and blameworthy things than God allowed me. Henceforth I shall have need nevertheless to seek to gain the protection of you, the holy King of heaven, in these transitory days and to look to and strive for that life after this other, so that gracious God may then bestow upon me there joy everlasting and grant me life, even though I made amends for my sins more tardily than were the commands of the saintly host of heaven. You have indeed vouchsafed me many favours here. Fix my trust, my timid expectations, upon yourself so that it may stand securely founded. Exalt my mind, God and King of spirits, in ready wisdom. I am coming now questing to you, Father of mankind, from out of this world, now I know that I must, in a very short time. Receive me then, Ruler of destinies, into your glorious joy and let me die, Lord of your loved ones, Succourer of my spirit. When too many adversaries are assigned to their malicious tasks, then I shall get comfort from the Lord, even though earlier in time I merited few mercies. Let angels bring me nevertheless into your presence, redeeming King and ordaining Lord, for your compassion's sake. Though throughout my days I have done many crimes, even so do not let the devil take me, your offspring, on that loathsome journey in case they should be enabled to take delight in that estimation

according to which they considered themselves better, those presumptuous angels, than the everlasting Christ. In that belief they were deceiving themselves; because of it, they have long had to suffer, as beings accursed, banishment.

59   Stand by me and when the storm closes in upon my spirit, steer it; then, mighty Lord, succour my soul, preserve it and sustain it, Father of mankind, and save it as being intended for celestial light, eternal God, ordaining Lord strong in might; for my spirit is stained with sins now and I am sometimes afraid for my soul. Although you have granted me many mercies in this world – thanks be to you for all the bounties and favours which you have granted me – not any of them were through deserving it; but from all this I will take courage to myself and rejoice and rest my hope in and array myself for the spiritual road and address myself to that journey which I must travel and make ready my soul and suffer all this for God in cheerful mood, now that I am firmly chastened in my spirit. The Lord indeed knows of certain sins in me which I cannot prudently discern myself. I have angered God, mankind's King, and because of that I have come to be thus cruelly tormented in respect of this world, according as my transgressions were great in the sight of men, to the extent that I am undergoing profound martyrdom.

82   I am not a man prudent in his judgments and wise in front of a crowd; in my spirit, therefore, I have eagerly spoken these words according as from the start poverty proved to be my lot upon the earth so that each year – thanks be to God for it all – I have always suffered more heartfelt hardships and dread than there was in other people; for I am driven, impoverished, away from my place of birth.

89   A man on his own, deprived of the pleasures of community, a friendless exile, cannot carry on much longer when the ordaining Lord is angry with him, in his youth he grieves and at every season people patronize him and add to his poverty, and all this, people's taunting, he suffers and always his mind is

mournful and his heart sick at the break of day. This sorry tale I most decidedly tell concerning myself, and I speak about a journey, eager with longing, and I think about the ocean. My mind does not know with what I may buy a boat on the sea, a vessel on the ocean stream. I do not have a lot of gold, nor indeed of friends that might help me on to the journey since I myself, because of my poverty, cannot carry out my desire.

105   A tree is allowed to flourish while awaiting its destiny and to spread its branches; I, because of the reproach, may not in my heart love any mortal man in my native land. Ah, my Lord, mighty Succourer; in so far as I am sick at heart and bitterly distressed the remedy is with you, after this life. In this existence I may in no way inhabit the earth without hardships, a destitute man; while I maintained an affection, a pleasant relationship, towards strangers, anxiety was always constantly mine as reward for my love, as I just now conceded. It is still the best thing, since a man may not himself avert his destiny, that he should therefore suffer it well.

The Descent into Hell

[The Exeter Book, fol.119^b–121^b]

Because the action of the poem shifts quickly to hell at the time of the harrowing, and remains there, the opening scenario of the Marys journeying to Christ's sepulchre has sometimes been deemed a false start. Yet it may be seen to have a plausible thematic and didactic purpose. The visit to the sepulchre was evidently a highly popular theme in the AS religious imagination. It was a recurrent subject of MS illumination (see, for example, London, BL Additional 49598 [The Benedictional of St Æthelwold]; Rouen, Bibl. Publ. Y 7 [The Benedictional of Robert of Jumièges]) and, highly significantly, it was dramatized in the Benedictine liturgy for Easter Day in the renowned form of the *Quem quaeritis?* dialogue (*Regularis Concordia*, ed. T. Symons, London 1953, pp.49–51). The essential dynamic of the episode which makes it so suitable for drama is the reversal of the protagonists' expectation and mood, following a discovery: the discovery is that of Christ's resurrection, the reversal is from despair at the apparent victory of death and the grave to Christian hope in personal resurrection and life beyond the grave.

In the historic event itself, the Marys were understood to represent all righteous Christian souls. Gregory the Great says so explicitly in his *Homilia 21 in Evangelia* for Easter Day which is still part of the Roman liturgy for Easter: 'Moreover, those women who came with spices saw angels – obviously because those souls which through divine longings set out towards the Lord with the spices of their virtues will gaze upon the citizens of heaven' (*PL* 76, *XL Homiliarum in Evangelia, Liber secundus*). In the poem, the symbolic suggestion that the Marys are all righteous souls journeying towards the grave is reinforced, according to the reading adopted here, by the use of the word *hinsið*, 'going hence', to denote their journey – a term elsewhere used as a euphemism for the soul's journey at death – and confirmed by the concluding prayer of Adam that he be released from death and hell by the sacrament of baptism which Christ and John had offered to the whole world. Thus the singular scriptural-historical events of the first Easter – the happy reversal of fallen humankind's condemnation and despair, experienced by the Marys and exemplified in the harrowing of hell – are presented here as archetypes of the experience mystically repeated thereafter in the life of each righteous soul which resolves, like the Marys, to journey towards the grave and the Lord, aided by baptism and bringing its virtues like spices. This distinctive philosophy of the suprachronological import of scriptural-historical events seems to operate in most OE scriptural-based poetry, notably in *Chr I*, *DrR* and *Exo*; while the specific point of doctrine, that fearsome death is truly the door to the heavenly paradise, is matched in *Phx*.

The apocryphal topic of the harrowing of hell was evidently no less popular than that of the visit to the sepulchre. An AS prose translation of the Latin version survives; it is the subject of AS homilies; there are references to it in *Chr I*, *Chr II*, *XSt*, *Glc B*, *Phx*, *Pnt*, *Rdl 55*, *Ele* and *DrR*; and it features in MS illustration, notably in London, BL Cotton Tiberius C vi, where a fine drawing shows Christ stooping to raise Adam and Eve from hell's gaping mouth. The common source is the *Gospel of Nicodemus* (M. R. James, *The Apocryphal New Testament*, Oxford, 1924). The poem does not give the full account. It omits the confrontation with Satan; thus its emphasis is upon the forgiveness of fallen humankind and the transcendence of death. The rhetoric is formal and strongly reminiscent of *Chr I*. Dramatic immediacy is conferred by the extensive use of direct speech.

Damage to the MS necessitates a few speculative readings in the text.

In the dawning they started, those noble women, preparing themselves for the visit. The band of men knew that their Prince's corpse had been enclosed in an earthy vault.

4   They meant, those desolate women, to mourn for a while with weeping and to bewail with lamentation their Prince's death. The grave was grown chill; it was a cruel journey there: but dauntless were the men whom they, overjoyed, would meet at the tomb.

10   In the daybreak she came, the grieving Mary, and summoned the other woman with her. Sorrowing, these two sought God's victorious Son, alone in that earthy vault where they previously knew that the men of the Jews had hidden him. They had imagined that he would have to bide in the tomb alone in that Easter eve. Something different indeed from this those women would know when they turned on their way.

17   For in the dawning there came a throng of angels; the rapture of those hosts surrounded the Saviour's tomb. The earthy vault was open; the Prince's corpse received the breath of life; the ground shook and hell's inhabitants rejoiced. The young man awoke dauntless from the earth; the mighty Majesty arose, victorious and wise.

23   The man John explained to hell's inhabitants; dauntless, he spoke rejoicing to the multitude about his kinsman's coming:

26   'Our Saviour promised me, when he willed to send me on this journey, that he, Lord of all the people, would seek me out after six months. Now that time is fled away, I most surely

expect and truly believe that today the Lord himself, God's victorious Son, will seek us out.'

33   Then the Lord of mankind hastened to his journey; the heavens' Protector would demolish and lay low the walls of hell and, most righteous of all kings, carry off the stronghold's populace. For that battle he gave no thought to helmet-wearing warriors, nor was his will to lead armoured fighting men to the stronghold gates. But the locks and the bars fell from those fortifications and the King entered in; onward he advanced, Lord of all the people, the multitudes' Bestower of glory. The exiles came crowding, trying which of them might see the victorious Son – Adam and Abraham, Isaac and Jacob, many a dauntless man, Moses and David, Isaiah and Zacharias, many patriarchs, likewise too a concourse of men, a host of prophets, a throng of women and many virgins, a numberless tally of people.

50   John then saw the victorious Son of God come with kingly majesty to hell; the man of sorrowing heart then recognized the coming of God's own self. He saw the doors of hell brilliantly gleaming which long since had been locked and shrouded in darkness; that servant was in ecstasy.

56   Boldly then, and undaunted before the multitude, the leader of the stronghold's inhabitants called out and spoke to his kinsman and with these words greeted the longed-for visitor:

59   'Thanks be to you, our Prince, because you were willing to seek out us sinful men since we have had to languish in these bonds. Although the traitorous devil – he is an enemy abroad – ensnares many a brotherless exile, that man is not bound so closely beneath oppressive locks nor so cruelly beneath painful fetters that he may not quite easily acquire courage, when he trusts in his Lord's good faith, that he will ransom him from those bonds. Thus we all trust in you alone, my precious Lord. I have endured much since you first came journeying to me when you gave me sword and breastplate, helmet and fighting-gear – this I have constantly held fast until now – and you made

known to me, Joy of royal majesties, that you would be my preserver.

76 'O Gabriel, how discerning and keen-witted you are, how gracious and thoughtful and humane, wise in your intellect and prudent in your words. This you made plain when you brought that boy to us in Bethlehem. So long we have waited and dwelt amid sorrows, filled with the desire for peace, happiness and hope as to when we might hear God's word uttered from his own mouth.

84 'O Mary, you bore us a brave king indeed when you brought us forth that child in Bethlehem. We, thus trembling behind hell's gates, were cruelly bound to abide in bonds. The destroyer was enjoying his work; our ancient enemies were all in ecstasies when they heard how we, penitent and mourning, lamented for our race – until you, victorious Lord God, bravest of all kings, were incarnate among us.

95 'By our greedy mind we have betrayed ourselves; therefore we deliver those sins in our hearts into the destroyer's hands and likewise to our foes we are forced to supplicate for peace. Alas, Jerusalem in Judea, fixed indeed you remain in that place: not all those living and dwelling in the earth, who sing your praise, may go about you. Alas, Jordan in Judea, fixed indeed you remain in that place: neither may you flow among earth-dwellers nor they enjoy the delights of your water.

107 'Now, deep in tribulations, I entreat you, our Redeemer – you are Christ the Lord – that you have mercy upon us, Creator of men. For the love of men you yourself sought your mother's womb, Lord God triumphant – not for your own need, Ruler of nations, but for the sake of those mercies which you have frequently shown mankind when it had need of grace. You are able to embrace all the habitations of the peoples; likewise, mighty Lord, you are able to count the sands of the sea, Best of all kings. Likewise I entreat you, our Redeemer, by your infancy, Best of kings, and by that wounding, Lord of hosts, and by your resurrection, Joy of princes, and by your mother,

Mary by name, whom all those lodged in hell exalt and praise, and by the angels which stand about you, whom you let sit at your right hand when you, the Lord of hosts, willed at your own discretion to seek us in this exile, and by Jerusalem in Judea – that city shall nonetheless henceforth await your coming again, beloved Prince – and by Jordan in Judea – we both bathed together in that stream: with that water besprinkle, Lord of hosts, in gracious mood all those lodged in this stronghold just as you and John happily inspired this whole world by the baptism in Jordan. For this, thanks be to the ordaining Lord for ever.'

Alms-giving

[The Exeter Book, fol.121ᵇ–122ᵃ]

Much AS religious poetry concerns personal salvation – by faith (*DrR*) and by deeds of valour against the devil (*Sfr*, *Glc*). *Alm* commends Christian generosity as proof of righteousness. As the lengthy chapter on alms in the *LSc* indicates (XLVIIII), concern for the poor was recognized as a social obligation endorsed by the Scriptures and the Fathers.

Since both wealth and poverty are ordained by Providence (*FtM*) it is the duty of the rich to relieve the poor, as Isidore says, according to their means (*LSc*, p.159). The *LSc* cites both likely sources for this poem: the general precepts of Tobit 12:8–10 – alms-giving is in effect the salve which cures Tobit's blindness, just as in this poem it is a salve for souls – and the specific idea in Ecclesiasticus 3:30. The poet could also have culled the sentiment from sermon usage. It occurs in sermon 30 of Caesarius of Arles (Sister M. M. Mueller, tr., *Saint Caesarius of Arles: Sermons* (New York, 1956), vol.I, p.152). Compare the charm 'For unfruitful land' for a rather more mercenary claim upon the credit of alms-giving.

It shall be well for the man, the mortal of righteous intent, who has within him a generous heart. Before the world this will prove his most esteemed remembrance and before our Lord the most favourable judgment. Just as with water he will quench the billowing flame that it may no longer, bright and blazing, damage dwellings, so with alms he will expunge all sins' wounds and salve souls.

Pharaoh

[The Exeter Book, fol.122ª]

8 verse lines. A dialogue is here used as the means of conveying received wisdom in question and answer form, as in the arcane *SnS*. The question: 'How many men in Pharaoh's army, pursuing God's folk?' The answer: 'Six hundred [or six hundred thousand; the text is damaged], I think.' The destruction of the Egyptians apparently alluded to here (but some words are lost) was interpreted as a symbol with far-reaching implications in Christian history and living (see *Exo*), so the information doubtless seemed less trifling to the poet than it may to us.

The Lord's Prayer I

[The Exeter Book, fol.122ª]

11 verse lines. This version of the Paternoster, without the concluding doxology, is only modestly elaborated in paraphrase, compared with *LPr II* and *LPr III*.

Homiletic Fragment II

[The Exeter Book, fol.122ª–122ᵇ]

20 verse lines. The poem is an exhortation addressed to 'you', the audience, to rejoice in spirit and to take the Lord and the certainties of the Faith to your comfort, and to let your light shine before men, though faithful friends prove false in this transitory world. It is a quite complex, compact and surely complete little poem, which discerns a model for the microcosmic individual Christian in the macrocosmic perspectives of divine history.

Riddle 30b

[The Exeter Book, fol.122ᵇ]

9 verse lines. This is the same riddle, with a few minor variants, as *Rdl 30a* on fol.108ª.

Riddle 60 (Reed-pen? Rune-stick? Gospel-book?)

[The Exeter Book, fol.122ᵇ–123ª]

A riddle by Symphosius with the solution '*Harundo*' ('Reed, cane' or 'Flute or pen of reed') has been offered as a source. But also attractive is the solution 'Wood inscribed with runes', while not implausible is the AS word *Boc* – not only 'Beech-tree' but also 'Book' and sometimes 'The Book' as in *Cristes boc* (the Gospels). This last interpretation would tend to strengthen the case, allowed by the codex layout, for linking *Rdl 60* with the following poem, *HbM*, as some scholars have wished. In the *HbM* too the speaker-persona is a message-bearer, at the literal level an inscribed piece of wood but symbolic, perhaps, of the Book of the Gospel, the good news. *Rdl 60* then, if related at all to *HbM*, may either be its opening or a separate riddle grouped by thematic association adjacent to *HbM*. See the headnotes to *Rdl 1–59*.

I used to be by the sand, close by the sea-cliff at the ocean's edge; firm in my first state I stood. It was few only of human-kind that observed my dwelling-place there in solitude but with each dawn the tawny wave would lap me with watery embrace. Little I imagined that early or late I should ever speak, mouth-less, across the mead-bench, and communicate words. It is something of wonder, perplexing to the mind of him who knows nothing of such, how the point of a knife and the right hand, a man's ingenuity and the point together, deliberately pricked me so that I should confidently declare a message in the presence of us two alone, so that no more people might gossip our converse further afield.

The Husband's Message

[The Exeter Book, fol.123ª–123ᵇ]

HbM and *WfL* are not adjacent in the codex, but still it is hard to resist considering them in the relationship which their (modern) titles suggest, even though *HbM* is as riddlingly allusive as *WfL*.

The speaker-persona – not the 'husband' but the instrument of the message – says that the message embodies an immutable covenant by which an 'ancient vow', made before a feud intervened and caused the lord to be cast out by his own people, will be honoured. The spouse is called upon to voyage to the lord across the ocean to another country where he rules, where wealth abounds but where earthly treasure will be superseded by the all-sufficient joy of reunion according to the covenant.

The runic clue at the end suggests an interpretation: 'sun' is con-joined with 'road' to make 'sun-road', that is 'heaven', and with 'earth' and 'joy' and 'man' to witness the fulfilment 'by his living self' of the covenant. If these are tokens of what is conjoined in the incarnate, resurrected and ascended Redeemer then the message affirming them is perhaps 'the good news', that is the Gospel or the whole Bible – the *boc* of *Rdl 60*?

St Caesarius (*c*. 470–542), an authority often cited in *LSc*, is elo-quent witness to the early currency of the idea that the Scriptures are a letter inviting exiled humankind home: 'Notice carefully, beloved brethren, that the sacred Scriptures have been transmitted to us like letters from our heavenly country. Our country is paradise, and our parents are the patriarchs, prophets, apostles and martyrs; the angels are its citizens, Christ is our King. When Adam sinned, we were all as though thrown into the exile of this world. However, since our King is more kind and merciful than can be imagined or expressed, He deigned to send us through the patriarchs and prophets sacred writings as letters of invitation summoning us to the eternal and excellent country.' (Sister M. M. Mueller, tr., *Saint Caesarius of Arles: Sermons* (New York, 1956), vol.I, Sermon 7, p.46).

HbM would thus stand in a larger context than any that can plausibly be found for it in secular legend. Its motif of seafaring towards a ready home in another country would relate to the meaning as well as to the language of *Sfr*; and its concern with the covenant – tenuously observed in faith and hope through the history of the Old Testament, awaiting the consummation of charity in the age of the New – would be shared with the poems of the Junius MS. In so far as the stoic endurance, the hope of retribution and the unceasing longing of the woman in *WfL* may represent faith and hope glimmering in the pre-Messianic age of exile, that poem too would belong in the context established for *HbM*: the message would be that, in answer to the faithful longing, love has called Jerusalem (the Church, the soul of man) to what is duly hers in heaven by virtue of espousal to Christ. Note Isaiah 54:4–7, and see the headnote to *WfL*.

But here as in *WfL*, *WlE* and *Sfr* the literal level of the poem is vivid, specific and circumstantial, and arguably self-sufficient as a poetic topic, without symbolic interpretation. The MS has suffered damage at this point and lines 2–8 (in which the speaker-persona refers to his origin as a tree, to frequent journeys by ship, to another country, and to his lord who sent him forth) and 36–41 are too much marred to allow satisfactory reconstruction.

I

8   Now in privacy I will tell you . . . (8) Now I have come here in a ship and now you shall know how you may think in your mind of my lord's heartfelt love. I dare promise that you will find there a covenant immutably glorious.

II

13   See, he who inscribed this wood instructed me to beseech you that you, the jewel-spangled, yourself recall into mind the spoken vows which you two often voiced in earlier days, while you were allowed to occupy a dwelling-place in the festive cities, inhabit the one country, and forward your friendship. A feud drove him away from his conquering people. Now he himself has bidden me gladly inform you that you should ply the ocean once you have heard on the cliff's edge the melancholy cuckoo calling in the thicket. Thereafter let no man living deter you from the journey or hinder your voyage.

III

26   Look to the ocean, the seamen's domain; take to the ship so that southward hence you may meet the man beyond the ocean-way where your lord is expecting you. Not a wish in the world more greatly in his thoughts may be realized for him, according to what he told me, than that all-wielding God should grant that you two together may thereafter distribute treasure, bossed circlets, to men and to comrades. He has plenty of burnished gold . . . though he holds his domain within another country, a lovely land . . . of trusty heroes, even though here my lord . . . impelled by necessity launched his ship and upon the motion of the waves had to journey alone upon the sea-road, swirling the ocean currents, eager for the onward way. Now the man has prevailed above his anguish. He has no need of desirable things, not of horses nor treasures nor the pleasures of mead nor any of the noble stores of wealth upon earth, O prince's daughter, if he may possess you in accordance with the ancient vow of the two of you.

49   I conjoin S (sun) together with R (road) (sun-road, heaven) and EA (earth) and W (joy) and M (man) to declare on oath that he would fulfil, by his living self, the pledge and the covenant of friendship which in former days you two often voiced.

The Ruin

[The Exeter Book, fol.123ᵇ–124ᵇ]

Damage to the MS, some apparent carelessness in the copying of the text, and the occurrence of words not known elsewhere in AS render *Rui* an incomplete and partially unintelligible work. Nonetheless it is remarkable as an early descriptive poem and as one which features a city rather than a natural landscape. Its haunting mood is achieved by the accumulation of closely focused detail; its powerful rhetoric involves some use of internal rhyme – a device rare in surviving AS poetry. If, as has been suggested, the poem refers specifically to *Aquae Sulis* (Bath) then it may be thought to articulate an historic sense of AS inferiority to the admired and emulated Romans. But read in the context of *Wan* and *Sfr* it should perhaps be judged a didactic rather than a purely descriptive poem. The decay of earth's cities and societies is taken in *Sfr* as a symptom of the decline of the whole world, while time itself runs out and the Judgment approaches. The ruined city of earth, like its reciprocal, the ineffable city of God, is a scriptural and patristic topos. Augustine (*CG*, Bk.II, ch.2), for example, cites Ps. 46 where these motifs occur in one complex: 'There is a river whose streams gladden the city of God . . . God is in that city; she will not be overthrown . . . Nations are in tumult, kingdoms hurled down . . . Come and see what the Lord has done, the devastation he has brought upon earth . . . Let be then: learn that I am God, high over the nations, high above earth. The Lord of Hosts is with us, the God of Jacob our high stronghold.' As Augustine says elsewhere (op. cit., Bk.XV, ch.1) the city of earth, though doomed and dangerous, may serve beneficently to prefigure the City of God. It may be, then, that *Rui*, like *Wan* and *Sfr*, dwells on the details of the world's decline in order to move its audience to seek the point-for-point reciprocal majesty, security and stability of the heavenly Jerusalem where earthly yearnings for noble fellowship and matching dignity of environment are fulfilled, free from the world's mutability.

The enigmatic nature of the poem may be no accident: is *Rui* perhaps a kind of *aenigma* belonging with the riddles which now follow in the MS? There would be room in the damaged ending for a formula challenging the audience to explain the circumstances described.

Wondrously ornate is the stone of this wall, shattered by fate; the precincts of the city have crumbled and the work of giants is rotting away.

3   There are tumbled roofs, towers in ruins, high towers rime-frosted, rime on the limy mortar, storm-shielding tiling scarred, scored and collapsed, undermined by age. An earthy grasp holds the lordly builders, decayed and gone, the cruel grip of the ground, while a hundred generations of humanity have passed away. Often has this wall, hoary with lichen, stained with red, lasted out one kingdom after another, left upstanding under storms: lofty and broad, it fell. Still the rampart, hewn by men, crumbles away . . . they were joined together . . . cruelly sharpened . . . shone . . . skilful work ancient structure . . . a ring with encrustations of soil prompted the mind and drew forth a swift idea. Ingenious in the making of chains, the bold-minded man amazingly bound together the ribs of the wall with cables.

21   There were bright city buildings, many bathhouses, a wealth of lofty gables, much clamour of the multitude, many a mead-hall filled with human revelry – until mighty Fate changed that. Far and wide men fell dead: days of pestilence came and death destroyed the whole mass of those renowned swordsmen. Their fortress became waste places; the city rotted away: those who should repair it, the multitudes, were fallen to the ground. For that reason these courts are collapsing and the wide red roof of vaulted beams is shedding its tiles. The site is fallen into ruin, reduced to heaps, where once many a man blithe of mood and bright with gold, clothed in splendours, proud and flown with wine, gleamed in his war-trappings, and gazed upon treasure, on silver, on chased gems, on wealth, on property, on the precious stone and on this bright citadel of the broad kingdom; and the stone courts were standing and the stream warmly spouted its ample surge and a wall embraced all in its bright bosom where the baths were, hot at its heart. That was convenient. Then they let pour . . . the warm streams across the grey stone . . . until the round pool hotly . . . where the baths were. Then is . . . It is a fitting thing how the . . . city . . .

Riddles 61–95

[The Exeter Book, fol.124^b–130^b]

See headnotes to Riddles 1–59.

Riddle 61 (Embroidered Shirt? Helmet?)

[The Exeter Book, fol.124^b]

Editors, varying in their suggestibility, have accordingly found the riddle indecent or innocuous. It is taken here to belong to the 'keyhole' division of the 'key/keyhole' group of riddles exploiting sexual innuendo.

Often a noble woman, a lady, has locked me up tight in a chest. On occasions she would pull me out in her hands and deliver me to her lord and loyal master, as she was bidden. Then he would poke his head inside me. From below, I being upturned, he would conjoin with me in a tight fit. If the recipient's strength kept up, some sort of hairy thing would be bound to fill my ornamented person. Interpret what I mean.

Riddle 66 (Creation)

[The Exeter Book, fol.125^a–125^b]

This brief exploitation of paradox is related to *Rdl 40*, a much lengthier poem on the Creation beginning 'Eternal is the Creator'. The hundred *Aenigmata Aldhelmi* strategically conclude with the riddle '*Creatura*'.

I am greater than this world, smaller than a tick, brighter than the moon, swifter than the sun. The seas, the ocean-floods, are all in my embrace, and this expanse of earth, the green plains: I reach to their foundations. I stoop below hell, I mount above the heavens, the glorious homeland, and extend abroad over the angels' abode. I fill the earth, the aged world and the ocean streams, amply with my own self. Say what I am called.

Riddle 69 (Ice)

[The Exeter Book, fol.125^b]

A wondrous thing happened at sea: the water turned to bone.

Riddle 76 (Hen?)

[The Exeter Book, fol.127^a]

I saw a solitary woman, sitting.

Riddle 86 (One-eyed Seller of Garlic)

[The Exeter Book, fol.128^b–129^a]

Perhaps the most renowned AS riddle, with its absurdly arbitrary-seeming solution – which nonetheless derives from Symphosius ('*Luscus allium vendens*').

A creature came slinking where men were sitting, many of them in council, men shrewd in mind. It had one eye and two ears and two feet, twelve hundred heads, a back and a belly and two hands, arms and shoulders, one neck and two sides. Say what I am called.

COTTON VITELLIUS
A xv

The Beowulf Manuscript

[London, British Library, Cotton Vitellius A xv]

The *Beowulf* MS, like the Vercelli Book, contains both poetry and prose. In two contemporary hands of the late tenth or early eleventh century, which change at line 1939 of *Bwf*, are a prose homily on St Christopher, a prose text of *Marvels of the East* with coloured drawings, the prose *Letter of Alexander to Aristotle*, and the poem *Jud*. The order of items has been changed by reconstruction of the book at some unknown date in its history, and it is conceivable that it originally contained more items than have survived. Very little is known of the early life of the MS but it was acquired by Sir Robert Cotton (d. 1631) whose great collection of MSS was partially destroyed and damaged by a fire at the Cottonian library in Westminster in 1731. The *Bwf* MS was charred, but survived – though the damage it suffered has made editors of both *Bwf* and *Jud* dependent for many readings on the testimony of earlier readers who saw the MS in a better state.

The texts between them make up a most extraordinarily eclectic gathering so that a convincing reason for the particular selection is hard to find, unless it is the compiler's interest in the fabulous, the exotic and the monstrous. St Christopher is a giant won over to the service of Christ; in the *Marvels* the wonders and extremities of God's creation are shown to include a man-eating monster whose portrait could well have realized the *Bwf*-audience's notion of Grendel; the *Letter* is a link with the corpus of fabulous tales of Alexander's conquests in the East and his encounters with the marvels there; and Holofernes is a physical and moral monster in an exotic Hebrew legend. Perhaps, then, the compiler sought to make a *Liber monstrorum*, or, more appositely, a prototype 'Beowulf and its analogues', documenting the types of good and evil in *Bwf* with other examples – for these and all the world's wonders and monstrosities were amenable to a didactic, moral interpretation according to commonplace Christian scholarship of the age.

No one doubts that here again a book has been put together from pre-existing materials, perhaps of great antiquity, not from literature newly composed nor even, in this case, from pre-existing texts creatively edited in order to bring out thematic correspondences between them. Compared with the dynamic relationships of the poems in Junius 11, or the many-faceted prescription for Christian living offered by the Exeter Book, or the consistently religious penitential, devotional tone of the Vercelli Book, this rationale of wonders, if that is what we have, looks trivial and smacks, perhaps, of the late AS literary taste for romance exemplified in the translation of *Apollonius of Tyre*.

Nevertheless, the codex preserves the finest poem surviving from the AS period and, in *Jud*, another of the very best.

Beowulf

[London, British Library, Cotton Vitellius A xv, fol.132ᵃ–201ᵇ]

The date of the poem remains an unsettled problem. A *written* version of it preceding the uniquely surviving MS may safely be postulated; and beyond doubt is the likelihood that a form of the poem was in circulation among poets of the *oral* tradition for some centuries before the known MS version was made. Indeed, the principal motifs of the poem's plot are motifs of widespread folklore, and parts of the story, and the figures of Beowulf and of the monsters, have analogies elsewhere in the ancient literature of North-West Europe. But the story as it survives embodies, unless we have misunderstood it, a strikingly sophisticated and deliberately structured philosophical statement which is surely the construct of one creative mind presiding in literary manner over the traditional material.

Concern with locating the elements of this traditional material in the context of early Germanic culture has characterized the preliminary stages of *Bwf* criticism; but it is the location of that artistically and didactically sovereign mind in a plausible intellectual and social milieu within the evolving culture of the Anglo-Saxons to which much *Bwf* scholarship continues to address itself. Though it is conventional to regard the poem as early – first, because of the obvious antiquity of some of the traditional content, then because the relatively clear landmarks of the age of Bede, or of Offa's Mercia, or of Rædwald of East Anglia and the Sutton Hoo ship-burial inevitably tempt scholars to take all other bearings from them – the early dating has always had its strenuous opponents. It must indeed be acknowledged that the arguments insisting on a seventh- or eighth-century date remain, after all the discussion, barely more absolute and compelling than arguments placing the poem after the start of the Danish invasions, in the ninth or tenth century, or even as late as the likely date of the unique MS itself, which palaeographers place about the year 1000. It is well to bear in mind what the very nature of the oral mode of transmission of poetry makes probable: that the broad narrative of *Bwf* had served many generations as a vehicle for their current values and tastes long before a version was composed in writing, and that however ancient in origin the narrative may be, however antique some of the elements surviving from earlier stages, the particular re-telling recorded in the Cotton MS may have been shaped to articulate philosophical and literary purposes much more 'modern' than the world of ship-funerals and dragon-tales preserved in its plot. What we can most confidently say of the poem as we have it is that it represents a literary judgment of the late tenth or early eleventh century.

Over generations of critical attention, *Bwf* has proved its stature as a literary classic – as a major monument to an historic culture and as a visionary statement of issues of abiding relevance to people living in community at any time. The literary appreciation of the poem benefited little from nineteenth-century scholars who quarried it for Germanic antiquities, or subjected it to drastic editorial restoration in quest of a prototype text, or used it as grist to the mills of anticlericalism, of nationalism, and of the cult of Aryanism. It fared little better when early twentieth-century critics tested it by standards of classical literary structure and taste, and found it wanting. But what scholars of that period derided as the chimera of a 'literary' *Bwf* has since been claimed by many to be a substantial reality – though even if there is wide agreement that the surviving version is the creative work of a single poet, and is therefore amenable on that basis to literary critical analysis and judgment, the poem continues to speak differently to different readers. One may do worse than look back for guidance to the pioneering assessment of the Dane, N. F. S. Grundtvig – largely ignored, particularly by English scholars, in his day – who published a Danish translation and a study of the poem in 1820, not long after the first printed edition of the whole text had been made, in 1815, by the Icelander, G. J. Thorkelin, on behalf of his Danish patron.

The language of the poem, Grundtvig says, is of the finest, compared with any other example of the rich corpus of early Germanic poetry. Though the poem's structure, he thought, was not so beautifully coherent as that of Greek epic poetry (but later critics have drawn attention to the differently conceived, but nonetheless distinctive structural principles of *Bwf*, to the symmetries, parallels and contrasts, large and small, of theme, imagery and diction), the English poem had in his view far more to say. He found it a poem whose liveliness and entertaining qualities enhanced its high ethical integrity. He evidently understood it to speak from deep poetic insight about humanity, not merely about men and women. He identified in it a fundamental religious tone, and saw that the poet desired to represent his hero's struggles as being part of the cosmic contest between good and evil which is a characterizing element in the Christian view of history. He recognized that the monsters represented the powers of darkness striving against the light with which God penetrated the primordial darkness; and he understood the stakes to be the survival and thriving of human community, through which mankind had best hope of realizing the Godward-aspiring part of its flawed human nature. He acknowledged the sombre view taken by the poet, who chose no refuge in literary escapism, but compelled his audience to contemplate the sacrifice when heroes lay down their life for their friends. But Grundtvig found final optimism in the poem, an optimism determined not by literary convention but by Christian philosophy: that though the powers of darkness are potent to kill mankind's worthiest champions, God will not let such champions bear witness in vain. In Grundtvig's view, Beowulf *succeeds* in saving the dying life of the community.

Thus, Grundtvig's reading implies, sacrifice of oneself for the life of civilized community, imperfect though it may be, is not an act of vain and self-deluding heroics, but a responsibility which the strong and the gifted may not repudiate, and which is in itself a victory against anarchy and elemental evil; such is the poet's understanding of the testimony of history, and he endorses his view by appeal to divine authority. We may cite St Augustine in his support: 'It is wrong to deny that the aims of human civilization are good, for this is the highest end that mankind of itself can achieve. For, however lowly the goods of the earth, the aim, such as it is, is peace.' (CG, Bk.XV, ch.4, pp.419–20).

Such a reading gives full credit to the secular heroic material of the plot, which the poet has evidently drawn from Germanic tradition. But it does not see these elements as bringing with them the heathen implications which no doubt many of them had when first they were coined. They are rather exploited so as to express in terms challengingly meaningful to an audience nurtured on secular heroic narrative poetry the larger philosophy of Christianity – at least as it related to questions of heroic altruism in defence of the common good, and of the virtues of (Christian) civilization, specifically defined in the poem as awareness of the source of good and of happiness, sanctity of familial bonds and the brotherhood of nations, mutuality of respect between ruler and ruled, communality, order, harmony, beauty, peace, the innocent pursuit of happiness, generosity, magnanimity and wisdom.

The prescriptions and warnings of this highly ethical work speak relevantly to any period of AS history one chooses to consider; and they remain a preoccupation of significant literature through the whole English literary tradition.

The sectional numbering used here follows that of the MS, repeating its error rather than arbitrarily adopting one of the hypothetical solutions. There are 43 sections or 'fitts' in the whole poem. The first is not numbered. The second to the twenty-ninth are numbered I-XXVIII. The thirtieth is unnumbered. The thirty-first, which according to the foregoing system ought to have been numbered XXX, is actually numbered XXXI, thus bringing the numeration into accord with the actual number of fitts. Thereafter the numbers XXXII–XLIII follow consecutively (though the number is missing from the thirty-ninth) to the forty-third and last section.

The language of *Bwf* is densely textured: a slightly more expansive manner of translation has therefore been adopted for it.

Listen! We have heard report of the majesty of the people's kings of the spear-wielding Danes in days of old: truly, those princes accomplished deeds of courage! Many a time Scyld Scefing dispossessed the throngs of his enemies, many nations, of their seats of feasting and struck awe into men of stature, after he had first been found, scantly provided. For that, he was to meet with consolation: here below the skies he flourished and prospered in estimations of his worth until each one of his neighbours across the whale-traversed ocean had to obey him and yield him tribute. He was a good king.

12   Later an infant son was born into the world to him, whom God sent as a comfort to the people. He came to understand the tormenting distress they had once suffered, being for a long while without a leader; for this the Lord of life, heaven's Ruler, granted him worldly renown. Beowulf, son of Scyld – far and wide his glory spread – was famed through the lands of Scandinavia. Just so ought a young man by his integrity, by generous gifts of treasure whilst in his father's guardianship, to bring it about that later, when he is of age, willing comrades will be at hand when war comes, and will support their prince. By praiseworthy actions a man will thrive in any nation.

26   Then at his appointed time Scyld, the man of abounding vigour, passed away, to journey into the keeping of the Lord. They who were his dear comrades then carried him to the seashore as he had himself commanded while he, the Scyldings' friend and lord, owned the power of speech: beloved founder of the land, he had ruled it long.

32   There in the harbour lay a ship with curved prow, ice-encrusted, eager to be outward bound – the prince's vessel. So they laid the beloved king, the ring-giver, the famous man, amidships, by the mast. A great number of treasures and trappings from far-away regions was transported there. I have not heard of a ship more splendidly bedecked with weapons of war and battle garments, swords and mail-coats. Amidships lay a multitude of treasures which were to travel far away with him into the possession of the ocean. By no means did they furnish him less with gifts, riches from the communal treasury, than did those who in the first place had sent him forth alone across the waves being still an infant. Furthermore, they set up a golden standard high above his head; they let the sea bear him off, and gave him over to the icy ocean. Their spirit was melancholy, their heart grieving, within them. Those men who dispense wisdom in the hall, worthies here below the heavens, were unable to say in truth who received that cargo.

I

53   Thereafter, Beowulf of the Scyldings, a beloved people's king, was for a long period held in esteem by the communities in their strongholds – his venerable father had departed from the earth to some other place – until to him in his turn was born the illustrious Healfdene.

57   Healfdene governed the contented Scyldings as long as he lived, aged and yet still fierce in battle. To him, the leader of armies, four children in succession were born into the world, Heorogar and Hrothgar and Halga the Good. I have heard that the fourth child was the queen and loved consort of Onela the Heatho-Scylfing.

64   To Hrothgar next, military success was granted, and esteem of his worth in war, so that his friends and kinsmen readily obeyed him, until his troop of young men grew into a great retinue of warriors.

67   It came into his mind that he would command a hall-building to be made, a banqueting-chamber, greater than the children of men had ever heard tell of, and that there inside it he would share out to young and to old all of such as God gave to him – that is, everything but communal property and human lives. I have heard that this labour of embellishing a place of the people was proclaimed far and wide to many nations throughout this earth. In due course, quickly in the sight of men, it came to pass that it was brought to final completion, the greatest of hall-buildings. He devised the name Heorot for it, he who far and wide exercised the authority of his word. He did not leave unfulfilled his vow: he shared out rings and jewels at the feasting. The hall towered aloft, high and wide-gabled: it awaited the upheavals of war and malicious fire, but it was not yet that time when violence was to break out between men bound by their sworn oaths, following a murderous attack.

86   Then that obdurate being – the one which waited in placcs of darkness – suffered tormentedly for a time because each single

day he heard the loud noise of happiness in the hall: the lyre's music was there, and the clear singing of the poet. He who was skilled in recounting the creation of men in time distant declared that the Almighty made the earth, a plain radiant to look upon which water encircles; he, taking delight in his achievement, established the sun and the moon, those luminaries, as light for those living in the world; he embellished the earth's surfaces with branches and with leaves; life too he created in each of those species which go their vital ways.

99   So the men of that community lived happily, blessedly, until one being, a fiend in torment, began to perpetrate outrages. That savage visitor was called Grendel, a notorious prowler of the marches, who patrolled moors, swamp and impassable wasteland. For a long while the unblest creature had inhabited the territory of a species of water-monsters since the Creator had proscribed him along with the stock of Cain. The everlasting Lord avenged that murderous act by which he slew Abel. He enjoyed no benefit from that violent assault, for God the Ordainer exiled him for that crime far away from humankind. From him all misbegotten things were born – ogres and elves and hellishly deformed beings such as the giants who fought for a long while against God: for that he paid them their due.

II

115   When night was come, then, he set out to investigate the lofty hall, as to how the mail-wearing Danes had organized it after the beer-drinking. Within it, then, he came across a company of noblemen sleeping after the banquet. They did not know grief, humanity's misfortune. This creature beyond redemption, savage and voracious, fierce and violent, was instantly prepared, and from their resting-place he snatched thirty thanes. From there, exulting in his plunder, he went journeying back homewards, seeking his lairs with that feast of carrion.

126 ·   Then in the half-gloom just before daybreak Grendel's fighting strength was made plain to people. Then was raised up, in the wake of the feasting, the sound of weeping, a great

noise with the morning. The famed king, a nobleman of integrity proved before this, sat cheerlessly; mighty in strength of numbers, he suffered, and experienced grief for his thanes, after people had scrutinized the trail of that loathsome, accursed being.

133   The struggle was too intense, too loathsome and too enduring. It was no longer a space of time but a single day before he perpetrated more acts of murderous destruction, aggression and violence, and felt no compunction for them: he was too addicted to them. After that the man was easy to find who looked for a place to lie down somewhere else more distant, a bed among the subsidiary chambers, once the hall-thane's hatred was signalled and unequivocally declared to them by clear token; he who had escaped the foe thereafter kept himself further away and safer. So he prevailed and, in defiance of right, he contended with them, one against all, until that finest of halls stood useless.

146   It was a great while: for a space of twelve years the friend and lord of the Scyldings suffered pain, every kind of misery and profound grief. It therefore became plainly known to the sons of men, lamentingly, by means of lays, that Grendel had contended for a long time against Hrothgar and sustained his spiteful attacks, violence and aggression and ceaseless strife for many years: for a settlement with any man of the pick of the Danes, to abandon that deadly work of destruction, to negotiate compensation, he had no wish; and none of the counsellors there had grounds to hope for gleaming gold in reparation at the hands of the killer. Instead, the monster, a dark death-shadow, went on harrying seasoned warriors and youthful ones alike: he would lie in wait for them and ambush them. Night after night he tyrannized the misty moors: men cannot know where those in conspiracy with hell may make their way in their roamings.

164   Thus the enemy of humankind, the hideous creature which walked alone, repeatedly perpetrated many violent deeds and

cruel humiliations. Heorot, that hall agleam with riches, he took over in the black nights – yet, thanks to the ordaining Lord, he was not allowed to come near that precious thing, the gift-throne, nor did he understand its purpose.

170 That was a great anguish and affliction of the heart for the friend and lord of the Scyldings. Many a gifted man sat time and again in deliberation; they would be weighing up advice as to what it was best for men stern of temperament to do in the face of the sudden terrors. On occasions they offered homage to idols at pagan shrines and prayed aloud that the slayer of souls might afford them help against their collective sufferings. Such, the optimism of heathens, had become their practice – they recalled things infernal to mind; they did not acknowledge the ordaining Lord, the Judge of deeds; they were oblivious of the Lord God nor indeed had they power to praise the Protector of the heavens, the Ruler of glory. Calamity will befall him who, because of cruel affliction, is impelled to thrust his soul into the fire's embrace, to hope neither for easement nor for there to be any change at all. Well shall it be for him who upon his death-day is permitted to seek the Lord and to supplicate for refuge in the embraces of the Father.

III

189 So Healfdene's kinsman agonized unceasingly over those lasting cares. The wise man was unable to avert those griefs: the struggle which had befallen the people was too intense, too loathsome and too enduring, an inexorable persecution, savage through envy, the grossest of acts of destructive malice under cover of night – until a thane of Hygelac, a worthy man, heard in his homeland among the Geats of Grendel's doings. He, Beowulf, was in strength the sturdiest of humankind at that time in this mortal existence, nobly born and of a physique beyond the ordinary. He ordered a good sea-going boat to be prepared for him. He declared that he wanted to go seeking the warrior-king, the famed prince, across the swan-road, since he was in need of men. Men of wisdom hardly cavilled at him over

that expedition, though he was dear to them; they encouraged him in his braveness of purpose and watched for the favourable signs. The worthy man had chosen soldiers out of the keenest that he could find among the Geatish people. As one of fifteen, he made his way to the timbered vessel; the man, being a person familiar with the ocean, led them to the limits of the land.

210   Time passed on. The buoyant vessel was waiting on the waves in the lee of the land. Accoutred heroes stepped aboard the prowed ship – the currents swirled, sea against sand – into the ship's hold soldiers carried gleaming pieces of equipment, magnificent fighting-gear. The men pushed off their boat of braced timbers upon that willing enterprise. Then the buoyant vessel with foam about its neck set off across the heaving ocean, exhilarated by the wind just like a bird, until at the due time on the second day the ship with curved prow had made such progress that the voyagers spied land, the coastal promontories gleaming, steep cliffs, wide headlands. So, with the ending of the voyage, the ocean had been successfully navigated. From there the Weder-Geatish people quickly stepped ashore and secured the timbered vessel – their mail-coats, their battle-clothing, jingled – and they gave thanks to God because the sea-roads had been easy for them.

229   Then the sentinel of the Scyldings, who was required to keep guard over the sea-cliffs, observed them carrying gleaming shields and serviceable fighting-gear down the gangplank. An urgency to know what men these might be obsessed his thoughts. Hrothgar's thane, then, went riding down to the shore on horseback, forcefully brandished the sturdy wooden shaft in his hands and demanded with formal words:

237   'What sort of armour-bearing men are you, protected by corslets, who have come here in this manner, steering your tall ship over the seaways and over the deeps? I have long been the installed custodian of the land's extremity and maintained the coast-guardianship so that no enemy with a ship-borne army might cause damage within the land of the Danes. No

shield-bearing warriors have ever arrived here more openly. Yet
you were not absolutely sure of the permission and consent of
the warrior-kinsmen. Never have I seen a greater nobleman on
earth than is that notable person in your midst, that man in his
accoutrements. He is no ordinary member of the hall enhanced
by his weapons: may his face, a peerless countenance, never
belie him.

251   'Now I must know your extraction before you go any further
beyond this point into the land of the Danes as dissembling
spies. Now, you inhabitants of far-off places, you voyagers of
ocean, listen to my straightforward mind: haste is best in
declaring what lies behind your coming here.'

IV

258   The chief, the leader of the contingent, answered him and
opened a treasury of words:

260   'We are by extraction out of the Geatish people and the
companions of Hygelac, sharers of his hearth. My father was
well known among the nations, a nobly born man of foremost
rank called Ecgtheow. He lived for many years until as an aged
man he passed away out of the world: surely every wise man far
and wide throughout the earth remembers him readily.

267   'Out of loyal purpose we have come seeking your lord,
Healfdene's son, the people's protector: be generous of advice
to us. We have an important mission to the famed ruler of the
Danes. A certain matter there must, as I imagine, be no secret.
You will know – if it is as we have heard honestly told – that in
the midst of the Scyldings an enemy, of what sort I do not
know, a mysterious perpetrator of acts of hate, manifests in a
fearful way incomprehensible malice, humiliation and slaugh-
ter. In this matter I can teach Hrothgar sound advice from a
generous spirit as to how he, the wise and the good, may
overcome the fiend – if the affliction of those baleful injuries
ever should of necessity change for him and a cure follow after
– and how those seething griefs of his might grow more cool:

but otherwise he will ever hereafter endure a lifetime of misery and inexorable suffering, as long as that best of halls remains there in its eminent position.'

286   The sentinel, a man fearless in fulfilling his duty, spoke from where he sat on horseback:

287   'The shrewd warrior who reflects sufficiently must know the difference between words and actions. I accept that this is a party of men loyal to the ruler of the Scyldings. Proceed, bearing weapons and armour. I shall guide you. I shall also order my warrior-thanes honourably to guard your vessel, your new-tarred boat on the beach, against every enemy, until that timbered ship with its curving prow carries a cherished hero back over the tides of ocean to the Weder-Geatish shore: to such a benefactor it will be granted that he will survive the onslaught of battle unharmed.'

301   So they proceeded to journey on. The buoyant vessel rested peacefully secure on its anchor; the broad-beamed ship rode quietly upon its mooring rope. Above their vizors shone images of the boar: that pugnacious beast, ornamented in gold, gleaming and tempered in the forge, afforded vital protection to warriors in their fury. The men went briskly on, marching together until they were able to make out a timber-built hall, magnificent and agleam with gold: of buildings here below the heavens this one in which the great ruler lived was the most eminently celebrated among earth's inhabitants. The lustre of it cast light over many lands.

312   Then the brave soldier directed them to that dazzling court of men of courage, so that they might get to it directly. The distinguished warrior turned his horse about and then spoke these words:

316   'It is time for me to go. May the Father and Ruler of all in his loving-kindness keep you safe in your undertakings. I will go back to the sea, to keep guard against any hostile band.'

V

320   The road, paved with stone, gleamed; the route guided the men grouped together – battle corslet shone, tough, with rings interlocked by skilful hands; shining iron link jangled in their mail-coats. As soon as they came marching up to the hall in their combat-gear, the sea-wearied men deposited their broad shields, their targes of extreme toughness, against the wall of the building. Then they seated themselves on a bench; their mail-coats, the men's battle-equipage, shafts of ashwood grey at their tips, stood stacked together – the iron-clad troop were done credit by their weapons.

331   There a proud and mettlesome man next questioned those campaigners about their parentage.

333   'From where do you come conveying gold-ornamented shields, grey mail-coats and vizored helmets, and that heap of war-spears? I am an envoy and court-officer of Hrothgar: I have not seen so many men from another nation looking more intrepid. I would guess that you have come seeking Hrothgar out of a proper pride – not because of misfortunes of exile, but out of majestic qualities of courage.'

340   The proud leader of the Weder-Geats, renowned for his valour, answered; looking stern in his helmet, he said these words in reply:

342   'We are the companions of Hygelac, sharers of his table. Beowulf is my name. I wish to tell my mission to Healfdene's son, the famed prince your lord, if he will grant us that we be allowed to greet him, generous man that he is.'

348   Wulfgar spoke out: he was a prince of the Wendels and his courageous temperament, martial prowess and wisdom were familiar to many:

350   'I will consult the friend of the Danes, the ruler of the Scyldings and giver of rings, the famed prince, in this matter

concerning your enterprise, just as you, as supplicant, have requested, and I will make the answer quickly known to you, which the worthy man sees fit to give me.'

356 Briskly, then, he went off to where Hrothgar, aged and quite white-haired, was sitting among the retinue of his earls; the man of renowned valour advanced, so that he stood right in front of the ruler of the Danes – he knew the mode of conduct proper to a noble society. Wulfgar made address to his friend and lord:

361 'There are some Geatish people here, come voyaging from far away across the ocean's ambit; these campaigners call the senior one among them Beowulf. They are supplicants, my lord, asking that they might be allowed to exchange words with you: do not deny them the substance of your conversation, gracious Hrothgar. They seem by their fighting-gear to be worthy of the earls' esteem. The leader who guided these battle-warriors here is indeed a man to depend on.'

VI

371 Hrothgar, protecting lord of the Scyldings, spoke forth:

372 'I knew him when he was a boy. His father was called Ecgtheow, to whom Hrethel of the Geats gave his only daughter in marriage; now his sturdy son has come here and sought out a loyal friend. Those seafarers who transported there precious gifts for the Geats as a token of esteem used to say that he, a renowned soldier in combat, has the potent strength of thirty men in his hand-grip. Holy God of his loving-kindness has sent him to us Danes – this I believe – against the violence of Grendel. I shall offer the worthy man treasures for the impetuosity of his courage. Be quick; summon this company of kinsmen to enter, all of them together, to see me, and also say to them explicitly that they are welcomed by the Danish people.'

389 So Wulfgar went to the hall door and declared these words from within:

391   'My victorious lord, king of the Danes, commands me to tell
you that he is familiar with your parentage and that you men of
stern determination are welcome here from over the surging
seas. Now you may enter in your fighting gear wearing your
warlike vizors, to see Hrothgar; leave your battle-shields and
death-dealing wooden spears here, to await the outcome of
your discussions.'

399   So the great leader arose and many a soldier round about
him – a majestic troop of thanes. Some remained there, to
guard their accoutrements of war, as the stern man had
instructed them. Together, as the man conducted them, they
passed quickly beneath the roof of Heorot; the warrior, look-
ing stern in his helmet, walked on until he was standing inside
the hall.

405   Beowulf spoke out – on him the mail-coat shone, an intricate
mesh linked together by the ingenious arts of the smith:

406   'Hail to you, Hrothgar! I am a kinsman and thane of
Hygelac. In my youth I have undertaken many famous
exploits. The affair with Grendel became openly known to me
on my native soil: seafarers say that this hall, this most excel-
lent building, stands desolate and useless to every warrior, once
the evening sun becomes hidden below the vault of the sky.
Thereupon my people, the most excellent of them, the men of
wisdom, advised me, king Hrothgar, that I should visit you –
for they were familiar with the force of my strength. They
witnessed for themselves the occasion when, stained with the
blood of my adversaries, I escaped from them and their snares.
Five of them I fettered there, and ravaged that family of giants;
and amid the waves, by night, I slew water-monsters, put up
with severe privation, took vengeance for the malice inflicted
upon the Weder-Geats and completely destroyed their enemies
– they asked for trouble – and now, alone, I must settle the
affair with that giant, the monster Grendel.

426   'Now, therefore, sovereign lord of the glorious Danes, prince
of the Scyldings, I want to beg a single favour from you: that

you do not deny it me, refuge of warriors, noble friend of the people, now that I have thus come from far away, that I be allowed to cleanse Heorot alone, without even my retinue of noble soldiers, this troop of hardy men. Furthermore, I have learned by hearsay that this monster does not bother with weapons in his recklessness: then in order that Hygelac, my lord, may be approving of me in his heart I shall disdain to carry a sword or broad shield, a yellow targe, into the encounter; but rather by wrestling shall I tackle the adversary and fight for life, foe against foe. In that event, the one whom death carries off must acknowledge the judgment of the Lord.

442 'I imagine that, if he is allowed to prevail, he will fearlessly devour the Geatish people, the flower of those victorious people, in the battlefield of the hall, as he has often done already. You will have no need to bury my body, for he will look after me, stained with dripping gore, if death carries me off; he will bear away the bloody carrion and have in mind to devour it. Remorselessly the lone prowler will eat it and stain his marshy haunts: you will have no need at all to worry any longer about the disposal of my corpse. If combat carries me off send to Hygelac the battle-garment, the best of its kind, a most excellent mail-coat, which protects my breast: it is an heirloom from Hrethel, the work of Weland. Providence will ever proceed as it must.'

VII

456 Hrothgar, protecting lord of the Scyldings, spoke out:

457 'Beowulf, my friend, out of obligations to friendship's bond and out of loving-kindness you have come to visit us.

459 'Your father precipitated an extremely serious feud. He became responsible for the hand-to-hand killing of Heatholaf of the Wylfings; after that his own people were unable to look after him, for fear of war. From there he made an approach to the Danish people, the honourable Scyldings. Already at that

time I governed the Danish people and. though still in my youth, I held charge of the wealthy kingdom and the stronghold full of treasure and fine men. Heorogar, Healfdene's son, my elder brother, was dead and lifeless then: he was a better man than I. Subsequently I settled the feud by a payment: I sent ancient treasures to the Wylfings over the ocean ridge and he swore me oaths.

473   'It is a grief to me in my heart to tell any man what Grendel with his hate-filled thoughts has perpetrated against me, by way of humiliations within Heorot and sudden vicious attacks. My hall-company, my warrior-band, is diminished: Providence has swept them away under Grendel's terrorism. God can easily cut off this presumptuous destroyer from his doings.

480   'Very often, men-at-arms grown heady with beer have pledged over the ale-cup that they would await Grendel's attack in the beer-hall with terror-dealing onslaughts of swords. Then in the morning as the day grew light, this mead-hall, this princely house, would be covered with gore; all the bench-boards would be drenched with blood and the hall with gore violently spilt – and I would have the fewer loyal men and cherished retainers by those whom death had carried off.

489   'Now, sit down to the feast and unfold to the men what you are deliberating, a glorious victory, as your spirit prompts you.'

491   So a bench was cleared in the beer-hall for the Geatish soldiers grouped together; there those men of stout heart went to sit, proud in their strength. A thane who bore in his hands the ornate ale-cup observed his office and poured out gleaming mead. Sometimes a poet sang clear in Heorot. Happiness was there, the happiness of heroes, a great host of the nobility of the Danes and Geats.

VIII

499   Unferth, Ecglaf's son, who sat at the feet of the lord of the Scyldings, spoke out and unloosed provocative imputations.

To him the enterprise of Beowulf, the courageous seafarer, was a great insult because he did not allow that any other man on earth might ever gain more glories beneath the heavens than he himself.

506　'Are you that Beowulf who pitted himself against Breca, and competed at swimming in the open sea, where out of pride the two of you tackled the ocean and for the sake of a foolish boast risked your lives in deep water? No one, friend nor foe, could dissuade you from that adventure fraught with anxiety as you swam out to sea. There you covered the flowing tide with your strokes, you spanned the seaways, you hauled yourselves along with your hands, and vanished across the icy ocean. The deep was surging with waves, with the turbulence of winter.

516　'For seven days the two of you toiled in the water's grasp. He outstripped you in swimming: he had the greater strength. Eventually the sea carried him ashore early one morning in the territory of the Heatho-Reamas. From there he made his way to his beloved homeland – he being held dear by his people – to the land of the Brondings and the handsome refuge and stronghold where he had people, a stronghold and treasures. The son of Beanstan certainly fulfilled his whole pledge against you. Therefore I anticipate an even worse outcome for you – though you may always have proved competent in the onslaughts of battle and fierce fighting – if you dare to await Grendel at close quarters for the duration of a night.'

529　Beowulf, son of Ecgtheow, spoke out:

530　'Well now, Unferth, my friend, you have had a lot to say about Breca and to tell about his enterprise, for one who is heady with beer. I consider the truth to be that I had more strength in the sea and difficulties to face in the waves than any other man. As boys we two would declare and vow – we were both still in our youth – that we would risk our lives out upon the icy ocean, and we did that. We had a tough naked sword in our hand as we swam off into the ocean – we intended to protect ourselves against whales. Neither was he at all able to swim away from me, far off on the swelling waves, as being faster in the open sea, nor did I wish to swim away from him. So we remained at sea together for the duration of five nights until the swell, the surging waters, the most freezing weather and darkening night drove us apart and a north wind fierce as the fray of battle turned upon us.

548   'Rough were the waves, and the anger of the fish of the deep was aroused. There my mail-shirt, tough, with rings inter-locked by skilful hands, afforded me help against adversaries; the meshed battle-garment decorated with gold covered my breast. One detested fiend of an attacker dragged me to the bottom – the fierce thing had me fast in its grip; but it was granted me that I might get at the monster with my sword-point, my fighting blade. The onslaught of battle carried off the mighty sea-beast by my hand.

IX

559   'Repeatedly, spiteful adversaries harassed me hard. I minis-tered to them with my excellent sword as was appropriate. The perpetrators of evil did not have the pleasure of that feast – of devouring me as they gathered around their banquet at the bottom of the sea; rather, next morning, hacked by blades, they were lying stranded along the shore slain by swords, so that henceforth they would never hinder sea-goers in their passage over the deep ocean-crossing.

569   'Light came from the east, God's bright token. The surf-waves abated so that I was able to see headlands, wind-beaten bastions. Often Providence will protect a man, so that he is not doomed to die, when his courage holds firm – at any rate, it happily turned out for me that I killed nine water-monsters with my sword. Never have I heard of a harder fight by night here below heaven's arch, nor of a man more pitiable amid the ocean-streams; and yet I escaped from my foes' grasp with my life, though exhausted by the adventure, when the sea, the

flood tide and the surging waters, carried me along the coast into the land of the Finns.

581 'I have heard nothing of such skilfully waged encounters, such terror-dealing use of swords, told about you. Never did Breca, nor either of you, achieve with gleaming swords a feat so brave in the contest of battle – I do not boast of it unduly – although you did become the killer of your brothers, your chief kindred: and for that you must endure damnation in hell, resilient though your conscience may be.

590 'I tell you for sure, son of Ecglaf, that Grendel, the terrible monster, would never have perpetrated so many violent outrages against your lord, and humiliations within Heorot, if your mind and heart were as fierce for the fray as you yourself reckon: but he has discovered that he need not have very much fear of the hostility, the terrible sword-fury of your people, the victorious Scyldings. He goes on taking his toll; to none of the Danish people does he show mercy. Rather, he pursues his lust; he slays them and despatches them. Opposition he does not look to find at the hands of the warrior-Danes.

601 'But now I shall shortly proffer him the strength and the courage of the Geats in combat. He who has the right to it shall go once more to the mead-drinking with confident heart, after the morning light of another day, the sun clothed in ethereal radiance, shines from the south upon the children of men.'

607 By now the distributor of treasure, white-haired with age and renowned in warfare, was in a state of rejoicing; the lord of the glorious Danes put his trust in this help as he, shepherd of the people, listened to the resolute sense of purpose informing Beowulf. The laughter of heroes was there – the clamour resounded cheerily – and their words were full of joy. Wealhtheow, Hrothgar's queen, came forward, a lady thoughtful in matters of formal courtesy. The beautiful woman, bejewelled with gold, greeted the men in the hall and first of all gave a cup to the guardian of the Danish homeland and wished him, loved

as he was by the people, to be of good cheer at the beer-drinking. With pleasure he shared in the banquet and the hall-cup, a king whose renown rested on being victorious.

620   The lady of the Helmings, then, went around every group of seasoned and of youthful retainers and offered the precious chalice until the due time arrived when the ring-bejewelled queen, distinguished for the quality of her mind, carried the mead-cup to Beowulf. She greeted the chief of the Geats and, being of wise understanding, gave thanks to God because her desire – that she might put her trust in some noble warrior for help against the violent outrages – was realized.

628   He, the fighter of deadly ferocity, received the cup at Wealh-theow's hands, and then, filled with eagerness for the encounter, he made a solemn declaration. Beowulf, Ecg-theow's son, spoke out:

632   'I resolved, as I put to sea and manned the ocean-going boat with a company of my men, that I should either accomplish totally the will of your people or else die in the place of battle, held fast in the enemy's clutches. I shall perform a deed of courage befitting a noble warrior, or else within this mead-hall live my last day.'

639   These words, the Geat's pledging-speech, pleased the lady well. The people's queen, beautiful, bejewelled with gold, went to sit at her lord's side.

642   So, once again just as before, the word of valour was spoken inside that hall, there was fellowship in happiness, there was the clamour of exultant people, until Healfdene's son desired to go forthwith to his night's rest. He was sure that a fight at the lofty hall would have been purposed by the monster from the time they could see the light of the sun until they could see night growing darker over everything and the creatures of the con-cealing shadows came stalking, dusky beneath the clouds.

651   The whole company rose. Then the one man saluted the other; Hrothgar saluted Beowulf and wished him success, supremacy over the festive-hall, and delivered these words:

652   'Never since I could raise hand and shield have I previously entrusted the splendid hall of the Danes to any man except here and now to you. Now have and hold the best of dwellings. Set your mind on glory, manifest your mighty courage, keep watch against foes. There will be no stinting of your wishes, if you survive that act of courage with your life.'

X

662   Then Hrothgar, shelterer of the Scyldings, went with a retinue of his men, out from the hall. The war-lord wished to join Wealhtheow, his wife, in bed. The heaven-King, so people heard, had appointed against Grendel a hall-guard who had a special duty towards the lord of the Danes: he kept guard against an ogre. And certainly the Geatish leader readily trusted in his own intrepid strength and the protection of the ordaining Lord, when he took off his iron mail-coat and his helmet from his head, gave his ornamented sword, the most select of weapons, to his servitor-thane and enjoined him to take care of his battle-gear.

675   Then that worthy, Beowulf of the Geats, before he climbed into bed, made a notable pledge:

677   'I do not reckon myself inferior in my prowess in physical feats of combat any more than Grendel does himself. Accordingly, I do not want to kill him, deprive him of life, by means of the sword, although I perfectly well could. He does not understand the good of exchanging sword-blow for sword-blow with me, of hewing at a shield, even though he is renowned for his malicious acts of aggression. Instead, we shall both of us forgo the sword tonight – if he dares to seek battle without a weapon – and then let wise God, the holy Lord, decree the glory to whichever side seems meet to him.'

688   The brave soldier laid himself down, then; the pillow cushioned the noble man's face, and many a brisk seaman about him took to his resting-place in the hall. Not one of them thought that he would ever find his way back to his own beloved land, to his people and to the noble stronghold where he had been nurtured, for they had heard that death by violence had already carried off too many by far of the Danish people in that wine-hall. But the Lord granted them, the nation of the Weder-Geats, a destiny inwoven with martial successes, and help and succour so that by the strength of one man and his own resources they might all overcome their enemy. It is a truth made manifest that mighty God has governed mankind through all time.

702   Through the black night he came making his way, the being which haunted the shadows. The warrior-bowmen whose duty it was to occupy the horn-gabled hall were sleeping – all except one. It was well known to people that this wicked spoiler was not allowed to drag them down into the shadows when the ordaining Lord did not will it; and so, watching in a mood of hostility against the foe, he, the one man, waited in ebullient mood for the issue of battle.

XI

710   So from the moor Grendel came advancing under the banks of mist: he bore upon him God's anger. The nefarious spoiler meant to snare a certain one of the human stock in the lofty hall. On he stalked beneath the clouds to where he knew with perfect familiarity the wine-building stood, the people's hall for the giving of gold, gleaming with plates of precious metal. Though that was not the first time he had visited Hrothgar's home, never in all the days of his life, before nor after, did he encounter hall-thanes with harsher consequences.

720   To the hall, then, the aggressor came making his way, cut off from the things that give joy. The door, secured with forged metal bands, yielded at once when he touched it with his hands.

So, now that he was in frenzied mood, obsessed with violence he swung open the entrance to the building. After that the fiend stepped swiftly on to the brightly coloured floor. Irascible of temper, he advanced; from his eyes there flashed a hideous light, most like a flame. In the hall he saw the many soldiers, the fraternal company, sleeping, a throng of young fighting-men gathered together. His heart jubilated then; the hideous monster meant, before day came, to part life from body of each single one of them, since the prospect of gorging himself full had presented itself.

734   It was no longer to be his lot beyond that night to be allowed to devour any more of humankind: strong and mighty, Hygelac's kinsman was observing how the nefarious spoiler would proceed in the course of this precipitate assault. The monster did not intend to delay, but as a start he hastily grabbed a sleeping soldier, tore him apart without any trouble, chewed his joints, drank the blood out of his veins and gulped him down in gobbets. Soon he had consumed the whole of the lifeless man, even his feet and hands. Forward and nearer he stepped; then with his hand he seized the unflinching soldier on his bed. With his claw the fiend clutched at him – he, with astute presence of mind, quickly grabbed hold of it and braced himself against the arm. Straightway that master of violent deeds discovered that nowhere in the world, nowhere on the plains of earth, had he met in any other man a greater hand-grip. He grew afraid in heart and in spirit but none the sooner for that could he get away. His instinct was urging him to be off; he wanted to escape into the darkness, to join the flock of devilish creatures. This present experience of his was not such as he had encountered before in all the days of his life.

758   Then that worthy man, Hygelac's kinsman, bore in mind his speech of that evening. He stood upright and grappled tightly with him. His fingers were at cracking point. The ogre was edging his way outwards; the noble warrior kept moving forward step by step. The notorious creature meant to go leaping off to a safer distance if he could, and flee away from there into

his fen-haunts. It was a bitter foray on which the malignant spoiler had journeyed to Heorot.

767   The lordly hall rang with the din. For all the Danes dwelling in the fortress, for those earls and for every brave man it was the bitter dregs of the ale. The two furious defenders of the hall were both enraged. The building resounded. It was a great wonder that the wine-hall withstood the fierce combatants and that the beautiful residence did not collapse to the ground, but it was sufficiently secured inside and out by straps of iron, cunningly smithied. Many a mead-bench embellished with gold was wrenched from its footings, so I have heard tell, where the ferocious adversaries fought together. Knowledge-able men among the Scyldings had not previously believed of it that any person could ever by ordinary means wreck that excellent hall clad with bracing timbers, or reduce it to ruin by cunning – unless fire's embrace should engulf it in its blaze.

782   A noise, a strange noise, rose up repeatedly. In the Danes a terrible fear sprang up, in each one of them who from the rampart heard a wailing, heard God's adversary howling a terrible war-chant, a song of victory lost, hell's prisoner moan-ing over his wound. The man who was in strength the sturdiest of people at that time in this mortal existence, held him fast.

XII

791   Beowulf, shelterer of earls, was not willing on any account to release the murderous intruder alive for he did not reckon that the days of his life were to anyone's advantage. Repeatedly, one of Beowulf's earls would draw his ancient sword there, wanting to protect the life of their lord and famed prince wherever they could. There was something they did not know when they joined in the struggle, those sternly motivated fighting-men, and thought to chop at him from every side and seek his life: no battle-blade nor any iron sword, not the choicest on earth, would touch that evil spoiler, for he had made himself impervi-ous by magic to weapons customarily victorious, to any sword

whatever – yet his severance from life at that time in this mortal existence was to be a wretched one and this alien being was to journey far away into the power of devils.

809   Then he who hitherto perpetrated much heartfelt affliction and violence against humankind – he being antagonistic towards God – found that his body would not perform for him, for Hygelac's courageous kinsman was restraining him by means of his hands. Each was loathsome to the other as long as he remained alive. The terrible monster suffered a bodily wound – in his shoulder a great lesion became conspicuous. The sinews were snapping apart, his joints were bursting. To Beowulf was granted the battle-triumph; Grendel was forced to flee from there mortally wounded, to make his way to a comfortless dwelling-place under cover of the marshy slopes – he was all the more clearly aware that the end of his life and the full span of his days had been reached. For the Danes as a whole an ambition had been realized in consequence of that fatal combat.

825   So the man who had earlier come from afar, a man both intelligent and stout of heart, had purged the hall of Hrothgar and liberated it from malice. He was well pleased with that night's work, with the glories of that deed of valour. The leader of the Geatish men had fulfilled his pledge to the Danes, and by the same token he had remedied all the distress of mind and spitefully inflicted sorrow, and the pain, not inconsiderable, which they had previously suffered and which they had been forced by crushing necessity to endure. The proof was plain to see, when the brave warrior hung up the hand, the arm and the shoulder – the whole grasp of Grendel was there, complete – beneath the broad roof.

XIII

837   Then, in the morning, as I have heard, there was many a fighting-man round about the hall. Leaders of the people journeyed from far and near along widely flung ways to gaze upon

that wondrous sight, the tracks of the hated enemy. His sever-
ance from life did not seem a painful thing to any of those
people who gazed on the humiliated creature's trail – how,
making off from there weary at heart, defeated in the hos-
tilities, he had extended the tracks of his life-blood, doomed
and routed, to the mere of the water-monsters. There the water
was foaming with blood; the hideous heaving of the waves, all
mixed with hot blood, foamed with violently-shed gore.
Doomed to death, he was in hiding when, in his lair in the fens,
the melancholy creature laid down his life and his heathen soul.
Thereupon, hell received him.

853   From there they turned back from sportive pursuit, old
companions and many a young man likewise, men of spirit
riding from the mere upon glossy-coated horses. There
Beowulf's glorious exploit was related; repeatedly, many a
man declared that south or north throughout the mighty earth
amidst the encircling oceans there was no other shield-bearing
man beneath the bright sky's vault more noble, more worthy of
dominion; only they did not in the least derogate their friend
and lord, the gracious Hrothgar, for he was a good king.

864   From time to time these men renowned for their pugnacity
would give their yellow-golden horses rein to gallop, to run in
competition wherever the ways seemed to them agreeable and
recognizable for their preferred qualities. From time to time a
thane of the king, a man fraught with exultant words, his mind
full of songs, and who had in memory a great multitude of tales
of antiquity – one word would conjoin with another, accu-
rately linked – this man cleverly set about reconstructing
Beowulf's exploit, and successfully recited a skilful narrative,
achieving variety with his words. Almost everything that he
had heard said about Sigemund he told; about his deeds of
courage and much that was unfamiliar, the struggle of this son
of Wæls – the wide wanderings, the feuds and the crimes – of
which the children of men were not entirely aware, except for
Fitela who was with him when he was inclined to tell him
something of such matters, as an uncle to his nephew, since in

every hostility they had always been comrades in need. For Sigemund there sprang up a great reputation following his death, after he, a stern man when it came to fighting, killed the reptile guardian of a treasure-hoard. Alone he, son of a prince, ventured upon the dangerous deed beneath the grey rock – Fitela was not with him – but yet it proved his good fortune that his sword passed clean through that prodigious reptile so that the lordly weapon of iron stood fast in the rock-face. The dragon died from the injury. By his courage the ferocious adversary had brought it about that he was free to make use of the hoard of rings at his own discretion. The son of Wæls loaded an ocean-going boat and carried shining ornaments into the ship's hold. The fiery reptile burned itself out. Of men in exile he, that protective lord over warriors, was the most famed throughout the nations on account of his courageous deeds – by such he had achieved greatness – after the pugnacity, strength and courage of Heremod went into decline.

902   Along with the giants, Heremod was seduced into the power of devils and was swiftly sent to perdition. For too long disturbing anxieties rendered him incapable of action; he became a cause of life-and-death concern to his people and to all his nobles. Often, moreover, on earlier occasions, many a shrewd man had expressed regret at what was becoming of the fierce-minded Heremod – many a man who had believed in him as the cure against evils, and that this son of a prince should have prospered, inherited the noble qualities of his forebears and looked after his people, the treasury and the sheltering stronghold, the realm of heroes, the native land of the Scyldings. There the kinsman of Hygelac gained yet greater approbation from his friends and from mankind: the other violent sin invaded.

916   Then again they would go racing with their horses along the sandy-yellow road. By then the morning sun had been set moving and hastening on. Many a subject was going to that lofty hall in a spirit of confidence, to look upon that monstrous tool of treachery: the king too, guardian of the ring-filled

treasuries, himself came striding out from the royal couple's
bedchamber together with a large retinue, a man secure in his
glory, renowned for his noble qualities, and with him his queen
came wending along the approach to the mead-hall with an
escort of young girls.

XIV

925　Hrothgar spoke out — he had reached the hall and was
standing on the steps and viewing the overhanging roof agleam
with gold, and the hand of Grendel:

928　'For this sight let thanksgiving to the Ruler of all forthwith
take place. Much hatred and many sorrows I have endured at
Grendel's hands, but God, heaven's Shepherd, is ever able to
work wonder upon wonder. It was not long since that I
despaired of finding for myself any cure for those miseries
during my lifetime, when the best of halls was standing agleam
with blood, covered with violently shed gore — a misery far and
wide thrust upon every one of my advisers, who despaired of
ever protecting the capital fortress of the nation from hostile
demons and evil spirits. Now, through the might of the Lord, a
retainer has done that deed which before we had all of us been
unable by our own skills to contrive. Truly, what woman
soever that bore this son after the way of humankind, the same
may say, if she is still living, that the Lord, provident of old, was
benevolent to her in her child-bearing.

946　'Now, Beowulf, most excellent man, it is my will to embrace
you in my heart as a son to me: henceforward foster this new
kinship as befits. Not one of your desires shall be lacking in life,
where I have authority. For less than this I have often enough
bestowed rewards, ornaments from the treasury, upon a hum-
bler fighting man, less strong in the strife of battle. By your
deeds you have achieved it for yourself that your reputation
will live for evermore. May the all-ruling Lord repay you with
good as he has just now done.'

957　Beowulf, Ecgtheow's son, spoke:

958   'With great feelings of goodwill we carried through the contest, that act of courage, and risked the dangerous strength of the unknown. I should rather have wished that you could have seen the enemy himself in his trappings, exhausted and dying. I had meant to pinion him swiftly about with such hard clinches upon his death-bed, that he would have to remain in my grasp struggling for life – unless his body should give me the slip. But since the ordaining Lord did not will it, I was not able to cut him off from escape; I did not cling to my mortal foe well enough for that – the fiend was too overwhelmingly powerful, once he was on the move. All the same, as the means of saving his life he left behind his hand to cover his line of retreat – and his arm and shoulder; and even so the empty-handed creature has bought no respite there. The bringer of hatred will live none the longer, tormented by his sins, for his wound will perforce have taken him over in its inexorable grip and deadly fetters; and so, potent in wickedness and stained by it, he must await the great Judgment, as to how the pure Ordainer will sentence him.'

980   One man, Ecglaf's son, was rather quieter in his bragging talk of warlike deeds after those aristocratic people, thanks to the noble man's strength, had taken a look at the hand up against the lofty roof, and at the fiend's fingers. Each finger at its tip, every place where the nails should be, was a claw, a horrible spike in the hands of the belligerent heathen, most like steel. Each man declared that no iron sword, though belonging to tough warriors and efficacious in the past, that may have been meant to take off the monster's bloody weapon of a hand, would have touched him.

XV

991   Then the bidding went forth that they should quickly turn their hands to redecorating Heorot within; there was a multitude of them, men and women, who made ready that wine-building and guest-hall. Tapestries agleam with gold glinted along the walls, a host of wondrous sights for any person to see,

who contemplates such things. That glorious residence, all secured within by iron straps, was nevertheless much damaged and its door-hinges were shattered; the roof alone survived completely unharmed when the monster, guilty of violent deeds, turned to flight, despairing of his life. That is a condition not easy to avoid; whoever so wishes may try, but still he will have to go to that place prepared and inexorably ordained for the soul-bearing sons of men dwelling here in earth, where his corpse, imprisoned in the grave, will sleep after life's banquet.

1008   By now it was due time and occasion for Healfdene's son to go to the hall; the king himself wished to share in the banquet. I have not heard that that people in a greater throng ever more fittingly rejoiced about their lord and giver of treasure. So those triumphant folk settled down on the benches and enjoyed the feast. Many a mead-cup their kinsmen, Hrothgar and Hrothulf, confident of mood, gracefully accepted in the lofty hall. Within, Heorot was filled with friends. The Scylding community was not as yet engaged in the intrigues of treachery.

1020   Then the warlike son of Healfdene gave Beowulf a gilded banner as a reward for victory, an ornate battle-standard, and a helmet and mail-coat. The many onlookers saw a famed treasure of a sword presented to the hero. This plenitude Beowulf accepted from the floor of the hall – in the eyes of fighting-men he had no cause to feel embarrassed at the lavish gift-giving. I have not heard of such a multitude of men at the ale-bench bestowing upon another four gold-ornamented treasures in a fashion more friendly. Upon the crown of the helmet a head-guard wound about with wires excluded violent death, so that fierce swords could not do very much harm to the helmet, toughened as it was against the rain of blows falling on it, when the fierce shield-bearer had to sally forth against savage enemies.

1035   After that, Hrothgar, shelterer of earls, ordered that eight horses, with bridle plated with gold, should be led within those protective walls, on to the hall floor. On one of them a saddle lay, made resplendent by cunning artistry, enhanced by rich adornments. It had been the high king's battle-seat, when the son of Healfdene had wanted to engage in the contest of swords: never had the widely-renowned warrior's pugnacity at the battle-front faltered, when the slain were falling. And so the protective lord of the Ingwine conveyed to Beowulf the owner-ship of each, of both steeds and weapons, and enjoined him to use them well. In such a fashion as befits humanity the famed prince, treasure-holding lord of heroes, recompensed with horses and with precious things the storms of battle, so that no one who is inclined in fairness to speak the truth may ever denigrate them.

XVI

1050   To those, also, who had undertaken the sea-voyage with Beowulf the lord of earls gave precious gifts, to each an heir-loom; and he directed that recompense in gold should be made for the one whom Grendel had earlier criminally killed – as he would have killed more of them if watchful God and the courage of that man had not prevented that outcome. The ordaining Lord had control over all members of the human race just as he still does now. For this reason, spiritual under-standing and forethought are the best thing at all times. Much of pleasure and of pain a man must live through, who for any length of time partakes of this worldly existence here in these days of strife.

1063   There in the presence of Healfdene's son, the battle-leader, singing took place to the accompaniment of music; the beguil-ing wooden lyre had been plucked and often a lay recited, when the time came for Hrothgar's poet to relate along the mead-bench something to beguile the hall.

1068   By the hands of the sons of Finn, the Danish hero Hnæf of the Scyldings was supposed to have perished in the Frisian mas-sacre when that act of precipitate violence claimed them. Yet neither did Hildeburh have cause to commend the good faith of the Jutes: for no fault of hers, she was bereft of those she loved in that armed contest, sons and brothers. They had fallen, according to their predestined lot, wounded by the spear. She was an unhappy woman. Not without reason did she, Hoc's daughter, mourn over the decree of Providence when morning came: then, under the brightness of the heavens, she could survey the slaughter wreaked upon the members of her family, there where she had once enjoyed the greatest worldly happiness.

1080   The fighting had carried off all but a solitary few of Finn's thanes so that he was quite unable to battle out the fight with Hengest, thane of the prince Hnæf, in that place of confrontation, nor was he able to dislodge the survivors of that evil calamity. Instead, the Frisians offered them terms for negotiation: that they should make vacant for the Jutes another complete place – a hall and a high-seat; that they must assign to the Jutish people a half share of power; and that at distributions of money the son of Folcwalda, Finn, should on every occasion honour the Danes, and should behave hospitably towards Hengest's party, with rings and rich treasures of plated gold, to the same extent as he would want to hearten the Frisian folk in their beer-hall.

1095   Then on both sides they put their trust in a firm compact of peace. Boldly and unreservedly Finn declared to Hengest upon oath that he would treat the survivors of that calamity honourably, in accordance with the judgment of his counsellors; that no one there should breach the compact by words or deeds, nor out of considered malice ever make mention of it, even though, bereft of their prince, they were serving the slayer of their ring-giving lord, since they had been constrained to do so; and that if any of the Frisians kept alive the memory of that murderous hostility, then it should be a matter for the sword-edge.

1107   The oath-taking was completed and splendid gold was brought up from the treasury. The finest fighting-man among the warlike Scyldings was ready for cremation. Upon the pyre the mail-coat was plainly to be seen, stained with blood, the swine-likeness gilded all over, the iron-tough likeness of the boar, and many a noble man, mutilated by wounds: notable men had fallen in that carnage.

1114   Then Hildeburh commanded her own sons to be committed to the flames, their bodies to be burnt and consigned to cremation at their uncle's side. The woman grieved and keened her lamentations. The warrior was raised up on to the pyre. That most enormous fire made of human carrion went whirling up to the clouds and roared in front of the burial mound. Heads melted, deep wounds, malignant sword-bites in the corpse, burst open when the blood spurted out. Fire, greediest of spirits, swallowed up all those of both nations whom the fighting there had carried off: their glory had slipped away.

XVII

1125   Then the Frisian soldiers left to go, bereft of their friends, to their townships, to visit the countryside, the homesteads and the hill-top strongholds of Frisia. But throughout that slaughter-stained winter Hengest still remained with Finn – in an utterly disastrous plight. He dwelt in his mind upon his homeland, and yet he was unable to sail his ship with curved prow upon the ocean. The deep surged in the storm and struggled against the gale. Winter locked the waves in icy bondage – until another year arrived among the earth's habitations, just as it still does even now, and those times of heavenly bright weather which always observe their proper season.

1136   Winter, then, had slipped away; the lap of the earth was grown beautiful. The exile and alien yearned to be away from those habitations. He was more preoccupied with vengeance for his injuries than with the sea-crossing – as to whether he would be able to contrive a bitter confrontation in which he might clear his conscience towards the sons of his enemies. So he did not prevaricate over his worldly duty when Hunlafing laid in his lap a gleaming sword, the finest of blades, whose edges were familiar to those enemies. Accordingly, a cruel death by the sword subsequently befell the bold-tempered Finn in his own home, when Guthlaf and Oslaf, after journeying over the sea, complained to him of the savage ambush and of their grievances, and blamed on him the full extent of their sorrows – and he was unable to contain his irascible temper within his breast. Then the hall was reddened with the lives of the conflicting warriors; Finn, the king, was killed among his bodyguard, moreover, and the queen was captured. The Scylding bowmen ferried to their ships all that was in the king's household, whatever they were able to find in Finn's home by way of jewelled ornaments and skilfully chased gems. The royal woman they ferried across the seaways to Denmark and delivered her to her own people.

1159   The minstrel's lay, his poem, had been sung to its end. The sound of revelry rose up again; the clamour from the benches grew distinct – stewards were serving wine in marvellous chalices. Then Wealhtheow stepped forward and went, wearing a gold crown, to where those two worthy men were sitting, uncle and nephew: at that time, the loving bond between them was still intact and each was true to the other. Unferth, adjutant of the king, also sat there immediately below the Scyldings' lord; every one of them believed in his integrity, and that he had much courage – even though he had not been unwaveringly honourable towards his kinsmen in a contest of swords.

1168   Then said the lady of the Scyldings:

1169   'Accept this cup, my noble lord, the giver of treasure. Be happy, generous friend to your people, and speak to the Geats with kindly words as is the proper thing to do. Be grateful towards the Geats, bearing in mind what gifts from near and far you yourself now own.

1175   'I have been told that you would like to have this fighting-man for your son. Heorot, the gleaming treasure-house, is cleansed. Make us, while you may, of its many guerdons, and when you are constrained to go forth to face the decree of Providence, leave the people and the realm to your kinsmen. I know my Hrothwulf is grateful, so that he will wish to treat these young ones honourably if you, lord and friend of the Scyldings, depart from the world sooner than he. I believe that he will repay our sons with beneficence if he remembers all that we two have previously done for him by way of honours, for his pleasure and for his dignity, during his childhood.'

1188   She turned then to the bench where her children, Hrethric and Hrothmund, and the sons of thanes, the contingent of youth, were gathered. There the worthy man, Beowulf of the Geats, was sitting, between the two brothers.

XVIII

1192   To him a cup was carried and offered with words of friendly invitation, and coiled gold was bounteously proffered: two decorative armbands, a cloak and collars – the greatest torque of any I have heard tell of on earth. Under the bright sky I have heard of no finer piece of jewellery from the treasury of heroes, since Hama carried off that ornament made by the Brisings – the neck-piece and its precious casket – to the excellent stronghold: he was fleeing from the malicious schemings of Eormanric. He died, and sought the eternal remedy.

1202   That collar Hygelac of the Geats, grandson of Swerting, had with him on his last expedition when, beneath his standard, he protected that treasure, and defended what was to become the spoil of slaughter. Fate took him off when in his pride he went looking for trouble and feuding into Frisia. He had come wearing that adornment, those precious stones, over the fullness of the rolling ocean, a powerful prince; he perished beneath his shield. So the person of the king passed into the clutches of the Franks, together with the armour protecting his breast and the torque: meaner warriors plundered the slain after the carnage of battle. Geatish people remained in occupation of that place of dead bodies.

1214   The hall was filled with the sound of exclamations. Wealh-theow spoke out and in the presence of that great assembly said:

1216   'Enjoy in good fortune, Beowulf, beloved young warrior, this torque, and make use of this cloak, a treasure from the communal hoard, and may prosperity rightly be yours. Distinguish yourself by your strength, and be kindly disposed towards these boys in giving them good counsels. I shall keep your reward for this in mind. You have brought it about that through all mortal time men will speak your praise far and near, even as widely as the sea, dwelling-place of the wind, flows round earth's ramparts. Blest may you be, prince, as long as you live. I sincerely wish for you a wealth of treasures. Having happiness yourself, be good to my sons in the things you do for them. Here every earl is true to the other, gentle of disposition, and loyal to his lord. The thanes are obedient, and the people are entirely at the ready: the men of this court, having drunk to it, will do as I bid.' Then she went to her seat.

1232   The banquet there was of the choicest; men were drinking wine, unaware of destiny, the grim preordained decree, as it was to befall many of the earls after evening came and the great Hrothgar withdrew to his apartment to bed. A countless number of earls occupied the hall as they had often done before; they cleared the boards where the benches had stood and it was overspread with mattresses and pillows. A certain one among those convivial thanes went to his bed a dying and doomed man.

1242   By their heads they set their battle-targes, shining shields of wood. There on a bench above each noble, plainly to be seen, was a helmet burnished for battle, a ring-sewn mail-coat and a splendid wooden spear. It was their practice that they should be constantly on the alert for warfare both at home and on active service, or on any such occasions whatever, as need befell their lord: it was an excellent community of men.

XIX

1251 So they settled down in sleep. A certain one paid sorely for his night's rest – just as had so often been their lot when Grendel had haunted the gold-endowed hall and maintained his pursuit of lawlessness, until the end arrived, death as the wages of his sins. It became evident and widely recognized by people that an avenger still lived on after the adversary, a long while after the distress of the fight: Grendel's mother. This woman, this female monster, brooded upon her misery – for she had to inhabit the fearsome fens and their chilling currents, in as much as Cain had become the killer of his own brother, his kin by the same father, and consequently, outlawed, marked with murder, he had gone fleeing from the happiness of human society and had settled in the wilderness. From him was born a multitude of beings preordained of old. One of these was Grendel, the bloody outcast full of hate, who at Heorot had met with a man watching and waiting for the fight. There the monster had fallen to grappling with him, but he bore in mind the potency of his strength, the liberal gift which God had granted him, and he entrusted himself to the grace of the one Lord, to his mercy and help: thus he had overcome the fiend and put down the being from hell. So the enemy of humankind, humiliated, cut off from happiness, went away seeking a place to die. And yet his mother, rapacious and desperate of mood, meant to make the journey that was to prove full of misery for her; she meant to avenge her son's death.

1279 She came, then, to Heorot where the mail-wearing Danes were asleep through the hall. Then there was soon a reversal of fortune for those earls, once Grendel's mother had made an incursion. Her violence, the violence of a woman in battle, was the lesser – by just as much as the strength of females is, compared with a male when the embellished sword, forged by the hammer, the blood-stained blade, durable of edge, shears through the opposing boar-image above the helmet.

1288 Then in the hall the hard-edged sword was snatched from over the seats and many a broad shield raised tight in people's grips – to helmet or ample mail-coat no one gave a thought when the horror of it seized him.

1292   She was in a hurry; she wanted to be out of there to save her life now that she had been discovered. In a moment she had one of the noble men securely ensnared, then she made off to the fen. Of all the heroes of the rank of companion between the oceans, he was the one most loved by Hrothgar, the mighty shield-warrior and man of secure renown whom she had killed in his bed.

1299   Beowulf was not there, for other lodgings had been previously provided for the famed Geat, following the treasure-giving. The sound of lamentation arose in Heorot. She seized the hand she had recognized, beneath the blood. Grief was come again, renewed, to those mansions. That was no good bargain, that on both sides they had to trade in the lives of friends.

1306   The old king, the grey-haired fighting-man, was in anguished mood then, when he knew his foremost thane was no longer alive, the man dearest to him dead. Hastily Beowulf, the man blest with victory, was fetched to the bedchamber. With the first light before the dawning, that earl among earls, the noble warrior, went in person together with his companions to where the sagacious man waited to see whether the Ruler of all would ever bring about a change of fortune for him, following the grievous news. Across the floor, then, the battle-honoured man walked with his personal retinue – the hall timbers re-echoed – so as to address his greetings to the wise lord of the Ingwine. He asked whether, in view of the urgent summons, his night had passed agreeably.

XX

1321   Hrothgar spoke, protector of the Scyldings:

1322   'Do not ask after matters of weal: woe has come afresh upon the Danish people. Æschere is dead, Yrmenlaf's elder brother, my privy adviser and my counsellor, a comrade at my shoulder when we defended our heads in the fray, when infantry-men clashed and crushed the boar-crested helms. Such ought an earl to be, a noble man proved worthy of old, such as Æschere was. Inside Heorot and by her own hand an irascible and carnivorous creature was his murderer. I do not know whether the terrible thing has made her way back home again, proud of a corpse and brought to fame by a killing. She has avenged that bloody deed by which you last night slew Grendel in violent fashion with your tough wrestling-holds, because for too long he had diminished and destroyed my people. In combat he fell, guilty of capital crime – and now another mighty and wicked predator has come. She meant to take vengeance for her kinsman and indeed she has gone far towards avenging the bloody deed, as it may seem to many a thane who, in cruel affliction of spirit, weeps in his heart for that treasure-giver: that hand now lies dead which served you unfailingly in all your desires.

1345 'I have heard people of mine, those dwelling in the countryside and those serving in the hall as counsellors, say that they have seen two such huge prowlers of the marches patrolling the moors, alien intruders. One of them, as far as they could make out with complete certainty, was in the likeness of a woman; the other ill-formed creature stalked such paths as outcasts go, in the shape of a man – except that he was huger than any other mortal. In days long ago the inhabitants of this region named him Grendel; they neither know of his father, nor whether any unknown creatures have been born to him in the past. They haunt an uncharted territory – wolf-infested hillsides, windy crags and the perilous waterways of a sump, where a mountain stream, a torrent, goes down beneath the gloom of the crags, underground. It is not many miles distant from here that the tarn is to be found. Above it hang rime-encrusted thickets; the firmly rooted trees overshadow the water. There each night is to be seen a sinister spectacle: fire on the pool. Among the children of men there is no one living so wise that he knows its depth. Though the heath-roving deer, the strong-antlered hart, harassed by the hounds and having been chased from a long way off, may be making for the forest, he will first yield up his life and being on the bank, before he will dive in to protect his head. It is not a pleasant place. From there, when the wind whips up foul weather, the turmoil of the waves mounts up dark to the clouds until the air grows thick with murk and the skies weep.

1376 'Now the remedy rests once more with you alone. As yet you do not know her lair, the perilous place where you will be able to find the grossly sinful creature. Seek it out if you dare. I shall reward you for this act of vengeance with wealth, with antique treasures, and with coiled gold, as I did before, if you get away.'

XXI

1383 Beowulf, son of Ecgtheow, spoke:

1384 'Do not, as a man of reason, give yourself up to grief. It is a finer thing in any man that he should avenge his friend than that he should unduly mourn. Each one of us must live in expectation of an end of life in this world: let him who can gain good repute before death – that is the finest thing thereafter for the lifeless man.

1390 'On to your feet, guardian of the realm. Let us go immediately and have a look at the trail of Grendel's female kin. I promise you this: she shall not escape, neither in the highest peak nor in the womb of the earth, neither in the mountain forest nor in the watery depths, go where she will. For today, have patience in every affliction, as I have come to expect of you.'

1397 The old man jumped up then and thanked God, the mighty Lord, for what that man had declared. Then a horse was harnessed for Hrothgar, a steed with plaited mane. Handsomely arrayed the wise king set out; a contingent of shield-bearing foot-soldiers marched with him. Broad tracks were to be seen along the forest paths – her trail over the ground. She had gone straight across the murky moor, carrying lifeless the finest of those thanes who together with Hrothgar had looked after domestic affairs.

1408   So the son of princes traversed steep rocky screes, narrow paths and ways constricted to single file, an unknown road, precipitous crags and many water-monsters' lairs. As one of a few experienced men, he went ahead to spy out the place – until suddenly he encountered some mountain trees, a wood devoid of any pleasant aspect, overhanging a grey rock; there was water standing below it, bloody and disturbed. For all the Danes – for the leaders of the Scyldings and for many a thane – it was an anguish to be suffered in the heart, a painful thing for every one of the earls, when, on the cliff bordering the lake, they came upon Æschere's head. The people stared at the watery expanse: it was welling with blood, with warm gore.

1423   A horn sang out at intervals its heartening battle-call. The whole contingent of foot-soldiers settled down, then they observed the multitude of a species of serpent, strange sea-dragons taking to the water, as well as amphibian monsters lying on the slopes of the cliff – reptiles and savage beasts which often at their morning mealtime make their woe-fraught way into the path of sail-driven ships. Aroused and puffed up with anger they plunged away: they had registered the clarion sound of the battle-horn crying out. One of them, the prince of the Geats by means of his bow parted from its life of battling the waves, for the hard war-arrow pierced it to the vitals: that one, which death carried off, was the slower for that at swimming in the lake. Swiftly it was hard assailed among the waves with deadly-barbed boar-spears, assaulted with vicious attacks, and hauled up on to the clifftop – an extraordinary master over the watery element. The men stared at the terrifying outlandish thing.

1441   Beowulf clad himself in trappings fit for a lord: he did not fret about survival. His battle-corslet, hand-meshed, copious and gleaming with craftsmanship, would have to probe the deeps – a corslet which was capable of protecting his ribbed chest in such a way that an aggressive grasp could not harm his vital spirit, nor the spiteful clutch of a furious enemy his life. And the silver-white helmet, which would have to disturb the depths of the tarn and quest into the troubled swirl of the waters, protected his head, embellished with precious ornament, braced about with sturdy bands, just as the weapon-smith had fashioned it in days far past and marvellously furbished it and set it about with impressions of boars, so that hereafter neither broadsword nor battle-blade could bite into it.

1455   Not the meanest among his mighty aids was that which Hrothgar's adjutant loaned him in his need. Hrunting was the name of that hilted sword. It was unique among things old and treasured; the edge was iron, agleam with the deadly branching patterns of damascene, tempered in the blood of warfare. Never in battle had it failed any man who brandished it with his hands and who had the daring to embark on terrifying exploits in the mustering place of enemies. It was not the first time that it was going to have to execute a deed of courage. Yet Ecglaf's son, albeit mighty in physical strength, did not remember what he had said before, drunk with wine, as he now lent that weapon to a worthier swordsman. He himself had not the daring to risk his life beneath the waves' turbulence, to live up to a lordly standing: in that he forfeited his repute and renown for courage. It was not so with the other, once he had clad himself for the fray.

XXII

1473   Beowulf, son of Ecgtheow, spoke:

1474   'Be mindful now, Healfdene's famous son, wise king, people's generous friend, now that I am set upon this exploit, of what we earlier spoke about: that if I should lose my life in the cause of your need you would always be in the stead of a father to me, being departed. Be a protecting hand to my retainers, to my right-hand men, if battle carries me off; the treasures too which you gave me, beloved Hrothgar, send them to Hygelac. Then the lord of the Geats will be able to understand by that gold, and Hrethel's son see when he gazes upon that wealth, that I have found a ring-giver virtuous in his generosity and had the joy of it while I was allowed. And let Unferth, a man known far afield, have the ancient heirloom, my rarely-ornamented sword of ripple-patterned damascene, hard of edge. With Hrunting I shall achieve renown, or else death will carry me off.'

1492 After these words the prince of the Weder-Geats pressed on with courage and would not even wait for a reply. The troubled water of the lake engulfed the warrior. Then it was a good part of the day before he was able to discern the bottom. She who for a hundred seasons, ravenous for blood, savage and greedy, had tyrannized over the watery regions soon discovered that some man was probing from above into the lair of alien creatures: so she made a grab at him and seized the warrior in her hideous clutches. But not that way would she harm his body unscathed within: on the outside, chainmail shielded it about so that she was unable to poke her loathsome fingers through his soldier's armour, the corslet of interlocked rings.

1506 So, when she had reached the bottom, this she-wolf of the water carted the mail-protected prince into her hall, because, although he had the courage for it, he was unable to wield weapons, for such a host of extraordinary creatures constricted him in swimming: many a sea-beast with fighting-fangs tore at his soldier's mail-coat; monsters menaced him. Then the man recognized that he was in some kind of abode of evil where no water harmed him at all and the current's sudden clutch was unable to touch him because of the roofed abode. He saw a fiery light, a lurid gleam glowing brightly. Then the virtuous man recognized the damned creature of the deep, the brawny water-hag. He gave his battle-blade a mighty impetus – his hand did not hold back the stroke – so that the ring-ornamented sword sang out a greedy war-cry on her head.

Then the visitor discovered that the gleaming weapon would not bite and damage her vitals, but the edge cheated the prince in his need. Many confrontations hand-to-hand it had sustained before this, had often sliced through a helmet, a doomed soldier's battledress: this was the first time for the precious treasure that its reputation failed.

1529   Even then he was single of purpose, nor did he lose courage: Hygelac's kinsman had glorious accomplishments in mind. So, angered, the assailant tossed aside the twist-patterned sword, fastened about with gems of artistry, so that it lay, sturdy and steely-edged, on the ground, and he trusted to his strength and the main force of hand-to-hand wrestling. A man must act so, when he means to gain long-lasting fame in the fight: he will not be obsessed with survival.

1537   So the leader of the warfaring Geats, who felt no compunction in the feud, grabbed Grendel's mother by the shoulder; then, ruthless in the struggle, for he was now enraged to bursting, he threw the life-menacing foe so that she fell to the floor. She sharply gave him quittance again with savage clutches, and she made a grab at him. Then, desperate of mood, she tripped the man fighting on foot, strongest of warriors, so that he was prostrated; then she pinned down her hall-visitor and dragged out her broad, bright-edged knife: she meant to avenge her child, her only son. Across his shoulder lay the meshed mail-shirt: it saved his life and resisted penetration by point or edge. Ecgtheow's son, the Geatish campaigner, would have perished then down in the vast deep, had not his battle-corslet, his sturdy soldier's mail-coat, afforded him help; and were it not that holy God held sway over victory in war. The wise Lord, arbiter of the heavens, easily determined the matter on the side of right as soon as he got up again.

XXIII

1557   Then, among some trappings, he saw a blade blessed with success, an ancient, gigantic sword, excelling in its edges, a thing to lend prestige to warriors. It was the choicest of weapons – except that it was huger than any other man would be able to carry into the cut and thrust of battle – efficient and beautiful, the work of giants. So, bold hero of the Scyldings, fierce and deadly grim, he grabbed the bound hilt, unsheathed the ring-embellished sword and, not expecting to survive, struck angrily – so that it caught her hard on her neck and smashed the rings of bone: clean through her doomed flesh clove the blade. She fell dead to the floor. The sword was bloody. The man felt pleased at his achievement.

1570   A radiance gleamed forth and a light appeared therein, even as the sun, candle of the sky, shines brilliantly from heaven. He gazed about the hall, then he set off alongside the wall. Hygelac's thane, angry and single of purpose, raised the weapon, gripped hard by the hilt, on high. The sharp-edged sword was not without further usefulness to the warrior, for he meant to repay Grendel smartly for those many assaults which he made upon the West-Danes – much more often than on that one expedition when he slew members of Hrothgar's household during their night-rest, devoured as they slept fifteen men of the Danish nation, and carted out and away as many again, as his loathsome spoil. For this, Beowulf, fierce campaigner, paid him reward – so efficaciously that on a bed he beheld the battle-weary Grendel lying lifeless, following the damage which the struggle at Heorot had done him. Wide open split his corpse as, after death, he suffered a blow, a hard swingeing sword-stroke – and Beowulf cut off his head.

1591   Soon the experienced men who with Hrothgar were watching the lake saw that the choppy surface was all suffused and the water dyed with blood. Grey-haired old men declared to each other that from now on they held out no hope for the prince that he might come jubilant in victory to visit their renowned lord, for it occurred to many that the she-wolf of the water had destroyed him.

1600   So the ninth hour of the day arrived. The bold Scyldings left the clifftop, and Hrothgar, a gold-giving friend to people, went away homewards. The Geatish visitors sat, sick at heart, and stared at the tarn. They wished, but they held out no hope, that they would see their friend and lord himself.

1605   Meanwhile the sword, the warring blade, began to waste away because of the gore from the fighting and the battle-spilt driblets of blood. It was a remarkable phenomenon how it entirely melted away – just like ice when the Father looses the fetters of frost and frees the shackles on the water – he who has disposal over times and seasons: he is the true ordaining Lord. The leader of the Weder-Geats did not take more of the precious possessions in those haunts, although he saw many there, only the head and the richly embellished hilt with it. The sword had already dissolved, the damascened blade had corroded away, so hot was the blood and so venomous the alien being which had perished within that place. He set out swimming forthwith, the man who had lately survived his enemies' defeat and death in the struggle. Upwards through the water he launched himself: its choppy expanses and vast tracts were completely cleansed since that alien being had left behind the days of her existence and this ephemeral creation.

1623   So the seaman's protective lord came swimming stout-hearted to shore; he was pleased with the spoils from the lake, the heavy load of the things which he had with him. Then they went to meet him and gave thanks to God, a majestic-looking troop of thanes. They were elated over their prince, because they had been allowed to see him unharmed. Then helmet and corslet were briskly unstrapped from the brave hero. The lake stilled, the water beneath the mists, dyed with blood shed in violence. From there they journeyed on, happy in their hearts, along the trodden tracks, and traced the overland way, the familiar road. From the craggy margin of the water, men of regal courage – toilsomely for each one of them, surpassingly spirited heroes – carried the head. Four men were needed laboriously to cart Grendel's head on a spear-shaft to the hall of gold-giving, until suddenly they had arrived at the hall, fourteen Geats marching, vigorous and soldierly bold; and with them their lord, proud in their midst, walked over the lawns about the mead-hall.

1644 So the thanes' prince came striding in, a man daring in action, enhanced by his repute, a hero brave in the fight, to greet Hrothgar. Then, by the hair, the head of Grendel, fearsome thing, was borne into the hall where people were drinking, into the presence of the earls and of the queen in their midst, a rare spectacle; the men stared at it.

XXIV

1651 Beowulf spoke forth, son of Ecgtheow:

1652 'See, son of Healfdene, king of Scyldings! We have with pleasure brought you these spoils of the deep which you here look upon, as a token of victory. Not without trouble, I escaped with my life from a fight underwater; with some difficulty I hazarded the task: had God not shielded me, the fight would have been over straightway. With Hrunting I could achieve nothing at all in battle, although the weapon itself was doughty; but the Ruler of men granted me that I should catch sight of a handsome, huge antique sword – time after time he has guided the friendless – so I unsheathed that weapon. Then, now that circumstance was in my favour, I dealt the final blow in that struggle to the keepers of the lair. Then the battle-blade, the damascened sword, corroded away as the blood spurted – the most reeking kind of combat sweat. The hilt I have taken away from there, from those adversaries: I have avenged their violent deeds, the killing of the Danes, as was fitting.

1671 'So now I promise you this, that you may sleep in Heorot free from anxiety, together with the company of your men and every one of the thanes among your subjects, seasoned warriors and youthful ones, and that you, prince of the Scyldings, need not fear on their behalf deadly malice against the carls from that quarter, as you did before.'

1677   Then the golden hilt, the ancient work of giants, was given into the hand of the old fighting-man, the white-haired battle-lord. After the annihilation of the demonic monsters it passed – the handiwork of marvellous smiths – into the ownership of the lord of the Danes; and when the cruel-hearted creature, God's adversary, quitted this world, guilty of murder, and his mother too, it passed into the possession of the best of the kings of the world amid the surrounding oceans, the best of those who have portioned out their wealth in Denmark.

1687   Hrothgar spoke forth. He was scrutinizing the hilt, the antique relic. On it was engraved the beginning of the age-old war; subsequently, the Flood, an overwhelming deluge, killed the race of giants – they had behaved wickedly. It was a people alienated from the eternal Lord; because of this the Ruler gave them final payment in the rising of the water. Also on those shining plates of bright gold it was duly recorded in runic letters, set down and declared, for whom that sword, a most select iron weapon, with twist-formed hilt, dragon-decorated, was first forged.

1698   So the wise son of Healfdene spoke, and all kept silence:

1700   'One who furthers truth and justice among the people, an aged guardian of the homeland who remembers everything from far back, is surely entitled to say this: that this earl was born a superior being. Your renown is exalted by far-flung ways, Beowulf, my friend, among every nation. All this physical strength you govern restrainedly with discretion of mind. I shall make good my affection for you just as we earlier discussed together.

1707   'You must come to be a truly long-enduring comfort to your people, a support to men. Not so was Heremod to the descendants of Ecgwela, the honourable Scyldings: he grew up to be not the fulfilment of the Danish people's hope, but their slaughter and mortal destruction. In frenzied mood he would murder the companions of his table and the comrades at his side, until he passed on from the pleasures of human existence, a king notorious and alone. Even though mighty God exalted him in power and in the joys of strength and advanced him above all men, nevertheless the heart in his breast grew bloody and cruel of spirit, and he did not give the Danes treasures in pursuit of high esteem. Joyless he lived to suffer pain, the people's long-enduring malice, because of that antagonism. Take example to yourself by this; know what makes for human excellence. For your sake I have told this tale, as one grown wise with the years.

1724   'It is a marvellous thing to tell, how mighty God in his infinite wisdom dispenses to mankind intelligence, land and lordship: he has power over all things. Sometimes in his love he allows the will of a man of renowned family to be realized; he gives him earthly happiness for the keeping, a sheltering stronghold full of men, within his native land; he also makes subject to him portions of the world, a broad kingdom, so that the man himself, in his folly, cannot imagine its end. He continues in a state of well-being; sickness and age distract him not at all, nor does pernicious anxiety cast its gloom upon his spirit, nor does strife anywhere bring about armed hostility, but the whole world wends according to his will.

XXV

1740   'He is unaware of the worser part – until within him a deal of presumptuousness grows up and flourishes while the soul's protector and guardian sleeps. Too sound is that sleep associated with worldly busyness, and very near is the destroyer who shoots from his bow with fiery darts. It is then that he is struck under his guard with a stinging arrow in his bosom – he is ignorant of protecting himself – by the perverse horrid promptings of the evil spirit.

1748   'What he has long enjoyed seems to him too little. Ruthless of purpose, he grows greedy; he gives out no gold-ornamented rings in lavish style and he forgets and repudiates his future destiny because God, heaven's ruler, has already given him his share of honours. Then in the final stage, it comes to pass that his perishable mortal frame decays and sinks down doomed. Another succeeds him, one who ungrudgingly shares out precious things, the man's formerly hoarded wealth, and repudiates terror.

1758   'Guard yourself against this insidious evil, dear Beowulf, most noble man, and choose for yourself the better part, everlasting gains; repudiate presumptuousness, renowned warrior. For a while now the splendour of physical strength is yours; then it will soon come about that sickness or sword strips you of vigour – or the clutch of fire or the water's surge or the blade's bite or the flight of the spear or repulsive senility – or the sparkle of your eyes will grow dim and become extinct: suddenly it will come about that death overpowers you, the warrior. I, likewise, for fifty years ruled the mail-clad Danes here below the skies and protected them in warfare by spears and by swords from many people throughout this earth, so that I did not count anyone beneath the circuit of the sun my adversary. But see: the reverse of that befell me within my native land, misery following mirth, when Grendel, the ancient enemy, became an intruder upon me. I endured unceasingly much anxiety of mind on account of that struggle. Thanks be to the Ordainer, to the everlasting Lord, for what I have lived to experience – that after ancient strife I might gaze with my own eyes upon that head, gory with blood.

1782   'Now, go to your seat and enjoy the pleasures of the banquet as one honoured for his prowess. A very great quantity of treasures is to change hands between us when morning comes.'

1785   The Geat was cheerful of mood. He went forthwith to seek his seat as the wise man had bidden. So, once again just as before, food was handsomely furnished anew for the men, famed for valour, occupying the hall. The helm of night spread its dark gloom over the warriors. The whole company rose up; the old, white-haired Scylding wanted to go to his bed. The

Geat, famed shield-warrior, was very well pleased to rest. At once a hall-thane who for courtesy's sake attended to all a thane's needs, such needs as seafarers were supposed to have in those days, escorted him away, a man far-travelled and tired out by his exploit.

1799   So, commodious of heart, he took his rest. The hall towered aloft, wide-gabled and gleaming with gold; within, the guest slept until the black raven, blithe of heart, heralded heaven's delight, the sun, when it came shimmering, a bright radiance, in the wake of the shadows. The warriors bestirred themselves. The high-born heroes were eager to voyage back to their people: the man who had come with spirit roused wanted to get back to his ship, a long way off from that place. The hardy warrior, then, enjoined them to bear Hrunting to Ecglaf's son and enjoined him to receive back his sword, a precious weapon; he declared his gratitude to him for the loan, said he regarded that friend in battle as an efficient one, strong in the fray, and did not outspokenly denigrate the blade's edge: he was a magnanimous man. And so the soldiers, keyed up for the journey, were ready in their armour. The one prince precious to the Danes went to the high-seat where the other was; the hero brave in battle greeted Hrothgar.

XXVI

1817   Beowulf, Ecgtheow's son, spoke forth:

1818   'We seafarers, having journeyed from afar, wish to say now that we are setting out to return to Hygelac. We have been well and willingly looked after here; you have been abundantly kind to us. If on earth hereafter I may by martial deeds gain a jot more of your heartfelt love than I have already done, then, lord of men, I shall at once be ready. If, across the ambit of the oceans I hear that surrounding nations menace you with fearsome threats, as enemies have at times done to you, I shall bring a thousand thanes and heroes to your help. As for Hygelac, lord of the Geats, though he, the people's guardian, is young, I know that he will support me in words and in actions so that I may well express my esteem for you and bring to your assistance spear and the aid of physical strength, when you have need of men.

1836 'If hereafter Hrethric, the king's son, determines to come to the courts of the Geats he will be able to find many friends there: far-distant lands are more profitably visited by one who is himself fitted for it.'

1840 Hrothgar spoke forth in reply to him:

1841 'These utterances the wise Lord sent into your mind. I have not heard a man speak more discerningly at so young an age. You are strong in physical might, mature in mind, prudent in your utterances. I hold it a likely thing – if it happens that spear, war fierce and cruel, sickness or sword of iron carries off from you Hrethel's son, your lord, the people's guardian, and you are alive – that the seafaring Geats would have no better man than you to choose as king and keeper of his men's treasure-store, if you are willing to govern your kinsmen's realm.

1853 'Your courageous spirit pleases me all the more as time goes on, dear Beowulf. You have brought it about that between the nations, the Geatish people and the spear-wielding Danes, there shall be a mutual peace, and the strife and the spiteful hostilities in which they have once engaged shall sleep; and that while I rule the wide realm treasures shall be shared, and many a man shall greet another with generous gifts across the gannet's dip; the curved-prowed ship shall bring across the ocean presents and tokens of love. I know that nation as one firmly disposed towards both foe and friend, faultless in each point, by long-standing tradition.'

1866 Then the earls' protective lord, Healfdene's son, gave him besides twelve precious gifts and bade him journey safely back to his beloved people with those presents, and quickly come again. Then the king, noble by virtue of his lineage as a prince of the Scyldings, kissed that most excellent thane and clasped him about the neck; tears fell from the white-haired man. To him, being old and wise with age, there was a possibility of two alternatives – the one of them more compelling: that they would never be allowed to see one another again, as men of integrity in converse together. This man was so dear to him that he could not restrain the turmoil in his heart but, bound fast by his heart-strings in his bosom, a hidden longing for the cherished man burned in his blood.

1880 Beowulf went marching away over the grassy ground, a soldier taking pride in the gold and delight in the treasure. The ocean-roving ship which rode at anchor was awaiting its owner and master. During the journey Hrothgar's liberality was often spoken of with praise. He had been a peerless king, without defect in any point, until old age, which has often crushed many, stripped him of the joys of physical strength.

XXVII

1888 So the troop of surpassingly brave young men arrived at the ocean; they were wearing chain-mail, the link-forged coat. The coastguard observed the men's return journey, just as he had done before. Not with aggression from the brow of the cliff did he greet the visitors: rather he went riding towards them and declared that they went aboard ship as warriors in shining armour whose return would be a joy to the Weder-Geatish people. Then on the beach the capacious ship with curving prow was loaded with battle-garments, horses and precious gifts; the mast towered above riches from Hrothgar's treasury. Beowulf gave to the boat's guardian a sword bound about with gold, so that henceforth he was thus much the more esteemed on the mead-bench for the precious gift, an heirloom; and, once aboard the ship, off he went, rippling the deep water, and left behind the land of the Danes. By then the sail, a shroud for use on the open sea, was secured by a rope to the mast; the wooden vessel reverberated with noise. No wind against waves hindered the billow-borne ship in its course. Onwards went the ocean-rover; forth it floated, foamy-prowed, stem braced about, over wave and over the currents of the deep until they could descry the Geatish cliffs and the familiar headlands. The keel, impelled by the wind, drove ashore and came to rest on the land.

1914   Quickly to hand at the seashore was the harbour-guard, who for a long time previously had kept watch far and wide at the water's edge, anxious for those dearly regarded men. The broad-beamed ship he securely moored with anchor-ropes to the beach, lest the majestic power of the waves should drive the winsome wooden vessel away from them. Then he ordered that wealth of princes, the rich adornments and plated gold, to be carried ashore. From there it was not far for them to seek the dispenser of treasure, Hygelac, son of Hrethel, where he dwells in residence, himself together with his companions, close to the sea-cliff.

1925   Surpassingly noble was the building, of royal renown the high king within the hall, and Hygd, daughter of Hareth, very young, yet wise and well-accomplished even though she had passed only a few years within the stronghold: despite that, she was not niggardly nor over-frugal towards the Geatish people in gifts and precious treasures.

1931   Modthryth, an assertive queen of the people, practised a fearsome brutality. Not one brave man among the close companions, but only the supreme lord himself, dared venture to look her in the eyes even by day, or else he could count on cruel chains, hand-twisted, being prescribed for him, and swiftly upon his arrest the sword would be ordained so that the damascened blade might settle the matter and publicize the capital offence. Such is not a queenly custom for a woman to follow, even if she is unmatched in beauty, that the peace-weaver should exact the life of a dearly esteemed man on account of an imagined insult. Nevertheless, a kinsman of Hemming, Offa, made light of that, and men supping their ale told another story: how she desisted from offences against the people and from acts of malice – once she, being loved by that prince, had been given, gold-bedecked, to the youthful conten- der, and when, at her father's exhortation, she had made her way to Offa's hall across the tawny ocean. From then on, renowned for her goodness, she used well as long as she lived the fortunes of life upon the throne there. She cherished a deep love for the heroes' king – the noblest man, I have heard tell, of all the mighty race of mankind amidst the encircling oceans, for Offa was a man of martial courage, widely esteemed for his gifts and his battles; in wisdom he ruled his native land. To them was born Eomer, kinsman of Hemming, grandson of Garmund, to be the help of heroes, accomplished in warlike deeds.

XXVIII

1963 So across the sand he went, the hardy Beowulf himself, together with his close following, marching upon the foreshore and the broad beaches. From the south the onward-moving sun, candle of the world, was shining. They continued on their way and pressed on in eagerness to where within the fortified mansions they had heard the earls' protecting lord, Ongen- theow's slayer, a good young warrior-king, was sharing out rings. To Hygelac, Beowulf's progress was swiftly reported – that there within the township, alive and unharmed by the cut and thrust of battle, the protecting lord of his fighting men and of his shield-bearing companions was coming marching to the court. Hastily the hall-floor was cleared within, as the ruler commanded, for the approaching warriors.

1977 So the one who had survived the strife was seated beside the ruler himself, kinsman beside kinsman, after he had greeted his gracious lord with imposing words in a formal speech. Through the hall Hæreth's daughter wended with draughts of mead; she treated the people with affection and delivered the drinking-cup into the hands of the Hæthnas.

1983 Hygelac began courteously to question his companion in that lofty hall: his curiosity overcame him, as to what the Sea-Geats' experiences had been:

1987   'How did it turn out for you on your voyage, beloved Beowulf, when you suddenly determined to go looking for strife and battle far away over the salt water at Heorot? And did you at all remedy for Hrothgar, the renowned prince, his widely notorious affliction? I have been in anguish with the melancholy surges of heartfelt anxiety, because of the misgivings I had over the venture of a man dear to me. Long I urged on you that you should not confront that murderous creature, that you should leave the South-Danes to settle the fight with Grendel themselves. I declare thanks to God that I have been allowed to see you safe again.'

1999   Beowulf, son of Ecgtheow, spoke up:

2000   'It is no secret, Lord Hygelac, but an encounter famed among many men, what an occasion of conflict it was between Grendel and me upon that site where he wreaked very many sorrows and no end of misery upon the conqueror-Scyldings. All that I avenged, so that none of Grendel's kindred on earth, nor that one of the loathsome family that shall live the longest, entrammelled in evil, will have grounds to brag about that clash in the half-light.

2009   'I had previously come there, to that ring-giving hall, to greet Hrothgar. At once the renowned kinsman of Healfdene, when he knew my mind, proffered me a seat beside his own sons. The company was in a cheerful state; not in my lifetime have I seen among hall-inhabitants under heaven's vault greater merrymaking over the mead. From time to time the renowned queen, the people's pledge of peace, wended through the entire hall, and heartened the young men; often she presented the round wreathed goblet to some man before she went to her seat. From time to time Hrothgar's daughter would bring the ale-cup before the contingent of seasoned retainers, to the earls in their part of the hall – her I heard those occupying the hall, where she presented the precious riveted cup to the heroes, call Freawaru. She is promised, young and gold-bedecked, to Froda's gracious son, Ingeld. The friend and lord of the Scyldings, guardian of the realm, has been instrumental in this, and he holds it sound policy that through this woman he should abate a number of slaughterous feuds and conflicts. Of rare frequency is the case where, after a nation's defeat, the destructive spear lies in submission for any length of time, even though the bride may be adequate.

2032 'It may then rankle with the prince of the Heathobards and with every one of the thanes of those people, when the Danish bridal escort walks with the woman into the hall, attended upon by senior retainers – upon whom gleam heirlooms, the tough ring-patterned property of the old Heathobards as long as they had been allowed to wield those weapons, until they brought to armed contest and to extinction beloved comrades and their own lives.

[XXIX]

2041 'So, during the beerdrinking, some old spear-warrior will speak out, who is eyeing one precious object, and who remembers everything, the men's slaughter by the spear – bitter is the heart within him. Brooding in spirit he sets out to try the young soldier's temper and provoke some evil act of war by the thoughts from out of his breast, and he speaks these words: "Can you recognize that blade, my friend, the precious iron sword which your father carried into battle on his last expedition in vizored war-helmet – where the Danes killed him, and the bold Scyldings, once Withergyld lay dead, prevailed over the field of slaughter, following the heroes' defeat? Now the son of one or other of those killers walks into the hall taking delight in his adornments, brags of the murder and wears that treasure which by right you should possess."

2057 'Thus he keeps hinting and reminding upon every occasion with painful words until the time comes when for the deeds of his father the woman's thane will sleep blood-stained after the bite of a sword, deemed answerable with his life; the other man escapes from there alive – he knows the country well. Then the earls' sworn oaths will be broken on both sides. Thereupon, mortal hates will surge up in Ingeld and love for his wife will grow cooler in him after the upsurgings of anxiety. Therefore I do not reckon the loyalty of the Heathobards, their part of the national alliance, to be free of treachery towards the Danes, nor their friendship firm.

2069 'I must carry on telling about Grendel once more, so that you may clearly know, treasure-giver, what the heroes' hand-to-hand onslaught subsequently came to. After heaven's jewel had glided across the terrestrial plains, a visitant came enraged, a horrible night-attacking adversary, to seek us out where safe and sound we were guarding the hall. The combat there was the downfall of Hondscio, and the mortal ruin of the doomed man: he, a girded soldier, was the first to lie dead. Grendel was the renowned young thane's killer, using his mouth: he completely gulped down the dear man's body.

2081 'Even then the bloody-toothed killer, obsessed in mind with evil-doing, was unwilling to leave the gold-hall so soon, empty-handed, but he, notorious for his strength, tackled me: deft of hand, he made a grab. His glove was hanging down, capacious and extraordinary, secured with ingenious fastenings; the whole thing had been fashioned by cunning, with the skills of a devil and out of dragon-hides. Ferocious as perpetrator of these deeds, he wanted to put me inside it, one innocent among many; he was not able to do so, once I was standing upright in anger.

2093 'It is too long to recount how I paid that scourge of the people quittance for every one of his evils; there, my prince, I did your nation credit by my achievements. He got away; for a little while he went on enjoying the pleasures of living. But his right hand remained in Heorot as a pointer, and from there, wretched and miserable in mood, he went down to the bottom of the lake.

2101 'For that mortal onslaught the friend and lord of the Scyldings rewarded me handsomely with hammered gold and many precious things when morning came and we had settled down to a banquet. There was singing there, and music. The aged descendant of Scyld, having heard tell of many things, recounted matters from long ago. Sometimes the courageous soldier would touch the beguiling wooden lyre in cheerfulness; sometimes he would utter a true and painful lay; sometimes, according to what was fitting, the commodious-hearted king would recount an extraordinary story; sometimes again the old warrior shackled with age would lament for his youth and its battle-strength. His heart was turbulent within him as, old in years, he called many things to mind.

2115 'In this way we made our entertainment in there the whole day long, until another night overtook mortal men. Then promptly after that the mother of Grendel was ready for revenge; she set out, fraught with misery – death, the martial implacability of the Weder-Geats, had taken her son away. She avenged her child, this monstrous woman. Valorously she killed a man: the life which departed there was that of Æschere, a wise old counsellor of long standing. And when the morning came, the Danish people were not permitted to cremate him, being dead, by fire nor to lay the beloved man on the funeral pyre: she had carried off the corpse in her devil's clutches down beneath the mountain stream. To Hrothgar this was the bitterest of the sorrows which had long beset the people's lord. Then, sorrowful of mood, the prince implored me upon your life that I should acquit my warrior-standing, venture my life and achieve glory in the crush of the waters; he promised me reward.

2135 'So, as is widely known, I sought out the grim and terrible guardian of the depths of that seething lake. There for a while it was hand-to-hand combat between us; the water seethed with blood and I sliced off the head of Grendel's mother in the hall of battle, with the edges of a sword unwontedly huge. I escaped from there – but not easily – with my life, for I was not yet ordained to die; instead, the earls' protector, Healfdene's kinsman, once again gave me an abundance of treasures.

XXXI

2144　'In this manner the people's king lived, according to worthy customs: I had by no means forgone those compensations, the reward for my strength – rather he, Healfdene's son, gave me treasures at my own choosing. These, warrior-king, I want to bring and present to you as loving gifts. Still the fulfilment of my joys depends upon you: I have few close kinsmen but you, Hygelac.'

2152　So he commanded the boar to be carried in, the high standard, the helmet towering in battle, the grey mail-coat and the splendid war-sword; then he completed his story:

2155　'Hrothgar, the discerning king, gave me this battle-gear and by his especial word he urged me that I should first explain to you the loving-kindness of the gift: he said that king Heorogar, prince of the Scyldings, owned it for a long while, but that none the less he did not want to give it, that breast armour, to Heorogar's son, the brave Heoroweard, although he was loyal to him. Use all this well.'

2163　I have heard that there followed closely upon those precious adornments four horses, all alike in being swift and tawny-dappled: he presented to him the loving gift of horses and treasures. So ought a kinsman to act, and not weave a web of malice for the other, with concealed cunning, nor devise the death of his close companion. His nephew was extremely loyal to Hygelac, a man severe in his enmities, and each was mindful of the other's welfare.

2172　I have heard that the torque, the remarkable and impressive treasure which Wealhtheow had given him, he bestowed upon Hygd, daughter of a prince, together with three horses, graceful and agleam in their harness. After the receipt of that necklet her bosom was then worthily decked.

2177　So Ecgtheow's son, a man famous for his military exploits, manifested his courage in good works and lived in pursuit of honourable reputation. He did not strike down his household comrades, being drunk: his was not a savage mind, but rather, he who was ferocious in warfare restrained his strength, the greatest among mankind, the liberal gift which God had bestowed on him. He had long been disregarded, for the men of the Geats had not reckoned him a man of integrity, nor had the lord of the Weder-Geats been willing to do him much honour on the mead-bench; they had strongly believed that he was indolent, a prince without vigour. There came a turnabout in each one of his troubles for this man blessed with glory.

2190   Then the protecting lord of earls, the king renowned in warfare, commanded a gold-decorated blade, a legacy from Hrethel, to be fetched in – at that time there was no finer treasure among the Geats in the category of sword. This he laid in Beowulf's lap, and granted him seven thousand hides of land, a hall and a prince's throne. Within that nation, land – a domain and hereditary rights – lawfully belonged to both of them alike, though pre-eminently – the kingdom at large – to the one who was of nobler rank there.

2200   Afterwards in later days it came about amid the strident sounds of battle, when Hygelac lay slain and battle-swords had been the means of Heardred's death beneath the sheltering shield after the warlike Scyldings had sought him out, a sturdy soldier in the midst of his victorious people, and assailed the nephew of Hereric with hostile attacks, that the broad kingdom passed into the hands of Beowulf.

2208   He ruled it well for fifty years – by then he was a wise old king, the aged guardian of his native land – until a lone being began to tyrannize in the dark night, a dragon who kept watch over a hoard within his lofty dwelling-place, a high stone burial chamber. Beneath it lay a path not known to people: into it some man or other had gone who had got within reach of the heathen hoard. His hand . . . [*Damage to the MS makes some readings irrecoverable between lines 2215–18 here, and 2227–31 below*] . . . gleaming with costly ornament . . . This he later . . . although he had been cheated while sleeping by the cunning of a thief; the people, the neighbouring community of warriors, came to realize that he had been infuriated.

XXXII

2221   Not at all with deliberate intentions nor of his own volition did he break into the reptile's hoard, this man who grievously molested him, but out of harsh necessity. The retainer of some worthy man or other, he was running away from an angry beating, this guilt-harassed man, and, lacking shelter, stumbled into that place. As soon as he looked inside, a horrid fear beset the intruder; nevertheless, the wretched man . . . when the terrible sight seized him. A precious vessel . . . Of such ancient riches there was a profusion in that earth-house, just as in days of old some man or other, lost in thought, had hidden them there, costly treasures, the mighty relics of a noble race. All of those people death had carried off at previous times and now this one man still remaining from the flower of the nation, the one there who had longest survived, a sentinel mourning for his friends, expected the same thing – that he would be allowed to enjoy the long-lived riches for a short time.

2241   A burial-chamber was waiting all ready on open ground near the ocean-rollers, new-built close by the cliff, secured by ingenious devices. Into it the custodian of the rings carried a hoarded and cherished quantity of riches fit for earls and uttered a few words:

2247   'You earth, may you now keep the earls' possessions, now that heroes could not. Indeed, good men got it from you in the first place. Death in war, savage and mortal injury, has carried off every one of the men of my nation who has yielded up his life: they knew the happiness of the hall. I have no one to bear the sword or burnish the gilded chalice, the costly drinking-vessel: a noble community has flitted elsewhere. The tough helmet shall be shorn of its plates, ornamented with gold: the burnishers are sleeping who should polish the battle mask. And likewise the war-dress which, amid the splintering of shields, has stood the bite of iron swords in the skirmish will rot away with the warrior, nor may the mail-coat's mesh journey afield with the war-leader alongside heroes. The pleasure of the harp is no more, the joyous sound of the singing wood, nor does the noble hawk sweep through the hall, nor does the swift horse gallop through the township. Violent death has dispatched hence many of mortal kind.'

2267   So, mournful of mood, he gave voice to his pain, the one left behind by them all; miserably he wept by day and by night – until the flux of death touched at his heart. The pleasure of that hoard an ancient twilight enemy found standing open – the one who, aflame, seeks out burial chambers, the naked evil dragon who flies by night, enveloped in fire. Him the land's inhabitants greatly dread. He is impelled to seek out the hoard in the earth where, ripe in years, he will keep guard over heathen gold, and will be not a whit the better for it.

2278   For three hundred years this enemy of the people, grown excessively cunning, thus kept this particular hoarding-place in the earth – until a lone man angered him in his heart. He carried the gilded chalice to the prince and pleaded with his lord for reconciliation. So now the hoard had been rifled, the hoard of treasures reduced and concession granted to the destitute man; the lord looked for the first time upon the antique work of men.

2287   When the reptile awoke, strife started all over again; truculent at heart, he forthwith went smelling along the rock and found the trail of the enemy's foot – for he had advanced with stealthy skill right up close to the dragon's head. Thus a man not ordained to die, who retains the favour of God the ruler, can easily survive sorrow and exile. Eagerly the guardian of the hoard went searching along the ground. He wanted to find the man who had done him an injury in his sleep. Smouldering and ferocious of mood, repeatedly he roamed around the whole outside of the tumulus. There was no one there in that wasteland; but he was relishing a fight, some aggressive action.

Eventually he returned into the burial-chamber and looked for the precious vessel. At once he discovered that some man had interfered with the gold and the superb treasures.

2302 The guardian of the hoard could hardly wait until evening came. By then the keeper of the burial-mound was swollen with fury; the malignant creature intended to recompense the costly drinking-vessel with flame.

2306 Then to the reptile's satisfaction the daylight was sped. He did not mean to wait inside the earthwork any longer but sallied forth with a blaze, imbued with fire. The beginning was terrible for the people in the land, just as it was soon to be ended in tragedy for their treasure-giving lord.

XXXIII

2312 So this visitant started vomiting fiery gobbets and burning up splendid buildings; the glare of the conflagration was a source of terror to mortals. The malignant creature flying aloft did not mean to leave anything living there. Wide afield, near and far, the reptile's belligerence, the malice of an intransigent foe, was evident, and how the warlike ravager hated and held in contempt the Geatish people. Then back to the hoard he hurried, to his secret princely dwelling before it was time for day. He had surrounded the land's inhabitants with fire, with blazing heap and flaming brand. He put his trust in the burial mound, in combat and in the earthwork: this hope deceived him.

2324 Swiftly and accurately then the horror was communicated to Beowulf that the best of buildings, his own home and the gift-throne of the Geats, was crumbling away in blazing billows of fire. To that virtuous man this was a heartfelt grief, the greatest of anxieties upon his mind. The wise man imagined that in breach of ancient law he had severely provoked God the ruler, the everlasting Lord; his breast was turbulent within with dark thoughts as was not usual with him.

2333　　With flaming gobbets the fiery dragon had razed the secure interior region of the nation and the coastal lands without, the whole of that part of the world: for this the warrior-king, prince of the Weder-Geats, planned a revenge upon him. So the warriors' protector, lord of the earls, commanded them to construct him a remarkable shield wholly of iron; he was well aware that linden wood from the forest could not afford him help against fire. The prince, proved virtuous of old, was to play out the ending of his borrowed days of life on earth – and the reptile with him, although he had long held the wealth of the hoard.

2345　　The ring-rich king then disdained to seek out the wide-roaming winged beast with an army, an extensive force; for his part he did not fear the fight, nor did he make much of the reptile's belligerence, strength and courage, because, risking the danger, he had survived many attacks and martial clashes ever since he, the man blessed with victory, had cleansed Hrothgar's hall and in the fight had grappled to the death with the kindred of Grendel's loathsome stock.

2354　　Not the least of those hand-to-hand encounters was that in which Hygelac was killed when in warfaring forays in Frisian territories the king of the Geats, lord and friend of the people, Hrethel's son, died from the blood-drenching strokes of the sword, beaten down by the blade. From there Beowulf escaped by his own strength; he made use of his skill at swimming. This one man had on his shoulder thirty sets of battle-gear when he launched out to sea. The Hetware, who came carrying their shields into confrontation with him, had no cause to be jubilant over the standing skirmish – a handful escaped again from that warrior to make their way home.

2367　　Ecgtheow's son, then, a miserable and lonely man, swam over the expanse of waters back to his people. There Hygd offered him treasure-store and kingdom, rings and royal throne; she was not confident of her son, that he would be able to maintain ancestral sovereignties against alien armies, now

Hygelac was dead. None the sooner for that were these necessitous people able to get consent from the prince that he should be lord above Heardred or that he was willing to accede to the kingdom. However, by his friendly counsels he supported him, lovingly and with respect, among the people until Heardred grew older and commanded authority in the Weder-Geats.

2379   Him some exiled kinsmen, the sons of Ohthere, Eadgils and Eanmund, came seeking across the sea: they had rebelled against the sheltering lord of the Scylfings, Onela, noblest of those sea-kings who dispensed treasure in the kingdom of the Swedes, a renowned prince. It proved to be the end of Heardred; for this hospitality Hygelac's son incurred a mortal wound from the blows of a sword, and when Heardred lay dead Ongentheow's son, Onela, set off again to make his way home, and left Beowulf to hold the royal throne and rule the Geats. He was a good king.

XXXIV

2391   He kept retribution for the prince's death in mind through later days. He befriended the necessitous Eadgils; he supported him across the wide sea with an army, with soldiers and with weapons. Then he took vengeance for those bitter occasions of grief; he deprived the king, Onela, of his life.

2397   Thus the son of Ecgtheow had survived every attack, fierce battle and valorous action until that particular day on which he had to measure up against the reptile. So as one of twelve the lord of the Geats went, bursting with anger, to face the dragon. By then he had heard when this feud had arisen, this violent hatred of men: the infamous precious vessel had come into his keeping through the finder's hand. The one who had brought about the beginning of the strife was the thirteenth man in the contingent, a gloomy-minded prisoner: abject, he was obliged to set off thence and point out the place. Against his will he went on until he perceived the solitary earth-house, the tumulus beneath the turf, close by the heaving ocean and the welter of

the waves, which was filled inside with gems and filigree orna-
ments. The ancient monstrous custodian, a ready combatant,
was guarding the gold treasures under the earth: the getting of
it was no easy transaction for any man. The king, a hardy man
in conflict, seated himself then on the headland while he,
generous friend and lord of the Geats, bade farewell to his
household companions. His spirit was melancholy, restless,
prepared for death, and that eventuality was immeasurably
close, which was to come upon the old man, seek the treasure-
store of his soul and part asunder life from body; not for long
after that was the prince's life clothed in flesh.

2425   Beowulf, son of Ecgtheow, spoke out:

2426   'Many warfaring forays and times of strife I survived in my
youth: I remember it all. I was a seven-year-old when the ruler
rich in treasures, lord and friend of the people, received me
from my father. King Hrethel kept me and looked after me,
gave me riches and feasting, and was ever mindful of our
relationship. Throughout his life I was not a whit less dear to
him as a young man within his dwellings than was any of his
sons, Herebeald and Hæthcyn or my own Hygelac. For the
eldest one, undeservedly, a violent grave was strewn, through
the actions of a kinsman, when Haethcyn hurt his lord and
friend with an arrow from his curved bow; he missed his mark
and shot his kinsman – one brother shot the other – with
blood-stained missile. It was an unatonable assault that was
emphatically a culpable one – wearying to mind and to spirit:
the prince, notwithstanding, had to lose his life unavenged.

2444   'So too it is a melancholy thing for an old man to experience,
that his young child should swing upon the gallows. Then he
will give vent to lamentation and agonized plaint, when his son
is hanging at the raven's pleasure and he, aged and senile,
cannot afford him any help. Always each morning his son's
departure to another place is remembered afresh; he does not
care to wait for another heir within his dwellings now that
this one has experienced the full consequence of his actions

through pain of death. Grieving and distressed he surveys his
son's apartment, the abandoned wine-hall, a lodging-place for
the wind, devoid of cheer; the heroes and the horsemen sleep in
the grave, the music of the lyre is there no more nor the sound
of joy in the courts, as once they were there.

XXXV

2460 'So he takes to his bed and sings a song of his distress, a
lonely man singing for his only son; fields and towns, every-
thing seemed to him too spacious.

2462 'So too the sheltering lord of the Weder-Geats, king Hrethel,
laboured under the distress for Herebeald welling in his heart.
He was quite unable to make good the act of violence upon the
killer, but none the sooner for that was he able to show hate for
the warrior in hostile deeds, even though he was not dear to
him. Then, on account of the grief which had cruelly befallen
him, he renounced mortal happiness and acceded to the light of
God. When he departed from life he bequeathed the land and
its strongholds to his sons, just as a happy man does.

2472 'Then there was feuding and strife between Swedes and
Geats, mutual recrimination across the wide water and stern
warfare, after Hrethel had died. Besides, Ongentheow's sons
were vigorous and full of martial zeal; they had no desire to
keep the peace across the seas but would frequently commit
some terrible and malicious killing about Hreosnabeorh. For
this, for the aggression and the violence, my dear kinsmen took
revenge, as was common knowledge, although another of them
bought that revenge with his life, a hard bargain; the battle was
the downfall of Hæthcyn, lord of the Geats. I have heard that
afterwards, on the morrow, with the edges of his sword one
kinsman avenged the other upon his slayer, where Ongen-
theow encounters Eofor. The battle-helmet split and the old
Scylfing, Ongentheow, sank down pallid from sword-wounds.
Eofor's hand was remembering violent outrages in abundance:
he did not hold back the fatal stroke.

2490 'Those treasures which Hygelac gave me I paid him back in battle, as it was granted me, by my bright sword. He had given me land, a domain, the joy of hereditary possession. It was not necessary for him to have to go to the Gifthas or the Spear-Danes or to the kingdom of the Swedes, looking for some inferior warrior and buying him for money. I was ever willing to go ahead of him among the footsoldiers, alone in the van-guard, and I shall go on doing battle in this way throughout my life, as long as this sword endures. Early and late it has often done its duty by me, ever since I became the slayer of Dæghrefn, the Frankish warrior, by hand-to-hand combat in front of the armies. He was unable after that to take to the Frisian king rich trappings and breast-ornaments, for he fell courageously in the struggle, this prince, the guardian of the standard. The sword was not his slayer; rather a pugnacious clinch crushed his heart's pulsings and his bone-framed body.

2508 'Now blade's edge, hand and tough sword, will have to fight for the hoard.'

2510 Beowulf spoke out and uttered pledge-plighting words for the last time:

2511 'I ventured into many battles in my youth; once more, grown old as the people's guardian lord, I will face up to a feud and accomplish a famous exploit – if the evil ravager comes out of his earth-house to face me.'

2516 Then for the last time he greeted each one of the bold, helmet-wearing men, his dearly-held companions:

2518 'I would not wish to carry a sword as weapon against the reptile if I knew how, otherwise, I could to my renown wrestle with the monster, as once I did with Grendel; but here I anticipate the heat of fierce fire and venomous breath. Because of this I have on me a shield and a mail-coat. I do not mean to fall back a foot's length from the guardian of the burial-mound, but hard by the earthwork we shall both fare exactly as the ordaining Lord of every man settles a destiny for us. I am confident in my heart that I shall be left possessing the renown against the winged adversary. You men in armour, protected by mail-coats, wait on the burial-mound and see which of us two better overcomes his wounds, following the deadly on-slaught. This undertaking is not yours, nor is it proper for any man, except myself alone, to put his strength against the mon-ster and live up to his lordly standing. Either I shall gain gold by my courage or else battle, savage and mortal injury, will carry off your lord.'

2538   So the famous fighter, sturdy beneath his helmet, got up with the aid of his shield and advanced, wearing his sword-proof mail-shirt, in front of the stone chamber. He was relying on the strength of a single man: such an undertaking is not that of a coward.

2542   This excellently virtuous man, who had survived so many fights and loud battles when infantry-men clashed, then saw in front of the earthwork a stone arch from which a stream came bursting out of the burial-mound. The bubbling surge of that brook was hot from fierce fires; he would not be able to survive the cavern close to the hoard for any length of time without being scorched up, because of the dragon's flame.

2550   Then, because he was now swollen with fury, the prince of the Weder-Geats let loose a cry from out of his breast; truculent of heart he bellowed aloud. His voice, challenging and clear, went reverberating within, under the grey stone. Fury was provoked: the hoard-guardian recognized the voice of a man. There was no more time to sue for peace. First the monster's breath came issuing forth from the stone, a hot harmful vapour: the ground rumbled. The man in front of the burial-mound, the lord of the Geats, swung up his round shield against the horrible attacker when the serpentine creature's heart was aroused to face up to the fight. The good warrior-king had already drawn his sword, the ancient heirloom very sharp in its edges. In each of the would-be destroyers a fear of the other prevailed. Resolute of mood, the lord of his loving people braced himself against his towering shield as the reptile quickly coiled himself together; in his armour he waited. Then, aflame, the coiled thing came slithering – and rushing towards his doom. His shield adequately protected the famous prince in life and limb for a shorter space of time than his purpose required in that moment, when for the first time he had to fight on without Providence having ordained for him the victory in the battle.

2575   The Geatish lord swung aloft his hand, and with his splendid ancestral sword struck at the creature guilty of raising terror, with the result that the gleaming edge was blunted on the bone and bit less keenly than the people's king, overloaded with difficulties, needed of it. Then, after that fierce stroke, the guardian of the burial-mound was in savage mood. He scattered deadly fire; attacking flames leapt in all directions. The generous lord of the Geats did not boast the glories of victory. His unsheathed battle-blade failed him in the struggle as it should not have done, an iron sword esteemed of old. It was no easy departure this, that Ecgtheow's famed son was about to relinquish the plain of earth: he was going to acquiesce in taking up an abode elsewhere: in such a manner every man ought to resign his borrowed days of life.

2591   It was not long then before these terrible adversaries closed with each other again. The guardian of the hoard, whose breast heaved with his breathing, had taken heart afresh; enveloped in fire, the man who once had ruled a nation suffered severe distress. Nor were his close comrades, the sons of princes, taking their stand about him as a group in the noblest traditions of warfaring: instead they retreated into a wood and looked to their lives. In one of them alone was a mind welling with feelings of remorse. Nothing at all can thrust aside the bond of kinship in one who thinks aright.

XXXVI

2602   He was called Wiglaf, Weohstan's son, a much-loved soldier, a prince of the Scylfings, a kinsman of Ælfhere. He saw his lord in his battle-mask enduring the heat. He remembered those gracious gifts which he had once bestowed on him, the prospering settlements of the Wægmundings and every one of the public rights which his father had possessed. After that, he could not hold back: his hand grasped the round shield of yellow linden-wood and he drew an ancient sword which was known among men as an heirloom from Eanmund, Ohthere's son, of which friendless, banished man Weohstan had been the killer, by the sword's edges, and had carried off to his kinsmen the burnished, gleaming helmet, the ring-linked mail-coat and the ancient sword forged by giants. Onela made him a gift of it – the battle-clothing of his own nephew, Eanmund, armour in fighting trim; nor did Onela have anything to say about the violent deed even though Weohstan kept the ornate equipment, the sword and the mail-coat, until his son could live up to his noble rank as his father before him. Later, when he departed, an old man, along the road leading on from life, he gave his son, then with the Geats, a number beyond tally of every kind of battle-clothing.

2625   For the young warrior this was the first time that he was to support an onslaught in battle alongside his noble lord. His sense of purpose did not melt away nor did his kinsman's legacy flinch at the fighting. The reptile found that out, once they had come together. Wiglaf spoke out and voiced many truthful remarks to his companions; his spirit was melancholy:

2633   'I remember the time when, as we drank mead there in the beer-hall, we would promise our lord, who gave us these treasures, that we would repay him for these battle-accoutrements, the helmets and the tough swords, if a need such as this should befall him. For this reason, from among the army he chose us, of his own free will, for this expedition, esteemed us worthy of its glories and gave me these treasures, because he counted us good spear-wielding warriors, bold helmeted soldiers – even though the lord and protector of the people meant to perform alone this courageous task for us, because he of all men has performed the most feats of glory and daring deeds.

2646 'Now the day has come when our lord is in need of the strength of good battle-warriors. Let us go to him and help our war-leader as long as the heat continues, the grim terror of smouldering fire. As for me, God knows that it is much more agreeable to me that smouldering fire should engulf my body alongside my gold-giving lord. To me it does not seem fitting that we should go carrying our shields back home unless we can first bring down the foe and defend the life of the prince of the Weder-Geats. This I know full well: his past achievements have not been such that among the multitude of the Geats he ought to be suffering torment alone and going under in the struggle. Sword and helmet, mail-coat and armour shall be shared between us both.'

2661 Then he strode through the deadly reek and went wearing his helmet to the help of his lord. He spoke a few words:

2663 'Dear Beowulf, see the whole thing through properly, in keeping with what you declared long ago in the days of your youth, that while you lived you would not let your reputation fail. Now, resolute prince, renowned for your deeds, you must defend your life with all your strength. I shall support you.'

2669 After these words the reptile, hideous malevolent being, came angrily on a second time, aglow with flaring flames, to attack his enemies, loathed mortals. The fire advanced in waves and burned Wiglaf's shield to the boss. His mail-coat could not afford the young armed warrior safety but the young man bravely carried on under cover of his kinsman's shield when his own had been destroyed by the fiery gobbets.

2677 Still the warrior-king kept his mind on matters of glory: in the might of his strength he struck with his battle-blade so that, given impetus by his hatred, it stuck fast in the head.

2680 Nægling broke; Beowulf's old and grey-coloured sword failed him in the struggle. It was not allotted him that the edges of iron weapons could assist him in the fight; that hand of his which, as I have heard, asked over much of every blade in the wielding, was too strong when he carried the weapon toughened by bleeding wounds into the struggle, and he was none the better off.

2688   Then for a third time the ravager of the nation, the ferocious and fiery dragon, determined upon aggressive moves, and when the opportunity offered itself to him he rushed, hot and fierce in the assault, upon the renowned man and grabbed him right round his neck with his cruel tusks. Beowulf was smothered with blood, his life-blood; the gore welled out in pulsing streams.

XXXVII

2694   I have heard that then, in the people's king's time of need, the earl at his side displayed courage, skill and daring, as was instinctive in him. He did not bother about the head but the brave man's hand was burnt as he helped his kinsman in that he, this man in his armour, struck the spiteful creature some-what lower down, so that the sword, gleaming and gold-plated, plunged in; and forthwith the fire began to abate.

2702   Still the king himself was in command of his senses; he unsheathed a deadly knife, cruel and sharp in conflict which he was carrying in his mail-coat. The protective lord of the Weder-Geats slashed the reptile apart in the middle. They had felled the foe – their courage had ousted his life – and the two of them together, noble kinsmen, had destroyed him. A man, a thane, ought to be like this in time of need. For the prince this was his last occasion of victory by his own deeds and his last achievement in the world.

2711   Then the wound which the dragon from under the ground had earlier inflicted on him began to grow inflamed and swollen. Soon he found that the poison inside him was welling up with deadly malignancy into his breast. The sagely reflect-ing prince then went and sat down on a plinth beside the earthwork. He was looking at the work of giants, how the ages-old earth-dwelling held within it the stone arches secure upon columns. Then with his own hands the thane, good beyond measure, bathed with water his famous prince, bloody from the fight, his lord and friend worn out by warfare, and loosed his helmet.

2724   Beowulf held forth; despite his injury, the grievous mortal wound, he spoke. He was well aware that he had outlived the span of his days and this world's happiness; now the whole tally of his days had slipped away and death was close beyond measure:

2729   'Now I should have wished to give my battle-clothing to my son, had it been so ordained that any heir engendered of my body should have followed me. I have ruled this nation for fifty years. There has been no people's king, not one of those border-ing us about, who has dared to challenge me to arms or threaten me with terror. I have bided the decrees of Providence in their own good time, at home; I have ruled well over my own, I have not gone looking for contrived quarrels nor have I sworn lots of oaths perjuriously. Sick as I am with a mortal wound, I can take comfort in all this, for the Ruler of men will have no cause to accuse me of the violent killing of kinsmen when my life slips away from my body.

2743   'Now, beloved Wiglaf, quickly go and view the hoard beneath the grey rock, now that the reptile lies dead, and sleeps, sorely wounded, deprived of treasure. Make haste now so that I may see the ancient wealth, the store of gold, and gaze well on gleaming skilfully chased jewels, so that because of this wealth of riches I may the more peacefully depart from my life and from the nation I have long ruled.'

XXXVIII

2752   I have heard that upon the utterance of these words Weohstan's son then speedily obeyed his wounded lord, sick from fighting, and went wearing chain-mail, his meshed battle-shirt, beneath the roof of the burial-mound. Then when he had gone by the plinth, jubilant in his achievement the brave young thane saw a multitude of precious jewels, gold lying glittering on the ground, wonderful things on the wall, and the lair of the reptile, the ancient being that flew in the twilight; he saw cups, the drinking-vessels of men long gone, standing there lacking the burnishers, shorn of their ornaments by decay. Many a helmet was there, old and rust-eaten, a multitude of arm-rings ingeniously fastened. Treasure, gold in the ground, can easily turn any man's head, hide it who will. He also saw hanging high above the hoard a standard all of gold, a thing supreme among marvellous artefacts, woven with the skills of agile fingers. From this a radiance gleamed so that he could see the open expanse of the floor and scan the ornate objects. There was nothing to be seen of the reptile there, for the knife-edge had carried him off.

2773　　I have heard that, single-handed, the man then plundered the hoard within the tumulus, that ancient construction of giants, and heaped up chalices and dishes in his arms, at his own discretion. The standard, too, he took, the most dazzling of banners. The aged lord's blade, whose edge was iron, had lately mutilated the creature who had for a long while been the custodian of those treasures, and who, for the sake of the hoard, had waged terror by scorching fire, deadly turbulent at the mid-hour of the nights, until he died a violent death.

2783　　The emissary made haste, anxious to be on his way back, and speeded by the ornate objects. An urgency obsessed him, bold-hearted man, to know whether he would find the prince of the Weder-Geats, stricken through doing deeds of courage, alive in the open place where he had lately left him. Then he with the treasures came upon the famous prince, his lord, bleeding and at the end of his life. Again he took to splashing water on him until the first sign of speech burst from his heart.

2792　　So the hero spoke, the old man in his pain; he surveyed the gold:

2794   'With these words I will say my thanks to the Lord of all, the King of glory, the everlasting Lord God, for these ornate treasures on which I am gazing here, because I was allowed to gain such things for my people before my dying day. Now that I have traded my old life for a hoard of treasures, you must now fulfil the people's need. I cannot be here any longer.

2802   'Command men famous as fighters to build a burial mound, a conspicuous one, on the ocean bluff, following the cremation. It must tower high on Hronesnæs as a reminder to my people, so that seafarers who from afar come navigating their tall ships over the gloom of the waters may thereafter call it Beowulf's Barrow.'

2809   From his neck the intrepid prince took the gold collar and gave it, and his helmet agleam with gold, his ring and his mail-coat to the young spear-wielding warrior, his thane, and charged him to use them well:

2813   'You are the last survivor of our line, the Wægmundings; Providence has lured away all my kinsmen, those earls in their valour, to their appointed destiny. I must follow after them.'

2817   This was the last word from out of the thoughts of the old man's heart before he ascended the funeral pyre, the scorching, surging destructive flames: but the soul departed from him to seek the glory of those steadfast in the truth.

[XXXIX]

2821   It went hard with the young man then, when he saw the one dearest to him faring so grievously on the ground at his life's end. The killer too, the terrible dragon from under the earth, lay robbed of life, overcome in the fighting. No longer would the coiling reptile be allowed to lord it over the ring-hoards; instead, iron blades, the tough, battle-scarred legacy of the smith's hammer, carried him off so that the wide-roaming winged beast had crashed to the ground, motionless from his wounds, near to his dwelling with its hoard. Neither would he wheel flapping through the air at the mid-hour of the nights nor flaunt his presence, proud of his rich possessions; instead, he had fallen to the earth through the handiwork of this warrior-prince. Few indeed of the able-bodied men in the land, so I have heard, daring though he might be in every one of his doings, had succeeded in charging against the breath of the poisonous ravager or in disturbing the treasure-house with his hands, if he encountered the wakeful guardian occupying the barrow. By Beowulf his share of the princely treasures was paid for in death. Each had journeyed to the end of his transient life.

2845   It was not long then before those sluggardly soldiers left the wood, ten faint-hearted faith-breakers together, who had not dared before to brandish their spears in their lord's time of great need; but skulking they came wearing shields and fighting-dress, to where the old man lay, and stared at Wiglaf. He was sitting exhausted, this fighter on foot, by his lord's shoulders; he was trying to revive him with water but he was having no success at all. Much as he wished to, he could not keep on earth the vital spirit within his leader, nor alter anything belonging to God the Ruler. The decree of God was pleased to govern every man's doings as it still does now.

2860   It was easy then for the young man to find a stern response to the man who had lately lost his valour. Wiglaf, Weohstan's son, spoke out, sad and grieved in spirit, and eyed the despised men:

2864   'Any man who means to speak truth may well say that the lord who gave you those precious things, the soldierly trappings in which you are standing there – as he often did bestow on those seated in hall, as a prince to his thanes, helmet and mail-coat at the ale-bench, according as he could find the most splendid ones for you, far or near – that he had utterly thrown away that fighting-dress, to his own hardship when war came upon him. The people's king had no cause to boast of his comrades in arms; nonetheless God the disposer of victories granted him that he should avenge himself, he alone with his sword, since there was a lack of valour in his support. I was barely capable of rendering him aid for his survival in the struggle and even so I set about helping my kinsman beyond my capacity. Once I had stabbed the life-menacing enemy with my sword he grew steadily feebler and the fire billowed less fiercely from his head. There were too few defenders clustered about the prince when the crucial moment came for him.

2884　'Now the receiving of riches, the giving of swords, the whole satisfaction of an ancestral heritage, the cherishing of a home-land by this people of yours, must sink into subjugation. Each and every person in the nation must become a vagrant stripped of his land-right, once princes from afar have heard of your desertion and your disreputable deed. Death is a better thing for any man than a lifetime of scorn.'

XL

2892　Then he commanded the outcome of the fight to be reported to the encampment high up on the sea-cliff where the contingent of shield-equipped soldiers, melancholy of mood, had been sitting all morning long in anticipation of both possibilities: the final day of the cherished man and his coming back. He left little of the new tidings unspoken, the man who rode to the headland, but truthfully declared in front of them all:

2900　'The gracious benefactor of the nation of the Wederas, the lord of the Geats, now lies unmoving on his deathbed and occupies the resting-place of the slain through the reptile's deeds. His mortal enemy lies alongside, stricken with knife-wounds; his sword was unable by any means to inflict a wound upon that monster. Wiglaf, Weohstan's child, is sitting beside Beowulf, earl beside lifeless earl; in weariness of heart he is keeping watch by the loved head and by the loathed. Now there exists for the nation the probability of a period of war, once the king's death gets revealed abroad to the Franks and Frisians.

This harsh state of hostilities with the Hugas was caused when Hygelac went to invade Friesland with a military fleet, where the Hetware attacked him in battle and with their superior strength did valiantly so that the mail-clad aggressor had to succumb, and fell among the footsoldiers: no ornate equipment did that prince hand over to his army. Since then, the favour of the Merovingian king has always been withheld from us.

2922　'Nor do I at all expect peace or good faith from the Swedish nation, for it was widely known that Ongentheow robbed Hæthcyn, Hrethel's son, of his life at Hrefnawudu, when the Geatish people in their presumption first attacked the warlike Scylfings. Promptly the aged father of Ohthere, Ongentheow, old and fearsome, delivered a blow in retaliation: he killed the leader from over the water and rescued his wife, the mother of Onela and Ohthere, an elderly woman despoiled of her gold. And then he pursued his mortal enemies until with difficulty they escaped, lordless, into Hrefnesholt. Then with a huge army he besieged the survivors of the sword, exhausted as they were from their wounds. All night long he repeatedly threatened woe to the wretched troop and said that in the morning he would dispatch them, some by the sword's edge, some on gallows-trees, for the birds' entertainment. Relief came again to their anxious minds with the first light of day when they recognized Hygelac's horn and trumpet and their call, as that worthy king came with an army of his people, advancing in their wake.

XLI

2946　'The bloody trail of the Swedes and the Geats, the human carnage of the onslaught, was everywhere evident, and with what effect these peoples had awakened the feud between them. So the worthy and shrewd old man, the earl Ongentheow, together with his comrades withdrew, greatly regretful, to return to his stronghold; he veered off because he had heard of Hygelac's fighting skill and of the proud man's cunning in battle. He was not confident of his ability to resist, nor that he would be able to fend off those men of the sea, the ocean voyagers, or protect his treasury, his children and his wife; so the aged man once more fell back from there behind the earthen rampart.

2957 'Then harassment was shown towards the Swedish people, and Hygelac's banners swept onwards over that place of sanctuary once the Geats, Hrethel's people, had thronged into the encampment. Then by the sword's edges white-haired Ongentheow was forced to a stand with the result that the people's king was to submit to the single-handed judgment of Eofor. Wulf, Wonred's son, lunged furiously at him with his weapon so that blood from his veins was spurting out under his hair from the stroke. But even so the old Scylfing was not daunted but once the people's king had wheeled round to face him he soon paid Wulf back for the murderous blow with a worse one in exchange. The nimble son of Wonred was not able to give the old man a knock in return, for Ongentheow had already sliced through the helmet on his head so that he was forced to fall back, blood-stained, and collapsed on the ground; he was not ordained to die yet and he recovered although the wound hurt him. Now that his brother was down, Hygelac's tough thane, Eofor, managed with his broad blade, a gigantic ancient sword, to smash Ongentheow's giant helmet above the barrier of his shield: then the king, the people's protective lord, fell back — he had been vitally hit.

2982 'There were men in plenty then who bandaged his brother Wulf and quickly lifted him up, when the way had been cleared for them so that they could take control of the site of the slaughterous battle. Meanwhile the warrior stripped his opponent; he took from Ongentheow his iron mail-coat, his tough hilted sword and his helmet as well, and took the white-haired man's armour to Hygelac. He accepted the ornate equipment and handsomely promised him rewards in the presence of the people and this he fulfilled accordingly. When he had returned home, the lord of the Geats, son of Hrethel, recompensed Eofor and Wulf for their impetuous fighting with lavish treasures: to each of them he gave one hundred thousand sceattas-worth of land and of rings joined together – no one on earth had cause to criticize him for those rewards since they had fought their way to those honours – and to Eofor he afterwards gave his own daughter, to the honouring of his household and as a pledge of his favour.

2999   'This is the feud and this the hostility, the murderous hatred between men, which the Swedish nation will visit upon us, according to the premonition I have, when they hear our lord is dead who once guarded the treasury, the kingdom and you brave shield-warriors against enemies, following the heroes' fall, who furthered the common weal and who ever more completely lived up to his lordly standing.

3007   'Now haste is the best thing, so that we may pay our respects to the people's king there, and escort him who gave us rings on his journey to the funeral pyre. It shall not be some single thing that burns together with the brave man, for there is a hoard of treasures there, gold beyond measure, cruelly purchased, and rings now paid for at the last by his own life. These flame shall devour and fire consume. No man shall wear these treasures as a memento, no beautiful girl shall have one as a flattering necklace about her throat; instead, melancholy, robbed of their gold, each of them shall wander an alien land, not once but often, now that the leader of armies has laid aside laughter, revelry and mirth. Because of this, many a spear cold with the chill of morning shall be grasped in the fist and raised up in the hand; nor shall the music of the lyre awaken the fighting men; instead, the black raven, greedy after men ordained to die, will croak a great deal, telling the eagle how well he had fared in his feasting as, with the wolf, he scavenged among the dead bodies.'

3028   In such a manner the brave man talked of the unwelcome tidings; he did not prevaricate over the facts or his words. The whole troop got up and went disconsolately with welling tears under Earnanæs, to view the awful sight. Lifeless on the sand, then, keeping his bed of rest, they found him, the one who in former times would give them rings. By then the final day was come for that virtuous man, the day on which the warrior-king, prince of the Weder-Geats, perished by an awful death.

3038   But first they had seen there a more extraordinary creature, a loathsome reptile lying opposite him there on the open ground: it was the fiery dragon, the grim creature guilty of raising terror, charred by its smouldering fires. He was fifty feet long as he lay; once he had enjoyed the delights of flying by night, then he would descend again to return to his lair; now he was constrained in death and he had used his earthen caves for the last time.

3047   Beside him chalices and bowls were standing and dishes and precious swords were lying, rusty and eaten through as though they had rested there against the bosom of the earth for a thousand years. During that time the enormous legacy, the gold of men long gone, was wound about with a spell so that nobody could have touched the ring-filled chamber had not God himself, the true King of victories, granted it to the man whom he preferred — God is the overseer of men — to open the hoard, to such a man, that is, as seemed to him fitting.

XLII

3058   It was plain then that his way of life had not benefited the one who had wrongfully kept ornate treasures hidden down inside the earthwork. The guardian had first killed the one man out of the few, and then that deed of violence had been furiously avenged. It is a thing inscrutable, where a warrior renowned for his courage may meet the end of the ordained days of his life, when a man may no longer go on living in the mead-hall among his kinsmen. So it was with Beowulf when he went to face the barrow's guardian and his malignant tricks. He himself did not know by what means his departure from the world would be brought about, since the glorious princes who put the treasure there solemnly stipulated it until the Day of Judgment,

that the man would be deemed culpable for his sins, impris-
oned in the haunts of devils, fast bound in the bonds of hell and
foully tormented, who plundered that place. But Beowulf was
not avaricious after gold; rather, he had lately revealed his
liberality as its owner.

3076 Wiglaf, Weohstan's son, spoke up:

3077 'Often many a man has to endure misery through one man's
will, as has now happened to us. We could not persuade our
cherished prince, the kingdom's protector, to accept any advice
that he should not approach the guardian of the gold, that he
should let him lie where he long had been and keep to his
haunts until the world's end; he remained obedient to his
exalted destiny. The hoard stands revealed – having been pain-
fully won; the lot which urged the king towards it was too
severe. I have been in there and surveyed the whole mass of
precious objects in the chamber once the path was cleared for
me and a way conceded, by no means amicably, in under the
earthwork. In haste I grabbed a great, hefty load of hoarded
treasures in my hands and carried it out here to my king. He
was still alive then, conscious and in command of his senses.
The old man said many things in his pain and told me to greet
you and commanded that you should build the high barrow on
the place of the pyre, in keeping with his deeds as a friend and
lord – great and glorious, since he was the most honourable
soldier among men far and wide throughout the earth while he
was allowed to enjoy the prosperity of his townships.

3101 'Now, let us hurry to see and search for a second time the
mound of skilfully chased jewels, a sight to marvel at, under the
earthwork. I will guide you so that you may look at close
quarters over rings in plenty and abundant gold.

3105 'Let the bier, made quickly ready, be fully furnished by the
time we come out and then let us carry this cherished man our
lord to where he long shall remain in the keeping of God the
ruler.'

3110   So Weohstan's son, the brave hero of the fight, commanded
them to proclaim it to the many men having rule over a hall that
they, the people's rulers, should come carrying wood for the
pyre to the good man's side:

3114   'Now the smouldering fire shall feed, and the dark flame
flourish, on the warriors' tower of strength, who has often
endured the rain of iron when a storm of darts sped by the
bowstrings came flying over the shield-wall, when the impetu-
ous shaft with its feather fitments did its job and lent its aid to
the arrow.'

3120   Sure enough, the prudent son of Weohstan called together
the king's seven best thanes and went as one of that group of
eight warriors in under the unfriendly roof; one of them, who
walked ahead, carried in his hand a blazing torch. After that it
was not according to lottery who plundered the hoard, once
the men had seen that any quantity of it remained, without a
guard, lying about the chamber, going to waste. Little com-
punction did any of them feel because they were hurriedly
making off with the precious treasures. Also, they shoved that
reptile, the dragon, over the ramparts of the cliff and let the
waves carry him away and the water close over the hoarder of
riches meant for adornment. Then coiled gold quite beyond
estimation was loaded on to a wain, and the prince, the grey-
haired warrior, was borne to Hronesnæs.

XLIII

3136   Then the Geatish people erected for him a funeral fire on the
ground, one not mean, but hung about with helmets, with
battle-shields, with bright mail-coats, as he had asked. Then in
the midst lamenting men laid the famed prince, their cherished
lord. And so the warriors proceeded to kindle upon the hill-top
a most mighty funeral pyre. Smoke from the wood climbed up,
black above the blaze, and roaring flame, mingled with weep-
ing, until, when the swirling of the turbulent air died down, the
fire had by then destroyed his bone-framed body, scorched to

its core. Contrite in their thoughts, they voiced their heart's grief, the death of their lord. A Geatish woman also, with tresses bound up, anxious in her grief, sang over and again a melancholy tale, how she for her part sorely dreaded evil days, a multitude of violent deaths, public panic, humiliation and captivity. Heaven swallowed up the smoke.

3156   Then the Weder-Geatish people built a resting-place on the headland, which was high and broad and widely visible to those journeying the ocean; and over ten days they constructed the monument of a man renowned for his striving. The remnants from the flames they built around with a wall in a way men of foremost skill could most worthily devise it. Within the barrow they placed rings and jewels, all such adornments as the hostile-minded men had previously seized from the hoard. They consigned the earls' wealth to the earth to keep, the gold into the ground, where it yet exists, still as unusable by men as it was at that former time.

3169   Then brave soldiers, princes' sons, rode round the burial mound, twelve in all. They wanted to utter their grief, to lament the king, to tell aloud his story and to talk about the man. They praised his heroism and his valorous accomplishments; in seemly ways they glorified him as it is proper that a man should, extolling his friend and lord by his words, embracing him in his heart, when he must submit to be led forth from out of his bodily exterior.

3178   So the Geatish nation, the companions of his hearth, mourned the death of their lord. They said that among the kings of this world he had been the most compassionate of men, and the most humane, the most kindly to his people and the most eager for good repute.

Judith

[London, British Library, Cotton Vitellius A xv, fol.202ᵃ–209ᵃ]

Attempts to associate the composition of *Jud* with some contemporary event or personage in AS history have not proved widely persuasive and are probably unnecessary. The Old Testament Book of Judith – received as canonical by the Anglo-Saxons – is the poet's starting-point with its central theme: 'Thou seest the Assyrians assembled in their strength . . . and putting their faith in shield and javelin. . . They do not know that thou art the Lord who stamps out wars. . . They have planned to desecrate thy sanctuary. . . Shatter their pride with a woman's hand. For thy might lies not in numbers nor thy sovereign power in strong men; but thou art the God of the humble, the help of the poor, the support of the weak, the protector of the desperate, the deliverer of the hopeless. . . Give thy whole nation . . . the knowledge that thou alone art Israel's shield' (ch.9). The potential relevance of such a text to AS England in the time of the Danish wars is plain – but so too is its timeless message to the Christian soul beleaguered by evil in any form; and it is this aspect that the poet explicitly develops out of the scriptural source-material. With deliberate anachronism he gives Judith a prayer to the Trinity, and with calculated exploitation of conventional diction and imagery he characterizes her as a virginal saint and saviour of the godly city of Bethulia. Holofernes he characterizes as the moral monster of the poem, the reckless lord over cities of earth, spiritually blind, arrogant, drunk, lecherous, and at the last a satanic figure plunged into a familiar hell. Thus Judith joins those 'men of old' who stand on record for their faith and manifest in defiance of God's adversaries 'the righteousness which comes of faith' (Hebrews 11:2, 7), like the heroes of the poems *Gen*, *Exo* and *Dan*. Grace is a theme here as it is in a number of OE poems such as *Wan*, *Jul* and *Glc*; and here as in *Exo* an earthly reward of treasures to the chosen people, of spoils from the defeated foe, prefigures the giving and taking away of wealth in the Day of Judgment.

It is now generally thought doubtful that *Jud* was ever substantially longer than the surviving text, though certainly the opening is missing. The poet has exercised aesthetic and didactic choice in dramatizing the narrative of the killing of Holofernes and the triumph of the Hebrews, and in reducing the cast-list of the scriptural account to the three principal personages of the poem. Stylistic features have suggested a tenth-century date which would preclude ascription to Cynewulf as favoured by some critics. But without doubt *Jud* is the work of an individualistic poet of rare talent. His capacity for characterization, scene-setting and story-telling is outstanding. The heroic diction used throughout is conventional enough, but when it is applied to the feminine and vulnerable Judith its effect is startling and aptly suggestive of extraordinary stature conferred in answer to the prayer of the righteous; when it is applied to Holofernes and the Assyrians its juxtaposition with gross behaviour effects not compliment but sardonic ridicule; and when it is applied to battle it matches in vitality the best battle-poetry in this long tradition and gives dynamic expression to the concept of God's unrelenting vengeance upon the unrighteous. The poet's relish in his subject and in his art is everywhere evident in this distinguished poem.

. . . she was suspicious of gifts in this wide world. So she readily met with a helping hand from the glorious Prince when she had most need of the supreme Judge's support and that he, the Prime Mover, should protect her against this supreme danger. The illustrious Father in the skies granted her request in this because she always had firm faith in the Almighty.

7   I have heard, then, that Holofernes cordially issued invitations to a banquet and had dishes splendidly prepared with all sorts of wonderful things, and to it this lord over men summoned all the most senior functionaries. With great alacrity those shield-wielders complied and came wending to the puissant prince, the nation's chief person. That was on the fourth day after Judith, shrewd of purpose, the woman of elfin beauty first visited him.

X

15   So they went and settled down to the feasting, insolent men to the wine-drinking, all those brash armoured warriors, his confederates in evil. Deep bowls were borne continually along the benches there and brimming goblets and pitchers as well to

the hall-guests. They drank it down as doomed men, those celebrated shield-wielders – though the great man, the awesome lord over evils, did not foresee it. Then Holofernes, the bountiful lord of his men, grew merry with tippling. He laughed and bawled and roared and made a racket so that the children of men could hear from far away how the stern-minded man bellowed and yelled, insolent and flown with mead, and frequently exhorted the guests on the benches to enjoy themselves well. So the whole day long the villain, the stern-minded dispenser of treasure, plied his retainers with wine until they lay unconscious, the whole of his retinue drunk as though they had been struck dead, drained of every faculty.

32   Thus the men's elder commanded the hall-guests to be ministered to until the dark night closed in on the children of men. Then, being wickedly promiscuous, he commanded the blessed virgin, decked with bracelets and adorned with rings, to be fetched in a hurry to his bed. The attendants promptly did as their master, the ruler of armoured warriors, required them. They went upon the instant to the guest-hall where they found the astute Judith, and then the shield-wielding warriors speedily conducted the noble virgin to the lofty pavilion where the great man always rested of a night, Holofernes, abhorrent to the Saviour.

46   There was an elegant all-golden fly-net there, hung about the commandant's bed so that the debauched hero of his soldiers could spy through on every one of the sons of men who came in there, but no one of humankind on him, unless, brave man, he summoned one of his evilly-renowned soldiers to go nearer to him for a confidential talk.

54   Hastily, then, they brought the shrewd lady to bed. Then they went, stout-hearted heroes, to inform their master that the holy woman had been brought to his pavilion. The man of mark, lord over cities, then grew jovial of mood: he meant to defile the noble lady with filth and with pollution. To that heaven's Judge, Shepherd of the celestial multitude, would not

consent but rather he, the Lord, Ruler of the hosts, prevented him from the act.

61   So this species of fiend, licentious, debauched, went with a crowd of his men to seek his bed – where he was to lose his life, swiftly, within the one night: he had then come to his violent end upon earth, such as he had previously deserved, the stern-minded prince over men, while he lived in this world under the roof of the skies.

67   Then the great man collapsed in the midst of his bed, so drunk with wine that he was oblivious in mind of any of his designs. The soldiers stepped out of his quarters with great alacrity, wine-glutted men who had put the perjurer, the odious persecutor, to bed for the last time.

73   Then the glorious handmaid of the Saviour was sorely preoccupied as to how she might most easily deprive the monster of his life before the sordid fellow, full of corruption, awoke. Then the ringletted girl, the Maker's maiden, grasped a sharp sword, hardy in the storms of battle, and drew it from its sheath with her right hand. Then she called by name upon the Guardian of heaven, the Saviour of all the world's inhabitants, and spoke these words:

83   'God of beginnings, Spirit of comfort, Son of the universal Ruler, I desire to entreat you for your grace upon me in my need, Majesty of the Trinity. My heart is now sorely anguished and my mind troubled and much afflicted with anxieties. Give me, Lord of heaven, victory and true faith so that with this sword I may hew down this dispenser of violent death. Grant me my safe deliverance, stern-minded Prince over men. Never have I had greater need of your grace. Avenge now, mighty Lord, illustrious Dispenser of glory, that which is so bitter to my mind, so burning in my breast.'

94   Then the supreme Judge at once inspired her with courage – as he does every single man dwelling here who looks to him for

help with resolve and with true faith. So hope was abundantly renewed in the holy woman's heart. She then took the heathen man firmly by his hair, dragged him ignominiously towards her with her hands and carefully laid out the debauched and odious man so as she could most easily manage the wretch efficiently. Then the ringletted woman struck the malignant-minded enemy with the gleaming sword so that she sliced through half his neck, so that he lay unconscious, drunk and mutilated.

107   He was not then yet dead, not quite lifeless. In earnest then the courageous woman struck the heathen dog a second time so that his head flew off on to the floor. His foul carcass lay behind, dead; his spirit departed elsewhere beneath the deep ground and was there prostrated and chained in torment ever after, coiled about by snakes, trussed up in tortures and cruelly prisoned in hellfire after his going hence. Never would he have cause to hope, engulfed in darkness, that he might get out of that snake-infested prison, but there he shall remain for ever to eternity henceforth without end in that murky abode, deprived of the joys of hope.

XI

122   Judith then had won outstanding glory in the struggle according as God the Lord of heaven, who gave her the victory, granted her. Then the clever woman swiftly put the harrier's head, all bloody, into the bag in which her attendant, a pale-cheeked woman, one proved excellent in her ways, had brought food there for them both; and then Judith put it, all gory, into her hands for her discreet servant to carry home. From there the two women then proceeded onwards, emboldened by courage, until they had escaped, brave, triumphant virgins, from among the army, so that they could clearly see the walls of the beautiful city, Bethulia, shining. Then the ring-adorned women hurried forward on their way until, cheered at heart, they had reached the rampart gate.

141   There were soldiers, vigilant men, sitting and keeping watch in the fortress just as Judith the artful-minded virgin had

enjoined the despondent folk when she set out on her mission, courageous lady. Now she had returned, their darling, to her people, and quickly then the shrewd woman summoned one of the men to come out from the spacious city to meet her and speedily to let them in through the gate of the rampart; and to the victorious people she spoke these words:

152   'I can tell you something worthy of thanksgiving: that you need no longer grieve in spirit. The ordaining Lord, the Glory of kings, is gracious to you. It has been revealed abroad through the world that dazzling and glorious success is impending for you and triumph is granted you over those injuries which you long have suffered.'

159   Then the citizens were merry when they heard how the saintly woman spoke across the high rampart. The army was in ecstasies and the people rushed towards the fortress gate, men and women together, in flocks and droves; in throngs and troops they surged forward and ran towards the handmaid of the Lord, both old and young in their thousands. The heart of each person in that city of mead-halls was exhilarated when they realized that Judith had returned home; and then with humility they hastily let her in.

171   Then the clever woman ornamented with gold directed her attentive servant-girl to unwrap the harrier's head and to display the bloody object to the citizens as proof of how she had fared in the struggle. The noble lady then spoke to the whole populace:

177   'Victorious heroes, leaders of the people; here you may openly gaze upon the head of that most odious heathen warrior, the dead Holofernes, who perpetrated upon us the utmost number of violent killings of men and painful miseries, and who intended to add to it even further, but God did not grant him longer life so that he might plague us with afflictions. I took his life, with God's help. Now I want to urge each man among these citizens, each shield-wielding soldier, that you

immediately get yourselves ready for battle. Once the God of beginnings, the steadfastly gracious King, has sent the radiant light from the east, go forth bearing shields, bucklers in front of your breasts and mail-coats and shining helmets into the ravagers' midst; cut down the commanders, the doomed leaders, with gleaming swords. Your enemies are sentenced to death and you shall have honour and glory in the fight according as the mighty Lord has signified to you by my hand.'

199   Then an army of brave and keen men was quickly got ready for the battle. Renowned nobles and their companions advanced; they carried victory-banners; beneath their helms the heroes issued forth straight into battle from out of the holy city upon the very dawning of the day. Shields clattered, loudly resonated. At that, the lean wolf in the wood rejoiced, and that bird greedy for carrion, the black raven. Both knew that the men of that nation meant to procure them their fill among those doomed to die; but in their wake flew the eagle, eager for food, speckled-winged; the dark-feathered, hook-beaked bird sang a battle-chant.

212   On marched the soldiers, warriors to the warfare, protected by their shields, hollowed linden bucklers, they who a while previously had been suffering the abuse of aliens, the blasphemy of heathens. This was strictly repaid to all the Assyrians in the spear-fight once the Israelites under their battle-ensigns had reached the camp. Firmly entrenched, they vigorously let fly from the curved bow showers of darts, arrows, the serpents of battle. Loudly the fierce fighting-men roared and sent spears into their cruel enemies' midst. The heroes, the in-dwellers of the land, were enraged against the odious race. Stern of mood they advanced; hardened of heart they roughly roused their drink-stupefied enemies of old. With their hands, retainers unsheathed from scabbards bright-ornamented swords, proved of edge, and set about the Assyrian warriors in earnest, intending to spite them. Of that army they spared not one of the men alive, neither the lowly nor the mighty, whom they could overpower.

236   Thus in the hour of morn those comrades in arms the whole
time harried the aliens until those who were their adversaries,
the chief sentries of the army, acknowledged that the Hebrew
people were showing them very intensive sword-play. They
went to inform the most senior officers of this by word of
mouth and they roused those warriors and fearfully announced
to them in their drunken stupor the dreadful news, the terror of
the morning, the frightful sword-encounter.

246   Then, I have heard, those death-doomed heroes quickly
shook off their sleep and thronged in flocks, demoralized men,
to the pavilion of the debauched Holofernes. They meant to
give their lord warning of battle at once, before the terror and
the force of the Hebrews descended upon him; all supposed
that the men's leader and that beautiful women were together
in the handsome tent, the noble Judith and the lecher, fearsome
and ferocious. Yet there was not one of the nobles who dared
awaken the warrior to inquire how it had turned out for the
soldier with the holy virgin, the woman of the Lord.

261   The might of the Hebrews, their army, was drawing closer;
vehemently they fought with tough and bloody weapons and
violently they indemnified with gleaming swords their former
quarrels and old insults: in that day's work the Assyrians'
repute was withered, their arrogance abased. The men stood
around their lord's tent, extremely agitated and growing
gloomier in spirit. Then all together they began to cough and
loudly make noises and, having no success, to chew the grist
with their teeth, suffering agonies. The time of their glory, good
fortune and valorous doings was at an end. The nobles thought
to awaken their lord and friend; they succeeded not at all.

275   Then one of the soldiers belatedly and tardily grew so bold
that he ventured pluckily into the pavilion as necessity com-
pelled him. Then he found his lord lying pallid on the bed,
deprived of his spirit, dispossessed of life. Straightway then he
fell chilled to the ground, and distraught in mind he began to
tear his hair and his clothing alike and he uttered these words to
the soldiers who were waiting there miserably outside:

285   'Here is made manifest our own perdition, and here it is imminently signalled that the time is drawn near, along with its tribulations, when we must perish and be destroyed together in the strife. Here, hacked by the sword, decapitated, lies our lord.'

290   Then distraught in mind they threw down their weapons; demoralized they went scurrying away in flight. The nation magnified in strength attacked them in the rear until the greatest part of the army lay on the field of victory levelled by battle, hacked by swords, as a treat for the wolves and a joy to the carrion-greedy birds. Those who survived fled from the linden spears of their foes. In their wake advanced the troop of Hebrews, honoured with the victory and glorified in the judgment: the Lord God, the almighty Lord, had come handsomely to their aid. Swiftly then with their gleaming swords those valiant heroes made an inroad through the thick of their foes; they hacked at targes and sheared through the shield-wall. The Hebrew spear-throwers were wrought up to the fray; the soldiers lusted mightily after a spear-contest on that occasion. There in the dust fell the main part of the muster-roll of the Assyrian nobility, of that odious race. Few survivors reached their native land.

311   The soldiers of royal renown turned back in retirement amidst carnage and reeking corpses. That was the opportunity for the land's in-dwellers to seize from those most odious foes, their old dead enemies, bloodied booty, resplendent accoutrements, shield and broad sword, burnished helmets, costly treasures. The guardians of their homeland had honourably conquered their enemies on the battlefield and destroyed with swords their old persecutors. In their trail lay dead those who of living peoples had been most inimical to their existence.

323   Then the whole nation, most famous of races, proud, curled-locked, for the duration of one month were carrying and conveying into the beautiful city, Bethulia, helmets and hip-swords, grey mail-coats, and men's battle-dress

ornamented with gold, more glorious treasures than any man among ingenious men can tell. All that the people splendidly gained, brave beneath their banners in the fray, through the shrewd advice of Judith, the courageous woman. As a reward the celebrated spear-men brought back for her from the expedition the sword and the bloodied helmet of Holofernes as well as his huge mail-coat adorned with red gold; and everything the ruthless lord of the warriors owned of riches or personal wealth, of rings and of beautiful treasures, they gave it to that beautiful and resourceful lady.

341 For all this Judith gave glory to the Lord of hosts who granted her esteem and renown in the realm of earth and likewise too a reward in heaven, the prize of victory in the glory of the sky because she always had true faith in the Almighty. Certainly at the end she did not doubt the reward for which she long had yearned.

346 For this be glory into eternity to the dear Lord who created the wind and the clouds, the skies and the spacious plains and likewise the cruel seas and the joys of heaven, through his peculiar mercy.

Poems from Other Manuscripts

The Battle of Finnsburh (The Finnsburh Fragment)

[London, Lambeth Palace Library 487 (now lost)]

By rare chance, and with interesting literary-critical implications, the story of the fight at Finnsburh preserved in this fragmentary text has survived elsewhere: the poet of *Bwf* uses it (lines 1063–1159) as an exemplum, backing up the foreground themes of his narrative, to suggest a universal pattern in the behaviour of people in community – a tendency for the lives and works of worthy men to be wasted in the clash of (merely) human ethical imperatives. The poet of *Fnb*, then, shares with the *Bwf*-poet and with the poet of *Wds* (see in particular the first cluster of rulers and nations named there) a special interest in the legend-history of the peoples of North-West Europe and Scandinavia; and *Fnb* is, or was, the story in a full epic form such as the *Bwf*-poet in his allusiveness relies on his audience to know.

Finn, king of the Frisians, marries Hildeburh, Hoc's daughter, a princess of the Jutes or Danes, to end a long-standing feud between the two nations. But when Hoc's son Hnæf comes with a company of Jutes as guests to Finnsburh, the feud proves more powerful than the compact, and the Jutes are attacked in their guest-hall (the episode apparently preserved in *Fnb*). Hnæf is killed; so is a son of Hildeburh's and Finn's union. But neither side prevails. Hengest takes on leadership of the Jutes, fetches reinforcements from home, breaches the truce and takes revenge by killing Finn. Hildeburh, who went forth as peace-weaver, returns a widow, mourning the violent deaths of brother, son and husband.

But if the *Bwf*- poet uses the story of Finn to illustrate a discrepancy between human and divine imperatives, there is no hint in the surviving fragment of *Fnb* that this recension of the story was intended as anything but a thoroughly secular poem, celebrating courage and stoicism in the context of a grim blood-feud. Cautiously, we may speculate that this is what AS heroic poetry was like before it adopted a Christian perspective upon human motivations; and that this absence of Christian thought and the detailed remembrance of continental Germanic legend may point to a very early date for the poem – though, as usual, the MS text of it appears to have been a late one. Since the single folio once kept in Lambeth Palace (London residence of the archbishops of Canterbury) has been lost, knowledge of the text rests upon a copy printed by George Hickes in 1705.

It has been speculated that the Hengest of this poem might be identifiable with the Hengist, a grandson of Woden, who, with his brother Horsa, was said to have led to Britain soon after the year AD 449 that contingent of AS mercenaries which eventually seized power from their employer, the British king Vortigern (*HE*, Bk.I, ch.15). In terms of cultural context, characterization, motivation and role, the literary Hengest could well be the kind of projection which oral poetic transmission would make of the historical personage of Hengist, leading migrant Jutes and Angles down through Frisia, and engaging in alliances and combat before crossing over to the province of Britain, then abandoned by the Romans. Were this so, *Fnb* would be all the more remarkable as a surviving memory, however dim and reshaped, of the period of the AS conquest of Britain – a period which must have offered countless incidents for AS poets to celebrate, yet of which no English poetic accounts have come down to match the Welsh elegiac *Gododdin* and its moving commemoration of defeat at the hands of the heathen English.

'. . . the gables will never burn.'

2   Then the king, a youngster in war-making, spoke:

3   'This is not the day, dawning from the east, nor is there a dragon flying here, nor are the gables of this hall burning here, but they are advancing here in arms: the birds of carrion will be calling, the grey-pelted wolf baying, the wood battle-spear thudding, the shield echoing to the shaft.

7   'Now the moon gleams, drifting behind the clouds; now evil deeds are afoot, which will set forward that people's enmity. But now, my warriors, awake, take up your linden shields, set your minds upon courage, turn to the front and be resolute.'

13   Then many a gold-clad thane rose up and girded himself with his sword; then the noble soldiers Sigeferth and Eaha went to the door and drew their swords and so did Ordlaf and Guthlaf at the other door, and Hengest himself followed in their footsteps.

18   Meanwhile, Guthhere was urging Garulf that he, so excellent a soul, should not at the first onset go wearing his armour to the door of the hall, now that a man stern in his enmity meant to deprive him of it. But, bold-spirited hero, he asked openly, over it all, who was keeping the door.

24   'Sigeferth is my name' he declared. 'I am a prince of the Secgan, an adventurer famed abroad. I have survived many adversities, many stern battles. Whatever you yourself insist on seeking at my hands, it is assured you right here.'

28   There was the din of murderous blows then in the hall. The spike-bossed shield in the hands of fierce men, the skull-guarding helmet, were to be shattered, the floor of the stronghold resonated, until Garulf, Guthlaf's son, fell in the fight, first among all those dwellers upon earth. About him perished a host of good and lively men. The raven hovered around; dark and dusky-gleaming light from swords flashed as though all Finnsburh were in flames. Never have I heard of sixty victors in a battle between men behaving more nobly and more worthily, and never of youths better repaying shining mead than his young warriors paid Hnæf. Five days they fought and not one of the retainers in their company fell, but they went on holding the doors.

43   Then a hero came walking away wounded; a man of action in his military trappings, he said that his mail-coat was hacked to pieces and his helmet was holed too. Then the guardian lord of the people asked him at once how the combatants were coping with their wounds, or which of the young warriors . . .

Waldere

[Copenhagen, Royal Library, Ny kongelige Samling 167b]

The two fragments of *Wld* may stand as a symbol of the unhappy fate of many another AS manuscript damaged or destroyed by neglect, accident or wilful action over many centuries. It is likely that the two complete leaves of vellum found in the Royal Library in 1860 had been used, perhaps several centuries earlier, to pad the binding of a printed book – of which we might have gladly foregone half a dozen copies in exchange for the whole of the MS used to wrap it. The handwriting suggests a date in the late tenth or early eleventh century, but the history of the MS is a blank.

The sequence in which the two leaves belonged is only to be conjectured, but enough indications remain in the sixty-three (when printed) completely or partially decipherable lines of alliterative verse to establish that this is part of an expansive treatment of the legend of Walter of Aquitaine. Of this legend, once widespread through the Germanic world, various fragmentary versions and summaries survive in Middle High German, in Latin and in Icelandic, though no other reference to Waldere has been identified in OE poetry. The plot implications of this English version seem broadly to agree with the tenth-century Latin redaction of the legend, *Waltharius*, written by Ekkehard of St Gall. Waldere and Hildegyth were hostages in the court of Attila king of the Huns and were plighted to each other. Eventually, Waldere was obliged to escape. Hildegyth resolved to flee with him, taking a quantity of treasures with her. At length they were overtaken and cornered by two warriors, a reluctant fellow-hostage Hagena and a loot-seeking king Guthhere. Waldere freely offered a share of the wealth but fighting was not averted. In several encounters all the men received serious wounds. They agreed to cease their hostilities and Waldere returned to his original home where, married to Hildegyth, he ruled for thirty years.

The first passage seems to be spoken by Hildegyth to Waldere, encouraging him and commending him to God in conventional heroic terms; the second opens with an unidentified speaker, guessed in this translation to be Hildegyth or Waldere, and concludes with Waldere entrusting the outcome of battle, as Beowulf does, to God.

The rhetorically spacious and noble speeches leave little doubt that a fine poem, probably of wholly secular scope, has been lost.

... eagerly she emboldened him:

2   'Certainly a thing of Weland's making will not fail anyone
who can hold the hardy Mimming: often in battle, blood-
stained and wounded by this sword, one man after another has
faltered. Do not you, a soldier of Attila's vanguard, yet awhile
allow your courage to falter, nor your dignity today. Son of
Alfhere, the day is now come when you must simply do one of
two things: let go your life or have lasting fame among men.

12   'By no means do I chide you, my friend, with my words, that
I have seen you shrink from fighting anyone out of cowardice
at the sword-encounter, or flee into shelter and save your skin,
even though many foes were hacking at your mail-coat with
swords; but rather you have looked ever further afield for the
fighting, for a target beyond the front line. Because of this, I
have dreaded your destiny, in that you have too outrageously
looked for a fight at the entrenchment, on the other man's
condition of battle.

24   'Do yourself honour with good deeds, while God takes care
of you. Have no misgivings as regards your sword: it was
granted you, the choicest of treasures, to our succour; with it
you shall put down the boasting of Guthhere because he first
unjustly looked for this strife. He refused the sword and the
precious cups and a profusion of rings; now he must face about
from this battle, ringless, and return to his lord and his ancient
homeland, or else die here first, if he . . .'

*   *   *

'. . . a better one – except for the one which I have besides,
quietly concealed in an earthenware vessel. I know that
Theodoric conceived of sending it to Widia himself and also a
great wealth of treasures along with that sword in order to
clothe with gold many of the rest along with him. This reward
for former service he received because he, Nithhad's kinsman,
Widia, son of Weland, released him from out of his difficulties:
he sped thence away through the giants' realm.'

11   Waldere spoke out, a warrior strong in courage – he held in
his hands the comforter in battle, in the brandishing of war-
blades – and uttered these words:

14   'Listen, lord of the Burgundians; you thought no doubt that
the hand of Hagena would have done battle upon me and
eliminated me from the standing fight. Fetch, if you dare from
one so wearied in combat, this grey coat of mail. Here on my
shoulders lies Alfhere's legacy, good and broad-fronted,
enhanced with gold – a prince's garment not utterly ignomini-
ous to have when hand defends life's treasury from foes. It will
not prove ill-disposed towards me when men again assail and
meet each other with swords, as you have done towards me.

25   'But he is empowered to award the victory who is swift and
sure of judgment in every righteous cause. He who trusts to the
Holy One for help, to God for aid, will readily find it there if he
has first devised ways of deserving. Then men of mettle will be
able to give out wealth and have rule over riches; that is. . .'

Maxims II

[London, British Library, Cotton Tiberius B i, fol.115ª–115ᵇ]

There is a view that the compiler of the codex saw a didactic associa-
tion between *Mxm II* and the texts which sandwich it, namely the
Menologium (a versified calendar of the Church's holy days from
Christmas to Christmas) and the C-version of the *Anglo-Saxon
Chronicle*. *Mnl* defines the process of the liturgical year, by which men
may make the purposive orderliness of sacred history the organizing
principle of daily living; *Mxm II* offers general precepts about the
divinely ordained laws of the natural world and of the human hier-
archy; and the *Chronicle* keeps the historical record of the actual vicis-
situdes of governing and being governed in an imperfect and transient
world. Certainly, all three texts, like *Mxm I* in the Exeter Book, are the
expression of a mentality which seeks order, rationality and purpose

in the human experience of this world. Many of the proffered truisms of the *Mxm* are to be found widely spread through OE poetry.

The king must rule over a realm. Cities are conspicuous from afar, those which there are on this earth, the ingenious constructions of giants, ornate fortresses of dressed stones. The wind in the sky is the swiftest thing and thunder in its seasons is the loudest. The powers of Christ are great; Providence is the most compelling thing.

5   Winter is the coldest time, spring the frostiest – it is cold the longest. Summer is the most sunshiny – the sun is hottest – and autumn the most gloriously abundant – it brings men the fruits of the year, which God sends them.

10   Truth is a very fickle thing; treasure, gold, is the costliest thing to every mortal; and the old man is the most knowing, the one grown wise through far-off years who has already experienced much. Grief is a strangely clinging thing; but clouds will glide by.

14   Good comrades must encourage a young nobleman to war-making and to ring-giving. In a warrior belongs courage; the sword must experience battle, blade opposing helmet. The hawk belongs on the glove to which, though wild, it must get accustomed. The wolf belongs in the forest, a wretched loner; the boar belongs in the wood, secure in the strength of his tusks; a good man belongs in his native land, forging his reputation.

21   The javelin belongs in the hand, the spear gaudy with gold. The gem belongs on the ring, standing proud and broad. The stream belongs among the waves, mingling with the ocean-flood. The mast belongs on the ship, swaying there as a sailyard. The sword belongs in the lap, a lordly iron weapon. The dragon belongs in its barrow, canny and jealous of its

jewels. The fish belongs in the water, spawning its species. The king belongs in his hall, sharing out rings.

29   The bear belongs on the heath, old and awesome. The river must run from off the upland, a grey spate. The army must hold together, a legion of men assured of glory. In a man there must be faith, in a mortal wisdom. The tree belongs in the soil, burgeoning with leaves. The hill belongs on the earth, standing firm and green. God belongs in the heavens, the Judge of deeds.

36   The door belongs in the hall, the building's wide mouth. The boss belongs on the shield, the fingers' safe protection. The bird belongs aloft, flying in the sky. The salmon belongs in the pool, gliding with the trout. The tempest must come from out of the heavens, churned by the wind, into this world.

42   The thief must go forth in murky weather. The monster must dwell in the fen, alone in his realm. The female, the woman, must visit her lover with secret cunning – if she has no wish to prosper among her people so that someone will purchase her with rings.

46   The sea needs must surge with salty water, and round about each one of all those lands the over-canopying air and the streaming ocean must needs flow, and the mountainous waters. Cattle must needs bring forth and multiply upon the land. The star must needs shine brightly in the heavens, as the ordaining Lord enjoined it.

51   Good must needs contend with evil; youth must needs contend with old age; life must needs contend with death, light must needs contend with darkness, army with army, one foe with another, enemy with enemy contend over land and impute to each other the guilt. The prudent man must always consider the quarrelsomeness of this world; the criminal must hang and fairly pay the recompense because he previously committed a crime against mankind. The ordaining Lord alone knows to where that soul will subsequently depart and all those spirits

who depart into God's presence after their death-day, and await the judgment in the Father's embrace. The shape of the future is obscure and unknowable; the Lord alone knows it, the redeeming Father. No one returns here below the heavens who might tell people for certain what it is like, that creation of the Lord, the habitations of his victorious people where he himself abides.

The Battle of Brunanburh

[Cambridge, Corpus Christi College 173, fol.26ᵃ–27ᵃ
and three other MSS of *The Anglo-Saxon Chronicle*]

Brb is the annal for 937 in four of the seven *Chronicle* MSS, the other three of which have corresponding entries couched in the terse and relatively uncircumstantial prose which characterizes the majority of *Chronicle* annals. Some fourteen other passages in annals of the tenth and eleventh century share with *Brb* the metrical and alliterative features of poetry to an equal or lesser degree. But it is a pity that when at last a fairly precise dating is available we cannot be confident that their authors conceived of these pieces as formal poetry. The relationship of these written records to the traditional mode of poetic composition and delivery is still far from clear. The prose sermons and homilies of Ælfric and Wulfstan, composed for oral delivery to a congregation, manifest a similar poetic rhetoric as though stylistically the upper range of prose rhetoric became poetry without crossing any formally recognized barrier. And since no distinction of layout was observed between prose and poetry in AS manuscripts it is hardly less arbitrary to print the annal for 937 according to the typographic conventions of poetry than it would be to print large tracts of Wulfstan (to whom authorship of some *Chronicle* 'poems' has been attributed) in the same way. In these circumstances, it is an unwarranted critical assumption to take this *Chronicle* 'poetry' – not all of which achieves the literary distinction of *Brb* – as the representative poetry of its day; and it is a mistake of methodology to build upon the assumption an evolution-modelled thesis of spontaneous degeneration of the species Poetry in the late AS period.

Brb itself is by far the most poetical of the annals. Its author is clearly indebted to the traditional formulaic diction of heroic poetry and he has accepted the challenge of a strict traditional metre. He succeeds in expressing infectiously the not-undignified exhilaration of victory – which stands in noteworthy contrast to the eloquence of defeat, loss and exile in such poems as *Mld*, *Bwf*, *Sfr* and *Wan*. Interestingly, and in this point too differing from the *Mld*-poet, he chooses to establish only a vague context of Christian militancy for the battle, even though Athelstan, grandson of king Alfred, was a notable patron of the Church, and gifts from him and his queen at the shrine of Cuthbert are still to be seen among the saint's relics in Durham Cathedral. Instead, historical perspective is given to the battle and a secular patriotism is celebrated in terms deliberately redolent of antique themes of heroism. Athelstan and his brother Edmund, leading the armies of Wessex and Mercia against an alliance of Norsemen, Britons from Strathclyde, and Scots, further consolidated by this victory the political claim of the house of Wessex to sovereignty over the one kingdom of England; the poem may well have been intended to serve as propaganda for this claim. Tennyson did a fine re-rendering of the poem.

At this time king Athelstan, lord over earls and his warriors' ring-giver, and his brother too, the prince Edmund, won by the edges of their swords life-long glory in battle about Brunanburh.

5   They sliced through the shield-wall and hacked the linden battle-targes with swords, the legacies of hammers, these sons of Edward, since it was inborn in them from their forbears that they should often, in warfare against every foe, defend land, treasure-hoard and homes. The aggressors yielded; Scots and vikings fell dying. The field grew wet with men's blood from when in the morning-tide that glorious star, the sun, glided aloft and over earth's plains, the bright candle of God the everlasting Lord, to when that noble creation sank to rest.

17   There lay many a man picked off by spears, many a Norseman shot above his shield and Scotsman too, spent and sated

with fighting. Onwards the men of Wessex in their contingents all day long pursued the trail of the enemy peoples, and from the rear harshly hacked down fugitives from the army with stone-sharpened swords. Nor did the men of Mercia stint of tough hand-combat any of those worthies who with Olaf came questing ashore across the waves' welter in the bosom of the ship, as dying men to battle. Five young kings lay on the battle-field, put to rest by swords, and seven of Olaf's earls too and a countless number of the array of vikings and of Scots.

32　There the Norsemen's chief, driven by necessity, was sent fleeing to his ship's prow with a puny retinue; the vessel crowded afloat; the king embarked upon the tawny ocean and saved his life. And there too the prudent Constantine went in flight north into his own land; the hoary warrior had no cause to crow over that mating of swords. He was pruned of his kinsmen and of friends felled on the field of battle, struck down in the strife; and he left behind his sons on the site of slaughter, young men mangled by wounds at the fray. The grey-haired warrior, the old villain, had no cause to brag of the sword-encounter, no more did Olaf. In the midst of the remnants of their army they had no cause to scoff that they were superior in martial deeds on the battle-field, in the clash of standards, the meeting of spears, the conflict of men, the exchange of weapons, according as they contended on the field of slaughter with Edward's sons.

53　So the Norsemen set forth, a dreary remnant left over by the javelins, in their riveted ships upon Dingesmere, to find their way to Dublin across the deep water, back to Ireland, humiliated.

56　Likewise those brothers, the two together, king and prince, headed for home, the land of the West Saxons, vaunting their valour. Behind them they left sharing out the corpses the dark-plumaged, horny-beaked black raven, and the dun-plumaged white-tailed eagle enjoying the carrion, the greedy war-hawk and that grey beast, the wolf of the forest.

65   Never yet within this island has there been a greater
slaughter of folk felled by the sword's edges before this one,
according to what books tell us, and ancient authorities, since
when from the east the Angles and Saxons arrived here, sought
out Britain across the broad ocean, proud craftsmen of war,
overcame the Welshmen and, being men keen after glory,
conquered the country.

The Battle of Maldon

[British Library, Cotton Otho A xii (burnt)]

The unique MS of the poem was destroyed in 1731 in the fire at
Ashburnham House, Westminster, in which the *Bwf* MS was charred
and others in Sir Robert Cotton's seventeenth-century collection lost
and damaged. All editions stem from John Elphinstone's transcript of
about 1724. The beginning was then already missing; so was the
ending, though the final remark comparing the two Godrics, one of
whom treacherously flees, the other of whom stays and dies with
Byrhtnoth, appositely states the choice that is at the heart of this poem
and, perhaps, of the whole AS heroic ethos.

The annal for 991 in the *Anglo-Saxon Chronicle* (versions C, D, E,
F) recording the death of Byrhtnoth, ealdorman of Essex, in a skirmish
with a Danish raiding-force at Maldon in Essex, is laconic and maybe
ironic in its juxtaposition of his death with the first payment, later that
year, of Danegeld. Behind it, perhaps, lay the disquiet which called
forth the poem. Since there was no discernible strategic gain, was not
the loss of so distinguished a servant of the Crown and protector and
benefactor of the Church, with so many soldiers, an insupportable
price to pay for a gesture of outmoded heroics? Subsequent legend-
history did not see it so. The Latin *Life of Oswald*, composed prob-
ably at nearby Ramsey within a decade of the battle, represents
Byrhtnoth as an Old Testament patriarch in bearing and as a Christian
martyr in his death. The Latin *Book of Ely*, compiled in Ely about
1170 but based upon an older work and ultimately, it seems, upon
oral tradition, bids so far for Byrhtnoth's reputation as to feature two
battles at Maldon, the first a triumphant victory over the heathens, the
second a fortnight-long struggle against overwhelming odds. In both

works are the makings of a martyr-cult; Ely in fact claimed possession of the body of Byrhtnoth and owned a tapestry depicting his deeds, made by his widow Ælflæd in commemoration of his probity. Nor, presumably, would archbishop Wulfstan of York have deemed Byrhtnoth's death futile. In his *Sermon of Wulf to the English* (1014) he castigates the English for stampeding like sheep before a handful of Danes and, so that God may have cause to revoke the curse he has loosed upon them, he urges them to return to old ideals of public and private integrity, since mutual good faith between kin and kin and lord and retainer and subject and sovereign is one with good faith between man and God which will surely win its reward. There is, then, as various annals expressively confirm over these years, a polemical and propagandist context current, treating the Danes as a trial of the nation, into which it is not implausible to fit the poem.

The poet's case is plainly that this strategic defeat of the English was a victory of the national spirit. Byrhtnoth testifies to his oneness with his people, with his land, with his lord the king; he witnesses to his Christian faith in defiance of heathendom and, dying, commends his soul to God. His men in turn testify to their oneness with him and thereby witness to their participation in the same total integrity of secular and spiritual values. Thus is defined an exemplary dynamic of warfare – one, we might note, which is far more complex than that attributed by Tacitus to the Germanic world in the first century after Christ, where the retainers fought for the chieftain, the chieftain for victory. If the *ofermod* in which Byrhtnoth yields equal footing to the Danes is 'pride', the poet is far from seeing it as the sin of Lucifer: it is nearer Beowulf's *wlenco*, a superb *superbia*, derided by Unferth who explicitly lacks it, but a pride justified when Beowulf backs up words with deeds. In this respect the values of the poem are traditional, secular and heroic, as quintessentially declared in Byrhtwold's speech (lines 312–19). But though, perhaps for calculated propagandist reasons, the poet appeals to the heroics of Germanic antiquity – and thus sends scholars looking to the *Germania* of Tacitus – he is even more strikingly forward-looking, even medieval, in his integration of these heroics with the motives of Church, Crown and country.

. . . should be broken. Then he commanded each one of the soldiers to set his horse loose, to drive it far away and to proceed on foot, and to turn his mind to his hands and a doughty disposition. As soon as Offa's relative observed that the earl was not willing to put up with slackness then from off his hand he let his beloved hawk fly towards the forest and addressed himself to the fighting. By that it could be understood that the young man had no intention of flinching at the fray when he took up weapons. Besides him, Eadric too had a desire to serve his chief and lord in the conflict, so he proceeded to carry his spear forward into battle. He was possessed of a doughty will – as long as he was able to hold with his hands shield and broad sword: he was fulfilling a pledge when he was called on to fight in front of his lord.

17   Then Byrhtnoth began to place the men in array there; he rode about and gave instructions, taught the soldiers how they were to stand and maintain the position and urged them that they should hold their shields properly, securely with their fists, and that they should not feel scared at all. When he had suitably placed the army in array he then dismounted among the people where it pleased him best to be, where he knew his troop of household retainers to be most loyal.

25   Then there appeared at the waterside and fiercely shouted out a messenger from the vikings who swaggeringly announced a message from the ocean-wanderers to the earl where he was standing on the foreshore.

29   'Bold seamen have sent me to you. They have bidden me tell you that you must speedily send rings in return for protection and it will be better for you that you should buy off this armed assault with tribute than that we should participate in such cruel conflict. There is no need for us to kill each other: if you are wealthy enough for the purpose, we are willing to fix a truce in exchange for the gold. If you, who are most influential here, decide upon this, that you are willing to ransom your people, pay the seamen a sum of money – upon their own assessment – in exchange for quiet, and accept peace at our hands, we will take to our ships with the levied moneys, set sail and keep the peace with you.'

42 Out spoke Byrhtnoth; he lifted his shield, shook his slim ash spear, held forth with his words and, angry and single-minded, gave him answer:

45 'Do you hear, sea-wanderer, what this nation says? They will give you spears as tribute, the poison-tipped javelin and ancient swords, those warlike accoutrements which will profit you nothing in battle. Seamen's spokesman, report back again; tell your people much more distasteful news: that here stands a worthy earl with his troop of men who is willing to defend this his ancestral home, the country of Æthelræd, my lord's nation and land. The heathens shall perish in battle. It seems to me too despicable that you should take to your ships with our riches, unfought, now that you have intruded this far hither into our country. Not so smoothly shall you get gold. First point and edge shall sort things out between us, the fierce exchange of fighting, before we pay tribute.'

62 Then he commanded the soldiers to advance, bearing shields, so that they were all standing on the river bank. The one troop was unable to get at the other on account of the water there, where the flood tide came flowing after the ebb: streams of water cut them off. Too long it seemed to them until the time they should carry spears against each other. There they stood by the River Pante in a state of uproar, the spearhead of the East Saxons and the ship army: none of them was able to harm another unless someone took his death from the flight of an arrow.

72 The flood tide went out. The seafarers were standing ready, many vikings eager for war. Then the lord of the English heroes commanded a warrior hardy in war to hold the causeway – he was called Wulfstan, a man valiant by virtue of his family. He was son of Ceola who with his spear fatally shot the first man who very rashly stepped on to the causeway there. With Wulfstan there stood two brave undaunted warriors, Ælfere and Maccus, who had no intention of making a retreat at the water-crossing, but rather they strove steadfastly against the enemy as long as they were able to wield their weapons.

84   When they realized this and clearly saw that they had encountered there furious guardians of the causeway, the despicable strangers began to cheat: they demanded that they should be allowed to have access to go leading their soldiers across the ford.

89   Then the earl, because of his extravagant spirit, yielded too much terrain to a more despicable people. Across the chill water, then, Byrhtelm's son called out – the men listened:

93   'It is cleared for you now; come on quickly to us, you men, and to the battle. God alone knows who will be allowed to control the place of slaughter.'

96   The slaughterous wolves advanced; they gave no heed to the water, that troop of vikings. Westwards across the Pante, across the gleaming water they carried their shields; the men from the fleet bore their linden targes ashore. There, confronting the fierce foe, Byrhtnoth stood ready with his men. He ordered the army to form the defensive barrier with shields and to hold steadfastly against their enemies.

103   The fighting was now imminent, glory was at hand; the time was come when doomed men were to perish there. A din was upraised there; ravens wheeled about, and the eagle greedy for carrion. There was uproar on the earth.

108   Then from their fists they let fly spears hard as a file, cruelly sharpened javelins. Bows were busy, shield caught point. The onslaught was furious. Warriors fell, soldiers lay dead on either side. Wulfmær was wounded. He had chosen death in battle, this relative of Byrhtnoth, son of his sister: he was violently hacked down by swords. Retribution was paid to the vikings for that. I heard that Eadweard violently struck one with his sword – he did not skimp the blow – so that the doomed fighter fell dead at his feet; for this his lord declared his thanks to the chamberlain when he had the chance.

122   So they stood firm, stubborn soldiers in battle; eagerly they set their minds on seeing who there could first win the life of a doomed man with his spear, those soldiers with their weapons. The slaughtered man would fall on the ground. Steadfast they stood; Byrhtnoth was in command of them; he urged that each soldier should set his mind on the warfare, who wanted to gain glory by fighting against the Danes.

130   Then one ruthless in warfare advanced, raised up his weapon and his shield for protection and moved towards that man. Just as resolutely the earl went towards the commoner: each of them intended harm to the other. Then the seaman dispatched a spear of southern design so that the warriors' lord was wounded. Then he gave a thrust with the shield so that the shaft broke and he shattered the javelin so that it sprang back out. The warrior was enraged; with a spear he stuck the presumptuous viking who had given him the wound. He was experienced, that soldier: he made his lance pass right through the man's neck; his hand steered it so that he struck the vitals in his sudden assailant. Then he rapidly hurled a second, so that the mail-coat burst: he was wounded in the breast through the linked rings – at his heart stood the poisonous point. The earl was all the happier; he laughed then, a man of spirit, and said thanks to the Ordainer for the day's work the Lord had granted him.

149   Then one of the viking warriors let go a spear from his hands, let it fly from his fist so that it went all too deeply into Æthelræd's noble thane. By his side a youth not grown to manhood was standing, a boy in the battle, who very bravely plucked the bloody spear out of the man, the son of Wulfstan, young Wulfmær. He made the extremely hard spear return again. The point penetrated so that he who had just now severely struck his lord lay dead on the ground.

159   Then an armed fellow went towards the earl – he wanted to take the man's valuables, his armour, and rings, and ornamented sword. Then Byrhtnoth drew sword from sheath,

broad and bright of blade, and struck against the corslet. All too quickly one of the shipmen hindered him, since he crippled the earl's arm. The golden hilted sword then fell to the earth: he was unable to hold the hard blade, or wield a weapon. Even then, the grey-haired warrior delivered a harangue, emboldened the young men and urged them to press onwards as good comrades. Then he was unable to stand steadily on his feet any longer. He looked up to the heavens.

173   'I thank you, Ruler of nations, for all of those joys which I have experienced in the world. Now, merciful Ordainer, I have the greatest need that you should grant my spirit the benefit that my soul be allowed to journey to you, into your keeping, Lord of the angels, to pass in peace. I beseech you that hellish assailants be not allowed to harm it.'

181   Then heathen warriors hacked him down, and both the men who were standing by him, Ælfnoth and Wulmær both lay dead, who gave up their lives at the side of their lord.

185   Then those who had no will to stay there made off from the conflict. The sons of Odda first took flight there; Godric took flight from the battle and deserted the good man who had often given him many a horse. He leapt on to that mount which belonged to his lord, into those trappings, as it was not proper for him to do, and both his brothers ran away with him, Godwine and Godwig: they had no taste for fighting, but turned away from the battle and made for the forest; they fled into that secure place and saved their lives – and more men than it was in any way fitting, if they had called to mind all the favours which Byrhtnoth had done for their benefit. Offa had said as much to them earlier that day in the place of assembly when he had held a council – that many there were speaking boldly who would later be unwilling to suffer at time of need.

202   So the leader of that people was laid low in death. Those of his personal retinue all saw that their lord lay dead. Then, proud thanes, they went on forwards; eagerly they pressed on,

men without fear. At that point they all desired one of two things – to render up their life or to avenge the man they had loved.

209   The son of Ælfric urged them onwards in these terms; a soldier young in years, he addressed his words to them. Ælfwine, then, spoke out and valiantly declared:

212   'Let us call to mind those declarations we often uttered over mead, when from our seat we heroes in hall would put up pledges about tough fighting; now it can be proved who is brave. I am willing to make my lineage known to all, that I was from a substantial family in Mercia. My grandfather was called Ealhelm, a wise nobleman blessed with worldly wealth. The thanes among that people shall not reproach me for my wanting to get out of this army, to make my way home, now that my leader is lying hacked down in battle. To me that is the greatest grief: he was both my kinsman and my lord.'

225   Then he moved forward and turned his attention to revenge, so that with his spear he struck a seaman among the army so that he lay dead on the ground, destroyed by his weapon. Then he exhorted his comrades, his friends and companions, that they should advance.

230   Offa spoke out and shook his ash spear:

231   'Yes, Ælfwine! you have exhorted all the thanes at time of need. Now that our lord the earl lies dead on the ground it is incumbent upon us all that each of us should encourage the others, as soldiers into battle, as long as he is able to keep and hold a weapon, a tough blade, a spear and a good sword. Godric, the cowardly son of Odda, has betrayed us all. Too many a man thought when he rode off on horseback, on that splendid mount, that it was our lord. Because of that the army here in the field was split and the shield barrier broken. May his conduct, in that he put so many a man here to flight, end wretchedly for him.'

244   Leofsunu spoke out and raised up his linden shield, his targe, as protection; he answered the warrior:

246   'I vow it, that I shall not retreat from here the space of a foot, but rather I mean to go on further, to avenge my lord and friend in battle. The stalwart men around Sturmer will have no cause to reproach me with their words, now that my lord has fallen, that I travel lordless home, and turn back from warfare; rather shall weapon dispatch me, spear point and iron sword.'

253   He pressed on, furious in the extreme, and fought resolutely: flight he scorned.

255   Then Dunnere spoke and brandished his lance; an elderly freeman, he called out above it all, and urged that each one of the warriors should avenge Byrhtnoth:

258   'He who thinks to avenge his lord upon that people, he may not flinch nor fret about his life.'

260   They pressed ahead then; they had no regard for life.

261   The men of the household, fierce spear-bearers, fought toughly then, and prayed God that they might be allowed to avenge their lord and friend, and wreak destruction upon their enemies. The hostage eagerly supported them; he was of sturdy stock in Northumbria, the son of Ecglaf: his name was Æscferth. He did not flinch in the give and take of battle, but he repeatedly fired off darts. Sometimes he landed a shot in a shield, sometimes he lacerated a warrior; constantly at brief intervals he inflicted some wound, as long as he was able to wield weapons.

273   Also in the spearhead stood Eadweard the tall, alert, and eager; he spoke words of declaration that he would not flee a foot's measurement of ground and fall back, since his superior lay dead. He broke through the shield-barrier and fought with the warriors until he had worthily avenged his treasure-giving lord upon the seamen, before he lay dead among the slain.

280 So too did Ætheric, an aristocratic companion, brother of Sibyrht; willing and eager to advance he fought zealously and very many another – they split the curved shield; the fierce men defended themselves. Shield rim smashed and mail-coat sang a certain terrible song.

285 Then in the fray Offa struck the sea-wanderer so that he fell dead to the earth; and there Gad's kinsman, Offa, found his way to the ground: he was rapidly hacked down in the battle. Nonetheless he had accomplished what he had promised his lord, according as he had previously pledged to his ring-giving master that they should both ride home sound to the manor or else both perish in war, to die from wounds in the place of carnage. He lay like a thane close to his lord.

295 Then there was a smashing of shields. The men from the sea advanced, infuriated by the fray. Spear often pierced the doomed man's body. Then Wistan went forward, the son of Thurstan fought against the men. He was the killer of three of them in the crush before Wigelm's son laid himself down among the slain. It was a stern encounter there. The soldiers stood firm in the struggle; fighting men dropped down dead, exhausted by wounds. The slain fell to the ground.

304 All this while both the brothers Oswold and Eadwold encouraged the warriors; by their words they urged their dear kinsmen that they should hold out there in the time of need and use their weapons unflaggingly.

309 Byrhtwold held forth, heaved up his shield – he was an aged companion – he shook his ash-spear. Most courageously he enjoined the warriors:

312 'Resolution must be the tougher, hearts the keener, courage must be the more as our strength grows less. Here lies our lord all hacked down, the good man in the dirt. He who now thinks of getting out of this fighting will have cause to regret it for ever. I am grown old in life. I will not go away, but I mean to lie at the side of my lord, by the man so dear to me.'

320   Æthelgar's son, Godric, also encouraged them all to the fray.
Repeatedly he let fly a spear, a murderous javelin among the
vikings. So he advanced, foremost into that body of men. He
hewed and struck until he dropped dead in the battle. He was
not that Godric who fled from the fray.

Judgment Day II

[Cambridge, Corpus Christi College 201, pp.161–5]

'Consummatio timoris dei sapientia. *Gefyllednyss eges godes ys wis-
dom* (The consummation of a fear of God is wisdom)'. This axiom,
attributed to Jesus son of Sirach (Ecclesiasticus) in the OE-glossed *LSc*
(p.67), states a central truth of a number of OE poems (*Wan*, *Sfr*, *Rsg*,
DrR, the epilogue to *Chr III*) whose mood is elegiac and penitential
and whose subject-matter concerns the grace of enlightenment which
follows a man's acknowledgment, through experience and contem-
plation, of a fear of God. 'Whoever fears the Lord receives his
guidance and whoever wakes to him meets with his blessing,' says
Defensor (*LSc*, p.67). Often this salutary fear of God is shown to be
stirred by God himself as an act of grace (see the headnotes to *Wan*),
and so it is in this poem. The narrator, the man set apart from worldly
obsessions who is so often the recipient of grace in Christian visionary
literature, is in a glade redolent of the Earthly Paradise when a rough
wind shatters its tranquillity, as man's first disobedience shattered the
tranquillity of Eden; and the narrator wakes to a consciousness of the
fallen state of Man, his mortality, the world's mutability, impending
Judgment – and a fear of God. Addressing his own will, his flesh, and
at last, out of his wisdom, all mankind, he pictures Doomsday, hell's
horrors and the ecstasies of heaven in a *tour de force* of compunction-
rousing imagery.

   The poet's chosen device of a first-person narrator – a device
enhanced in the live oral performance of the poem when the singer
assumes the narrator's identity – intensifies the emotive power of this
meditation, whose purpose is to open an audience to the grace of tears
– to tears of contrition before Christ the Saviour and the King and to

penitence before Christ the Physician and the Judge. 'Truly, penitence is the wound's medicament, the chance of deliverance; through it God is called to mercy,' quotes Defensor from Isidore, a chief authority for Bede and the Middle Ages (*LSc*, p.47); and the message of the poem also echoes Isidore: 'If in tranquillity we will not fear God, when his Judgment is at hand or we are trampled down by torments we shall be afraid' (*LSc*, p.68). Here, then, poetry serves as a conducted therapeutic exercise in meditation. *JgD II*, like *DrR* (though with a different story-line), amounts to an imaginative embodiment of the spiritual processing described by Gregory the Great (who sent Christianity to the English in 597 and was thenceforth a writer especially revered in England) in the third of his *Dialogues* (see introduction to *DrR*).

The poem, which bears little specific relation beyond theme to *JgD I* in the Exeter Book, is an anonymous creative translation of the Latin *De Die Judicii* traditionally attributed to Bede, whose authorship would well account for the patristic orthodoxy informing the work.

Listen! alone I sat within a grove canopied over with a sheltering roof in the forest's midst where the streams of water murmured and ran amid the glade, exactly as I say. There too delightsome herbs flourished and blossomed round about within that unparagoned place. And the trees stirred and murmured at the roughness of the winds, the sky was churned up and my miserable spirit was quite thrown into confusion. Then forthwith, frightened and unhappy, these fearsome verses I raised up in song, all as you declared it. I remembered my sins, the crimes of my life and the long-drawn-out time of dark death's advent upon earth, and I was afraid of the great judgment because of my wicked deeds upon earth, and I was afraid too of everlasting wrath from God's own self, upon me and each one of the sinful, and how the mighty Lord will divide and sentence all humankind according to his mysterious might. I remembered too the glory of the Lord and of the saints in the kingdom of heaven as well as the misery and the torment of those doomed to wretchedness. This I remembered within myself and I was greatly fearful and, grieving, I declared, troubled in spirit:

26   'You fountains all, I bid you now abundantly open with haste your well-springs, hot from the cheeks, to tears; then I shall smite with my fist and beat my sinful breast in a place of prayer and prostrate my body on the earth and invoke all my merited pains. I bid you now with supplications not a whit to be sparing of tears, but to drench with weeping my sorrowful cheeks and forthwith flood them with salty drops and reveal my wickedness to the everlasting Lord. Let there not be left within the den of my heart any jot of my abject guilts so that that which was concealed be not known to the light of day, nor all – of the breast, of the tongue, of the flesh alike – discovered in plain words. This is the one cure for the miserable soul, and for the grieving the best of hopes: that here, with weeping, he makes known his wounds to the celestial Physician who alone can heal by his virtue felonies slipped into and gloried in, and can swiftly unloose the enchained. Nor will the Ruler of the angels with his right hand crush the reckless spirit, nor will Christ the Ruler quench with water the feeble smoking of the frail flaxen wick. Did not the thief who was put to death on the cross with Christ create for you a telling example of how greatly avails and how glorious is true repentance of sins and of guilts? The thief on the cross was culpable and criminal, all burdened with wrongful deeds; and yet, close to death, he offered his prayers to the Lord with heartfelt intentions. With few but faith-filled words he instantly attained his cure and help and entered the peerless gates of Paradise with the Saviour.

65   Well then, wretched will, I ask you: why do you linger so long and not confess yourself to the Physician? And why, sinful tongue, do you keep silence now that you have available time for forgiveness, now the Almighty, heaven-kingdom's Keeper, will willingly listen to you with attentive ears? For the day is coming when God will judge the orb of earth. You shall, yourself alone, render in words an account to God the Creator, and duly repay the mighty Lord. I urge you anticipate with penitent tears and forestall the wrath of the eternal Judge. Why do you wallow in filth, my flesh, replete with crimes and with sins? Why do you not cleanse your mortifying sins with a flush

of tears? Why do you not pray for poultice and plaster for yourself, the physic of life, from the Lord of life? You must cry and shed tears now, while there is time and a season for weeping: it is a healthy thing that one does one's weeping here and now, and makes one's repentance to the Lord's delight. The Son of God will be gracious if you suffer remorse and condemn yourself for your sins on earth, nor will the God of heaven punish more than once the offences and guilts in anyone. You must not despise lamenting and weeping, and the time available for forgiveness.

92 Remember too in your mind how great is the punishment which is that of the wretched because of their former deeds; or how terribly and how awesomely the King of supernal majesty will here judge each single man according to his former deeds; or what portents will begin to occur and testify to Christ's coming upon earth. All the earth will tremble, and the mountains will crumble and collapse also, and the slopes of the hills will subside and melt, and the appalling tumult of the turbulent sea will greatly bewilder all men's minds. The whole firmament too will become black and bedimmed – very murky it will become – dark and drab of hue, and black as chaos. Then, loose from their places, the stars will fall and the sun will forthwith grow bedimmed, nor will the moon have any strength at all that it may chase away the shadows of night. Then too hitherwards from above, from out of heaven, shall come signs signalling death, and they shall terrify the wretched people. The heavenly hosts will come, a strong power stirred to action; all the squadrons of angels will hover about the eternal Lord and surround the glorious Ordainer with might and with majesty. Then the Lord of heaven, bright as the sun, will sit on the high throne, enhanced by a crown. We shall be brought before him forthwith, come from all quarters to his presence, so that each may undergo judgment according to his deeds, at the hands of the Lord himself.

123 I entreat you, man, to remember how great will be the terror before the judgment-seat of the Lord then; a most enormous

multitude will be standing disheartened and craven, confused and confounded, impotent and afraid, when all the squadrons of angels come together from the vault of the sky and array themselves about the eternal Lord. Then there will be a great summons and all the family of Adam will be commanded there, all earth-dwellers who were ever nurtured in the world or whom mother ever brought forth to human form, or who have existed or will exist, or who will at all be numbered in time to come. Then the secret thoughts of all will be revealed to all in that day: all the evil that heart has contemplated or tongue has spoken in malice, and all the wickedness that man's hand has perpetrated in these murky dens – all his enterprises upon earth. All of the guilty acts in the world which one was ashamed to reveal or declare to any man will then be together exposed to all, and likewise that will be admitted which one has long concealed.

145   On top of all this, all the upper air will furthermore be filled with venomous flame. Fire will spread overall; there will be no curb and no one will ever be able to oppose its might. The whole of that horizon which seems to us empty beneath the sky's expanse will thereupon be quite completely filled with red flame. Then the fiery flame will bluster and roar, red and fierce, and crackle and run apace, by which it will cause torment to the sinful. The avenging blaze will not spare nor show pity on anyone there, unless he is purged here of his defilements, and then arrives there rigorously cleansed. Then many nations, a countless tally of people, will violently beat with fist their sinful breast, afraid, because of their wicked lusts. Paupers will be there and kings of the people; the poor and the affluent all will be frightened. There the poor and the wealthy will have one law, for they will all be subject to fear together. That fierce flood will crackle with fire and cruelly burn those wretched souls, and worms will tear and shred them. No one there can be confident on account of his own achievements in the presence of the Judge, but terror will altogether pervade his heart's thoughts, and bitter grief; and there, grown rigid just like stone will stand the whole wicked throng, in anticipation of misery.

176   Alas, flesh! what will you do? What are you doing now? What can you achieve at that time by lamenting in distress? Woe to you now, you who serve this world and live happy here in wantonness and goad yourself with the unrelenting spurs of luxury. Why do you not fear the fiery terror, and dread for your own sake those excessive torments which the Lord ordained of old for the devils, those cursed spirits, as retribution for their sins? They outdo the understanding and the speech of any man in their enormity. There can be no speech on earth to recount in any sort of story the miserable torments, the foul places of burning in the abyss, which there were in the grim torture in hell. Mingled together there by way of affliction are the smoky flame and the rigours of ice, extreme heat and cold in hell's midst. At times the eyes weep there inordinately because of the furnace's blaze – it is quite full of things noxious. At times too the teeth of the people there gnash because of the great cold. This horrible alternation will go on happening to the wretches in there in an aeon of aeons, between bedarkened black nights and the misery and the smoke of seething pitch. There no voice stirs except violent weeping and lamentation – nothing else. Nor is there seen the face of any being except of the executioners who torture the wretched. Nothing is encountered therein except fire and cold and loathsome foulness: with their nose they can savour nothing except an overabundance of stench. There lamenting lips will be filled with the flame-spewing blaze of loathsome fire, and deadly fierce worms will shred them and gnaw their bones with fiery fangs.

213   On top of all this, the wretched breast will be terrified and tormented with bitter remorse as to why, during this perilous age, the offending flesh devised for itself so many sins that it came to be tortured in the prison where there are these horrible everlasting torments; where no tiny spark of light gives light to the wretched; where no pity nor peace nor rest give any cheer at all to the multitude of the weeping. Consolation will flee away; there will be no help there that can afford protection against those painful things. No face of any friendliness will be encountered there, but grisly terror will be there and fear and sorrowing

hearts and the violent grinding of teeth; there will every-where be cruel unhappiness, disease and fury, and weariness; and there too sinful souls will burn in the fire and roam about in the blind dungeon.

232   Then the damaging pleasures of this world will vanish hence and altogether pass away; then drunkenness will vanish along with banquets, and laughter and play will make off together, and lust too will pass hence away, and parsimony and niggard-liness will pass far away, and every culpable wantonness will go hastening then into the dark, and wretched degenerate sloth, slack with slumbering, will flee slinking away behind. Then at the last the wretch will have seen in the dark corrosive flames what is not in this present approved: the most cherished thing in life will then be loathsome, and these felonies will inexorably turn the weary mind with sorrows and with grief.

247   Ah! he is blessed and blessed again and the most blessed of beings in an aeon of aeons, who may happily escape with his health from such plagues and torments, and at the same time cheerfully perform all things in the world for his Prince and then be permitted to possess the kingdom of heaven: of all hopes, that is the greatest.

254   There night with its darkness never snatches away the radiance of celestial light; neither grief nor pain ever comes there, nor tormented old age. Nor does any toil ever exist there, nor hunger nor thirst nor abject sloth. No fever is there, nor disease nor sudden plague, no crackle of flame nor loathsome cold. There is not unhappiness nor weariness there, nor decay nor anxiety nor rough punishment. There is no lightning nor unpleasant storm, no winter nor thunder nor the least cold, nor are there hard hail-showers with snow. Nor is there poverty nor loss, nor the terror of death nor distress nor suffering nor any discontent; but there peace shall reign together with pros-perity, and pity and everlasting goodness, glory and honour, likewise praise and life and loving concord.

272 On top of all this, the everlasting Lord will graciously minister to them each and every benefit there where he, the Father ever-present, will honour and gladden and favour them all together, glorify them and cherish them well and adorn them in beauty and freely love them and place them upon a high celestial throne. His gentle Son, the Giver of victory, will grant to each one everlasting reward, heavenly treasure which is a sublime gift, in the midst of the peerless host of the angels and of the flocks and throngs of the holy. There they will be received among the peoples, among the patriarchs and the holy prophets, with exulting hearts, amidst the cities where are the apostles of almighty God, and among red heaps of roses where they will for ever shine.

290 There the virgin throng of the immaculate walks, hung about with blossoms, most radiant of hosts, all of whom God's peerless loved one leads – that woman who brought forth to us the Lord, the Ordainer, upon earth, the pure Virgin, that is Mary, most virtuous of maidens. Through the bright shining realms of the glorious Father, between Father and Son, in a noble throng, and amidst that everlasting celestial peace, she, most blessed of them all, leads mighty counsellors, the sentinels of the skies.

301 What can there be of hardship here in this life, if you will speak the truth to one who asks, set against this: that you be permitted to dwell, spotless, among that company in eternity and enjoy happiness upon the blessed thrones of those above, for ever more without end?

The Lord's Prayer, The Creed, Fragments of Psalms (The Benedictine Office)

[Oxford, Bodleian Library, Junius 121, fol.43ᵃ–47ᵃ]

Bodleian MS Junius 121 is one of a small group of related MSS which were evidently compiled and copied at Worcester about the time of the Norman Conquest. The codex contains documents of which the broad purpose was to regulate the government, liturgical practice and spiritual discipline of the English (Benedictine) monasteries, and perhaps of the English church more widely. Amid the penitentials, confessionals, canons, polities, homilies and pastoral letters occurs a text which has come to be called *The OE Benedictine Office* – with only approximate accuracy, since the work is not explicitly related to the Rule of St Benedict, nor does it set out to present a complete act of worship. It is in fact a rendering, not in Latin, but in OE prose and verse, of parts of the Latin liturgy of six of the Hours into which the monastic day's worship (the *opus Dei*, 'God's work') was divided. A second (incomplete) version of the *Office* survives in Cambridge, Corpus Christi College 201 (Ker 49B), which includes a longer treatment of the Lord's Prayer (*LPr II*) and a second text of the same Gloria (*Glo I*). Another, but much shorter, Gloria in OE verse (*Glo II*) occurs in British Library, Cotton Titus D xxvii (Ker 202); and a third, shorter, OE metrical Lord's Prayer (*LPr I*) is collected in the Exeter Book. In marked contrast with these poetic versions of liturgical matter are the dry academic expositions of the Lord's Prayer and the Creed in the form of a Latin dialogue between master and pupil in Oxford, Bodleian Library, Bodley 343 (Ker 310). Other metrical paraphrases and amplifications of the Psalms survive in the Paris Psalter, the sole extant AS collection of extensive translations of psalms into OE verse; and in British Library, Cotton Vespasian D vi (Ker 207), where a distinguished Kentish exposition of Ps. 50 (Vulgate; Ps. 51 in the *NEB*) is preserved.

The Lord's Prayer, the Creed, a selection of antiphons and one or two particular psalms were regarded from early times as a core of liturgical matter which even the most bucolic layman ought to know by heart. Caesarius, Bishop of Arles (*c.*470–542), wrote: 'Someone may say: I am a farmer and continually engaged in earthly matters; I can neither listen to nor read the divine lessons. How many men and women in the country remember and repeatedly sing diabolical, shameful love songs! Those things which the Devil teaches they can remember and say; are they unable to keep in mind what Christ shows them? How much more quickly and to better advantage, how much more profitably could these men and women from the farm learn the Creed, the Lord's Prayer, a few antiphons or the fiftieth and ninetieth Psalms? By getting and remembering these and saying them rather frequently they might have a means of uniting their soul to God and freeing it from the Devil. Just as shameful songs send a man into the darkness of the Devil, so holy songs show him the light of Christ. Therefore, let no one say: I cannot remember anything of what is read in Church.' (Sister M. M. Mueller tr., *Saint Caesarius of Arles: Sermons* (New York, 1956), vol. I, Sermon 6, p.40.)

The need not only to teach the laity these most important formulas of worship and prayer, but also to have available English renderings of them for the benefit of those not skilled in Latin, was evidently felt throughout the history of the AS church. Bede, whose last scholarly task was to translate St John's Gospel into English, had also prepared translations of the Lord's Prayer and the Creed for the instruction of layfolk; and of course he recorded with approval Cædmon's achievement in adapting traditional AS poesy to Christian purpose, as a means of popularizing scriptural (and therefore liturgical) matter in the native language. King Alfred deplored that at his accession few clerics south or north of the Humber could construe even the Latin of their Offices in English: so he launched his remedial programme of translations into English and proposed that schools be established for teaching suitable young men to read English. The early eleventh-century translation of the Gospels into West Saxon directly involved Englishing the scriptural versions of the Lord's Prayer, as had earlier glossing of the Latin Bible. Most pertinently, both Ælfric and Wulfstan, leading Benedictines of the late tenth and early eleventh century, in their turn approved of English renderings of the Lord's Prayer and the Creed for the laity's instruction. Indeed, it has been suggested that both of these men contributed to the making of the OE *Benedictine Office*, perhaps intending it for the use of the non-monastic clergy (see J. M. Ure, *The Benedictine Office: An Old English Text*, Edinburgh, 1957, especially pp.52–3, 62–3 and 72–5).

But the OE *Office* is no mere literal and academic crib for poor Latinists: rather, it amounts to an exposition of the fuller import of the elements of the liturgy. St Augustine of Hippo would perhaps have felt uneasy at the constraints imposed by OE metre upon the sense of the Latin texts (see *CI*, Bk.IV, ch.20, pp.209–10), but he would surely have found the authors' doctrinal aim in accord with his ideal of Christian teaching practice. This he summed up in a dictum of Cicero: 'that an eloquent man should speak in such a way that he "teaches, pleases, and persuades". Then he [the orator Cicero] added: "To teach is a necessity, to please is a satisfaction, and to persuade is a triumph." Of these three, the one mentioned first . . . depends upon what we say; the other two depend upon the manner in which we say it.' (*CI*, Bk.IV, ch.12, p.193.)

In particular, the *poetry* of this codex – heavily formulaic, with measured pace and spacious phrases – may well be intended by its manner of articulation to offer scope for semi-formal meditation upon the words of the hallowed texts. By its very structure it enhances the thematic extension of each Latin proposition into a more complex statement of doctrine and dogma; it offers homage to the sentiment of the Latin by adorning it in the colours of English poetic rhetoric; and it causes the mind and heart to dwell upon and contemplate the subject-matter, unfolding phrase by phrase.

Thus at the end of the AS period the ancient *ars poetica* of the English, still versatile, comes to serve a distinctively poetic function in giving worthy vernacular articulation to those ritualistic, sacred and central formulations of the liturgy which were habitually reserved elsewhere throughout Christendom to the Latin tongue. The composition of the *OE Benedictine Office* was just one among many dynamic and creative innovations of the Benedictine reformers who largely reshaped English culture in the tenth and eleventh centuries. It was to be many generations before the English church returned to exploring the place of vernacular poetry in the liturgy, or that of the liturgy in vernacular poetry.

The Office of Prime, in which LPr III, Crd and some of the FPs occur, is prefaced by an explanation in OE prose of the significance of the hour of Prime, then the Office proper opens with a Latin antiphonal verse from the Psalms (Ps. 70:1 in the NEB), together with its rendering in OE verse, as follows:

De prima hora
In the first hour of the day, that is at the sun's rising, we should praise God and eagerly pray him that he, out of his tenderness of heart, illumine our hearts with the illumination of the true Sun — that is, that he by his grace so illumine our inward thought that the devil may not through harmful darkness lead us astray from the right path nor too much impede us with the snares of sin.

Deus in adiutorium meum intende; domine ad adiuuandum me festina.
Be, Lord God, a noble helpmeet; look, Lord, upon me, and help me quickly then in my mortal need.

Next follows the Gloria patri (Glo I), a poem of fifty-seven OE lines based on the Latin phrases of the Gloria. Then comes the Latin hymn Iam lucis orto sidere *and another antiphonal verse from the Psalms (Ps. 54:1 in the NEB) with its rendering in OE verse:*

Deus in nomine tuo saluum me fac; et in uirtute tua libera me.
In your holy name, make me whole, O God; free me from foes through the power of your love.

Next comes the Capitulum (1 Tim 1:17) and the response, all in Latin, followed by further Latin versicles and responses and the Latin Gloria patri; then another citation from the Psalms (Ps. 44:26 in the NEB) with its OE verse rendering:

Exsurge domine adiuua nos; et libera nos propter nomen tuum.
Arise, Lord, now, and swiftly lend us trusty help; and save us from our enemies, for we earnestly love your name.

There follows the Kyrie eleison, and then the Lord's Prayer (LPr III) in OE verse:

Pater noster qui es in celis
I   Father of mankind, I pray you for solace, holy Lord, you who are in the heavens.

Sanctificetur nomen tuum

3   May this your name be hallowed now, fast fixed in our intellects, redeeming Christ, fast established in our bosoms.

Adueniat regnum tuum

6   May your kingdom now come to us mortals, Wielder of mighty powers, righteous Judge, and may your sublime faith remain in our hearts for the span of our lives.

Fiat uoluntas tua sicut in celo et in terra

10   And may your will be fulfilled among us in the habitation of the kingdom of earth as clear as it is in the glory of heaven, pleasingly beautified for ever into eternity.

Panem nostrum cotidianum da nobis hodie

14   Give us now today, Lord of men, high King of the heavens, our bread, which you sent into the world as salvation to the souls of mankind: that is the pure Christ, the Lord God.

Et dimitte nobis debita nostra

19   Forgive us, Guardian of men, our guilts and sins, and pardon our crimes, the body's wounds, and our wicked deeds, although we often offend against you, the almighty God, in your mercies.

Sicut et nos dimittimus debitoribus nostris

23   Just as we pardon on earth their crimes to those who often do wrong against us, and do not think to accuse them of their evil deeds, in order to merit eternal life.

Et ne nos inducas in temptationem

27   Do not lead us to punishment, into the grief of affliction, nor to the testing, redeeming Christ, lest we, devoid of grace, become out of enmity estranged from all your mercies.

Sed libera nos a malo

31　And also free us now from the evil of every fiend; we in our bosoms shall zealously speak thanks and glory, Prince of the angels, true Lord of victories, because you by your mighty powers mercifully freed us from the bondage of hell-torment.

Amen

37　Let this be.

After the Lord's Prayer come two more sets of verses from the Psalms (Ps. 119:175 and 119:176 in the NEB) together with their OE verse renderings, followed immediately by the Creed:

Uiuet anima mea et laudabit te; et iudicia tua adiuuabunt me.
My soul shall live and passionately praise you; and your decrees shall help me in my doings.

Erraui sicut ouis que perierat; require seruum tuum domine, quia mandata tua non sum oblitus.
I have gone astray like the foolish sheep that would indeed have perished; ah! zealously seek your servant, Lord, for I have never forgotten your glorious behests.

Credo in deum patrem omnipotentem

1　Almighty Father in heaven on high, who shaped and wrought this bright creation and founded this whole plain of earth, I confess and passionately believe you to be the only and everlasting God. You are the Lord of life, the Author of angels, the Ruler of earth, and you wrought the depths of ocean, and you know the myriads of the illustrious stars.

Et in Iesum Christum filium eius unicum, dominum nostrum

9　I believe in your righteous Son, the Saviour-King, sent hither from the realm of angels on high, whom Gabriel,

God's messenger, annunciated to Saint Mary's own self. Immaculate woman, she freely accepted the behest, and within her breast she brought forth you, the Father's own Self, as a child. There was done no sinful thing at the nuptials, but there the Holy Ghost gave the morning-gift and filled the virgin's bosom with rapture; and so she manifestly conceived for earth's inhabitants the illustrious Creator of angels, who came as a consolation to worldlings; and round about Bethlehem angels proclaimed that Christ was born upon earth.

Passus sub Pontio Pilato

25 　When Pontius Pilate wielded rule and judgment under the Romans, then the dear Lord suffered death – on the gallows he mounted – the Lord of mortals, whom Joseph, despondent of mood, buried: and from out of hell he fetched booty, from out of that hall of torment myriads of souls, and bade them seek their homeland on high.

Tertia die resurrexit a mortuis

33 　After that, upon the third day, the Ruler of the nations arose, Lord of might, straightway from the ground, and for forty days he comforted his disciples with mystic counsels; and then he went seeking to his kingdom, that homeland on high, and said that he would abandon no one who ever after that would follow him and with a steadfast spirit hold loyal to his friendship.

Credo in spiritum sanctum

41 　I embrace in hope the Holy Ghost, equally as eternal as is either the Father or the Son declared to be by the voices of the nations. These are not three Gods three times named, but this is one God who owns all these three names in the mystic conditions of circumstances, righteous and sure to prevail throughout the broad creation, the Giver of glory to the multitudes, superb and everlasting.

Sanctam ecclesiam catholicam

49   I also believe that they are beloved of God who with singular purpose praise the Lord, the exalted King of the heavens, during their life here.

Sanctorum communionem

52   And I trust in the illustrious fellowship of your saints during life here.

Remissionem peccatorum

54   I believe in the forgiveness of every sin.

Carnis resurrectionem

55   And I believe in the resurrection of all people, of the body upon earth, in that terrible hour,

Et uitam eternam

57   when you will apportion to all people life everlasting, according as each mortal here proves pleasing to the ordaining Lord.

The Office of Prime concludes with a series of thirty-five further citations from the Psalms together with their OE verse renderings, and a Latin collect.

The Metrical Charms

Out of the ninety-odd OE and Latin charms which have survived from the AS period some twelve metrical charms, often accompanied by a prose description of ritual to be followed in their application, are commonly identified among a slightly larger number which make use of alliteration. The oldest extant text is that of the charm *For the water-elf disease* (*ASPR VI*, Charm 7) in London, British Library, Royal MS 12D xvii, which comprises three mid-tenth-century collections of AS medical recipes, probably compiled at Winchester (Ker 264).

From the second half of the tenth century survives one of the texts translated below, *For unfruitful land* (*ASPR VI*, Charm 1), which is written on three folios added, probably contemporaneously, at the end of a MS containing the Old Saxon religious poem *Heliand* (Ker 137).

Five more metrical charms occur in another medical manual, London, British Library MS Harley 585, from the turn of the tenth-eleventh century, following upon an OE translation of the *Herbarium* attributed to Apuleius (born about AD 130), scholar of Carthage and Athens. Though doubtless spurious, the attribution serves as a reminder that much AS scientific (and 'pagan') lore derives from Roman and Greek sources. These five are *The nine herbs charm*, *Against a dwarf*, *For a sudden stitch*, *For loss of cattle*, and *For delayed birth* (*ASPR VI*, Charms 2–6 respectively).

In the early eleventh-century MS, Cambridge, Corpus Christi College 41, of which the principal text is the OE translation of Bede's *HE*, and which also includes part of the text of *SnS*, are written into the margins four charms in the same hand as *SnS*, namely, *For a swarm of bees*, *For theft of cattle*, *For loss of cattle*, and *A journey charm* (*ASPR VI*, Charms 8–11 respectively). Other entries in this MS include, interestingly, masses and other liturgical forms as well as Latin charms (Ker 32). Contemporary Latin and English inscriptions state that the MS was among those bequeathed by Leofric (d.1072) to his cathedral at Exeter (see headnotes to the Exeter Book).

The latest recorded AS metrical charm, *Against a wen* (*ASPR VI*, Charm 12), is inserted in a mid-twelfth-century hand in the tenth-century MS, London, British Library, Royal 4A xiv, containing Latin scriptural commentary and a sermon attributed to St Jerome.

Most, perhaps all, of these MSS were made for monastic use and kept in monasteries; but it remains highly likely that the charms recorded in them have a remote and actively heathen origin, despite their later Christian trimmings – and in so far as they do preserve the supposedly effectual formulas of pre-Christian religious practice they may be regarded as virtually the only truly pagan poetry, as distinct from the simply secular, to survive in OE. *The nine herbs charm* attributes to Woden the revelation of the nine herbs named as being particularly efficacious against poisons, and in the charm *For unfruit-ful land* the invocation to a 'mother of earth' seems to preserve the name of some lost goddess, Erce (if this is not rather some ancient bidding cry); while in both of these as in several other charms, allusions to warlocks, witches, elves and gods testify to the superstitious survival of pagan religious notions – indeed, not all of the references to the Lord are necessarily, in origin, Christian. The use made of Christian liturgical formulas is hardly less superstitious, and in this respect the charm *For unfruitful land* in particular may offer a complex comment on the purpose, the form and the spirit of the OE metrical renderings of liturgical items in the *OE Benedictine Office*. The invocation beginning 'East-facing I stand' achieves a certain impressive sonority of diction, metre and alliteration which matches the genuine liturgical poetry; but on the whole the charms evidently use verse primarily for mnemonic purposes, and they do not belong, as regards technique, among the more aesthetically sophisticated accomplishments of the AS poets.

For Unfruitful Land

[London, British Library MS Cotton Caligula A vii, fol.176ᵃ–178ᵃ]

In the following translation, the metrical passages are distinguished by indentation.

Here is the remedy, how you may restore your fields if they will not crop well, or where some untoward thing is done upon them by warlock or witchcraft.

By night, then, before it begins to grow light, take up four turfs in the four quarters of the land, and mark how they were positioned before. Then take oil and honey and barm, and milk of each of the livestock which are on the land, and a piece of each species of tree which has grown on the land, except for hardwood trees, and a portion of each plant of known name, excepting only buckbean, and then put in holy water, and then drip this three times on the underside of the turfs, and then say these words, 'Crescite, grow, et multiplicamini, and multiply, et replete, and fill, terre, the earth. In nomine patris et filii et spiritus sancti sit benedicti' and say the Paternoster as often as this other. And afterwards carry the turfs to the church and let the priest sing four masses over the turfs, and let the grass be turned towards the altar. And afterwards let the turfs be brought to where they previously were, before the setting of the sun. And let there be made for them four Christ-symbols of rowan, and write on the end of each 'Matheus' and 'Marcus', 'Lucas' and 'Iohannes'. Lay the Christ-symbol at the bottom of the hole, then say 'Crux Matheus, crux Marcus, crux Lucas, crux sanctus Iohannes'. Then take the turfs and place them there on top, and then say the 'Crescite' words nine times and the Paternoster as often, and then turn yourself towards the east and bow nine times humbly and then say these words:

> East-facing I stand. I invoke favours for myself. I invoke the illustrious Domine; I invoke the great Lord; I invoke the holy Keeper of the heaven-kingdom. Earth I invoke and heaven on high and the righteous Saint Mary and the might of heaven and that sublime abode; so that by the Lord's grace I might speak from my teeth this spell with unwavering will: to germinate these crops for our worldly use, to fill these lands by steadfast faith, to render beautiful these meadow-turfs, even as the prophet said — that he would gain favour in the earthly realm who judiciously distributed alms for the Lord's sake.

Then turn yourself round three times sunwise, then stretch yourself prostrate and recite the litanies there, and then say 'Sanctus, sanctus, sanctus' to its ending. Then sing the Benedicite with outstretched arms, and the Magnificat and the Paternoster three times, and offer this to Christ and to Saint Mary and to the holy Cross in praise and in honour, and in favour of him who owns the land and of all those who are subordinate to him. When all this is done, then one should take unspecified seed from almsmen, and give them twice as much as one receives from them, and gather together all one's ploughing-gear, then drill frankincense and fennel and hallowed salve and hallowed salt into the plough-tree. Then take the seed and set it on the body of the plough, then say:

> Erce! Erce! Erce! Mother of earth! May the Ruler of all, the everlasting Lord, grant you fields sprouting and shooting, increasing and strengthening, tall stalks, shimmering crops and broad barley crops and glistening wheat crops and all the crops of the earth! May the everlasting Lord and his saints who are in the heavens grant him that his tilth be protected against any and every foe, and defended against each and every evil thing, from the witchcrafts sown across the land! Now I invoke the Ruler who shaped this world, that there be no woman so skilled in conjuration and no man so cunning that they may avert the words thus spoken.

Then let the plough be driven forwards and the first furrow opened up, then say:

> Hale may you be, earth, mother of mortals! Grow pregnant in the embrace of God, filled with food for mortals' use.

Then take flour of each sort, and let a loaf be baked as big as the hollow of the hands, and knead it with milk and with holy water, and lay it under the first furrow. Then say:

> Field full of food for humankind, brightly burgeoning, may you be blessed in the holy name of him who shaped the sky and the earth on which we live. The God who wrought the depths grant us increasing grace, so that each kind of corn may turn out to our profit.

Then say 'Crescite . . . in nomine patris . . . sit benedicti' three times, and the Amen and the Paternoster three times.

A Journey Charm

[Cambridge, Corpus Christi College MS 41, pp.350–3]

There are many problems of interpretation in this text. Some pre-Christian magic perhaps survives in the function of the rod or staff – within which, according to one possible translation, the speaker 'embodies' himself. But it has been suggested that this rod is meant to be a crucifix; and certainly the tone and content of the charm are in all other respects inoffensive to Christian orthodoxy. There are echoes of Ephesians 6:10–18 in the invocation of the evangelists; and perhaps, as this translation proposes, there is an allusion to the Israelites' safe crossing of the Red Sea, in the obscure lines 35–7.

By this rod I protect myself and commend myself into God's keeping – against that wounding stab, against that wounding blow, against that fierce horror, against that great terror which is hateful to everyone, and against everything hateful that comes into the land.

6   A charm of overcoming I chant; a rod of overcoming I carry – overcoming by word, overcoming by deed. May this avail me so that no nightmare upsets me nor my belly afflicts me nor fear for my life ever arises; but may the Almighty save me, and the Son and the Holy Ghost, the Comforter, the Lord worthy of all glory, inasmuch as I have obeyed the Creator of the heavens.

13   Abraham and Isaac and such men, Moses and Jacob and David and Joseph and Eve and Anna and Elizabeth, Sarah, and Mary too, mother of Christ, and also the brothers Peter and Paul, and also a thousand of your angels I call to my aid against all foes. May they lead me and protect me and preserve my going, keep me entirely and rule over me, guiding my work. May God, the Hope of heaven, and the array of the saints and the multitude of those renowned for overcoming, of those steadfast in truth, and of the angels, be a hand over my head. I

entreat with willing heart that Matthew be my helmet, Mark my mail-coat, radiant, confident of life, Luke my sword, sharp and of shimmering edge, John my shield, and the Seraph, created beautiful in heaven, my spear.

31   Forth I go: may I meet with friends, with all the inspiration of the angels and the counsel of the blessed. Now I invoke the God of overcoming, the grace of God, for a good journey and mild and light winds upon the coasts. I have heard of the winds rolling back the water, of men constantly preserved from all their foes. May I meet with friends, so that I may dwell in the safe-keeping of the Almighty, protected from the loathsome enemy who harasses my life – firm-founded in the inspiration of the angels and within the holy hand of the puissant Lord of the heavens, the while that I am allowed to dwell in this life. Amen.

A Check-list
of Old English Poetry

A Check-list of Old English Poetry

Each entry comprises: the title given as in *ASPR* and printed in small capitals if the poem is wholly or partly translated in the present volume; citation of the MS source(s); item number(s) in Ker's *Catalogue* for a description of MSS and other contents; volume number in *ASPR* for a printed text; and column number(s) in *NCBEL*, vol.1 for a bibliography. Where several MS sources exist, the one used as basis for the *ASPR* text is cited first and Ker items are listed in corresponding sequence. CCCC is Corpus Christi College, Cambridge; Cotton, Harley, Royal and Additional MSS are in the British Library, London; Junius, Hatton and Rawlinson MSS are in the Bodleian Library, Oxford. Hickes refers to G. Hickes, *Linguarum Veterum Septentrionalium Thesaurus*, Oxford, 1705. Title abbreviations are those proposed by Magoun (see p.xxiv) and utilized (with some slight modifications) in J. B. Bessinger and P. H. Smith, *A Concordance to ASPR* (Ithaca and London, 1978), here designated *CASPR*.

Chr I	ADVENT LYRICS – see CHRIST I.
Ald	Aldhelm – CCCC 326 (pp.5–6) – Ker 61 – *ASPR* VI – *NCBEL* 237.
Alm	ALMS-GIVING – Exeter Book (fol.121ᵇ–122ᵃ) – Ker 116 – *ASPR* III – *NCBEL* 237.
And	ANDREAS – Vercelli Book (fol.29ᵇ–52ᵇ) – Ker 394 – *ASPR* II – *NCBEL* 237.
Aza	Azarias – Exeter Book (fol.53ᵃ–55ᵇ) – Ker 116 – *ASPR* III – *NCBEL* 239.
Brb	BATTLE OF BRUNANBURH – CCCC 173 (fol.26ᵃ–27ᵃ); Cotton Tiberius A vi, Cotton Tiberius B i, Cotton Tiberius B iv – Ker 39; 188, 191, 192 – *ASPR* VI – *NCBEL* 239, 295.
Fnb	BATTLE OF FINNSBURH – Hickes, printed from London, Lambeth Palace 487 now lost – Ker 282 – *ASPR* VI – *NCBEL* 240.
Mld	BATTLE OF MALDON – Rawlinson B 203, transcript by J. Elphinstone of Cotton Otho A xii subsequently destroyed in Ashburnham House fire 1731 – Ker 172 – *ASPR* VI – *NCBEL* 241.

BDS   BEDE'S DEATH-SONG — Switzerland, St Gallen Stiftsbibliothek 254 (p.253); Durham, Univ. Lib. Cosin V.II.6 and many other MSS — Ker App.25; 88, 104, 110, 152, 273, 306, 321, 356, 386; App.1, 2, 12, 13 — *ASPR* VI — *NCBEL* 243.

       BENEDICTINE OFFICE POEMS — see CREED, FRAGMENTS OF PSALMS, Gloria I, LORD'S PRAYER III.

Bwf   BEOWULF — Cotton Vitellius A xv (fol.132ᵃ–201ᵇ) — Ker 216 — *ASPR* IV — *NCBEL* 244.

BCr   Brussels Cross — Inscription on cross reliquary, Cathedral Church of SS Michel and Gudule, Brussels — *ASPR* VI — *NCBEL* 267.

Cæd   CÆDMON'S HYMN — Cambridge, Univ. Lib. Kk.5.16 (fol.128ᵇ) and many other MSS — Ker 25; 23, 32, 121, 122, 180, 304, 326, 341, 351, 354, 356, 357, 396; App.8 — *ASPR* VI — *NCBEL* 268.

CFB   Capture of the Five Boroughs — CCCC 173 (fol.27ᵃ); same MSS as BRUNANBURH — Ker 39; 188, 191, 192 — *ASPR* VI — *NCBEL* 269, 295.

Chr I   CHRIST I (ADVENT LYRICS) — Exeter Book (fol.8ᵃ–14ᵃ) — Ker 116 — *ASPR* III — *NCBEL* 269.

Chr II   CHRIST II (THE ASCENSION) — Exeter Book (fol.14ᵃ–20ᵇ) — Ker 116 — *ASPR* III — *NCBEL* 269.

Chr III   CHRIST III (THE JUDGMENT) — Exeter Book (fol.20ᵇ–32ᵃ) — Ker 116 — *ASPR* III — *NCBEL* 269.

XSt   CHRIST AND SATAN — Junius 11 (pp.213–29) — Ker 334 — *ASPR* I — *NCBEL* 270.

EgC   Coronation of Edgar — CCCC 173 (fol.28ᵇ); Cotton Tiberius A vi, Cotton Tiberius B i — Ker 39; 188, 191 — *ASPR* VI — *NCBEL* 271, 295.

Crd   CREED — Junius 121 (fol.46ᵃ–47ᵃ) — Ker 338 — *ASPR* VI — *NCBEL* 271.

Dan   DANIEL — Junius 11 (pp.173–212) — Ker 334 — *ASPR* I — *NCBEL* 272.

DAl   Death of Alfred — Cotton Tiberius B i; Cotton Tiberius B iv (fol.70ᵃ) — Ker 191; 192 — *ASPR* VI — *NCBEL* 273, 295.

EgD   Death of Edgar — CCCC 173 (fol.28ᵇ–29ᵃ); same MSS as Coronation — Ker 39; 188, 191 — *ASPR* VI — *NCBEL* 273, 295.

DEw   Death of Edward — Cotton Tiberius B i (fol.160ᵃ); Cotton

Tiberius B iv – Ker 191; 192 – *ASPR* VI – *NCBEL* 295.

Deo   DEOR – Exeter Book (fol.100ᵃ–100ᵇ) – Ker 116 – *ASPR* III – *NCBEL* 273, 276.

DHl   DESCENT INTO HELL – Exeter Book (fol.119ᵇ–121ᵇ) – Ker 116 – *ASPR* III – *NCBEL* 273.

DrR   DREAM OF THE ROOD – Vercelli Book (fol.104ᵇ–106ᵃ) – Ker 394 – *ASPR* II – *NCBEL* 275.

Drm   Durham – Cambridge, Univ. Lib. Ff.1.27 (p.202); Hickes, printed from Cotton Vitellius D xx, severely damaged in Ashburnham House fire 1731 – Ker 14; 223 – *ASPR* VI – *NCBEL* 276.

      Durham Proverbs – Durham, Cathedral Lib.B.III.32 (fol. 43ᵇ–45ᵇ) – Ker 107A – Not in *ASPR* nor in *CASPR*; printed O. S. Arngart, *The Durham Proverbs*, Lund 1956 – *NCBEL* 276.

Ele   ELENE – Vercelli Book (fol.121ᵃ–133ᵇ) – Ker 394 – *ASPR* II – *NCBEL* 277.

ECL   Exhortation to Christian Living – CCCC 201 (pp.165–6) – Ker 49A – *ASPR* VI – *NCBEL* 278.

Exo   EXODUS – Junius 11 (pp.143–71) – Ker 334 – *ASPR* I – *NCBEL* 278.

FAp   FATES OF THE APOSTLES – Vercelli Book (fol.52ᵇ–54ᵃ) – Ker 394 – *ASPR* II – *NCBEL* 279.

FtM   FORTUNES OF MEN – Exeter Book (fol.87ᵃ–88ᵇ) – Ker 116 – *ASPR* III – *NCBEL* 280.

FPs   FRAGMENTS OF PSALMS – Junius 121 (fol.43ᵇ, 44ᵇ, 45ᵃ, 45ᵇ–46ᵃ, 47ᵃ–50ᵇ, 51ᵃ, 52ᵃ, 53ᵇ) – Ker 338 – *ASPR* VI – *NCBEL* 271, 280.

FrC   Franks Casket – Inscriptions in runes on front and right side panels of casket in the British Museum – *ASPR* VI – *NCBEL* 280.

Gen   GENESIS – Junius 11 (pp.1–142; GENESIS A lines 1–234, 852–2936; GENESIS B lines 235–851) – Ker 334 – *ASPR* I – *NCBEL* 281.

GfM   GIFTS OF MEN – Exeter Book (fol.78ᵃ–80ᵃ) – Ker 116 – *ASPR* III – *NCBEL* 284.

Glo I   Gloria I – Junius 121 (fol. 43ᵇ–44ᵇ); CCCC 201 – Ker 338; 49B – *ASPR* VI – *NCBEL* 271, 284.

Glo II   Gloria II – Cotton Titus D xxvii (fol.56ᵃ–56ᵇ) – Ker 202 – *ASPR* VI – *NCBEL* 284.

Glc	GUTHLAC − Exeter Book (fol.32ᵇ–52ᵇ; GUTHLAC A lines 1–818; GUTHLAC B lines 819–1379) − Ker 116 − *ASPR* III − *NCBEL* 284.
Hom I	Homiletic Fragment I − Vercelli Book (fol.104ᵃ–104ᵇ) − Ker 394 − *ASPR* II − *NCBEL* 285.
Hom II	Homiletic Fragment II − Exeter Book (fol.122ᵃ–122ᵇ) − Ker 116 − *ASPR* III − *NCBEL* 285.
HbM	HUSBAND'S MESSAGE − Exeter Book (fol.123ᵃ–123ᵇ) − Ker 116 − *ASPR* III − *NCBEL* 276, 285.
InC	Instructions for Christians − Cambridge, Univ. Lib. Ii.1.33 (fol.224ᵇ–227ᵇ) − Ker 18 − Not in *ASPR* (abbreviation supplied from *CASPR*); printed J. L. Rosier, 'Instructions for Christians: a poem in Old English', *Anglia* 82 (1964) and 84 (1966) − *NCBEL* 286.
JgD I	Judgment Day I − Exeter Book (fol.115ᵇ–117ᵇ) − Ker 116 − *ASPR* III − *NCBEL* 286.
JgD II	JUDGEMENT DAY II − CCCC 201 (pp 161–5) − Ker 49A − *ASPR* VI − *NCBEL* 286.
Jud	JUDITH − Cotton Vitellius A xv (fol.202ᵃ–209ᵃ) − Ker 216 − *ASPR* IV − *NCBEL* 287.
Jul	JULIANA − Exeter Book (fol.65ᵇ–76ᵃ) − Ker 116 − *ASPR* III − *NCBEL* 288.
KtH	Kentish Hymn − Cotton Vespasian D vi (fol.68ᵇ–69ᵇ) − Ker 207 − *ASPR* VI − *NCBEL* 288.
LEP	Latin-English Proverbs − Cotton Faustina A x (fol.100ᵇ); Royal 2 B v (f.6ᵃ) − Ker 154A; 249 − *ASPR* VI − *NCBEL* 288.
LdR	Leiden Riddle − Leiden, Rijksuniversiteit, Vossianus Lat.Qto 106 (fol.25ᵇ) − Ker App.19 − *ASPR* VI − *NCBEL* 288.
LPr I	Lord's Prayer I − Exeter Book (fol.122ᵃ) − Ker 116 − *ASPR* III − *NCBEL* 289.
LPr II	Lord's Prayer II − CCCC 201 (pp.167–9) − Ker 49B − *ASPR* VI − *NCBEL* 289.
LPr III	LORD'S PRAYER III − Junius 121 (fol.45ᵃ–45ᵇ) − Ker 338 − *ASPR* VI − *NCBEL* 271, 289.
Mxm I	MAXIMS I − Exeter Book (fol.88ᵇ–90ᵃ Group A; 90ᵃ–91ᵃ Group B; 91ᵃ–92ᵇ Group C) − Ker 116 − *ASPR* III − *NCBEL* 289.
Mxm II	MAXIMS II − Cotton Tiberius B i (fol.115ᵃ–115ᵇ) − Ker 191

– *ASPR* VI – *NCBEL* 290.

Mnl   Menologium – Cotton Tiberius B i (fol.112ᵃ–114ᵇ) – Ker 191 – *ASPR* VI – *NCBEL* 290.

MBo   Metres of Boethius – Cotton Otho A vi (fol.1ᵃ–129ᵇ including prose sections) – Ker 167 – *ASPR* V – *NCBEL* 290.

MCh   METRICAL CHARMS – Cotton Caligula A vii (fol.176ᵃ–178ᵃ: FOR UNFRUITFUL LAND); Harley 585 (fol.160ᵃ–163ᵇ Nine herbs charm; 167ᵃ–167ᵇ Against a dwarf; 175ᵃ–176ᵃ For a sudden stitch; 180ᵇ–181ᵃ For loss of cattle; 185ᵃ–185ᵇ For delayed birth); Royal 12 D xvii (fol.125ᵃ–125ᵇ For the water-elf disease); CCCC 41 (p.182 For a swarm of bees; 206 For theft of cattle; 206 For loss of cattle; 350–3 A JOURNEY CHARM); Royal 4 A xiv (fol.106ᵇ Against a wen) – Ker 137; 231; 264; 32; 250 – *ASPR* VI – *NCBEL* 291.

MEp   Metrical Epilogue (of scribe) – CCCC 41 (pp.483–4) – Ker 32 – *ASPR* VI – *NCBEL* 292.

PCE   Metrical Epilogue to the Pastoral Care – Hatton 20 (fol.98ᵃ–98ᵇ); CCCC 12; Junius 53, transcript by Junius of Cotton Tiberius B xi, damaged 1731, destroyed 1864; Cambridge, Trinity Coll.R.5.22 – Ker 324; 30, 195, 87 – *ASPR* VI – *NCBEL* 292.

MPD   Metrical Preface to Gregory's Dialogues – Cotton Otho C i, vol.2 (fol.1ᵃ) – Ker 182 – *ASPR* VI – *NCBEL* 292.

PCP   Metrical Preface to the Pastoral Care – Hatton 20 (fol.2ᵇ); same MSS as Metrical Epilogue to PC – Ker 324; 30, 195, 87 – *ASPR* VI – *NCBEL* 292.

OrW   Order of the World – Exeter Book (fol.92ᵇ–94ᵃ) – Ker 116 – *ASPR* III – *NCBEL* 293.

Pnt   PANTHER (PHYSIOLOGUS) – Exeter Book (fol.95ᵇ–96ᵇ) – Ker 116 – *ASPR* III – *NCBEL* 293, 294.

PPs   Paris Psalter – Paris, Bibliothèque Nationale Fonds Lat.8824 (fol.64ᵃ–175ᵇ) following prose versions of Psalms 1–50 in fol.1ᵃ–63ᵇ) – Ker 367 – *ASPR* V – *NCBEL* 293.

Ptg   Partridge (PHYSIOLOGUS) – Exeter Book (fol.97ᵇ–98ᵃ) – Ker 116 – *ASPR* III – *NCBEL* 293, 294.

Phr   Pharaoh – Exeter Book (fol.122ᵃ) – Ker 116 – *ASPR* III – *NCBEL* 293.

Phx   PHOENIX — Exeter Book (fol.55ᵇ–65ᵇ) — Ker 116 — *ASPR* III — *NCBEL* 294.

POEMS OF THE AS CHRONICLE — see BATTLE OF BRUNAN-BURH, Capture of the Five Boroughs, Coronation of Edgar, Death of Edgar, Death of Alfred, Death of Edward (annals for 937, 942, 973, 975, 1036 and 1065 respectively). Other entries marked by poetic rhetoric, not printed in *ASPR*, are 959 (prospect of Edgar's reign), 975 (anti-monasticism in Edward's reign), 979 (murder of Edward at Corfe), 1011 (seizure of archbishop Ælfheah of Canterbury by Danes), 1057 (return from exile of Edward Ætheling), 1067 (Margaret's vow of virginity), 1075 (two epigrams on a wedding conspiracy against William), 1086 (the harsh character of William), and 1104 (epigram on the evils and miseries of Henry's reign). For texts see C. Plummer, *Two of the Saxon Chronicles Parallel* (Oxford, 1892); and for translations G. N. Garmonsway, *The Anglo-Saxon Chronicle* (London, 1953, revised ed. 1954).

Pra   A Prayer — Cotton Julius A ii (fol.136ᵃ–137ᵃ); London, Lambeth Palace Lib. 427 (fol.183ᵇ) — Ker 159; 280 — *ASPR* VI — *NCBEL* 295.

Prc   Precepts — Exeter Book (fol.80ᵃ–81ᵇ) — Ker 116 — *ASPR* III — *NCBEL* 295.

PrW   A Proverb from Winfrid's Time — Vienna, Nationalbibliothek 751 (fol.34ᵇ–35ᵃ) — Ker App.37 — *ASPR* VI — *NCBEL* 296.

Psm 50   Psalm 50 — Cotton Vespasian D vi (fol.70ᵃ–73ᵇ) — Ker 207 — *ASPR* VI — *NCBEL* 296.

Rsg   RESIGNATION — Exeter Book (fol.117ᵇ–119ᵇ) — Ker 116 — *ASPR* III — *NCBEL* 276, 296.

Rdl   RIDDLES — Exeter Book (fol.101ᵃ–115ᵃ; 122ᵇ–123ᵃ; 124ᵇ–130ᵇ) — Ker 116 — *ASPR* III — *NCBEL* 296.

Rim   Rhyming Poem — Exeter Book (fol.94ᵃ–95ᵇ) — Ker 116 — *ASPR* III — *NCBEL* 299.

Rui   RUIN — Exeter Book (fol.123ᵇ–124ᵇ) — Ker 116 — *ASPR* III — *NCBEL* 299.

Run   Rune Poem — Hickes, printed from Wanley's transcript of Cotton Otho B x (fol.165ᵃ–165ᵇ), destroyed in

Ashburnham House fire 1731 – Ker 179 – *ASPR* VI – *NCBEL* 300.

RCr   RUTHWELL CROSS – Inscription in runes on the East and West faces of the cross in the church at Ruthwell, Dumfries – *ASPR* VI – *NCBEL* 300.

Sfr   SEAFARER – Exeter Book (fol.81^b–83^a) – Ker 116 – *ASPR* III – *NCBEL* 301.

SFt   Seasons for Fasting – Additional 43703 (fol.257^a–260^b), transcript by Nowell of Cotton Otho B xi, badly damaged in Ashburnham House fire 1731 – Ker 180 – *ASPR* VI – *NCBEL* 303.

SnS   Solomon and Saturn – CCCC 422 (pp.1–6, 13–26 with intervening prose dialogue) and CCCC 41 (pp.196–8) – Ker 70A and 32 – *ASPR* VI – *NCBEL* 303.

SlB I   Soul and Body I – Vercelli Book (fol.101^b–103^b) – Ker 394 – *ASPR* II – *NCBEL* 304.

SlB II   SOUL AND BODY II – Exeter Book (fol.98^a–100^a) – Ker 116 – *ASPR* III – *NCBEL* 304.

SmP   Summons to Prayer – CCCC 201 (pp.166–7) – Ker 49A – *ASPR* VI – *NCBEL* 304.

Thr   Thureth – Cotton Claudius A iii (fol.31^b) – Ker 141 – *ASPR* VI – *NCBEL* 305.

Vgl   Vainglory – Exeter Book (fol.83^a–84^b) – Ker 116 – *ASPR* III – *NCBEL* 305.

Wld   WALDERE – Copenhagen, Kongelige Bibliotek, Ny kongelige Samling 167b (two loose folios) – Ker 101 – *ASPR* VI – *NCBEL* 305.

Wan   WANDERER – Exeter Book (fol.76^b–78^a) – Ker 116 – *ASPR* III – *NCBEL* 276, 306.

Whl   WHALE(PHYSIOLOGUS) – Exeter Book (fol.96^b–97^b) – Ker 116 – *ASPR* III – *NCBEL* 294, 308.

Wds   WIDSITH – Exeter Book (fol.84^b–87^a) – Ker 116 – *ASPR* III – *NCBEL* 308.

WfL   WIFE'S LAMENT – Exeter Book (fol.115^a–115^b) – Ker 116 – *ASPR* III – *NCBEL* 276, 310.

WlE   WULF AND EADWACER – Exeter Book (fol.100^b) – Ker 116 *ASPR* III – *NCBEL* 276, 296, 311.